THE NEW NATURAL

A SURVEY OF BRITISH NA

GRASSHOPPERS & CRICKETS

THE NEW NATURALIST LIBRARY

GRASSHOPPERS & CRICKETS

TED BENTON

Collins

This edition published in 2012 by Collins,
An imprint of HarperCollins Publishers

HarperCollins Publishers
77–85 Fulham Palace Road
London W6 8JB
www.collins.co.uk

First published 2012

© Ted Benton, 2012

A cip catalogue record for this book is available
from the British Library.

Set in FF Nexus

Edited and designed by
Patricia Briggs

Printed Hong Kong by Printing Express

Hardback
ISBN 978-0-00-727723-0

Paperback
ISBN 978-0-00-727724-7

Contents

Editors' Preface

Following his earlier New Naturalist, *Bumblebees*, we are delighted that Ted Benton has shared his enthusiasm for another familiar and well-loved group of insects that contribute greatly to the sights and sounds of summer – grasshoppers and crickets. As well as dealing with identification, he considers the natural history of the British species and their conservation, and discusses their distribution, their polymorphisms and the timing of their life history stages in relation to the changing climate. He shows how studies of their bizarre behaviour contribute to our understanding of the evolution of reproductive strategies, and illustrates their songs and dances in the accompanying DVD, an innovation for this series. The fruit of many years of careful observation, photography, filming and recording, this book will surely bring many fresh converts to the study of Orthoptera.

Author's Foreword and Acknowledgements

My semi-retirement from the 'day job' as professor of sociology at the University of Essex has given me more free time (but not so much as might be hoped!) to indulge in the delights of field natural history. As I explained in the foreword to my previous New Naturalist (*Bumblebees*, 2006), it took me longer than it should have to see the connections between my work as a sociologist and my passionate interest in natural history and wildlife conservation. In the bumblebee book the links were made in several ways, including a thoroughgoing treatment of the bees as social animals, and the use of some ideas from critical political economy, political sociology and planning law in thinking about the causes of bumblebee decline and prospects for reversing it. I hope that in this book, my background in philosophy and social science also gives a distinctive perspective that justifies its publication, even though the topic is so brilliantly covered by several other works.

Having observed the astonishing and puzzling antics of courting male rufous and mottled grasshoppers, I began to research the literature on mating systems, sexual selection and sexual conflict. The history of this topic engaged my sociological interests, as there are striking parallels between the emergence of these issues in the human social sciences and their resurgence in the life-sciences literature – both in the wake of 'second-wave' feminism. After quite a struggle, I managed to cut the treatment of these issues down to a mere three chapters (4 to 6), but echoes will be seen through the accounts of particular species, as well as in some of the video clips. As in the bumblebee book, I have tried to reflect on the relationships between shifting ways of conceptualising behaviour, the posing of questions for research, and the elusive activities of the insects themselves. A historical perspective on the topic often helps to bring out the always provisional character of our current ways of understanding nature, and the ways in which social and cultural processes play their part in shaping and focusing scientific practice.

Since very early in life, I have been aware of grasshoppers and their allies as abundant denizens of the wild places I inhabited as a 'feral' child in south Yorkshire. However, their coming to attention as topics for special study by an amateur naturalist required reliable, accessible literature. David Ragge's wonderful Wayside and Woodland *Grasshoppers, Crickets and Cockroaches of the British Isles* (1965) provided this and much more – real inspiration! What finally consolidated the interest for me was helping Alan Wake to map the Orthoptera of Essex, for his excellent 1997 book on the topic. We traversed the lanes and byways of our much-maligned county on battered old push-bikes – and had more laughs than we deserved. By that time, Ragge's great work had been complemented by another: Judith Marshall and E.C.M. Haes's *Grasshoppers and Allied Insects of Great Britain and Ireland* (1988). More recently, Tim Gardiner's research on ecology and conservation – much of it conducted also in Essex – as well as his generosity in sharing his great expertise, has been a further stimulus to my own interest. Finally, the excellent *Photographic Guide to the Grasshoppers and Crickets of Britain and Ireland* (2007), by Martin Evans and Roger Edmondson, updated previous literature and included excellent photographic images of the British species.

Having agreed to write a New Naturalist on the Orthoptera, I was somewhat awed by the inevitable comparisons with these works, and concerned that my own contribution should have something new and different to offer. As both Ragge and Marshall & Haes had included excellent sound recordings, it seemed there would be little point in repeating the exercise, so, in a moment of madness, I suggested that I might provide a DVD film of orthopteran behaviour. As a well-known technophobe, with no experience whatsoever of film making, this was, indeed, a rash offer! So it turned out! There was a very steep learning curve just to operate the camcorder and then edit the tapes. However, by far the greatest challenge was to capture relevant sequences of behaviour in the field. It soon became clear that a tripod was needed, and this meant filming from a fixed location, as any movement immediately 'spooked' the insects. The best I could do was to make an informed guess as to likely vantage points, and wait for something to happen. I guess the patience involved is comparable to that needed by anglers. I was given indispensable help by Roy Cornhill and John Dobson, both of whom also had their patience tried to the extreme, spotting singing insects, pointing out examples of behaviour I would otherwise have missed, and generally keeping me company on many occasions. Alan James (of Secondsight Productions) turned my crude editing into something like a real film – but even he could not correct all the many limitations that you will observe when you view the DVD. For all the frustrations of the work of filming, I have no doubt it immeasurably enhanced my appreciation of these fascinating insects. Being forced to stand and watch for many hours allowed me to witness so much more than would be observed by casually walking by.

Many other people contributed in numerous ways to the production of this book. First mention goes to my consistently amazing life-partner, Shelley Pennington, without whom nothing. Even after her encounter with a stray camel cricket in the shower, she generously bought lettuce for its companions. Shelley, Rowan, Linda and Jay have combined amused tolerance of my obsession for insects with gentle reminders of (what they continue to imagine is) a more normal world occupied by other humans. John Kramer, whose obsession for insects has rivalled my own during a friendship that stems from primary-school days, offered great help and support in the rescue of camel crickets and the search for scaly crickets on bleak Chesil beach. The search for the camel crickets was greatly aided by correspondence with Maggie Frankum, Helen Iken and Glenys Panter, while the management at the former Derbyshire garden centre both encouraged the crickets and aided our rescue attempt. Roy Cornhill and John Dobson have given generous, patient and convivial companionship on countless field trips, and unstinting support in many ways. Mike Edwards gave of his expert knowledge and practical work with the field crickets, but, most of all, has been an inspiring example. Bryan Pinchen, too, shared his expert knowledge of mole crickets, and introduced me to some unique habitats in the New Forest. Adrian Kettle and Roy Cornhill took care of the rescue population of camel crickets while I was on holiday, and Tracy Kettle supplied valuable observational details of the nocturnal courtship and egg-laying activities of the crickets.

John Kramer and long-term friend, Simon Randolph, helped with encouragement, bibliography and critical reading. My editor at HarperCollins, Sally Corbet, was, as always, a supportive, thorough and critical reader of complete drafts of the book. Other experts gave freely of their time to read and comment on drafts, so saving me from numerous errors – David Robinson, Bryan Pinchen, Karim Vahed, Berthold Hedwig, Mike Edwards, Peter Sutton, Andrew Cherrill, Judith Marshall, Tim Gardiner and Marion Hall. Marion Hall, especially, gave serious thought to the task and provided incisive and insightful criticisms that were decisive in making me re-think the organisation of chapters 4 to 6. However, none of the above should be held responsible for any failings on my part.

Judith Marshall helped in many other ways, by giving me access to the NHM collections, sharing some of her great expertise, and generously hosting the annual orthopterists' workshops. These events were indispensable, providing a forum for presentations and discussions of so many aspects of the biology and natural history of these fascinating insects. Attendance at these meetings gave me the opportunity to meet and learn from such leading researchers as Karim Vahed, Berthold Hedwig, Andrew Cherrill, Tim Gardiner, Marion Hall, Patricia Ash, David Robinson and the legendary David Ragge, as well as Judith Marshall herself.

Although I have never met Darryl Gwynne, his writings were a great stimulus, and he provided advice and much-needed photos by email correspondence.

Nick Owens sent me valuable information on colour morphs of the mottled grasshopper, and provided convivial company 'in the field'. Michael Chinery helped with literature, and shared an enjoyable day out in the brecks. David Baldock helped with the inspiration of his own books, as well as the loan of others. Judith Marshall helped with identification of my photos of European species, as did Dragan Chobanov. Tim Bernhard provided convivial company, and his superb drawings of great green bush cricket, field crickets, slender groundhopper and stripe-winged grasshopper. For other illustrations, I am very grateful to: Marion Hall, Scott Sakaluk, Dave Funk, Bryan Thomas, John Dobson, Roy Cornhill, Tim Gardiner, Daryl Gwynne, David Rentz, Bryan Pinchen, Adrian Kettle, Karim Vahed, Andrew Cherrill, Peter Sutton and Nick Owens.

Peter Sutton gave valuable advice and comment, as well as working with Bjorn Beckmann at the Biological Records Centre to produce the up-to-date distribution maps. Particular thanks to Bjorn also for his help with presentation of the data.

The work of the Biological Records Centre, which is co-funded by the Natural Environment Research Council (through the Centre for Ecology & Hydrology) and the Joint Nature Conservation Committee is very much appreciated. Records are exchanged with the Irish National Biodiversity Data Centre (www.biodiversityireland.ie), and readers are encouraged to send in records of their sightings, including common species, to the Orthoptera Recording Scheme's website (www.orthoptera.org.uk), or to the above centres, or to the UK national recorder, Peter Sutton (petersutton@freeuk.com). The maps include records submitted and processed up to March 2012, but should be interpreted with care. To a considerable extent they reflect the level of recording activity, and absence of records should not be taken automatically to imply the absence of the species from a given area. It should also be noted that the maps present only presence or absence of species at vice-county level for the two date-classes. This is liable to give an exaggerated impression of the distribution of scarce or more localised species, as presence in just one site will be represented by colouring of the whole vice-county. It is hoped that with increased recording effort, an Atlas of Orthoptera of Britain and Ireland at 10 km square resolution will soon be produced.

Several other organisations have provided encouragement and resources that made the work on the book possible. These include the membership of the unequalled Colchester Natural History Society, its president, Joe Firmin and chair, Darren Tansley, the Essex Field Club, Essex Wildlife Trust, Chris Gibson and Natural England, and, not least, Essex University. My own department has been extraordinarily tolerant of my deviant interests, while the Albert Sloman Library, and especially the inter-library loans service, has been indispensable: a model of public-sector efficiency, flexibility and helpfulness. Terry Tostevin, formerly of the library staff, devoted time and energy to rooting out many fascinating literary references to grasshoppers and crickets. I have made use of some of these, but unfortunately did not have space for all.

Finally, I thank Julia Koppitz for her unfailing kindness and conviviality, despite great pressures of work, Myles Archibald for his continued encouragement, and the rest of the 'team' at HarperCollins.

CHAPTER 1

Introduction

And here, if you like, the Cricket DID chime in! ... The kettle had had the last of its solo performance. It persevered with undiminished ardour; but the cricket took first fiddle and kept it. Good Heaven, how it chirped! Its shrill, sharp, piercing voice resounded through the house, and seemed to twinkle in the outer darkness like a star ... Yet they went very well together, the Cricket and the kettle. The burden of the song was still the same; and louder, louder, louder still they sang it in their emulation ... There was all the excitement of a race about it. Chirp, chirp, chirp! Cricket a mile ahead. Hum, hum, hum-m-m! Kettle making play in the distance like a great top. (Dickens, 2004 [1845])

Many of Dickens's readers would have recognised from their own experience his description of the singing of the 'cricket on the hearth'. Unfortunately this once-familiar songster is now rarely heard, except, perhaps, in the homes of keepers of reptiles, who use them to feed their pets. However, another group of insects, the grasshoppers, continue to contribute their songs to the soundscape of the British summer. Although the use of sound for communication is not universal among grasshoppers, crickets and their allies, it is very widespread. And it is this feature that above all others attracts the attention of passers-by, as well as poets, musicians and scientists. An ear-opening introduction to contemporary creative uses of insect sounds can be accessed from the website www.pestival.org, a festival celebrating insects in art and the art of being an insect. Particularly interesting is Chris Watson's installation 'whispering in the leaves' at the Royal Botanical Gardens, Kew (for related events and recordings, visit: www.chriswatson.net).

Scientists have been interested in the nature of the insects' musical instruments, the messages they communicate in their songs, and the responses of their intended listeners. Although the song of the male may play its part in making known to any interested female both his presence and his readiness to mate, it may also give away his location to a less welcome eavesdropper in the shape of a potential predator or parasite. Dickens's emphasis on the competitive performance of his cricket is more accurate than he may have realised. It is now recognised that the calling songs of grasshoppers and crickets communicate information between the males themselves and are involved in their competitive interactions and spatial distribution. The extraordinary complexity and diversity exhibited by grasshoppers and crickets in their reproductive behaviour has stimulated a great body of research, some of which will be introduced in Chapters 4, 5 and 6.

The songs of crickets and bush-crickets, especially, have proved so attractive in some cultures, notably in China and Japan, that these insects are caged and kept for their song (Jin, 1994, in Gwynne, 2001; Pemberton, 1990). In China, not only is there a long tradition of breeding crickets that are selected for their aggression and fighting ability (Jin & Yen, 1998), but they were also a symbol of fecundity (Meng, 1993, in Gwynne, 2001). Elsewhere, grasshoppers and crickets are assigned a great variety of other symbolic meanings. According to Kevan (1979) species of bush-crickets were feared in Navaho native American culture as they were thought to be associated with spirits and attracted to corpses. The great Cuban dancer, Carlos Acosta, tells us that while he was a disruptive schoolboy his father had told him of a dream.

> *Last night I had a magnificent dream … You were dancing in a majestic theatre in another country and suddenly a cricket landed on your shoulders … Don't you realise, the cricket represents hope. It means you are going to be great one day.*
> (Acosta, 2007: 76)

In stark contrast, Arundhati Roy uses the image of swarms of grasshoppers as an omen of genocide. She reports the account given by a friend of the sole survivor of the massacre of Armenians that took place in Anatolia in 1915.

> *She was ten years old in 1915. She remembered the swarms of grasshoppers that arrived in her village, Dubne, which was north of the historic Armenian city of Dikranagert, now Diyarbakir. The village elders were alarmed, she said, because they knew in their bones that the grasshoppers were a bad omen. They were right; the end came in a few months, when the wheat in the fields was ready for harvesting.* (Roy, 2009: 133–4)

A rather different moral is perpetuated in the story of the ant and the cicada, originally told by Aesop, but later transmuted into the encounter of ant and grasshopper. Either way, the message is the same: the grasshopper/cicada spends the summer in song, with no thought of tomorrow, while the industrious ant makes preparation for the bitter weather to come. Then, the destitute songster comes to beg or borrow from the ant, who replies: 'You used to sing! I'm glad to know it. Well, try dancing for a change' (Fabre, 1917: 1). Not every commentator finds the moral of this tale convincing. Fabre disputes its claims on behalf of the ant, while, in one of his short stories, Somerset Maugham (1963: 101–4) declares: '... I could never quite reconcile myself to the lesson. My sympathies were with the grasshopper and for some time I never saw an ant without putting my foot on it.' To underline the point, the story goes on to describe the contrasting lives of two brothers, Tom, a carefree and disgraceful hedonist, and George, a hard-working, prudent and faithful husband and father. Just as George is expecting to get his reward and watch the descent of his profligate brother into the gutter, Tom marries a rich and elderly lady, who dies and leaves him everything.

Visitors to the City of London might be surprised to see a number of representations of grasshoppers distributed in this citadel of international finance: on the weather vane and embossed on a wall of the Royal Exchange, and suspended over the pavement in Lombard Street. In apparent defiance of the fabled image of the grasshopper as hedonistic songster, these representations refer us to the long association of the Gresham family with finance and banking. Perhaps the best-known Gresham is Sir Thomas (1519–71), merchant and

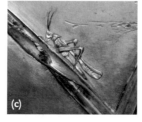

FIG 1. The Gresham grasshopper: (a) Lombard Street, City of London; (b) Gresham House, Cambridge; (c) Gresham Palace, Budapest; (d) The Royal Exchange, City of London.

financier, and financial agent to several English monarchs, including Elizabeth I. He was founder of the Royal Exchange, and his legacy was devoted to the establishment of Gresham College. The grasshopper motif figures above the Gresham family coat of arms, and legend has it that the founder of the family, Roger de Gresham, was abandoned as a new-born baby in long grass, only to be discovered by a woman whose attention was drawn to him by a grasshopper. The grasshopper motif is to be found on the exchange in Boston, in the bar of the spectacular art nouveau Gresham Palace in Budapest (originally owned and commissioned by the Gresham Life Assurance Company), in the car park of Gresham House in Cambridge, and elsewhere. Apparently, in the system of English heraldry the grasshopper symbolised wisdom and nobility. In view of our current experience of the financial services, perhaps the original association of the grasshopper with short-term profligacy might be reinstated!

More material relations between human societies and grasshoppers and crickets include actual and potential uses of orthopterans as food sources, and, more dramatically, the economic impact of locusts and other migratory species. Fabre (1917) extols the virtues of the 'locusts' (that is, what we would call grasshoppers) as important food for turkeys, guinea fowl and red-legged partridge, and so, indirectly, as contributing to human diets. He is more hesitant about the desirability of grasshoppers as direct culinary fare, but cites the gospel according to St. Matthew as evidence that the diet of St. John the Baptist was 'locusts and wild honey' during his time in the desert, and an Arab author to the effect that the wives of the Prophet were sent grasshoppers as gifts, and that the Caliph of Omar once declared: 'would that I had a basket of them to eat'. Gwynne (2001) mentions 4,000-year-old cave deposits in Wyoming that contained evidence of cooked bush-crickets, as well as more recent accounts of the roasts, soups and 'cricket cakes' prepared by native Americans. Still more recently, farming and eating insects has been advocated as a contribution to the growing crisis of global food production. A feature in *The Guardian Weekend* (Bailey, 2010) claimed that 1,400 insect species are eaten in over 80 per cent of nations. The UN's Food and Agriculture Organisation held a workshop in Thailand in 2008 to highlight the idea, and our own Oxford Museum of Natural History hosted a 'Banquet of Bugs' in April 2011 to promote insects as an environmentally sustainable alternative to meat. Grasshopper salsa tacos, cricket tostados, and cricket fried rice were among the delicacies on offer.

Less benign are the ravages to crops that orthopterans can cause in some parts of the world as a result of the formation of dense migratory aggregations. Locusts are especially notorious for their recurrent outbreaks in parts of Africa and Australasia. Two species in particular (*Schistocerca gregaria* and *Locusta*

FIG 2. *Locusta migratoria.*

migratoria) have been the most frequent research subjects. In these species a change of 'phase', from solitary to gregarious forms, underlies the tendency to form massive aggregations. Gregarious forms often differ in colour and structure as well as in their behaviour. The change of developmental pathway that produces the gregarious forms may be triggered by degenerating habitat conditions, or by increased population density, and is mediated by pheromonal communication. Plagues and outbreaks of dense clouds of flying insects that descend to feed as they move can cover tens to hundreds of square kilometres. A radar station in south eastern Australia monitored the passage over a 1 km line of two million locusts per night for six nights in November 1979 (Farrow, 1990). A similar pattern of aggregation and migration is found in other groups of orthopterans. Gwynne (2001) describes huge bands of so-called mormon crickets (*Anabrus simplex*) and coulee crickets (*Peranabrus scabricollis*) that form in western USA. The nymphs of these bush-crickets (or 'katydids' as they are known in America) form dense marching bands numbering many millions, up to 16 km long and 2 km wide. Although, as Gwynne points out, these species are less damaging to crops than has been assumed, drastic control measures have been used against them. Other bush-crickets that form aggregations under some conditions cause economically significant damage to forest trees in south and central America, to coconut palms and banana crops in Papua New Guinea and to grain in Ethiopa (Barrientos & Montes, 1997; Solulu *et al.*, 1998; Rentz & Gurney, 1985). The variegated grasshopper (*Zonocerus variegatus*) of western and central Africa periodically forms large aggregations and was known as a minor pest of plantation crops such as coffee, pineapple and banana from early in the 20th century. However, in the 1970s and 1980s it became a much more abundant and serious pest, possibly owing to a combination of deforestation and increased cultivation of cassava as a subsistence crop (Chapman *et al.*, 1986).

THE GRASSHOPPERS AND CRICKETS
AND THEIR RELATIVES

Although, as we have seen, the lives of humans and those of grasshoppers and crickets are and have been intertwined in many ways, the lives and interactions of these insects have a fascination in their own right and this will be the focus of the rest of this book.

The insect order to which the grasshoppers and crickets belong is the Orthoptera (from the Greek, 'straight winged'). Often the orthopterans are treated alongside closely related groups (as in Ragge, 1965 and Marshall & Haes, 1988). These relatives of the Orthoptera include cockroaches and mantids (order Dictyoptera), earwigs (order Dermaptera) and stick insects (order Phasmida). Taken together, these groups are often known as 'orthopteroid' insects. In this book we will be concerned more narrowly with the Orthoptera in the strict sense, but first it is necessary to give brief indications of those characteristics that mark out the Orthoptera from their relatives.

The stick insects (Phasmida) will be familiar to most readers, with their long, roughly tubular bodies, and three pairs of legs that are more or less equal in length. The tarsi have five segments. There are no native species, although a small number of species, probably escapees from domestication, or deliberate introductions, have established themselves in England – mostly in the south-west peninsula. Some tropical species are winged or elaborately spined, but those found in England conform to the characteristic stick shape.

The cockroaches (Dictyoptera) are flattened dorsoventrally, like beetles. However, in winged forms the fore wings overlap along the midline of the insects' dorsal surface, and are not shell-like as in beetles. The cerci that project

FIG 3. A stick insect, *Parachymorpha zomproi*.

from the rear end of the abdomen
are simple, and the tarsi have five
segments. Although the hind legs
may be longer than the fore and mid
legs, they show no obvious adaptation
for jumping. The large common or
oriental cockroach (*Blatta orientalis*) is
probably the best known, but, owing
to its pest status, it is now rarely
encountered in Britain. It and other
non-native species are often kept as pet
food, and may occasionally establish
temporary colonies outdoors. However,
they do not generally persist except in artificially heated buildings or refuse tips.

FIG 4. The Australian cockroach, *Periplaneta australasiae*, an alien species sometimes found in artificially heated buildings in Britain.

There are three native cockroaches. These are much smaller than the oriental cockroach, and rather inconspicuous. The dusky cockroach (*Ectobius lapponicus*) inhabits scrubby habitats, and is found mainly in south central England; the tawny cockroach (*Ectobius pallidus*) inhabits both heath and downland in southern England; while the lesser cockroach (*Ectobius panzeri*) is a predominantly coastal species of southern England, west Wales and East Anglia.

The mantids are included with cockroaches in the order Dictyoptera. The image of the praying mantis (*Mantis religiosa*) is well-known and quite representative of the group, with its powerful and spiny fore legs adapted for catching its prey. There are no native British species, although occasional escapees may be seen. There are up to 15 European species (Battiston *et al.*, 2010), but, with the exception of the praying mantis, these are mainly southern in distribution.

FIG 5. Two native British cockroaches: the dusky cockroach, *Ectobius lapponicus* (left), and the tawny cockroach, *Ectobius pallidus* (right).

FIG 6. A large mantid, *Sphodromantis viridis*, which occurs in southern Spain.

FIG 7. The common earwig, *Forficula auricularia.*

Earwigs (order Dermaptera) are small, dorsoventrally flattened insects. Their distinguishing feature is the modification of the cerci at the tip of the abdomen to form curved pincers, or forceps, that can be used as defensive weapons. They may be with or without wings. In the winged forms the fore wings are reduced to short, hardened flaps that cover the folded-up hind wings when the insects are at rest. As in the other groups discussed so far, the hind legs are not modified for jumping. There are four probably native species, together with a small number of aliens that have become established in Britain (see Marshall & Haes, 1988).

Now to the Orthoptera! Fossil evidence indicates that this is one of the oldest of the insect orders, dating from the late Carboniferous period as much as 300 million years ago (Sharov, 1968; Gorochov *et al.*, 2006). Perhaps the most well-known feature of the grasshoppers, crickets and their allies is that their hind legs are longer than the other two pairs, and adapted for jumping. This is indicated

FIG 8. The male stridulatory apparatus of (left) the speckled bush-cricket, *Leptophyes punctatissima*, and (right) the southern field cricket, *Gryllus bimaculatus*.

in an older name for them: the 'saltatoria'. Another very widespread, but not quite universal, characteristic is the use of sound communication. The males of most species (and the females of some) have specially adapted structures for the production of sound. These are generally body parts so modified that when they are rubbed together a sound is produced, the repetition rate or frequency composition of which is usually distinctive for each species. In some groups there are structures modified to act as resonators which amplify the sound, while some others use vegetation or a chamber in a burrow for this. Most species also have specialised hearing organs, sometimes tuned to the dominant frequency of the song. Receptive females use the song of the male to move towards him, an activity known as 'phonotaxis'. In a few species it is the male that moves to the female. The structures concerned in both sound production and hearing differ very markedly among the different groups of Orthoptera, suggesting that sound

FIG 9. The tibial 'ear' of a bush-cricket, *Phaneroptera falcata*.

communication may have evolved independently several times in the order.

Like other orthopteroids, orthopterans pass through a series of stages in their development from egg to adult. Unlike orders such as Lepidoptera (butterflies and moths) and Coleoptera (beetles), which have a distinct larval (caterpillar) stage followed by a 'resting' pupal stage, the juvenile developmental stages of the orthopteroids resemble smaller versions of the adults. The wings develop externally, and can be seen as small flaps in the nymphal stages (hence the term 'exopterygote' which is used to describe this sort of developmental pattern). What distinguishes the Orthoptera is that in the winged forms (including most of the short-winged, or brachypterous species) the developing wing buds are inverted in the final two nymphal stages. This does not occur in the development of the winged forms in the other orthopteroid orders.

There are believed to be over 25,000 species of Orthoptera worldwide (Orthoptera Species File: http://Orthoptera.SpeciesFile.org), and some 650 in Europe (www.ortheur.org gives 1040, but the geographical scope of this site is wider than that of other estimates). However, partly because of our northerly climate, and partly because of the brief period during which the insects were able to colonise the British Isles, the number of British native species is small: some 28 species. There are also two long-established aliens that remain closely associated with human activity, and a small number of recent additions that appear to be establishing themselves. However, despite the small number of species, the British orthopteran fauna is very diverse both in the range of taxonomic groups that are represented, and in terms of habitat and mode of life.

FIG 10. A final instar nymph of the grey bush-cricket, *Platycleis albopunctata*, showing inverted wing-stubs.

THE SUBDIVISIONS OF THE ORTHOPTERA

The Orthoptera are divided into two main suborders: the Ensifera and the Caelifera.
The Ensifera includes the true crickets (Gryllidae), bush-crickets (Tettigoniidae) and mole-crickets (Gryllotalpidae), as well as more exotic groupings including the ambidextrous crickets (Haglidae), Jerusalem crickets (Stenopelmatidae), king crickets, ground and tree weta (Anostostomatidae), camel-crickets and cave crickets (Rhaphidophoridae), cooloola monsters (Cooloolidae), raspy and leaf-rolling crickets (Gryllacrididae), scaly crickets (Mogoplistidae), splay-footed crickets (Schizodactylidae) and ant-crickets, or ant's nest crickets (Myrmecophilidae). The earliest orthopterans were Ensiferans belonging to groups that are now extinct.

Various authors differ on the higher-level classification of these groupings, and as the majority of families do not have British representatives, it is not necessary to enter too far into taxonomic controversy here. However, several families usually grouped together in the superfamily Stenopelmatoidea, although strictly beyond the scope of this book, are especially interesting, and exhibit characteristics relevant to one of our principal themes. This large and diverse grouping includes predominantly flightless cricket-like species with vernacular names such as cooloolee and dingo monsters, Jerusalem crickets, king crickets and raspy crickets (see Field (Ed.), 2001). As a group they are very widely distributed globally, and have radiated especially in the southern hemisphere. Research on these insects has been slow to develop, but knowledge of them is rapidly expanding. One particularly well-researched grouping are the 'weta' of New Zealand. The term weta is the Maori name given to them. The group shows great disparities between males and females, with males often having enlarged heads and tusk-like mandibles. The ground weta (*Hemiandrus* species) are distinctive in their extensive use of chemical communication, but it is the tree weta (*Hemideina* species) that have attracted most research attention by virtue of their distinctive reproductive behaviour. Males are aggressive, and occupy holes in trees where they gather together 'harems' of females. We will return to a detailed discussion of their extraordinary lifestyle in the chapters on mating systems and sexual selection (Chapters 4, 5 and 6).

The term Ensifera refers to the sword shaped ovipositors possessed by the females of the suborder, although it is not an accurate characterisation of the ovipositors of female crickets. These are variously described as spear or needle shaped. Nevertheless, the general point is valid. Prominent and elongated ovipositors projecting from the rear of the abdomen are almost universal among the females of the suborder. Another characteristic feature, and one present in both males and females, is the pair of long, flexible filamentous antennae. In many species these are as long as or even much longer than the body. As well as providing multi-modal sensory information, the antennae are used extensively in courtship. There are internal anatomical features and DNA evidence that support the view that the different subdivisions of the Ensifera belong together as a natural grouping (Gwynne, 2001).

The other suborder of the Orthoptera is the Caelifera. This suborder evolved later than the Ensifera, probably during the early Triassic, and is likely to have evolved from earlier ensiferans (Gorochov *et al.*, 2006). The term Caelifera may refer to the inconspicuous chisel-shaped ovipositors of the females (in contrast to the sword shaped ones of the Ensifera) (Marshall, pers. corr.). The Caelifera also have shorter, relatively stiff, parallel sided or clubbed antennae, quite different in appearance to the long filamentous and tapering antennae of the Ensifera. By far the greatest number of species worldwide are grasshoppers, or grasshopper-like insects that are assigned together under the superfamily grouping 'Acridomorpha'. This grouping is further subdivided into seven superfamilies, only two of which are represented in the European fauna. These are the Acridoidea and the Pyrgomorphoidea. The latter superfamily is represented in Europe by one genus only: *Pyrgomorpha*, characterised by a distinctive profile, in which the dorsal surface of the head rises from its junction with the pronotum, rather than continuing in the same plane as is usual in grasshoppers.

The superfamily Acridoidea includes eleven families, only two of which are represented in Europe. One of these, the Pamphagidae, includes some of the largest orthopterans in Europe, but their distribution is limited to the extreme south.

The other family is the Acrididae, the principal grasshopper family. Worldwide some 25 subfamilies are distinguished (Orthoptera Species File:

FIG 11. The grasshopper *Pyrgomorpha conica*, from southern Europe.

FIG 12. (left) The Egyptian grasshopper, *Anacridium aegyptium*.

FIG 13. (below) A melanopline grasshopper, *Miramella alpina*, and an acridine grasshopper, *Acrida ungarica*.

http://Orthoptera.SpeciesFile.org), but most of the European species and all of those that are native to Britain belong to just two: the Oedipodinae and the Gomphocerinae.

Other subfamilies with some European species include the subfamily Cyrtacanthacridinae to which belongs the well-known Egyptian grasshopper (*Anacridium aegyptium*), vagrants or escapees of which are frequently reported in Britain.

The subfamily Melanoplinae includes a distinctive group of several mostly brachypterous (short-winged) species that occur in the European mountain ranges, and the subfamily Acridinae includes the elongated, twig-like *Acrida ungarica*.

In addition to the Acridomorpha, there are two further extant superfamiles of the suborder Caelifera. These are the Tridactyloidea and the Tetrigoidea. The Tridactyloidea includes sandhoppers and pygmy mole-crickets and is represented in Europe by just two species (in the family Tridactylidae), *Xya pfaendleri* and *X. variegata*. These are scarce, small southern species that inhabit unvegetated margins of rivers and lakes. They feed on algae, and dig long, winding galleries in the earth where they take refuge in bad weather (Bellmann & Luquet, 2009).

The other caeliferan superfamily is the Tetrigoidea, and it is represented in both Britain and Europe by several members of the family Tetrigidae. In English they are known variously as groundhoppers, pygmy grasshoppers and grouse-locusts. They look superficially like very small grasshoppers, but are distinguished by the extension of the pronotum back over the dorsal surface of the abdomen. Britain has three species, all included in the genus *Tetrix*.

ORTHOPTERANS AND THEIR ENEMIES

One stimulus to the study of diseases, parasites and predators of grasshoppers and crickets has been the hope of biological control over the populations of pest species such as locusts. However, despite the fact that some of their enemies can cause high death rates, the scientific view seems to be that the population dynamics of orthopterans are not, in general, greatly affected (see below and Chapter 9).

Predators of orthopterans include many species of birds, small mammals (especially bats) and reptiles, but they are also highly vulnerable to a range of invertebrate predators, most notably spiders and robber-flies (Diptera: Asilidae), as well as other orthopterans, such as the carnivorous wartbiter bush-cricket. Belwood (1990) describes predation on bush-crickets by forest gleaning bats in South America (see Chapter 5), while Robinson (1980) mentions four British species of bats that pick insects from vegetation, and whose hearing is in the frequency range of the speckled bush-cricket. Gwynne (2001) describes the remarkable convergence of predators on marching bands of mormon crickets in western USA: gulls, lizards, rodents, badgers, over two dozen bird species – and even fish, as the 'katydids' raft over rivers. Even in the absence of such huge concentrations of orthopterans in temperate climates, orthopterans can still constitute important components of the diet of birds – including threatened farmland species, and game birds such as pheasant and partridge (see Chapter 9).

Spiders are serious predators of orthopterans at all developmental stages. Early instar nymphs suffer very high mortality from 'wandering' spiders of family Lycosidae (see Oedekoven & Joern, 1998; Cherrill & Begon, 1989b). Adults and late instar nymphs frequently fall victim to large web-weaving spiders such as the labyrinth spider (*Agelena labyrinthica*), the garden spider (*Araneus diadematus*) and the four-spotted spider (*Araneus quadratus*). The wasp spider (*Argiope bruennichi*), a recent addition to the British spider fauna, is another effective predator of orthopterans.

The females of several species of solitary wasp, the most widespread of which is *Tachysphex pompiliformis*, collect and paralyse grasshoppers. These are carried back to a burrow, where the wasp lays an egg on the underside of the

FIG 14. A wasp spider, *Argiope bruennichi*, with grasshopper prey.

FIG 15. A solitary wasp, *Tachysphex pompiliformis*, with field grasshopper, *Chorthippus brunneus* nymph as prey. (© N. Owens)

thorax between the first and second pairs of legs. Early in the season up to ten grasshopper nymphs may be used to provision a single brood cell, but later a single large nymph may be sufficient. The newly hatched wasp larva feeds on the grasshopper body contents, and emerges from the burrow about a week later. A range of grasshopper species are attacked, including *Chorthippus* species, *Stenobothrus lineatus* and *Myrmeleotettix maculatus* (Edwards (Ed.), 1998; Baldock, 2010; Owens, pers. corr.).

Grasshoppers and bush-crickets are also threatened by a range of invertebrate parasites and parasitoids. One of the most fully studied is the parasitoid fly *Blaesoxipha plumicornis* (Diptera: Sarcophagidae). The female fly gives birth to tiny larvae which she deposits on the abdomen of a grasshopper. The fly larva burrows through the cuticle and feeds on the host's body tissues until it is full grown. It then emerges from the membrane between the grasshopper's head and pronotum, and pupates in soil. Up to four fly larvae have been recorded from a single grasshopper, but more usually only one larva is deposited per host (Richards & Waloff, 1954). Usually it is females that are targeted by the fly, possibly because they are more readily detected as they move toward singing males, or because they are a more nutritious host for the larva. The host grasshopper invariably dies when the fly larva has completed its development.

The eggs of grasshoppers and bush-crickets are also vulnerable to parasitism, especially by wasps of the genus *Scelio* (Hymenoptera: Scelionidae). Richards and Waloff (1954) estimated the level of parasitism in eggs of *Chorthippus parallelus* and *C. brunneus* at their study site as between 19 and 28 per cent of egg pods, with most eggs in each parasitised pod being affected (see Chapter 9 for more detail). A study cited by Brown (1983) reported four out of ten pods of *C. brunneus*, and three out of thirteen of *C. parallelus* affected, but only seven or eight percent of eggs were parasitised. A chalcid wasp (Hymenoptera: Chalcidae) is reported as an egg parasite of the short-winged conehead (*Conocephalus dorsalis*) (Blair, 1948).

Orthopterans are also parasitized by nematode worms, and are very vulnerable to various pathogenic fungi and bacterial diseases. Grasshopper victims of the fungus *Entomophthera* can sometimes be seen with their legs wrapped around the stems of grasses (Marshall & Haes, 1988). Streett & McGuire (1990) give a wide-ranging review of the diseases of grasshoppers.

The calling song of male orthopterans provides one important means by which potential predators and parasites are able to locate them. Such 'acoustically orienting' enemies have hearing that is sensitive to the frequency range of their host species. Belwood's study, mentioned above, details predation by acoustically orienting bats, and birds such as screech owls, as well as carnivorous bush-crickets and mantids, which prey on bush-crickets of the subfamily Pseudophyllinae in South American forests. Flies of the widespread family Tachinidae are well-known parasitoids of other insects, and some (tribe Ormiini) parasitise crickets, mole-crickets and bush-crickets. Like the females of *Blaesoxipha*, the flies deposit their young larvae on the abdomen of their host. The larva goes on to consume the body tissues of the host ensiferan, emerging when fully grown, and pupating outside the host's body. The flies use the calling song of the male orthopteran to locate it, so it is mostly males that are parasitised (Cade ,1975; Allen, 2000; review in Robinson & Hall, 2002).

Under selection pressure from intense predation and parasitism, orthopterans have evolved numerous defensive strategies. Primary defences are ones that operate independently of the actual presence of a potential threat. Most grasshoppers and crickets are cryptically coloured, and often have shapes that mimic the structures of vegetation such as leaves or twigs (for example, the leaf mimics of the Pseudophyllinae, see Gwynne, 2001, plates 10 to 13). A few species (but none of the British ones) have adopted bright 'aposematic' colour patterns that are believed to act as a warning to potential predators, and a few are mimics of other invertebrates – notably spiders and ants. Marshall & Haes

FIG 16. Spider-like early instar nymph of the dark bush-cricket, *Pholidoptera griseoaptera*.

(1988) give as an example of the former the similarity of early nymphs of the dark bush-cricket (*P. griseoaptera*) to a lycosid spider, and the greenhouse camel-cricket (*D. asynamorus*) is also remarkably spider-like. The early instars of the south east Asian conocephaline bush-cricket *Macroxyphus sumatranus* look and behave in ways that closely resemble ants (Gwynne, 2001). These are presumably adaptations that offer some protection against visual predators.

If a potential predator or parasite is detected, one option is to remain perfectly still on the expectation that camouflage will be effective. However, if the threat appears urgent (as when approached by large mammals such as humans – see below) the main alternatives are to dive deep into long grasses or other deep vegetation, or to jump or fly. The first of these is available only in some microhabitats, but it is very effective. Jumping or flying has several disadvantages. First, it attracts attention, offsetting its value as a means of escape; second, it is energetically costly; and, third, it runs the risk of blundering into a spider's web. However, the jump/fly response is often effective if, as very often seems to be the case, the fugitive is able to 'disappear' by landing on a suitable background and remaining motionless. In a few species, potential predators are greeted by a defensive 'startle' behaviour, often combining a distinctive threat posture with an aggressive stridulation. Some of the most striking examples are provided by the giant and tree weta of New Zealand (Field & Glasgow, 2001).

Acoustically orienting predators and parasitoids exert selective pressures on songsters – predominantly males. However, singing is likely to have been evolved by sexual selection through competition with other males and the need to attract potential mates. There is thus some tension between pressures to enhance reproductive success and the heightened vulnerability to predation and parasitism that song brings with it. Possible defences include developing the ability to detect a potential enemy before it becomes an immediate threat, singing at times when potential enemies are not active, or switching to a different call frequency (or even to an alternative channel of communication, such as vibration ('tremulation')). Ceasing to call as a potential predator approaches is another tactic (ter Hofstede *et al.*, 2008), as is simply calling briefly and intermittently, so that an enemy does not have time to effectively locate the caller.

Assuming that there is a trade-off between the reproductive success of males and the increased vulnerability to predation or parasitism imposed by their calling song, it is to be expected that natural selective pressures will have influenced the pattern of acoustic communication in species that suffer from acoustically orienting enemies.

It may be speculated that the very brief and intermittent chirps of the speckled bush-cricket (*Leptophyes punctatissima*), together with the call-and-response pattern established when a willing female answers a male chirp, could be a system that has evolved in response to predation or parasitism from acoustically orienting hunters (Robinson, 1980; Robinson *et al.*, 1986; Robinson, 1990). A recent case of 'evolution in action' is reported from a Hawaiian island on which males of the cricket *Teleogryllus oceanicus* have suffered intense selective pressure from a parasitoid tachinid fly (*Ormia ochracea*). In a few generations most of the males have evolved as flat-winged forms, no longer able to sing. This is despite the fact that females continue to show preference for calling males (Zuk *et al.*, 2006; Bailey and Zuk, 2008. See Chapter 5 for more details).

THE BRITISH ORTHOPTERA

The 28 British native species, together with the two long-established aliens and two recent colonists, include representatives of five families of the Ensifera (Rhaphidophoridae, Tettigoniidae, Gryllidae, Mogoplistidae and Gryllotalpidae) and, among the Caelifera, the Tetrigidae and two subfamilies of the Acrididae. Detailed accounts of the appearance, life history, behaviour, habitat and distribution of the individual species will be given in Chapters 7 and 8. This section will provide an introduction to the main distinctive features of each family or subfamily grouping.

ENSIFERA

1. Rhaphidophoridae (camel-crickets)
The greenhouse camel-cricket (*Diestrammena* (formerly *Tachycines*) *asynamorus*) is a long-established alien, now occurring rarely in heated greenhouses. It is the

FIG 17. The greenhouse camel-cricket, *Diestrammena asynamorus*, female.

only established breeding species of this family in Britain. The camel-crickets are wingless and also lack either hearing organs or means of stridulation. However, they do have vibration receptors (subgenual organs) in the tibiae. The females have long, slightly up-turned ovipositors. The antennae are especially long, often several times the length of the body, and the legs are also long and spindly, giving a spider-like appearance. They live in caves or other dark, humid places, and are often gregarious, interacting frequently by stroking one another with their antennae.

2. Tettigoniidae (bush-crickets)

The bush-crickets are also sometimes referred to as long-horned grasshoppers, and in America and Australasia are commonly called 'katydids', a word thought to be an onomatopoeic representation of the song of an American species, *Pterophylla camellifolia* (Gwynne, 2001: 18–19). Fossil remains of ancestral bush-crickets date from at least the mid Triassic (although Gwynne (2001), following Sharov (1968), places them as early as the late Permian – some 250 million years ago). There are ten native British species, and two recent colonists.

The bush-cricket body is roughly tubular (that is, not dorsoventrally flattened), the antennae are long and filamentous, the hind legs are long and adapted for jumping, and the tarsi have four segments. The pronotum is saddle-shaped, with the rear edge of the dorsal surface curved. In fully winged species the wings are folded back over the dorsal surface of the abdomen when the insect is at rest. The males of most species produce sound by rubbing together their fore wings (tegmina). These are structurally modified for this function,

FIG 18. (top) Female great green bush-cricket, *Tettigonia viridissima*, a fully winged species; (left) male dark bush cricket, *Pholidoptera griseoaptera*, showing fore wings (tegmina) reduced to stridulatory apparatus only.

and in the males of some species with reduced wings the stridulatory apparatus comprises most of the wing. In bush-crickets the sound is produced by scraping the left tegmen over the right. In just two species that occur in Britain there is no stridulation, but the males produce a sound by drumming with one leg against a substrate. The specialised hearing organs consist of a pair of 'ears' each located in a fore tibia, just below the knee. The tibial ears are linked internally by extended tracheal tubes to a pair of auditory spiracles located on the sides of the first segment of the thorax (see Chapter 2 for more details).

The females have conspicuous ovipositors that project from the rear of the abdomen. Although the ancestors of bush-crickets are believed to have laid their eggs in the soil, the majority now lay their eggs (singly or in small batches) in plant tissue. The straight or sickle-shaped ovipositors are used to insert the eggs into the appropriate substrate. The ovipositor is made up of three pairs of

TABLE 1.1. Oviposition substrates used by British bush-crickets (adapted from Gwynne, 2001, Table 3.1)

Species	Leaf tissue	Leaf sheaths	In pith of stems	Dry plants	Bark crevices	Soil
Phaneroptera falcata	X					
Leptophyes punctatissima				X	X	
Meconema thalassinum					X	
Conocephalus discolor		X	X			
Conocephalus dorsalis		X	X		X	
Tettigonia viridissima						X
Decticus verrucivorus						X
Platycleis albopunctata		?	X			
Metrioptera brachyptera		X				X
Metrioptera roeselii		X	X	X		
Pholidoptera griseoaptera		X	X			X

articulated valves, through which the eggs pass, singly, into the selected medium. In a few species that lay their eggs in tough plant tissue (such as the bark of trees – e.g. M. thalassinum) the material may be excavated or softened by chewing first. Some species that lay their eggs in plant stems, such as Roesel's bush-cricket (M. roeselii) and the short-winged conehead (C. dorsalis), nibble holes in the outer cuticle of the stem prior to piercing it with their ovipositors (see the DVD selections on these species).

Variation in the shapes of ovipositors may be related to the kind of substrate used and also the ovipositing technique employed. The robust, straight ovipositors of the great green bush-cricket (T. viridissima) and the wartbiter (D. verrucivorus) are supposed to be an adaptation to their habit of ovipositing in soil. The short, stubby ovipositor of the sickle-bearing bush-cricket (P. falcata) is adapted for its habit of laying its eggs between the epidermal layers of leaves.

The males have a pair of cerci that are used to grip the female during mating, and, in some cases, to prolong copulation by constraining her movements. A general feature of the mating systems of the bush-crickets (shared with a few other orthopteran groups) is that during mating the male transfers not just the sperm and associated fluid to the female, but also a gelatinous mass, known as the spermatophylax. The female subsequently eats this, and the function of these 'nuptial gifts' has inspired a great deal of fascinating research and controversy

FIG 19. (a) Ovipositor of a female warbiter, *Decticus verrucivorus*; (b) female wartbiter egg-laying in the ground; (c) eggs of the short-winged conehead in stem of the sea clubrush, *Bolboschoenus maritimus*; (d) ovipositor of the short-winged conehead, *Conocephalus discolor*.

(see Chapters 4 and 6). The bush-crickets are usually omnivorous or vegetarian, but a few are predatory carnivores, feeding on small invertebrates. As the English name implies, the bush-crickets generally live among vegetation, although a few have become secondarily adapted for life on the ground. Depending on species, there are from four to eight nymphal instars, and the life cycle may be annual or, in some species, may be prolonged by an extended embryonic period in the egg for two or more years (up to seven years). The wing stubs in winged species are inverted for the final two instars (see Chapter 3).

3. Crickets (Gryllidae)

Although ancestral gryllids were present from the mid- to late-Triassic period, the true crickets did not make an appearance until the early Cretaceous (some 130 million years ago). The British gryllid cricket fauna is very limited, with only two native species, and one established alien. The antennae are long and filamentous, the body is flattened dorsoventrally, and the dorsal surface of the pronotum is rectangular. The hind legs are longer than the fore and mid legs, but not so markedly as in the bush-crickets. The hind legs are also sturdy, and not spindly, as in the bush-crickets. Both males and females have long straight cerci, and the ovipositor of the females is straight with a pointed swelling at the tip, and projects backwards from the rear end of the abdomen. Males have rows of spines facing outwards from their hind tibiae.

In fully winged species the hardened tegmina are folded back and around the sides of the abdomen when the insect is at rest. Males of most species are able to produce sounds by stridulation. As in the bush-crickets, the sound is produced by scraping one tegmen over the other, but in the gryllid crickets, it is the right tegmen that is moved over the left. The 'ears' of the crickets are, like those of the bush-crickets, located on the fore tibiae, and linked to auditory spiracles on the first thoracic segment. However, there are some structural differences, and it is believed that hearing evolved independently in the two families.

The life cycles differ greatly from species to species, and sometimes within a species, depending on climate. Eggs are usually laid in the soil rather than in plant material, and there may be from eight to eleven nymphal instars. As in other orthopterans, the wing stubs (in winged species) are inverted for the final two instars. Several of the structural features of the crickets can be seen as adaptive for life on the ground, rather than in vegetation, and most species take shelter in holes or under leaf litter, while others (such as the field cricket, *Gryllus campestris*) dig burrows.

FIG 20. Female field cricket, *Gryllus campestris.*

4. Scaly crickets (Mogoplistidae)

The family is widespread globally, but only one British species is known. Formerly considered a subfamily of the Gryllidae, the scaly crickets are so called because their body surface is covered with minute fragile scales, giving them a rough, granular appearance. The body is flattened dorsoventrally, and wings are entirely absent in most species. There are no stridulatory organs, and no tibial hearing organs. The antennae are used constantly in communication with conspecifics and in monitoring the environment. Both sexes have long, tapering cerci, and there are three tarsal segments. The hind legs are shorter than in most other Ensifera, but the crickets retain the ability to jump. The female ovipositor is spear-shaped, as in the true crickets.

FIG 21. Female scaly cricket, *Pseudomogoplistes vicentae*.

5. Mole-crickets (Gryllotalpidae)

It seems that the mole-crickets evolved somewhat later than the Gryllidae, during the Cretaceous period. There is just one British species, which is close to extinction, although there are relatively frequent reports of accidental imports of alien species in plant material. The most striking feature of the mole-crickets is the enlargement and structural modification of the fore legs

FIG 22. The mole cricket, *Gryllotalpa gryllotalpa*. (© B. Pinchen)

for digging. Together, the head and pronotum form a smoothly tapering egg shape, and the hind legs are secondarily reduced in size, so that the overall shape of the insect is modified for its mainly subterranean habit. The antennae are short, compared with those of the other ensiferan groups, and there is a pair of long, straight cerci at the tip of the abdomen. The hind tarsi have three segments. The short tegmina are hardened and, in the males, structurally modified for stridulation, with the hind-wings furled over the abdomen as in winged species of true crickets. The females lack the prominent ovipositor characteristic of other ensiferans. Females remain in their burrows with the eggs and are almost unique among the Orthoptera in showing maternal care of the eggs and early instar nymphs.

CAELIFERA

1. Groundhoppers (Tetrigidae)

The groundhoppers are small relatives of the grasshoppers. The antennae are short and the long hind legs are adapted for jumping. The most obvious difference between them and the grasshoppers is the backward extension of the pronotum over the dorsal surface of the abdomen, and in some species beyond its tip. The fore wings are reduced to small lateral flaps, while the hind wings are fan-folded under the pronotum. There are two segments in the tarsi of the fore and mid legs, three in the tarsi of the hind legs, and there is no arolium (small pad or swelling) between the claws. There appear to be no stridulatory or hearing organs. The eggs are laid in batches in the soil or among low-growing plants, and the resulting nymphs pass through five instars in the male, six in the female. There are three British species.

FIG 23. The common groundhopper, *Tetrix undulata*.

2. Grasshoppers (Acrididae)

The grasshoppers are the most familiar of the orthopteran groups. They are common, and sometimes abundant, in a range of grassland types. The antennae are short and either parallel-sided or thickened towards the tip – sometimes club-tipped (as in butterflies). The pronotum is saddle shaped and has several features that are important for identification. When viewed from above, the rear edge of the pronotum is curved outwards, but does not project back over the abdomen as in the groundhoppers.

There is a fine longitudinal ridge, or keel, along the midline of the dorsal surface of the pronotum (the 'discus'). There are two more longitudinal keels, one on each side of the discus of the pronotum. These may be straight and almost parallel, more or less strongly curved inwards, or angled inwards ('indented'). There is also a fine groove ('median suture') that runs transversely across the discus.

Most species are fully winged, with the tegmina hardened, and both pairs of wings folded back over the abdomen when the insect is at rest. Some species (including one British species, *Chorthippus parallelus*) have their wings markedly reduced, although in some such species there are long-winged forms. The hind legs are long, and grasshoppers are generally very effective jumpers. Fully winged species are able to supplement their jumps with flights of ten metres or more.

Most species have a distinctive song produced by the male, and sometimes also by the female. There are two subfamilies with representatives among the British species. In subfamily **Oedipodinae** sound is usually produced by scraping a ridge on the hind femur over a prominent vein in the tegmen. In the one native British oedipodine grasshopper (*Stethophyma grossum*) a series of sharp clicking sounds is made by flicking a hind tibia against the adjacent wing tip (see DVD).

FIG 24. The common field grasshopper, *Chorthippus brunneus*, male.

FIG 25. Dorsal surface of the pronotum of grasshoppers, showing the shape of the lateral keels: (a) lesser marsh grasshopper, *Chorthippus albomarginatus*; (b) meadow grasshopper, *Chorthippus parallelus*; (c) common green grasshopper, *Omocestus viridulus*; (d) field grasshopper, *Chorthippus brunneus*.

Most British species belong to subfamily **Gomphocerinae**, and in this group sound is produced by scraping a row of tiny pegs on the hind femur against a prominent (radial) vein on the flexed tegmen. Both hind femora are used, often to some extent out of synchronisation with one another. Some species have elaborate courtship performances, including both song and dance. The hearing organs are a pair of distinct auditory cavities located at the sides of the first abdominal segment.

The female ovipositor is short, with two pairs of valves, whose shape is useful in the identification of some species. Males have an up-turned subgenital plate at the tip of the abdomen, and different profiles of the abdomen tips are useful in distinguishing males from females. Both sexes have a pair of short cerci.

The eggs are laid in batches among grasses or in the soil. They are surrounded by a secretion that hardens into a pod. In temperate climates the winter is usually spent in the egg stage, the nymphs hatching the following

FIG 26. Tip of the abdomen of male (left) and female (right) of the lesser marsh grasshopper, *Chorthippus albomarginatus*.

spring and passing through four or five nymphal instars. As in other winged orthopterans, the developing wing pads are inverted in the final two nymphal stages. There are eleven British species (with a further two that occur in the Channel Islands).

WHERE ARE HOW TO FIND GRASSHOPPERS AND CRICKETS

A glance at the distribution maps for the British species reveals one very clear pattern: more than a third of the native species occur only south of a line between southern coastal districts of Wales, the Bristol Channel and the Wash. The distribution of others reaches not much further north, while even the hardy species that are widespread throughout mainland Britain often become noticeably more localised northwards. Ireland, while not significantly different climatically from the rest of the British Isles, has only twelve species. D. Ragge (1963, 1965, 1988) has provided a powerful explanatory framework for this pattern. His analysis combines historical climates, geological formations and vegetation cover, together with understanding of the habitat requirements and climatic tolerances of our orthopteran fauna. Conditions prior to the retreat of the ice at the end of the last glaciation (approximately 12,000 years ago) were too cold for all of the species that currently occur here. At that time, the lowering of the sea level due to the formation of the ice cap had allowed the formation of a land bridge between the British and continental mainlands, and another between the west of northern Britain and the north of Ireland.

As the climate continued to warm, and the ice to retreat, orthopteran species began to colonise what eventually became southern Britain. Cold-tolerant species such as the common field grasshopper (*C. brunneus*), the common green grasshopper (*O. viridulus*), the common groundhopper (*T. undulata*), the speckled bush-cricket (*L. punctatissima*) and the oak bush-cricket (*M. thalassinum*) are likely to have been the first to colonise. These would have spread northwards and, together with the mottled grasshopper (*M. maculatus*), the large marsh grasshopper (*S. grossum*), the lesser marsh grasshopper (*C. albomarginatus*), and the mole-cricket (*G. gryllotalpa*), would then have crossed the land bridge between mainland Britain and Ireland. By the onset of the Boreal period (some 9,000 years ago) sea-level rise cut off Ireland and the Isle of Man from the British mainland, preventing any more orthopteran species from colonising Ireland from the rest of the British Isles. Some time later (Ragge suggests between 9,000 and 8,000 years ago) further sea-level rise isolated the British mainland from continental Europe, preventing further colonisation of Britain from the rest of Europe. This historical sequence helps to explain why species that endure more hostile climates in northern Europe, and probably could survive in Britain, still do not occur here. It seems that their post-glacial northward migration through what is now France took place too late for them to cross the land bridge.

Ragge's account makes good sense of the absence of the meadow grasshopper (*C. parallelus*) from Ireland and the Isle of Man: its inability to fly may have slowed down its range expansion into northern Britain, so that it arrived at the land bridge too late to colonise them. However, as he acknowledges, his account has difficulty in making sense of the isolated population of the lesser mottled grasshopper (*S. stigmaticus*) on the Isle of Man. Did it formerly have a more widespread distribution in England? If so, what explains its extinction everywhere else? On the assumption of a north-western land bridge to Ireland, the presence there of highly localised populations of the dark bush-cricket (*P. griseoaptera*) and Roesel's bush-cricket (*M. roeselii*) also seems puzzling. Although Roesel's bush-cricket has recently extended its British range both northwards and eastwards, its known historical range was far distant from the land bridge to Ireland. The dark bush-cricket's current range does reach to south-west Scotland, but its known distribution in Ireland is confined to restricted areas in the south and west. It is, of course, possible that the geographical gaps in the currently known distribution of these species were filled in previous, warmer epochs, with subsequent contraction leaving isolated relict populations.

With the climatic warming that took place following the arrival of the native orthopteran fauna came also a rapid spread of forest cover. This would have severely limited range extensions on the part of almost all species, and it seems likely that they remained confined to small areas of open ground, perhaps on the coasts, river margins, and adjacent to early human settlements. On Ragge's account, deforestation would have begun in earnest from around 5,000 years ago in Neolithic times, when the East Anglian Brecks and southern downlands were cleared. By the end of the Roman occupation only half of the forest remained, and orthopterans would have had much greater opportunities for dispersal. However, their subsequent patterns of dispersal would have been limited both by a climate that was by now cooler in the summers, and by features of geology, land forms and vegetation cover.

Ragge's analysis focuses on the Hampshire basin – including the New Forest, the Isle of Purbeck and the Isle of Wight. This remains the richest area in Britain for Orthoptera. The sands and clays of the New Forest and the heaths of north Purbeck are fringed by calcareous downland ridges. The acidic sandy soils are nutrient poor, and so do not support luxurious vegetation, while the valley bottoms have become waterlogged because of the underlying clay. These conditions support the boggy hollows where species such as the large marsh grasshopper (S. grossum) and bog bush-cricket (M. brachyptera) thrive, while on drier heathland and scrubby woodland occur the woodland grasshopper (O. rufipes) and the wood cricket (N. sylvestris), as well as small populations of the rare heath grasshopper (C. vagans). On the warm, south-facing slopes of the downland can be found the great green bush-cricket (T. viridissima) and stripe-winged grasshopper (S. lineatus). A similar pattern of wet and dry heathland and chalk downland is to be found to the north and east, in the London basin, in the shape of the North Downs, South Downs and Surrey heaths.

These areas remain prime hunting grounds for Orthoptera enthusiasts, but there are many opportunities for the study of these fascinating insects elsewhere. Some species are to be found in a wide range of coastal habitats, while others can still be found in the wider countryside, and in urban locations where intensive agriculture or excessive tidy-mindedness have so far failed to eliminate them. As will be discussed at greater length in Chapter 9, the post-war transition to more intensive agriculture over large areas of southern and central England must have devastated populations of the commoner grasshoppers and bush-crickets. Orthoptera are virtually absent from intensive arable cropland, while the nutrient enrichment and commercially dictated cutting regimes of hay meadows allow the survival of no more than two or three very resilient species of grasshopper. Lightly grazed pasture seems to be favourable to a few more common species. Loss of hedgerows and copses, too, will have eradicated much of the habitat of species such as the oak, speckled and dark bush-crickets on farmland.

However, there are some compensations. Fragments of suitable habitat do persist – often unintentionally – in intensively managed farmland. Some

FIG 27. New Forest wet heath, habitat of the large marsh grasshopper, *Stethophyma grossum*, and the bog bush-cricket, *Metrioptera brachyptera*.

hedgerows and woodland have survived, and are increasingly valued by many farmers and other land managers. Alongside hedgerows there are often footpaths, bridleways and cart tracks, and these, together with ditches, continue to provide habitat for as many as eight or nine species. Other patches of suitable habitat for several species are incidental products of modern infrastructures such as coastal flood defences, the cuttings and embankments of motorways, the verges of lanes and roads, open areas in forestry plantations and margins of reservoirs. Special mention here should be made of many so-called brownfield sites, former industrial land that has benefited from neglect of formal management and has acquired a rich botanical diversity and invertebrate fauna. Such sites are frequent targets for developers, and need to be actively advocated and defended.

Many areas set aside for public recreation, such as urban parks and gardens, country parks, and rural 'visitor attractions' such as stately homes and gardens, have a good range of Orthoptera species, and it is well worth surveying them and highlighting their value to owners and managers. Finally, alarm about the loss of biodiversity associated with agricultural intensification and urbanisation has led to a shift of policy in the direction of conservation. Land managers can apply for

FIG 28. A so-called 'brownfield' site on Canvey Island, Essex, with an exceptionally rich invertebrate fauna.

government funding to set aside land from commercial production in favour of habitat provision. In addition both statutory and voluntary bodies have established nature reserves where the interests of biodiversity conservation are given (or *should* be given) priority in the management regime. Such measures have undoubtedly been to some degree beneficial, but newer approaches that conceptualise nature conservation at the level of whole interconnected landscapes may offer more promise for the future if adequate funding can be gained.

The above discussion should provide some suggestions as to *where* to look for grasshoppers and crickets, but not necessarily *how* to do so! Often, if the day is warm, and the observer is possessed of good hearing, the general location of a suitable site to survey can be made on the basis of the songs of the grasshoppers. Otherwise, experience soon enables one to spot a potentially suitable patch of habitat. Having found such a place, perhaps the simplest method is to walk slowly through the area, watching out for the insects to jump or briefly fly as they attempt to escape. Even then, locating the insect is not always easy. A grasshopper will often touch a grass stem before it lands, and while its hunter is distracted by the movement, it will have disappeared a few inches further on. While some species remain motionless and perfectly camouflaged once they land, others dive down into the depths of vegetation.

Even when located, grasshoppers and bush-crickets keep a close watch, and even a slow, gentle approach to get a close look at structure or markings will often trigger another jump. Alternatively, the insect will swivel around the grass stem so that only its feet are visible. A hand passed around the other side of the stem will sometimes persuade it to swivel back again – but only sometimes! The method of walking slowly and searching visually when they jump or fly is probably the best way of locating groundhoppers, as they make no sound. Here, some experience of their favoured habitats and geographical distribution is a most useful aid.

With experience, and good hearing, it is possible to locate and identify many species by noting distinctive features of their song. For those of us with a deteriorating ability to pick up high-frequency sounds, a bat detector is invaluable. Again, some experience is necessary to recognise the modified sounds of the different species, but when this can be done the detector is a great help with surveying for bush-crickets, especially. Speckled bush-crickets, the coneheads, grey bush-crickets, wartbiters and, for some of us, even Roesel's bush-crickets, are very difficult or outright impossible to hear unaided. Surveying in Essex using a bat detector has revealed that the speckled bush-cricket, for example, is far more widespread then would have been guessed from visual sightings. Even those with exceptionally acute hearing still may benefit from the use of bat detectors (Baldock, 1999; Gardiner et al., 2010).

The oak and southern oak bush-crickets do not stridulate, and I have no evidence that the sound of their drumming can be used by humans to locate them. Several methods are recommended. They fly at night, and the oak bush-cricket comes to light, often entering lighted rooms, or intervening during moth-trapping sessions. It is said they may be found as road casualties after being dislodged from their perches by high winds. Another method, which is hard work but moderately successful for both species, is beating the lower branches of deciduous trees, while holding a purpose-made beating tray, or inverted umbrella, below. This seems to be more effective as a means of finding nymphs than adults – either simply because they are more numerous, or, possibly, because the adults tend to live in higher foliage. Finally, shining a torch on the trunks of trees at night is said to be an effective method of finding the females (Hawkins, 2001) – although in some areas this might put one at some personal risk from other humans!

Surveying the range of Orthoptera inhabiting particular sites can be very valuable if evidence is needed to defend an area from unsuitable development, or give advice on management. Despite their lack of gaudy decoration, grasshoppers and crickets are very beautiful animals, and make excellent photographic subjects. Photography is also an extremely useful aid to identification for the beginner. Although very high-quality photographs can now be taken using low-priced cameras, it is helpful to be able to obtain a large image while working at some distance from the subject. A macro lens (e.g. 200 mm) or camera with a macro setting is therefore advisable. For identification from photographs it is important to get a clear view of the diagnostic features. So, for example, a dorsal view of the side keels of the pronotum together with a lateral view showing the leading edge of the fore wing in focus are required for the identification of many grasshoppers. A clear view of the shape of the ovipositor in female bush-crickets is another example.

Filming the fascinating behaviour of orthopterans can also be a great source of interest and information. As I found, for someone without experience of filming, there is initially a very steep learning curve! Even with a degree of ability to work the technology, the problems of filming in the field are legion. As the subjects necessitate use of macro settings, filming without a tripod is impossible, even for those with a very steady hand. This means that filming has to be done from a static viewpoint, given the disturbance caused by attempting to move a tripod around in long grass, scrub or heath. This problem can only be addressed by getting to know the site very well before beginning filming. With experience it is possible to get a sense of exactly where and when during the day certain species come to bask, or sing, or carry out their courtship. Then it is a matter of setting up the tripod and camera, and waiting quietly in the hope that something will happen. Often it doesn't, and the main reward of a day's fieldwork will be aching legs and a liberal covering of insect bites. However, the satisfaction to be gained when things do happen, and one can view the results on a TV screen in the evening, is ample compensation. I guess the required attitude of mind is very similar to that needed for angling.

For more help with identification as well as scientific research projects, sound recording of orthopteran songs has a most important role to play. Pioneering work by D. W. Ragge in field recording of the songs of grasshoppers and crickets has contributed to the taxonomy of European species by showing how song is often a key element in the development of reproductive isolation between populations and the differentiation of species. In grasshoppers and bush-crickets the frequency spectrum of the song seems to be less significant than the rhythmic pattern of sound intensity. This has been represented by Ragge and others in the form of oscillograms which are distinctive for each species, and also show some revealing differences within species. Ragge describes the technique, and provides song analyses and oscillograms for the western European species in Ragge & Reynolds (1998).

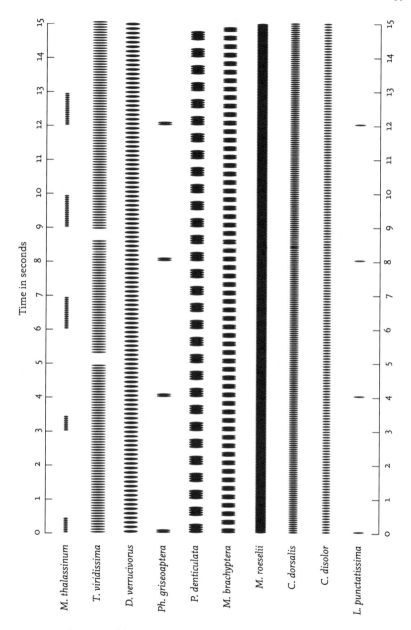

FIG 29. Song diagrams of the British Orthoptera, drawn from oscillograms by D. Ragge (reproduced from Ragge 1965, figs 38 and 58, with permission).

Finally, for some purposes it is important to be able to estimate the size of orthopteran populations in a given area. Several methods have been used. These include catching, marking and releasing insects. Subsequently samples are recaptured, and overall population size can be calculated from the proportions of marked to non-marked individuals among the new sample. Other methods include using a sweep-net and passing it through vegetation in a standardised way, counting insects in quadrats laid out at intervals across a site and walking a standard transect across a site, counting the insects flushed as one walks. Pit-fall traps are also sometimes used, although these are more useful for indicating the presence or absence of species than for estimating population sizes. Each of these survey techniques has its advantages and disadvantages, and these vary according to the purpose of the research and the nature of the habitat under study. An excellent critical review is Gardiner *et al.*, 2005.

ABOUT THIS BOOK

Chapter 2 is about 'mechanics'. It gives an account of the main external features of the orthopteran body, together with brief introductions to the basic mechanisms underlying sight, hearing, and the chemical senses. The processes involved in generating the distinctive motor responses to these sensory inputs are also described, for example, how orthopterans achieve their extraordinary leaps, fly and steer their phonotactic movements.

Chapter 3 introduces some of the diversity of orthopteran life cycles. Two key themes are the focus of the chapter. One is the various ways in which grasshoppers and crickets can vary the timing of the different phases of their life cycle in relation to the seasons, or to deal with adverse climatic conditions. The other theme is the phenomenon of alternative developmental pathways that are available within populations of some species. The most widely known examples are, of course, the phase transitions of locusts, but the production of minorities of long-winged forms in normally short-winged species is observed in a few British species. The coexistence in populations of many species of a variety of colour forms also poses puzzles that have been addressed in the scientific literature.

Chapters 4, 5 and 6 should be taken together, as they deal with aspects of a common theme: the reproductive behaviour of orthopterans. As almost all species reproduce sexually, reproduction involves at least these necessary stages: locating a potential mate, getting up close, persuading him or her to cooperate, and mating (in fact, as we shall see, there are more). It is commonly assumed that sexual reproduction is a cooperative process, in which both partners share an interest. However, it has long been recognised that conflict is also involved: males often compete for females, and females frequently reject the advances of males. Darwin went so far as to suggest that inheritable differences that conferred advantages in the struggle for sexual partners constituted a distinct evolutionary mechanism – sexual selection – alongside natural selection. Chapter 4 traces some of the history of debate about this idea, and more recent developments which emphasise the asymmetry of male and female interests and the evolutionary significance of sexual conflict. Chapter 5 is concerned mainly with the first steps in the reproductive process: how males signal their presence to potential mates, how rival males react to this 'advertisement', and how receptive females recognise and respond to it. The focus, then, is on the use of song, and the extent to which females exhibit preferences on the basis of its quality or persistence. Chapter 6 reports on further phases in the encounter between male and female, including courtship, mating, the transfer of sperm and the methods by which males attempt to ensure that it is their sperm that fertilises the female's eggs. The diversity of behaviour exhibited across the different orthopteran groups is astonishing – from the elaborate song-and-dance routines of some grasshoppers, to the provision of gelatinous 'nuptial gifts' by male bush-crickets and the guarding of harems in holes in trees by male tree weta of New Zealand. The chapter draws on a selection from the vast international literature that describes and attempts to interpret these 'mating systems' in terms of the ideas of sexual selection and conflicts of interest between males and females.

Chapters 7, 8 and 9 deal exclusively with British species (including a small number that are not, or not yet, fully resident, but may occasionally be found here). Species and varieties found in the Channel Islands but not in mainland Britain are not included (see Evans & Edmondson, 2007). Preceding this group of chapters is an identification key to the British species (pp. 217–238). The aim is to enable identification on the basis of clear photographs, without the need to catch or kill specimens. A few structural features that may be difficult to see in a photograph are mentioned for confirmation of the identification of some species. Chapter 7 consists of species accounts for the British Ensifera (bush-crickets, crickets and the mole-cricket). Photographs and descriptions are given for each species, together with accounts of the main variant forms, methods for distinguishing it from lookalikes, and details of behaviour, life cycle, habitat, British distribution and any conservation issues. Chapter 8 repeats the exercise for the Caelifera (groundhoppers and grasshoppers).

Chapter 9 brings together material from previous chapters to inform a general discussion of the habitats, distribution and conservation issues concerning the British Orthoptera.

CHAPTER 2

Orthoptera: structure and function
Singing, hearing, jumping and flying

Subsequent chapters will be devoted to the natural history of orthopterans – their adaptations to their habitats and modes of life, their reproductive interactions, methods of avoiding predators and parasites, and so on. This chapter aims to provide a brief outline of the mechanisms underlying these different activities. Grasshoppers, crickets and their relatives are equipped with specialised sensory organs that detect vibration, sound, moisture, taste and smell. They also have well-developed visual acuity. Sensory inputs from this range of sources are processed in the nervous system and issue in nervous and hormonal messages, which in turn trigger motor activities such as feeding, flying, mating, egg-laying and jumping. There is space here to deal with only some of these sensory and motor activities, and only in a summary way. However, there should be enough information to give the reader a sense not only of how these insects achieve such remarkable feats of, for example, direction-finding, thermoregulation, or escaping, but also of their limitations and vulnerabilities. Because of the special place of sound communication in the lives of most orthopterans, the mechanisms involved in this will be explored in a dedicated section.

The chapter begins with a brief guide to the main bodily features of grasshoppers and crickets, and this will be referred to in other chapters. Some knowledge of this is essential for identifying specimens, as well as for understanding many descriptions of their behaviour.

EXTERNAL FEATURES

There are features of structure and associated sensory and motor abilities that are widely shared across the order.

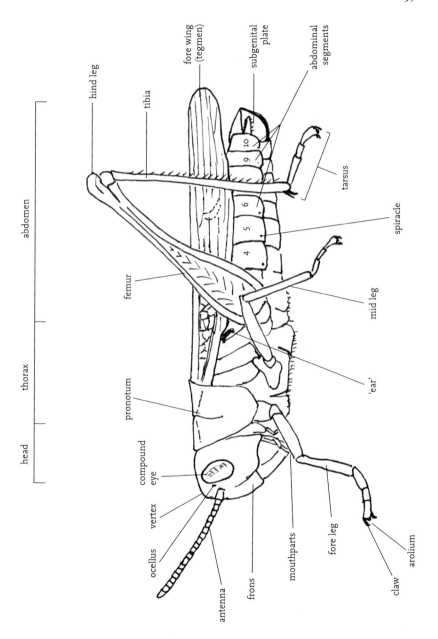

FIG 30. External structures of a male grasshopper.

(a)

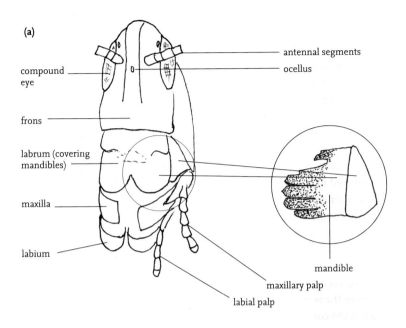

antennal segments

ocellus

compound eye

frons

labrum (covering mandibles)

maxilla

labium

mandible

maxillary palp

labial palp

(b)

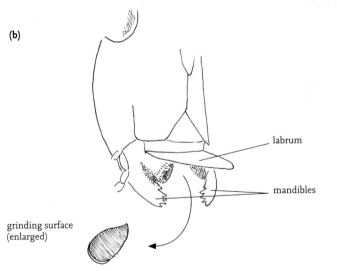

labrum

mandibles

grinding surface (enlarged)

FIG 31. (a) Head and mouthparts of a grasshopper, with (right hand side) right mandible (hidden behind the labrum in the main drawing); (b) Mouthparts of a groundhopper, with labrum raised to reveal mandibles, with flattened grinding surface.

The body is divided into three sections: head, thorax and abdomen. The main features carried on the head are the two large, prominent compound eyes, the antennae, and the mouthparts with their associated sensory organs, the palps. Most species also have three tiny simple eyes situated on the 'forehead' (frons), between the compound eyes. The mouthparts are adapted for biting and chewing, and consist of an upper 'lip' or labrum that covers a pair of mandibles. The mandibles are used for biting. They open and close laterally, and usually have a serrated outer edge. Below these are the maxillae, used for chewing. The maxillae and the 'lower lip' (labium) bear fine, jointed projections, the palps. These are important sense organs, and are closely involved in detecting and selecting food, as well as being involved in chemical communication between the sexes, especially in bush-crickets. The antennae project from the forehead. They consist of a variable number of ring-like segments, and are covered with sensory hairs (sensilla) that give the insect both tactile and chemical information about its environment. The head also contains the brain ('cerebrum'), and another neural complex, the suboesophageal ganglion. These receive sensory inputs directly from the eyes, antennae, mouthparts and alimentary canal, as well as receiving and processing neural inputs from the rest of the body. Close by in the head are two pairs of endocrine glands, the corpora allata and corpora cardiaca, whose secretions play a range of crucial roles in metabolism, behavioural readiness and development.

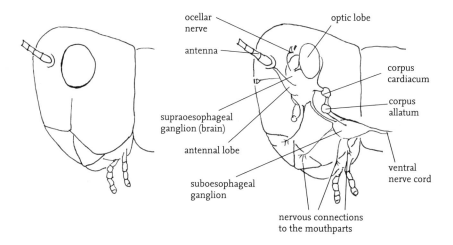

FIG 32. Side view of the head of a grasshopper, showing (right hand side) the internal nervous and endocrine organs (schematic).

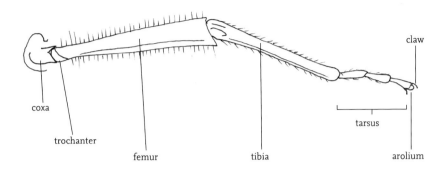

coxa

trochanter

femur

tibia

tarsus

claw

arolium

FIG 33. Mid leg of a grasshopper.

The thorax is composed of three segments. A pair of legs is attached to the lower part of each of these thoracic segments, and, in winged species, the wing-bases stem from the upper part of the second and third thoracic segments. The dorsal plate on the first thoracic segment (the pronotum) is saddle-shaped (except in the mole-crickets), and covers the wing-bases. The shape and structural features of the pronotum give useful clues to the identification of species, especially in the grasshoppers. The legs articulate with their respective thoracic segment by way of short sections known as the coxa and trochanter, while the longest sections (the femur and tibia) are joined to one another by knee-like joints. Each leg ends in a foot, or 'tarsus', which usually consists of three or four segments, the terminal one of which bears a small claw. The legs are used in locomotion, but also play a role in regulating body temperature, enabling the insect to lift itself from, or press its body down on its substrate. The fore legs are also used for manipulating food items, and may be extensively modified for digging, especially in burrowing species. In most groups of the Orthoptera the hind legs are much longer than the other two pairs, and the femora are packed with powerful muscles that are involved in jumping. In some groups, notably the mole-crickets, the hind legs are secondarily reduced, but in almost all species some ability to jump is retained. In some species there are sharp spines on the hind legs that are used in aggressive encounters, or for defence.

In winged species there is usually a marked structural differentiation between the fore and hind wings. The former are relatively narrow and to some degree hardened, and termed the 'tegmina' (singular: tegmen). When the insect is at rest the fore wings are held back over the abdomen, and provide a protective cover for the more delicate hind wings, which are folded fan-like between the tegmina and the abdomen. The thorax in fully winged orthopterans is packed

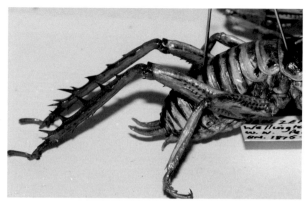

FIG 34. Hind legs of tree weta, *Hemideina crassidens*, showing spines on the tibiae (collection of the Natural History Museum, London).

with powerful flight muscles, and each segment has a complex of nerve cells (ganglion) that is involved in the control of flight and the movements of the legs, sometimes directly responding to external stimuli, but also under the control of the coordinating function of the brain. Except in populations undergoing range extension, and in migratory species, such as the locusts, orthopterans rarely fly or jump spontaneously. These activities are costly in energetic terms, and tend to be used only in cases of emergency, typically in escape from predators. Some species, notably the groundhoppers, but also some grasshoppers (see Gardiner, 2009e) are able to use their legs to swim.

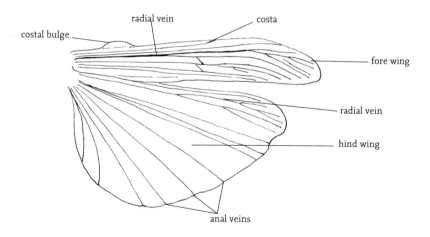

FIG 35. Extended wings (right-hand side) of the field grasshopper, *Chorthippus brunneus*, showing the principal veins and costal bulge.

FIG 36.
(top) Groundhopper
with wings extended
(© Roy Cornhill);
(left) slender
groundhopper, *Tetrix
subulata*, swimming.

　　The abdomen consists of eleven segments, but these are not always clearly
visible, as terminal structures are considerably modified for reproductive
functions. Each segment has pair of spiracles, or breathing pores, which allow the
exchange of gases involved in respiration, but also play a role in maintaining the
water-balance of the body. Towards the tip of the abdomen is a pair of projections
(cerci), which may be modified in the case of males to constrain females during
mating (see the Key, Fig K5, p. 231). Towards the tip of the female abdomen is a
genital opening into which sperm pass during or after mating, and a complex
structure used for egg-laying (the ovipositor). The shape and structure of the
ovipositor can be a useful aid to identification, especially among the bush-crickets
(see the Key, Fig K3, p. 230). At the tip of the abdomen, the ventral portion of
the segment is termed the subgenital plate. The shape of this is also useful in
the identification of some species. The contents of the abdomen include the
hindmost sections of the digestive system, terminating in the anus at the tip of the
abdomen, the rear portion of the longitudinal ventral nerve chord, together with
a series of ganglia distributed along it, and some glandular structures associated
with the formation of the eggs (and in some groups egg pods) in females, and
sperm, plus ancillary substances secreted along with the sperm, in males.

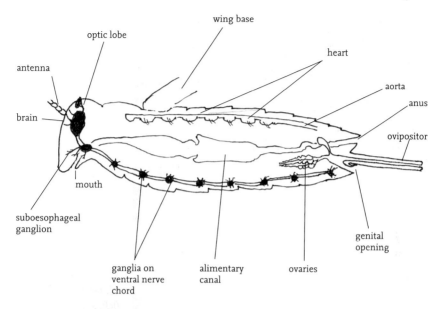

FIG 37. Schematic representation of the principal internal organs of a female cricket.

ORTHOPTERAN SENSES

Orthopterans are able to monitor a wide range of aspects of their environment by means of both specialised organs and numerous minute projections from the body surface known as sensilla. The main specialised organs are the eyes, hearing organs and vibration detectors. The sensilla are distributed over the whole body surface, but are especially concentrated in certain areas such as the palps, mouthparts, antennae and, in females, the ovipositor.

The reception of sound and vibration will be dealt with separately below. The organs of visual perception are the two compound eyes, combined with three simple ocelli arranged on the front of the head. The compound eyes give a 360° field of vision, with a relatively small area of frontal overlap. This enables binocular vision in front of the insect, and so the distance of a fixed object can be judged by parallax. Each of the facets and associated structures (ommatidia) that form the compound eye receives light from a narrow field, and the associated sensory cells are linked to neurones that synthesise the multitude of sensory inputs into a single image. This does not give the insect clear vision of detail, but broad patterns of shape, contrast, and especially movement can be detected.

Light receptor cells grouped within each ommatidium contain specialised areas ('rhabdomes') that contain pigments, and variations in these are responsible for colour vision. The ocelli are believed to function mainly to monitor light-levels, and may be important when light intensity is low. Orthopterans such as locusts that engage in long-distance flights, as well as others involved in dispersal during range extension, or simply moving to favoured parts of a local habitat, require directional information to aid navigation. This is provided by specialised ommatidia in the dorsal rim of each compound eye, enabling detection of light polarisation. This has been studied in the locust (*Schistocerca gregaria*), but the adaptation seems to be present in a wide range of other species (Zufall *et al.*, 1989; Labhart, 1999; Labhart & Meyer, 2002)

The senses of touch, taste and smell, as well as the ability to monitor temperature and moisture levels, are all mediated by sensilla. These are variously shaped outgrowths of the cuticle that enclose a variable number of nerve-cells whose dendrites are adapted to respond to specific stimuli and which transmit sensory information via their axons to the ganglions of the central nervous system. Sensilla that respond to chemical stimuli, as well as those used to detect moisture levels, have pores in their cuticles. The olfactory sensilla (responsible for the sense of smell) have numerous pores that allow in airborne molecules, while those responsible for the sense of taste (contact chemoreceptors) have a pore at the tip. Chemically sensitive sensilla are especially densely concentrated

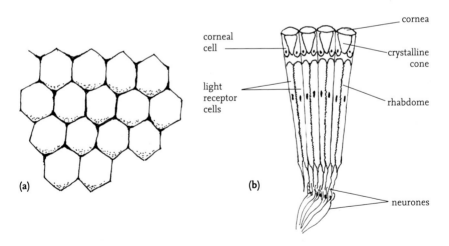

FIG 38. (a) Surface of part of a compound eye, showing hexagonal facets; (b) section through a compound eye showing four ommatidia (simplified).

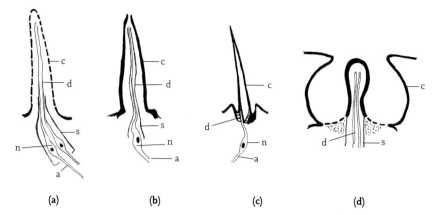

FIG 39. Cuticular sensilla (diagrammatic): (a) olfactory sensillum; (b) contact chemosensory ('taste') sensillum; (c) mechanoreceptor; (d) coeloconic thermo/hygro receptor. (Key: a: axon; c: cuticle; d: dendrite; n: nerve cell; s: sheath.) (Adapted from Chapman & Joern 1990.)

on the antennae, and, as the antennae are used especially for distance reception of scents, the olfactory sensilla predominate. However, there are also numerous touch- and taste-sensitive sensilla on the antennae.

The concentrations of sensilla on the palps and mouthparts are mainly concerned with providing sensory information relevant to choosing and processing food items. The tips of the palps are equipped with large numbers of sensilla that are sensitive to taste, the physical properties and surface odours of potential foods. These sensilla continue to be involved in transmitting information as the palps repeatedly tap a food item (palpation) while the insect bites and chews (Blaney & Duckett, 1975; Chapman & Sword, 1993). The mouthparts themselves are also provided with dense patches of contact chemoreceptors and these continue the process of evaluating food as it is being consumed. The fore and mid legs are also endowed with sensilla that are sensitive to the surface chemistry of food substances, as well as with helping to hold and guide the food to the relevant mouthparts (see the DVD).

Most research on the chemical senses of orthopterans has focused on selection of food and feeding behaviour. Comparative research has shown that there are variations in the numbers and role of sensilla that are related to the dietary patterns of the species concerned (e.g. Chapman & Thomas, 1978). In general, grass-feeders have relatively fewer sensilla than species that feed on broad-leaved plants, and those with highly specialised diets also have fewer than food-generalists, in ways that relate to the respective differences in the requirements to identify plants that are either good to eat or not good to eat. Even species thought to be food-generalists ('polyphagous') reject some plants, and demonstrate preferences between the range of plant species that they will eat. An experimental study on feeding and survival among last instar nymphs of *Schistocerca americana* showed that rejection of plant materials on the basis of detection of deterrent chemicals played an important part in food selection, along with learnt aversions resulting from ingestion of toxins (Chapman & Sword, 1994).

Much of the above information has come from the study of acridids, especially locusts, but broadly similar sensory patterns are present in the various groups of ensiferans (Gwynne, 2001; Bland & Rentz, 1991). The role of chemical communication in other aspects of the lives of grasshoppers and crickets has been less thoroughly researched. In locusts, pheromones are known to play a part in aggregation, maturation, oviposition and phase-transition (Fuzeau-Braesch *et al.*, 1988; Norris, 1970; Okelo, 1979; Schmidt & Osman, 1988; Whitman, 1990), while a role for pheromones in mate-recognition in grasshoppers is suggested by the presence of greater numbers of chemoreceptors in the antennae of males (Blaney & Simmonds, 1990). More recent research has established a crucial role for chemical communication in the reproductive behaviour of crickets (see Chapter 6 for more detail).

The relatively impermeable cuticle of orthopterans presents problems for maintaining physiologically optimal body temperatures and fluid content. Regulation of body temperature is critical both for development (see Chapter 3) and for maintenance of normal functioning in adults. Orthopterans appear to have little ability to generate heat internally, but are seriously affected by overheating and by cooling. To some extent the insect's body temperature is regulated by convection currents and by heat transfers from surrounding air or solid substrates. Evaporation through the cuticle and spiracles also may have a small effect. Colour, too, may affect the ability of insects to absorb or reflect heat energy (Joern, 1982). At least one species has the ability to change colour in response to changes in ambient temperature (Key & Day, 1954). Perhaps the most important means of maintaining body temperature within the necessary range is by various behavioural strategies – the body can be pressed down onto the substrate or raised up on stretched legs as appropriate; the body can be oriented to incident solar radiation ('flanking': Chappell & Whitman, 1990) so as to maximise heat gain, or the insect can avoid overheating by retreating to the shelter of dense vegetation. The ability of different species of grasshopper to raise their body temperature above the ambient by these means varies considerably and is a significant determinant of their habitat requirements and geographical distribution (Willott, 1997). Water regulation is achieved mainly by food selection and by varying the water content of faeces, although direct drinking of water has also been noted.

LOCOMOTION: JUMPING AND FLYING

Jumping

The ability to jump long distances relative to their body-size is very widespread in the Orthoptera, and especially well-developed in the grasshoppers and groundhoppers, although most crickets and bush-crickets are also able to jump if provoked, and the long-established British alien, the greenhouse camel-cricket (*Diestrammena asynamorus*) has a prodigious leap. However, jumping is highly expensive energetically, and tends to be used only as a response to disturbance. Even then, it is frequently augmented by flight once the jump has commenced.

The mechanics of jumping in grasshoppers have constituted a challenge to researchers, and our understanding of the anatomical and physiological processes involved owes much to the extensive studies of the locust (*Schistocerca gregaria*) by H. C. Bennet-Clark (e.g. Bennet-Clark, 1975, 1976, 1990). The initial take-off is powered by opening of the angle between femur and tibia of each hind leg. The muscles involved are packed into the swollen femur, and are attached at their distal end (the 'knee') to the tip of the tibia. The largest of the muscles in the femur is called the 'extensor tibiae', and its contraction pulls on the ligament by which it is attached to a flexible area of cuticle at the tip of the tibia, so straightening the leg and exerting force on the substrate, via the tarsi.

However, this is by no means the whole story, as the power required to propel the insect into the air for a distance up to 0.8 metres is far more than can be mobilised by the simple contraction of the extensor muscle. To understand the source of this extra power, other features of the femur's structure have to be introduced. Running alongside the extensor muscle, ventrally to it, is another muscle, the 'flexor tibiae'. This is attached ventrally to the joint between tibia and femur, and has a pocket close to the point of attachment that fits over an inward projection of the cuticle of the femur ('Heitler's lump'). When the flexor muscle is contracted, the angle between femur and tibia is locked closed by the connection between the lump and pocket, but when it is relaxed, the femur and tibia can swing apart. Two other types of structure are also present in the femur. Towards the tip of the femur are two 'semilunar' processes, attached at one end to the wall of the femur and at the other to a ligament of the extensor muscle. The extensor muscle, as well as being attached along the inner and dorsal walls of the femur, also has attachments along a blade-like structure, the 'apodeme', which, at the distal end, forms the ligament that attaches the muscle to the tip of the tibia.

Now, if the extensor muscle is flexed while the flexor muscle is also flexed, locking the tibia in place, the semilunar processes, the flexible cuticle of the tibial attachment, and the apodeme of the extensor muscle, are subject to powerful stresses. If the flexor muscle is then relaxed, the energy stored in the apodeme and sublunary processes is released, as in the action of a steel spring, or catapult. This 'storage-release' mechanism augments the power of the extensor muscle tenfold. According to Bennet-Clark, the tensile stress of the apodeme material is similar to that of silk, and its energy storage about five times that of steel (Bennet-Clark, 1990: 182)! Anatomical studies by Bennet-Clark (1975) of other grasshoppers as well as the common groundhopper (*Tetrix undulata*) indicate that this mechanism is common to at least the Caelifera.

Studies of the nervous pathways between the metathoracic ganglion and the muscles of the femora, and the patterns of their excitation during jumping, have given support to the above account of the mechanisms involved in jumping in locusts (Hoyle & Burrows, 1973; Heitler & Burrows, 1977a, 1977b).

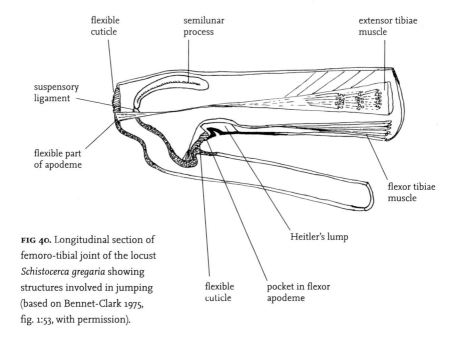

FIG 40. Longitudinal section of femoro-tibial joint of the locust *Schistocerca gregaria* showing structures involved in jumping (based on Bennet-Clark 1975, fig. 1:53, with permission).

Flying

In fully winged grasshoppers and crickets jumping is frequently supplemented by flight. It seems that ancestral orthopterans were flightless, but the ability to fly has evolved as a feature of many species of both Caelifera and Ensifera. However, in numerous species the wings of one or both sexes have become reduced, with associated loss of the ability to fly. In some of these ('brachypterous') species varying proportions of some populations develop as fully winged ('macropterous') forms that are capable of flight. These macropterous forms are responsible for colonisation of new habitat patches, and are probably important for range-extension in response to favourable climatic or general environmental changes (see Chapters 3 and 9).

As flight is dependent on high thoracic temperatures, and is very demanding in terms of energy expenditure, it tends to be used rather sparingly in cooler, temperate climates. In some species of grasshopper, there are short flight-displays that play a part in their reproductive behaviour, and in other species flight is commonly a 'last-resort' means of escape from predators when temperatures are sufficiently high. British species such as the common field grasshopper, stripe-winged grasshopper, large marsh grasshopper and common green grasshopper fly readily when alarmed, but their flights are relatively short (10 to 15 metres) and show only slight manoeuvrability.

As an escape tactic this relies on the ability of the insect to adjust its landing position. The landing process itself appears to be achieved by a coordinated set of reflexes (and is not dependent on visual inputs), and may be adapted to lessen the physical impact of the landing on a hard surface. However, it also could be that in facing the original source of disturbance the insect may benefit from being able to visually monitor the predator (Kral, 2010).

It also seems likely that there is considerable spontaneous flight activity between local habitat patches, but much greater publicity and research attention has been paid to larger-scale migratory and swarming phenomena that are more characteristic of species of the tropics and subtropics. Although large-scale migratory activity is usually associated with locusts, it is also a feature of the behaviour of numerous other acridid species, and some ensiferans such as the mormon cricket, *Anabrus simplex* (see Gwynne, 2001). The ability to migrate by flying considerable distances is an adaptation to a variety of environmental exigencies – most notably to ephemeral habitats and to regular climatic and seasonal changes that render particular habitat patches unfavourable for survival or development at certain times of year. In semi-arid grassland systems of tropical and subtropical Africa, Australia, the Middle East and India, large-scale grasshopper and locust migrations are common in relation to seasonal changes.

The insects generally take to the wing at dusk and continue their flights for several hours into the night and, with ground-speeds of from 20 to 50 km per hour, can cover from 60 to 250 km in a night.

Brief flights initiated by the threat of predation, or performed as part of a visual display, require availability of immediately accessible energy sources to feed the intense activity of the flight muscles. In grasshoppers the initial fuel is carbohydrate in the haemolymph, and glycogen deposits in the muscles themselves. However, because the circulatory system is 'open', and the haeomolymph washes over internal organs (rather than being carried in vessels as in vertebrate systems) diffusion is relatively inefficient. An adaptation to this situation is that carbohydrate is present in the haemolymph in very high concentrations in the form of trehalose, which is broken down into glucose at the muscle site by enzyme activity. However, in species such as locusts, which are capable of sustaining prolonged flights, a supplementary source of energy is needed. For longer-distance flights (i.e. after 4 to 5 minutes), locusts draw on energy stored in their fat-body in the form of triacylglycerides. These are metabolised under hormonal control to form diglycerides that are then oxidised to provide energy over prolonged periods of muscle activity (Goldsworthy, 1990).

SINGING AND HEARING: SOUND COMMUNICATION IN ORTHOPTERANS

The songs of grasshoppers on summer days are among the most evocative of wildlife sounds. Many other groups of animals make use of sound communication, but no other insect group compares with the Orthoptera for the sheer variety and complexity of their uses of sound. Because of this, and because of the deep embedding of sound communication in their modes of life, this has been overwhelmingly the most popular topic in scientific research on the order (see, for example, Hartley & Robinson,1976; Hartley, 1993; Greenfield, 1997; Ragge & Reynolds, 1998; Hartley et al., 2000; Robinson & Hall, 2002; Gerhardt & Huber, 2002; Drosopoulos & Claridge, 2006; Bailey & Zuk, 2008; Nityananda & Balakrishnan, 2009).

Some groups of Orthoptera, such as groundhoppers (Tetrigidae) and camel-crickets (Raphidophoridae), lack specialised hearing organs. In some species this seems to be the ancestral condition, while in others the ability to hear has been lost in the course of their evolution. However, all species have the ability to detect low frequency vibration by means of specialised organs (the subgenual organs) located in the tibia of all three pairs of legs, and in the Ensifera (crickets and their allies) the organs that are specialised for hearing may have evolved from the subgenual organs in the fore tibia. It seems likely that hearing evolved prior to the ability to produce sounds, probably as a means of detecting predators. Although the neural basis for hearing is very similar in all groups of Orthoptera, it is thought that the specialised hearing organs evolved separately in the Ensifera and the Caelifera (grasshoppers and their relatives). It also seems likely that the ability to produce sound by stridulation also evolved independently several times in various orthopteran groups as the mechanisms involved differ considerably (Gwynne, 1995, 2001).

If sound communication evolved separately several times during the evolution of the Orthoptera, and remains almost universal across the main subdivisions of the order, this raises the question of why this particular channel of communication is favoured against other possible ones (see Robinson 1990).

First, orthopterans are relatively heavy, large-bodied insects that are vulnerable to a range of parasites and predators. Their ability to jump or fly is an important means of escape, but is generally used as a tactic of last resort. Compared, for example, to relatively small-bodied groups, such as butterflies, the agility of orthopterans in flight is very limited. Butterflies use flight not only as a means of escape, but also in mate location. Moreover, they use the colour patterns of their large wings in courtship, to communicate species identity and to deter or distract predators from vulnerable body parts. Relatively sedentary orthopterans tend to rely on cryptic colour patterns and body structures and the ability to remain motionless when approached by predators. If showy colours are ruled out, then some other channel of communication is needed.

Second, many species (especially among the ensiferans) are active at night as a predator-avoidance adaptation and this, too, rules out visual communication. Of course there are nocturnal predators, but a variety of defensive adaptations have evolved in response to these (see below). Also, chemical communication can be used effectively at night over long distances, as demonstrated by night-flying moths. There is a growing recognition that chemical communication plays a significant part in the reproductive activities of many orthopterans, although usually for interactions at close quarters.

Third, they are relatively immobile insects with dispersed populations living in structurally complex environments, so visual communication is likely to be ineffective. Orthopterans that lack, or have lost, the ability to communicate using sound (such as camel-crickets and groundhoppers) are generally ones that live in dense aggregations, and therefore can rely on tactile or chemical communication.

Fourth, the medium of sound has several variable parameters, enabling a large amount of information to be encoded – the location, species, sex, mating readiness and quality of the caller.

FIG 41. Vivid upperside (left) and cryptic underside (right) of small tortoiseshell butterfly, *Aglais urticae.*

Fifth, sound can be switched off as soon as a potential predator is detected (ter Hofstede *et al.*, 2008), although something comparable is possible with visual stimuli as when brightly coloured butterflies snap their wings sharply together to expose cryptic undersides.

Orthopterans may use sound to deter predators, and many aspects of sound communication are likely to have been shaped by selective pressure from parasites and predators. However, the main uses of sound communication across the different subdivisions of the order are linked to their reproductive activity, in ordering the interactions between males, in attracting potential mates and in close-quarters courtship behaviour. These aspects of the behaviour of grasshoppers and crickets will be the focus of Chapters 4, 5 and 6, and the natural history of acoustic communication, especially, in Chapter 5.

In this section the emphasis will be on the various mechanisms that have evolved for hearing and for the production of sound in the different orthopteran groups. The ways in which acoustic information is processed and responded to by the insects concerned is a fascinating topic that is being addressed in current research. Unfortunately there is space here to offer only a brief glimpse of this.

Hearing

In **bush-crickets** (Tettigoniidae) the 'ears' are located in the tibiae of the fore legs, just below the joint between tibiae and femora. Each ear consists of two thinned areas of cuticle (the tympana). In some species (such as, for example, the speckled bush-cricket, *Leptophyes punctatissima*) the tympana are exposed on the surface of the tibia, but more often they are partially enclosed by folds in the cuticle, so that from

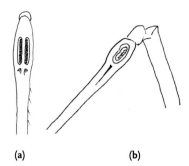

FIG 42. Fore tibiae of bush-crickets, showing tibial 'ears': (a) long-winged conehead, *Conocephalus discolor*, anterior view (tympana hidden); (b) speckled bush-cricket, *Leptophyes punctatissima*, side view (tympana exposed).

(a)   (b)

the external view they are hidden behind slits in the tibial wall. There are numerous grades of elaboration of the surrounding structure, including, in some species, an external structure almost resembling the mammalian ear (Bailey, 1990).

Internally, each pair of tympana is linked by an elongated tracheal tube to a spiracle on the side of the first thoracic segment, close to, but distinct from, the ventilatory spiracle. The auditory spiracle varies considerably in shape and size both within and between species, and acuity of hearing in females has been shown to be linked to size of the spiracle in some species (Bailey, 1998).

It is generally accepted that the main point of entry of sound is the spiracle. Interior to the spiracle, the trachea is expanded to form an auditory vesicle (the 'bulla'), which acts to amplify the incoming sound. The sound waves are transmitted along the trachea to the tibia. Here, the trachea divides into two sections, each terminating at one of the paired tympana. The resulting vibrations of the tympana are mediated by the two parts of the trachea and the membrane separating them, and registered by a row of receptor cells that make up an organ called the crista acoustica, attached to the dorsal surface of the anterior of the two sections of the trachea. Neither the tympana nor the tracheae are directly responsible for perception of the frequency spectrum of incident sound and it seems that this is achieved by the arrangement of the auditory receptor cells on the crista acoustica – the largest cells, toward the proximal end of the organ, being sensitive to lower frequencies.

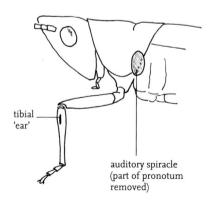

tibial 'ear'

auditory spiracle (part of pronotum removed)

FIG 43. External features of the hearing system of a bush-cricket, *Conocephalus dorsalis*.

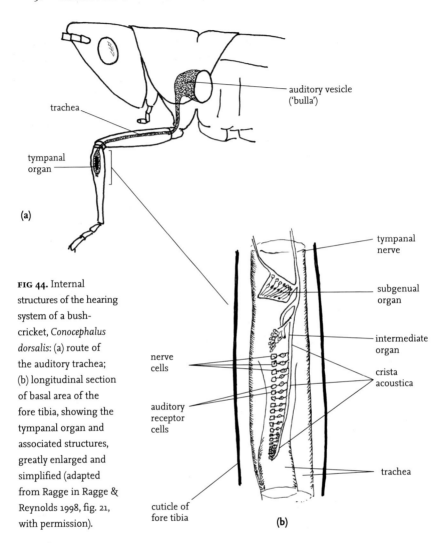

(a)

FIG 44. Internal structures of the hearing system of a bush-cricket, *Conocephalus dorsalis*: (a) route of the auditory trachea; (b) longitudinal section of basal area of the fore tibia, showing the tympanal organ and associated structures, greatly enlarged and simplified (adapted from Ragge in Ragge & Reynolds 1998, fig. 21, with permission).

(b)

Although it seems to be generally agreed that the main point of entry of sounds is via the acoustic spiracle, there remains some uncertainty about the role of the tympana and their exposure to incoming sound through the tibial slits. This may vary among different bush-cricket groups, and resonance in the cavity formed around the tympana may play a role in directional perception (Robinson & Hall, 2002: 14).

All three pairs of legs bear tibial organs, although only the fore legs have tympana and sensory receptors for sound. However, the tibial organs of all three pairs of legs possess a subgenual organ, which is sensitive to substrate vibration, and an 'intermediate' organ, which harbours vibratory receptor cells.

The hearing organs of **crickets** are believed to have evolved independently from those of the bush-crickets from common origins in the subgenual organs of their common ancestor. Like bush-crickets, crickets also have a 'tracheal-tibial' hearing system, but there are some differences of structure and function. The anterior tympanum in each tibial ear is reduced in size and not functional in hearing, and the septum between the left and right tracheae is thin, giving good sound transmission between the two sides of the system.

Other ensiferan groups, including Gryllotalpidae, Haglidae and Anostostomatidae, share broadly similar tibial-tracheal hearing systems, but with considerable variation in details of structure. However, some groups appear to have no hearing organs and are presumed deaf to airborne sounds.

In **grasshoppers** the hearing organs are located on each side of the first abdominal segment. The thin membranous tympana lie within depressions in the abdominal cuticle, and are in some species partially covered by flaps. Internally, the tympana are connected to closed air-sacs that are linked, so that sound waves from each side of the insect are transmitted to both tympana. Unlike the bush-cricket tympana, those of grasshoppers show different modes

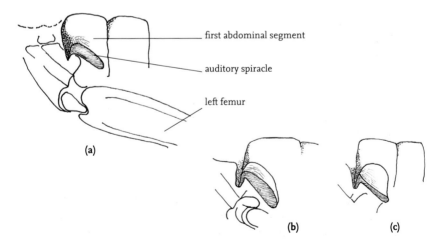

first abdominal segment

auditory spiracle

left femur

(a)

(b)

(c)

FIG 45. Side view of the auditory spiracle and nearby structures of two grasshopper species: (a) lesser marsh grasshopper, *Chorthippus albomarginatus*, female; (b) stripe-winged grasshopper, *Stenobothrus lineatus*, male; (c) stripe-winged grasshopper, female.

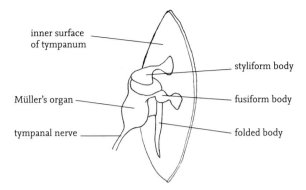

FIG 46. Inside view of the tympanum and associated structures of a grasshopper (redrawn from Ragge, in Ragge & Reynolds 1998, fig 23, with permission).

of vibration at different points on their surface, and these are detected by different groups of sensory cells (scolopidia) which are tuned to different sound frequencies. It seems that the receptor cells respond to a complex combination of inputs from different parts of the tympanum and the associated motions of the relevant ganglion (Müller's organ) (Robinson & Hall, 2002).

Production of sound

With some exceptions, the mechanism used for sound production is the scraping of one part of the hardened cuticle against another, and this is termed 'stridulation'. However, the various subgroupings within the Orthoptera have rather different structural modifications for stridulation, indicating that sound-communication may have evolved independently several times.

Stridulation in male **bush-crickets** (Tettigoniidae) involves scraping the modified left fore wing (tegmen) over the right. The right tegmen has an area of thin, resonating membrane, the mirror, near the wing-base, and, on its dorsal surface, a projection called the scraper or plectrum. The left tegmen has a toothed vein, called the file, on its lower surface. As the wings are opened and closed, the file is drawn over the plectrum and vibrations are communicated to the frame of the mirror on the right tegmen, so amplifying the sound. In many species the tegmina are reduced or absent, and in the males of some species, such as the speckled bush-cricket (*L. punctatissima*), they are retained as little more than the sound-producing mechanism. Prior to stridulation, the insect warms up, with rhythmic muscular contractions. The wings are raised to allow the file and scraper to come into contact, and repeatedly opened and closed. In most cases, sound is produced mainly or wholly by the wing closure, to yield a single sound pulse, or 'syllable'. In some species, however, sound is produced by both opening and closing the tegmina, and, in a few, the sound is produced by the opening movement. A sequence of several rapidly repeated syllables followed by an interval will be heard by humans as a single chirp or buzz, sometimes termed an 'echeme'. Echemes may be further organised into more complex song structures in many species. The sounds produced by bush-crickets have carrier frequencies that vary from 600Hz at the lower end, up to as high as 135 kHz. Although most have broad frequency spectra, with peaks at several points within the range, some sing with relatively pure tones. As well as the role of the mirror in amplifying sound, the air space between the tegmina and the abdomen also has a role, although precisely what this is remains controversial (Robinson & Hall, 2002).

In most bush-crickets only the males stridulate. However, in some subfamilies (notably Phaneropterinae and Ephippigerinae) the females have a responding chirp. In the speckled bush-cricket, the very brief female chirp is produced, as in the male, by left-over-right movements of the greatly reduced tegmina, but the plectrum is on the lower surface of the left tegmen and the toothed structure that serves as the file is on the upper surface of the right tegmen.

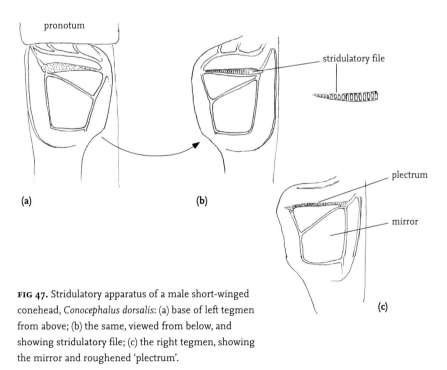

FIG 47. Stridulatory apparatus of a male short-winged conehead, *Conocephalus dorsalis*: (a) base of left tegmen from above; (b) the same, viewed from below, and showing stridulatory file; (c) the right tegmen, showing the mirror and roughened 'plectrum'.

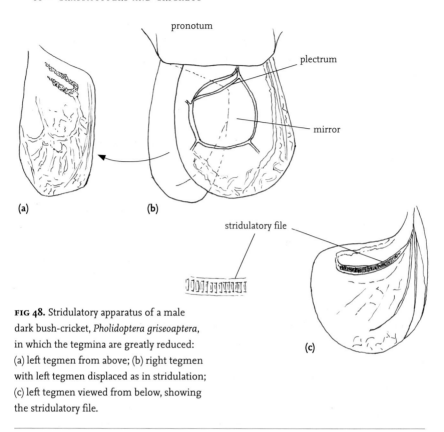

FIG 48. Stridulatory apparatus of a male dark bush-cricket, *Pholidoptera griseoaptera*, in which the tegmina are greatly reduced: (a) left tegmen from above; (b) right tegmen with left tegmen displaced as in stridulation; (c) left tegmen viewed from below, showing the stridulatory file.

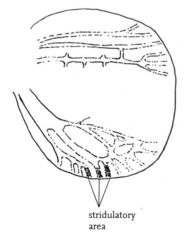

FIG 49. Right tegmen of a female speckled bush-cricket, *Leptophyes punctatissima*, showing stridulatory area (redrawn from Ragge in Ragge & Reynolds 1998, fig. 10, with permission).

In some bush-cricket subfamilies the ability to produce sound by tegminal stridulation has been lost, but in one group (Australasian giant leaf bush-crickets, *Phyllophora* species) sound can be produced by a quite different mechanism – scraping a file on the hind coxa (first leg segment) against a ridge on one of the ventral plates of the thorax.

The British species, the oak bush-cricket (*Meconema thalassinum*), produces sound by drumming with one hind leg on the leaf it is standing on. The resulting sounds are said to be audible some metres away, but the action also produces substrate vibration which may be important in enabling females to locate a drumming male.

Secondary loss of the ability to stridulate has occurred in a number of **cricket** (Gryllidae) species, but in the ones that have retained it, sound is also produced by rubbing together modified basal areas of the tegmina. However, in crickets, the usual mechanism is movement of the right over the left tegmen. Both wings are similar in structure, with a file of teeth formed from a vein (the Cu2 vein, as in bush-crickets) on both tegmina, and each forming one side of a roughly triangular resonating membrane: the harp. During stridulation the file of teeth on the underside of the right tegmen is passed over a plectrum on the upper side of the left tegmen. The file communicates vibrations to the harp and an adjacent thin membranous area, the mirror, on the right tegmen, while the similar harp and mirror on the left wing also resonate in phase with those on the right. The frequency of the sound produced is determined by a combination of the rate at which the teeth of the file are plucked by the plectrum, and the resonating frequency of the harp and mirror areas on the wings. The larger these are, in general, the lower the frequency of the song. Compared with most bush-crickets, the resulting song is more musical, with relatively pure tones. As with the bush-crickets, there is some dispute as to the role played by the semi-enclosed air-space that is formed below the tegmina when the cricket raises them in order to sing. It is noticeable that the males of the field cricket (*Gryllus campestris*) produce their calling song with the wings held high, but lower them when producing the distinct, quieter courtship chirps and clicks at close quarters (see the DVD).

Mole-crickets (Gryllotalpidae) also usually stridulate by passing the right over the left tegmen. The structural adaptations for stridulation are less developed than in the true crickets, with a less clearly defined harp, and no mirror. However, mole-crickets are able to amplify their songs by using their burrow as an effective secondary resonator, tuned to the frequency of their song.

The New Zealand **weta** (Anostostomatidae) have evolved their astonishingly diverse modes of sound production in isolation from the other groups of Orthoptera. Systematic research by L. H. Field and co-workers over more than thirty years has revealed much of this structural diversity and its related behavioural complexity (see, for example, Field & Bailey, 1997; Field, 1982; Field & Sandlant, 1983; Field & Rind, 1992; Field (ed.), 2001; McVean & Field, 1996; Kelly, 2006, 2008; see also Chapter 6 for more detail on the reproductive behaviour of some of these insects).

Lacking wings, the weta share a common elementary mode of sound production that is complemented in some species by a range of other methods. The common pattern is patches or rows of projections on the sides of one or more abdominal segments that are rubbed or scraped against variously shaped projections on the inner surfaces of the hind femora. Although this basic femoro-abdominal mechanism is shared by all weta species, it has undergone great diversification in the different genera and species. The ground and tusked weta (genus *Hemiandrus*) have the most elementary version, with patches of pegs or short spines on three abdominal tergites, and patches or rows of pegs on the femora. As these insects appear to have no ability to hear airborne sounds, it seems that their sound production functions solely in defence against would-be predators. The tree weta (*Hemideina*) generally possess a file on each side of the second abdominal tergite, with patches of blunt pegs on the femora. The latter project towards the leading edge of the file so that the two structures engage when femora and abdomen move against one another. The femoro-abdominal structures are very diverse in the giant weta (*Deinacrida*), including, in one group, crescent-shaped and grooved ridges on the second abdominal tergite that connect with a radial arrangement of pegs and spines on the femora, making multiple engagements with the ridges as they are drawn over them.

Stridulation in the giant weta appears to be used solely as a defensive response, but the tree weta (*Hemideina* species) also use stridulation in aggressive encounters with other males, in response to rejection of mating attempts and as a calling song. In defensive stridulation, the hind legs are drawn down against projections on the abdomen, while in other contexts the insect rocks forwards and draws the abdomen upwards against the hind femora.

Three other sound-producing structures have been evolved in a few species of weta, in addition to the shared femoro-abdominal one. The tusked weta have curved forward-pointing 'tusks' on the mandibles. These cross over towards the tips, and have lines of oval tubercles on mutually facing surfaces of the tusks. Sound is produced as these scrape against one another when the mandibles are opened. Another mechanism (also present in a few bush-crickets) is pleuro-coxal stridulation, in which patches of spines on the underside of abdominal segments one to three rub against small spines on the dorsal surface of the coxal segments of the hind legs. The third mechanism is 'tergal-tergal' stridulation. Several species of *Deinacrida* have blunt pegs on the underside of the rear edge of some dorsal plates of the abdomen that engage with dense patches of spines on the upperside of the leading edge of the one behind. Sounds are produced when the insect 'telescopes' its abdomen, scraping the abdominal plates against one another.

Most **grasshoppers** use a quite different mechanism. The hind femora of the male each have a file formed by a row of tiny pegs on the inner surface. In stridulation the hind legs are moved up and down so that the file on each hind femur rubs against a prominent vein (the radial vein) in the (flexed) fore wing on that side of the body, usually producing a louder sound on the down-stroke. In most species the legs move independently of one another and slightly out of phase during stridulation. Among British species this is most marked in the stripe-winged grasshopper (*Stenobothrus lineatus*) (see DVD). The file in this

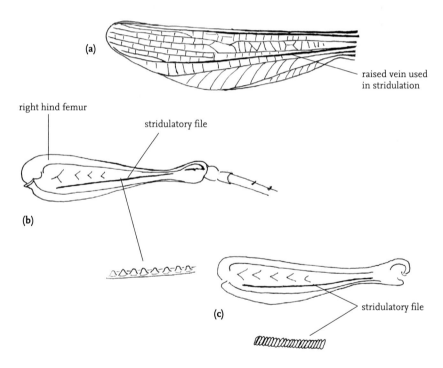

FIG 50. Stridulatory apparatus of two grasshopper species: (a) right fore wing (tegmen) of a male woodland grasshopper, *Omocestus rufipes*; (b) right femur of the same insect, showing the stridulatory file; (c) right femur of a male stripe-winged grasshopper, *Stenobothrus lineatus*, showing more densely toothed file.

species is exceptionally long and dense, and the amplitude of the leg movement very wide. The stridulatory movement is thus unusually slow, and the lag between left and right leg-movements is obvious (see DVD). However, males of this species, along with most others, frequently lose one of their hind legs, and continue to stridulate quite effectively with the other.

Females of many grasshopper species are able to stridulate, and the stridulatory mechanism and the pattern of the song usually resemble that of the male. However, the stridulatory pegs on the hind femora are formed from the surrounding cuticle of bristles, rather than the bristles themselves, as in males. Female stridulation is usually much quieter than that of males, and much less often heard, as sexually receptive females are very quickly located by males (see brief female stridulation in the courtship sequence of the mottled grasshopper on the DVD).

Grasshoppers belonging to the subfamily Oedipodinae are represented in Britain only by the large marsh grasshopper (*Stethophyma grossum*), although another, the blue-winged grasshopper (*Oedipoda caerulescens*) occurs on the Channel Islands, and could well colonise mainland Britain. In this group, there are no stridulatory pegs on the hind femora, and stridulation is usually effected by the scraping of a ridge on the hind femur over a file of teeth on a prominent vein in the fore wing, although the large marsh grasshopper has yet another method.

PATTERN RECOGNITION, LOCALISATION OF SOUND AND PHONOTAXIS

Bush-crickets have several ways of determining the direction of a sound source. First, the delay in reception of sound travelling through the trachea and across the septum dividing right and left sides causes a difference in phase between sound waves making contact with the tympana externally and from within. Second, with sounds of sufficiently high frequency relative to the size of the insect's body, a 'sound shadow' is produced on the side of the body facing away from the sound source which can be detected in species with enlarged tracheal vesicles. In crickets, the thin septum between the tracheae on each side of the body allows for effective transmission of sound impulses between the two sides. Detection of phase and pressure differences impacting on the tympana from the two sides of the body provides a further means to locate the source of sound.

Hedwig and his co-workers are conducting on-going research to analyse the neural processing of sound information in relation to the phonotaxis of female crickets, notably the southern field cricket, *Gryllus bimaculatus* (Hedwig

& Poulet, 2004, 2005; Poulet & Hedwig, 2005; Hedwig, 2001, 2006). Impulses from acoustic receptors in the ears are transmitted by afferent neurons to the first thoracic ganglion. One pair of neurons (two pairs in bush-crickets), termed omega neurons because of their similarity in shape to the Greek letter Ω, play a key role in processing the incoming information, and are, in the species studied, most sensitive to the carrier frequency of the species-specific song. The anterior pair of omega neurons inhibit one another in ways that enhance the contrast between sensory inputs from the two sides of the body, supporting directional auditory processing. Other neurons are involved in transmitting information both backwards and forwards. The ascending auditory neurons transmit nerve impulses forwards to the brain for further processing.

However, for (usually) females to be able to respond effectively to the (usually) male calling song, it is necessary not only for the source of the sound to be located, but also for the identity of the caller to be recognised (Gerhardt & Huber 2002). The processing requirements of these two achievements are different, and it seems that different neural pathways are involved. Sound localisation requires comparison of inputs from the two sides, whereas pattern recognition involves integration of information from both sides.

Early work (e.g. Huber, 1964) supposed that pattern recognition preceded the phonotactic response. However, more recent experimental work on crickets has demonstrated that the steering response of the receptive insect begins in response to the first syllable of the male song and then continues as a series of reflex-like responses to successive sound pulses. The neural pathway here seems to be a circuit involving the first thoracic ganglion independently of any higher level processing of sound in the brain. The processing involved in pattern recognition takes place in the brain on the basis of impulses transmitted forwards from the first thoracic ganglion, with walking and steering commands then being transmitted back to the thoracic ganglion. The interaction between these processes is not yet fully understood (Hedwig, pers. corr.).

In the speckled bush-cricket (L. punctatissima) the problems posed by sound location and phonotaxis are still more challenging than for ground-dwelling crickets. In this species it is the male that moves towards the female. The first extra problem is that localisation of the source of sound has to be made on the basis of extremely brief and infrequent chirps. The second is that the species inhabits structurally complex environments, in which the caller may be located either above or below the hearer, or to the left or right. The first problem is addressed by the male calling and the female responding within a narrow time-window, followed by an increased rate of calling and responding (see Chapter 5 for more detail).

The problem posed by the requirement to locate a sound source in three-dimensional space is solved very effectively by male speckled bush-crickets. In experiments conducted by Rheinlaender *et al.* (2007) using a walking frame and artificial female calls located on the horizontal as well as at 45° above or below males, the latter chose a path very close to the shortest one in all trials. The researchers hypothesised that the information underlying this ability must be detection of changes in the differential sound intensity across the two ears as the insect approached the sound-source. However, this would not enable discrimination between a source located above the approaching insect and one located below. It seems that this discrimination is achieved by a twisting movement of the body, which the researchers term 'tilting', that is performed at the start of phonotaxis (Kostarakos *et al.*, 2007). The ability of the males to locate sound sources at various displacements from the horizontal becomes less reliable above 60°, and confusion sets in towards a 90° elevation or depression (Ofner *et al.*, 2007).

CHAPTER 3

Life histories

The life history of all orthopterans takes the form of a series of stages marked by successive skin moults. This relatively simple and gradual process of development is sometimes called 'hemimetabolous', or 'exopterygote' to contrast it with the pattern of development of such insect groups as Lepidoptera or Diptera, in which there are structurally very different larval and pupal stages. The early stages (instars) are very similar in structure to the adults, with the exception of the genitalia, the ovipositor in females, and the wings in winged species. These features of the adult become increasingly prominent as development proceeds. The initial egg stage is succeeded by a brief worm-like or 'vermiform' pre-nymphal phase. The resulting nymphs grow and develop by periodically shedding their chitinous skin, or 'exoskeleton'. Immediately after shedding its skin the nymph is soft-bodied, pale and highly vulnerable, but soon the skin hardens and acquires its usual coloration, revealing a larger and, depending on the stage reached, more developed nymph. The number of instars through which the developing insect passes varies greatly across the different groups of orthopterans, and may even vary within a species.

This chapter will concentrate on the main groups of orthopterans that have established populations in Britain, focusing especially on the bush-crickets (Tettigoniidae), and the grasshoppers (Acrididae). These two families have been most fully studied, and variations in their life histories illustrate much of the diversity in the Orthopera as a whole. However, some brief mention will be made of key features of the life histories of the other families.

Two themes have been evident in much of the life history research. One is the way the timing of developmental processes in many species has evolved in response to climatic variables. Periods of suspended or delayed development or maturation occur in some species during periods when weather conditions are adverse. This may occur in very hot or dry seasons in warm climates (Masaki, 1980), or there is usually a suspension of development at one stage or another during the winter months in cooler, temperate climates. In some cases, the slowing down or suspension of activity or development ('quiescence') may be a direct response to adverse conditions. Frequently, however, periods of suspended development are a part of the developmental biology of a species. For example, in some species suspension of development anticipates the onset of adverse conditions – in British species, usually the winter – and development is resumed when environmental changes trigger its resumption in the spring. This sort of suspended development is termed 'diapause', and it may be 'obligatory' and general to the whole population, or 'facultative'. In the case of facultative diapause the progeny of a species may or may not enter diapause, depending, for example, on the date when eggs are laid. As we shall see, among the British Orthoptera diapause is a common developmental strategy for overwintering eggs, preventing the premature hatching of eggs laid late in the summer, when there is too little time for them to complete their nymphal development before winter.

A second theme has been the availability in some species of alternative developmental pathways, leading to adults with some structural or physiological differences as well as behavioural ones ('polymorphism'). The most striking examples of polymorphism are provided by locusts, and also by some bush-crickets, such as the mormon and coulee crickets (*Anabrus simplex* and *Peranabrus scabricollis*) of the USA, which respond to environmental conditions – usually population density – by undergoing physiological, structural and behavioural changes (Gwynne, 2001; Loher, 1990; Dale & Tobe, 1990). The associated processes of 'gregarisation' and the formation of vast marching bands or flying swarms of insects do not occur in Britain or the rest of Europe, where population densities of orthopterans are much lower than in some tropical and subtropical regions.

However, less dramatic and less economically significant alternative developmental pathways do occur among the British Orthoptera, and they have attracted considerable research interest. The first of these is the production, in some species, of adults with markedly different wing-lengths and associated musculature. The notable expansion of geographical range that has occurred in recent decades in two species of bush-cricket has almost certainly been aided by the prevalence in some populations of long-winged (or extra long-winged) forms. The second case has to do with the persistence of a range of different colour forms in many species. Many questions have arisen as to how this colour-pattern polymorphism is maintained in each population, how and why ratios between the different morphs change, and what developmental or genetic mechanisms are involved in producing them.

ENSIFERA

The bush-crickets (Tettigoniidae Kauss, 1902)

The eggs and embryonic development

The eggs of the bush-crickets vary considerably in shape, reflecting partly the shape of the ovipositor, and partly the nature of the substrate into which they are laid. The eggs of the short-winged conehead, for example, are long and narrow, and inserted lengthways within the plant stem, parallel to the grain of the plant tissue. Eggs of other species, laid in soil or bark crevices, may be more rounded in shape (Hartley, 1964).

To complete the life cycle, each species requires a combination of sufficient warmth, moisture and nutrition to pass through all its developmental stages. However, in most parts of the world, periods suitable for growth and development are punctuated by more adverse periods when it is, for example, too hot, too cold, or too dry. In some geographical areas there are also unpredictable periods in which conditions are inhospitable – in the event of occasional fires, or droughts, for example. In general, the developmental rhythms of each species are adapted to local seasonal changes, and many species also have variably extended life cycles so that a single catastrophic event, or exceptionally inclement weather, does not wipe out the whole population.

The most fully studied adaptations to seasonal variation are periods of dormancy – particularly in the egg stage. Development is suspended when conditions are adverse – as, for example, during the winter in temperate climates such as Britain, or central and northern Europe – and then resumed when favourable conditions return. These patterns of stop-start development vary from one species to another, and also for the same species under different conditions. This raises many questions. For example, how can we explain the differences among the different species? What mechanisms are involved? What triggers them?

Observation of populations in nature can help us to pose these questions, but clear answers to them require experimental studies on animals that can be kept under controlled conditions. Much of what we now know on this topic has come from ingenious experimental studies carried out by Hartley, Ingrisch and their colleagues from the early 1960s onwards. This work established the developmental sequence of bush-cricket embryos during the egg stage and, on that basis, it was possible to research the relationship between phases of dormancy and the various developmental stages.

In one series of experiments, Ingrisch subjected the eggs of 21 species of European bush-crickets to periods of warmth of various temperatures and duration, alternating these with one or more cold periods, and he also examined the influence of varying day length (Ingrisch, 1986a). His results indicated three broad patterns of development among the species studied. These were: (1) an annual life cycle; (2) an annual life cycle with an 'optional' second (or third) year; and (3) an 'obligatory' two-year (or more) life cycle (up to eight years).

Bush-crickets of the first group include the short- and long-winged coneheads and the grey bush-cricket. In these species embryonic development generally begins without a resting period, and continues until either it is reduced or stopped by the onset of cold conditions, or until a late stage of development is reached, when an obligatory resting stage, or diapause, sets in. Either way, development does not recommence until warmer conditions return. A short period of time is then required for embryonic development to be completed before the nymph emerges from the egg and continues to develop to adulthood before the onset of the following winter.

The second group includes species that are capable of completing an annual cycle if they have enough time with warm temperatures to reach a late stage of embryonic development before they encounter cold weather. However, if there is insufficient time, or not enough warmth, they become dormant with the onset of cold conditions at an early or median stage of embryonic development. Embryonic development then continues during the following warm period to a late stage, whereupon the embryo enters into a final diapause for a second cold period (i.e., in wild populations, winter) and hatches when the warmth returns. Ingrisch divides this group into two subcategories: fast- and slow-developing species. The oak bush-cricket and Roesel's bush-cricket belong to the former, and the speckled and dark bush-crickets to the latter. In Roesel's bush-cricket, eggs that are laid early in the summer develop rapidly to a late embryonic stage, before entering into winter diapause and then hatching the following summer. However, eggs laid later in the year (i.e. when days are shorter) enter into a diapause at an early stage of development, and require a further year to complete their embryonic development (Ingrisch, 1984b).

In central Europe (and Britain) the more slowly developing species in this group, such as the dark bush-cricket (8–12 weeks at 24°C), do not usually have sufficient time to reach the stage of embryonic development that would enable hatching after just one winter. In cooler climates, therefore, their life cycle normally takes two years (or possibly more) (Hartley, 1990; Hartley & Warne, 1972, 1973). However, in southern Europe some individuals may be able to achieve an annual cycle.

The third broad developmental pattern involves 'obligate' egg diapause at an early stage of embryonic development for the first winter. On the return of warmer weather, embryonic development may continue until near-maturity, at

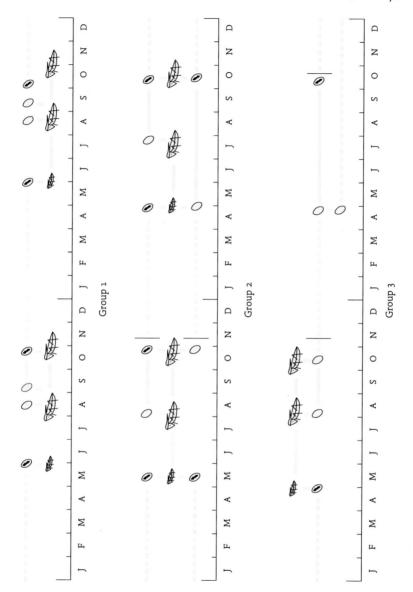

FIG 51. Life cycles of bush-crickets in southern Britain: Group 1: the annual life cycle of the long-winged conehead, *Conocephalus discolor*; Group 2: the annual or biennial life cycle of Roesel's bush-cricket, *Metrioptera roeselii*; Group 3: the biennial life cycle of the wartbiter, *Decticus verrucivorus*, with 'optional' extension of second diapause for up to seven years.

which point the embryo enters another diapause, for a second winter. Hatching and further development to adulthood take place during the following spring and summer. However, further development of the embryo following the first winter may be delayed, and the first diapause extended for as many as seven years. Species with this developmental rhythm therefore always have a cycle lasting two years or more – up to eight years. The ability to 'spread one's bets' in this way may be an adaptation to harsh or very variable climates, allowing compensation for poor conditions in any one year.

British species that have this developmental pattern include the great green bush-cricket and the wartbiter, both of which lay their eggs in the soil, and have slowly developing embryos.

To test for the influence of day length at the time when eggs were laid, Ingrisch carried out further experiments on 13 species (Ingrisch, 1986b). It was already known that day length influenced the development of the eggs of Roesel's bush-cricket, with a higher proportion going through a second winter before hatching when eggs were laid during relatively short periods of daylight (later in the summer), compared with those laid during periods with longer days. Interestingly, Ingrisch showed that when eggs were laid during short photoperiods in captivity, but maintained at high temperatures for prolonged periods (eight weeks rather than four at 24°C), the proportion hatching after the first period of cold greatly increased. The effect of photoperiod on development seems to have been overridden by the duration of favourable temperatures. The speckled bush-cricket showed a similar pattern, but in the dark bush-cricket a significant minority of eggs required a second cold treatment before hatching, even if laid during periods of extended photoperiod. The one species of group 3 that was tested required two periods of cold to complete embryonic development, regardless of photoperiod. In the case of the wartbiter, the influence of photoperiod depended on the latitude of the source populations: more northerly ones required two cold treatments for full development, irrespective of photoperiod, but a majority of the more southerly ones hatched after the first cold treatment if laid during extended photoperiod and allowed eight weeks at 24°C (Ingrisch, 1984b, 1986b).

Dormancy may also be triggered by high temperatures. A summer diapause has been established in both the dark and Roesel's bush-crickets. For Mediterranean species a summer diapause is presumably an adaptation to drought or excessive heat, but for species of cooler climates it appears to be a mechanism for preventing overwintered embryos from developing to reach maturity in high summer, which appears to be unfavourable for the late-stage embryos. This may explain the significant proportion of eggs of the dark bush-cricket laid during periods of long days (i.e. early summer) that still entered into early diapause (Ingrisch, 1984a, 1986b).

A further environmental condition that affects embryonic development is the uptake of water. Eggs at the earlier stages of embryonic development tend to be more resistant to drought, while for most species studied, up-take of water at late stages is necessary for completion of development. Ingrisch (1986c) discovered that drought slowed down embryonic development, and also prevented it from reaching the final stage. Lack of water at the time when hatching should take place may have the effect of reduced survival, or, alternatively, it may induce a further period of dormancy so that hatching takes place the following year (or subsequent years). For those species (the third group discussed above) that may take from two to eight years to complete the life cycle, there is always a scattering of hatching across successive years. However, in any one year, lack of water increases the proportion that continue in diapause rather than completing their development and hatching.

In general, it seems that the ability of bush-crickets to vary the rate or periodicity of their embryonic development in relation to the direct effect of environmental conditions, or to token stimuli such as day length that induce diapause, enables them not only to synchronise their development through cyclical climatic patterns but also to deal with unpredictable exigencies such as drought or fire.

In the more equable climates of the tropics and subtropics, many species do not have seasonal cycles, so that all developmental stages can be present together throughout the year. However, even here, some species retain annual or other seasonal developmental rhythms that may be related to the risk of drought, or the occurrence of rainy seasons (see, e.g. Ingrisch, 1996).

Nymphal development
After hatching from the egg, and freeing itself from the material in which the egg was laid, the nymph begins to feed and grow. The relatively inelastic exoskeleton has to be periodically shed to allow for growth, and the nymph may undergo a series of from four to nine moults before finally reaching the adult stage. The number of moults (ecdyses) required for the nymph to reach full adulthood varies from species to species, and, in a few cases, within the same species. Of the British species Roesel's bush-cricket has six nymphal stages, or instars, while the wartbiter has seven. The long- and short-winged coneheads may have either five or six instars depending on regional climates in Europe. Apparently they are able to develop with fewer stages where the season favourable to development is relatively short, for example in mountainous areas. There are also sex-related variations in

some species, some with more developmental stages in the females, and others in which a minority of males go through an extra stage (Gwynne, 2001: 57–8).

Unlike many insects that develop through distinct larval and pupal stages (the endopterygote groups such as Lepidoptera and Hymenoptera), the larvae (or nymphs) of the orthopterans resemble the adults in general external appearance. In winged forms, the wings are represented by small flaps in early-stage nymphs, and develop with each successive stage. In the final two instars prior to emergence as an adult the wing stubs are inverted, with the costal margins facing upwards, and the hind wings lying outside the fore wings. This is a general feature of the development of all the winged Orthoptera.

In a few species there are more striking differences of appearance between nymphs and adults, as, for example, in species that have evolved to mimic

FIG 52. Developmental stages of the short-winged conehead, *Conocephalus dorsalis*, normally a brachypterous species: (a) eggs; (b) first instar nymph; (c) third instar nymph, female, showing stub of the ovipositor; (d) final instar nymph, female, showing inverted wing stubs and developed ovipositor; (e) adult, female.

poisonous or distasteful insects as a predator avoidance strategy. One example is the astonishing resemblance of the nymph of the south-east Asian bush-cricket (*Macroxiphus sumatranus siamensis*) to an ant (Helfert & Sänger, 1995, cited in Gwynne 2001).

When about to moult, the nymph usually hangs below a twig or other perch, and the 'skin' splits from the head-end first, under pressure from the haemolymph ('blood'). The emerging insect is initially quite soft and pale, but when its exoskeleton has fully hardened and acquired its typical coloration, the insect is noticeably larger than it was before the moult, and, in winged forms, more closely resembles the adult. Around the time of ecdysis the nymphs are particularly vulnerable to predation, and in general mortality rates during the nymphal stages are high. In the strongest British population of wartbiters

FIG 53. Developmental stages of the great green bush-cricket, *Tettigonia viridissima*, a fully winged species: (a) early instar nymph; (b) female nymph (?6th instar) showing stub of the ovipositor; (c) penultimate (?7th) instar nymph, female, showing inverted wing stubs and developing ovipositor; (d) penultimate (?7th) instar nymph, male; (e) final instar female nymph; (f) final instar male nymph; (g) adult male.

FIG 54. Newly emerged adult bush-cricket, wings fully extended.

(*Decticus verrucivorus*), their density fell by 99.3 per cent between hatching and final moult in 1988 (Cherrill & Brown, 1990a). Many species make a meal of their cast-off 'skin', leaving no trace of their developmental history.

Like embryonic development, the rate of growth and development through the nymphal stages can be significantly affected by environmental conditions. The availability of food and moisture are, of course, important, as is temperature. Nymphs have optimal temperature ranges for their development, and, for some species at the northern edge of their range in Britain, this may impose important habitat requirements. In their studies of the development of wartbiters in East Sussex, Cherrill and Brown found changes in the habitat preferences of nymphs at different stages. First-instar nymphs were concentrated in areas of short turf with bare ground, with later instars spreading to denser, taller grassland, and adults associated with dense, tussocky patches. Although the concentration of first-instar nymphs could be to some extent explained in terms of the ovipositing preferences of the adult females, subsequent distributions suggested the importance of warm microclimates in the short-turf patches for nymphal development. Retreat to taller, tussocky areas in late-instar nymphs and adults could be explained in terms of predator avoidance and (in males) adoption of singing 'perches', but even here, loss of warmth could be compensated by basking on the warmer edges of the tussocks (Cherrill & Brown, 1992a).

The crickets (Grylloidea)

As among the bush-crickets, the life cycles of crickets vary greatly between species, and in some cases, within species. All species pass through a series of nymphal instars, which may vary between species from five to fourteen. It has been shown that diet, as well as day length, can influence both the rate of growth and the number of instars. For example, the southern field cricket (*G. bimaculatus*) develops quickly through eight instars on a high protein diet,

FIG 55. Late instar nymph of the southern field cricket, *Gryllus bimaculatus*, showing developed wing stubs.

but slowly and through ten instars on low protein (Walker & Masaki 1989). In winged species, the tiny wing pads appear in early instar nymphs, but are reversed in orientation (as in other orthopteran groups) for the final two instars, and assume their adult form at the final moult. Males and females can usually be distinguished once the ovipositor begins to be visible in females, usually during the middle instars. The hearing organs (tympana) appear on the fore tibia only with the final moult.

As in other groups of Orthoptera, the timing of the developmental stages is generally adapted to seasonal cycles, except for species that have not evolved in seasonal environments, such as species of the moist tropics, or those that live, for example, in caves, where environmental conditions may vary much less. These species reproduce continuously without any clear demarcation between generations – the house cricket (*A. domesticus*) being one example. Species that have to fit their developmental processes into favourable periods have, like the bush-crickets, the ability to suspend development at various stages (Masaki, 1987).

In temperate climates, the most common pattern is an annual life cycle, with the winter spent in the egg stage. Where there are insufficient numbers of days above a critical temperature threshold for metamorphosis to be completed in a single summer, development may take two or three years, often with variable patterns of embryonic development that depend on day length at the time when the eggs were laid. In the case of the field cricket (*G. campestris*), eggs laid when days are long (i.e. early in the season under natural conditions) produce nymphs that develop slowly, while eggs laid when photoperiods are short give rise to fast-developing nymphs, so both groups reach the overwintering stage at the appropriate time.

FIG 56. Late instar nymph of the field cricket, *Gryllus campestris*, in Autumn.

FIG 57. Late instar nymph of the wood cricket, *Nemobius sylvestris*.

Some of this variation is represented among the small number of native British species. In the wood cricket (*N. sylvestris*) the eggs undergo a winter diapause, giving rise to nymphs the following spring. These continue to develop during summer and autumn, and pass the winter in a late nymphal stage (usually the fifth). In their second spring they complete their nymphal development (eight instars in all), becoming adult during the summer. These adults mate and lay eggs, and some adults survive through yet another (third) winter. Both adults and nymphs can be found at any time of year.

The field cricket (*G. campestris*) mates and lays its eggs from May to July. The resulting nymphs go on to develop through summer and autumn, usually reaching their tenth (penultimate) instar by this time. The late-instar nymph digs a burrow in which it spends the winter, and emerges the following spring to complete its development.

The scaly cricket (*P. vicentae* – now assigned to a distinct grylloid family, Mogoplistidae) has a particularly complex developmental pattern, disentangled by Sutton (1999). Based on evidence of co-existence of various developmental stages at various times of year, Sutton postulates a three-year life cycle, with overwintering as egg, early-stage nymph or adult (see species account for more detail).

FIG 58. Developmental stages of the scaly cricket, *Pseudomogoplistes vicentae*: (a) eggs; (b) first instar nymph; (c) late instar male; (d) adult male.

The mole-crickets (Gryllotalpidae Leach, 1815)

The native British species of mole-cricket (*G. gryllotalpa*) spends most of its life underground. The eggs are laid in clutches of up to 300 in spring in underground chambers, and they are regularly tended by the female to prevent the growth of mould. The eggs hatch in two to four weeks, and the newly emerged nymphs are also cared for. The first winter is spent in one or other of the nymphal instars. Full development takes two or more years. This is one of the very few examples of parental care among the insects.

Raphidophoridae (Walker, 1871)

The greenhouse camel-cricket (*Diestrammena* (*Tachycines*) *asynamorus*) is an introduced species in Britain, and the only one of its family likely to be found here. The eggs are laid singly or in small groups of up to eight, in loose soil. They are grey-white and slightly flattened ovoid in shape, 2–2.5 mm long, and 1–1.2 mm wide. Depending on temperature, they take from 8 to 10 weeks to hatch. They pass through 8 to 11 instars, each stage lasting some 3 to 5 weeks, with complete development taking from 6 to 10 months. Individuals from a single population develop at very different rates, and there is no diapause. There are no wings, and after each moult the nymphs consume the cast-off skin. In females, the

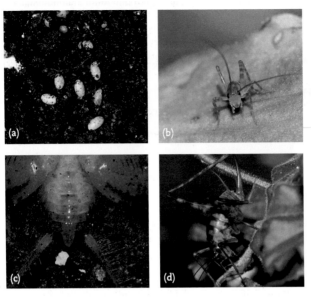

FIG 59.
Developmental
stages of the
greenhouse camel-
cricket, *Diestrammena
asynamorus*: (a) eggs;
(b) newly hatched first
instar nymph;
(c) underside of
abdomen of third
instar female nymph,
showing stub of the
ovipositor; (d) adult
female.

ovipositor is just visible at the third instar and grows with each subsequent moult (2 mm in the fifth instar, 13 mm in the adult). However, it is difficult to recognise the developmental stage of males except by size. The antennae vary from four to five times the total body length throughout development.

CAELIFERA

Groundhoppers (Tetrigidae Serville, 1838)

The three British groundhoppers have similar patterns of development. The eggs are laid in batches of 10 to 20 in soil or among mosses, often stuck together, but not enclosed in a protective pod (as in Acrididae). The eggs hatch in three to four weeks, and the resulting nymphs pass through five (males) or six (females) instars before emerging as adults. The wings are present as tiny pads (but hidden by the pronotum) in the early instars. Their orientation is reversed in the final two nymphal instars, but set back to the adult position in the final moult.

In the common groundhopper (*Tetrix undulata*), adults and nymphs of various stages of development can be found together at any time of year. Populations of Cepero's and slender groundhoppers (*T. ceperoi* and *T. subulata*) appear to have more synchronised life cycles: nymphs develop during spring and summer, and overwinter as late instar nymphs or immature adults.

FIG 60. Groundhopper nymphs: (left) common groundhopper, *Tetrix undulata*; (right) slender groundhopper, *Tetrix subulata*.

Grasshoppers (Acrididae MacLeay, 1821)

The grasshoppers are believed to all have an annual life cycle in Britain. Eggs are laid during the summer or early autumn and the winter is passed in the egg stage. In the following spring (generally during April, but sometimes later, depending on the weather and species concerned) the eggs hatch and the resulting nymphs go through a series of moults before emerging as adults in early to mid-summer. All adults die off before the onset of winter.

Fertilised females lay their eggs in batches of up to 14 in repeated egg-laying events through their adult lives. Some species lay their eggs in the soil, in bare ground or sand (sometimes in ant-hills) or among grass roots. Others, notably those (such as the lesser and large marsh grasshoppers,

C. albomarginatus and *S. grossum*) that tend to prefer more moist, densely vegetated habitats, lay their egg batches in grass tussocks among the bases of grass stems and blades. When each egg batch has been laid, the female secretes a frothy substance around it. This soon hardens and forms a tough protective 'pod', often incorporating particles of soil or vegetation. The numbers of eggs in each pod, and the size and shape of the pod vary from species to species (and, to some extent, among different populations of the same species).

FIG 61. Female common field grasshopper, *Chorthippus brunneus*, laying its eggs in the ground.

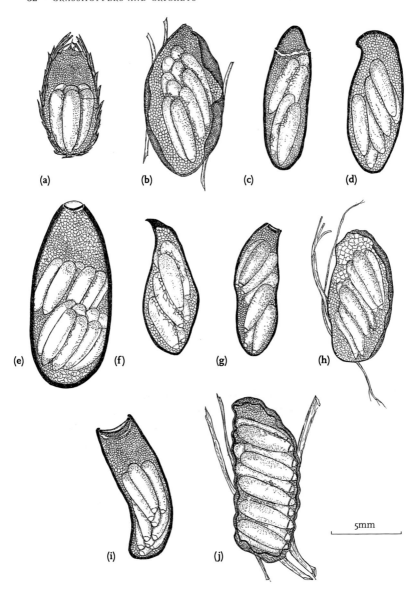

FIG 62. Egg pods of British grasshoppers (from Waloff 1950): (a) *Stenobothrus lineatus*; (b) *Omocestus viridulus*; (c) *Omocestus rufipes*; (d) *Myrmeleotettix maculatus*; (e) *Chorthippus brunneus*; (f) *Chorthippus parallelus*; (g) *Chorthippus vagans*; (h) *Chorthippus albomarginatus*; (i) *Gomphocerippus rufus*; (j) *Stethophyma grossum*.

Usually (and especially in eggs laid early in the season) embryonic development continues within the egg shell until a late stage. At this point the embryo enters a diapause until later in the year, when the winter temperatures are too cold for further development. With the arrival of warmer weather in spring, the eggs hatch. As in the other groups of Orthoptera, the hatchling is enclosed in a fine membrane, and looks worm-like. It wriggles its way out of the egg shell, and (in eggs laid in the soil) up to the surface. Very soon afterwards the membrane is shed, and the first nymphal stage is reached. Most British grasshoppers go through a series of four nymphal instars, before reaching adulthood with their final moult. The nymphs are like smaller versions of the adults, but the wings are present as small flaps, or buds. The size and orientation of these vary from one stage to the next, and so are very useful in identifying the developmental stage of grasshopper nymphs. In first

FIG 63. Life history stages of the lesser marsh grasshopper, *Chorthippus albomarginatus*, a fully winged species: (a) first instar nymph; (b) second instar nymph; (c) third instar nymph; (d) fourth instar nymph; (e) adult male.

and second instars the wing stubs are very small and hang down at the sides from the second and third thoracic segments, while in the two final instars they are progressively larger, and their orientation inverted – with the leading edge of the wings uppermost, and the hind wings visible in side view, largely concealing the fore wings. With the final moult the wings are fully developed and the orientation is reversed yet again, with the leading edges facing down along the sides of the insect, and fore wings concealing the hind wings (Hassall & Grayson, 1987; Schädler & Witsak, 1999; Collins, 2001, 2003; Cherrill, 2004; Cherrill & Haswell, 2006).

One significant variation in this life-history pattern occurs in at least four British species (the common field and meadow grasshoppers, *C. brunneus* and *C. parallelus*; the lesser mottled grasshopper, *Stenobothrus stigmaticus*; and the large marsh grasshopper, *S. grossum*). These species (like the coneheads,

FIG 64. Life history stages of the common meadow grasshopper, *Chorthippus parallelus*, normally a brachypterous species: (a) first instar nymph; (b) second instar nymph; (c) third instar nymph; (d) fourth instar nymph; (e) female adult.

Conocephalus) can add an extra instar to their development. In these grasshoppers the extra stage is intermediate between stages II and III, but has the wing bud characteristics of the first two instars, and so is referred to as instar IIa (the use of Roman numerals to designate nymphal stages is now a convention). Further south in Europe more species exhibit this flexibility in their development, and the variation may occur in both males and females of some species. This is now known to be the case with the large marsh grasshopper, but in the meadow and field grasshoppers, it appears to be only the females that are able to add an extra developmental stage. For some field research topics it is relevant to be able to decide whether a particular female has passed through four or five nymphal stages, and careful study, notably by Collins (2006), has revealed that this can be done by counting antennal segments. At each moult, the number of segments

FIG 65. Life history stages of the common field grasshopper, *Chorthippus brunneus*, with 'optional' five instar nymphal development: (a) first instar; (b) second instar; (c) third instar; (d) fourth instar; (e) fifth instar female (unusual purple colour form); (f) adult.

in the antennae increases. As a result adult females that have included stage
IIa in their development have more segments than those with the 'standard'
four instars. Adult females with 22 or 23 segments in the antennal flagellum are
products of a four-stage development, while those with 24 result from a five-stage
sequence (see Collins, 2001, 2003, 2006; Cherrill & Haswell, 2006)

Within this broad pattern (in Britain) of an annual life cycle with
overwintering in the egg stage, there is still considerable variation between
species and between different populations of the same species. Research has
focused on the common field grasshopper (*C. brunneus*), which is both common
and widespread in Britain, as well as being relatively easy to rear under laboratory
conditions. On theoretical grounds, it is generally assumed that insects will
be endowed with 'developmental strategies' that maximise their chances of
surviving and reproducing (e.g. Forrest, 1987). These strategies will be related to,
among other things, seasonal availability of food, opportunities for mating and/
or ovipositing, risks of inclement weather (cyclical changes or unpredictable
events), and risks of mortality or loss of fitness due to predation or parasitism.
As we saw above, the ability to slow down or halt development at particular life
history stages, as, for example, by entering into diapause, is widespread, and
can be seen as a developmental strategy that helps insects deal effectively with
seasonal changes that limit periods favourable to different activities, as well as
with unpredictably occurring adverse environmental conditions or events.

Such developmental strategies will generally involve complicated trade-offs
between different aspects or features of the life cycle. Indeed, the effort involved
in reproduction itself involves a trade off with survivorship (for evidence of
this in *C. brunneus*, see de Souza Santos Jr. & Begon, 1987). Seasonality, too,
imposes constraints on life cycles that necessitate trade-offs between different
features. For example, we might expect that, other things being equal, a species
whose adult reproductive period is limited by a brief summer/autumn season
would evolve to reach maturity early in the year so as to benefit from as long a
reproductive period as possible. However, there is also evidence to suggest that
for both males and females there is a reproductive advantage associated with
large size (e.g. Forrest, 1987; Honěk, 1993; Telfer & Hassall, 1999). So, it might
benefit smaller individuals with the 'option' for rapid development to maturity
in spring to invest instead in further growth even at the cost of arriving at sexual
maturity later. Similar considerations apply to such aspects as size and number of
eggs, embryonic and nymphal developmental rhythms, number of instars, and, of
course, courtship and mating strategies (see Chapters 4, 5 and 6).

Sibly and Monk (1987) produced a complex mathematical model of the factors
that might influence the trade-off between grasshopper egg size and time taken up

in nymphal development the following spring. Hypothetically, larger eggs carry more provisioning for the embryo, enabling more rapid nymphal development, and hence a longer adult breeding 'window'. However, other factors will influence this relationship: size has implications for the number of eggs that will be laid in each clutch, and the resulting eggs will be liable to varying mortality rates, as will the resulting nymphs. The period of time over which females lay their egg clutches, the frequency with which they lay, and the life chances of the offspring of eggs laid at different times during the season are also to be taken into account. The authors applied their model to the progeny of females of two species of grasshopper (*C. brunneus* and *C. parallelus*) taken from three different sites, but reared under common laboratory conditions. As the insects were reared in the laboratory, some of the factors that would have affected fitness under natural conditions were not applicable. However, the experiment did confirm the predicted relationship between egg size and nymphal development time for insects sourced at the three sites. Smaller but more numerous eggs were produced by females from sites with longer adult reproductive seasons. Development times were longer for this group, suggesting an adaptive linkage of smaller egg size and longer period of nymphal development with the locally available longer adult reproductive season. Larger egg sizes, with associated costs to egg number, but greater provisioning for the offspring, should shorten nymphal development time, and so enable adults to reach reproductive age early in the shorter season at their source locations. In fact, these expectations were borne out in the case of *C. brunneus*, but, on the assumptions made in the model, *C. parallelus* populations at the study site appeared to have suboptimal reproductive strategies.

However, drawing on a larger data set for *C. brunneus*, from 28 sites in Britain, and field data on several other species, Grant *et al.* (1993), found no correlation between egg weight (measured by hatchling weight) and rate of nymphal development. They also modified Sibly & Monk's model in the light of well-established generalisations positing a positive relationship between size of adult female insects and their fecundity (see for example Honěk, 1993), a relationship for which there is specific evidence in British grasshoppers, and in *C. brunneus* in particular (Richards & Waloff, 1954; Wall & Begon, 1987).

Using evidence-based estimates of the likely numerical values of the various life-history variables for British grasshopper populations, and their modified version of the model produced by Sibly and Monk, Grant *et al.* concluded that the two main influences on reproductive success were juvenile mortality rates and development time from hatching to first oviposition. These results appeared to challenge Sibly & Monk's emphasis on the limitations posed by the length of the season available for reproductive activity – at least in the British context. Grant *et al.* acknowledge that length of season is clearly limiting in the sense that at these latitudes it precludes multiple generations in a single year. However, since the adult lifespan of individual grasshoppers is small in relation to the duration of the season within which reproductive activity can occur, it seems unlikely that reproductive success is strongly affected by the length of the season. This conclusion gets intuitive support from the fact that grasshopper populations have already declined greatly before inclement winter weather sets in.

Grant *et al.* also calculate the implications of the ability of *C. brunneus* females to include an extra instar (IIa) in their development. Since all growth takes place during the nymphal stages, and there must be a mechanical limit to the amount of size increase conferred at each moult, the main determinant of adult size can be assumed to be the number of instars (the pattern of size increases between moults is given by 'Dyer's rule', and the adaptive value of size increases relative to food availability and numbers of moults is discussed in Hutchinson *et al.*, 1997). The data for *C. brunneus* provided by Grant *et al.* do confirm a strong correlation between the frequency of the IIa stage in a population and their index of growth (ratio of mature weight to hatchling weight). Assuming that increasing the number of instars results in larger adults, but also prolongs development time, there will be a trade-off between greater fecundity of the larger adults and the increased risk of mortality during the developmental stages. Other things being equal, under conditions that favour rapid development and low juvenile mortality, the five-stage development 'option' will confer greater reproductive success. Again, Grant *et al.*'s model suggests that the duration of the season is relatively unimportant as a limiting factor, compared with climatic variables such as warmth and amounts of sunshine. However, they do concede that length of season would be a limiting factor if, contrary to fact, it was very short, or the weather conditions were so poor as to greatly prolong juvenile development to the point that few individuals reached maturity.

An implication of Grant *et al.*'s model is that the inclusion of the extra nymphal stage IIa should be more common in warm, dry and sunny sites (or seasons), and rarer where summers are cooler, wetter and cloudy. Under the latter conditions, rapid development to sexual maturity would be favoured, even at the cost of smaller adult size and reduced fecundity. In fact, the proportion of females undergoing the five-instar development path did show great variation between source locations, reaching up to 90 per cent in the warmer, sunnier sites. The extra instar can also be induced under laboratory conditions by higher rearing temperatures (Hassall & Grayson, 1987).

Telfer and Hassall (1999) provide a further analysis of the large data set from the samples of *C. brunneus* referred to by Grant *et al.* The insects were drawn from a large number of sites in Britain and Ireland, incorporating a wide range of both latitude and longitude, and associated climatic conditions. The insects were used to establish laboratory populations and these were subsequently bred under standard conditions through three generations. Despite differences between the model proposed by Sibly and Monk and that of Grant *et al.*, especially with respect to the importance of season length, these authors point out that both models predict a trade-off between earlier maturation followed by slower reproduction and slower development followed by faster reproductive output. Where there are conditions such as longer seasons for nymphal development, and warmth and plenty of sunshine that enable faster growth, selective pressures will favour larger adult size, with associated greater fecundity. Under harsher climatic conditions and shorter seasons, the pressures would be for shorter development times, and smaller adult size. Additionally, other things being equal, adverse climatic conditions would be expected to favour larger eggs, with larger hatchling size, and so potentially faster development to adulthood (although note that this association between size and development rate was not found in the laboratory study reported by Grant *et al.*).

The results reported by Telfer and Hassall suggest significant variation in several life-history traits in relation to climatic conditions. Since different climatic factors are frequently interrelated it was not possible to distinguish with precision, for example, between the effects of warm winter temperatures, seasonal incidence of sunshine, or summer temperatures. Nevertheless, some very significant broad generalisations were possible on the basis of their study of *C. brunneus*: that both growth and nymphal development were more rapid in the populations drawn from the more northerly, cooler locations, with shorter seasons. The adult size in these populations was also smaller, and the frequency of females including the extra IIa stage in their development was much lower. Hatchling size was also, as predicted, larger in the insects sourced from the more northerly sites.

The above variations in developmental strategies in relation to climate and latitude might be expected to be also reflected in responses to varying environmental conditions through the year in single populations. Adults, including egg-laying females, of *C. brunneus* can be found from June through to the end of October (depending on location). The conditions for growth, development and reproduction of hatchlings are likely to vary considerably depending on the dates at which egg batches are laid. In general, the hatchlings from eggs laid early in the season will hatch earlier the following spring and will experience more favourable conditions than those hatching later. They will also have potentially more time for reproduction once they reach adulthood.

Cherill (2002, 2005) studied a single population of *C. brunneus* in the field to find out if hatching date was, indeed, correlated with differing life-cycle patterns. He was able to show that eggs laid later in the season were larger (with larger, later-emerging hatchlings), and that early-hatching nymphs developed more slowly and to a larger adult size than did late-hatching ones. Moreover, equipped with Collins's criterion for separating the females that had developed through five nymphal stages from those resulting from four (in terms of numbers of antennal segments), Cherrill was able to demonstrate that the proportion of females including the extra IIa stage was higher among the earlier-hatching individuals, and declined as the season progressed. In general, the variations in developmental strategy relating to seasonality closely mirrored those reported by Telfer and Hassall in relation to broad climatic and latitudinal parameters.

So far this discussion of developmental strategies has focused on the development of nymphs, but implicit in it have been assumptions about embryonic development. As we saw in the above discussion of embryonic development in bush-crickets, the timing of embryonic development in grasshoppers is also affected by environmental conditions, most especially seasonality. A key feature of these strategies is the ability to slow down or halt embryonic development to deal with adverse climatic or other environmental conditions. In climates such those encountered in Britain and Europe, the most usual form taken by this ability is an 'obligatory' diapause during the winter months. Embryonic development ceases once a certain late stage (usually IVd) (see Chapman & Whitham, 1968 and Cherrill, 1987), called the 'diapause stage', is reached. Development is resumed to completion and hatching only after a period of time at low temperatures (eight weeks at 4°C for *C. brunneus* under laboratory conditions – see Moriarty, 1969a and 1969b, and Cherrill & Begon, 1989a). However, there is evidence from laboratory studies and theoretical considerations (Hilbert *et al.*, 1985) that some species of Orthoptera show flexibility in their embryonic development and can avoid diapause under some conditions. Cherrill and Begon (1991) were able to demonstrate this in a naturally occurring population of *C. brunneus*. By taking samples of eggs from a population at intervals during their development they discovered that eggs laid early in the summer developed through to the diapause stage and then ceased development, resuming and completing their development the following spring. Hatching in these egg batches was relatively synchronised early in spring. However, eggs laid later in the season did not reach the diapause stage before winter weather set in. Their subsequent development was slowed down, presumably by the direct effect of low temperatures, and development then continued in spring, without diapause and with a later and more dispersed period of hatching.

LIFE HISTORIES · 91

Taken together, these studies indicate a range of variation in developmental strategies available within a single species. These appear to be adaptive in relation to variations in climate, latitude and oviposition date. Eggs laid early in the season in favourable climates (or further south) are prevented from premature hatching by the winter diapause, after which fitness may be enhanced by more extended development resulting in larger, more fecund adults, aided, in the case of females, by the ability to add an extra instar in their nymphal development. However, the ability to avoid diapause enables late-laid eggs to hatch the following year, despite their immature developmental stage at the onset of winter. Late hatchlings tend to be larger and develop more quickly, allowing them to reach adulthood in time to reproduce before the end of the season. This is achieved at the cost of smaller adult size (and, in the case of the females, a lower probability of including the IIa nymphal stage). These later-maturing females tend to lay larger eggs in smaller batches, possibly as an adaptive response to the relatively poorer environmental conditions and shorter seasonal 'window' for development that is likely to be experienced by the resulting (late-hatching) nymphs. Individual females also tend to increase egg size, but reduce clutch size as they age. This seems to be widespread among grasshoppers (Cherrill, 2002).

The developmental plasticity illustrated in the case of *C. brunneus* (and probably present in many other species) confers on individuals and local populations a high degree of adaptability to a wide variety of environmental conditions. In some cases there appear to be alternative developmental pathways that can be triggered by direct experience of the relevant environmental conditions, such as cumulative days of sunshine, day length, or maximum or minimum temperatures. However, the study conducted by Telfer and Hassall is of particular interest, since it shows adaptive differences in developmental strategies on the part of differently sourced populations of the same species after standard treatment over three generations. This is highly suggestive of genetic adaptation to local environmental conditions on the part of different subpopulations of a single species.

A further topic of considerable practical as well as biological interest is the effect of competition induced by population density on developmental outcomes. In one laboratory study carried out by Wall and Begon (1987), again with *C. brunneus* as the 'guinea pig', individual differences in weight and rate of development in the first two nymphal instars were noted, and these were unaffected by population density. However, in the later instars, density had marked effects. Increased density (crowding) led to greater variation in body size between individuals in the population, presumably a result of differential individual success in competing for limited resources. However, in still higher

densities, these differences became less marked and the population became
more uniform in weight. This was a consequence of higher density-dependent
mortality rates among the smaller individuals, which developed more slowly
and failed to reach a critical weight for transition to the adult stage. This critical
weight is much greater for females than for males (70 mg and 45 mg respectively).

ALTERNATIVE DEVELOPMENTAL STRATEGIES: POLYMORPHISMS

Much more marked examples of alternative developmental strategies include
the process of 'gregarisation' associated with swarming in locusts and similar
changes associated with aggregation in some species of bush-crickets, such as the
mormon and coulee crickets of North America (Gwynne, 2001, and see Chapter 1).
These fascinating phenomena are beyond the scope of this book, but comparable,
although less dramatic, alternative developmental pathways are found in some
British species. These include the production of a minority of long-winged,
dispersive forms in otherwise wingless or brachypterous species. This is a
familiar feature in several native British species, including Roesel's bush-cricket,
the short-winged conehead, and the common meadow grasshopper, and is more
rarely reported in the bog bush-cricket. A related phenomenon is the production
of a minority of 'extra-macropterous' forms of the normally macropterous
long-winged conehead. Yet another sort of diversity among the adults of single
species is colour polymorphism. Many species of orthopterans occur commonly
in two alternative colour forms (usually green and brown). Common green and
stripe-winged grasshoppers, and the long-winged conehead are examples of
this. However, other species display a seemingly indefinite variety of colour
patterns within a single population. Research into these polymorphisms has
been concerned with their relevance to the adaptation of the species concerned
to features of their habitats, to population dynamics, dispersal and changes of
range, as well as with the external cues for divergent developmental pathways,
the developmental stage at which they operate, and the internal physiological
processes that bring them about.

1. Wing-length dimorphism
Populations of many brachypterous or wingless species may include small
minorities of long-winged, or 'macropterous' forms. As noted above, the British
orthopteran fauna includes several bush-crickets and one grasshopper that
have this capacity for divergent developmental pathways. It is usually supposed

that the macropterous individuals play the main role in dispersal across long distances, and there is evidence of this in the case of Roesel's bush-cricket, where increases in the proportion of macropters in the population have been associated with recent dramatic range extension. The same may be true of the long-winged conehead (see Chapter 9).

Wing-length polymorphism is widespread across a number of insect orders, but so far as the Orthoptera are concerned, the most systematic research has been focused on a small number of cricket species. One key generalisation that seems to apply across the insect orders, including the crickets, is that among females, macroptery is associated with later sexual maturity and lower fecundity – in other words, there is a trade-off between the ability to fly and reproductive output. It is usually supposed, but has only been fully demonstrated in a small number of cricket species, that withdrawal of resources necessary for developing wings and wing muscles reduces those available for the formation of the eggs and ovary (Roff, 1984). In the case of *Gryllus rubens*, the wing muscles of brachypterous females weigh 24 mg less, and the ovaries 67 mg more, than those of macropterous females of similar body mass. This does suggest a redistribution

FIG 66. Normal and macropterous forms of Roesel's bush-cricket, *Metrioptera roeselii*: (a) final instar male nymph, normal form; (b) final instar male nymph, macropterous form; (c) adult male, normal form; (d) adult male, macropterous form.

of resources from reproduction to flight in the macropterous form, but the decreased ovarian weight is clearly much greater than the increase in wing muscle weight. Subsequent research on this species indicates that extra resources are required in the macropterous form not just to produce the wings and flight muscles, but also to maintain them, and there is a further metabolic demand to produce a store of flight fuel. This difference expresses itself in much higher resting respiration rates in macropters (Zera & Denno, 1997).

The loss of reproductive potential associated with macroptery in females is well established. Does a similar trade-off occur among males? There has been less research on this question and its results have been equivocal. It may be that the trade-off is less significant in the case of males, or it may be that the reduced reproductive success of males is less easily detected or measured under laboratory conditions. Studies of macroptery in male bush-crickets might shed some light on this question, especially in the case of those species in which there is considerable investment in the spermatophylax. Supporting evidence for this (albeit based on a small sample) comes from a study by Simmons and Thomas (2004) on the long-winged conehead. Spermatophylaces of extra-macropterous males were significantly lighter than those of normally macropterous ones.

The critical developmental stage at which an individual is determined to develop as one or the other adult morph varies among different insect groups. If the critical stage occurs early in development, it has the advantage of preventing the (partial) development of structures that turn out to be inappropriate. Alternatively, if the critical stage comes late in development, it enables development to respond flexibly to the current environmental cues. In the crickets that have been most closely studied (*G. rubens* and *G. firmus*) the switching-point occurs early to mid-way into the final nymphal instar. The mechanism so far identified in both species supports the longstanding assumption that the juvenile hormone (JH) is intimately involved. Two hormones are known to be involved in both moulting and transition from final instar nymph to adult. These are JH and 20-hydroxy ecdysone (20-OH ecdysone). High concentrations of JH initiate moulting from one nymphal instar to the next, but with the final instar, JH concentrations fall and 20-OH ecdysone levels are raised, promoting moulting and completion of metamorphosis (Zera & Denno, 1997).

Research on the physiological processes leading to the production of the two morphs in the cricket *G. rubens* found that persistence of high concentrations of JH during the final nymphal instar was implicated in the production of brachypterous adults. In nymphs destined to become macropterous adults, there were high concentrations of an enzyme (juvenile hormone esterase, JHE) that degrades JH, resulting in lower concentrations of JH in the haemolymph

(Zera *et al.*, 1989). Similar results were obtained for the sand cricket, *G. firmus*. In this study, separate lineages of the crickets had been bred over more than 30 generations, some selected for macroptery, others for brachyptery and others as unselected controls. The resulting laboratory populations showed radically different proportions of macropters according to the principle of selection, indicating substantial heritability of the traits (Roff *et al.* 1999). Physiological analysis yielded similar relationships between JH and JHE concentrations at a critical phase during the final instar and the resulting wing-length morph to those established for *G. rubens* (Fairbairn & Yadlowski, 1997). This study was also able to illustrate shifts both in the levels of activity of the hormones and enzymes and in the threshold concentrations leading to either morph. The lineage that had undergone selection for macroptery showed higher mean levels of JHE (and so lower levels of JH) as well as lower thresholds for production of macropters, indicating that both the liability to produce the macropterous form and its physiological threshold may be affected by selective pressures. Fairbairn and Yadlowski also took into account other traits – such as fecundity, muscular development and flight-propensity – that are correlated with wing morphs and collectively termed 'migratory tendency'. Their hypothesis is that these constitute a single phenotypical syndrome mediated by juvenile hormone levels.

In many insect groups the production of long-winged forms is associated with declining habitat quality or with crowding, with a suggested adaptive value in these circumstances for ability to disperse, leading to potentially better habitat patches or reduced intraspecific competition for resources. However, in the case of two British bush-crickets – the long-winged conehead (*C. discolor*) and Roesel's bush-cricket

FIG 67. Forms of the normally macropterous long-winged conehead, *Conocephalus discolor*: (left) normal form; (right) extra-macropterous female.

(*M. roeselii*) – there is substantial, if rather circumstantial, evidence that increased macroptery is associated with favourable climatic conditions, and some more systematic evidence that it is associated with lower population densities (Simmons & Thomas, 2004; Gardiner, 2009b). A laboratory study of the common meadow grasshopper (*C. parallelus*) also found increased macroptery to be correlated with extended day length (possibly related to higher temperatures or opportunities for basking) (Ritchie *et al.*, 1987). In the two bush-crickets, greatly increased proportions of macropterous individuals were present in newly-established populations at the margins of their expanding ranges (see Chapter 9), compared with populations closer to the range core. In addition, descendants of specimens drawn from these different locations, but reared under common conditions, also showed differential proportions of macropters. Interestingly, in experiments to determine the flight ability of the morphs of the long-winged conehead, it was discovered that the extra-macropterous forms drawn from sites at the edge of the range flew for four times as long as the same morph drawn from closer to the range-core. In other studies it has been shown that non-dispersive macropters can redistribute resources from wing-muscles by histolysis to partially restore fecundity at the adult stage (Zera & Denno, 1997). It might be speculated that macropters of the long-winged conehead at the range-core also have this ability – although they are externally (extra) long-winged, they may have traded off wing muscle for greater reproductive potential.

A promising explanation of these findings is that climate change may be increasing the availability of suitable habitat that is not yet colonised. This would select for dispersal ability, counterbalancing the physiological costs of migratory tendency. However, once a new population is established, the selective pressures reverse, with more fecund, less dispersive brachypterous forms being favoured. In the study by Simmons and Thomas (2004), populations at sites that were known to have been colonised from 5 to 10 years previously had reverted to proportions of macropters close to those at the core of the range. The case of the common

FIG 68. Forms of the common meadow grasshopper, *Chorthippus parallelus*: (left) normal form of the male; (right) macropterous male.

meadow grasshopper remains puzzling, as it appears that the macropterous form is incapable of flight. Ritchie *et al.* (1987) speculate that the ability to produce this morph might be considered a 'genetic relic', whose environmental threshold is rarely encountered in the habitats it now occupies.

2. Colour polymorphism

A striking feature of many species of Orthoptera is the wide range of variation of colour pattern that can be seen in some species, frequently within a local population. In addition to the colour transformations associated with phase transition in locusts and other swarming and migratory species, there are also colour differences between the sexes of some species and other differences associated with maturation. In the large marsh grasshopper (*Stethophyma grossum*),

FIG 69. Colour forms of grasshoppers and bush-crickets: (a) green form of *Conocephalus discolor*; (b) brown form of *C. discolor*; (c) green form of *Omocestus viridulus*; (d) brown form of *O. viridulus*; (e) uncommon purple form of *Gomphocerippus rufus*.

for example, the usual form of the female is a dull olive-green, while the male is usually bright apple green. In the woodland grasshopper (*Omocestus rufipes*) the ground colour of the females is variable, but in males it is predominantly black. In several species of grasshopper (*O. rufipes, Stenobothrus lineatus, Stenobothrus stigmaticus* and *Myrmeleotettix maculatus*) adult maturation is associated with reddish coloration of parts of the abdomen and/or hind tibiae.

Yet another sort of colour polymorphism is evident in many species whose populations include a range of colour forms unrelated to sex or stages of maturation. Perhaps the most common of these is the presence within the same species of alternative green or brown forms. This is found in British species such as Roesel's bush-cricket (*Metrioptera roeselii*), the long-winged conehead (*Conocephalus discolor*), and the stripe-winged and common green grasshoppers (*Stethobothrus lineatus* and *Omocestus viridulus*). In some species there are relatively rare variant colour forms that appear to be present in only some populations. Examples include the uncommon purple forms of the large marsh grasshopper and rufous grasshopper (*Gomphocerippus rufus*). The rare wartbiter bush-cricket (*Decticus verrucivorus*) has even rarer grey and purple/yellow forms, the latter known from only one UK site (Cherrill & Brown, 1991a; Sutton & Browne, 1992).

Some species display even greater degrees of variation in colour pattern. This variation may include a range of different ground colours combined with differently coloured patches, stripes or markings variously distributed over different body surfaces. Among the British species such high levels of colour polymorphism are found in several species of grasshopper (notably *Chorthippus brunneus, Chorthippus albomarginatus, Chorthippus parallelus* and *Myrmeleotettix maculatus*) and three species of groundhopper (*Tetrix ceperoi, T. subulata* and *T. undulata*). For beginners in 'orthopterology', who often try to identify species on the basis of colour pattern, this can be very confusing! Several attempts have been made to classify the different colour forms. Perhaps the most influential was devised by E. J. Clark (1943), and consisted of a string of symbols denoting the colours of each of the body parts in sequence. This was used in the classic study by Richards & Waloff (1954) of grasshopper ecology (see Chapter 9), distinguishing, for example, 32 colour forms of *C. brunneus*! However, for convenience, they simplified the problem by reducing the diversity into a smaller number of named forms: 'green brown legs', 'dorsal stripe', and so on. In his major work on the British grasshoppers, Ragge (1965) modified Clark's system, as well as classifying the main variants of each species using descriptors such as those developed by Richards and Waloff. This method of classifying colour morphs has been generally adopted by researchers.

The phenomenon of colour polymorphism has posed several puzzles for researchers. What are the developmental processes that lead to these different

FIG 70. Some similarly coloured forms of four different grasshopper species: (a) lesser marsh grasshopper, *Chorthippus albomarginatus*; (b) common field grasshopper, *Chorthippus brunneus*; (c) common green grasshopper, *Omocestus viridulus*; (d) common meadow grasshopper, *Chorthippus parallelus* (macropterous female).

outcomes? To what extent are they under environmental or genetic control? Do the various morphs differ in their fitness? How is this high degree of intra-specific variation maintained? These questions still command active research attention, and there are as yet no clear or general answers to them.

There is strong evidence that in some species colour patterns are under quite rigid genetic control. In species such as *C. parallelus* and *C. brunneus* the considerable diversity in colour forms appears to be under genetic control, but in a complex way, involving several alleles at numerous loci (14 and 20 respectively for the above two species), and with interaction or linkages between alleles at different loci (Gill, 1981). However, for other species, the developmental processes that lead to the deposition of pigment are sensitive to various environmental cues, so that an individual has the potential to follow different developmental pathways. This poses questions concerning the sorts of habitat or associated selective pressures that might lead to the production and maintenance of a plurality of genetically determined colour patterns in a population, as against genotypes that respond developmentally to environmental cues.

FIG 71. Some named colour forms of the mottled grasshopper, *Myrmeleotettix maculatus* (following key in Ragge 1965): (a) black; (b) brown green sides; (c) mottled; (d) semi-mottled; (e) plain; (f) purple; (g) striped; (h) green.

Dearn (1990) reviewed evidence on the environmental factors involved in determining colour patterns in grasshoppers. These include humidity and moisture content of food, the colour of the background against which they develop, temperature and population density. In some grasshopper species with environmentally cued green and brown forms, development into the brown morph is associated with low humidity or low moisture content in food. This might be an adaptive response giving better colour matching to the substrate in dry habitats. A similar result occurs in species that are able to change colour to match their background. This ability is mediated by grasshoppers' visual perception, and affects deposition of black pigment, together with yellow and orange where these are present in the environment (Rowell, 1971).

A very striking phenomenon that has been a source of controversy is known as 'fire melanism'. Colour-polymorphic species, such as the mottled grasshopper (*M. maculatus*), which occupy habitats that are vulnerable to fire, often show marked shifts in the ratios between the colour forms after such episodes. For example, D. Baldock reported 'virtually all' the *M. maculatus* population in an area of heathland after a fire were of the black form (Sutton, 2003c).

There is some ambiguity as to whether such colour-switches occur during the adult stage, or whether the flexibility is a response to cues experienced at earlier stages of the life-history. An alternative possibility in the case of some species is that high ratios of cryptically coloured morphs are the result of differential predation on genetically fixed colour forms.

Owens (2010) reports an interesting study of the response of mottled grasshopper populations to the effects of fire on a Norfolk heath. His study compared the proportions of colour morphs at several locations: one of these sites had been burnt the previous year, another two years previously, and three other sites had no recent history of fires. This study reduced complexity to just two classes of colour morphs: 'not green' (mainly black or dark/mottled morphs) and 'green' (including all morphs with at least some green pigment). 'Not green' morphs comprised 75.5 per cent of the population collected from the site that had been burnt the previous year, compared with less than 50 per cent on those sites without a recent history of fire.

There are (at least!) three possible ways of accounting for this apparent shift in the ratios between the different colour morphs. One is that differential predation on cryptically coloured morphs might have produced the result in a single generation. A second possibility is that this species (like some of those discussed in Dean's review) has the ability to change at least some aspects of its colour pattern in response to its surroundings, either as an adult, or during the course of its development. Phenotypic plasticity in this respect could be highly adaptive for a species liable to be exposed to rapid environmental change. The third possibility is that the different colour morphs have a behavioural disposition to migrate to microhabitats that match their coloration.

Interestingly, the following Spring (2011), the ratios of the different colour morphs among the early instar nymphs were very close to those of the adults the previous year (Owens, pers. corr.). This appears to tell in favour of the genetic determination of colour forms, and against phenotypic plasticity, leaving open the possibilities that differential predation and/or behavioural dispositions might explain this case of fire melanism. An observation by Gardiner (2011) on mottled grasshopper colour morphs following another heath fire adds a further piece of evidence. In his study, third and fourth instar mottled grasshoppers were collected on 30 May at a site damaged by fire on 22 May – only some ten days previously. More than 90 per cent of these were non-green, compared with less than 17 per cent non-green at a nearby site with no recent history of fire. This suggests either very intensive and rapid selective pressure from predators, or that the nymphs are disposed to move to habitat patches that match their colour. Of course, these observations constitute highly perceptive responses to *ad hoc* situations rather than fully controlled experiments. However, they are highly suggestive, and deserve to be followed up. The classification of colour patterns is notoriously difficult, and it may be that some features are, while others are not, open to environmental influences during development.

In some species of grasshopper colour is affected by temperature, with cooler temperatures favouring shifts to darker colours. This may be relevant to the ability of the species concerned to regulate body temperature, given the greater capacity of darker surfaces to absorb solar radiation. Species with this ability would presumably be better able to survive in cooler climates, and might also do better in zones with unpredictably variable climates.

There are likely to be fitness trade-offs between colour patterns that confer protection from predators, for example, and those that confer benefits in terms of thermoregulation, and the balance of advantage may vary depending on features of the habitat, climate, and type and degree of predation. In species whose various colour patterns have been shown to be directly heritable there is considerable debate about how this genetic polymorphism is maintained in the population. Models consider the possible role of specialisation of different morphs to different microhabitats, in which selective pressures operate to maintain the overall genetic diversity of the population, as well as the possibility that mating preferences serve to ensure genetic diversity in the offspring as a way of bet-hedging where future environmental conditions are unpredictable. However, it seems that the combinations of genetic predispositions and environmental cues that trigger different developmental outcomes are as yet not fully understood – and are very likely to differ from species to species.

This last point is illustrated by on-going research into the colour polymorphism evident in populations of groundhoppers (Tetrigidae). Three species in the genus *Tetrix* (*subulata, undulata* and *ceperoi*) figure in recent research, much of which has been conducted on the assumption that colour patterns in these species are heritable. This seems reasonable, as early research on related tetrigids (Nabours, 1929; Fisher, 1930b, 1939) is taken to have established this. Much more recent studies carried out in Sweden by Forsman, Caesar, Ahnesjö and others have shown that colour morphs differ not just in their colour patterns, but also in a group of other traits, including body size, fecundity, body temperature preferences, thermoregulatory behaviour and microhabitat selection (e.g. Forsman, 1997, 1999a and 1999b; Ahnesjö & Forsman, 2006). Moreover the values of these traits are correlated with the colour patterns. In the case of the links between colour morph and body size, and between morph and thermoregulatory behaviour, different morphs from the same egg clutch and reared under constant conditions still show the expected associations of traits. This is supporting evidence for the likelihood of a genetic contribution to the correlations.

However, Caesar and colleagues, working on the hypothesis that colour morphs were indicative of co-adapted gene complexes, tested the expectation that distinct colour morphs might mate assortatively, that is, show mating preferences for morphs similar to themselves (Caesar *et al.*, 2007). This would prevent the break-up of the hypothesised advantageous genetic linkages. An alternative possibility was that they might mate disassortatively as a strategy for ensuring their progeny were heterogeneous, at least some of them having traits that would be adaptive whatever (unpredictable) conditions they experienced. In this case the study species was *Tetrix subulata*. Both field observation and laboratory experiments indicated that females are polyandrous, but that they appear to mate randomly with respect to colour morph. That is, they show neither preference for potential mates coloured like themselves, nor aversion to potential mates similar to themselves or their previous partner.

This result is capable of a number of different interpretations, but is at least consistent with the hypothesis that colour morphs may not be strictly genetically determined after all. An experiment conducted by Hochkirch *et al.* (2008a) using samples of both *T. subulata* and *T. ceperoi* set out to test the common assumption (e.g. Paul, 1988) that colour patterns are subject to direct genetic determination. Recent work on pigmentation in the fruit-fly *Drosophila* suggests that it is affected by gene-regulation during development. Hochkirch *et al.* argue that if the regulatory genes are activated by environmental cues, then colour morphs might be subject to environmental influences during development (Pool & Aquandro, 2007). The observed variability of colour forms might then be due, at least in part, to environmental heterogeneity, with selection operating on the genetic basis for the ability to alter coloration, rather than on discrete colour morphs.

Hochkirch *et al.* (2008a) reared split broods of both species from eggs, some on a substrate of light coloured sand, the others on dark. In both species the colour morphs of the first instar nymphs did not differ in frequency between the two treatments. However, from the second instar onwards, the dark-coloured nymphs (black and olive-brown) became more frequent at successive instars on the dark substrate, while the light instars became more frequent on the light substrate. Monochrome forms were also more frequent on the dark substrates,

FIG 72. Some examples of colour forms of the common groundhopper, *Tetrix undulata*, matching their immediate surroundings: (a) black, from recently burnt heath; (b) autumn leaves; (c) fawn; (d) green mottled; (e) straw striped.

and colour shifts were observed not just following each moult, but also within instars as well as at the adult stage. Interestingly, while substrate colour did affect the basic colour of the nymphs, the pattern of markings on the pronotum did not show any significant relationship to colour of the substrate (although it did change during development). However, there was some effect on the colour of the pattern in *T. ceperoi*, with black patterning becoming more frequent on dark substrate, brown more frequent on pale background.

The authors conclude that there is an environmental as well as a genetic influence during development on the basic colour in these species, and on the colour of the markings in *T. ceperoi*, but the pattern of pronotal markings appears to be genetically fixed (or, perhaps, does not vary with background colour). Hochkirch *et al.* argue that this finding requires reinterpretation of some previous studies on colour polymorphism that assumed genetic fixity of the distinct colour morphs. For example, colour patterns of adults may in part be expressions of microhabitats occupied during nymphal development, possibly reinforced by microhabitat preferences of adults. They cite an astonishing study by Gillis (1982) in which the area around the eyes of a sample of colour morphs of a grasshopper that occurs in Colorado, *Circotettix rabula*, were painted red or green to match red or green painted surroundings. The grasshoppers chose to settle on backgrounds that matched the colours they could see on their own cuticle near the eyes. Still more surprising, when painted with a novel blue colour they preferred to settle on blue rather than red substrates!

A subsequent study of *Tetrix subulata* carried out by Karlsson *et al.* (2009) appears to contradict the conclusions of Hochkirch *et al.* Their study also involved split-brood rearing and involved larger numbers of insects. To make their study relevant to the phenomenon of fire mimicry they reared nymphs on crushed charcoal and on white aquarium gravel. Their study revealed no significant effects of substrate on the colour or patterning of the resulting adults. They point to methodological controls used in their study, as well as the larger sample size and lower nymphal mortality rates, compared with the study by Hochkirch *et al.* However, some of the latter's results seem hard to explain in these terms, and the two studies are not strictly comparable in several respects. It seems likely that the complex of issues surrounding colour polymorphism remain to be fully disentangled.

CHAPTER 4

Introduction to mating systems and sexual selection

A major stimulus to research on grasshoppers and crickets has been the striking diversity of their reproductive activities, and the opportunities they therefore offer to investigate some of the most challenging questions of evolutionary theory. The feature of orthopteran reproductive behaviour that has attracted most attention from researchers is the use of sound signalling – 'stridulation' or just 'song'. Although this is not universal among orthopterans, it is widespread, and, as the mechanisms used for both producing and hearing the signals differ considerably from group to group within the order, it is thought that this means of communication has evolved independently more than once. But as well as utilising different mechanisms, sound communication may play several different parts in the mode of life of a single species, as well as functioning differently in the lives of different species. So, for example, many species that communicate by projecting their songs over considerable distances – calling songs – also produce softer songs for communication at short distances (courtship songs). In most species that use sound communication it is the male that sings, while the female is attracted by the male's song and uses it to approach him ('phonotaxis'). This usually signals that the female is sexually receptive to the male. Sometimes a call-and-response pattern (duetting) is used by the male to locate the female (as in the British speckled bush-cricket, *Leptophyes punctatissima*), while in other species it is the female that approaches the male.

Another interesting variation involves the interaction between the songs of nearby males that sing either in unison or in alternate discrete chirps. In these cases the timing of each male's singing is altered in response to the other's efforts. But larger aggregations of singing males may also be heard, a phenomenon known as chorusing. This is often compared to the 'lekking' behaviour of some bird species, such as grouse and peafowl. The lek is an area of ground within which congregating males compete for sites from which they perform displays to females who are drawn to them. Dominant males occupy central positions where they secure greater mating success. The location of the lek is supposed not to be a source of resources important to the females independently of the presence of the lekking males. How well this analogy works, and the part played by aggregation and chorusing in males among the Orthoptera remains controversial, and probably varies from species to species.

In considering the use of sound communication it is important to bear in mind that although it may serve to bring male and female together, it may also involve an exchange of messages among the males. Sometimes it may take the form of a competitive interaction, or sometimes a cue that enables males to space themselves out across their habitat.

However, song is not the only aspect of the reproductive activity of orthopterans that is of interest to us. Some species (including some that do and others that do not also communicate using sound) communicate by inducing vibrations that are conducted through the substrate on which they are standing. This might be bare ground or, very often, vegetation that has a complex structure. The vibration may help the potential mate (usually the female) to orient herself and find her way to the vibrating male. Because the vibrations fall away in intensity relatively quickly, this form of communication operates over short distances only. Depending on the nature of their habitat, much the same may apply to visual communication. Visual cues are used extensively in communication between orthopterans at close quarters. Sudden flicks of one or both hind legs may function as antagonistic signals between potentially rival males, or, again, may simply work as means of gender recognition. In groups (notably the groundhoppers, *Tetrix* species) that do not stridulate, males may perform simple courtship movements before attempting to mate, but even in some species that make use of sound communication, the males have evolved elaborate visual 'dance' displays that they perform while continuing to sing at low intensity (elaborate examples are the displays of the mottled and rufous grasshoppers (*M. maculatus* and *G. rufus*) among the British species). Females may appear completely unresponsive, or, in some species, re-orient their legs or bodies either to enable or to prevent mounting by the male. Rejection often takes the form of the male receiving a sudden kick by a hind leg of the female!

Tactile and chemical stimuli appear to be very important in the courtship of many species, but especially in the Ensifera (crickets, bush-crickets and their allies), which use their long, thread-like and highly mobile antennae in an elaborate 'fencing' engagement, often for very extended periods of time before any attempt at mating. Typically among these groups, the male has to turn his back to the female and encourage her to mount him in order for mating to take place. At this stage there is further tactile communication, especially 'palpation' (in which the female repeatedly probes the dorsal cuticle of the male with her palps), as well as chemical communication *via* cuticular pheromones emitted by the male. In general, although it is now established that chemical communication is involved in close-quarters mating behaviour, this aspect of communication in orthopterans is the least fully researched.

In yet other species there appears to be no courtship behaviour at all, with males grasping and mounting females, often against strong resistance. In some examples of such 'coercive copulation', the male has powerful cerci with which he grips the female, sometimes piercing her external skeleton.

Most of the variety in mating patterns mentioned so far concerns species in which the males make no contribution other than delivery of sperm to the female. However, this is by no means universal among orthopterans. In some groups of the Ensifera, especially among the bush-crickets, the males supply what is often called a 'nuptial gift' in the shape of an enlarged spermatophore. This structure consists of an 'ampulla', which contains the ejaculate, including the sperm, together with a gelatinous mass, known as the 'spermatophylax'. The whole spermatophore is transferred to the female during copulation, and remains attached to the tip of her abdomen. After copulation she curves her body round to bite off parts of the spermatophylax, which she eats while the sperm enter her abdomen. As we shall see, interpretations of this pattern of behaviour vary greatly.

These more complex interactions between males and females may include a variety of other ways in which either may secure reproductive advantage. One of these is 'mate-guarding' in which a male may follow a female around for some time after mating to limit her chances of mating with another male. In the case of the relatively recently studied tree weta of New Zealand, males control resources in the form of holes in trees. These provide shelter from predators and males attract females into them, so attempting to secure mating priority over a number of females. Some of these species have highly developed weapon-like mandibles and vigorously defend their harems. However, other males have an alternative strategy of attempting to waylay stray females wandering outside the burrows.

In other burrowing species (notably field crickets (*Gryllus*) and mole-crickets (*Gryllotalpa*)), burrows may be used for shelter from predation, but also as resonators, enhancing the power of the male's song. In some species males and females appear to cohabit for considerable periods of time, but the significance of this behaviour is not clear. In most orthopteran species the fortunes of the future offspring after the eggs have been laid are left to chance (and whatever prior 'investment' they contain). However, in a few species of burrowing crickets, ground weta and mole-crickets the females stay with their eggs, protecting them from fungal growth and other dangers, and even continue to show maternal care of the nymphs during their early stages (see Chapter 6).

Such diversity in the mating systems among the Orthoptera provides students of the nature and evolution of reproductive behaviour with exceptionally rich subjects for research. Comparative study of closely related species that differ in their reproductive behaviour is a particularly rewarding means of testing rival evolutionary hypotheses.

SEXUAL SELECTION

Almost all orthopterans reproduce sexually, so their reproductive behaviour necessarily involves members of each sex finding and mating with one or more members of the opposi sex. To this extent reproductive behaviour is cooperative, as, if mating never took place, neither sex would succeed in passing on genetic information to subsequent generations. Until relatively recently, this was the prevailing assumption made by evolutionary biologists in understanding sexual reproduction. However, as we shall see, more recent developments in evolutionary theory have placed more emphasis on the role of individual competition, the significance of reproductive outcomes at the genetic level, and the likelihood of asymmetrical and even conflicting reproductive interests between sexual partners.

The past 30 to 40 years have witnessed a great flowering of interest, theoretical model-building and empirical investigation into the structural and behavioural adaptations exhibited by males and females that are related specifically to success in mating, and, more broadly, to securing their distinctive reproductive interests. There are several different sorts of questions that are addressed in this research. First, careful study of the details of the interactions at species level is essential. This descriptive task is intrinsically demanding, and is a prerequisite for any valid attempt at comparative analysis or theoretical interpretation. Second, there are questions about how the insects are able to perform the various activities that go to make up their mating systems. These 'how' questions may include, for example, the mechanics and physiology underlying stridulation, the sensory apparatus that enables perception of the sounds that are produced, the neural mechanisms involved in recognition of the identity, direction, distance and so on of the source of the sound, and the motor mechanisms involved in the stimulation and adjustment of the phonotactic response. These mechanisms are often referred to as the 'proximate causes' of the behaviours they explain, and they are the focus of much important research. Unfortunately much of this is beyond the scope of this book (but see Chapter 2 for basic accounts of sound production, hearing and phonotaxis in the main groups of orthopterans).

However, much of the more recent fascination and controversy surrounding insect mating systems derive from the challenges they pose to newer versions of evolutionary theory. These challenges concern the answers to questions about 'ultimate causes'. What sorts of selective pressure, sometimes acting differently on males and females of a species, could have produced the distinctive structures and patterns of interaction characteristic of the mating system of that species? What pressures might be at work in maintaining it under more recent conditions?

In fact questions about 'ultimate' and 'proximate' causes turn out to be closely related to each other, as any plausible interpretation of the way a particular species' mating system operates has to be able to stand the test of how it might have arisen and been preserved in the face of the selective pressures operating in its past history. However, this test should be used with caution for several reasons. One is that a behavioural or structural trait that was adaptive in the past may have ceased to be so under changed environmental conditions. Another is that species are not mere contingent bundles of traits that can be limitlessly modified in response to selective pressures. There may be constraints imposed by developmental processes, and also genetic mutations with multiple phenotypic effects, some of whose adaptive potential might be outweighed by adverse consequences of others. Given the evolutionary lineage of any population, there will be constraints on its potential for further adaptive modification that are imposed by its past history. So, any proposed 'ultimate' explanation of a trait must also be viewed in the light of the constraints implicit in the evolved biological character of the species, and the available genetic variation within its population.

With these provisos in mind, we can go on to consider the implications of the questions posed above about choice and competition in mating and reproductive strategies. Perhaps the most obvious characteristics that call for such consideration are ones that differentiate the sexes. If the sexes of a species differ markedly from one another this is a sure sign of the past operation of selective pressures bearing differently on males and females. The concept that has been most used to capture (most of) these pressures is that of 'sexual selection'. A brief account of the history of this concept, and the transformations through which it has passed, might be helpful in understanding current approaches and the light they shed on the often puzzling 'antics' of grasshoppers and crickets.

The legacy of Darwin and Wallace

Charles Darwin introduced the concept of sexual selection in his *On the Origin of Species* as a way of accounting for inheritable differences between males and females of a species which otherwise shared the same 'habits of life':

> *Thus it is, as I believe, that when males and females of any animal have the same general habits of life, but differ in structure, colour, or ornament, such differences have been mainly caused by sexual selection; that is, individual males have had, in successive generations, some slight advantage over other males, in their weapons, means of defence, or charms; and have transmitted these advantages to their male offspring.* (Darwin, 1968 [1859]: 138)

The structural and behavioural traits – such as offensive weaponry and pugnacity – that would confer an advantage to males in fighting for possession of females would be likely to be advantageous in the general struggle for life. On this assumption, sexual selection might be understood as simply reinforcing natural selection in enhancing 'fitness'. However, the gorgeous plumage of birds of paradise, the extreme development of the peacock's tail, or the 'strange antics' performed by the males of some species, could not be explained in the same way. In these cases, we seem to be witnessing the effects of active female preferences over many generations for the males who could put on the most impressive or beautiful display.

Darwin makes use of the same analogy with the practices of selective breeders of domestic breeds that he drew on for the concept of natural selection, suggesting that if breeders can modify domestic species in line with their standard of beauty,

> *... I can see no good reason to doubt that female birds, by selecting, during thousands of generations, the most melodious or beautiful males, according to their standard of beauty, might produce a marked effect.* (Darwin, 1968 [1859]: 137)

FIG 73. Portrait of Charles Darwin seated in a chair (from an engraving by Thomas Johnson, c. 1874, private collection, © PoodlesRock/Corbis).

Viewed in the context of mid-Victorian sexual morality, this attribution of active choice to the female can be seen as a bold move on Darwin's part. Even more remarkable (and, it turned out, controversial) was his willingness to attribute choice on the basis of a species-specific 'standard of beauty' to non-humans.

Darwin's collaborator and co-originator of the concept of natural selection, Alfred Russel Wallace, was initially inclined to accept the value of the concept of sexual selection, but mainly in its application to the struggles between males for possession of females. While sometimes acknowledging a role for female preference in producing male adornment, his extensive work on the evolutionary significance of colour patterns emphasised other causes (for examples, Wallace, 1875a, 1875b, 1875c). What seem to be gaudy exhibitions when taken out of context can often be cryptic when viewed in the natural habitat of a species. Bright colours can also be a form of protection from predators, warning of toxicity or distastefulness. Particularly in the cases of birds with brightly coloured males and dowdy, inconspicuous females, Wallace offers an ingenious explanation in terms of natural selection. The 'habits of life' of the two sexes are not, after all, the same. Where females incubate the eggs on exposed nests, cryptic coloration would have evolved by selective pressure from potential predators. The explanatory priorities are reversed: suppose that bright colours are the normal result of physiological processes, and it is the dowdy colours of the females that stand in need of explanation!

FIG 75. Satin Bowerbird (*Ptilonorhynchus violaceus*, male) arranging blue ornaments to impress the female in a bower, Victoria, Australia (© Konrad Wothe/Minden Pictures/FLPA).

FIG 74. Asian Paradise-flycatcher (*Terpsiphone paradisi*, male), Ussuriland, Far East of Russia (© ImageBroker/FLPA).

However, the differences of emphasis between the two men developed into a sharper theoretical disagreement at the beginning of the 1870s. Partly in response to Wallace's shocking declaration of the insufficiency of the concept of natural selection to explain the origin of uniquely human traits, Darwin delivered his much-awaited tome on the *Descent of Man* in 1871. His argument makes important uses of the idea of sexual selection in explaining aspects of human uniqueness, and as if to justify this, many chapters of the book are devoted to a wide-ranging survey of sexual dimorphism and the role of sexual selection across the animal kingdom. In the course of this work Darwin elaborates on his concept, posing the question why it is generally males that compete for females, with sexual selection therefore pressing most powerfully on males, and coming close to a solution to this puzzle that is generally accepted today. Unlike Wallace, whose research was mainly limited to divergences of colour pattern, Darwin identifies a wide range of characters that might be modified by sexual selection:

FIG 76. Alfred Russel Wallace, aged 24 (image from *My Life*: London, 1908).

> [T]he weapons of offence and means of defence of the males for fighting with and driving away rivals – their courage and pugnacity – their various ornaments – their contrivances for producing vocal or instrumental music – and their glands for emitting odours, most of the latter structures serving only to allure or excite the female. (Darwin, 1874 [1871]: 210–11)

Of interest to our theme here is that Darwin notes the special adaptations of some insect groups – notably the cicadas and orthopterans – to produce sounds that have a role in attracting the opposite sex. He notes that it is generally the males that sing to attract the females (failing to notice that this is an exception to his general rule that it is the male that moves to the female), but that in a few species both sexes sing to one another. Pointing out that in three major sub-divisions of the Orthoptera the mechanisms for producing sound are

(a)　　　　　　　　　　　　　　(b)

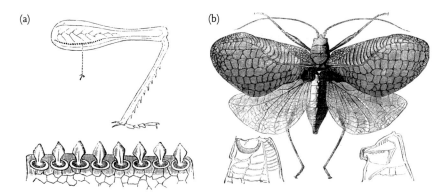

FIG 77. (a) Stridulatory mechanism of male grasshopper; (b) bush-cricket and its stridulatory mechanism (both from Darwin, *The Descent of Man and Selection in Relation to Sex*).

quite different, he suggests that this cannot but impress upon us the 'high importance' of these structures to the males. Interestingly, in discussing cicadas (but not orthopterans) he mentions rivalry in song between two or more males, suggesting that song functions not only to enable the females to find them, but also to choose between them: '… they are excited or allured by the male with the most attractive voice.' (Darwin, 1874 [1871]: 282)

In much of his discussion, Darwin supposes that the male traits that confer advantages in the struggle for mates are likely also to advantage them in the general struggle for life. This is even so with those traits such as beautiful plumage and vigorous display. If these are correlated with male fitness, then in choosing males that are most attractive, females will also be selecting those with heritable traits that will advantage their offspring in the struggle for life. However, in relation to the more exaggerated male ornamentation (and weaponry) Darwin makes two important points. First, these traits must impose on the male some cost in terms of natural selection. To some extent, the accumulated consequence of sexual selection may run counter to natural selection. To that extent, the advantage to a male in obtaining mates and siring offspring may outweigh adaptation to his general conditions of life. Darwin's second point concerns the extremities to which the pressure of sexual selection may drive the development of some traits. Here is another contrast with natural selection – modifications produced by natural selection will gravitate towards a definite limit (optimum adaptive value), whereas there is no fixed outer limit – save that imposed by the operation of natural selection – to the evolution of traits acquired by the preferences of successive generations of females.

Both in his review of *The Descent of Man*, and in subsequent writings (notably Wallace, 1871, 1889), Wallace developed a sustained critique of what we might call 'female choice' sexual selection, and provided alternative explanatory hypotheses for sexually dimorphic traits. Wallace's critique includes four main arguments in addition to those implicit in his earlier papers:

(1) There are many examples in nature of brilliant colours and apparently functionless structures that can have nothing to do with sexual attraction. The caterpillars of many species of butterflies and moths must have some other function – such as mimicry or warning.

(2) While it may make sense to imagine that female birds exercise choice on the basis of standards of beauty, this can hardly be plausible in the case of insects and other invertebrates. Moreover, in many species mating is coercive, leaving very little room for female choice.

(3) Evolutionary change implies a constant direction of change over many generations. How could the vagaries of female choice operate consistently to produce long-term directional change? It is possible that Wallace is here giving way to contemporary gender stereotyping, but Darwin admits there is a difficulty: he has not offered an explanation of female preferences.

(4) The most persuasive argument, however, takes up Darwin's own speculation about the possibility that sexual and natural selection might pull in opposite directions. If, Wallace argues, we suppose that females make choices based on the quality of the males' displays or ornaments, then there are two possibilities. Either these traits are or they are not correlated with heritable traits that confer advantages in the struggle for life. If they are so correlated, then female choice is simply treating attractiveness as an indicator of fitness, and sexual selection is reduced to a special case of natural selection. If, on the other hand, attractiveness is not correlated with fitness, females that mate with males they found most attractive would be mating with the less fit males, and their preferences would be eliminated by natural selection.

By the late 1880s, Wallace was taking a firmer stance against the Darwinian view of sexual selection, adding to his earlier alternative explanations of colour patterns in terms of natural selection another important hypothesis (Wallace, 1889). This is that distinctive colour patterns have evolved to enable members of each species to recognise and locate members of their own species and to distinguish the sexes. Such 'markers' might be important in the case of gregarious species in keeping the group together to avoid predation, but, more importantly, they are crucial for avoiding the 'evils of infertile crosses'. Wallace

FIG 78. Remarkable ornament and colouring of the caterpillar of the sycamore moth, *Acronicta aceris*.

emphasises that the functions of recognition and location of potential mates are distinct from any notion of mate-choice, and the relevant markers can be fully explained in terms of natural selection. Wallace also recognises that some species that are active at night, or that have cryptic colour patterns, will have evolved other media to enable distinctions of sex and species to be made: differences of 'form, motions, stridulating sounds and odours' have the same function in such species as have colour patterns in others.

The disagreements between Darwin and Wallace were not resolved in their life times. As we shall see, subsequent developments in evolutionary theory and in understanding of the mechanisms of both embryonic development and inheritance settled some, but certainly not all, of the issues posed by their work. However, it is worth reviewing the enormous explanatory achievements contained in their different contributions. First, a huge range of otherwise unexplained phenomena – immense diversity of colours, patterns, structures and behaviour across the animal kingdom; divergences between the sexes of many species in structure, colour pattern, display, song, and odour – were all carefully logged and subjected to interpretation in terms of rival versions of evolutionary theory. Colours and patterns of marking were explained in terms of natural selection as functioning for protection by concealment from, or warning to, potential predators, or, along with song and the emission of distinctive odours, to enable potential mates both to locate and to recognise one another. The possession by males of weapons of offence and defence, as well as their dispositions for pugnacity, were explained in terms of an uncontroversial application of the idea of sexual selection according to which either it was a form of natural selection, or it merely reinforced it.

The more extreme forms of sexual dimorphism in adornment and display were subject to continuing disagreement, but the disagreement itself provided important new insights and theoretical developments. Darwin drew attention to the potential evolutionary significance of choice of mates, suggesting that female choice might select characters that worked against the grain of natural selection. In rejecting this, Wallace developed a view of male secondary sexual characteristics as indicators of male fitness. Both lines of thought have survived into our contemporary research and debate about male/female relationships. Finally, in their different ways, both thinkers drew attention to the question (which is still a matter of debate) of how far constraints in embryonic development and laws of inheritance might set a limit to the power of selective pressures – whether natural or sexual – to transform organisms.

Vicissitudes of the idea

Wallace's increasingly sceptical view of the role of female choice of mates as an evolutionary mechanism seems to have won the day – and, indeed, to have obtained through most of the following century (see Cronin, 1991). Male competition for mates was generally accepted, since the pugnacity, vigour and other adaptations involved in the struggles between rival males could be seen either as enhancing general fitness, or as indicators of fitness (Hingston, 1933; Huxley, 1938). However, the sorts of extreme male adornment and display that had at first seemed to Darwin to require some special form of explanation could not be so easily dismissed. There were three broad approaches, all of them consistent with natural selection as the explanatory mechanism, and all avoiding recognition of female choice. The first two were elaborations of Wallace's arguments: many sexual dimorphisms could be explained in terms of ecological differences between male and female, while the importance of external markers of sex and species were seen as of great evolutionary importance, especially during speciation. Related to this, visual signals or advertisement songs might be necessary for potential mates to locate one another – something that would prompt selection independently of any role in mate-choice.

The third hypothesis followed from observations of courtship performances (especially among some bird species) that persisted after pairs had been formed.

The relevant displays could be understood as maintaining pair bonds, or as evoking physiological or motivational changes in favour of mating on the part of the female (Huxley, 1914; Huxley, 1938).

Sexual selection – back in fashion

One of the key contributors to the modern synthesis of evolutionary theory, R. A. Fisher, proposed two feasible models of female-choice sexual selection (Fisher, 1915, 1930a). The first of these is consistent with Wallace's line of argument. On this model, the inheritable male traits preferred by females correlate with general fitness, and so serve as indicators that the male has 'good genes'. Female choice on this model would serve to reinforce the spread of survival-related traits among her offspring, and would not run counter to natural selection. However, Fisher's alternative model was and is more controversial. He resolves the question of consistency of female choice over generations by simply supposing that females inherit a sensory bias, possibly from their feeding preferences or from some other source. If their preference for males with heritable traits consistent with that bias is continued through a succession of generations, the result will be to spread that trait within the population of males because males possessing the trait will be more successful in gaining mates. On this model, sexual selection could augment the preferred male traits either indefinitely, or at least until checked by the operation of natural selection when the (survival) fitness costs of exaggerated male traits outweigh the reproductive advantages they confer. This notion of 'runaway' sexual selection relies on the idea that the reproductive interests of females might be served by having offspring that inherit their male partner's sexual attractiveness, independently of his 'fitness' in other respects. This is sometimes referred to as the 'sexy sons' model of sexual selection, and has become associated with Fisher's name, although it is close to Darwin's original use of the idea to explain extreme male adornments.

It was, however, not until the 1970s that the concept of sexual selection returned to centre-stage in biological theorising and empirical research. At this time there was a marked shift in evolutionary thinking to the analysis of processes at the level of individual organisms and, still lower, to the genetic level, along with a renewed tendency to emphasise competition rather than mutualism in the interactions between organisms. It is possible that the simultaneous rise to dominance of neo-liberalism in economic and political thinking played a part in this shift, but the emergence of 'second wave' feminism may have also contributed to the focus of this broader shift in emphasis on the question of asymmetrical and even conflicting reproductive interests of the sexes (Cronin, 1991; Arnqvist & Rowe, 2005).

A purely behavioural-statistical interpretation of female preference dispensed with some Wallacean objections to the idea of female choice, and the newer approaches were open to recognition of it as causally active in evolution. Surveys of empirical research also amply confirmed the widespread significance of sexual selection. A review of studies of 186 species – mainly of insects, birds, fish and amphibians – found that mechanisms of sexual selection, involving either female choice (the majority) or male competition were identified in each case (Andersson, 1994; Andersson & Iwasa, 1996).

Key developments in the revival of interest in sexual selection are attributed to work by Trivers, Emlen & Oring, and Parker in the 1970s. R. L. Trivers (1972) argued that males and females will typically have asymmetrical reproductive interests because of their different contributions. Usually it is females who make the greater reproductive investment in the production or survival of the offspring, while males make relatively little. However, this difference in 'parental investment' may be exaggerated or to some extent reversed in ways that can explain the great variety of male and female roles in the mating systems of different species, and the implications for the sexual selection of sex-specific traits. So, for example, the usual expectation that males have a greater reproductive interest in multiple matings, making females the 'choosy' sex, may be partially reversed in those species in which the males make more reproductive investment than mere delivery of sperm. If males supply scarce resources in the form of shelter from predation, or nutritional 'gifts', then they, too, may be the choosy sex. Emlen and Oring, (1977) addressed Darwin's puzzle concerning sex ratios. Even in species that produce equal numbers of males and females, there may be unequal numbers of each sex present and willing to mate at any particular time and place. It is the 'operational sex ratio' in this sense that can make choice by one sex a selective force *vis-à-vis* the other. Finally, G. A. Parker (1979) brought together both empirical evidence and theoretical insights to focus on the significance of conflicts of reproductive interest between males and females. He applied this idea beyond the influences on mating success to consider the role of female choice and male counter-adaptations in relation to fertilisation. Multiply-mated females may evolve mechanisms to affect which male's sperm fertilises the eggs they go on to lay, while males may evolve ways of increasing the likelihood that eggs laid by a female with whom they mate are fertilised by their sperm. The mechanisms involved may be behavioural, as in mate-guarding, or forced prolongation of copulation, or physiological and bio-chemical, as in the transfer of behaviour-modifying compounds in the ejaculate. The associated concepts of 'sperm competition' and 'sexually antagonistic co-evolution' substantially extend and complicate the way biologists understand the overall patterns of interaction through which males and females of each species have evolved their distinctive 'mating systems'.

In empirical research and discussion on sexual selection, the emphasis has been on the two main mechanisms recognised by Darwin: male competition for possession of females, and female preference for male ornament or display. However, Andersson and Iwasa (1996) have argued that this emphasis has led to neglect of other mechanisms that are likely to be highly significant. These include:

(1) 'scrambles': strategies that enhance the chances and efficiency of encountering individuals of the opposite sex. These include early maturation, as well as highly-developed sensory and locomotive abilities. In sound-signalling orthopterans, for example, the ability to detect, recognise and locate the source of sound, as well as to orient to it rapidly and accurately in 'phonotaxis', are likely to significantly affect the chances of mating success.
(2) 'endurance rivalry': the ability of individuals to maintain reproductive activity for extended periods of time through the season.
(3) coercion: various male strategies and adaptations to overcome female resistance, such as forced copulation, harassment, or physical isolation of females from other males.
(4) sperm competition: a variety of post-mating strategies used by either males or females to control fertilisation.

Andersson and Iwasa also argue that the more familiar two categories of sexual selection – male contests and female choice – are both more diverse and less easily distinguished than has often been recognised. For example, lekking behaviour in which males congregate and display simultaneously may involve either female mate choice or male rivalry (or both!). Also, smaller or less powerful males may compete successfully by adopting strategies that avoid direct confrontation with superiors. Silent male bush-crickets ('satellites') that lie in wait close to a singing male to waylay approaching females might be an example of this. Mate choice, too, as we have seen, may be shaped by offers of various resources by individuals of the opposite sex, as well as by preferences for exaggerated ornament or display.

Since the resumption of interest in sexual selection and its mechanisms in the 1970s, theorists have developed elaborate mathematical models to investigate possible scenarios in which Fisherian 'runaway' selection or alternative 'indicator' or 'good genes' sexual selection might have occurred. The details of these models are beyond the scope of this short chapter, but they suggest that the outcomes of sexual selection are highly sensitive to quite small variations in the behavioural and ecological contexts in which it occurs. It seems, for example, that Fisherian runaway sexual selection depends on the costs of mate choice being relatively slight. Also, models of indicator sexual selection suggest that this, too, might produce marked sexual dimorphism and the sort of exaggerated male traits that first puzzled Darwin.

FROM SEXUAL SELECTION TO SEXUAL CONFLICT

The realisation that males and females may have reproductive interests that differ has given rise to a recent shift of emphasis in thinking about and researching mating systems. That both sexes have a mutual interest in mating and producing offspring is accepted, but it does not follow that their interests correspond in all respects. Sexual selection may exert pressures on either sex that take it away from its 'reproductive optimum'. This theoretical approach shifts the focus of analysis away from the assumption of essentially cooperative relationships between the sexes towards the identification of points of conflict. Arnqvist and Rowe (2005) begin their influential advocacy of this approach by drawing attention to the common observations of coercion, manipulation, deceit and actual harm as features of male/female interactions in nature. This seems to support the expectations on theoretical grounds that there may be conflicting reproductive interests between males and females over a wide range of structural or behavioural traits. The selective pressures resulting from such conflicts may lead to adaptations and counter-adaptations in dynamic 'evolutionary chases', and this, they argue, has potentially important implications for such topics as the evolution of mate choice, sexual dimorphism, reproductive isolation and speciation. However, as they acknowledge, despite the great increase in empirical research, many of the emerging issues remain unresolved. Obtaining clear-cut empirical tests for alternative theoretical interpretations is often very difficult.

Arnqvist and Rowe (2005) distinguish three main phases of reproductive activity during which sexual conflict may arise: the interactions leading up to mating, after mating, and in the allocation of parental care (for those species in which this occurs). Given the rarity of parental care among Orthoptera, the former two phases are of greatest interest here. Sexual conflict prior to mating is evidenced in the frequently observed female resistance to the courtship and mating attempts of males. If females, as is usually the case, derive less benefit from multiple matings than do males, or derive no benefit, then resistance to subsequent matings may be explained in terms of the costs of mating: increased risk of disease transmission, greater exposure to predation, or loss of time for foraging, egg-laying, etc. Resistance is also implicit in the exercise of mate choice by females – preference for certain male traits implies rejection of 'inferior' males. However, resistance itself also carries costs, in terms of expenditure of energy, disruption of other activities, and the risk of harm – from persistent males, for example. Male persistence traits, too, may evolve as a counter to female resistance, potentially leading to an 'evolutionary chase'.

Perhaps the greatest diversity of forms taken by pre-mating sexual conflict have to do with female resistance and male counter-adaptations. In some species males emit toxins that anaesthetise females, while in others dominant males attempt to monopolise mating opportunities by controlling 'harems' and sequestering females from other males. Male guarding of females prior to their reaching full maturity, and the development of means of physically grasping and securing the female are other widespread male reproductive strategies. Clasping structures on the male abdomens of many species of bush-crickets fall into this category. However, given the often high costs to females in resisting male harassment, an alternative strategy is simply to acquiesce to male advances, especially if the costs to the female of mating are relatively slight. Mating systems with this feature are termed 'convenience polygyny'. The mating systems of the UK species of groundhopper (*Tetrix* species) seem to fit this description.

Where mate choice relates to some particular trait in the opposite sex – such as male preference for larger females in bush-crickets, or female preference for large 'nuptial gifts' – sexual selection may lead to the evolution of 'deceptive' appearances such as inflatable abdomens or the presentation of non-nutritional 'gifts'. As Arnqvist and Rowe (2005) acknowledge, empirical evidence on the evolution of such mating systems is lacking, but the observational data are certainly challenging.

Some of the most significant considerations to come from the newer focus on conflict have to do with processes that occur during and after mating. Where there is post-mating competition between males for fertilisation of a female's eggs, this is known as 'sperm competition', and the counterpart to it, the female's ability to determine which male's sperm effect fertilisation, is known as 'cryptic female choice'. Chemical, physiological or anatomical processes internal to the female may be involved, as well as overt behaviours, such as males guarding females after mating, and/or during egg-laying (see Eberhard, 1991, 1997).

Arnqvist and Rowe (2005) argue that many of these aspects of mating systems may be outcomes of sexually antagonistic co-evolution of male and female traits, although they concede that it is generally very difficult to provide decisive empirical support for this interpretation in specific cases. One suggestive line of investigation has to do with the chemical analysis of male ejaculates. These are usually very complex, and include compounds that give nutritional or other support to sperm. However, they also generally include substances that affect female reproductive physiology. In insects, seminal fluid includes both juvenile hormone (JH) and a chemical compound that stimulates synthesis of this hormone in the female. The effects of juvenile hormone include egg maturation and oviposition so enhancing the reproductive rate of the female. This form of manipulation of the female reproductive rate is likely to favour the male's reproductive interests, and may be at a cost to the female.

In species with polyandrous mating systems, ejaculates from two or more males may be present simultaneously in the reproductive system of a female. In this situation 'sperm competition' ensues, and numerous male adaptations to success in fertilisation can be related to it. So-called 'offensive' adaptations are those that enhance the male's ability to mate with previously mated females, and/or to displace the sperm from previous matings. These adaptations may be chemical or physiological, such as provision of more numerous or more active and 'efficient' sperm, or the ability to destroy or incapacitate the sperm of rival males. Alternatively, they may be behavioural, such as the ability of male dragonflies to physically remove sperm from previous matings before depositing their own. 'Defensive' adaptations are those that reduce or delay future matings on the part of the female, or prioritise the current male's sperm against any deposited later. Again, these adaptations are very diverse, and include chemical substances transferred in the seminal fluid that induce reluctance to re-mate on the part of the female, or promote early oviposition, as well as behavioural adaptations such as prolonging copulation by using hooks, barbs or other 'locks', or mate-guarding after copulation.

If such male adaptations are deleterious to the reproductive interests of the females, the expectation is that the females will have evolved various counter-adaptations. The generally hostile chemistry of the female reproductive tract, as well as the demonstrated ability of females of many species to metabolise substances in the male ejaculate that would otherwise modify their reproductive behaviour in the interests of the male, can be interpreted as forms of female resistance, or as counter-adaptations to those of the male.

Conflicts of interest between males and females over the duration of copulation may also be widespread. Mating is costly for both sexes, with costs likely to increase in line with its duration. Generally males benefit more than females from the prolongation of copulation, partly because more sperm can be transferred and partly because it delays opportunities for females to re-mate. Acquisition of enough viable sperm to fertilise the eggs of the female may be achieved more rapidly, and so females will often have an interest in terminating copulation earlier than the males. Armaments such as spines, clasps and the like can be seen as adaptations by which males prolong copulation despite female resistance. This latter often takes the form of physical struggles, and, in several insect groups, the female may use her rear legs to kick the male away (this is a common form of female resistance to unwelcome mating attempts in grasshoppers). As is commonly the case, this form of resistance is capable of more than one interpretation. Is the female using resistance as a way of testing the male's persistence, and so exercising choice in favour of 'high-quality' males, or is she (the sexually antagonistic interpretation) resisting a costly (to her) prolongation of copulation?

No less controversial is the interpretation of the nuptial gifts presented by males to females as a key part of the mating systems of some species – including insects of several orders as well as very commonly among ensiferan Orthoptera (reviewed in Vahed, 1998). A widely accepted interpretation has been that the nuptial gift is a form of male parental investment or 'reproductive effort' – providing nutrients to the female with a pay-off for the male in terms of higher female fecundity or better-nourished offspring. However, chemical analyses of the gifts frequently show them to have very little nutritional value, and other interpretations of the part played by this feature of ensiferan mating systems have been devised and tested empirically, as we will see in Chapter 6.

In this chapter we have encountered some of the complexities, controversies and sheer diversity of issues concerning the evolution of mating systems, the role of sexual selection, and conflicts of reproductive interest between males and females. In many particular cases it will be difficult to decide between rival interpretations, as sexual conflict, sexual selection for 'quality' mates, and forms of sexual dimorphism that enable correct identification of the species of potential mates will often yield closely similar expectations. Accordingly, much of the literature on the topic is theory-driven, and there is room for contributions to be made on the basis of field observations. It should be kept in mind that each species is the outcome of its unique history of interaction between its ancestral populations and their successive environmental conditions of life. The implications of general theoretical models need to be adapted to an understanding of the limits and opportunities of that history if they are to give us insights into the behavioural repertoires of any particular species. Moreover, field observation reveals, even in the case of relatively 'simple' species such as the orthopterans, there is a high degree of flexibility in the behavioural interactions of individuals. Far from a fixed sequence of stereotyped stimuli and responses, the mating systems of most species are highly variable. Nevertheless, the recent recovery and further development of Darwinian insights into mating systems, sexual selection, and sexual conflict, together with their role in speciation, offers a great deal to the field naturalist. Our eyes are opened to aspects of interaction that we might not have noticed, and puzzling sequences of behaviour can at least be made sense of in a provisional way by the new theoretical ideas.

ANALYSIS OF MATING SYSTEMS:
THE MATING SEQUENCE

The following two chapters will illustrate some of the enormous variety of mating systems that have evolved among the Orthoptera – a variety that has inspired a great deal of research activity devoted to understanding in greater depth the processes involved in sexual selection and their consequences.

The reproductive behaviour involved in orthopteran mating systems can be analysed in terms of a sequence of phases leading to copulation, and sometimes with post-copulatory behaviour (such as the consumption of the spermatophylax in bush-crickets). At each stage in the process, the sequence can be terminated by rejection on the part of one or other of the potential mates, or by interference from rival males or predators.

Alexander *et al.* (1997) use the term 'mating sequence', and distinguish eight phases, although not all phases will be present in every species. The discrete character of each phase is considered to be the outcome of a distinct pattern of natural and sexual selective pressures. These include the impact of predation and parasitism, adverse general environmental conditions, competition with rivals of the same sex for mating opportunities, and resistance or rejection on the part of potential mates. These pressures are likely to operate differently at each phase of the mating sequence.

Phase one is termed 'rapprochement', and involves the formation of pairs by some process of location of, and approach to, a potential mate. This might occur as a contingent effect of the clustering of both males and females in response to some environmental stimulus, such as presence of a food resource or pattern of vegetation cover. Alternatively, members of one sex may actively search for a potential mate, or signal or call to the other. For reasons given in Chapter 5, it is most commonly the males that do the searching or signalling – although there are interesting and important exceptions.

Phase two, 'courtship', follows success in phase one. Both male and female are within range of one another by way of at least one sense, and at least one of them is responding both sexually and positively to the other. One partner to the interaction (usually the male) behaves in such a way as to lessen the resistance of the other (usually the female) to copulation, by changing her motivational state, or by displaying qualities that may bias her toward mating with him rather than other potential mates. Usually courtship is taken to refer to pre-copulatory behaviour, but as females may exercise cryptic choice, males may continue to seek to influence events during and even after copulation – hence the term 'copulatory courtship' to characterise male behaviour during or even after successful mating.

Phase three is copulation itself, and involves the physical connection of male and female, generally involving engagement of the genitalia. In some species copulation occurs with little or no overt 'courtship' behaviour, while in others seemingly interminable male performances still meet with eventual rejection.

Phase four, insemination, involves the passage of sperm into the body of the female – generally into a sperm-storage organ, the spermatheca. This may occur during or after copulation, as in the case of many bush-crickets, where the sperm take time to flow into the female from a spermatophore that the male attaches to the female. Ensuring that this process is not disrupted or terminated is clearly in the reproductive interest of the male.

Phase five includes a range of behaviours after copulation, or between repeated copulations, by means of which males may influence the probability of their sperm fertilising the ova of their mates. This might include such devices as prolonged engagement of the genitalia after insemination has occurred, application of mating plugs, transfer of substances that delay the readiness of the female to re-mate, or induce egg-laying, nuptial feeding and mate-guarding behaviour.

Phase six is fertilisation of the ova. Generally among the Orthoptera this occurs at the time of egg-laying, with sperm released from the spermatheca as the egg passes by its opening.

Phases seven and eight involve the various interactions and 'investments' made by either or both parents in the offspring that result from development of the fertilised ova. Cooperative care for the offspring is rare among insects, but there are some orthopteran examples, as well as a few in which one parent devotes some care to the eggs and early nymphal stages (see Chapter 6). The eighth phase, involving 'bonding' ceremonies, occurs where there are long-term partnerships between parents. This phase is common among birds and mammals but probably absent from Orthoptera.

The distinctive role of sound communication in most groups of orthopterans has been a major focus of research, with a particular concentration on the part played by calling songs in mediating the interactions between males, and in bringing together males and females. The next chapter will provide an introduction to both the theoretical ideas and empirical research surrounding the first, rapprochement, phase in the mating sequence. The questions posed by the great variety of orthopteran behaviours that follow once male and female have come into close contact will be addressed in Chapter 6.

CHAPTER 5

Calling, chorusing and competing: insect songsters

This chapter is mainly concerned with the first of the eight phases of the mating sequence outlined at the end of the previous chapter. This phase – rapprochement – involves the location and coming together of potential mates. Across all the main groups of Orthoptera, communication by sound is the principal means by which this is effected. In some species sound communication did not evolve, while in others it has been lost. Generally, these are species that have changed little from the ancestral forms of the Orthoptera, or ones that live in aggregations that make location and attraction at a distance unnecessary. The mating systems of some of these species will be discussed in the next chapter.

For those species that make use of sound communication in pair formation, it is usually the male that advertises his presence and readiness to mate by a calling, or advertisement song. As well as playing a role in attracting a willing female, and, perhaps, in influencing her choice of potential mates, the calling song is also involved in mediating the competitive interactions among rival males. Further, both the calling male, and the potential mate, of whichever sex, that travels to the other will be exposing themselves to increased risk of predatory or parasitic enemies. The different patterns of calling song and response that have evolved are thus the outcome of complex and cross-cutting combinations of both natural and sexual selection pressures (Hoy 1992).

THE MALE CALLING SONG

Since it is almost always the male who utters the calling song, and the female who (initially at least) moves towards the male, it is supposed that singing entails higher risks and costs than phonotaxis towards the singer, although considerable risks and costs must be involved in both. Viewed from the standpoint of its role in the mating system of a species, the function of song is generally thought to be to bring the female to the male. However, the male's broadcasting of his song has other consequences. It makes him highly vulnerable to predators and parasites that locate prey or hosts by sound, but also the stridulatory movements themselves may provide a cue for visual predators. The male's song also puts him into a competitive relationship with other males who may be present, either singing or not, who are potential rivals for the attentions of arriving females. Both of these aspects, along with selective pressures exerted by the females, are likely to have played a significant part in the formation of the great variety of singing behaviour and song characteristics to be found among the Orthoptera.

Both male songsters and females moving towards them are more vulnerable to visually hunting predators and parasites than they otherwise might be. Darwin's advocacy of sexual selection in the case of the peacock and birds of paradise provided an explanation of the gaudy colour patterns and vivid displays of the males. However, where the medium of communication is sound, as in many orthopterans, the tendency has been towards cryptic coloration in both sexes, and relatively slight sex differences in appearance. If sexual selection favours development of singing ability in males, natural selection favours adaptation to offset the greater exposure to predation that the advertisement song brings with it.

An astonishing example of rapid evolutionary change in the balance of sexual and (survival-related) natural selection is provided by a population of the Polynesian field cricket *Teleogryllus oceanicus*. On the Hawaiian island of Kauai, where males were subject to attacks by an acoustically orienting parasitic fly

FIG 79. *Teleogryllus oceanicus*, male. (© D. Rentz)

(*Ormia ochracea*), a flat-winged mutation that rendered the crickets unable to sing spread to 90 per cent of the males in 15 to 20 generations, despite strong selective pressure in favour of songsters from female preferences (Zuk *et al.*, 2006; Bailey & Zuk, 2008; Tinghitella *et al.*, 2009).

Where and when to sing

The conflicting pressures from predation risk and the reproductive interest in being heard by a receptive female combine to affect the male's preference for his song perch. Males of many species that live among herbaceous vegetation tend to sing from the cover of dense tufts of grasses or small shrubs. In this way they can increase the distance over which their song carries, compared with ground-level emission, while benefiting from concealment. The great green bush-cricket (*Tettigonia viridissima*) tends to sing from perches at a greater height than surrounding vegetation. One study showed that the transmission of the song of this species increased with the height of its song perch above the ground (Römer, 1992). However, despite their large size and loud song, male great green bush-crickets are astonishingly difficult to locate visually. Males of the meadow grasshopper (*Chorthippus parallelus*) generally sing from much lower (less than 20 cm above ground) perches, presumably to avoid predation from birds and spiders (Gardiner & Hill, 2005b). In some species, males sing from the outer edges of grass tufts, but are ready to freeze and/or suddenly dive down into tangled vegetation when alarmed. British examples of these strategies include the wartbiter (*Decticus verrucivorus*), the grey bush-cricket (*Platycleis albopunctata*) and the bog bush-cricket (*Metrioptera brachyptera*). Other species, especially those ground-living species that inhabit more open and sparsely vegetated habitats, may typically utter one bout of song only from each perch, quickly moving on to another. This is a common behaviour among males of the British mottled grasshopper (*Myrmeleotettix maculatus*) and the common field grasshopper (*Chorthippus brunneus*). The common green grasshopper (*Omocestus viridulus*) and stripe-winged grasshopper (*Stenobothrus lineatus*) also usually utter just one burst of song before moving on to another perch. Species that typically inhabit bushes or trees combine cryptic colour patterns and shapes with a tendency to sing from the cover of dense vegetation (see the DVD for several examples of these tactics).

However, in all these cases it seems likely that the adaptation to avoidance of predation has been achieved at some cost to the reproductive function of the calling song. Where males move position after each burst of song, or where they sing from dense and structurally complex vegetation cover, the difficulties faced by females in locating the sound source and then moving towards it are considerable. Often, deviations from the standard model of male calling and female phonotaxis have evolved in response to these challenges. For example, males that call and search simultaneously are generally ones that take on the risks associated with both calling and searching while the females remain static. In a small number of other examples, notably the speckled bush-cricket (*Leptophyes punctatissima*), females reply to the male's chirps, and the male's location of, and movement towards, the female is achieved by a finely adjusted call-and-response sequence.

This means of pair-formation is rather rare. It appears to be limited to a small number of bush-crickets. These include members of three European genera of ephippigerine bush-crickets and some phaneropterine bush-crickets, notably the British speckled bush-cricket. Among the ephippigerines, in some species the female moves to the male, while in others either sex may undertake the risks of phonotaxis (Hartley 1993). In *Steropleurus stali* the male approaches the female if she delays phonotaxis, which she is more likely to do the more previous matings she has had (Bateman, 2001). This is presumably a case of different male/female reproductive interests shifting the burden of phonotaxis between them. Among the phaneropterine bush-crickets, it is usually the male that moves to the female, a reversal of the more general pattern among signalling Orthoptera.

The signalling system of the speckled bush-cricket has been the subject of extensive observational and experimental research (e.g. Hartley & Robinson, 1976; Robinson, 1980, 1990; Robinson *et al.*, 1986; Zimmermann *et al.*, 1989; Robinson & Hall, 2002; Rheinlaender *et al.*, 2007; Ofner *et al.*, 2007; Kostarakos *et al.*, 2007). The calling song of the male consists of an extremely brief chirp, emitted at irregular intervals. It consists of 5 to 8 rapid pulses (each lasting

FIG 80. Stridulatory apparatus of the speckled bush-cricket: (left) male and (right) female.

approximately one millisecond), the whole chirp lasting for no more than 10 to 13 milliseconds. A responsive female answers with a chirp at the same high frequency (in the ultrasonic range of around 40 kH), that is even shorter than the chirp of the male, often consisting of only a single pulse. Experimental studies carried out by Robinson and others have demonstrated that a male begins to move towards a female only if she replies within a definite time window of 35 milliseconds, placed between 25 and 55 milliseconds after the start of the male call. Subsequent location of the female is enabled by exchanges of chirps between the pair. The use of ultrasonic frequencies means that communication can take place only at quite close quarters, as these sounds attenuate with distance faster than

FIG 81. Tibial 'ears' of the speckled bush-cricket: (top) male and (above) female.

those of lower frequency. In fact, it seems that although the female can hear and respond to the call of the male at a distance of up to seven metres, her song is more subdued and cannot be heard by the male at that distance. Male phonotaxis takes place only when the pair are separated by quite small distances of up to five metres (M. Hall, pers. comm.), the male response being limited by the intensity of the female's response, or by a combination of that together with the length of the pause before he hears her response.

It seems likely that this system has evolved under powerful predation pressures, with call and response kept to a minimum to limit the ability of enemies to eavesdrop. Males also increase their calling rate once a female responds, confining energy expenditure and predation risk to times when the chances of mating are increased. It seems likely that the critical time window for the male to respond to the female chirp helps in identifying her response by enhancing the signal-to-noise ratio. Not only is the speed of sound-processing in this species quite exceptional, but the ability of the male to locate the female despite the brevity of her responses is also remarkable. As this species may occupy perches at widely varying heights up to at least 10 metres (Ash & Robinson, unpub.; Robinson *et al.*, 2009) in herbaceous or woody vegetation, males have to locate the source of the female chirps both vertically and horizontally. Detailed studies of phonotaxis in the males of this species have shown that they use a combination of their binaural hearing system with regular stops to alter their bodily posture, rolling from side to side, turning on the spot, and tilting their head and thorax downwards (Kostarakos *et al.*, 2007; Ofner *et al.*, 2007; Rheinlaender *et al.*, 2007. See also Chapter 2).

The time of day when the males sing may also be seen as a compromise between reproductive advantage and predation risk and other cost factors. In general, we would expect males to sing in areas and at times when they are most likely to attract willing females, consistent with minimising the costs and risks of calling. One frequent compromise is to sing at night when visually hunting predators and diurnal sound orienting ones are not active. This has the benefit for the males of both enhancing the transmission of their song, as the sound conductivity of the air is greater at night, and reducing the energetic cost of calling. This latter cost is very significant. The calorific cost of calling averages ten times the normal metabolic rate in orthopterans, but in some cases it has been estimated to be as much as 35 times that of a resting male (Prestwich, 1994; Walker, 1983a). Females, too, may benefit from reduced predation risk as they move towards singing males under cover of darkness. Calling early in the night has the added advantage that ambient temperatures have cooled only slightly.

However, this strategy also has its downside: the threat from nocturnal predators! A detailed study by Belwood of nocturnal bush-crickets in the forests of Peru and Panama gives excellent insights into the complexity of the interactions involved (Belwood, 1990). Forest-gleaning bats, ovenbirds and tropical ant birds were all found to be major predators on bush-crickets, along with tropical screech owls, titi monkeys and spiders. In the face of such powerful selective pressures from nocturnal predators it seems that a variety of adaptations to song and singing behaviour have evolved. Some highly palatable species sing later in the night when bats are less active while those species that sing just after sunset formed the bulk of the prey in her study. The character of the song itself also appears to be adaptive to nocturnal predator avoidance. Individual chirps are very short (up to one second), and issued infrequently. The song is at a very high (ultrasonic) frequency, and the insects actually sing for only a small part of the song period. It seems that the sporadic nature of the emission of sound does limit the ability of bats to locate the calling bush-cricket, as does the tendency of these species to sing in choruses. Belwood suggests that chorusing might confuse predators and so make it more difficult for them to locate individual prey (see later in this chapter).

But there is a trade-off between predator avoidance and effective calling of potential mates. Adaptations that make songsters difficult for predators to locate may also have the disadvantage of making them difficult to locate by approaching females. Belwood suggests that there are two sorts of counter-adaptation that address this. One is fine-tuning of ear morphology and song structure to the detection of sporadic calls. The other is the use of vibratory signals that are not detectable by the bats. In two groups of bush-crickets she studied (copiphorine and pseudophylline species) calling was accompanied by complex up/down movements of the body with all legs firmly planted on the substrate. This tremulation produces airborne vibrations and vibrations in the substrate that females can use to locate the calling male. However, an added layer of complexity is provided by the fact that although bats cannot detect the vibratory signals, predatory spiders can. But, as bush-crickets are provided with highly sensitive detectors of vibration (the tibial subgenual organs) it seems likely that they can detect the approaching spiders (as well as other enemies) by vibration. Belwood also notes that the very long antennae of pseudophylline bush-crickets are kept in constant circular motion round their bodies while they are active, with the possibility that this might help to detect approaching spiders (see also Heller, 1995).

Song structure and what it communicates

As a form of communication the calling song conveys information both to potential mates and to other males. There are five variable aspects of the sound produced by orthopterans that, either separately or in combination, can convey such information. These are: the frequency or pitch of the sound; the pattern of rise and fall of pitch ('frequency modulation'); sound intensity or loudness; the pattern of increase or decrease in sound intensity ('amplitude modulation'); and the sequencing of sound patterns through time (different sorts and lengths of buzzes, chirps, trills, etc. and the intervals between them). However, the nature of the environmental conditions when the song is emitted and the relative location of the hearer both have consequences for the effectiveness of the communication of information. In general, the interference provided by the songs of other males of the same species, sounds made by members of other species (see clips of male songs of stripe-winged and common green grasshoppers on the DVD), as well as non-biotic sounds, such as the wind, can all serve to obscure aspects of the song structure. Also, the greater the distance between source and receiver, the more likely it is that the signal will be degraded. Although song intensity may make a difference to how far it transmits, other things being equal, the information content carried by it is limited by the fact that it varies with distance. Similarly, pitch may be varied by conditions of transmission, so it seems likely that for most species the most reliable information is carried by the sequential patterns of sounds through time.

Unfortunately there is no international consensus among researchers on how to classify the various elements of the song structure. The most basic element is the sound produced by a single up-and-down stroke of the hind leg against the wing in grasshoppers, or by the opening and/or closing of the tegmina in crickets and bush-crickets. This is sometimes referred to as a 'phonotome', but Ragge and Reynolds (1998) prefer the term 'syllable'. A series of syllables forming a single unit of sound is termed an 'echeme', and, in turn, a series of these forming a repeating unit is termed an 'echeme sequence'. However, the analysis of a song involves more complexities – for example, some species produce sounds in both directions of movement of the stridulatory mechanism, others only one ('diplosyllables', 'hemisyllables') and there are numerous different ways of sequencing echemes through time. The complexity of the song may be even greater than this – with some species interspersing incomplete syllables among the complete ones, and sometimes combining echemes into second-order repeated units. For some purposes, too, it is useful to include the silence between buzzes or chirps in the definition of the song unit – so the repeated unit is the period taken up by the chirp together with the interval of silence before the onset of the next chirp.

Finally, of course, some species have prolonged, continuous calling songs, and in cases such as these – for example, the great green bush-cricket (*T. viridissima*), long-winged conehead (*Conocephalus discolor*), and Roesel's bush-cricket (*Metrioptera roeselii*) – the song can be given structure by variations in intensity or frequency. On a longer time scale, most species have favoured periods of day or night during which they sing. The daily pattern of these periods is known as the 'duty cycle'. Generally, of course, males do not sing continually throughout even their duty cycle. The timing of duty periods during day or night varies very much among orthopteran species, in relation to predation risks, maturation times of females, temperature, and other factors as noted above (see, for example, Walker 1983a). For deeper understanding of these issues than can be provided here, see Ragge and Reynolds (1998), who also describe the techniques for producing and interpreting oscillograms to represent the structures of songs visually. For many more informal purposes, descriptive terms that indicate the pattern of sounds as they are heard by humans (unaided or with the use of such devices as bat detectors) – such as 'buzz', 'trill' or 'chirp' – have a reasonably clear meaning.

The issuing of the calling song by the male indicates to any female in hearing distance that he is ready to mate, and also provides cues to his location. A receptive female will turn towards the sound and make her way to its source. With hearing organs on both sides of the body, comparison of inputs from the two sides provides the female with cues as to the general direction of the sound. However, this is no simple matter, as both horizontal and vertical dimensions of location have to be combined, and she may have to surmount intervening obstacles, or deal with the branching structure of a bush or other complex perch. Experimental studies have shown that orthopterans cannot locate a sound from a source that is head-on to them, and so their movement towards the sound source takes the form of a succession of turns with subsequent corrections. The resulting course, even in the absence of obstacles, has a zig-zag character, as the insect responds to the relative direction of successive pulses of sound (Rheinlaender & Römer, 1990; Oldfield, 1980; Bailey & Stephen, 1984). The localisation of calling males by females attracted to them seems to improve with the height of their path above the ground, where there are fewer echoes and so improved directionality of sound (Rheinlaender & Römer, 1990), but this is likely to render them more vulnerable to predation. The neural processes involved in both recognition of the species-specific song pattern by a female, and location of the singing male, have been studied experimentally by Hedwig and colleagues. Directional location requires processing of inputs from each ear separately, while recognition of the song involves summation of inputs, but both aspects have to be integrated for phonotaxis to operate. Considerable progress has been made in identifying the neural structures involved in these feats in the case of crickets – especially *Gryllus bimaculatus* (see Hedwig, 2001, 2006, 2007; Hedwig & Poulet, 2004, 2005; Poulet & Hedwig, 2005; see also Chapter 2).

In many species, especially where males sing from perches in shrubs or dense vegetation, the fine tuning of location is achieved by the female detecting the vibrations of his perch that are caused by the male's stridulation. Kalmring *et al.* (1990) report experiments showing that the locating ability of females of two European bush-cricket species (*Tettigonia cantans* and *Ephippiger ephippiger*) is

FIG 82. A female
Ephippiger ephippiger,
a species that makes
use of vibratory as well
as auditory cues in
phonotaxis.

FIG 83. European
species of *Poecilimon*:
(top) *P. thoracicus*,
female, and (below)
P. brunneri, male.
(Bulgaria).

enhanced if vibratory signals are given in addition to auditory ones. In the case of
E. ephippiger the males cease stridulating when they detect an approaching female.
Greenfield (1990) describes the use of vibratory signals by the males of the genus
Neoconocephalus in addition to stridulation as an aid to females in locating their
perches at close quarters. British coneheads of the genus *Conocephalus* also use
vibratory signals (see the example of *C. dorsalis* on the DVD). There is evidence
that visual clues are also helpful in mate location for some species. For example,
the bush-cricket *Poecilimon affinis* is a species in which the male approaches a
female who responds to his brief chirp within a definite time window. A study
by von Helversen and Wendler (2000) showed that males were able to locate
a responding female by sound alone, but only by way of a round-about route.
However, when visual cues were added, their performance was much improved.
It seems that they first establish the direction of the female from her response
chirp, but then use visual landmarks to maintain a direct route to her.

   In those species that locate potential mates by way of acoustic
communication, the calling song must carry information about not only the

location of the caller, but also his species. In crickets, whose songs often include 'pure' notes, and in some bush-crickets, it seems that the frequency spectrum of the song plays an important part both in locating the singing male and in recognising his species (e.g. Oldfield, 1980). In bush-cricket species such as *Tettigonia cantans*, *T. viridissima* and *Ephippiger ephippiger* and *E. discoidalis*, in which the males sing from tall grasses or shrubs, females use the frequency composition of the song in identifying the singer. This is possible as the different sound frequencies attenuate at different rates with distance, so that the changing relative intensities of the different frequency components of the song will provide clues to both the distance of the singer and his species (Kalmring *et al.*, 1990). However, for grasshoppers, and other bush-crickets, whose songs tend to include broad frequency bands, it seems that the song structure is the main feature used by females to identify the species of singing males. For many species it has been shown that the calling song of the male is the main means by which females recognise the species of potential males, so that song plays an important part in reproductive isolation.

The distinctiveness of the male calling song is particularly significant where several species occur in the same habitat, and sing at the same times. Ability to occupy a distinct acoustic transmission channel in such orthopteran communities may be an important source of competition between species, and so may influence the species composition in the habitat (Bukhvalova, 2006). The reverse may also be true: the species composition of a habitat may influence song structures. Jang and Gerhardt (2006) compared aspects of song structure in two species of American crickets (*Gryllus fultoni* and *G. vernalis*). In areas where both species occurred, chirp rate and pulse rate of the songs were divergent. In locations occupied by only one of the species, both aspects of song overlapped. The characteristics of the calling song are likely to have played a significant part in the formation of new species (see Heller, 2006), and comparison of the songs of closely related forms gives useful evidence for classification, as well as providing the basis for speculation about their evolutionary origins. Ragge (1987) and Ragge and Reynolds (1998) have shown the value of oscillograms representing the song structures of European

FIG 84. A male *Tettigonia cantans* singing from his perch (Swiss Alps).

species for both these purposes. Ragge argues that given the role of song in species recognition, it is probable that where two forms have identical or very closely similar calling songs they should be regarded as belonging to the same species, even if there are minor morphological differences. Equally, differences in the calling song can justify separation of forms as distinct species even though they may be inseparable on the basis of morphological characters. Puzzles in the taxonomy of closely related species of *Chorthippus* and *Euchorthippus* among European grasshoppers, as well as bush-crickets in the genus *Metrioptera*, have been resolved on the basis of song comparisons (Ragge, 1987).

However, the calling song of the male does not always provide definitive clues to its identification, and there are instances where females may be attracted by the songs of males of species other than their own. Often this does not result in wasted effort under natural conditions, as many such species pairs do not inhabit the same localities (even though their distributional range may overlap considerably). An experimental study by Morris and Fullard (1983) of song recognition in three American species of the genus *Conocephalus* produced some interesting results. Males of all three species aggregate and sing in unsynchronised choruses (see below), and have similar broad frequency bands in their songs. Females of one species, *C. nigropleurum*, moved towards recordings of random noise, noise combined with songs of single males or choruses of males of their own species. They also appeared not to discriminate between songs of males of their own species and those of *C. attenuatus*. However, they did not respond to males of *C. brevipennis*, whether presented singly or along with males of their own species, even when the song of *C. brevipennis* was modified to make it more similar to the male of their own species. Although all three species have overlapping ranges, only *C. nigropleurum* and *C. brevipennis* occur in the same habitats (although as adjacent populations rather than intermingled).

Morris and Fullard suggest that females of *C. nigropleurum* may have undergone selection to recognise and ignore the songs of male *C. brevipennis*, rather than to identify the song of their own species. The failure to discriminate between conspecific males and those of *C. attenuatus* is not mal-adaptive as the two species do not occur together. According to Morris and Fullard, a wide range of continuous sounds of roughly the right frequency range will be sufficient to induce positive phonotaxis, with more precise species-recognition taking place at close quarters. They cite a parallel with the two related crickets, *Gryllus campestris* and *G. bimaculatus*, where females of the latter species appear to discriminate *against* songs of male *G. campestris*, rather than *in favour of* the songs of conspecific males.

In general it seems that where the songs of two species are very similar they tend to occur in different habitats, or call in different seasons or at different times

FIG 85. (a) A male *Allonemobius fasciatus*, singing (© D. Funk); (b) A male *Tettigonia viridissima*, showing stridulatory apparatus; (c) A female *Tettigonia cantans*, liable to confuse the song of *T. viridissima* with that of her own species.

of day (Schatral 1990). However, this is not always the case, and in the example of two North American ground crickets (*Allonemobius fasciatus* and *A. socius*), females of each species seem to be unable to distinguish the songs of the other from their own, despite actual differences in the songs. Doherty and Howard (1996) argue that in this case heterospecific mating is not necessarily mal-adaptive as there appear to be post-insemination barriers to hybridisation, costs to the females involved in mating are likely to be low, and they gain from nuptial feeding whichever male they mate with (see Chapter 6). The females of the bush-cricket *Tettigonia cantans* will respond to the songs of males of *T. viridissima*, especially if they are closer and so perceived as louder (Schul *et al.*, 1998). This phenomenon of imperfect separation of the reproductive behaviour of closely related species (called 'reproductive interference') is of considerable interest, and we will return to it in the following chapter with reference to three groundhoppers (*Tetrix* species).

Female preference and the calling song
These exceptions aside, the calling song of the male typically enables females to locate the singer, and to identify his species as the appropriate one. If a female is willing to mate, the song also stimulates her to move towards her potential mate. However, in many species there is evidence that the song has a third function: that of allowing the female to discriminate between rival males. As we saw in the

previous chapter, the question of female choice in non-human animals has long been a source of controversy. However, if there are systematic differences in appearance or behaviour between the two sexes in a species, it seems likely that sexual selection has played a part in their evolution. As we saw, sexual selection can take the form of competition between males for access to females or of the exercise of choice on the part of females. Often, however, it is difficult to distinguish between these when we analyse the mating systems of particular species. As we shall see, males of some species of Orthoptera form aggregations and sing in chorus, so that it is difficult to decide whether mating success is a function of competition within the aggregation, or of female choice from among the assembled songsters.

However, there is now good evidence to suggest that females of at least some species show preferences for certain features of the song performance of some males, as against others (see reviews in Zuk & Simmons, 1997; Gerhardt & Huber, 2002; Robinson & Hall, 2002). Female choice may be classified as active or passive. Passive choice refers to the tendency of females to move towards the male that happens to be closest or sounds the loudest, and can be considered simply as contingent (i.e. the 'choice' just reflects the chance spatial relationship between singer and hearer) or as an aspect of competition among the males to project their song to receptive females. Where choice is active, however, females show preferences for the song characteristics of one male rather than another, in the absence of other means of differentiating them. Such preferences have been demonstrated experimentally for a range of species across the different sub-groups of the Orthoptera, and in some cases backed up by field observation. The calling songs of a New Zealand weta, *Hemideina crassidens,* are delivered from the entrances to holes, or 'galleries', in tree trunks, and are reported to have patterns specific to each individual (Field & Sandlant, 1983). It may be that these differences inform female choice of potential mates.

Theoretical considerations suggest that these female preferences may have evolved because they correlate with immediate or with genetic benefits to the female of mating with a male with the preferred trait, rather than with a rival. Immediate benefits might include mating with minimal predation risk (mating with the closest male if phonotaxis is risky might confer this benefit), mating with a large male who can provide a substantial nuptial gift (see next chapter), or with an energetic male whose powerful song implies that he is free of parasites. Genetic benefits, as we saw in the previous chapter, can be of two main sorts – the probability of producing offspring with 'good genes', or the likelihood of producing male offspring that will be attractive to females ('sexy sons').

One commonly reported example of female preference is for the first song heard when more than one male is singing within earshot of the female.

This leading call preference has been shown to be widespread among bush-crickets, as well as some crickets and grasshoppers – extending even to frogs. The central American bush-cricket *Neoconocephalus spiza*, for example, exhibits this preference, even when the second male sings for longer and (within limits) more loudly. Snedden and Greenfield (1998) established that this is a result of a neurological mechanism that temporarily suppresses the animal's response to a second sound. However, although this preference may not have evolved as part of the mating system, it does have consequences for it: if males' mating success is influenced by their ability to be the lead caller, then males calling close to each other will be constrained to compete to be perceived as the lead caller, or adopt an alternative strategy. Studying a species of *Mecopoda* bush-cricket in southern India, in which females prefer leading male callers, Nityananda and Balakrishnan (2008) explored the availability of such alternative male strategies. They found that generally leading callers sang louder than followers, and that spacing did not compensate for the disadvantage of being a follower. However, a majority of follower males did sing when leaders were silent, and it was found that leading was a function of chirp rate, itself a consequence of contingent factors such as, in their view, male condition (but see Hartbauer *et al.*, 2006). As leader and follower roles were not played consistently from night to night, it seems likely that this is not a heritable trait.

In some species the males stake out and defend song perches as territories. Occupants of such territories inhibit singing in males that cannot acquire or have not yet gained a territory, and such silent males are sometimes termed 'satellite' males. In her study of the north American meadow bush-cricket *Orchelimum nigripes*, Feaver (1983) observed that females only mate with singing males. In this species, the male territories are grouped together, and females show a preference for males among groups, as against lone singers. Even among grouped singers, the females (who mate only once) move from male to male over many hours before finally making their choice of male. Greater choosiness on the part of females is to be expected in species where the females mate only once.

Although experimental studies have revealed female preferences in a wide range of species, the nature of the preferences varies greatly from species to species. As well as lead callers, males may be preferred because they sing more loudly, or with higher, or in some cases, lower, frequency, greater rate of syllable repetition, more syllables per chirp, higher chirp rate and other song features (Gwynne & Bailey, 1988; Simons, 1988). A further influence on female choice in some species is an indication from the male call of structural asymmetry. In the European bow-winged grasshopper *Chorthippus biguttulus*, females discriminate against male songs that include gaps of more than 4 milliseconds. This generally

TABLE 5.1. Some parameters of the male advertisement call for which female choice has been demonstrated (modified and reproduced from Robinson & Hall, 2002).

Parameter of call	Example of species showing female mate choice based on parameter	Reference
Lower frequency	*Requena verticalis*	Schatral, 1990
	Oecanthus nigricornis	Brown *et al.*, 1996
Higher frequency	*Kawanaphila nartee*	Gwynne and Bailey, 1988
Loudness (intensity)	*Amblycorypha parvipennis*	Galliart and Shaw, 1996
	Requena verticalis	Bailey *et al.*, 1990
Higher chirp rate	*Gryllus lineaticeps*	Wagner and Hoback, 1999
More syllables per chirp or phrase (longer chirp/phase durations)	*Acheta domesticus*	Gray, 1997
	Gryllus lineaticeps	Wagner and Hoback, 1999
	Scudderia curvicauda	Tuckerman *et al.*, 1993
More pulses per trill and shorter interpulse intervals	*Gryllus texensis*	Wagner *et al.*, 1995
Longer chirps	*Phaneroptera nana*	Tauber *et al.*, 2001
Shorter pulses	*Gryllodes sigillatus*	Champagnon & del Castillo, 2008
Symmetry in maximum frequency and chirp duration between chirps produced by different legs	*Myrmeleotettix maculatus*	Møller, 2001
Leading call (start of call not overlapped by another call)	*Neoconocephalus spiza*	Snedden and Greenfield, 1998
	Amblycorypha parvipennis	Galliart and Shaw, 1996
	Ephippiger ephippiger	Greenfield *et al.*, 1997
	Ligurotettix planum	Minckley and Greenfield, 1995
	Ligurotettix coquilletti	Greenfield *et al.*, 1997

is the outcome of loss of one of the male's hind legs, and is thought to indicate some form of developmental deficiency (von Helversen & von Helversen, 1994).

Some of these features of the calling song can be construed as reliable indicators of male fitness – both in the common-sense meaning of the term and in its more technical meaning in evolutionary theory (genetic constitution conferring high probability of survival and reproduction). Other things being equal, ability to sing loudly, as lead caller, with more signal content per unit time, as well as ability to sing for prolonged periods, indicate an energetic male, one that has out-competed rival males, is resistant to parasites and, in general, possesses 'good genes'.

Females of *Orchelimum nigripes* use song characteristics to discriminate in favour of larger and older males (Feaver, 1983; Gwynne, 2001). Favouring older males might seem adaptive for the females since this is a species with a high rate of mortality among young males, suggesting that any male that has lived long enough and succeeded in gaining and holding a territory has good genes. However, in other species, a preference for younger males has been observed. Reasons for this may have to do with expected reductions in the fertility of older males through declining sperm quality, or insufficient sperm numbers (Velando *et al.*, 2008). Verburgt *et al.* (2011) showed that, in *Gryllus bimaculatus*, various aspects of song performance changed with age, probably because of declining power in the flight muscles. These changes in the song would enable females to detect the age of potential mates and to exercise the preference of the females of this species for younger males.

There is more recent evidence that female preferences and the intensity of selection may be to some extent a function of female acoustic experience, rather than being under direct genetic control (Wagner *et al.*, 2001; West-Eberhard, 2003). The case of the Polynesian field-cricket *Teleogryllus oceanicus*, in which the majority of males in one population lost their ability to call (see above), provided a unique opportunity to explore phenotypic plasticity in female responses to male song. In this species, females generally show a preference to a song structure containing more long chirps. Bailey and Zuk (2008) conducted a rearing experiment in which some females were reared in silence (replicating common acoustic experience on Kauai) while others were played recordings of a range of male songs. When mature, the former group were both more responsive and less discriminating in their responses to male songs than females reared with relevant acoustic experience. This suggests that variability in female response to male song characteristics on the basis of experience during development may enable adaptation in a situation

FIG 86. (left) *Orchelimum nigripes*, male (© D. Funk); (right) stridulatory apparatus of *Gryllus bimaculatus*.

of radical environmental change, as on Kauai. Another implication is that the intensity of sexual selection on male song may also vary in relation to the acoustic experience of females. In general, it may be that mate-choice is likely to be less significant in low-density populations, or in complex environments, where locating any mate at all is relatively rare (Robinson, pers. comm.).

Findings on female preference for large males are more clear-cut. Generally, there is a close relationship between the vigour of the male song – its chirp rate, intensity, persistence, etc. – and male size. In turn, size is a good indicator, for many species, of fecundity (the female can expect sufficient sperm to fertilise her eggs), and also of male competitive success against other males. This is particularly so in the case of males, such as those of *Orchelimum*, that defend territories. Tuckerman *et al.* (1993) showed female preference for songs to be indicative of male size in the north American bush-cricket *Scudderia curvicauda*. Similarly, Champagnon and del Castillo (2008) found that in the widespread tropical cricket *Gryllodes sigillatus*, females preferred males who delivered songs with short pulses. This trait is associated with large size, but males did not show significant genetic variance in those size parameters that were measured. As the authors point out, this could be the outcome of sexual selection depleting genetic variation in a characteristic relevant to male mating success. In the tree cricket, *Oecanthus nigricornis*, females show a preference for lower-frequency songs which are, in turn, indicative of larger male size. In this species, larger males are the ones that tend to win fights with other males, and females who mate with larger males produce more eggs (Brown, 1999). Some burrowing species, such as mole-crickets, use specially shaped 'horns' at the entrance to their burrows that amplify the sounds of their songs. Some South African tree crickets are also reported to amplify their songs by making holes in leaves of the right shape to fit their vibrating tegmina (cited in Ragge & Reynolds, 1998: 33).

FIG 87. Male *Gryllodes sigillatus*, singing. (© D. Funk)

A further reason for thinking that females might have evolved a preference for larger males is that in some species the larger males are able to supply greater direct benefits – such as access to good egg-laying sites, protective shelters, or, as in some bush-crickets, a nutritious nuptial gift. There is some evidence to suggest that female preference for song features that indicate large size may be associated with variations in the size of the male nuptial gift in those species that have this as a part of their mating system. In the European bush-cricket *Poecilimon zimmeri*, for example, females use song to locate and choose males. Where they have a choice, they prefer song features that are associated with male size, and this, in turn, is associated with spermatophylax size (Lehmann & Lehmann, 2008). In the tree cricket *Oecanthus nigricornis*, there is no correlation between female choice and spermatophylax size. However, larger males had more protein in the relevant glands, indicating that nutritional quality of the spermatophylax may be important, not just size (Bussière *et al.*, 2005a, 2005b). However, for one well-studied species, the Australian bush-cricket *Requena verticalis*, the evidence is equivocal, and there may be no correlation between male size and either quality or size of the nuptial gift (see Schatral, 1990; Bailey *et al.*, 1990. See also Chapter 6 for further discussion).

An experimental study of two US species of mole-crickets reported by Forrest (1983) indicated a strong female preference for loud-calling males. Males were placed in soil-filled buckets, surrounded by traps to collect others attracted by their songs. In fact, both males and females were attracted, but in both species the louder of two males placed within 20 metres of one another was far more successful in attracting females. In one calling bout, a male of *Scapteriscus ascletus* attracted 24 females, while his less vocal competitor attracted only one. In the case of the other species, *S. vicinus*, the figures were even more stark: 27 to none. However, as the acoustic horns these species construct to amplify their songs are more effective in damp soil, it could be that loudness of song is an indicator of a suitable site for oviposition, rather than (or perhaps as well as?) the size and fitness of the male.

Evidence of female preferences on the basis of male song has generally come from experimental designs that vary particular aspects of song that are associated with size, fecundity or some other male trait. However, some recent work has shown that at least in some species, female preferences are more complex than this assumes. Studies of the calling and phonotactic behaviour of the Australian field cricket *Teleogryllus commodus* analysed variation in five distinct features of song structure (Brooks *et al.*, 2005; Bentsen *et al.* 2006). Females showed preferences for specific combinations of values of these aspects of song structure. These preferences are considered 'stabilising', as selection is away from extreme values of the structural features concerned. However, in field trials it was also shown that females preferred males that repeated their bouts of calling more frequently. As this is an open-ended variable, female selection on this aspect of male performance (indicative of male effort or condition) is directional. To make matters even more complex, it seems that there is an interaction between female preferences for particular structural characteristics of song and for male calling effort. Bentsen *et al.* conclude that studies that manipulate only a single dimension of male signalling may underestimate both the strength and complexity of selection. A study of female preferences of components of male song in *Teleogryllus oceanicus* by Bailey (2008) even showed that female preferences for different song components exercise selection pressures in contrasting directions!

Most of the studies of female preferences and sexual selection cued by male song have examined the effects of features of the male calling, or advertisement song. However, in many species of crickets, males have two versions of their song – a calling song and a courtship song, delivered at close quarters. There is evidence that for at least some species the calling song functions mainly to indicate the location and species of the male, while the courtship song may give more particular information about the quality of the male. A study by Zuk *et al.* (2008) gives support to this in *Teleogryllus oceanicus*. Like Bentsen *et al.*, these authors distinguished a number of structural elements in the song – in their case, eight in number. As would be expected on the hypothesis that female choice is related to features of the courtship song, it was discovered that, among different males, the courtship song varied more than the calling song did in five out of eight elements.

CALLING SONG AS A MESSAGE TO OTHER MALES

The calling songs of males do seem to play an important part in the formation of pairs for courtship and mating in many species. However, in others, as we have seen, the calling songs appear to play a lesser role in male-to-female communication, and much research attention has been paid to the role of song in the mediation of the relationships among males. Indeed, sound communication between males appears to be no less significant a component of orthopteran mating systems than that between males and females.

It is commonly observed that populations of various species of orthopterans appear to be concentrated in small areas within wider stretches of apparently suitable habitat. It may be that this pattern of distribution is related to subtle differences in food availability, micro-climate, soil properties, or physical aspect. However, whatever their underlying causes, the existence of such aggregations invites questions as to how individual insects distribute themselves spatially within them. There is considerable evidence that the calling song of males is the main mechanism by which such spatial relationships are established and maintained. In the case of the mole-crickets studied by Forrest (1983), the male calling song also attracts other males and, as with the females, the louder song attracts the most males. Forrest's hypothesis is that males may benefit from being drawn to other singing males either because this brings them to superior sites already colonised by other males, or because as satellite males they may be able to intercept females that are attracted to the initial songster. A further possibility, to be considered further below, is that aggregations as such confer benefits on the males that participate in them.

Like those of the mole-crickets, the calling songs of male field crickets also attract both males and females. However, within a certain distance adjacent males repel one another (Boake, 1983). The effect of these mutual responses to song on the part of males is to distribute them spatially into what are sometimes called 'acoustic territories'. Within an aggregation, the spacing of singing males can be very uniform, and, at least in some species, it is mediated wholly by sound communication. This was demonstrated for the western Australian copiphorine bush-cricket *Mygalopsis marki* by Bailey and Thiele (1983). Experimentally deafened males were introduced into an area that had been cleared of normal males and their distribution compared to that of a control group over a period of six days. The spatial distribution of the control group was similar to that of undisturbed populations, but the deafened males remained in close proximity to one another. In another experiment, males with tegmina trimmed to reduce the intensity of their songs were released, and their spatial distribution measured. In this experiment, the males distributed themselves evenly, but their mean distance apart was significantly less than that of undamaged males. The study also revealed that in addition to moving closer or further apart in response to the sound intensity of their neighbours, males could also move up or down in the shrubby vegetation to adjust their relative positions. This response enabled males to maintain their acoustic distance while remaining on the same bush. In this species, males show strong fidelity to their song sites, with some males retaining their positions on the same bush for more than 30 days.

A similar study of the spatial distribution of males of a Colombian subtropical bush-cricket, *Panacanthus pallicornis*, in two types of forest habitat demonstrated that male spacing behaviour is mediated by sound communication. Artifically deafened males tended to aggregate, while the control group, with hearing intact, spread through the forest (Chamorro-R *et al.*, 2007)

Like males of *Mygalopsis*, those of the mainly tropical and sub-tropical species of the genus *Neoconocephalus* also show strong fidelity to particular song sites, which they may occupy for several weeks (Greenfield, 1990). Regular spacing of singing males within a wider aggregation is also a feature of these species, and intruding males are repelled by a distinct contact call. Greenfield argues that discontinuous song structures may have evolved in some species with dense populations so that males have an 'acoustic window' between chirps to monitor the songs of adjacent males. In the case of species with a continuous song, it is possible that males are able to periodically close off the broad-spectrum tracheal hearing input so as to focus on the more finely tuned inputs from their tibial hearing organs (Bailey & Thiele, 1983). In common with other orthopteran groups, non-territorial, non-singing satellite males are often interspersed among the songsters. Among British species of the related genus *Conocephalus* there is evidence of territorial defence of song perches. Males of the short-winged conehead *Conocephalus dorsalis* appear to scent-mark leaves, and intruding males are driven off. However, in this species the song is continuous, and contact between males takes the form of intense antennation, aggressive bodily postures and kicking with the hind legs (see DVD). Males of another British species, Roesel's bush-cricket (*Metrioptera roeselii*) also compete for favoured song perches. Rival males produce short bursts of song, unlike the continuous stridulation of the calling song, and lunge at one another until one retreats (personal observation; see DVD). Males of the meadow grasshopper (*Chorthippus parallelus*) also compete for favoured song-perches by posturing together with brief bursts of stridulation (see DVD).

It seems likely that spacing behaviour among males in many species represents a compromise between whatever benefits may accrue to individuals from being part of an aggregation, on the one hand, and avoidance of the costs of possible damage and heightened risks of predation that would be associated with direct physical conflict, on the other (Bailey & Thiele, 1983; Greenfield, 1990). However, the spacing of males within aggregations need not be even. If there are definite advantages to be gained from occupying some particular song perches rather than others, perhaps because of greater height, better protection from predators, or greater likelihood of encountering females, there may be intense competition between males within an aggregation to occupy particular sites. This will also be true where there is significant variation among males in their fitness, energy or aggressiveness. In these cases, the mutual monitoring of calling songs may provide information that enables each male to assess the likelihood of success in direct conflict. However, in many species, males also have a distinct aggressive song. In the New Zealand stenopelmatid *Hemideina crassidens*, the aggressive song is emitted when two males encounter one another, but it may also be used when courtship is interrupted, and before, during or after actual conflict between males (Field & Sandlant, 1983; Field, 2001). Greenfield and Minckley (1993) describe the alternation of graded aggressive songs between rival males of the American tarbrush grasshopper *Ligurotettix planum*. Males of this species compete to call from shrubs whose foliage is a favoured food source for females, and females may use the male call either as an indicator of his quality, or as a short cut to assessing the shrub he occupies as a food source (or both). For males to establish relations of dominance in this way, each must have a reliable indicator of the combat fitness of his rival. Greenfield (1997) argues that neither intensity nor frequency of the song will satisfy this criterion, and in fact individual males that win such stand-offs are normally ones that call faster or call for longer. This is the case in *L. planum*, and other species such as *Gryllus bimaculatus* and *Hemideina crassidens*.

Singing together

In addition to the male calling song's role in mediating the spatial relationships and relations of dominance between males, there appear to be other sorts of information conveyed, and other dimensions of behaviour altered. By far the most dramatic and puzzling of these forms of behaviour are the 'awesome' chorusing episodes referred to in a classic article by R. D. Alexander (1975). These included 'a massive synchrony extending several hundred meters, from one end of the forest to the other' produced by cicadas, and another of 'synchronised alternation' exhibited by a population of katydids (bush-crickets) in the Appalachians. However, as Alexander acknowledges, these events are rare, and often not observed even by close students of the species concerned. It is thus unlikely that they form part of the evolved mode of life of the species, but rather should be seen as incidental effects of their normal behaviour under unusual conditions. Nevertheless, there are many species that do have as a regular feature of their behaviour periods when numerous males sing more or less simultaneously, and often modify their song in response to that of others in the same general area. This phenomenon of chorusing in orthopterans, as in some other groups of insects, amphibians and birds, has long been a topic of discussion and controversy. Wynne-Edwards (1962) offered a group-level explanation in terms of males monitoring and regulating population size, and Alexander himself in his earlier work offered a variety of explanations, some depending on physiological constraints that rendered some male song as an unavoidable response to that of a neighbour.

Alternating or synchronising

However, the more recent focus on the operation of selective pressures at or below the level of individual organisms, and the associated tendency to look for adaptive explanations of behaviour, have shifted attention from the group level of interaction to that of pairs of interacting individuals. These are now generally thought to form the basis of the larger-scale chorusing phenomena.

Alexander provides some interesting experimental evidence that, in the case of at least some species, the response of one male to the song of a calling neighbour is an incidental effect. Such 'captive phonoresponders' may be trapped into responding to the song of another by the way they have evolved to maintain the rhythm of their own song by monitoring it through their own hearing organs. However, he acknowledges that regular interaction in the singing of adjacent males is such a widespread and ingrained feature of the calling behaviour of many species that it is likely to have arisen, or at least become intensified, by selection – whether natural or sexual. In line with much contemporary thinking, Alexander postulates that these interactions are best understood as forms of male rivalry in the competition for mating opportunities.

If we consider the situation of two males singing within hearing distance of one another, Alexander argues that two of the obvious responses are likely to be maladaptive. Retreating to another song site is likely to incur risk of predation, may lead to a less favourable location, and will involve a loss of time and energy that might have been put into effective calling. The alternative of staying and fighting is also likely to be very costly, also involving risk of damage or even death, increased risk of predation, and diversion of time and energy. The adaptive alternative is likely to be to stay in position but out-sing the rival: 'acoustic competition'.

Sometimes this results in the superior singer inhibiting the song of his rival. Greenfield (1990) gives the example of the inhibition of the discontinuous song of *Neoconocephalus spiza* by any continuous sound within the frequency range of its song. In this species, subordinate males confine their chirps to gaps in the song of continuous singers, or sing at another time of day.

Alternatively, male songsters may stimulate the competitive responses of others. The consequences of this will differ as between different sorts of song structure. Alexander discusses the likely outcome of male-to-male competitive phonoresponse for three common types of song structure. Where the normal song is a prolonged trill, composed of rapidly delivered pulses, a competing male can either start first, or continue after his rival has stopped. The result would be extended and overlapping songs produced by adjacent males. Alexander gives the tree crickets *Oecanthus* species as examples, and among the British species we might include the long-winged conehead (*Conocephalus discolor*) and Roesel's bush-cricket (*Metrioptera roeselii*).

In species whose male calling song is a series of short chirps, and in which the key recognition pattern for females is the pulse rate, number or pattern within the chirp, the maximally effective strategy for a male will be to chirp in the interval between his rival's chirps. This pattern of alternation is widespread among male Orthoptera. The north American bush-cricket *Pterophylla camellifolia* is often cited (e.g. Greenfield & Shaw, 1983), as are such British species as the grey bush-cricket (*Platycleis albopunctata*), the dark bush-cricket (*Pholidoptera griseoaptera*) and grasshoppers such as the common field (*Chorthippus brunneus*) and the common meadow (*Chorthippus parallelus*) (see DVD). In the case of the

FIG 88. Male long-winged conehead singing – note the partly exposed mirror of the right tegmen.

FIG 89. Male grey bush-cricket singing.

dark bush-cricket, the temporal frequency of chirps is increased during bouts of alternation, and when alternating at close quarters (less than three metres) the length of each chirp is increased (Young, 1971, cited in Greenfield & Shaw, 1983). As Robinson and Hall, (2002) point out, this raises interesting questions about how species in which mutual location and phonotaxis depends on exchange of chirps between males and females manage to avoid obscuring the responding chirps of females by acoustic interactions between males. In the European bush-cricket *Phaneroptera nana* the frequency spectra and temporal patterns of the male and female songs are different, and males respond in a very brief time window to the female reply, but delay their response to an alternating male (Tauber, 2001).

If the key communicative unit is the pattern formed by slowly repeated chirps and the interval between each and the next, then alternation on the part of males would produce the effect of a more rapidly repeating pattern than is characteristic of the species. In such a situation, the species-specific pattern for female recognition could only be preserved if the males synchronise their chirps. Presumably sexual selection would tend to produce synchronised chirping in such species.

However, some authors (unlike Alexander) postulate 'spoiling' tactics on the part of competing males. As we have seen, even in synchronising species chirps are not delivered exactly in unison. There is a leader/follower pattern in *Neoconocephalus*, in which the follower, in beginning the repeating unit of the song slightly later than the leader, will obscure the ending of the latter's chirp or buzz (Greenfield, 1990). This may be significant if the ending of song units is used by females or other males in identifying the caller (Greenfield & Shaw, 1983; Greenfield, 1990). Greenfield *et al.* (1997) have provided a model which would explain both synchronisation and alternation of male calls as consequences of a mechanism in the central nervous system that regulates the rate of signalling. This might have evolved as a male competitive strategy in response to female preferences for leading calls, as in the south Indian bush-cricket *Mecopoda elongata* (Hartbauer *et al.*, 2006; Nityananda *et al.*, 2007). However, models provided by Nityananda and Balakrishnan (2009) for the sister species, *Mecopoda* 'chirper', suggest that in this species, in which males alter their chirp rate in response to one another, synchrony could not have evolved as a stable strategy unless aggregation preceded it. They argue that, at least in this lineage, aggregation may have conferred advantages in terms of protection from predation, or communication of intra-specific cues, with synchronised calling as a cooperative strategy being selected subsequently.

There are other, more complex interactions in which parts of rival male songs are obscured. Heller's study of a subdivision of phaneropterine bush-crickets (the Barbitistini) illustrates the diversity in this group of complex male song structures, including changes of amplitude of single syllables, combinations of different ('hard and 'soft') syllable types and fixed temporal sequences of syllables of each type. Females respond to specific elements in the male song, and Heller suggests that complexity has evolved in response to competitive interactions between males to obscure significant elements in one another's calls (Heller, 1990; Greenfield & Roizen, 1993; Minckley *et al.*, 1995; see also Bailey (2006) for a more detailed discussion of the evolution of signal complexity).

Alexander, too, argues that selective pressures arising from a range of different strategies used by males in addition to simple competitive calling may explain the evolution of more complex song structures. Since the formation of pairs is frequently disrupted by the intervention of competing males, more complex calling songs may have evolved to signal differentially to rival males, and/or to females at various distances. The latter may respond to different parameters of the song (intensity, lead frequency, rapidity of pulses, number of pulses in a chirp, and so on) at different

FIG 90. (above) *Neoconocephalus retusus*, male. (© D. Funk)

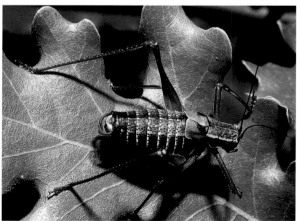

FIG 91. (left) *Barbitistes obtusus*, male (southern France), a species with a complex song structure (see Ragge & Reynolds 1998: 120–122).

distances. For example, males of the eastern US bush-cricket *Microcentrum rhombifolium* alternate two calls ('ticks' and 'lisps'). The 'lisp' when emitted at high intensity is a long-range signal, while at low intensity, females move towards the male. Females also reply to the series of ticks in the male song, also with ticks, and these enable the male to locate the female at short range. Males also use the ticking signal when attempting to interrupt a communicating pair (Alexander, 1960 and Grove, 1959, cited in Alexander, 1975).

The British short-winged conehead (*Conocephalus dorsalis*) also has a complex prolonged song in which two different sounds – described by Ragge (1965) as a 'hiss' and a rapid 'ticking' sound – alternate with one another every few seconds. His more detailed analysis (Ragge & Reynolds, 1998) reveals an alternating pattern of repeated echemes, each of which is made up of four syllables (the 'hiss' or 'rustle' component), and repeated single-syllable 'ticks', each sequence lasting several seconds. The significance of this degree of complexity is not clear. The mating system of this species does seem to involve territorial defence, and there is frequent antagonistic interaction between males. However, it is also the case that this species and the long-winged conehead (*Conocephalus discolor*) overlap in their habitat requirements and are frequently found in mixed communities. Superficially the songs of the two species are very similar (although hardly audible to the human ear without amplification), but in *C. discolor* the 'hiss' echemes are tri-syllabic. In general the song of *C. discolor* is uniform, without the regular alternation of ticking phases – although as Ragge & Reynolds show, some males of *C. discolor* do include brief interludes of ticking sounds in their song. It may be that this is a case where the key function of song complexity has to do with species recognition (see sequences of both species on the DVD).

Aggregation and chorusing

Alexander argues that many chorusing phenomena may simply be incidental consequences of competitive interactions between individual males. However, even this implies some degree of spatial aggregation of singing males and clearly aggregation and chorusing are closely related to one another. Aggregations, in the sense of patches of more densely concentrated subpopulations, may be, and usually are, based on the spatial distribution of some important resource. Aggregations of sexually active males are frequently associated with zones that contain resources important for females, especially safety from predators, feeding or egg-laying sites, or with areas where females are more likely to be encountered for other reasons, such as emergence sites. Groupings of males in such locations are referred to as 'resource-based aggregations'. Such aggregations may be the result of passive movements of males, in the sense that the aggregation is merely an incidental effect of a number of males independently finding or being drawn to them on the basis of the likelihood of finding willing mates. However, the evidence in many species is that males are attracted by the songs of males that are already aggregated. This could be understood as a behavioural disposition that has evolved from an original basis in passive aggregation.

More difficult to explain are aggregations of chorusing males that appear not to be centred around competition for or control over areas that are otherwise more likely to be favoured by females. As Alexander rightly points out, it can often be difficult for a human observer to be sure that such areas really do not include resources important for females. However, in those cases of chorusing that are presumed not to be resource based, this appears to be a form of cooperative behaviour among the males that are in other respects rivals. The current orthodoxy in evolutionary theory demands an explanation of how such cooperation could have evolved (and could persist) in terms of the reproductive interests of individual males (or their genes). There are two strong candidates to meet this challenge. One is that non-resource based aggregations offer protection from predation in some way. This could be because an approaching predator might be more easily detected, or, perhaps, because in some way potential predators are confused or intimidated by the size of the aggregation, or the volume of the sound, or the difficulty of locating individual sound sources. On the other hand, it might also be the case that aggregations of chorusing insects could actually attract the attention of predators and so increase predation risk, and there seems to be little evidence either way.

The other possible explanation advanced by Alexander draws on the idea of sexual selection by female preference. It could be in the reproductive interest of individual males to approach and call from an aggregation only if by doing so they were more likely to have mating (and fertilisation) success, than if they were to remain aloof and sing solo. This could be the case if chorusing groups attracted into their midst more sexually responsive females per member from outside their 'arena' than the average solo performer. In turn, this would be a likely scenario if females had evolved preferences for males singing in aggregations, compared with soloists. Females would be likely to evolve such preferences in polygynous species where the males offer little in the way of parental investment (such as control over resources, as in resource-based aggregations). In such species, females would be likely to express preferences for inheritable traits that are generally preferred by females of the species, or for phenotypic indicators of male 'quality'. Either way, female preferences for male traits could have selective effects only if females are able to compare the performances of a number of rival males, and also if this could be achieved with minimal additional cost or risk to the female over simply mating with the first male she encounters. Given these conditions, there would be strong sexually selective pressures on males to form chorusing aggregations. Such pressures would become still more powerful if females simply refused to mate with solo males, and they might even override any costs to both sexes from increased risk of predation.

This analysis draws on the analogy between insect chorusing and the lekking behaviour of some vertebrate species (see the previous chapter). Despite some disanalogies, such as the reuse of the same arena year after year by relatively long-lived individuals in the case of birds such as grouse and European ruff, the model does seem to work quite well for at least some chorusing behaviour of insects. However, there still is only limited empirical evidence of the relative mating success of different males within such insect choruses, or of any advantage accruing to male members of choruses compared with soloists.

T. J. Walker (e.g. 1983a) took this argument further, and provided some empirical confirmation. Using essentially the same model of sexual selection as Alexander, he emphasised the distinction between spatial aggregation and chorusing. While spatial aggregation is the key characteristic of leks, the relevant feature of orthopteran choruses is that they are concentrated in time. They are likely to occur during time periods when the maximum number of females is available, and, reciprocally, females are most likely to be active when numerous males are performing, enabling their displays to be compared. These are likely to be relatively brief periods during the day, and choruses as 'concurrent display' are the temporal equivalent of a lek – for which Walker coined the term 'spree'. Walker gives the examples of American short-tailed crickets (*Anurogryllus arboreus*) and mole-crickets of the genus *Scapteriscus* which chorus without aggregation, although it is difficult to see how chorusing could occur in the absence of at least some spatial aggregation (or indeed, how lekking could work without temporally simultaneous displays!).

In the case of *Scapteriscus* species, males chorus briefly just after sunset, and females fly to them. Flight entails potentially increased risk of predation, as well as significant energetic costs to the females. The adaptive 'trade-off' in this example is that males call and females fly to them at night, so avoiding visual predators, but this occurs just for a short period after sunset when ambient temperature is still high enough to minimise energetic costs. The spree is thus reinforced by males calling more profitably during this period, and females responding at a time when they have the best chance of comparing male calls. This pattern of chorusing – where most or all of the males in a local population sing together for limited periods, followed by extended periods of silence, is termed 'unison bout singing'. Where there is no consistent temporal relationship between song units delivered by individual males within the chorus, this is referred to as 'unsynchronised unison singing' (Greenfield & Shaw, 1983) or 'unsynchronised chorusing' (Otte, 1977). Examples mentioned in the literature include field crickets (*Gryllus* species), stripe-winged grasshopper (*Stenobothrus lineatus*) and *Neoconocephalus exiliscanorus* (see Robinson & Hall, 2002).

There appears to be rather little evidence that bears directly on the question whether individual males singing in choruses actually encounter more females, or acquire more mating opportunities than they would if they sang solo. Morris *et al.* (1978) reported a preference on the part of females of the north American bush-cricket *Conocephalus nigropleurum* for grouped males. However, studies on other species have failed to find evidence of this (Robinson & Hall, 2002).

In the absence of such evidence, the most likely explanation of much orthopteran chorusing is that it is an incidental effect of interactions among males that have become spatially aggregated. As noted above, resource-based aggregations, whether formed passively or by attraction of males to the calls of others already aggregated, are relatively easy to explain. Questions concerning the frequency and interpretation of purely mating aggregations and 'sprees' remain open to further research.

INSTEAD OF CALLING: OTHER MALE STRATEGIES

As we have seen, some groups of orthopterans do not use sound as a mode of communication. These are usually species that live in dense aggregations such that a distinct phase of rapprochement is unnecessary: males and females readily encounter one another in pursuit of their non-reproductive activities. However, even among species that do communicate by sound, and in which males have a distinct calling song, the calling song is by no means the only way that males find themselves potential mates.

One alternative male strategy, especially for smaller individuals or less powerful singers, is to adopt the role of silent satellite close by a male songster, and attempt to intercept females drawn to his neighbour. This is particularly common in males of species where there is male conflict over song perches or control of resources important to females, such as the British short-winged conehead and field cricket.

Defeated males in song contests over occupancy of bushes in the American tarbush grasshopper *Ligurotettix coquilletti* may increase their chances of mating by remaining on the bush even if the cost of doing so is to avoid direct conflict with the dominant male by remaining silent (Greenfield, 1997; see the next chapter for a fuller account of this mating system). Studies of satellite behaviour in several species suggest that playing this role is a consequence of prevailing conditions, and individual males may adopt either strategy, according to circumstances. For example, a subordinate male in a high-quality location may switch to calling when he shifts to a lower-quality location.

In at least some grasshopper species, it seems that the male advertisement has a relatively small role in the formation of courting or mating pairs. The males of the US band-winged oedipodine grasshopper *Trimerotropis maritima*, for example, engage in dramatic flights, in which they display the bright colouring of their hind wings and as they do so emit 'crepitation' sounds. However, a detailed observational study by Steinberg and Willey (1983) offered no evidence of females being attracted to such displays. As many as 162 instances of pair formation were observed, and all of them resulted from the searching activities of males on the ground.

In some circumstances, especially where population density is high, it may benefit males to modulate between singing and active visual searching. Males of the lesser mottled grasshopper (*Stenobothrus stigmaticus*), lesser marsh grasshopper (*Chorthippus albomarginatus*) and the mottled grasshopper (*M. maculatus*) are among those that often adopt this method of mate searching, spending much of their time moving rapidly around favoured areas of their habitat, emitting occasional bursts of stridulation (see the DVD).

In studies of a zone of overlap between the nominate sub-species of the meadow grasshopper and the Iberian sub-species, *C. parallelus erythropus* (Ritchie, 1990; Butlin & Ritchie, 1991; Neems & Butlin, 1992, 1995), females of each sub-species showed statistically significant preferences for males of their own sub-species. This suggests that female choice is influenced by aspects of male calling or courtship behaviour that differ as between the two sub-species. Behavioural studies in the zone of overlap between the two did show differences in the patterns of calling, courtship and search behaviour. *C. p. parallelus* males sang in longer bouts, with more songs per bout, than did *C. p. erythropus*. In addition, male *erythropus* songs had longer intervals between echemes, and between bouts of singing they moved actively in search of females. Males of *C. p. parallelus* more frequently remained inactive between bouts of singing. Although not discussed in Neems and Butlin, sub-species *erythropus*, unlike *parallelus*, has a well developed and distinctive courtship song (see oscillograms in Ragge & Reynolds 1998). The implication of these studies is that female discrimination and response in *C. parallelus parallelus* is primarily to acoustic cues in the male song, while in *erythropus*, the greater devotion to searching as against singing suggests a greater role for visual and chemical cues at close quarters (Ritchie, 1990). It seems likely that chemical cues in the form of pheromones play a significant role in orthopteran courtship generally. This topic has recently become the focus of more research, as we shall see in the following chapter.

CHAPTER 6

Courting, giving and guarding

The patterns of interaction through which reproduction is managed in each species are the outcome of the evolutionary history of their lineage, and bear the legacy of the responses of past generations to a great range of different sorts of selective pressure. These include climatic and other environmental conditions, together with predation and parasitism and other factors that affect survival chances. But these factors combine with and often modify the various ways in which the behaviour and condition of individuals of one sex influence the reproductive success rates of the other. While it is recognised that sexual reproduction necessarily involves cooperative interactions between males and females, it is also true that males and females frequently have asymmetrical and even conflicting reproductive interests. Since neither sex has complete control over the reproductive process, the mating and reproductive sequence of each species can be understood as embodying a (possibly still evolving) co-evolutionary compromise between male and female reproductive interests, modified and constrained in various ways by natural selection (refer to Chapter 4 for more on these ideas).

As we saw in Chapter 4, the sequence of interactions that make up the reproductive system of sexually reproducing species can be analysed as a series of eight distinct (but sometimes overlapping) phases, each the outcome of a distinct set of selective pressures (Alexander, *et al.* 1997): rapprochement, courtship, mating, insemination, post-copulatory behaviour, fertilisation (in Orthoptera, coinciding with egg-laying), care of offspring, and maintenance of long-term pair bonds.

The first of these phases – rapprochement – was the main topic of the previous chapter. However, in gregarious species, such as the greenhouse camel-cricket (*Diestrammena (Tachycines) asynamorus*) no distinct phase of pair formation is required. In many species of grasshoppers, populations are often so dense that active searching for females on the part of males is an advantageous alternative to the calling song, and in the case of groundhoppers it is the only available strategy.

The second, courtship, phase is initiated when a male and female are at close quarters, and at least one – usually the male – is showing some sign of sexual interest in the other. In some species there is a distinct courtship song, but this is often combined (as becomes possible when the pair are physically close) with other channels of communication – visual, chemical and tactile. The courtship phase is considered to function as a way of inducing in the female a motivational change so that she accepts the male's eventual mating attempt. Because even prolonged courtship often ends in rejection, and/or disruption and usurpation by rival males, it must also provide the basis for females to exercise choice (Robinson & Hall, 2002). Courtship songs and performances, therefore, should be understood as at least in part the outcome of sexual selection acting on ancestral populations. However, these and other pressures are likely to have worked to some extent in contradictory directions. As well as fixing the attention of the target female and influencing her physiological state, the male's courtship should avoid attracting the attention of rival males or predators. This may help to explain why courtship songs, in those species that have them, are generally delivered at much lower intensity than calling songs. There is no benefit to be gained from the energetic costs and risks associated with projecting their advertisement over long distances once there is a target female close by, and presumably there is an advantage to be gained from a discreet assignation that is not noticed by other males in the vicinity.

In a few species there is no courtship phase, and males forcibly mate with females. This reproductive strategy, 'coercive copulation', is an extreme expression of conflicting male and female reproductive interests. It is adopted

FIG 92. The alpine bush-cricket, male. (© G. Carron)

in some grasshopper species and, among the Tettigoniidae, in the Alpine bush-cricket *Anonconotus alpinus* (Vahed, 2002; Vahed & Carron, 2008).

In Orthoptera, as in most sexually reproducing species, there is usually a time lapse between copulation, insemination and actual fertilisation of the eggs. This lapse may allow females to choose which male's sperm will fertilise her eggs and also reflects her greater interest in the timing and placing of the fertilised eggs. As most of the female's strategies for controlling which male's sperm fertilise her eggs are internal, physiological processes, they are termed 'cryptic female choice' (Eberhard, 1991, 1997. See also Chapter 4). In many species, males have evolved strategies in response to this that commonly prolong copulation or, by various means, limit the probability that the female will mate with another male prior to laying eggs fertilised by him.

Phases three to six in the mating sequence (copulation, insemination, fertilisation and post-copulatory behaviour) often overlap with one another, and have provided many opportunities for conflicting reproductive interests between males and females to have evolved into a great variety of strategies and counter-strategies in the mating systems of different subgroups among the Orthoptera. Perhaps the most intriguing and challenging of these elements in orthopteran mating systems are the nuptial gifts, which are especially prevalent among bush-crickets. The often ingenious research effort that has focused on the exploration and interpretation of this phenomenon has addressed some of the most fundamental theoretical questions concerning sexual selection, conflict of reproductive interest, and the evolution of sexual difference itself.

The final two phases of the sequence of reproductive behaviour as listed by Alexander *et al.*, (1997) are rarely, if ever, encountered among orthopterans. The penultimate phase, cooperation between the sexes in care for the offspring, is found only in monogamous species, in which the male has equal interest in the welfare of the jointly produced offspring. A few groups of beetles and cockroaches exhibit joint care of the young, but there is as yet little or no evidence of this in any group of orthopterans. However, in some deep-burrowing species of crickets (*Anurogryllus* and *Gymnogryllus* species, for example), ground weta (*Hemiandrus*) and some mole-crickets (Gryllotalpidae), females take care of eggs and young nymphs. There is some evidence, too, that females of some of these species take over the underground chambers of males, and so may indirectly benefit from resources provided by them (Alexander & Otte, 1967; Walker, 1983b).

The many different groups of orthopterans have evolved strikingly divergent reproductive patterns, in which the various strategies mentioned above have been exemplified, and some of the sequential phases either omitted or collapsed into one another. This diversity has been a popular topic for researchers because it offers great opportunities to test the expectations derived from general evolutionary theory, as well as theoretical frameworks with a more specific focus on insects. What follows is a selection of case studies drawn from the vast literature on orthopteran reproductive behaviour. Some of these are readily understood in terms of theoretical expectations, while others remain puzzling and demand further research effort. The focus of this chapter will be on reproductive interactions following the successful completion of the rapprochement phase.

CAELIFERA

Examples of mating systems will be drawn from two major subgroups of the Caelifera: groundhoppers (Tetrigidae) and grasshoppers (Acrididae). The groundhoppers are of interest because their courtship and mating are conducted without the use of sound communication, but rely on visual (and probably chemical) signals. Another focus of research interest has been the incomplete development of signals to prevent mating between different species.

Grasshoppers exhibit a great variety of mating systems. Of particular interest are the sometimes highly elaborate courtship performances, including both song and dance, and the great persistence of male courtship in the face of repeated female rejection. In a small number of species there is evidence of male competition for, and defence of, territories holding resources attractive to females ('resource defence polygyny') – a pattern more frequently observed among the Ensifera.

In the Caelifera, mating involves the male mounting the female and curving his abdomen down and round so as to engage the female's genitalia with his own. The spermatophore is inserted directly into the genital opening of the female.

Groundhoppers (family Tetrigidae)

The groundhoppers superficially resemble very small grasshoppers. However, there are significant structural and behavioural differences (see the Key and Chapters 1 and 8). They have no stridulatory or hearing organs, although they do make use of vibratory communication, presumably mediated by the substrate. This group of orthopterans has attracted rather little research attention until quite recently, but during the last decade Axel Hochkirch, Julia Gröning and their associates and others including Anders Forsman, and Sofia Caesar have produced a series of remarkable studies on three species of European groundhopper that also occur in Britain – the slender (*Tetrix subulata*), Cepero's

FIG 93. Habitat (mid Essex) shared by both common and slender groundhoppers.

(*T. ceperoi*) and common (*T. undulata*). Several of their studies explore distinctive features of the reproductive behaviour of these species, and pose interesting questions about the lack of fully developed behavioural mechanisms preventing courtship and mating across the species divide (notably Hochkirch *et al.*, 2006; Gröning *et al.*, 2007; Hochkirch *et al.*, 2008).

Courtship, mating attempts and actual mating between males and females of different species are referred to as 'reproductive interference', and its persistence in this group of insects is puzzling from a theoretical point of view. Actual hybridisation has not been recorded, and apparently on genetic grounds is considered unlikely, so there are presumably post-mating barriers to fertilisation or embryonic development. As there are costs associated with interspecific reproductive activity – in terms of wasted time and energy, and unnecessary risk of predation – one would expect that better perceptual cues and communicative behaviours would have evolved to secure pre-mating reproductive isolation. Alternatively, one might expect that species lacking reliable means of discriminating between potential mates of their own and other species would either have evolved in discrete geographical zones, or, if overlapping in their ranges, would at least have diverged in their habitat preferences so that *de facto* encounters between individuals of the different species would be unlikely.

In fact, Hochkirch and his colleagues sometimes consider reproductive interference as a possible explanation for the rarity of shared habitat between pairs of groundhopper species, but in other discussions the problem is posed the other way round: how can we explain the fact that the species do coexist, despite failure to develop isolating mechanisms in their reproductive behaviour? *T. ceperoi* is a rare species in Britain, so the pattern of its coexistence with the other members of the genus is difficult to ascertain. However, careful searching of numerous sites where the slender groundhopper (*T. subulata*) occurs in my part of south-east England suggests that it commonly coexists in mixed communities with the common groundhopper (*T. undulata*). However, the common groundhopper does have a much wider ecological tolerance and is often found on dry heath and open grassland, by paths and so on, whereas the slender groundhopper does seem to be confined to damp or wet habitats.

All three species occur in rather dense aggregations, usually in open habitats with patches of bare ground or stones and plants such as algae, mosses and liverworts. Males are more active than females and move around their habitat, apparently in search of potential mates. They frequently interact with each other, sometimes signalling visually by raising one or both of the hind legs ('leg flick'). If this occurs, both males usually go their separate ways. However, males frequently mount other males, which usually provokes a sudden (and quite amusing!) vibratory response like a temper tantrum from the one mounted. This, again, usually leads to mutual separation. The vibratory signal is sometimes used in addition to the leg-flick signal between approaching males, and also by a male after dismounting from another male.

On approaching a female a male will usually stop, and, facing her, extend his antennae forwards, twirling them as he does so (see DVD). This strongly suggests some form of chemical communication, although there appears to be no research evidence to support this.

The next phase consists of a series of one or more bodily movements that appear to have a courtship function. The male of Cepero's groundhopper performs an antic referred to by Hochkirch *et al.* (2006) as 'pronotal bobbing'. He simultaneously dips his head and raises his hind legs, giving the impression of a very brief (0.8 of a second) and deep 'bow'. He then approaches the female directly and attempts to mate. In both the slender and common groundhoppers, there are also visual displays. However, these are less marked than those of Cepero's, and may be of two sorts. Sometimes a male will raise his body by stretching fore and mid legs, and swing his body

FIG 94. A male slender groundhopper detects a female.

FIG 95. A male slender groundhopper performing a 'frontal swing' signal.

forwards ('frontal swing'), or he may swing his body sideways by stretching his legs on one side. Both slender and common groundhoppers use these signals, so that there is no obvious visual differentiation between their courtship signalling.

Mounting and copulation in all three species are very similar. Males clamber onto the back of the female, often back-to-front and with a good deal of physical re-orientation. When appropriately perched on top of the pronotum of the female, facing the same way, and grasping her with his legs, the male, with genital valves open, probes between the near-side of the female's pronotum and her hind femur on that side. If she is receptive she allows this space to open up, and the male curves his abdomen down, twisting the tip sideways to make contact with the genitalia of the female from below. The process frequently involves antennal contact, the male lowering his towards the female, while she raises hers. Usually

FIG 96. (above) A male slender groundhopper begins to mount a female, and (right) now mounted, back-to-front.

mating is very brief – often no more
than a few seconds – but in cool or wet
weather a pair may remain *in copula* for
several hours.

The male quickly dismounts
and continues searching, frequently
re-mating soon afterwards. Similarly,
females may re-mate with a series of
males in rapid succession. However,
females also regularly reject males
in various ways, including simply
walking away, or walking over them.
More characteristically, however,
rejection takes the more passive form
of refusal to open sufficient space
for the male to push his abdomen
between her hind femur and pronotum.
Sometimes females will vibrate
their bodies violently to shake off
particularly persistent and unwanted
males. Occasionally, however, a female

FIG 97. (top) A mating pair of slender
goundhoppers; (above) a mating pair of
common groundhoppers, with surplus male.

approaches a male and appears to invite mating by performing the 'leg flick' signal
and waving her abdomen at the male. (The DVD shows examples of most of these
behaviours).

Gröning *et al.* (2007) carried out studies of heterospecific mating attempts
between *T. ceperoi* and *T. subulata* in both laboratory and field conditions. Their
results suggested that males of both species did not discriminate between
females of their own and those of the other species. Indeed, they even sometimes
attempted to mate with other males. However, females did discriminate between
con- and heterospecific males, rejecting the latter more frequently. The authors
suggest that the differences between the visual displays of the males of the
two species might enable females to identify the 'right' species. Gröning *et al.*
consider that coexistence between the two species despite lack of complete
reproductive isolation is possible because of differences in local population
density between them. Frequencies of mating attempts by males were correlated
with the number of encounters, irrespective of the species encountered, so if they
encountered mainly females of their own species this would reduce the frequency
of counter-adaptive mating effort being spent on the 'wrong' species.

Where the common (*T. undulata*) and slender (*T. subulata*) groundhoppers coexist, heterospecific courtship, mating attempts and actual mating are common. In laboratory studies by Hochkirch *et al.* (2008), females of each species were equally receptive to males of the other. Possibly, they argue, this may be to do with the similarity of the visual displays of the males of the two species. However, males of both species showed a preference for females of *T. undulata*. In fact, the preference of male *T. subulata* for females of *T. undulata* was so marked that in a mixed population experiment there were no conspecific *T. subulata* matings. The possible interpretation here is that the more bulky appearance of *T. undulata* females is preferred by male *T. subulata* in line with the common view that male insects tend to prefer larger females as they are likely to be more fecund.

However, filming at a site in Essex, where both species coexist, revealed frequent heterospecific courtship and mating between these two species and in both directions. In two of five filmed examples of male *T. subulata* attempting to mate with female *T. undulata* the male was successful. In three out of six examples of male *T. undulata* attempting to mate with female *T. subulata*, three were apparently successful. However, there was some evidence of conflict surrounding these mating attempts. Females of *T. subulata* sometimes resisted mating attempts by *T. undulata* males, in one instance by an episode of vibration. In two cases males of *T. subulata* attempted to disrupt mating between male *T. undulata* and female *T. subulata*, one of them by attempting to drag its rival off the female by grabbing its genital valves in its mandibles (see DVD). However, it is not clear whether these examples of competition between males or conflict between males and females are more common in relation to heterospecific mating attempts than they are in conspecific encounters. In both species, males frequently attempt to disrupt mating pairs of their own species. One common male tactic is to cling onto the opposite side of a female to the one already occupied by a rival male, and probe with his abdomen between his side of the female's abdomen and her near-side femur. This tactic is frequently successful, as the second male may be allowed to mate as soon as the first has departed.

Hochkirch *et al.* (2008) consider that these species may coexist despite incomplete behavioural reproductive isolation, because although their distributions and habitat preferences overlap, they are not identical. If the two species predominantly occupy different niches within the same habitat, reproductive interference will be minimised by the relative rarity of heterospecific encounters. However, while it is true that *T. undulata* can occupy a wider range of habitats than can *T. subulata*, populations of the two species interact freely where they overlap. My own observations in southern Britain suggest that this is a common situation. One possible explanation might be that

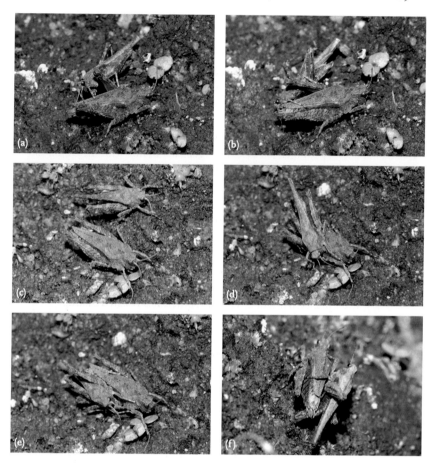

FIG 98. Heterospecific mating: male slender groundhopper with female common groundhopper: (a) male attempts to mount but is blocked by the raised left femur of the female, but the male clings on (b), then dismounts (c), and tries again (d), this time succeeding (e). (f) Rear view of mating attempt of slender with common groundhopper.

where population densities are high and males are persistent, the costs to females of resisting male harassment may be more than the costs of tolerating them, even when mating cannot lead to fertilisation. Although the minimal courtship displays described by Hochkirch *et al.* (2008) and Gröning *et al.* (2007) are often used as preludes to mating, males also proceed directly to attempted mountings and sometimes succeed in mating with no apparent courtship. This may be a measure of the intensity of male competition for mating opportunities.

Apparently the spermatophore transferred by male groundhoppers is relatively large (Farrow as cited by Marshall & Haes, 1988: 43) and consists mainly of protein. If, indeed, this constitutes a form of 'nuptial gift', it is surprising that male reproductive behaviour is so promiscuous, and that the refractory period between successive matings is virtually non-existent. Compared with most grasshoppers, among which it is quite rare to observe a female accepting a courting male under natural conditions, males of groundhoppers mate frequently, and females are also highly polyandrous. The relatively high success rate of males in persuading females to mate, which seems to characterise the mating systems of all three species, poses the question whether females may have evolved mechanisms of cryptic choice over which male's sperm fertilise her eggs. Equally, there is no obvious male counter-strategy to prolong copulation or limit female promiscuity as one might expect in a mating system involving significant male parental investment. Caesar & Forsman (2009) conducted a laboratory study of the effects of polyandry on offspring viability in *T. subulata*. Surprisingly the survival of the offspring of multiply-mated females was lower than those of monogamous females. However, these results differed considerably between nymphs reared in shaded versus sunny conditions, implying that any benefits that might accrue from multiple matings could depend on the environmental conditions to which offspring are exposed.

The instances of males mounting other males, and associated interactions, seem to be open to interpretation. Gröning *et al.* (2007) and Hochkirch *et al.* (2008) describe these as copulation trials and see this apparently homosexual behaviour as an indication of the promiscuous mating motivation of the males. Sometimes these homosexual mountings do seem similar to mating attempts, but often they appear to have the character either of antagonistic encounters, or merely contact behaviour. An alternative interpretation of the rather high frequency of physical contacts and non-sexual mounting between individuals in these species may be that they are mechanisms involved in maintaining mating aggregations. This may be important in species that lack acoustic or other means of communication over long distances.

Grasshoppers (family Acrididae)

Courtship among grasshoppers varies greatly from species to species. Even among the three common British species of the genus *Chorthippus* there is a great deal of variation not only between species, but also from population to population in response to such factors as climate and density. In the nominate subspecies of the common meadow grasshopper, *Chorthippus parallelus*, there appears to be no distinct courtship song, but instead the male continues to

produce the repeated buzz of the
calling song when at close quarters
to the female (see DVD). According to
Ragge (1965) a receptive female makes
soundless stridulatory movements in
response, and males may sometimes
make a sudden loud sound by a down-
stroke of the hind legs immediately
prior to mating. A close relative,
the common field grasshopper,
Chorthippus brunneus, also has no
distinct courtship song. However,
in this species, receptive females
also stridulate, in response to other
females as well as to males. Mating
occurs as the outcome of exchanges
of brief chirps between a male and a
responding female.

A third common British
species in this genus, the lesser
marsh grasshopper, *Chorthippus
albomarginatus*, has a courtship song
that is quite different from the calling
song. Once a male encounters a
female at close quarters he faces her
and begins a prolonged sequence of
stridulation that is repeated many
times. Ragge divides this into four
phases – a modified chirp, produced
by the vibrating hind legs held at a low
angle, almost parallel to the insect's
body, and ending with them held at

FIG 99. Courtship and mating in the lesser
marsh grasshopper: (a) phase 1 courtship,
legs held low; (b) phase 2 courtship, legs held
higher; (c) successful mating.

a more acute angle. The second phase is a more subdued sound produced with
the hind legs retained at this higher angle. The third phase consists of a variable
number of continuous repetitions of phase one. After a short pause (phase
four) the whole sequence is repeated (see clips on the DVD). Throughout the
sequence the sounds produced are much more subdued than the buzzing chirps
of the calling song, but even so they are frequently interrupted by the arrival of
competing males.

In all three species the courtship sequence may be repeated many times over before a male attempts to mate. A male that attempts to mount an unreceptive female may receive a sharp kick from one or both of the hind legs of the female, or, less decisively, will have his mating attempt obstructed by the female raising her hind femur on the relevant side. At any point in the courtship, a female may either jump clear, or simply move off and settle again nearby. In the latter eventuality, the male will often follow and resume his courtship.

These species frequently occur in quite dense populations, and it is relatively rare for males to be allowed to continue courtship without interruption by one or more rival males. Males that encounter one another in the course of searching behaviour will usually exchange a leg flick signal with one or both hind legs and move on their separate ways. However, in some species, notably *Chorthippus brunneus* (and, in other genera, *Omocestus stigmaticus* and *Myrmeleotettix maculatus*)

small clusters of two to four or five males may engage in collective chases of an unwilling female, often signalling to one another with hind leg flicks or brief bursts of stridulation as they do so. In *C. albomarginatus*, groups of up to ten individuals of both sexes gather together, with repeated direct mating attempts by assembled males, and leg-flick signals exchanged between them (see the species account and DVD clips).

Some species exhibit much more complex courtship routines (see Berger, 2008; Ostrowski *et al.*, 2009), and these include two species that occur in Britain – the rufous grasshopper, *Gomphocerippus rufus* and the mottled grasshopper, *Myrmeleotettix maculatus*. Males of the mottled grasshopper have a rather quiet calling song, which is often uttered at intervals as males run around patches of open habitat in search of females. As a female is encountered (either visually or by chemical cues) the male stops a short distance away, and begins his

FIG 100. Two males of the lesser marsh grasshopper compete for the same female: (top) one courts while the female blocks an attempted mounting by the other; (above) the rejected male departs, while the other attempts to mount from the rear.

FIG 101. A mating pair of mottled grasshoppers, with the female still courted by another male (and a common groundhopper looks on!). (© N. Owens)

elaborate courtship routine. This is characterised by Ragge and Reynolds (1998: 366) as one of the most complex so far known among the western European grasshoppers. The sequence consists of a series of three phases, the first two of which may be repeated many times over before a male makes a mating attempt. If he moves on from phase two to three, there is usually a mating attempt as the culmination of phase three. However, if this is unsuccessful, the male will usually return to phase one and continue the courtship.

Phase one takes the form of a prolonged (20 or more echemes) quiet stridulation, with the hind femora held relatively high, and describing a narrow arc as the sound is produced. The antennae are raised gradually with each stroke of the hind legs until they are raised vertically above the head, but spread out laterally in a wide 'v' shape. In the course of this phase, the insect sways both sideways and vertically by regular alteration of the angles of the various leg segments. These movements become more intense until phase one is terminated by a sudden swinging forward and back of the hind legs, sweeping back of the antennae and lifting of the face. Phase two continues with a new pattern of stridulation, in which the hind legs are vibrated alternately at low and higher angles in the production of each echeme. The antennae are kept raised during this phase, and the process of increasingly intense rocking, or swaying movements of the body is repeated as in phase one. This phase, too, is terminated by the sudden, jerky, throwing back of the antennae, facial movement and hind-leg swing. These phases may be repeated many times, but the routine culminates in a third phase in which the repetition rate of echemes is increased, giving a low-intensity continuous sound, while the rocking movements of the body are accompanied by a repeated sideways swivelling of the head. As this phase reaches a peak of intensity, the male lunges at the female.

Almost always this approach is rejected by the female. She may leap decisively away or, more usually, hop or walk a few centimetres away, and remain motionless. Invariably the male will follow and recommence the courtship routine. Sometimes the female, too, may issue a brief burst of stridulation, but this does not seem to indicate immediate readiness to mate. This 'cat-and-mouse' game can continue seemingly interminably – for 30 minutes or more – before the male gives up or succeeds in mating. Ragge and Reynolds note that the sequence in this species is not as stereotyped as in some others, with some variation in the passage between phases. Interestingly, the transition from phase two to three is variable, often being preceded by numerous repetitions of the first two phases. However, there appears to be a stage reached in the sequence when phase three follows 'automatically' from a final repetition of phase two. This is evidenced in a sequence (see DVD) in which a female leaps away from a courting male at the end of phase one, but he continues through phases two and three and finally lunges at the now absent female. He then appears to search the immediate vicinity as if confused by her absence. This seems to suggest that visual inputs after a certain point in the routine are not processed, or, at least, do not issue in appropriate motor responses to modify or terminate the routine.

The courtship of the rufous grasshopper (*Gomphocerippus rufus*) is, if anything, still more striking. It too can be conveniently analysed as comprising three phases. First, on encountering a female, the male faces her with antennae held low, and palps wide apart. He produces a low-intensity stridulation with the hind femora describing a narrow arc, and held low (i.e. almost parallel to the line of the body), and waves his antennae up and down, independently of one another. The next phase, which may or may not involve continued low-intensity stridulation, consists of side-to-side head-wagging, with the palps swinging conspicuously along with the head movements. This pattern is accelerated until phase three takes over. This is initiated by a sudden swinging back and then forward of the antennae, now spread wide, while the head-wagging is greatly speeded up and accompanied by an intense lateral shaking of the palps. This continues for approximately one second, after which the insect jerks back a few millimetres and repeats the exercise two or three times. These actions are accompanied by rapid vibration of the hind legs. Phase three usually culminates in the male lunging at the female, frequently hitting her sharply with his head. He may repeat this two or three times, unless the female departs (see DVD).

As with the mottled grasshopper, the first two phases may be repeated many times before a male moves into the final phase of the courtship and then, in the (usual!) event of the mating attempt failing, the whole performance is repeated. In one courtship sequence observed, the rebound from the violence of the male's

lunge at the female was sufficient to throw him off the dogwood leaf on which
both were perched. This male laboriously negotiated the complex shrub structure
to climb back and continue the courtship. As with the mottled grasshopper, a
female frequently departs during a performance, leaving the male to complete
'solo' and lunge at the space she had previously occupied. Again, the courtship
behaviour of the rufous grasshopper resembles that of the mottled in that
females show little sign of interest, if any, in the male performance, sometimes
leaping well away or, alternatively, making less decisive signs of rejection. In
the case of rufous grasshoppers, courted females frequently turn away from
their suitors, in which eventuality males usually manoeuvre so as to present
themselves frontally to the female (presumably to ensure that she has a good
view). Sometimes male attempts to mount are blocked by the simple expedient
of the female raising the relevant hind femur. Like males of the mottled
grasshopper, male rufous grasshoppers also continue at least to the end of the
current phase of the courtship routine, and often repeat it even if the female
jumps away. An experimental study by Riede (1986) designed to investigate the
control mechanisms of the courtship performance in this species showed that in
fact courting males can process visual inputs during most parts of the routine.
However, detailed visual cues are involved in the initial male orientation to the
female prior to courtship, and thereafter even replacement by a dummy does not
disrupt the courtship. Partially blinded males continue to repeat phases of the
courtship performance many times over in the absence of the female.

Another species with elaborate courtship behaviour is the north American
band-winged grasshopper *Trimerotropis maritima*. As noted in Chapter 5, despite
the vivid flight displays of the males, pairs are generally formed by male
searching behaviour, using visual or chemical cues. According to the detailed
study of the mating system of this species (Steinberg & Willey, 1983), males
respond to encounters with females either with a direct mating attempt, or by
embarking on a courtship routine. This begins with a signal they refer to as
'fluttering' (small-amplitude movements of the hind femora) followed by bouts
of courtship chirping, interspersed with periods of silence in which the male
continues to face the female. Signals used by the female include 'fluttering', as
well as what Steinberg and Willey refer to as 'femur raising' and 'waving off'.
The former, as the name suggests, involves raising the hind femur (or femora)
to 90 degrees or more, with the angle between tibia and femur open or closed.
'Waving off' consists in either a waving or a kicking movement of the raised hind
femur. These female responses appear to indicate unreceptiveness on the part
of the female, as a courting male never mounted after presentation of all three
signals by a female, and usually did not mount after the femur-raising or waving-

off responses. However, males did not abandon courtship after these signals from the females, and Steinberg and Willey suggest that they may even have the function of further stimulating the male's courtship activity. In seven out of eight cases of courtship leading to copulation, femur-raising and/or waving-off responses had occurred in earlier bouts. The number of bouts involved in the instances of courtship observed varied greatly, but in some cases males showed great persistence, in one case continuing a courtship for over 27 minutes. Courtships were terminated by males mounting females, but these often did not result in copulation, as females either did not open their genitalia, or revealed spermatophore mating plugs from previous matings.

This mating system has several interesting features. First, the ability of males to identify the sex of static females suggests a possible role for chemical communication in this mating system. Second, the role of various female signals in response to male courtship cuts against common assumptions about the passive character of female involvement in mating systems. Steinberg and Willey consider that courtship in this species may have several functions – enabling sex and species identification on the part of females, changing the motivational state of the females to overcome their resistance to mating, and displaying the 'fitness' of the male. It might not be easy to discriminate between the last two of these supposed functions, but possibly the persistence of male suitors despite repeated rejection signals is one way in which females may assess the fitness of individual males. Finally, a feature that defies easy explanation is that males frequently court nymphs. There is clearly no chance of copulation, and the visual appearance of the nymphs is quite different from that of adult females. Courted nymphs femur-raise and wave off males, and the males do not generally attempt to mount them.

The elaborate courtship performances that appear to be required by the females in each of these species are presumably the result of a long history of sexual selection acting on the males. This suggests an 'operational sex ratio' strongly biased against males. One possible explanation for this could be that the females mate only once, or very few times, so males get very few mating opportunities. Extremely elaborate and prolonged courtship could be explained either as a means whereby females assess the 'quality' of males by their vigour and persistence, or as the outcome of a 'Fisherian' process of sexual selection, through which female preferences for elaborate courtship routines co-evolve with the inherited ability of males to produce them (see Chapter 4). Either way, the extreme persistence of the males in the face of repeated apparent rejection by courted females suggests that persistence itself has been rewarded, with persistent males eventually mating successfully. Bull (1979) reported that only 10 per cent of 1,610 courtship routines initiated by males of M. maculatus actually reached the final phase, and mating attempts even then 'rarely succeeded'. The high energetic and other costs to the males of these prolonged performances do seem to imply a powerful role for sexual selection in defiance of survival-related selective pressures. In the virtual absence in the world of grasshoppers of vivid colours and eye-catching patterns, perhaps these elaborate and impressive courtship routines are the closest orthopteran parallel to the peacock or the bird of paradise?

The intensity and direction of sexual selection depends, among other things, on the relative frequency with which males and females mate, the common view being that it is usually in the reproductive interest of males to mate more frequently; females less frequently (See Chapter 4). However, very little is known about mating frequencies of grasshoppers under natural conditions. Reinhardt et al. (2007) carried out a field study to establish the mating frequency of females of C. parallelus. The population chosen was dense, with frequent encounters between males and females, but females were estimated to re-mate only every 6 to 7 days, compared with the greater frequency of once every 2.6 days when kept under confined conditions in captivity. This is interpreted as an effect of greater female control over courtship and mating under natural conditions. Nevertheless, it seems that females in this and many other grasshopper species are generally multiply mated, despite mating less frequently under natural conditions. It has been independently shown that multiple mating is not usually necessary to fertilise the complement of the female's eggs, so a question arises as to the potential benefits to females of multiple mating (in those species in which it occurs). One hypothesis is that sperm deteriorates in some way while it is stored in the spermatheca, with female re-mating explained in terms of the benefits of replenishing the store with fresh sperm. Reinhardt et al. (1999) compared singly with multiply-mated females, with respect to numbers of eggs per egg pod, fertilisation rates, hatching rate and sex ratios, and found no negative effect of single mating or age of stored sperm on any of these measures of fitness.

However, Reinhardt et al. did find that multiply-mated females produced heavier offspring. A possible explanation for this is that females derive some nutrients from the protein-rich spermatophore delivered by the male. Amino acids derived from spermatophores have been shown to be directly involved in the formation of the eggs in some grasshopper species, and there is associated evidence of increased fecundity of multiply-mated females as well as greater longevity (e.g. Butlin et al., 1987; Pardo et al., 1994, 1995; Belovsky et al., 1996). In C. parallelus, both singly and multiply-mated females were supplied with abundant food in the study by Reinhardt et al., suggesting that general shortage of nutrients was not the cause of willingness to re-mate. However, it could be that the male spermatophore delivers some specialised nutrients important for egg formation. In the north American migratory grasshopper *Melanoplus sanguinipes*, laboratory trials by Belovsky *et al.* (1996) indicated a female preference for males that fed more effectively. These males provided greater spermatophore mass. This result is consistent with female choice related to paternal investment, with poorer male foragers resorting to coercive copulation. However, in this study males that had recently mated and so produced smaller spermatophores were still preferred by the females.

The evidence of nuptial feeding and paternal investment in the offspring in grasshoppers is still rather limited, but, as we shall see, these aspects of bush-cricket mating systems have been intensively researched and discussed.

The transfer of nutrients along with the sperm presumably involves some additional cost to males, which, in any case, have a reproductive interest in increasing the probability that their sperm will fertilise the eggs of the female with which they have mated. This is a possible source of conflict of reproductive interest between the two sexes, and we might expect male strategies to have evolved that induce the female to lay eggs soon after mating, and/or to restrict her opportunities to re-mate with another male before laying her eggs. In *C. parallelus* (and probably most other grasshoppers), sperm from successive matings are not stored separately in the spermatheca. Clearly, the eggs laid by a female who has mated only once will all be fertilised by that male. However, assuming that not all the stored sperm from that mating are used up prior to a second mating, some of the first male's sperm are likely to fertilise at least some of the eggs laid after the second mating. On the theoretical assumption of free mixing of the sperm in the spermatheca, and no 'passive' loss of sperm (e.g. from leakage or absorption), the first male would have roughly half the paternity of eggs laid after the second mating.

In a study of *C. parallelus* and its relative *C. biguttulus* (Reinhardt, 2000) the proportion of eggs fertilised by a second male showed considerable variation among individual females of each species. In some females, the proportion of eggs fertilised by the second male was initially high, but declined over time (and successive egg pods). In others, the percentage of eggs fertilised by the second male remained high and constant at 80 to 90 per cent. In both species, significant passive loss of sperm was noted, contributing to the reduction in the first male's paternity, to an extent dependent on the time elapsing between first and second matings. The 'last male sperm precedence' shown in those cases where the second male continued to fertilise most of the eggs laid subsequently is consistent with a displacement model in which the sperm left over from the first mating are displaced by the second. Studies of other grasshoppers and locusts have indicated a range of strategies employed by females to control the process of fertilisation after mating, including ejection or dissolution of the spermatophore, and re-positioning of the sperm from different matings in relation to the oviduct (cited in Reinhardt, 2000), but so far the results of experimental studies are inconclusive.

There appears to be little research on male strategies to enhance paternity in grasshoppers, but it has been established that in some species chemical stimulants delivered by the male by way of the spermatophore are responsible for accelerated formation of eggs, stimulation of oviposition or increases in the numbers of eggs laid. Increased rates of oviposition in females of *Melanoplus sanguinipes* and the locust, *Schistocera gregaria*, were produced by implantation of male accessory gland secretions (Friedel & Gillott, 1976, 1977), and similar results were obtained for the migratory locust, *Locusta migratoria* (Lange & Loughton 1985). In other species (e.g. *Ailopus thalassinus*), volatile chemical secretions – pheromones – emitted from the male abdomen and detected by the female antennae can induce increased egg production independently of either visual or tactile contact with the male (Siddiqi & Kahn, 1981; Whitman, 1982; Schmidt & Osman, 1988; see also Whitman, 1990).

Among male grasshoppers, the most common type of mating system is that sometimes described as 'scramble competition'. However, a genus of gomphocerine grasshoppers, *Ligurotettix*, is very unusual in that the two recognised species, *L. coquilletti* and *L. planum*, exemplify the 'resource-defence polygyny' form of mating system (more frequent among the Ensifera). Aspects of acoustic communication in these species were introduced in Chapter 5, and here we consider other aspects of their mating systems, as studied by Greenfield, Shelly and others. Both species occur in desert ecosystems in southwestern USA. Their distinctive mating systems have probably evolved in the context of highly specialised food sources that are particularly important for females, giving selective advantages to males that can establish and maintain territories on those (relatively scarce) shrubs favoured by females. *L coquilletti* is associated with creosote bushes (*Larrea tridentata*) while *L. planum* is confined to bushes of tarbrush (*Flourensia cernua*). The nutritional value of individual shrubs varies greatly, and there are toxins in the less nutritious plants that inhibit growth. Both males and females in both species tend to congregate on the more nutritious shrubs, and males call, court and mate with females on a shrub that they may occupy persistently – for up to 21 days in the case of *L. coquilletti* males. A female approaches a shrub in response to the calling song of a territorial male, but once on the shrub, does not approach further. The male occupant uses visual cues to spot her, approaches, and proceeds to court her, often continuing to stridulate but also producing soundless hind leg movements. This usually leads to the male mounting the female, but if she is not receptive, he dismounts. One in three or four mountings leads to mating, which lasts from ten to fifteen minutes, depending on the species.

Males compete for territory on the more nutritious shrubs by a series of escalating behaviours. An intruding male is approached by the incumbent, and if the former does not retreat, a bout of competitive calling ensues, as a result of which the male who sustains a higher signal rate often succeeds in causing his rival to retreat or become silent. If he does not do so, then direct fighting ensues, involving kicking, grappling and biting. However, retreating to less favoured shrubs has disadvantages: defeated males may still remain on the same bush as silent satellites, and 'co-dominant' males might coexist, despite conflict, on the same bush. In *L. planum*, rather different ecological conditions have favoured a greater tendency for males to depart and move from shrub to shrub. Males on nutritious shrubs mate, on average, every five to ten days. Male encounter rates with females, and mating success, are higher for those congregating on nutritious bushes than for solitary males on less favoured perches.

This is clearly a system in which strong sexual selection is at work, but it is not clear whether females are attracted to calling males on the basis of their 'quality', or whether they, and possibly the males themselves, are independently attracted to the more nutritious shrubs because of the resources they offer. Ingenious experiments carried out by Shelly and Greenfield (1991) favour the interpretation that females of *L. coquilletti* were attracted to and settled on the more nutritious *Larrea* shrubs independently of the intensity and number of calling males, although they did not approach shrubs that lacked a calling male. However, some observational evidence suggested that females left shrubs when some occupant males left. Greenfield (1997) suggests that, once present on a shrub with one or more rival males, females would be well placed to evaluate male 'quality' on the basis of a wide range of characteristics, not just according to calling intensity or signal rate.

Evidence on whether males were attracted to the calling of other males was also rather equivocal, leaving open the question of whether males tended to congregate on and defend territories on nutritious shrubs solely on the basis of assessment of the quality of the shrubs, or whether they were also using the calls of incumbent males as a short cut to identification of shrubs offering favourable resources and/or more frequent mating opportunities. Given that males who maintained territories among congregations on the most nutritious shrubs were the ones with the highest mating rates, it seems likely that sexual selection would favour the male attributes that lead to successful holding of advantageous territories. In the case of *L. coquilletti*, prime among these attributes was the date at which they became adult, with early maturation linked to finding and maintaining favourable shrubs. Early occupants usually won subsequent conflict with potential usurpers. However, mating success does not necessarily imply successful fertilisation – and nothing is known about the ability of females of these species to evaluate the fecundity of rival males.

ENSIFERA

This diverse grouping includes the crickets, mole-crickets and their relatives (Grylloidea), bush-crickets (Tettigoniidae), camel-crickets (Rhaphidophoridae), New Zealand weta (Anostostomatidae), ambidextrous crickets (Haglidae), and others (see Chapter 1).

In the Ensifera, copulation is usually achieved by the male's courtship performance stimulating the female to mount him, although in some species that live among tall grasses or rushes, contact is achieved by mutual orientation from opposite sides of a plant stem. The active cooperation of the female is needed for successful mating in most species, and this is commonly associated with distinct courtship interactions. Generally, the Grylloidea have courtship songs, while the Tettigonioidea tend to rely more on chemical and tactile interactions, especially involving mutual antennation and palpation of body surfaces. However, more recent research has emphasised the multiplicity of the channels of communication involved in courtship, mating and post-copulatory behaviour in all subgroups of the Ensifera.

The sperm are contained in a spermatophore, which is attached to the genital opening in the abdomen of the female during copulation. Some time is taken for the sperm to pass from the spermatophore into the spermatheca of the female, where, in some groups, sperm from each mating are stored separately (Vahed, 2003a). In bush-crickets, camel-crickets and some gryllid crickets, the spermatophore includes not just an ampulla containing the sperm and seminal fluid, but also a large gelatinous spermatophylax. Much of the fascination of bush-cricket mating systems is associated with rival hypotheses about the role of the spermatophylax in relation to conflicts of reproductive interest between males and females. In most true crickets there is no spermatophylax, and the conflict of interest between males and females is played out in rather different ways, with various sorts of male coercion – including mate-guarding – often playing a greater role.

Stenopelmatoidea

Tree weta (Hemideina *species*)

Only relatively recently have the extraordinary mating systems represented among the Stenopelmatoidea been subject to close study, and their evolutionary relationships and classification remain controversial. Among the best-studied are the mating systems of the New Zealand tree weta of the genus *Hemideina* (family Anostostomatidae).

Two species, *H. femorata* and *H. crassidens*, have similar, well-studied mating systems. Both species are closely associated with 'galleries' – holes in trees of several species that are initially made by wood-boring beetles or moths, and subsequently widened or deepened by occupying tree weta. Occupancy of galleries is very variable. Many apparently suitable holes are not occupied, while others may contain solitary males or females, male/female pairs, or single males with 'harems' of up to as many as 13 females. Males compete aggressively for control over galleries containing females, and a case has been made for their mating system to be included, like that of the *Ligurotettix* grasshoppers described above, in the category 'resource-defence polygyny'. This is because the galleries are important means of shelter from a wide range of predators, and so are sought by females. Control over access to a large gallery would therefore increase the chances of a male encountering and mating with one or more females.

Adult males of both species have strikingly enlarged heads and mandibles, and these are used in conflicts between males over possession of galleries. Aggressive responses are graded, from a minimal palpation and antennation on the part of an intruding male who then departs, through kicking of the intruder by the occupant with his spined hind legs, and aggressive stridulation, to grappling, biting and lunging with gaping mandibles. The larger, better-equipped males more often succeed in these conflicts, and larger males tend to be the ones occupying the larger galleries with harems. It is supposed, therefore, that these males have greater reproductive success, and the large size and large heads and mandibles are secondary sexual characteristics that have evolved by sexual selection (Field & Sandlant, 1983; Field & Jarman, 2001).

There is no distinct courtship song, but a male tree weta approaches a female and at close quarters uses antennal contact and touching with the mandibular and maxillary palps prior to gripping the hind tibia of the female, and dragging her out of the gallery if necessary. He then curves his abdomen to probe various parts of the female's body. The response of the female involves various levels of resistance, such as reorienting her body, moving away, kicking the male or attempting to re-enter the gallery. However, these signs of apparent female rejection do not usually deter the male, who continues to 'court', with

variable eventual success rates (23
per cent successful in *H. femorata*;
64 per cent in *crassidens* are reported
– see Field & Jarman, 2001). Mating
behaviour in the male is triggered by
non-volatile chemicals present on the
cuticle of the female, but it is unclear
whether there are specific organs of
chemical sense in the male, as distinct
from widely distributed sensilla.
Copulation is usually achieved by the
male standing behind the female,
grasping her with one or more pairs
of legs, and curving his abdomen-
tip under hers. However, the 'female
on top' pattern that is more typical
among the Ensifera has also been
observed. The dorsal surface of the
ninth and tenth segments of the male
has a structure known as the 'gin trap',
which ensures genital connection
and transfer of the spermatophore.
Copulation in *Hemideina* is brief
(lasting 1.5 minutes, according to Field
& Jarman). However, complete transfer

FIG 102. A tree weta, *Hemideina crassidens*:
(top) a male, showing enlarged head and
mandibles; (above) a male making use of its
mandibles! (both photos © D. Gwynne)

of sperm may take as long as 5 hours (Kelly, 2008), and, in this group, males lack
the spermatophylax or other nuptial gift that might serve to distract the female
and prevent her from consuming the spermatophore before its contents have
been fully transferred.

One possible interpretation of the male occupancy of galleries is that it
enables them to guard females with which they have mated, ensuring both that
the full complement of sperm is transferred to the female, and also that she
has no opportunity to mate with other males prior to ovipositing. Evidence
that supports this interpretation is given by Jarman (1982) who observed male
guarding behaviour for an average of 36.5 minutes after copulation in *H.
crassidens*. However, males also sometimes react to female attempts to leave
during the guarding period with what appears to be aggressive behaviour, similar
to that shown in male-to-male encounters. This usually results in the departure
of the female and appears to contradict the reproductive interest of the male.

As previously demonstrated in an ecological study by Field and Sandlant (2001), many apparently suitable holes are not used, suggesting that galleries *per se* are not a limiting resource. Studies by Kelly (2006, 2008) suggest that females prefer otherwise unoccupied holes to ones already occupied either by other females, or by a male (or both). He explains this in terms of the hypothetical costs to females of cohabitation with males (or with other females whose presence is likely to attract males). These costs have to do with male harassment which, as we have seen, can involve high levels of male aggressive behaviour. This often damages the females and renders them less mobile. Also, according to Kelly's account, when matings occur at the entrance to galleries, males throw females off the tree after mating. This, along with other evidence on male aggression towards mates, tells against the interpretation of the gallery system simply as one adopted by males to monopolise mating opportunities with one or more females. The picture is further complicated by evidence that males are not in general more sedentary than females. Males do persist in a gallery for longer, the more females they have with them, but they and the females frequently depart without apparent usurpation by a competing male. Kelly interprets his findings as fitting the mating system of *H. crassidens* more with 'male dominance polygynandry' than with the usual model of resource-defence polygyny (Emlen & Oring, 1977). In male dominance polygynandry, both males and females mate multiply, and males compete for and mate with groups of females as they become receptive. On this interpretation, the males defend galleries only by virtue of the presence of females, and remain in charge of galleries in order to mate with the females, subsequently moving on to search for further mating opportunities.

The puzzling tendency of males to aggressively evict females after mating, throwing them off the tree onto substrate below, was confirmed in both field and experimental studies by Kelly (2008). One possible explanation for this is prompted by the novel observation that when females are confronted by a subsequent mating attempt, they consume the spermatophore from their previous mating. As other males are much less likely to encounter females that have been evicted in this way (because of the low population density), the eviction may serve the same function as mate-guarding. This leaves open the question of why a female consumes the spermatophore from a previous mating when she encounters a subsequent mating attempt. Kelly suggests that this may be because of the likelihood that a subsequent mating attempt will be made by a rival male who has successfully displaced her previous mate (Kelly, 2006). Spermatophore consumption, on this interpretation, would be an expression of female preference for a dominant male. The frequency with which females mate, their longevity (approximately one year as adults), and evidence from examination of wild-caught females that they store sperm, taken together suggest that the habit of spermatophore consumption imposes no risk that they will acquire too little sperm to fertilise their eggs.

It seems that the complexity of observed behaviour so far defies consistent interpretation in terms of prevailing theory. Even more demanding is the discovery that in *H. crassidens*, some males become sexually mature at an early developmental stage – in their eighth or ninth instar – rather than when fully adult (tenth instar). These males are smaller, with much smaller head and mandibles relative to total body size. They tend to occupy smaller holes than the larger males, and call from the entrances to their galleries. They do not compete aggressively with larger males, but attempt to mate with females as the latter move about outside galleries. Their mating success is supposed to be lower than that of the larger males, but ninth instar males are sometimes able to hold galleries with females. It may be that sexual selection has given rise to two alternative male mating strategies.

Finally, *H. femorata* provides an interesting example of potential 'run-away' sexual selection in favour of large heads and mandibles being off-set by natural selection. In the population studied by Field and Sandlant (2001), *H. femorata* galleries were almost exclusively made in the holes of a single species of wood-boring beetle, which, on emergence from the tree, leaves a hole of 10–13 mm in diameter. This diameter sets an outer limit to the head-size of *H. femorata* males, for if they were unable to enter these abandoned holes they would have no protection from predators and would be unable to establish harems. In fact, although large-headed males are dominant and probably have greater mating success, smaller males can occupy smaller galleries and avoid aggressive usurpations from larger males that are too big to enter their galleries.

FIG 103. (left) A female ground weta with her eggs; (above) and with newly hatched nymphs in an artificial chamber. (© D. Gwynne)

Ground weta (Hemiandrus *species*)

Unlike most weta, males of this group offer 'nuptial gifts' to females. These are delivered to a separate receptor-organ on the abdomen of the female. The ground weta are also unusual among the Orthoptera in that females take care of both eggs and early instar nymphs (Gwynne, 2004).

Hagloidea: Ambidextrous crickets (genus *Cyphoderris*)

The ambidextrous crickets belonging to the genus *Cyphoderris* (family Prophalangopsidae) are relics of an ancient grouping that may have been ancestral to the bush-crickets. Only three species that occur in north-western USA have been thoroughly studied, but even they remain somewhat mysterious. The calling and mating of *C. strepitans*, which inhabits sage bush meadows in mountainous regions of Colorado and Wyoming, takes place early in the Spring, just after snow melt. Males suffer the cost of having to sing at very low ambient temperatures, and it may be that this feature of the mating system has evolved as avoidance of temporal overlap between overt calling activity and peak activity of predators such as voles and owls (Sakaluk & Eggert, 2009). Males sing from perches at various heights, but often from the tops of sage bushes, from late afternoon into the night. They are equipped with powerful mandibles, and can show aggression to one another if crowded artificially, but under natural conditions they sing from evenly spaced-out perches. It seems that male song is involved in the spacing out of the males, but is also a means of attracting sexually receptive females. On locating a potential mate, the female mounts him. The male then ceases calling and spreads out his tegmina to expose the soft fleshy hind wings below. The female feeds on these, while the male attempts to connect his abdomen-tip with her genitalia, using a 'gin-trap' structure on his final abdominal segment. Females are able to prevent copulation, and extended periods

FIG 104. *Cyphoderris strepitans*: (a) a singing male; (b) a pair mating. (both photos © D. Funk)

of mounted females feeding from the males' wings without copulation are reported. However, receptive females copulate with the male, whereupon he makes pumping movements with his abdomen and a spermatophore, including a large spermatophylax, is attached externally to the female's genital opening. Copulation may last from one to five minutes, varying by species and in relation to the mating history of the individuals involved. Mating is terminated by the male, but females sometimes continue to feed on his wings and the haemolymph that flows from the exposed tissue. There is a considerable delay before the females consume the spermatophylax. Males begin to call again directly after mating, but re-mating in the same night has not been reported, and females appear not to mate again for some time, if at all.

This mating system appears to be unique in the provision by the male of a double nuptial gift. The high cost to the male of his role in the mating system has been assessed by changes in weight. Calling itself demands a high level of energy, and weight loss as a result of calling for just one hour was reported to be 1.9 per cent of the males' body weight (Dodson et al., 1998). Copulation, including the transfer of the nuptial gifts, was shown to be still more costly, with weight loss measured at approximately 10 per cent of body weight. The most plausible interpretation of the male nuptial gift in this case appears to be that it is a form of 'mating effort' on the part of the male, a result of sexual selection by females who benefit either in the form of nutritional input for themselves, or in the form of greater resources devoted to egg-laying (or both). If females do benefit from the transfer of the dual nuptial gift, then it is to be expected that they will prefer males that have more to offer. One obvious indication of this might be the relative mating success of 'virgin' males, with fully intact hind wings, and non-virgins, who will have less – or less that is palatable – to offer. An experimental study conducted by Morris et al. (1989) on a population of Cyphoderris strepitans confirmed the expectation that virgin males would be preferred. It was not clear how this discrimination occurred. It might have simply been a consequence of the depressed calling of just-mated males, who might have to be preoccupied with feeding or healing their wounds. Alternatively, females might detect wing damage in males, either by direct contact or by the small change in the character of the song caused by the reduced size of the hind wings.

Subsequent experimental work by Sakaluk and colleagues (Eggert & Sakaluk, 1994; Sakaluk et al., 2004) demonstrated that a distinct reduction in male mating success after their first mating was imposed by the loss of haemolymph, independently of the costs of restoration of the spermatophore. It was also shown that removal of the hind wings had no effect on the attractiveness of the male song, or of the willingness of females to mount males. However, males that were able to provide haemolymph feeding were more likely to succeed in transferring their spermatophore to the female. As males tend to withdraw from the female once the spermatophore is attached, it is supposed that the function of the haemolymph nuptial gift is to sustain copulation for long enough for transfer of the spermatophore to take place.

Tettigonioidea: the bush-crickets (Tettigoniidae)

Bush-crickets generally do not have a courtship song distinct from their calling song, although, in many species, courtship does include a subdued version of the calling song. Once a pair is formed – either by female phonotaxis towards a male calling song, or by mutual orientation through exchange of calls (sometimes aided by vibratory communication) – courtship is usually initiated with extended 'fencing' with the long, filamentous antennae. It is likely that chemical communication is also involved, either in the form of contact stimulants or volatile pheromones, although this has been fully demonstrated in only a few species. Where both male and female are receptive, they orient themselves in such a way to enable genital contact and 'locking' to take place. In some species (e.g. *Conocephalus discolor* – see DVD) this involves male and female passing each other in opposite directions on a plant stem, with the male curving his abdomen round in an effort to engage the female's genitalia as he passes. Even where both individuals appear to be receptive, this seems to be a difficult feat, as numerous repetitions are often required, and failure is frequent. In other species, the male has to persuade the female to mount him and curve her abdomen round to contact his genitalia. Often the mounting behaviour of the female appears to be stimulated by chemical secretions on the dorsal surface of the male abdomen, and a female can be observed to rapidly palpate or 'nibble' the male abdomen as she mounts

FIG 105. Courtship in Roesel's bush-cricket: (left) a male both sings and communicates with the female with his antennae; and (right) at close quarters continues to 'fence' with his antennae.

(Vahed, 1998. See this in *P. griseoaptera* on the DVD). In most species, genital locking is achieved by projections on the inner side of the male abdominal cerci fitting into pits on both sides of the female abdomen close to the genital plate. The eventual mating position varies – with the male curled up behind the female, facing in the opposite direction to her, and often clinging onto her ovipositor, or with the female mounted on the male (a more common pattern among the Gryllidae).

FIG 106. Male cerci of Roesel's bush-cricket. Note the sharp inner-directed points.

Although the pattern of courtship described above is very widespread among the bush-crickets, there is one genus in which the males of all species so far studied dispense with courtship entirely (Vahed, 2002; Vahed & Carron, 2008). In the genus *Anonconotus*, males stalk females silently, gradually closing in on them. After briefly contacting the target female with his antennae, the male usually leaps onto her back, curves his abdomen round and attempts to grip her abdomen with his sharp-pointed, pincer-like cerci. While holding the female in position he then re-positions himself in the standard bush-cricket copulatory posture – curved around behind the female, holding on to her ovipositor. Females frequently resist this form of 'coercive copulation' by jumping away when males attempt to mount them, kicking or attempting to shake them off, or even biting them. However, in *A*.

FIG 107. Female of *Poecilimon jonicus* (Macedonia) mounted on the male.

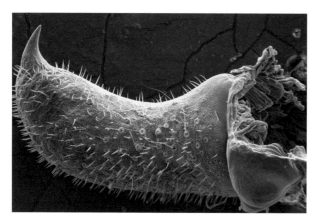

FIG 108. Scanning electron micrograph of a sharply pointed cercus of the alpine bush-cricket. (© K. Vahed)

alpinus, the male usually places his hind tarsi on the hind femora or tibiae of the female, apparently locking her hind legs into a posture that would prevent her jumping away or kicking back. Although not stridulating prior to mounting the female, males of these species do utter a 'disturbance' chirp while mounting, and also at intervals when provoked by movements of the female. In these species, males and females mate frequently, and sperm transferred per mating are relatively few in number. It may be that this unusual mating system has evolved under conditions of high population densities in open montane habitats where males encounter frequent mating opportunities.

In these and almost all other bush-crickets, once genital contact has been secured, the male attaches a spermatophore to the female's genital opening. This consists of an ampulla which contains the sperm and seminal fluid, together with a large, gelatinous mass (the spermatophylax) which is attached to the abdomen of the female, covering the ampulla. Sperm, together with seminal fluid, begin to flow into the female's spermatheca. One of the most dramatic early descriptions of this aspect of bush-cricket mating is provided by the great French naturalist, J. Henri Fabre. After observing the courtship of a pair of captive *Decticus albifrons* over several days, he finally witnesses their mating:

> *The two ventral extremities curve into a hook, seek each other, meet; and soon from the male's convulsive loins there is seen to issue, in painful labour, something monstrous and unheard-of, as though the creature were expelling its entrails in a lump.*
>
> *It is an opalescent bag, similar in size and colour to a mistletoe-berry, a bag with four pockets marked off by faint grooves, two larger ones above, and two smaller ones below ... The strange concern remains hanging from the lower end of the sabre of the future mother, who solemnly retires with the extraordinary wallet ... (Fabre, 1917: 153)*

FIG 109. *Decticus albifrons*, male.

But Fabre's shock at the sight of the spermatophylax is compounded by his observation of what happens next:

> *At intervals she draws herself up on her shanks, curls into a ring and seizes her opalescent load in her mandibles, nibbling it calmly and squeezing it … The huge, sticky mass is not let go for a moment, but is munched, ground and kneaded by the insect's mandibles and at last gulped down whole. (Fabre, 1917: 154)*

Initially Fabre saw this 'horrible banquet' as an aberration, but soon found similar patterns in other species – the 'green grasshopper' (*Tettigonia viridissima*), *Ephippiger vitium* (= *provincialis?*), the Alpine bush-cricket (*Anonconotus alpinus*), and the sickle-bearing bush-cricket (*Phaneroptera falcata*). Fabre's vivid descriptions of these events also anticipate the most widely proposed explanations of the role of the male's nuptial gift and its consumption by the female: as a 'fertilising capsule' the spermatophore is responsible for the transfer of sperm to the female, but is also 'possibly a powerful stimulant', as well as providing a 'source of life for the ovules'.

Studies carried out in the first decades of the 20th century in Germany by Gerhardt, and by the Russian, Boldyrev (cited in Gwynne, 2001: 123ff), yielded the hypothesis that the spermatophylax had evolved in various ensiferan groups primarily as a means deployed by males to ensure full transfer of sperm and seminal fluid from the ampulla to the female's genital tract. Boldyrev complemented his 'ejaculate-protection' hypothesis by observations on prolongation of copulation and post-copulatory guarding in some species that served the same function in preventing the female from prematurely consuming the ampulla and its contents. This hypothesis assumes that the

FIG 110. Female bush-crickets with spermatophylax attached: (a) *Tylopsis lilifolia*, green form; (b) *Tylopsis lilifolia*, brown form; (c) Roesel's bush-cricket (© J. Dobson); (d) long-winged conehead, female consuming the spermatophylax.

ancestral condition that led to the evolution of the nuptial gift was one in which the sperm capsule was not completely enclosed in the female genital cavity, while multiply-mated females would have benefited from consuming all or part of the nutritious capsule containing the sperm. Sexual selection would have led to the development of the spermatophylax as a counter-adaptation on the part of males.

The ejaculate-protection hypothesis has subsequently been extended by evidence that chemical substances transferred to the female either induce a period of reduced readiness for further mating ('refractory period') or stimulate her to lay eggs at an increased rate (or both). In many orthopterans, for example, males produce an enzyme (prostaglandin synthase) which is transferred to females in the ejaculate, and subsequently converts a fatty acid into prostaglandin. This compound is known to stimulate female reproduction, and so favours male reproductive interests (Arnqvist & Rowe, 2005). The combination of nuptial feeding together with hormonal modification of female reproductive behaviour can be understood as male strategies to enhance the likelihood of both insemination and fertilisation of the female's eggs. The other major hypothesis, hinted at by Fabre, is that the spermatophylax contains nutrients that enhance the fecundity of the female and/or increase the survival chances of the offspring of the pair. On this 'paternal-investment' hypothesis, the reproductive interests of both parents are served by the spermatophylax – possibly to a degree that the usual direction of sexual competition is reversed, and females compete with one another for the chance of sex with a good meal on offer.

Unfortunately it is not easy to design decisive tests for these rival hypotheses, and it may be that in some cases the spermatophylax serves both functions. Also, as Gwynne (2001) is careful to point out, explaining how and why the spermatophylax evolved is not the same thing as explaining how it functions now in the mating systems of existing species. In some lineages it could well have acquired new functions. In fact, nuptial gifts of various sorts are widespread among invertebrates, and broad comparisons are useful both in generating and in considering the plausibility of different explanatory possibilities (see Simmons & Parker, 1989; Vahed, 1998; Gwynne, 2008).

Comparative studies across a wide diversity of bush-cricket taxa have tended to confirm expectations based on the ejaculate-protection hypothesis. Wedell (1993, 1994) compared bush-crickets of 19 genera and discovered correlations between spermatophylax size, ampulla size and the length of the female refractory period. Using a different method of comparison, Vahed & Gilbert (1996) analysed the relationship between ampulla mass and spermatophylax mass in 43 European species, and added sperm number for 31 of these in which it was known. Their study, which controlled for overall male body size and for phylogenetic relationships, showed close correlation across species in the relationship between spermatophylax mass, ampulla mass and sperm number. On the assumption that spermatophylax mass is a reasonable indicator of the time a female takes to consume it, this is what might be expected if its function is to ensure complete transfer of the sperm, so both of these studies seem to support the evolutionary hypothesis of ejaculate protection. However, as Vahed and Gilbert note, these results do not rule out the paternal-investment hypothesis.

Other aspects of mating systems are highly relevant here. One important variable is the extent to which females are polyandrous, as this affects both the likelihood that a given male's paternal investment will be 'wasted' on the offspring of another male, and the risk that time and energy devoted to production of the spermatophylax might reduce his chances of mating with other females. Also relevant is information about the contents of both ampulla and spermatophylax. If the spermatophylax may be large but of little nutritional value, then this tends to support the ejaculate-protection hypothesis. However, it is not decisive: there may be small quantities of nutrients that have specialised importance for the fecundity of the female. Equally, highly nutritive spermatophylaxes may be required to keep the female distracted, or to enable her to delay seeking another nutritive gift from a subsequent male, quite independently of whether the nutrient content of the spermatophylax is involved directly in the formation of the eggs.

Alongside comparative studies aimed at investigating the rival evolutionary hypotheses, there are several detailed studies of the function of the spermatophylax in the mating systems of a number of particular species. These suggest that, although it may have evolved primarily as a male strategy to protect his paternity, and still has this function in many species, the function of the spermatophylax may have changed in a few lineages over evolutionary time. A study of the wartbiter (*Decticus verrucivorus*) by Wedell and Arak (1989) established that the average spermatophore was just large enough to distract the female while the sperm were transferred, to induce a refractory period of five days and to increase her rate of egg-laying. Smaller spermatophores would have resulted in incomplete insemination. Increasing the size of the male's gift had no detectable effect on the number or size of eggs produced by the female. Moreover, females of this species tend to re-mate before the nutritional content from the male's spermatophylax can be transferred to their eggs. Finally, the male wartbiter also has a high re-mating rate, and low protein content in his spermatophylax,

FIG 111. (left) A female wartbiter, laying her eggs in soil.

FIG 112. (right) Female *Leptophyes laticauda*, consuming the large spermatophylax. (© K. Vahed)

FIG 113. Mating sequence of the speckled bush-cricket: (a) a mating pair; (b) transfer of the spermatophylax; (c) female with attached spermatophylax; (d) female bites and pulls the spermatophylax. (© M. Hall)

indicating that his gift is relatively low-cost. All of this is consistent with the ejaculate-protection hypothesis for the wartbiter. Similar support for the ejaculate-protection hypothesis was provided by studies of two species of the genus *Leptophyes*. In the case of *L. laticauda*, neither food shortage in the female nor deprivation of the spermatophylax made any difference to the number or weight of eggs laid, despite the relatively large gift in this species (approximately one third of the male weight) (Vahed & Gilbert, 1997). In the speckled bush-cricket, *Leptophyes punctatissima*, multiply-mated females did lay more eggs than singly mated ones. However, artificial removal of the spermatophore from some of the females made no difference to the number or weight of the eggs laid (Vahed, 2003b).

The Australian listroscelidine bush-cricket, *Requena verticalis*, provides a marked contrast. In this species, the time taken by the female to consume the spermatophylax is very variable, but always as long as, or, usually, much longer than, is required for transfer of the ejaculate. In addition, gift size has been shown to significantly enhance egg size, over-wintering survival rates of eggs and growth rates of resulting nymphs. There is evidence that nutrients derived from the male are incorporated into the eggs, that females do not re-mate before the eggs from a prior mating have matured, and that females give sperm precedence to the first male they mate with (Bowen *et al.*, 1984; Gwynne, 1984a, 1988a, 1988b, 1990, 2001; Gwynne & Snedden, 1995; Simmons & Gwynne, 1991). These features of the mating system of this species strongly favour the paternal-investment hypothesis.

On the basis of a comparative study of 19 bush-cricket species from 14 genera, Wedell (1994) proposed that variations in the spermatophylax offering represented two distinct male reproductive strategies. In many species, a spermatophylax of low nutritional value serves to distract the female for just long enough to allow for (on average) complete transfer of the ejaculate. This is true of the wartbiter and other species that have been studied in sufficient detail, except for *Requena verticalis*. The latter species, on Wedell's account, belongs to a cluster of species in which the spermatophylax is relatively large and nutritious and has measurable impact on female fecundity (measured in Wedell's study as mass of eggs laid). Subsequent work has provided evidence in support of some element of paternal investment in several bush-cricket species, such as the European phaneropterine *Poecilimon veluchianus* (Reinhold, 1999) and the Australian pollen bush-cricket (Zaprochilinae) *Kawanaphila nartee* (e.g. Simmons & Gwynne, 1991; Simmons, 1994). In these species, it seems likely that the spermatophylax serves both to ensure paternity and to contribute to female fecundity and offspring survival.

Indirect comparative support for the ejaculate-protection hypothesis comes from the mating behaviour of some species of bush-cricket that have little or no spermatophylax. In at least some of these species, such as the southern oak bush-cricket (*Meconema meridionale*), males appear to be able to prolong copulation by grasping the female with their cerci while insemination takes place (Vahed, 1996). In one of the species of *Anonconotus*, *A. baracunensis*, the male copulates coercively, the spermatophylax is very small, and mating is very prolonged, possibly to give time for full insemination to take place. Evidence that it is the male that prolongs copulation is provided by the interesting example of inter-specific matings of *A. baracunensis* males with females of *A. pusillus*, a species in which copulation is much more brief. The duration of these interspecific matings was just as great as that of normal *A. baracunensis* matings (Vahed & Carron, 2008), implying male control over the duration of copulation in this species.

It seems that prolonged copulation, with duration under male control, may have evolved as an alternative male strategy to the provision of a substantial spermatophylax. A comparative study of pairs of closely related species drawn from a range of tettigoniid groups suggests that male genital structures may have evolved to secure such extended copulations. The inwardly directed spines on

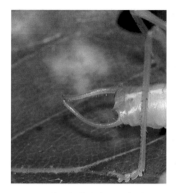

FIG 114. Cerci of male southern oak bush-cricket, which are used to constrain the female and prolong copulation.

FIG 115. Male large conehead. (© B. Thomas)

the cerci of *Anonconotus* males are used to grip – and often pierce – the cuticle of the sides of the female abdomen (see Fig 108), while some meconematines and phasmodines have extended linear cerci that powerfully encircle the female abdomen. In other cases (e.g some copiphorines), differently angled stiff points on the male cerci must also limit the ability of the female to break free. In each of these cases, the duration of copulation is very much extended compared with related taxa that lack these structural features (Vahed, in prep.)

In some other species that produce a small spermatophylax, it seems that the females do consume it, but that they delay feeding on the ampulla. The large conehead (*Ruspolia nitidula*) is one such species (Vahed, cited in Gwynne, 2001) and the unwillingness of the female to consume the ampulla may be explained by the finding that she is likely to mate only once. In singly-mated, or 'monandrous', species, the reproductive interest of the female requires that the ampulla remains in place until all the sperm have been transferred.

The number of times a female mates in her lifetime will significantly affect the balance of reproductive interests between the sexes. In monandrous species, females will tend to be 'choosy' in selecting a mate, and will seek to achieve full insemination of their eggs from one mating. In monandrous mating systems, where a male can be sure that his investment will benefit offspring he has fathered, selective pressures may favour the evolution of male parental investment. Arnqvist and Rowe (2005) therefore suggest that we should expect nutritional content of nuptial gifts to increase, as against substances that manipulate female reproductive rate, to the extent that mating systems approach monandry.

Assuming that males are polygynous, it is also to be expected that there would be a high degree of competition among males, and strong sexual selection acting on them. But what of species (probably the majority) in which females mate more than once? Recent research has focused on the degree of polyandry among bush-cricket females, and its relationship to male reproductive strategy. As we have seen, there is evidence that substances passed to the female in the ejaculate (and possibly in the spermatophylax) induce a refractory period during which the female is unreceptive to further male courtship. This refractory period is thought to be dose-dependent – that is, the greater the amount of seminal fluid transferred, the longer the refractory period (Simmons & Gwynne, 1991; Simmons, 1995; Vahed, 2006). This is generally understood to be an evolved tactic on the part of the male to increase the chances that his sperm fertilise the eggs laid by the female prior to her re-mating with another male. However, it also seems likely that induced refractory periods will affect the life-time number of matings of the females. A comparative study of 18 bush-cricket species conducted by Vahed (2006) revealed a significant negative correlation between the mass of the ampulla (relative to the body mass of the male) and the degree of polyandry of the females, by species. In general, the larger the ampulla – so, presumably, the greater the volume of ejaculate – the smaller the average number of female lifetime matings. This suggests (although not conclusively) that male manipulation of female receptivity reduces the degree of polyandry, possibly against the reproductive interests of the female.

However, it remains uncertain what the optimal number of matings for females might be. In the examples of coercive copulation exhibited by *Anonconotus* species, the lifetime mating frequency is estimated to be far higher than is usual for bush-crickets – between 18 and 34 for female *A. baracunensis*, compared with 2 to 4 in *Metrioptera roeselii*, or 1 to 7 in *Tettigonia viridissima* (based on numbers of spermatodoses in the spermathecae of field-caught individuals; Vahed, 2006). This suggests that the *Anonconotus* coercive mating system imposes higher than optimum mating frequency on the females. However, female resistance is often successful, which may provide some support for the alternative interpretation that the coercive behaviour of males is actually sexually selected by females.

A subsequent comparative study (Vahed *et al.*, 2011) has confirmed the expectation from theoretical models that the mass of male testes increases with the degree of polyandry. This might be expected on the basis of a greater frequency of male mating opportunities in species in which females mate more frequently. However, this study found no significant association between testis mass and sperm number per mating, and revealed a negative relationship between testis mass and ampulla mass. These findings are open to interpretation,

FIG 116. (left) *Platycleis affinis*, male. A species with exceptionally large testes mass relative to body weight (© Vahed 2011); (right) *P. affinis*, male, with dissected testes. (© K. Vahed)

but it may be that the high cost to males of large ejaculates (which are correlated with large spermatophylaces) also reduces their own re-mating rate. If so, smaller testes may still allow recovery of sufficient sperm in time for a repeated mating. As the non-sperm contents of the ejaculate are produced by other glands, there may also be increased investment in production of other contents of the ejaculate relative to sperm. Confirmation of the cost to males has been provided by another study by Vahed. Comparison across 23 species of bush-crickets showed that larger ejaculates and larger nuptial gifts were positively correlated not only with longer refractory periods in females but also with the duration of a male refractory period after each mating (Vahed, 2007; see also Vahed & Parker, 2012). This is virtually absent in species, such as *Anonconotus* species, that transfer a small or even no spermatophylax (Vahed, 2002; Vahed & Carron, 2008).

Another remarkable and puzzling feature of the mating system of at least some bush-crickets may also be connected to the provision of the nuptial gift. In most species of Orthoptera (as with other sexually reproducing species) males compete with one another for mating opportunities with females, while females either passively or actively choose successful male competitors, or ones with preferred traits. In some species of bush-crickets, at least some of the time, there is sex-role reversal. That is, females compete with one another to mate with males, and males choose from the available females. This is evidenced in the unusual sight of males rejecting the mating attempts of females (see the example of this in the dark bush-cricket (*Pholidoptera griseoaptera*) included in the DVD). The most fully studied species in which sex-role reversal has been observed is the Australian pollen bush-cricket *Kawanaphila nartee* (Simmons, 1990, 1994; Simmons & Bailey, 1990; Shelly, 1993; Gwynne *et al.*, 1998; Gwynne & Bailey, 1999). In populations of this species that occur in food-poor habitats, females approaching a calling male are observed to jostle one another, grappling with front legs and kicking. Even when a female has succeeded in mounting a male she could be displaced by usurping females. Even despite a male's attempts to remove a female that has made genital contact, she may continue to cling on, although without receiving a spermatophylax gift. By contrast, the sex-role behaviour of populations of the same species in food-rich habitats reverts to the norm, with males competing for females.

Reversal of sex roles has been reported in several other species, such as the European white-faced decticus (*Decticus albifrons*), the American mormon bush-cricket (*Anabrus simplex*), Australian *Metaballus litus* and *Requena verticalis*, and European species of *Ephippiger* and *Uromenus* (Hartley, 1993; Gwynne, 2001; Ritchie *et al.*, 1998). In some of these species, role reversal is observed in some sites and not in others and this has provided an opportunity to use experimental techniques to explore the conditions under which reversal takes place, and to test wider theoretical ideas about sexual selection and the evolution of sex differences.

Studies by Gwynne, Bailey, Shelly, Simmons and others of role reversal in the pollen bush-cricket *K. nartee*, the garden bush-cricket *Requena verticalis*, and the mormon bush-cricket *Anabrus simplex*, have yielded important insights into these topics. In these species, food-stress leads to relatively longer refractory periods for males between matings, presumably because of resource limitations on the ability to produce the spermatophylax. But food-stress increases the readiness of females to re-mate, presumably in response to their requirement for the nutritious content of the nuptial gift. So, combining these two effects, mating frequency in

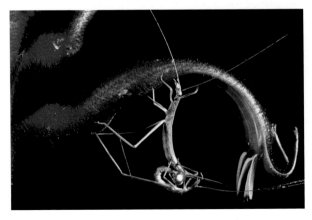

FIG 117. A male *Kawanaphila nartee* transfers his spermatophylax to his mate. (© D. Gwynne)

females is increased, but male mating frequency is reduced under conditions of food shortage. The consequence is female competition for mating opportunities and increased male choosiness. This might be explained in terms of the shift in balance of operational sex ratios – that is, the numerical proportions of sexually receptive females to receptive males. However, role reversal under these conditions may also be explained in terms of increased male choosiness in response to increased differences among the females in terms of their quality as potential mates. If females have to compete for food, and some are more successful than others, then the larger, presumably higher-quality (in the sense of more fecund) females are expected to be preferred by the males. This was, in fact, confirmed in the experimental studies. That female size is a cue for male choice, rather than an effect of greater mating success (and therefore more nutritional intake from consumption of male gifts), was demonstrated by measuring the pronotum length of the females, which does not alter after the final moult (Gwynne, 1984b, 1993).

FIG 118. (top) *Anabrus simplex*, female, with a spermatophylax (© D. Gwynne); (above) female *Ephippiger* species (Sardinia)

At least two of the most thoroughly studied role-reversal species have nutrient-rich spermatophylaxes and show paternal investment. In these species it might be expected that males would exercise choice over potential female recipients of a valuable and costly gift, and also that poorly fed females would compete for it. However, this is less clear in the case of species such as *Uromenus stali* or *Ephippiger ephippiger*, which have very large spermatophylaces that appear to be low in protein. It could be, as Gwynne suggests, that these apparently nutrient-poor gifts contain specialised nutrients that are important to the females. A study by Ritchie *et al.* (1998) suggests that this might be the case in *E. ephippiger*. On high-quality diets, females rejected males more frequently than males rejected females, but on low-quality diets the reverse occurred. In addition, on high-quality diets all conflict was among males, while on low-quality diet all conflict was among females. It seems hard to explain the persistence of this behavioural response to food shortage on the part of females, other than on the assumption that they gain some nutritional benefit from the male spermatophore.

In general, as the production of the spermatophylax is generally very costly to the male, and leads to a male refractory period of several days in some species, it seems likely that, even short of full sex-role reversal, males could be expected to exercise choice of female partners where these vary in fecundity (generally taken to be correlated with size).

Most comparative and species-focused studies of gift-giving species have found evidence of various sorts of male manipulation of female behaviour associated with the practice. These include distraction of the female for long enough for full insemination to take place, induction of a refractory period, or increased rate of egg-laying. However, in some species there is good evidence that the spermatophylax provides nutritional benefits that enhance female fecundity and the survival chances of the offspring, supporting the paternal investment interpretation of gift-giving in these species.

In those species, apparently the majority, where the spermatophylax appears to function primarily as a sperm-protection device, enhancing the reproductive interests of the male, there is good evidence of asymmetrical interests between the two sexes. What is less clear is whether a stronger thesis of sexual conflict is supported. Is female reproductive potential depressed, for example, by reduced opportunities to mate with other males? If the female derives no nutritional or other benefit, but only costs, as a result of the male manipulation of her behaviour, it might be expected that she would have evolved counter-strategies, such as disposing speedily of the gift without taking the time to consume it all.

Gwynne addresses this question in a review of nuptial gift-giving across a wide range of arthropod mating systems (Gwynne, 2008). He argues that most studies suggest that females obtain net direct benefits from nuptial gifts. These may be in the form of nutrients, or transfer of immune functions or other chemical defences. Indirect evidence is provided by increased mating frequency of females of some species when food from other sources is limited and by competition between females for mating opportunities in several bush-cricket species that exhibit sex-role reversal. The prolonged refractory periods in females following consumption of a nuptial gift do not necessarily imply a cost to females. An alternative explanation is that the nutritional contents of nuptial gifts take time to process. Complex interactions between food availability, nutrient content of the spermatophylax, operational sex ratios and other variables make it difficult to specify the optimum mating rate for females.

Gwynne (2001) considers the implications for sexual difference in bush-crickets of the possibility that role reversal has been a longstanding evolutionary trait in some species. If this were the case, we might expect sexual selection to have produced inverted sexual dimorphisms – that is, exaggerated traits in females that have developed as a result of successive generations of expression of male preferences. Although detailed studies are awaited, Gwynne lists: sex differences in size; sharper hearing in females, and associated differences in ear anatomy between males and females; modified genital holding adaptations in females of *Kawanaphila* species; exceptionally complex stridulatory organs on the tegmina of females in some species; and, finally, weapon-like facial horns in females of a few species. One of the few empirical studies of sexual selection on females in a role-reversing species is Robson and Gwynne (2010). In aggregations of mormon crickets (*Anabrus simplex*) where food is limited, females aggressively compete with one another and scramble for opportunities to obtain male nuptial gifts. Robson and Gwynne predicted that females equipped with larger head width, longer mandibles, and other traits that would be advantageous in competition for mates, would have greater reproductive success. The results were generally inconsistent with this expectation – females with smaller heads and shorter mandibles being favoured. Possible explanations of these puzzling results include trade-offs in male preferences between sexually selected ornamentation and fecundity, with males giving priority to the latter. This might provide a general explanation for the lack of exaggerated secondary sexual characteristics in females to compare with the weaponry and striking visual displays sometimes developed by males.

Grylloidea: Crickets

The family Grylloidea includes several subgroupings, with rather different characteristic mating systems. These include, among others, the 'ground crickets' (Nemobiidae), scaly crickets (Mogoplistidae), tree crickets (Oecanthidae) and field crickets and their allies (Gryllidae). Research into mating systems has tended to focus on the Gryllidae, and several *Gryllus* species, such as *G. bimaculatus*, in particular.

In the gryllids, pair formation and courtship commonly make use of acoustic communication, as in the bush-crickets and grasshoppers. However, in some species, notably those that live in dense aggregations, calling and courtship songs have been secondarily lost. In common with some grasshoppers, but unlike most bush-crickets, many crickets have distinct calling and courtship songs. There is also a high level of mutual aggression among males of many species, and this is often associated with a distinct aggressive stridulation. Females (as well as males in some species) are attracted to the conspecific calling song, while at close quarters male courtship frequently involves a distinct, usually more subdued, stridulation together with bodily movements, pheromonal communication and antennation. Male crickets have to induce females to mount them, and mutual alignment often involves close cooperation; courtship routines appear to play a decisive role in this.

Recent work on cricket mating systems has recognised the role of multiple sensory cues in courtship, mating and post-copulatory behaviour (Rence & Loher, 1977). An influential study by Tregenza and Wedell (1997) on *Gryllus bimaculatus* demonstrated a role for hydrocarbons on the cuticle of females in stimulating courtship singing in males. Some of the males courted dead females, but none did so after the compounds on their cuticles had been removed. Replacement of the compounds on the body-surfaces of the females led to renewed male courtship. Chemical analysis suggested that relative concentrations of different compounds were the cue for sex recognition, rather than any single 'sex pheromone'. Subsequent work, using similar techniques to those pioneered by Tregenza and Wedell, have shown that chemical cues are critically involved in the mating systems of other crickets – notably *Teleogryllus oceanicus* (Balakrishnan & Pollock, 1997; Murakami & Itoh, 2003; Thomas & Simmons, 2008, 2009) and the southern US decorated, or house cricket, *Gryllodes sigillatus*. In the latter species, experimental removal as well as chemical ablation of the antennae in males reduced the probability of production of the courtship song, or delayed it. Females deprived of their antennae or of their chemical sensory powers were less likely to mount males in response to the courtship song, and, if they did, responded more slowly than females with fully functional antennae (Ryan & Sakaluk, 2009). Removal and replacement of cuticular hydrocarbons on dead females had the same effects as in *G. bimaculatus*, while replacement of removed cuticular compounds with others removed from males produced only one male courtship (out of 120!).

However, this study showed that the antennae communicate tactile as well as chemical information, and this is particularly important in guiding the female in achieving the necessary alignment with the male for successful copulation. Visual perception of behavioural responses is also clearly involved, as, although some 25 per cent of males courted dead females with cuticular compounds intact, this is clearly far less than would court living ones. In some species the ability of males to produce the courtship song is also decisive. Crankshaw (1979) showed that artificially silenced males of the house cricket *Acheta domesticus* were unable to elicit mounting by females, despite being able to produce all other elements of the courtship behaviour (see also Hardy & Shaw, 1983).

Copulation requires the female to climb onto the back of the male (or he backs under her) to make genital contact. Once in the copulatory position the male attaches a spermatophore (already formed in the case of crickets) to the external genitalia of the female. Sperm and seminal fluid then pass into the female genital duct over a period of a few minutes to an hour, depending on species. In most gryllids, the spermatophore lacks the additional spermatophylax typical of the bush-cricket. In most species, females mate more than once, and this, combined with the absence of the distraction provided by the spermatophylax, puts males at the risk of failing to fertilise the eggs of their mates – either because the female consumes the spermatophore before complete transfer of the ejaculate, or because she re-mates with another male before egg-laying. Post-copulatory mate-guarding is a distinctive male reproductive strategy, widespread among the Gryllidae, that may be an evolved response to this risk. Various interpretations of this trait have been advanced and subjected to ingenious observational and experimental tests. Finally, in a few cricket species, notably the short-tailed crickets (*Anurogryllus*), the females tend their eggs and nourish the resulting nymphs. These are among the very small number of orthopterans that include in their reproductive behaviour any element of the

final phases listed by Alexander *et al.* (1997) – care of offspring following oviposition (see Chapter 4).

Rather different mating systems have been evolved in other groups of crickets. These include provision by males of a range of nuptial gifts other than the spermatophylax of the bush-crickets. Among the ground crickets, Nemobiidae, females of several species feed from male tibial spurs (e.g. *Allonemobius species*, see Fedorka & Mousseau, 2002), while those of the

FIG 119. (above) male wood cricket – glands in the fore wings are 'licked' by the female during copulation; and (left) *Allonemobius fasciatus*, pair mating, with the female feeding from the tibial spur of the male (© D. Funk).

British wood cricket (*Nemobius sylvestris*) receive double spermatophores and also feed from glands in the upper surfaces of the male fore wings, which may provide chemical cues rather than offer nutrition (Prokop & Maxwell, 2008. See species account for more detail). In the tree cricket genera *Oecanthus* and *Neoxabea*, males secrete a fluid into a hollow in the dorsal surface of the thorax, and females feed from this prior to, during and after extended copulation. There is evidence that nuptial gifts in at least some species play a part in mate choice (e.g. Brown, 1999; Bussière *et al.*, 2005a, 2005b).

Research on several species – *Acheta domesticus*, *Gryllus integer*, *G. bimaculatus*, *G. pensylavaticus*, *G. veletis*, *Aneurogryllus arboreus*, *Teleogryllus commodus*, *Gryllodes sigillatus*, and others – has discovered a variety of male traits that are apparently preferred by females: large size, age, symmetry and low parasite load. Males that have previously won competitive interactions with others are also more likely to win conflicts with other males and more likely to experience mating success. Some of these traits, presumed to be indicative of male quality, might be cued by features of song, such as intensity, duration, or other elements of courtship behaviour. (See review in Zuk & Simmons, 1997, and more recent work, e.g. Bailey, 2008; Bentsen *et al.*, 2006; Champagnon & Castillo, 2008; Holzer *et al.*, 2003; Hunt *et al.*, 2005; Simmons *et al.*, 2001; see also Chapter 5.) In the Polynesian field cricket, *Teleogryllus oceanicus*, aggressive interactions between males are common, and include antennal contact, kicking, loud chirping, lunging and biting (Burk, 1983). Fights produce a dominance hierarchy among males, and success in any particular encounter is a function of two factors: previous fighting success and burrow occupancy. Males defending a burrow were found to have an 84 per cent success rate in fights with intruding males. Dominant males also had a higher rate of mating success, too – but not as a direct result of female choice. Dominant males were more likely to produce the courtship song, and less likely to have their courtship disrupted by intruding males. Even without the courtship song, males were able to elicit responses from females to the early stages of courtship, but only males that produced the courtship song were allowed to mate. However, the recent loss of the ability to produce song on the part of most males in one population of this species has led to significant changes in both male and female reproductive behaviour (Zuk *et al.*, 2006; see also Chapter 5 for more detail).

A recent experimental study of aggressiveness in four species of north American *Gryllus* species found marked differences among species (Jang *et al.*, 2008). The research involved standardised encounters between males in a confined space, and aggressive responses were scaled, from antennation, through delivering an aggressive stridulation or flaring the mandibles, to grappling and pushing with heads or mandibles engaged. Two species (*G. fultoni* and *G. vernalis*) never reached the 'grapple' stage, while in the other two species (*G. rubens* and *G. pennsylvanicus*) most agonistic encounters escalated to that stage. The authors argue that the higher levels of aggression probably represent the ancestral condition, with subsequent reduction in aggressive tendencies in two species. One plausible explanation is that *G. rubens* occupies and defends burrows, and *G. pennsylvanicus* also shows evidence of territoriality. Aggressiveness in these species may be related to their predisposition to defend resources valued for obtaining mates, or for shelter from predators. By contrast, the other two species do not use burrows or occupy other sorts of territory.

Viewed in the light of this study, the British population of the field cricket *G. campestris* presents some puzzles. Males often sing from a platform at the entrance to a burrow, and this, together with reports of their aggressive tendencies (e.g White, [1789] 1937: 244, and Darwin, 1874, Ragge, 1965), has led to the supposition that they are strongly territorial. This might, for example, align their mating system to the 'resource defence polygyny' model, in which males fight to control resources attractive to females. However, a study of one remaining British colony revealed high rates of mobility from one burrow to another of both males and females (Edwards *et al.*, 1996). In undisturbed colonies, the fierce fighting between males reported by Gilbert White and others is not in evidence, and may have been an effect of attempts to introduce them into a different habitat, or keep males together in confinement. It is also possible that aggressive interactions are functions of population density or some other parameter. Although the study of American field crickets by Jang *et al.*, (2008) seems to have been designed to reveal innate differences in aggressiveness, the standardised conditions under which the test males were placed may have produced misleading results. Experience with *G. campestris* suggests that aggressive interactions are highly conditional on circumstances.

It seems likely that in *G. campestris*, the burrows function as shelters from predators in the open habitats that are characteristic of field crickets, but they also seem to play a key part in the post-copulatory behaviour. Courtship and mating usually take place close to the burrow entrance, with the male alternating between calling song and the less musical 'ticking' courtship stridulation. Depending on the receptivity of the female, the courtship can be very brief or apparently non-existent, or very prolonged. In prolonged courtship bouts the male faces the female with tegmina raised prominently, stridulating and 'fencing' with his antennae. Periodically he turns to present his rear end to her and backs towards her as if inviting her to mount. If she does not respond the whole sequence is repeated. However, a receptive female may arrive at the male's song platform and immediately mount him. During copulation the

FIG 120. (right) Burrow of the field cricket *Gryllus campestris*; (below) courtship in the field cricket.

male makes vigorous side-to-side motions. When the pair separate, the small white spermatophore can be seen attached to the underside of the female's abdomen (see the sequences included in the DVD).

Courtship and mating in *Teleogryllus oceanicus* is still more complex and precarious. The male initially crouches down, strokes the female with its antennae and jerks slowly back and forth. If she stays, he turns 180 degrees to face away from her and walks forward. She follows, touching his abdomen or cerci. The male then flattens himself against the substrate and spreads out his rear wings, enabling her to walk onto his back while he moves backwards. Only if she is positioned directly on top of him, and only if he sings during the courtship process will copulation ensue. If the angle is wrong, they may try again. It seems that a high degree of mutual cooperation is required. Attempted matings are frequently abandoned either because of obvious rejection by one or other partner, interruption by a rival male, or, apparently, by mere failure to get it right (Burk, 1983)!

In the field cricket (*G. campestris*) the female usually remains for some time after mating in, or close to the entrance of, the male's burrow. This is generally regarded as an example of 'mate-guarding', a common feature of gryllid mating systems. In *Gryllus bimaculatus, Teleogryllus commodus* and other species, mate-guarding is described as involving antennation, and various aggressive responses

FIG 121. *Teleogryllus oceanicus*, male. (© D. Rentz)

on the part of the male to female movement. Three main (but not necessarily mutually exclusive) hypotheses have been advanced that interpret mate-guarding as a predominantly male reproductive strategy:

(1) The first hypothesis (encountered already in connection with the reproductive behaviour of bush-crickets) is that, by preventing the female from premature consumption of the spermatophore, mate-guarding serves to protect the male's ejaculate for the period of time taken for insemination to take place after copulation. This hypothesis predicts that the duration of mate-guarding should correspond to the time it takes for the spermatophore to empty, and that spermatophore attachment should be prolonged in guarded females compared with unguarded ones.

(2) The second hypothesis is that guarding is a strategy of the male to secure repeated matings with the same female. On this hypothesis it would be expected that the male should continue to guard the female for at least as long as it takes for him to renew his capacity to re-mate and deliver a second spermatophore.

(3) The third hypothesis is that guarding is a male strategy to prevent or delay the female's re-mating with a rival male. On this hypothesis we would expect the duration of spermatophore attachment to be longer where males guard a previously mated female in the presence of a rival than when no rival is present.

The possible roles of mate-guarding should be understood in terms of the reproductive biology and behaviour of this group of crickets. Females of most species are polyandrous, and there is an extensive research literature on the benefits, if any, that females derive from multiple matings, and what difference it makes whether these are with the same male or several (reviewed by Simmons, 2005; see also the discussion of multiple mating in bush-crickets, above). A distinction is made between direct benefits (such as the life-time fecundity or fertility, or longevity of the female) and indirect benefits (fitness of the offspring). An experimental design pioneered by Tregenza and Wedell (1998) has been used in numerous studies to measure both direct and indirect effects of multiple mating of females with varying numbers of males. Multiple matings have generally been shown to increase the daily rate of egg production, life-time egg production, and the proportion of eggs that are fertile. Multiple matings, then, generally confer direct benefits on female gryllid crickets, either because of materials derived from the male during mating, or because the risks of incomplete fertilisation of the eggs, or deterioration of stored sperm are avoided. However, studies of a number of cricket species using Tregenza and Wedell's protocol have yielded very different results concerning indirect benefits. The most frequently used measures of offspring fitness have been the proportion of fertile eggs that hatch (a measure of embryonic survival), survival rate of early instar nymphs, or hatchling size. On these measures, polyandry, compared with multiple mating with the same male, resulted in increased offspring fitness in some species, but not in others. For example, indirect benefits from polyandry were reported for the southern field cricket *Gryllus bimaculatus* in the original study by Tregenza and Wedell (1998), but not for the decorated cricket, *Gryllodes sigillatus* in a study by Ivy and Sakaluk (2005). The positive finding of indirect benefits from polyandry in *G. bimaculatus* is consistent with experimental evidence that females of this species prefer novel partners over previous partners when they mate more than once (Bateman, 1998). Where there is evidence of increased offspring fitness associated with polyandry, it remains unclear how far this is a result of female cryptic choice in favour of preferred males ('good genes'), differences in compatibility between the genetic endowments of different males, or non-genetic maternal influences. An experimental study of the effects of polyandry in an Australian black field cricket, *Teleogryllus commodus*, reported by Jennions *et al.* (2007) yielded no evidence of either increased hatching of fertilised eggs or offspring survival. This is consistent with their finding that the identity of male partners in this species had no effect on offspring survival.

Studies of another gryllid, the US vocal field cricket (*Gryllus vocalis*), presented females with many more opportunities to mate with different males than in other studies of polyandry (Gershman, 2007, 2010). Virgin females were presented with different males each day for 5, 10 and 15 days. Females that were mated 10 times laid more eggs, and laid proportionally more fertile eggs, than those that were mated only 5 times. However, there was no significant increase in either effect from 10 to 15 matings. Comparison of the offspring hatching rates of females mated many times to a single male with that of females mated to numerous different males showed no benefits from polyandry. These studies suggest that females continue to obtain direct benefits from large numbers of matings, possibly in part because of replenishment of their sperm stores with fresher and more viable sperm. As in *T. commodus*, there may be no indirect benefit from polyandry, or, if there is a benefit, it is acquired with relatively smaller numbers of male partners than the 5 to 15 used in these studies.

In gryllid females, the sperm from successive matings is mixed in the spermatheca, and there appears to be no internal selection in the fertilisation of the eggs. In general, males whose spermatophore remains attached for longer, or who manage more matings with a given female than their rivals, are likely to have paternity over the larger proportion of offspring. In view of this, it might be expected that males will have been sexually selected to prolong spermatophore attachment, secure multiple matings with the same female, and resist the female's preference for mating with rivals. Females' reproductive interests may differ depending on whether they have mated previously. Virgin females may benefit from full sperm transfer at their first mating as an insurance policy in case they have no further matings. So, for a female's first mating there may be no conflict of reproductive interests between male and female. However, for subsequent matings, females may have an interest in mating with a rival male and/or prematurely detaching and consuming the spermatophore before full ejaculate transfer, either to obtain direct benefits or possibly as a method of exercising choice between different mates.

Experimental work involving various combinations of captive males and females of several species of gryllid crickets has produced rather different results, suggesting that mate-guarding has evolved to play different parts in the mating systems of diverse cricket species. It also seems probable that there is flexibility in behaviour within species, depending on contingencies such as population density. At least some of the diversity in the function of mate-guarding can be understood in terms of other aspects of the biology of the species concerned. Experimental studies of mate-guarding in several species have been consistent with the ejaculate-protection hypothesis. Hockham and Vahed (1997) studied a captive-reared population of the South African field cricket *Teleogryllus natalensis*. In this species (as in most gryllid crickets) there is no spermatophylax. In this study, presence or absence of a guarding male made no significant difference to the success of rival males in dislodging the spermatophore, the presence of a rival male did not affect the duration of spermatophore attachment, and males with continuous access to females ceased guarding long before the females were ready to re-mate. These results are interpreted as counting against both 'spermatophore-renewal' and 'rival-exclusion' hypotheses, while the ejaculate-protection hypothesis was supported by the prolongation of spermatophore attachment where females were guarded, and a significant positive correlation between guarding and spermatophore attachment durations. In addition, there were behavioural observations of the males responding aggressively to female movements toward consumption of the spermatophore. Studies have supported the ejaculate-protection hypothesis in some other species too, including *Gryllus campestris* and *Teleogryllus commodus*. Species comparisons give indirect support to the ejaculate-protection hypothesis, as in many (but not all – see below) species that have evolved a spermatophylax, mate-guarding has been lost. An alternative male strategy, as in some bush-crickets, is prolongation of copulation for as long as it takes for full insemination to be completed.

However, the other two hypotheses gain support from studies of two more crickets – the Asian and southern-US decorated cricket, *Gryllodes sigillatus*, and the southern field cricket, *Gryllus bimaculatus*. The decorated cricket is unusual in this group, as the male does transfer a spermatophylax, and this is large enough to distract the female while sperm transfer takes place. The interval before the male is ready to re-mate is prolonged in this species. This may be because the production of the spermatophylax is costly to the male, as indicated by a reduction in the male's immune response associated with spermatophore production (Kerr *et al.* 2010), although in this species the spermatophylax contains amino acids that stimulate a feeding response in females independently of nutritional value (Warwick *et al.*, 2009).

Despite the transfer of a spermatophylax, mate-guarding has been retained in this species. The ejaculate-protection hypothesis is not supported, as females do not remove the spermatophore more quickly if they are left unguarded. Also, the refractory period before the male is ready to re-mate is much longer than the

FIG 122. (left) A male *G. sigillatus* extruding the spermatophylax during copulation; (right) a female consuming the spermatophylax following copulation. (both photos © D. Funk)

duration of post-copulatory guarding, seeming to rule out the spermatophore-renewal hypothesis. However, spermatophore attachment is prolonged by guarding in the presence of rival males, supporting the rival-exclusion hypothesis in this species, the female of which is described as 'promiscuous' (Frankino & Sakaluk, 1994; Sakaluk, 1984).

The southern field cricket (G. bimaculatus) has been subjected to particularly intensive study, although there is some inconsistency in the findings of different studies. Simmons (1986) found that there was a correspondence between mean duration of guarding and the time taken for sperm to pass into the spermatheca of the female in this species – a finding that is at least consistent with the ejaculate-protection hypothesis. Simmons also detected two divergent patterns of female post-copulatory behaviour. Some females departed within 15 minutes, while others stayed with the male for the full guarding period of between one and two hours. Matings that occurred away from the burrow were not followed by guarding. Where females did not stay for the full guarding period, the spermatophore was removed and consumed more quickly than it was among those that were guarded. Simmons's studies also found that females were more inclined to leave the male the more closely related they were (Simmons, 1989), and also that females laid more eggs when allowed to choose their mates than when they were allocated a mate (Simmons, 1987). Also, the size of the male had a positive effect, although relatively small, on egg-laying (see also Parker & Vahed, 2010).

Some studies have shown female preference for larger males in this species, as evidenced by a tendency to reject small males or retain their spermatophores for a shorter time when they have prior mating experience with larger males (Bateman et al., 2001). However, a study by Wynn and Vahed (2004) detected no evidence of female preference for heavier males. Their study also discounted the ejaculate-protection hypothesis, as un-guarded females showed no inclination to premature detachment of the spermatophore, and in fact retained the spermatophore for longer in the absence of a guarding male. This was because of the frequency with which males dislodged the spermatophore in subsequent mating attempts (or females removed it in advance of repeat mating attempts by males). However, males did guard females for long enough to resume their ability to mate and transfer a spermatophore, a result consistent with the spermatophore-renewal hypothesis. Results of trials in which females were presented with rival males also supported the rival-exclusion hypothesis, as unguarded females re-mated with rivals more quickly than did ones whose original mate was allowed to continue guarding. Females showed a significant preference for the rival mate for their second copulation.

Wynne and Vahed's study is of particular interest in revealing a difference in the behaviour of virgin females compared with previously mated ones (also noted by Bateman *et al.*, 2001). As expected, virgin females tended to retain the spermatophore from the first mating for a longer period than that of subsequent copulations. Interestingly, this difference was consistent through each of the test-situations, indicating that females had a high degree of control over the duration of spermatophore attachment. This poses the further question how far mate-guarding is an example of males overriding the reproductive interests of females, and how far it might be understood as a form of cryptic female choice: if females are able to evade their guards, but do not do so, it may be that this is an expression of female mate choice – although there appears to be little clear evidence as to what male traits are preferred. In the case of the British field cricket, *G. campestris*, cohabitation between males and females after copulation appears to be consensual, as females may be observed to leave the male's burrow and explore the surrounding area only to return to his side (pers. obs.; see also DVD).

In most field crickets the females use their long, spear-shaped ovipositors to lay their eggs under the surface of the ground, or in crevices. However, in the short-tailed crickets (*Anurogryllus* species) the female lacks the elongated ovipositor of her relatives, and this is indicative of a quite different feature of the reproductive behaviour of this group, and probably other genera of the subfamily Brachytrupinae, such as *Gymnogryllus* (Alexander *et al.*, 1997). *Anurogryllus arboreus* (formerly *A. muticus*) is a widespread and often abundant species in the Americas, sometimes considered a serious pest. The calling and courtship behaviour of this species have been intensively studied, but what is of interest here is the exceptional role of maternal care of eggs and early-stage nymphs. Strangely, it seems that since the pioneering study by West and Alexander (1963) this aspect of reproductive behaviour has received only passing mention, with many publications concerned exclusively with pest control methods. Although most acoustic signalling and some courtship and mating take place in the open (Walker, 1983b), most of the lives of these insects is spent in underground chambers and tunnels. Burrows may be dug by both males and females, and usually consist of one or more short entrance tunnels leading to a shallow open chamber. Passing down from this is a longer 'retreat shaft', with one or more lower chambers at a depth of up to 50 cm, with offshoots where faeces, waste food and other debris are deposited (Weaver & Sommers, 1969). Mating is confined to a relatively brief season in spring and may occur in the burrow of either male or female, or in the open. Walker reports examples of mating occurring in male burrows, followed by the male leaving the female in occupation. In one instance a male that attempted to return was repelled by an aggressive display of 'gaping mandibles' (Walker,

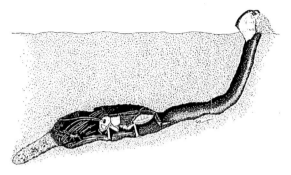

FIG 123. Aspects of the behaviour of *Anurogryllus muticus*, from West & Alexander, 1963. (a) Female of *Anurogryllus muticus* (De Geer) in brood chamber with new pile of cut grass stems. Note antennal contact between juvenile and female. Filled defecation chamber is at left. Egg pile is partly covered with sand near female's left front leg. Tunnels leading into the interior of the jar in which the female is confined begin directly on her right. The female burrowed up under chunks of apple, as shown, and plastered substrate particles being removed from the burrow alongside the apple, creating 'push-ups' of the sort indicated. The female's hind leg was lost while she was juvenile.

(b) Female ousting an intruding male from her burrow by kicking him after tearing off his right hind leg with her mandibles. Note the male's lop-sided position, and the retracted labrum and spread mandibles of the female.

(c) Female responding to bright light by rearing up, approaching the glass side of the brood chamber, pressing against it, and touching it with her forelegs and maxillary palps. Temperature change may be involved. Note egg pile between her front legs.

(d) Juvenile crickets (probably second and third instars) disturbed by breaking burrow above them. This is about the age at which the female dies and the juveniles begin to fend for themselves. These juveniles are more plump and soft-bodied than those of most other crickets.

1983b). There is some evidence that female occupation of male burrows, with food stocks, may constitute a form of male parental investment.

Fertilised females occupy a burrow and proceed to lay a batch of eggs. Weaver and Sommers (1969) counted eggs in excavated burrows at various dates, with numbers varying between 5 and 129, but with an average of 49 per burrow across 10 burrows at the peak of the egg-laying season in May. The eggs are kept in piles by the female, and are of two different sizes. The female tends the eggs, 'mouthing' them, presumably to clean them of fungi, until they hatch. The resulting nymphs compete intensely for the smaller, presumably infertile, eggs and eat them. The female forages on the surface and brings food items down into the brood chamber for the nymphs. These remain with their mother through the first three instars and disperse to form their own burrows when she dies – usually towards the end of June or early July (West & Alexander, 1963; Weaver & Sommers, 1969).

The mole-crickets (Gryllotalpidae)

The mole-cricket *Gryllotalpa gryllotalpa*, which once occurred quite commonly in Britain, is another species in which there is continued parental care of offspring after the eggs have been laid. The mole-cricket spends most of its life underground, and although males do sometimes sing from the entrances to their burrows it seems likely that most encounters between males and females take place underground (Pinchen, pers. comm.). In the presence of a female the male performs a courtship display, continuing to sing while lowering its hind wings at the sides of its body, and swaying from side to side. If the female is receptive she climbs onto his back, as in other ensiferans, and mating is completed by the transfer of a spermatophore.

The female lays her eggs in an underground chamber that may be just below the surface or up to a foot deep. The eggs are piled into heaps in the chamber, and are said to number from 100–300 normally, although up to 640 have been recorded. The female stands guard over the eggs, and mouths them from time to time as do female *Anurogryllus* crickets. This is presumed to protect them from fungal attack. The eggs hatch after two to four weeks, and the early instar nymphs remain in the chamber for several weeks, after which they come to the surface but continue to be guarded by the mother (Ragge, 1965; Pinchen, 2009).

Key to British Orthoptera

IF	▶ THEN GO TO
* Antennae long, tapered and thread-like, as long as or longer than the body, or, if shorter, with body flattened dorsoventrally.	▶ Ensifera: Key A
* Antennae relatively short and stiff, not tapered, but parallel sided or thickened towards the tip; body not flattened dorsoventrally.	▶ Caelifera: Key B

Key A. Ensifera (crickets, bush-crickets and relatives)

IF	■ THEN IT IS … *or*	▶ THEN GO TO
* Fore legs enlarged and adapted for digging (Fig. K.1); ovipositor of female inconspicuous.	■ mole cricket (*Gryllotalpa gryllotalpa*) (extremely rare, occasional imports)	
* Fore legs not enlarged and adapted for digging; ovipositor of female conspicuous and sword or needle shaped.		▶ A1

IF	■ THEN IT IS ... *or*	▶ THEN GO TO

KEY

A1   * Body shape roughly tubular (*i.e.* not flattened dorsoventrally); ovipositor of female long and straight or upturned, tapering towards the tip (sword shaped); head profile as in Fig. K.2a or b; tarsi with four segments.

▶ **A2**

* Body flattened dorsoventrally; ovipositor of female straight and parallel-sided, sometimes thickened at tip (spear or needle shaped); head profile as in Fig. K.2c; tarsi with three segments.   ▶ **A17**

A2   * Fully winged (when at rest, wings reach back to or beyond the tip of the abdomen).   ▶ **A3**

* When at rest, wings do not reach back to the tip of the abdomen (may be reduced to small flaps or completely absent).   ▶ **A11**

A3   * Head triangular in profile (angle between the frons and vertex 50° to 60°) (Fig. K.2a).   ▶ **A4**

* Head not triangular in profile (angle between frons and vertex approximately 70° or more, and transition between them smoothly curved) (Fig. K.2b).   ▶ **A6**

A4   * Large (30 mm plus), uniformly green, with pale band on the front of the head and a black line on each tibia.   ■ **large conehead**
(*Ruspolia nitidula*)
(very rare vagrant/early colonist in UK)

* Smaller (24 mm or less), brown or green, with brown stripe on dorsal surface of head and pronotum.   ▶ **A5**

A5   * Female with up-curved ovipositor (Fig. K.3a); male with pair of central projections on final abdominal segment and cerci sharply narrowed and up-turned towards the tips (lateral view) (Fig. K.4a).

■ **short-winged conehead**
long-winged form
(*Conocephalus dorsalis f. burri*)

| IF | ■ THEN IT IS ... *or* | ▶ THEN GO TO |

* Female with long, straight ovipositor (Fig. K.3b); rear margin of dorsal plate of final abdominal segment of male smoothly curved, and cerci taper evenly towards the tip (Fig. K.4b). ■ **long-winged conehead** (***Conocephalus discolor***)

A6 * When at rest, wings reach back well beyond tip of the abdomen, and hind wings protrude beyond the tip of the fore wings; body green with minute black spots; female ovipositor broad, short and strongly up-curved (Fig. K.3c); male cerci up-curved, tapering to a sharp point (Fig. K.5a). ■ **sickle-bearing bush-cricket** (***Phaneroptera falcata***) (very rare, recent colonist of Britain)

* Wings reach back approximately to the tip of the abdomen, or, if well beyond, fore wings as long as or longer than hind wings; body green or brown, without minute black spots; female ovipositor straight, or up-curved (Fig. K.3d, e, f, g, k); male cerci straight, slightly incurved or, if strongly incurved, not tapering to a sharp point (Fig. K.5b, c, g, i). ▶ **A7**

A7 * Wings do not reach as far back as the hind knees; robust, 'plump' build; median keel along the dorsal surface of the pronotum (Fig. K.6a); usually green, with variable black blotches; female ovipositor long and straight or slightly up-curved, minutely serrated towards the tip (Fig. K.3k). ■ **wartbiter (*Decticus verrucivorus*)** (very rare, in southern England only)

* Wings usually reach as far back as hind knees or beyond; lacking median keel along the dorsum of the pronotum (Fig. K.6b); may be slender or robust in build; green or brown, but without black blotches; female ovipositor straight or up-curved, lacking serrations (K3d, e, f, g). ▶ **A8**

A8 * Large species (40 mm plus); body and wings mainly green, but with variable brown dorsal markings; wings reach back well beyond the tip of the abdomen; female ovipositor straight or slightly down-curved (Fig. K.3d); male cerci long and moderately incurved (Fig. K.5b). ■ **great green bush-cricket** (***Tettigonia viridissima***)

IF	■ THEN IT IS ... or	▶ THEN GO TO

* Smaller species (30mm or less); body and wings green or grey/brown; if green, then lacking brown dorsal markings; wings reach back approximately to the tip of the abdomen, or, if well beyond, then brown; female ovipositor up-curved (Fig. K.3e, f, g); male cerci long and strongly incurved, or, if short, straight or only slightly incurved (Fig. K.5c, g, i). ▶ **A9**

A9 * Body and wings green, with small yellow and reddish markings on the dorsum of the pronotum; wings reach back approximately to the tip of the abdomen; female ovipositor long, slightly up-curved and mainly green (Fig. K.3e); male cerci long, thin and strongly incurved (Fig. K.5c).

■ **oak bush-cricket**
(**Meconema thalassinum**)

* Body and wings mainly grey/ brown (may have some yellow/green markings on the sides of the body, but wings always brown); wings reach back to the tip of the abdomen or beyond; female ovipositor markedly up-curved and dark brown or black (Fig. K.3f, g); male cerci relatively short and straight, or slightly incurved (Fig. K.5g, i). ▶ **A10**

A10 * Side plates of the pronotum with clear cream/yellow border (Fig. K.7b); body and wings mainly plain brown, or with greenish tints along the sides of the abdomen; wings may reach well beyond the tip of the abdomen; female ovipositor relatively short, markedly up-curved and dark brown (Fig. K.3f); female subgenital plate with deep median cleft (Fig. K.8a); male cerci slightly incurved, and with inner projection approximately two thirds along from the base (Fig. K.5g). ■ **Roesel's bush-cricket, long-winged form**
(**Metrioptera roeselii f. diluta**)

* Mottled grey/brown, without clear pale borders to the side plates of the pronotum; wings reach back approximately to the tip of the abdomen; female ovipositor longer, more gently up-curved and black (Fig. K.3g); female subgenital plate with slight median cleft (Fig. K.8c); male cerci with inner projection approximately half-way along, and slightly curved outwards toward the tip (Fig. K.5i). ■ **grey bush-cricket**
(**Platycleis albopunctata**)
(mainly coastal and southern)

IF	■ THEN IT IS ... *or*	▶ THEN GO TO

A11 * Wings absent; antennae extremely long (more than 2× length of the body); dorsal outline of the body markedly convex; palps, cerci and legs long relative to the body, giving a spider-like appearance; body pale brown with darker blotches.   ■ **greenhouse camel cricket** (***Diestrammena* (*Tachycines*) *asynamorus***) (only in artificially heated buildings)

* Wings present, even if vestigial; antennae long, but not more than twice the length of the body; dorsal outline of the body not markedly convex, and not spider-like in appearance; may be green or grey/ brown. ▶ **A12**

A12 * Head triangular in profile (angle between vertex and frons 50° to 60°) (Fig. K.2a); green with brown on the dorsal surfaces of head and pronotum; female ovipositor long, narrow and up-curved (Fig. K.3a); male with pair of central projections on the final abdominal segment, and cerci abruptly narrowed and up-turned towards the tip in lateral view (Fig. K.4a).
 ■ **short winged conehead** (***Conocephalus dorsalis***)

* Head not triangular (angle between vertex and frons 70° or more, and the transition between them smoothly curved) (Fig. K.2b); may be predominantly green or brown; female ovipositor broader and up-curved or, if long, narrow and up-curved, then the insect lacks brown markings on dorsal surfaces of head and pronotum, and wings are vestigial. ▶ **A13**

A13 * Wings vestigial; body mainly green. ▶ **A14**

* Wings short (approximately one-third to two-thirds of the length of the abdomen), or, if wings vestigial, grey/brown (not green). ▶ **A15**

A14 * Body and legs with minute black spots; female ovipositor relatively short, broad and strongly up-curved (Fig. K.3h); usually with a brown/purple median band on the dorsal surface of abdomen, and orange/brown wing-stubs in the male; male cerci relatively short, strongly incurved and tapering to a point at the tip (Fig. K.5d). ■ **speckled bush-cricket** (***Leptophyes punctatissima***)

* Body and legs pale green, without black spots; usually with a median yellowish line along dorsal surface of head, pronotum and abdomen, with a pair of reddish marks on the dorsal surface of the pronotum; female ovipositor long, narrow and gently up-curved (Fig. K.3i); male cerci long, incurved and not tapering to a point (Fig. K.5e).

■ **southern oak bush-cricket**
(*Meconema meridionale*)

A15 * Wings vestigial in female, reduced to stridulatory apparatus only in male; side flaps of the pronotum more or less evenly patterned, lacking clear pale border; male cerci straight, with small inner projection near the base (Fig. K.5f).   ■ **dark bush-cricket**
(*Pholidoptera griseoaptera*)

* Wings one-third to two-thirds of the length of the abdomen, more extensive than the stridulatory apparatus in the male; side flaps of the pronotum with clear pale border along at least one edge (Fig. K.7a, b); male cerci with prominent inner projection (Fig. K.5g, h).   ▶ A16

A16 * Pale border on the side plates of the pronotum on both front and rear edges (Fig. K.7b); paired yellow spots on the sides of the thorax; female ovipositor relatively short and strongly up-curved (Fig. K.3f); female subgenital plate with deep median cleft (Fig. K.8a); male cerci with inner projection approximately two-thirds along from the base (Fig. K.5g).

■ **Roesel's bush-cricket**
(*Metrioptera roeselii*)
(long grass)

* Pale border on the side plates of the pronotum on rear edge only (Fig. K.7a); lacks yellow spots on the sides of the thorax; female ovipositor longer and more gently up-curved (Fig. K.3j); female subgenital plate with shallow median cleft (Fig. K.8b); male cerci with inner projection approximately midway along (Fig. K.5h).

■ **bog bush-cricket**
(*Metrioptera brachyptera*)
(damp heath/ bog)

IF	■ THEN IT IS … *or*	▶ THEN GO TO

A17 * Entirely wingless; small (less than 15mm).

> ■ **scaly cricket**
>
> ***Pseudomogoplistes vicentae*)**
>
> (rare, under stones on shingle beaches)

  * Winged species (often wings reduced or vestigial). ▶ **A18**

A18 * Wings vestigial in female, reduced to stridulatory apparatus only in male; small species (less than 12mm); dark brown with pale 'y' marking on vertex.

> ■ **wood cricket**
>
> (***Nemobius sylvestris*)**
>
> (in leaf litter, southern)

  * Fully winged, or wings at least two thirds of the length of the abdomen; larger (14mm or more). ▶ **A19**

A19 * Pale brown with darker markings; folded wings extend well beyond the tip of the abdomen; without yellow patches at the base of the fore wings.

> ■ **house cricket**
>
> (***Acheta domesticus*)**
>
> (only in artificially warmed habitats; also similar species kept for the pet trade)

  * Body dark brown or black, with yellow patches at the base of the fore wings. ▶ **A20**

A20 * Wings reach back approximately to the tip of the abdomen (males), or are shorter (females). ■ **field cricket (*Gryllus campestris*)**

> (very rare, open sandy habitats)

  * When folded, wings reach back well beyond the tip of the abdomen.

> ■ **southern field cricket**
>
> (***Gryllus bimaculatus*)**
>
> (only occasional short-lived colonies in Britain)

Key B. Caelifera (groundhoppers and grasshoppers)

Note 1: Some characters used in this key apply to one sex only, or are clearer in one sex than in the other. The distinction between males and females in grasshoppers and groundhoppers is less obvious than in crickets and bush-crickets, as the female ovipositor is usually less prominent. Sex differences in the appendages at the tip of the abdomen, as seen from the side, are shown in Fig. K.9.

Note 2: The colour patterns of several species are highly variable, so identification depends largely on structural features. A small bulge towards the base of the leading edge of the fore wing is present in some species, and its presence or absence is often useful for identification (but often obscured in photographs). The shape of the side keels on the dorsal surface of the pronotum is another very important character. The key distinguishes between 'incurved' and 'inflexed' side keels. The former refers to a pattern in which the keels are smoothly curved, as distinct from the latter, in which the keels are inwardly angled. In a few species, this distinction may not be clear in all specimens, and for these cases the key is designed to work whichever option is taken.

IF	■ THEN IT IS … *or*	▶ THEN GO TO

* Pronotum projects back over the abdomen dorsally; fore and mid tarsi with only two segments (Fig. 10b). ▶ **B1**

* Pronotum saddle-shaped, with dorsal rear margin curved (*i.e.* not projecting back over the abdomen); all tarsi with three segments (Fig. K.10a). ▶ **B3**

B1 * Pronotum reaches back approximately as far as the hind knees, or less; median keel on dorsal surface forms a raised ridge, giving a markedly convex profile (Fig. K.11a); wings do not extend beyond the tip of the pronotum. ■ **common groundhopper (*Tetrix undulata*)**

* Pronotum reaches back beyond the hind knees; median keel on dorsal surface of the pronotum less prominent, giving straight or slightly convex profile (Fig. K.11b); wings extend beyond the tip of the pronotum. ▶ **B2**

KEY

B2   * Mid femur with both edges smoothly curved (Fig. K.12a); vertex is at least 1.5 times as wide as the eye (Fig. K.13a), and reaches forward beyond the front margin of the eyes (view from above), (this character is less clear in males); the angle between the vertex and frons (view from the side) is 90° or less (Fig. K.14a); edges of female ovipositor valves are densely and shallowly toothed (Fig. K.15a); dorsal ridge along the edge of the hind femur is straight (Fig. K.16a).   ■ **slender groundhopper**
(***Tetrix subulata***)

* Mid femur with wavy edges (Fig. K.12b); vertex is less than 1.5 times as wide as the eye, and the front edge is in line with the front margin of the eyes (view from above) (Fig. K.13b) (this character less clear in the males); the angle between the vertex and frons (view from the side) is more than 90° (Fig. K.14b); edges of the female genital valves have longer, less densely packed teeth (Fig. K.15b); dorsal ridge along the edge of the hind femur bends outwards towards the hind 'knee' (Fig. K.16b).

■ **Cepero's groundhopper**
(***Tetrix ceperoi***)
(rare, southern, often coastal)

NB: The groundhoppers are difficult to identify with certainty. The key is designed to work with adult specimens, not nymphs. The length of the pronotum is quite variable in both *T. subulata* and *T. ceperoi*, so this character alone should not be used to separate either from *T. undulata*. The distinction between *T. ceperoi* and *T. subulata* is particularly difficult. Viewing the mid femur with a hand lens is a useful guide, and the 'kink' in the dorsal ridge of the hind femur of *T. ceperoi* is also visible both with a hand lens and in a sharp photo. However, confident identification should be based on several characters. It is possible that *T. ceperoi* is under-recorded because of its similarity to *T. subulata*.

B3   * Side keels of the pronotum parallel or incurved (Fig. K.17a–g).
▶ **B4**

* Side keels of the pronotum inflexed (Fig. K.17h–k).   ▶ **B12**

B4 * Large species (usually 25 mm plus); hind femur greenish with black knees and red on the rear edge; side keels of the pronotum gently incurved, diverging towards the rear edge (Fig. K.17a); pale stripe along the leading edge of the fore wing; male lacks stridulatory file on the inner surface of the hind femur.

■ **large marsh grasshopper**
(***Stethophyma grossum***)
(rare, wetlands, southern)

* Smaller species (less than 25mm); hind femur not coloured as above; side keels of the pronotum parallel or incurved; in males a stridulatory file on the inner surface of the hind femur (Fig. K.18). ▶ **B5**

B5 * Side keels of the pronotum parallel or almost so, but often diverging towards the rear (Fig. K.17b); in females, the wings terminate just short of the tip of the abdomen, in males they reach the tip, or a short way beyond; often a prominent white stripe on the fore wing; there is a small bulge on the leading edge of the fore wing in females ('costal bulge') (Fig. K.19), inconspicuous or absent in males.

■ **lesser marsh grasshopper**
(***Chorthippus albomarginatus***)

*Side keels of the pronotum incurved (Fig. K.17c–g). ▶ **B6**

B6 * both sexes have costal bulge (Fig. K.19). ▶ **B7**

* no costal bulge in either sex. ▶ **B9**

B7 * Side keels of the pronotum slightly incurved (Fig. K.17c). ▶ **B8**

* Side keels of the pronotum more strongly incurved (or inflexed) (Fig. K.17d–g, i) ▶ **B12**

B8 * Wings reach back significantly beyond the tip of the abdomen; distinct costal bulge in males and females; hind knees usually black (rarely so in C. albomarginatus).

■ **common meadow grasshopper, long-winged form**
(***Chorthippus parallelus f. explicatus***)

* Wings greatly reduced in the female (half the length of the abdomen or less), and, in the male, falling short of the tip of the abdomen; bulge on the leading edge of the fore wing in both sexes; hind knees usually black.

> ■ **common meadow grasshopper**
> **normal form**
> (***Chorthippus parallelus***)

B9   * Wings do not reach as far back as the tip of the hind knees; pronotal side keels broadly outlined pale (Fig. K.17d); with a pale 'panel' at the front of the side plates of the pronotum (Fig. K.20); small species (15mm or less); in mature individuals often a red suffusion on the abdomen.

> ■ **lesser mottled grasshopper**
> (***Stenobothrus stigmaticus***)
> (in UK known only from
> Isle of Man)

* Wings reach back approximately to the tip of the hind knees or beyond; pale outlining of the pronotal side keels, if present, may be relatively broad or narrow (Fig. K.17e, f, g); side plates of the pronotum lack pale panel; larger species (usually more than 15mm).   ▶ **B10**

B10   * Chalk-white palps, contrasting with face, especially in the males; mature males with extensive red on the abdomen, and black head and pronotum; females green, brown or grey dorsally, with brown, grey/black or rust-coloured sides; side keels of the pronotum are strongly incurved (Fig. K.17e); except where obscured by dark coloration (especially in males), the side keels of the pronotum are narrowly outlined in white, and bordered by two prominent black wedges; female ovipositor valves smoothly curved to point at tip (Fig. K.21a).

> ■ **woodland grasshopper**
> (***Omocestus rufipes***)

* Palps may be pale but not chalk-white; mature males may develop reddish suffusion on the abdomen, but head and pronotum never black; side keels of the pronotum less strongly incurved (Fig. K.17f, g); female ovipositor valves as in Fig. K.21b or c.   ▶ **B11**

IF	■ THEN IT IS … *or*	▶ THEN GO TO

B11 * Enlarged cells in the fore wing have parallel cross veins, giving a ladder-like impression (Fig. K.22); pale outlining of the side keels of the pronotum is relatively broad (Fig. K.17f); mature specimens develop reddish tints to the tip of the abdomen (and hind tibiae in males); wings of mature specimens often black with white stripe and crescent marking; female ovipositor valves have acute dorsal projection (Fig. K.21b).   ■ **stripe-winged grasshopper** (***Stenobothrus lineatus***)

* Wing venation not as above; pale outlining of the pronotal side keels relatively narrow (Fig. K.17g); neither sex develops reddish tints on the abdomen; female ovipositor valves are unevenly curved, but lack a distinct dorsal projection (Fig. K.21c).   ■ **common green grasshopper** (***Omocestus viridulus***)

B12 * Antennae clubbed or distinctly thickened towards the tip.   ▶ **B13**

* Anennae not clubbed or thickened towards the tip.   ▶ **B14**

B13 * Pronotal side keels very strongly inflexed (Fig. K.17h); antennae clubbed in male, but only widened towards the tip in females, and not generally white-tipped (Fig. 23a, b).   ■ **mottled grasshopper** (***Myrmeleotettix maculatus***) (usually on bare ground or low vegetation)

* Pronotal side keels less markedly inflexed (Fig. K.17i); both sexes have white-tipped and clubbed antennae (Fig. K.23c, d).   ■ **rufous grasshopper** (***Gomphocerippus rufus***) (usually in taller grasses or low scrub)

B14 * Costal bulge present on fore wing (K19).   ▶ **B15**

* Lacking costal bulge on fore wing.   ▶ **B9**

B15 * The transverse sulcus on the dorsal surface of the pronotum is anterior to the mid point (K17j); wedge-shaped dark markings on the rear portion of the

IF	■ THEN IT IS ... *or*	▶ THEN GO TO

dorsal surface of the pronotum do not reach the rear margin (Fig. K.17j); the underside of the thorax is densely hairy.

■ **common field grasshopper
(Chorthippus brunneus)**
(widespread and common)

* The transverse sulcus on the dorsal surface of the pronotum cuts across at the mid point or to the rear (Fig. K.17k); wedge-shaped dark markings on the rear portion of the dorsal surface of pronotum reach back to the rear margin (Fig. K.17k); the underside of the thorax is sparsely hairy.

■ **heath grasshopper
(*Chorthippus vagans*)**
(very rare, on heaths in Dorset and Hampshire)

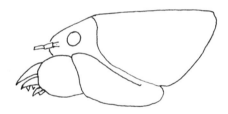

FIG. K.1 (left) Mole cricket: fore legs modified for digging.

FIG. K.2 (below) Profiles of heads: (a) conehead; (b) bush-cricket; (c) cricket.

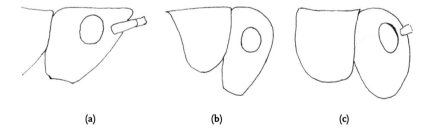

(a) (b) (c)

KEY

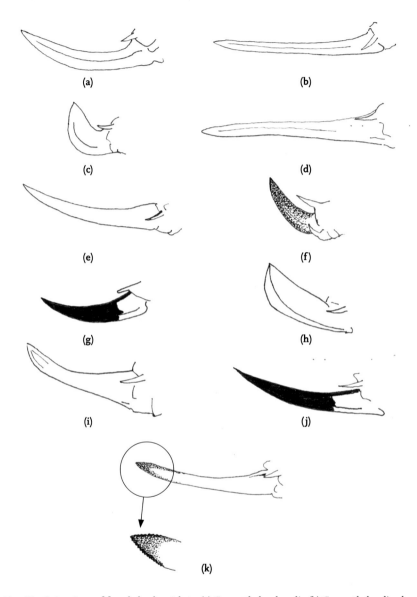

FIG. K.3 Ovipositors of female bush-crickets: (a) *Conocephalus dorsalis*; (b) *Conocephalus discolor*; (c) *Phaneroptera falcata*; (d) *Tettigonia viridissima*; (e) *Meconema thalassinum*; (f) *Metrioptera roeselii*; (g) *Platycleis albopunctata*; (h) *Leptophyes punctatissima*; (i) *Meconema meridionale*; (j) *Metrioptera brachyptera*; (k) *Decticus verrucivorus*.

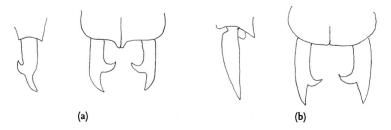

FIG. K.4 Male cerci and tip of the abdomen (lateral view and dorsal view): (a) *Conocephalus dorsalis*; (b) *Conocephalus discolor*.

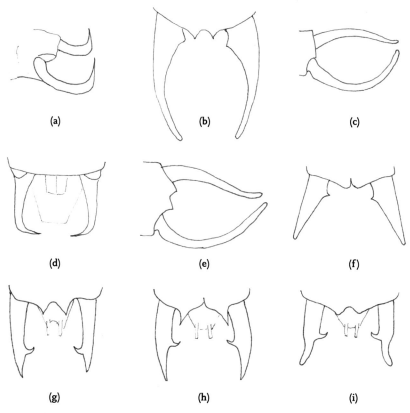

FIG. K.5 Cerci of male bush-crickets: (a) *Phaneroptera falcata*; (b) *Tettigonia viridissima* (dorsal view); (c) *Meconema thalassinum* (dorso-lateral view); (d) *Leptophyes punctatissima* (dorsal view); (e) *Meconema meridionale* (dorso-lateral view); (f) *Pholidoptera griseoaptera* (dorsal view); (g) *Metrioptera roeselii*; (h) *Metrioptera brachyptera*; (i) *Platycleis albopunctata*.

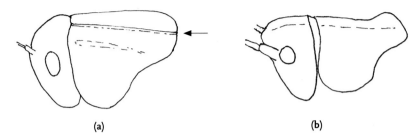

FIG. K.6 (a) Pronotum of *Decticus verrucivorus*, showing median keel on dorsal surface of the pronotum; (b) pronotum of *Tettigonia viridissima*: median dorsal suture, but lacking a keel.

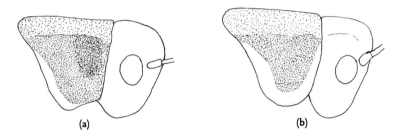

FIG. K.7 Side view of pronotum: (a) *Metrioptera brachyptera*; (b) *Metrioptera roeselii*.

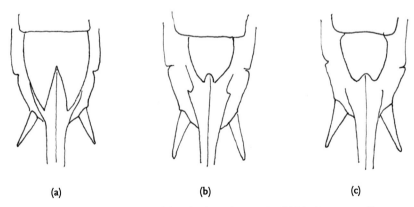

FIG. K.8 Female subgenital plates of three bush-cricket species: (a) *Metrioptera roeselii*; (b) *Metrioptera brachyptera*; (c) *Platycleis albopunctata*.

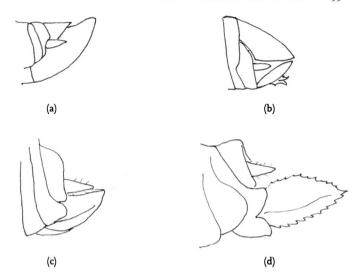

FIG. K.9 Tip of abdomen and associated structures in: (a) male grasshopper; (b) female grasshopper; (c) male groundhopper; (d) female groundhopper.

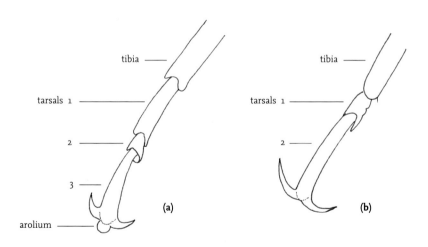

FIG. K.10 Tarsi of fore legs: (a) grasshopper (three segments and arolium); ((b) groundhopper (two segments, and arolium absent).

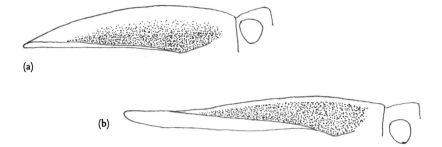

(a)

(b)

FIG. K.11 Side views of pronotum and head of groundhoppers: (a) *Tetrix undulata*; (b) *Tetrix subulata and ceperoi.*

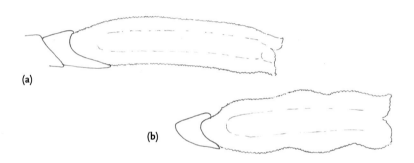

(a)

(b)

FIG. K.12 Mid femur: (a) *Tetrix subulata*; (b) *Tetrix ceperoi.*

(a)   (b)

FIG. K.13 Dorsal view of head of (a) *Tetrix subulata*; and (b) *Tetrix ceperoi* (females).

KEY

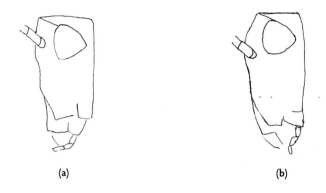

FIG. K.14 Side view of the head of (a) *Tetrix subulata*; and (b) *Tetrix ceperoi* (females).

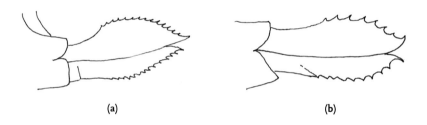

FIG. K.15 Ovipositor valves of females: (a) *Tetrix subulata*; (b) *Tetrix ceperoi*.

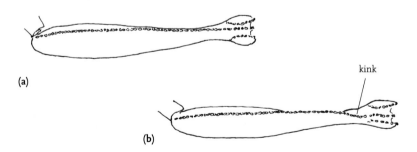

FIG. K.16 Dorsal view of hind femur: (a) *Tetrix subulata*; (b) *Tetrix ceperoi* (showing 'kink' in dorsal ridge).

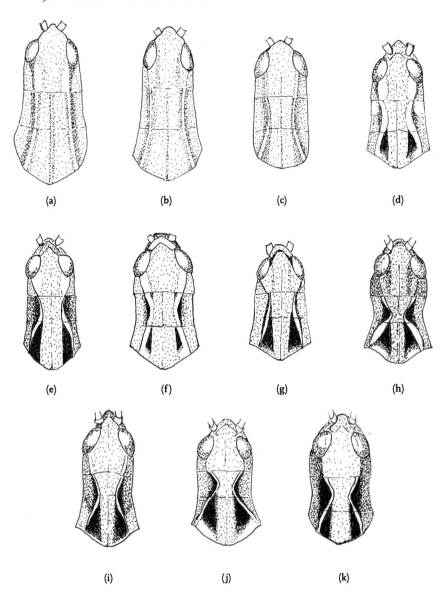

FIG. K.17 Dorsal view of pronotum: (a) *Stethophyma grossum*; (b) *Chorthippus albomarginatus*; (c) *Chorthippus parallelus*; (d) *Stenobothrus stigmaticus*; (e) *Omocestus rufipes*; (f) *Stenobothrus lineatus*; (g) *Omocestus viridulus*; (h) *Myrmeleotettix maculatus*; (i) *Gomphocerippus rufus*; (j) *Chorthippus brunneus*; (k) *Chorthippus vagans*.

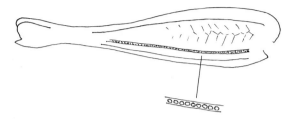

Fig. K.18 Inner surface of hind femur of male grasshopper (*Chorthippus brunneus*) showing stridulatory file.

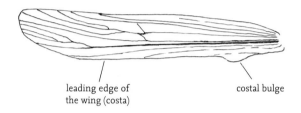

leading edge of
the wing (costa)

costal bulge

Fig. K.19 Fore wing of *Chorthippus brunneus*, showing costal bulge.

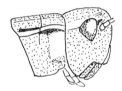

Fig. K.20 Side view of the head and pronotum of *Stenobothrus stigmaticus*.

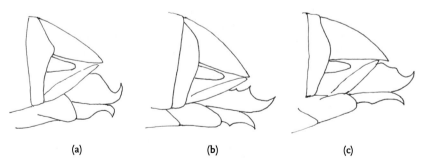

(a)   (b)   (c)

Fig. K.21 Ovipositor values of female grasshopper species: (a) *Omocestus rufipes*; (b) *Stenobothrus lineatus*; (c) *Omocestus viridulus*.

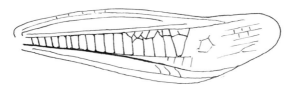

Fig. K.22 Fore wing of *Stenobothrus lineatus* (female).

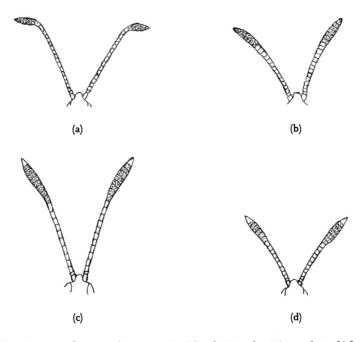

Fig. K.23 Antennae of two grasshopper species: (a) male *Myrmeleotettix maculatus*; (b) female *Myrmeleotettix maculatus*; (c) male *Gomphocerippus rufus*; (d) female *Gomphocerippus rufus*.

CHAPTER 7

The British species, part 1: Ensifera
Bush-crickets, crickets and their relatives

This large subdivision of the Orthoptera includes nine (or ten; see Gwynne, 2001 and Chapter 2) orthopteran families worldwide, of which only five are represented in the British fauna. These are: the Tettigoniidae (the bush-crickets or 'katydids'); the Gryllidae (the true crickets); Mogoplistidae (scaly crickets); Gryllotalpidae (mole-crickets); and the Rhaphidophoridae (camel-crickets and cave weta).

The derivation of the word 'Ensifera' suggests a reference to the sword-shaped external ovipositor that is a characteristic feature of the families belonging to the suborder (although the true crickets have more needle-shaped ones!). Another characteristic feature is the long – often much longer than the body – pair of filamentous antennae possessed by both sexes. There are also internal structural differences and characteristics of DNA shared by all groups within the suborder that justify their treatment as a single 'clade' (i.e. as sharing a common ancestor). The two families Raphidophoridae and the Tettigoniidae are generally classified together in the super-family Tettigoniodea, while the Gryllidae, Mogoplistidae and Gryllotalpidae are included together in the Grylloidea.

FAMILY RHAPHIDOPHORIDAE: THE CAMEL CRICKETS

Members of this family have much in common with the Tettigoniidae (bush-crickets), having long, filamentous antennae, four-segmented tarsi and sword-like ovipositors. They also resemble most bush-cricket species in their mating behaviour. During copulation the male transfers to the female a gelatinous spermatophore. This mass (which varies in size between species) contains both a sperm sac (ampulla) and an attached mass of edible material (the spermatophylax), which the female consumes while the sperm are transferred to her spermatheca (see Chapter 6).

The Rhaphidophoridae differ from most of the bush-crickets in being entirely wingless, and lack the hearing organ on the fore tibia. However, they do have a structure on the fore tibiae, called the subgenual organ, that enables the insects to detect substrate vibration. The pronotum is smoothly rounded, and both antennae and the cerci are much longer than is usual among the Tettigoniidae. There may be ten or more nymphal instars. Only one species has been established in Britain, probably introduced along with plants imported from southern China, although other accidental introductions of related species are occasionally reported.

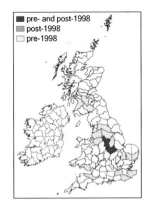

THE GREENHOUSE CAMEL-CRICKET

Diestrammena (formerly Tachycines) asynamorus (Adelung, 1902)

MEASUREMENTS: Male: 12–14 mm in length; female: 14–18 mm in length (excluding the ovipositor); ovipositor: 10–12 mm; antennae: 65–70 mm.

A

B

FIGS A–C. Male; male, dorsal view; female.

C

Description

The pronotum is smoothly rounded, and the convex outline of the back when viewed from the side may explain the vernacular name. The ground colour is pale brown, with darker mottling and banding, especially on the rear margins of the pronotum and abdominal segments. The legs are also pale with dark banding. There are no wings, and no hearing organs on the fore tibiae. The legs, antennae, abdominal cerci and palps are also very long in relation to the size of the body. The four segments of each tarsus are also elongated and there are sparsely distributed long bristles on the legs and cerci.

Similar species

There are no similar British species, although there are reports of occasional accidental introductions of related species such as *Dolichopoda bormansi* from Corsica (Evans & Edmondson, 2007).

Life cycle

In the artificially heated environments where this species breeds in Britain, the life cycle is continuous through the year. The eggs are approximately 2–5 mm in length by 1–1.2 mm, and are laid singly or in small batches of up to 8 in soil. The eggs hatch after 8 to 10 weeks, depending on temperature, and the resulting nymphs pass through 8 to 10 or more instars to reach adulthood. This takes 6 to 10 months. As breeding is not governed by seasons, and the rate of nymphal development varies considerably in the same population, adults and all nymphal stadia may be found together. Nymphs are whitish in colour immediately after moulting, but acquire the characteristic brown-blotched pattern in a day or so. The cast-off skin is rapidly eaten after each moult. The ovipositor appears as a very small projection at the third instar, and becomes longer at each successive stage (see Chapter 3, Fig 59 for images of key developmental stages).

Habitat

In Britain this species is confined to artificially heated environments, such as greenhouses, warehouses or even garages. However, most British records are from garden centres or glasshouses with exotic plants. The two recently reported populations were living in plant nurseries, under wooden staging or paving slabs close to hot-water pipes, as well as in storage cupboards. The mid-winter temperature in one case was between 13°C and 17°C (Panter, 2007; Sutton, 2007b; own observations). During daylight hours the insects tended to be found hidden away in groups in dark, moist and warm locations.

Behaviour

Camel-crickets are nocturnal, and hide in dark corners during the day. In the absence of stridulation and developed hearing organs, it seems likely that they communicate by vibrations of the substrate, but they also cluster together in dark and damp places during daylight hours, constantly touching one another with their exceptionally long antennae. Courtship and mating seem to occur mainly at night, and male and female adults have been observed with the male resting a fore leg on the pronotum of the female. Ragge (1965) describes the male as attempting to push his abdomen under the female from various angles until he is able to crawl backwards underneath her. Mating lasts for 2 to 4 minutes, and during it a spermatophore is placed at the base of the female's ovipositor. The spermatophore is white and gelatinous, approximately 3–4 mm in diameter, and is rapidly eaten by the female. The palps are used during feeding and general 'searching' behaviour, as well as by females in selecting suitable ovipositing sites. The female draws her ovipositor under her body so that it points directly down to the soil, moves slightly forwards and presses the tip into the ground. When it is fully inserted into the soil, egg-laying is indicated by a pumping motion of the abdomen (T. Kettle, pers. comm.).

Both sexes have very powerful back legs and can jump long distances when disturbed. They are therefore very difficult to catch. They are reputed to feed on other insects, including insect pests. However, staff at one plant nursery reported their penchant for the flesh of dead rats, and in captivity they ate rabbit flesh. Close observation of captive crickets by several observers produced no examples of them taking live prey. They appear to be generalised scavengers, feeding on a variety of plant material such as lettuce (where they bite holes in the leaf lamina), groundsel, carrot, apple, nectarine, as well as dead woodlice, mealworms and rabbit flesh. One instance was noted of a female feeding from the carcase of another camel-cricket. However, it seems likely that the 'victim' was either dead or moribund prior to being eaten! Early instars feed on small plants, including soil algae. At all stages, if provided with a range of 'options' for cover during the day, they will tend to roost together, and opt for the dampest situation.

History

Greenhouse camel-crickets were probably introduced into heated greenhouses in Britain (and much of the rest of Europe) in the latter part of the 19th century. In England the species has been recorded from widely scattered locations in Somerset, Sussex, Kent, Surrey, Middlesex, Suffolk, Cambridgeshire, Leicestershire, Derbyshire, Cheshire and Lancashire. It has also been recorded from Glamorgan, Glasgow, Edinburgh, Ayr and Dumfries. There are Irish records from Dublin. Post-1960 records given by Marshall & Haes (1988) include: plant nurseries at Canterbury (1962–5) and near Woking (1970–3); in the garage of a private house near Fleetwood, Lancashire (1975); and Dublin zoological gardens (1975).

The two most recent reports appear to be from a garden centre at Clowne, Derbyshire, where it was recorded in 2006 (and had been present, according to staff, for at least 10 years), and from another at Leicester (where it had been present for at least 15 years). In the face of the impending closure of the Leicester site, rescue attempts were made in December 2006 and January 2007 by G. Panter, H. Ikin, M. Frankum and P. Sutton. Small numbers of the crickets were retained in the hope that the population could be kept going in captivity, but these attempts proved unsuccessful in the long term. However, the Derbyshire population was fully recognised and positively valued by the centre management. John Kramer and the author visited the site on 8 December 2009, only to find that it, too, was due to close down. With the help and support of staff we collected as many of the crickets as could be found (causing some amusement and curiosity from customers). In all, we collected some 15 insects, several of them in various juvenile stages. These were kept in two old aquaria, in which they reproduced continuously, allowing several independent 'colonies' to be established during 2010, including a sample taken by Bristol Zoo. At the time of writing, one sample has reached a range of instars including adults in the third generation from the original stock.

Status and conservation

Accidental introductions with exotic plants imported from the Far East resulted in the spread of the camel-cricket throughout much of Europe in the 19th century. According to the owners of the garden centre in Leicester, their crickets had come in from plant stock imported mainly from Belgium, Holland and Denmark.

It seems quite possible that other populations of this species still survive in heated glasshouses somewhere in Britain, and efforts should be made to locate any other remaining populations. Meanwhile, a case could be made for a captive breeding programme to be established, using specimens from the known surviving British population.

References: Marshall & Haes, 1988; Ragge, 1965; Panter, 2007; Sutton, 2007b, 2011.

FAMILY TETTIGONIIDAE: THE BUSH-CRICKETS

Also known as 'long-horned grasshoppers' and, especially in North America and Australasia, as 'katydids', this family includes some of the most thoroughly studied of orthopteran groups. They number over 6,000 known species, and are distributed over the whole of the world, apart from Antarctica. The majority of species are nocturnal, and spend most of their time in vegetation. The females possess external sword-like ovipositors, which may be used for piercing plant tissue or, less commonly, for digging into soil. The antennae are long and filamentous and are used in an elaborate 'fencing' performance during courtship.

Along with crickets and grasshoppers, most species communicate by sound (see Chapters 2 and 5). In most species, males transfer an edible 'nuptial gift' to the female during mating, and this has provided researchers with a valuable way of exploring controversial issues in evolutionary theory, notably sexual selection and reproductive conflict between the sexes (see Chapters 4, 5 and 6).

The males sing by rubbing together their modified fore wings (or tegmina), as do the true crickets, but the bush-crickets are distinctive in scraping the left over the right tegmen. The songs of bush-crickets tend to be of a higher frequency than those of grasshoppers, close to, or above the limits of human hearing. The bush-crickets also have distinctive hearing organs, tuned to the frequencies of their songs, located on the basal area of the tibiae of their fore legs, and linked via an enlarged auditory vesicle to a spiracle on the thorax (see Chapter 2).

Many species in Britain have a life cycle lasting two or more years, with the first year (or more) spent in the egg stage. Most species pass through five or six nymphal instars, usually emerging as adults during mid to late summer. In winged species, the wing buds are inverted for the final two juvenile instars. In some species the wings are reduced, often, in males, consisting almost wholly of the stridulatory apparatus. Some species have both long- and short-winged forms.

Bush cricket (© Tim Bernhard)

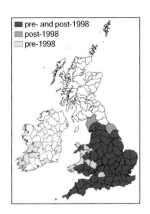

THE OAK BUSH-CRICKET
Meconema thalassinum
(De Geer, 1773)

MEASUREMENTS:
Male: 12–17 mm
in length;
female: 11–17 mm
in length.

A

FIGS A–B. Male; female.

B

Description

The oak bush-cricket is pale green in colour and rather delicately built. Both sexes have an indistinct yellowish stripe along the middle of the dorsal surface of the abdomen that is continued onto the pronotum and head. However, on the dorsal surface of the pronotum it is flanked by two small black and two chestnut brown markings. The hind margins of the wings (i.e. the 'ridge' of the tent-like shape formed when the wings are folded) are often narrowly brownish, and the eyes are pale lilac. In mature specimens, the tibiae and tarsi are yellowish green. The adults are fully winged, the wings reaching back to approximately the tip of the abdomen. The wings of the male are not modified for stridulation. The male has a pair of long, curved cerci at the tip of his abdomen, and the female has a long, slightly up-curved ovipositor, which is green, usually shading to yellow and finally brown towards the tip (see the Key, Figs K3e and K5c, pages 230–1).

Similar species

The great green bush-cricket (*Tettigonia viridissima*) is a much bigger and more sturdy insect, and is found in quite different habitats. The speckled bush-cricket (*Leptophyes punctatissima*) often occurs in the same haunts, but is a more compact insect, has only very tiny wing stubs, and, as the name suggests, is covered by minute black points. The southern oak bush-cricket (*Thalassium meridionale*) is a newcomer to Britain and a close relative of the oak bush-cricket. The two species look very similar, except that the southern oak has only very tiny wing stubs in the adult.

Life cycle

The eggs are laid from late summer to autumn, in crevices in the bark of trees, or under mosses or lichens. The eggs are buff-coloured, and approximately 3 mm by 1 mm in size. They may pass one or two winters in the egg stage, and hatch in late spring. The resulting nymphs pass through five nymphal instars to reach adulthood by late July or early August. The adults survive well into November in most years.

Habitat

They live among the foliage of trees – most commonly, as their vernacular name implies, in oak trees – but they can also be found in a wide range of other tree species as well as garden hedges and shrubs. There are even reports of their occurrence in reed beds (Haes, 1976). They are commonly found in urban and suburban parks and gardens.

FIG C. Characteristic 'Hindu' resting pose.

Behaviour

They are nocturnal, and during the day they rest on the underside of leaves, body pressed close to the leaf-lamina, and legs spread out in an angular pattern – rather resembling the image of a Hindu god. Even when present in gardens, they are extremely difficult to locate during daytime, but at night they are often attracted to light, and commonly enter houses, only to settle motionless on the ceiling.

When they are active, from dusk onwards, they walk about from leaf to leaf and onto the trunks or larger branches of trees. They can hop and also fly short distances. They feed mainly on small invertebrates, such as caterpillars and other larvae, aphids and even members of their own species. They will also consume some plant material but in captivity do not thrive on this alone.

There are some literature references to the males being able to produce a soft stridulation, but it seems that the main mode of communication is vibratory. The males issue a series of bursts of drumming on the substrate with one hind foot. This is Ragge's description of the process:

> Both pairs of wings are raised upwards until they are perpendicular to the body, and one of the hind feet is drummed on to the substrate (e.g. the surface of a leaf). The other hind leg is extended backwards to act as a support. The drumming is extremely rapid and is in very short bursts of less than a second. There are usually a number of these bursts, the first ones being of shorter duration than the remainder. The whole process lasts no more than a few seconds. During the drumming the abdomen also vibrates, but is held clear of the surface on which the insect is resting. (Ragge, 1965: 98)

Presumably females can detect the vibrations produced in this way and move towards the drumming male. During mating, the male encircles the female's abdomen with his long, curved cerci.

Oak bush-crickets can be found by shining a torch beam on tree trunks in the evening, when females may be seen laying their eggs. Alternatively, sharply beating the lower branches of trees during the daytime with a stick while holding a specially designed beating tray (or an up-turned umbrella) beneath will usually dislodge them from their resting places. This technique is more successful for finding nymphs during June or early July. After high winds they can often be found on the ground under trees, and they can also often be found in spiders' webs around outhouses and sheds. In gardens, if clippings from trees and shrubs are collected in garden bags, bush-crickets will find their way to the top within an hour or so and can be easily detected.

Enemies

It may be that they fall victim to nocturnal predators such as bats. In gardens, cats find and catch them, and they are frequently found in spiders' webs. Smith (1972) gave an account of a pair of goldcrests bringing 31 oak bush-crickets to feed their young in just three hours of observation (Ragge, 1973).

Distribution

The species is widespread throughout almost the whole of the European mainland. In Britain it is common and widespread in the southern and midland counties of England, becoming more localised further north, towards Yorkshire, Lancashire and Cumbria (Sutton, 2008a). It is widespread in Wales, and has a small number of known localities in Ireland.

Status and conservation

Although generally considered to be common and widespread, at least in the more southerly parts of Britain, some observers report that it has been less easy to find in recent years. It is difficult to see why this should be so, and it may simply represent a temporary cyclical contraction of the population.

References: Haes, 1976; Ragge, 1965, 1973; Smith, 1972; Sutton, 2008a.

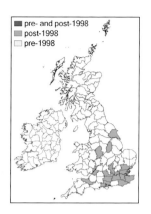

Meconema meridionale
(Costa, 1860)

MEASUREMENTS: Male: 11–15 mm in length; female: 11–17 mm in length.

A

B

C

D

FIGS A–D. Male; female; male and female; male, dorsal view.

FIG E. Dorsal view, female.

E

Description

This species is very similar in
appearance to the oak bush-cricket, but
the most obvious difference is the lack
of developed wings. In *M. meridionale*
the wings are reduced to small stubs in
both sexes. The body is mainly pale green, with a poorly defined yellowish stripe
along the dorsal surface of the body. This is flanked by two wedge-shaped brown
markings on the dorsal surface of the pronotum. In this species, where pairs of
black spots are also present, they are merged into the brown markings at their
anterior tips. The ovipositor is more distinctly up-curved towards the tip.

Similar species

The speckled bush-cricket (*Leptophyes punctatissima*) also has reduced wings and
a pale green ground colour, but it is a more robust insect, and is covered with
minute black points. The ovipositor of the female of the speckled bush-cricket is
wider and more strongly up-curved.

The oak bush-cricket (*M. thalassinum*) is fully winged. There are other, minor
differences: the eyes are usually cream to pinkish in *M. meridionale*, lilac in *M.
thalassinum*, and the ovipositor is more sharply up-turned towards the tip in *M.
meridionale*, regularly curved and slightly longer in *M. thalassinum*. Also, the patterns
on the rear of the dorsal surface of the pronotum differ. In *M. meridionale* the paired
black spots (where they are present) are fused with the brown wedges, but they are
distinct in *M. thalassinum*. The shape of the tip of the male abdomen between the two
cerci is also different in the two species, and the cerci of *M. meridionale* are slightly
longer than those of *M. thalassinum* (see the Key, Figs K5c and e, page 231).

Life cycle

The adults are found from late July onwards and it is believed that the life cycle is
closely similar to that of *M. thalassinum*. The eggs are laid in crevices in bark.

Habitat

The southern oak bush-cricket lives in oak trees as well as sycamore, elder, birch,
maple, bay, and a range of garden shrubs.

Behaviour

During the day they are inactive and remain hidden among foliage. Although they cannot fly, they can jump well and can successfully avoid capture. Like the oak bush-cricket, they are nocturnal, and feed on small insects. In captivity they are cannibalistic, in particular taking advantage of nymphs when these are vulnerable after moulting. The males drum with one hind foot, although the pattern of taps (from 3 to 7 in succession (Hawkins, 2001)) is somewhat different from that of the oak bush-cricket. Hawkins describes the mating posture: with the male on his back, facing away from the female, but with his head raised to grip the ovipositor of the female with his mandibles. As in other bush-crickets, an edible spermatophore is transferred to the female during mating.

They can be found by beating lower branches of trees as described for the oak bush-cricket, by shining a torch beam onto tree trunks, and also by waiting for them to climb up to the surface of garden bags after pruning.

Enemies

Given the similarity between this and the oak bush-cricket it seems likely that they are vulnerable to the same predators.

History

The species was first described from Italy, by Costa, in 1860. Prior to 1960 it was known also from eastern France and parts of Yugoslavia. Since 1960 its northward spread has been noted: from southern Germany and Austria and northern and eastern France to the Netherlands, Belgium and northern Germany in the 1990s. Between 1995 and 2001 it was recorded from more

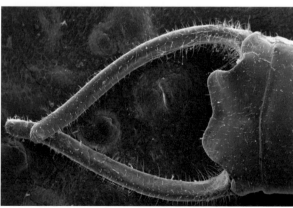

FIG F. Scanning electron microscope photo of male cerci, used to constrain the female during mating (see Chapter 6) (© K. Vahed).

F

than 20 sites in Normandy. Its imminent arrival in Britain was predicted (e.g. Widgery, 2001a: 360) and the first British specimen was found by R. D. Hawkins by beating a birch tree growing in a garden near Thames Ditton railway station on 15 September 2001. Alerted by this discovery, D. Coleman found the insect at another Surrey site in the London suburbs, and this time it was confirmed that an established breeding colony was present. On 20 October 2001 yet another discovery of the species, this time in a garden in Maidenhead, Berkshire, was made (Hawkins, 2001). Retrospectively, the insect was identified as having been present in a London garden in 2001 (Sutton, 2004d).

Since 2001, the spread of reported British sightings has been remarkable:

- Surrey and Maidenhead, Berkshire in 2001
- Another Surrey site 2002
- Hammersmith, w. London 2003
- Kent, Surrey 2005
- SW London, North Kent 2006
- East London, West London, Nottinghamshire, Sussex and Bristol 2007
- West and mid-Essex 2008
- North East Essex and Wiltshire 2009

Distribution
The southern oak bush-cricket now appears to be an established breeding species at numerous localities in Greater London, Avon, Somerset, Berkshire, Buckinghamshire, Hampshire, Surrey, Sussex, Kent, and Essex, with outlying records from Nottinghamshire, Staffordshire and Yorkshire.

Status and conservation
It is generally accepted that this species was incidentally imported into Britain in horticultural produce, and may have established itself in several localities independently. However, the pattern of records suggests that it is also spreading out from its original introduction. As there appears to be no winged form, the general assumption is that its rapid spread is aided by its hitching lifts on motorised transport. Support for this is provided by an observation of an especially tenacious specimen that attached itself to a car and remained in place over a 150-mile drive (Edmondson, 2011). It seems likely that this species will continue to spread out from its strongholds in several southern and south-eastern counties of England.

References: Edmondson, 2011; Hawkins, 2001; Sutton, 2003a, 2004d, 2005b, 2006b, 2007a, 2007d, 2008a, 2008c, 2010a; Widgery 2001a.

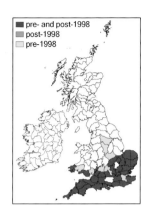

THE GREAT GREEN BUSH-CRICKET

Tettigonia viridissima
(Linnaeus, 1758)

MEASUREMENTS: Male: 40–50 mm in length; female: 40–55 mm in length.

FIGS A–C. Male; female; male, dorsal view.

A

B   C

Description

This is the largest of the British Orthoptera, green in ground colour, and fully winged. The wings extend back well beyond the tip of the abdomen in males, and as far as, sometimes beyond, the tip of the long, straight ovipositor in the females. The male fore wings are modified for stridulation, with a ridged basal area on the left fore wing and a toothed 'file' on the underside. The right fore wing has a clear 'mirror' basally, that is covered by the left fore wing when the insect is at rest.

There is an ill-defined brownish dorsal stripe along the abdomen, and another along the leading edges of the fore wings, including the stridulatory area in the male. The yellow to brownish stripe is continued on the dorsal surface of the pronotum, and on the head often becomes lilac in colour. The eyes, too, are lilac. Most abdominal segments have a narrow yellow lateral 'dash' marking towards the ventral surface, just above the spiracle. Often the abdominal segments are indistinctly bordered laterally with brownish or purple tints. The legs frequently are flecked with tiny purple-black points.

Similar species

This species is quite distinctive, but superficially resembles the oak bush-cricket. However, that species is much smaller and more delicately built, paler in colour, and unlikely to be found in the same habitat as the great green.

In the very few localities where the wartbiter (*Decticus verrucivorus*) still occurs, the great green bush-cricket may sometimes also be found. However, the wartbiter has a much more compact, 'chunky' appearance, shorter wings (relative to its body length), and a markedly angled pronotum (smoothly saddle-shaped in the great green bush-cricket).

The recently established sickle-bearing bush-cricket (*Phaneroptera falcata*) has, as its vernacular name implies, a very differently shaped ovipositor in the female. In general, this species has a more frail appearance, with relatively longer and more 'spindly' legs. It is also is covered in minute black spots.

Nymphs of the great green bush-cricket are also minutely covered in tiny purple-black spots and could be confused with nymphs or adults of the speckled bush-cricket (*Leptophyes punctatissima*), but the body shapes of the two species are quite different.

Life cycle

The eggs are laid in soil during the summer, and pass two or more winters before hatching in late April or May. The number of nymphal instars varies, with a range from six to nine recorded. The nymphs are bright green with an indistinct brownish dorsal stripe and are densely marked with tiny purple-black points, especially on the legs. In early stages the wing stubs appear as small lobes pointing down behind the rear edge of the pronotum. In the final two instars the wing-stubs are reversed, and slight indications of the future venation are perceptible. The ovipositor is visible in the final three or four instars of the female, increasing in length with each moult. The adults are usually present by mid-July (4 July in East Sussex in 2009 (Sutton, 2009) is exceptionally early) and can be heard until the end of October (see Chapter 3, Fig 53 for images of selected developmental stages).

Habitat

The characteristic habitat is rank grassland in the process of succession to scrub, with clumps of bramble, or low hawthorn bushes providing a favoured song perch for the males. Females, too, use the upper branches of bushes to bask on warm days. The insect may also be found on south-facing slopes of downland, in hedgerows, and in gardens. In coastal and estuarine sites it is often abundant among *Phragmites* reeds along ditches and dykes, and in neglected 'foldings' on the landward side of sea defences.

Behaviour

The great green bush-cricket is nocturnal, but the males often begin to sing from mid-afternoon onwards. The song is one of the loudest emitted by any British orthopteran, and can be heard at distances of several meters (Ragge, 1965, says 200 metres, but this is presumably for those with better hearing than mine!). The tone is slightly metallic and rasping, and is produced in continuous, prolonged bursts. While singing, the male appears to 'pump' his abdomen rhythmically – presumably to enhance respiration. Even when singing, the cryptic coloration of a male perched among vegetation makes it very difficult to locate. There is some competition between males for song perches, and where the population is dense one may nip an intruder with his mandibles. The latter will usually dive down into lower vegetation. The females are inactive during the day, spending much of their time basking on sunny days. They, too, are surprisingly difficult to find for such large insects. When approached, they tend to rely on their cryptic appearance for protection, and remain static. If disturbed in a more determined way, they tend, unlike most other bush-crickets, to climb upwards through the vegetation. Even then, their movements are slow and awkward. They can fly, but do so rather reluctantly, and usually only for short distances.

They are omnivorous, including in their diet both vegetation and invertebrates such as caterpillars, aphids, flies and other orthopterans – including members of their own species. The great French entomologist Henri Fabre

(1823–1915) recorded the feeding and courtship activities of this species in the south of France. This is his vivid description of the predation of the great green bush-cricket on a cicada.

> In the dense branches of the plane-trees, a sudden sound rings out like a cry of anguish, strident and short. It is the desperate wail of the Cicada, surprised in his quietude by the Green Grasshopper, that ardent nocturnal huntress, who springs upon him, grips him in the side, opens and ransacks his abdomen. An orgy of music followed by butchery. (Fabre, 1917: 276)

Fabre found that, in captivity, they would eat a range of vegetable matter, including fruit, insects such as cicadas, and other delicacies: 'The Green Grasshopper resembles the English: she dotes on underdone rump steak seasoned with jam' (Fabre, 1917: 289).

Fabre also described the courtship activity of specimens in captivity. Head-to-head they 'fenced' with their long antennae (as do most bush-cricket species), while the male gave brief stridulations occasionally. Fabre notes that the process seemed interminable, but when he looked the following morning, mating had clearly taken place and a 'green bladder-like arrangement' (the spermatophore) was hanging from the base of the female's ovipositor. After a couple of hours she consumed this, bit by bit.

Vahed & Gilbert (1996) measured the spermatophore in this species as weighing more than 22 per cent of the body weight of the male.

Enemies
Ragge (1973) refers to reports of this species being attacked by yellow buntings and by a house sparrow.

Distribution
The great green bush-cricket is widely distributed in Europe, North Africa and temperate Asia. In Britain it has a mainly southerly distribution, south of a line from the south Wales coast to the Wash.

Status and conservation
This species is very localised and is vulnerable to 'tidy minded' management of grassland. Its requirement for late succession patches and fringes with tall grasses and scrub can be accommodated by rotational management with long cycles.

References: Fabre, 1917; Ragge, 1965, 1973; Sutton, 2009; Vahed & Gilbert, 1996.

pre- and post-1998
post-1998
pre-1998

THE LARGE CONEHEAD
Ruspolia nitidula
(Scopoli, 1786)

MEASUREMENTS:
Male: 25–37 mm
in length; female:
25–45 mm in length;
ovipositor: 17–26 mm in
length (Harz, 1969).

A

FIGS A–B. Male; male,
showing stridulatory
apparatus (both photos
© B. Thomas).

B

Description
The large conehead is bright green, with a pale whitish line across the tip of its sharply conical head, and running back through the eyes. There is a fine black line along each tibia. The wings are very long, usually reaching back beyond the tip of the very long, straight ovipositor in females, and giving the insect a slender appearance. Brown and reddish forms are reported from mainland Europe.

Similar species
The great green bush-cricket (*T. viridissima*) is comparable in size, but the head shape of the large conehead is distinctive. The great green bush-cricket also has relatively shorter wings, and a dark band along the dorsal surface.

The long-winged conehead (*C. discolor*) is much smaller, and, like the great green bush-cricket, it has dark brown coloration on the dorsal surface, especially on the head and pronotum.

The song is loud and distinctive, enabling discovery and identification of the first British arrivals.

Life cycle
In southern Europe it has an annual life cycle, over-wintering in the egg stage. There is so far no clear evidence of its breeding in Britain, but occasional sightings indicate that the adults emerge relatively late in the year, from August onwards.

Habitat
In southern Europe its habitat is given as moist meadows and waste ground, but also dry fields with long grass (Bellmann, 1985; Bellmann & Luquet, 2009).

Behaviour
The spermatophylax 'nuptial gift' to the female is extremely small in this species (approximately 0.3 per cent of the male weight), and females, which mate only once, delay consumption of the ampulla (Vahed & Gilbert, 1996; Gwynne, 2001; see also Chapter 6).

The male song is a prolonged, continuous buzz that can last for 10 minutes or more. In this respect the song resembles that of *M. roeselii*, but it is an almost pure tone of about 13 to 20 kHz (Hathway *et al.* report a somewhat higher lead frequency), and is delivered almost exclusively at night (Ragge & Reynolds, 1998).

History
There are occasional reports of specimens incidentally imported in plant material (e.g. Nottingham and Northamptonshire, 2001 (Widgery, 2002)) but the

first reports of the species arriving in the British Isles apparently unaided were from the Isles of Scilly in August and September 2003. Males were heard singing and subsequently captured and definitively identified on two islands: St Marys and St Agnes (Hathway *et al.*, 2003; Sutton, 2003c).

A single male was located on Canford Cliffs, Poole, Dorset, in September 2005 and another at the same site in 2006 – suggesting the possibility of a breeding population (Sutton, 2006b).

Distribution
South and central Europe, Eastern Europe, North Africa and eastwards to Palaearctic Asia. It has been spreading northwards in mainland Europe in recent years, and was established in Normandy by 2002 (Sutton, 2003c).

Status and conservation
Given continued warming of the climate, it seems likely that this species will establish a breeding population in the British Isles (and it may have already done so).

References: Bellmann, 1985; Bellmann & Luquet, 2009; Evans & Edmundson, 2007; Gwynne, 2001; Hathway et al., 2003; Harz, 1969; Ragge & Reynolds, 1998; Vahed & Gilbert, 1996; Sutton, 2003c, 2006b; Widgery, 2002.

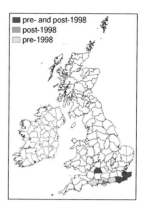

THE WARTBITER

Decticus verrucivorus
(Linnaeus, 1758)

MEASUREMENTS: Male: 26–34 mm in length; female: 27–42 mm in length.

A

B

C

D

FIGS A–D. Male; plain green female; male, showing dorsal surfaces of pronotum and stridulatory apparatus; female, dorsal view.

E

F

FIGS E–F. Female with black markings; rare yellow and purple form (© P. Sutton).

Description

The wartbiter is a robust, 'chunky' insect. The adults are fully winged, but the wings barely reach back to the tip of the abdomen. The wings of the males are modified basally for stridulation. The head and pronotum have a smooth, shiny appearance. The pronotum is strongly angled at the sides, and has a fine median longitudinal ridge. The ovipositor is long, relatively narrow and slightly up-turned.

The typical form is bright green, often with variable amounts of dark brown to black blotching on the wings. There is also often a black mark on the rear margin of some of the abdominal segments. The eyes are very dark – contrasting with the green of the head. The base of the ovipositor in females is beige, shading to dark brown towards the tip. The stridulatory area of the left fore wing in the male is irregularly ridged and brown in colour in fully mature individuals. The cerci are yellowish, and have an inward-projecting tooth. The ventral surfaces of the hind femora are yellow, and the hind tibiae are pale lilac.

There are other colour forms, which are very rare in British populations: a grey form (f. *bingleii* – sometimes described as 'brown') was discovered in the main Sussex population in 1987, while a remarkable form with purple sides and yellowish wings also formerly occurred there. Neither has been seen since, although a partially purple form does occasionally occur (Cherrill & Brown, 1991a; Sutton & Browne, 1992; Sutton, 2009).

Similar species

It would be difficult to confuse this species with any other. Our only other species of similarly large size is the great green bush-cricket (*T. viridissima*), which does occur on some of the few remaining sites for the wartbiter. However, the great green bush-cricket is rather more slender in build, and has significantly longer wings relative to its body. Also the great green's pronotum is smoothly rounded and saddle-shaped, contrasting with the strongly angled pronotum of the wartbiter.

The sickle-bearing bush-cricket (*Phaneroptera falcata*) is another large and fully-winged green bush-cricket. However, it is much more delicately built than the wartbiter, with long, spindly legs, and, in the female, a short, strongly curved ovipositor. So far, only one British locality is known for this species – one not shared with the wartbiter.

Life cycle

The greyish brown eggs are laid singly or in small batches in bare soil, or in short turf, to a depth of 0.5 to 2 cm from July onwards. They soon enter a resting stage, and remain in diapause until this is broken by cold winter weather. Embryonic development usually continues, with a further diapause which is broken by the onset of the next cold winter temperatures. The eggs thus usually hatch in the spring (early to mid-April) after their second winter. However, both in Britain and in mainland Europe this pattern is variable, and embryonic development can take up to seven years. There are seven nymphal instars. The rate of nymphal development is strongly dependent on sunny and warm weather, and the date at which development is completed varies from year to year. Usually adults appear from about the beginning of July and continue to emerge until the last week in July. However, adults have been recorded as early as mid-June, and in 1989 at the main Sussex locality, no nymphs were observed after 28 June. Development is slightly faster in males, which also have lower body weight. After the final moult both sexes increase in weight, especially females, which more than double their weight to an average of 2.1 grammes by late August. The weight gain in females is an indication of their fecundity, and as their weight increases with age, it is likely that they do not achieve their full reproductive potential if they encounter inclement weather in the latter part of their adult lives, or if poor weather in spring slows nymphal development. Depending on the weather in late summer and autumn, the adults can survive until mid-October.

Habitat

The wartbiter survives in a wide variety of habitat types further south in Europe, but in Britain it is at the northern edge of its range, and so has much more specialised requirements. The British populations are concentrated in a very small number of unimproved calcareous downland slopes, with one very precarious tiny population on grass/heather heathland. The downland population that has been most closely studied by A. Cherrill and colleagues has been shown to require a mosaic of dense tufts of tall grasses (*Brachypodium pinnatum* and *Bromus erectus* at the main study site) with areas of short turf and some bare ground. The short turf and bare ground are required for oviposition, and are also the habitat for early-instar nymphs. Sixth and seventh instar nymphs and adults are found more frequently associated with the tall grass tufts. In the few downland sites where they occur, population densities are greatest on south-facing slopes, compared with more easterly aspects where they also survive.

Their diet includes other invertebrates, and, not surprisingly, they are found in sites that are rich in other species of Orthoptera. On the south-facing slopes of their strongest British population they coexist with particularly large numbers of *M. roeselii* and *C. discolor*, along with *T. viridissima*, *S. lineatus*, *C. parallelus*, *C. brunneus* and *O. viridulus*.

In its heathland habitat the mosaic vegetation structure may be comparable to that on downland, with taller heathers interspersed with sedges and fine grasses.

Behaviour

In captivity, females have been observed to lay their eggs in soil, some of them showing a preference for short turf over bare ground. During oviposition the female inserts her ovipositor vertically into the soil, apparently testing for suitability of the substrate. When a suitable site is found, she presses the ovipositor fully into the soil, and usually lays one egg quickly afterwards. Most frequently only one egg is laid in one session but sometimes a small batch is laid (up to 13 have been recorded). After the egg (or final egg in a batch) has been laid, the female raises and lowers her ovipositor to fill in the space above the eggs, and, after removing her ovipositor, scrapes the soil surface around the oviposition site, so concealing it. There is evidence that warmer sites are selected for oviposition.

The adults are bulky animals, apparently rather poor climbers, whose typical responses to disturbance are to remain still and rely on their excellent camouflage, or to jump out of the way – usually into deep grass tufts. When they do this they have the appearance of small, plump green frogs. They are omnivorous, feeding on both vegetation and other invertebrates, including beetles and grasshoppers (see DVD sequence).

The adults, while tending to favour the shelter of the dense grass tufts, will bask in sunshine on the warmer aspect of the tussocks. However, as the microclimate is cooler in the tufts than in the shorter turf, it seems likely that the association with this vegetation structure on the part of adults and late instars is related to avoidance of predation. The tufts are also used by the males as song perches. Unlike many other bush-crickets, they sing most in the early part of the day – from mid-morning to early afternoon, and only during warm weather. The song is usually delivered from a perch on a grass tussock, and takes the form of prolonged bursts

FIG G. Head and pronotum of this female show signs of predator damage: possibly beak-markings of a bird.

G

of repeated high-pitched clicks. The rate of repetition increases to about 10 clicks per second within a minute or so of the start of the burst. The volume of the song is quite low, and for many observers a bat detector is needed to locate it at more than a few metres distance. Males are also reported to emit short isolated chirps.

Like most bush-crickets, the males produce a substantial spermatophore which includes a 'nuptial gift', the spermatophylax, which is bitten off and consumed by the female while sperm from the ampulla are transferred to her. In the wartbiter, literature sources give measurements of the mass of the spermatophore varying from approximately 6 per cent (Cherrill & Brown, 1990a) to 11 per cent of the body-weight of the male (Vahed & Gilbert, 1996).

Enemies

Cherrill & Brown (1992a) noted the presence at their study site of foraging foxes, badgers, kestrels, magpies, crows and starlings. The large size of the late instars and adults probably makes them an attractive food item for predators, and Cherrill (1997) found numbers of adults with severed legs, or hind femora, tibiae or ovipositors, and one female with a beak mark on her abdomen. Insects showing signs of past predator attacks were more common among adults and late instars.

However, mortality rates were shown to be much higher among the earlier nymphal instars, with population densities declining by 99.3 per cent from egg hatch to adult emergence, but remaining quite constant after that. Mortality arising from defective moulting between instars is known to be high, but various other causes including predation probably contributed to the high levels of pre-adult mortality (Cherrill & Brown, 1990a).

Distribution

The wartbiter is widely distributed in Europe and temperate Asia. As a species close to the northern edge of its range in Britain and northern Europe, it is especially vulnerable here to habitat change and inclement weather. There is evidence of decline in recent decades in the Netherlands, Belgium, Denmark and southern Sweden as well as in Britain.

In Britain it has always been a rare and highly localised species, confined to a few localities south of the Bristol Channel. These localites were in east Kent, Sussex, Hampshire (New Forest), the Isle of Wight, Dorset and Wiltshire. The majority of these populations have been lost as a result of urban development, agricultural change and changes in habitat management (in some cases enacted for conservation purposes!). Currently it is believed that the wartbiter is confined to no more than four of its original localities: two in east Sussex (including the largest, at Castle Hill National Nature Reserve), one on downland in Wiltshire, and the other a very small heathland population near Wareham. There is, however, at least one site, in Kent, where re-introduction of the species appears to have been successful.

Status and conservation

The wartbiter was scheduled in the Wildlife and Countryside Act, 1981, and included as 'Vulnerable' in the Nature Conservancy Council's *Red Data Books: 2. Insects* (Shirt, 1987). It was the subject of a Nature Conservancy Council/English Nature Species Recovery programme from 1987, with substantial research conducted by Andrew Cherrill, Valerie Brown and colleagues (the main basis of the above account), together with captive breeding and attempts at reintroduction. The captive breeding programme proved very demanding for several reasons. The nymphs had to be reared in separate containers because of cannibalism, they suffered from protozoan and fungal infections, as well as a high frequency of failed moults, and they required high-quality food (Pearce-Kelly *et al.*, 1998). The process was labour intensive, but produced enough late instars and adults for release into three sites, one of which, at least, still has a population of the species.

Adults of the British population are smaller than those from further south in Europe, and our populations are also much less dense. In Cherrill's view (1993), the species is capable of high reproductive success in Britain only in years when weather conditions are particularly favourable. Even then, it is dependent on appropriate habitat management on its predominantly south-facing grassland sites. A complex sward structure, with tufts of coarse grasses interspersed on a fine scale with short turf and bare ground, appears to be an essential combination of requirements for wartbiters during their developmental stages, and for thermo-regulation, shelter from predators, song perches, oviposition, and mate location for the adults (see also Chapter 9).

References: Cherrill, 1993, 1997; Cherrill & Brown, 1990a, 1990b, 1991a, 1991b, 1992a, 1992b; Cherrill et al., 1991; Haes et al., 1990; Ingrisch, 1984a; Pearce-Kelly et al., 1998; Sutton, 2009; Sutton & Browne, 1992; Vahed & Gilbert, 1996.

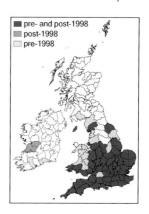

pre- and post-1998
post-1998
pre-1998

THE DARK BUSH-CRICKET

Pholidoptera griseoaptera
(De Geer, 1773)

MEASUREMENTS: Male: 13–20 mm in length; female: 13–20 mm in length.

FIGS A–C. Male; female; male, dorsal view.

A

B

C

FIGS D–F. Grey form; chestnut form; underside.

D

E

Description

This species has a robust build. The dorsal surface of the pronotum is smoothly curved with a fine median longitudinal ridge that extends forwards on the head. The side flanges ('paranota') of the pronotum are continuous with the dorsal surface, but form a definite angle with it. The males have small inner projections near the base of their cerci. The ovipositor in the female is relatively long, broad, and up-curved. There are no hind wings, and the fore wings in the male are greatly reduced to function solely in stridulation. The wings in the female are even more vestigial, being reduced to tiny flaps just visible at the rear of the pronotum.

F

The ground colour varies from pale grey to grey-brown, with darker grey or brown fine flecks and indistinct markings. There are often darker patches of grey-black, especially on the sides of the pronotum and on the outer surface of the hind femora. One striking form has sandy or chestnut brown coloration on the dorsal surface of head, pronotum and abdomen, contrasting with the paler sides. The ovipositor is usually darker than the rest of the body, especially towards the tip. The underside of the abdomen is yellow to yellowish green.

Similar species

There are three other medium-sized bush-crickets that could be confused with *P. griseoaptera*.

(1) The grey bush-cricket (*Platycleis albopunctata*) has a similar range of colour patterns, but is fully winged in the adults (the wings reaching back just beyond the tip of the abdomen). On closer inspection, the inner projections on the male cerci are mid-way along them, rather than close to the base as in the dark bush-cricket. The fine median ridge on the dorsal surface of the pronotum is

slightly more raised in the grey bush-cricket, present only on the rear portion of the pronotum, and divides at its anterior end to form a 'y' shape. In Britain the grey bush-cricket is rarely found more than a few kilometres from the coast.

(2) The bog bush-cricket (*Metrioptera brachyptera*) is usually short-winged, but its wings are not so greatly reduced as in the dark bush-cricket. Both sexes have wings that reach back about halfway, or a little more, along the abdomen. The male cerci are similar to those of the grey bush-cricket. Although the range of colour patterns overlaps, there is a partly green form of the bog bush-cricket, unlike any form of the dark bush-cricket. Bog bush-crickets also have a pale border to the rear of the side plates of the pronotum. Their habitat is damp heathland and bogs, and they do not commonly occur together with the dark bush-cricket.

(3) Roesel's bush-cricket (*Metrioptera roeselii*) is also usually short-winged, but with less markedly reduced wings than the dark bush-cricket. The side plates of the pronotum have strongly contrasting cream to yellow margins right round their edges, unlike any colour form of the dark bush-cricket.

Life cycle

The eggs are buff-coloured, 4 mm by 1 mm in size, and laid in crevices in bark or in rotting wood. They may hatch the following spring (in mid- to late April), but are more likely to over-winter twice, to give a two-year life cycle. There are six nymphal stages, with the tiny wing stubs of the males visible in the final two. The nymphs are more strikingly contrasting in their colour patterns than the adults. They are commonly pale brown with darker brown patterns and blotches, the latter frequently along the sides of abdomen and pronotum, and on the hind femora. They settle on exposed lower leaves of bramble and other shrubs on sunny days. The adults emerge from mid-July onwards, and survive later into the autumn and winter than most other species.

Habitat

Although sometimes found among tall grasses, they are rarely far from patches of low scrub, especially bramble clumps and rough hedgerows. They are apparently also found on exposed cliffs in the south-west (Marshall & Haes, 1988).

Behaviour

Like most other bush-crickets they are omnivorous and include other insects as well as small spiders in their diet. In captivity they will also consume earthworms (A. Kettle, pers. comm.).

They are mainly nocturnal, skulking among the branches of bramble scrub during the day. From mid-afternoon, especially late in the season, the females,

FIGS G–J. Early instar nymph; basking nymphs; late instar nymph, male; late instar nymph, female.

especially, spend long periods basking in sun spots. They alternate their posture between exposing each side to the sun, with the hind leg facing the sun lowered to expose more of the abdomen, and exposing their dorsal surface to the sun, hind legs stretched out behind. Both sexes frequently run their antennae through their mouthparts, presumably to clean them, although it is also possible that this behaviour is linked to the 'fencing' with their antennae during courtship, and involves chemical communication. Active preening of the fore legs with the mouthparts is also frequent. In cloudy or even wet weather the males may begin singing quite early in the day. Usually, however, they are heard from mid-afternoon onwards, and continue through the night.

They are gregarious, and from mid-afternoon into the evening often gather in groups of a dozen or more within a square metre on lower leaves and branches of the bramble. The group may include four or more males, each chirping, with females gathering from inner branches of the scrub. Although the females approach singing males they do not, at this time, show any interest in mating. However, prolonged 'fencing' with their antennae is noticeable.

The 'solo' song of the male is a brief, high pitched chirp repeated at variable intervals of a few seconds. However, several males are often singing in close proximity to one another, and sometimes this results in a regular pattern of alternation between two adjacent males. When more than two males sing together, their chirps still are generally emitted separately to produce a non-synchronous 'chorus' (Jones, 1963, 1966). The males can also emit a more prolonged chirp lasting approximately a second. This is considered to signify an aggressive interaction between males, but it is also occasionally emitted by males on the approach of females. In general, males do not appear to interact aggressively with one another. However, experimental work does show that the onset, termination, and timing of chirps are all affected by the stridulation of other males (see Chapter 5).

Courtship involves prolonged 'fencing' with the antennae between a male and female pair at close proximity. Eventually the female mounts the male from the rear, actively palpating the dorsal segments of his abdomen, presumably imbibing a chemical secretion. The male raises his hind legs to allow the female to mount, but may still reject her at this stage by a powerful back-kick of the hind legs. Males who do this continue to chirp, indicating continuing readiness to mate (see DVD). This somewhat puzzling behaviour is explained by Gwynne (2001) in relation to the mormon cricket (*Anabrus simplex*) in terms of the 'choosiness' of the male in view of the cost to him involved in the 'nuptial gift'. Apparently the males assess the weight of the females that mount them, accepting only the heaviest ones (presumably as these are most likely to lay more eggs). In the dark bush-cricket, the spermatophore weighs some 10.7 per cent of the male body weight (Vahed & Gilbert, 1996).

Enemies
They can be caught in the webs of larger spiders, most notably the wasp spider (*Argiope bruennichi*).

Distribution
The dark bush-cricket is widely distributed and generally common throughout most of Europe. In southern Britain it is perhaps our commonest bush-cricket, and has been recorded in almost every 10 km square south of a line from south-west Wales to the Wash. North of this, its known distribution is more scattered, but reaches as far north as north Yorkshire and south-west Scotland. It is also known from the south and west of Ireland.

Status and conservation
The dark bush-cricket remains common within its geographical range and thrives on small, neglected patches of habitat. Its only serious threat seems to be excessive tidy-mindedness that might disrupt that neglect.

References: Gwynne, 2001; Jones, 1963, 1966; Hartley, 1967; Vahed & Gilbert, 1996.

pre- and post-1998
post-1998
pre-1998

THE GREY BUSH-CRICKET
Platycleis albopunctata
(Goeze, 1778)

MEASUREMENTS: Male: 20–25 mm in length; female: 20–28 mm in length.

A

B

C

FIGS A–C. Male;
female; dorsal view,
male.

Description

The grey bush-cricket is sturdily built and medium sized. It is fully winged, with the wings extending back to a few millimetres beyond the tip of the abdomen. In the males, the anterior part of the leading edge of each fore wing is modified for stridulation. The male cerci have inwardly directed spines about halfway along.

The ovipositor of the female is broad, up-turned and black in fully mature specimens. In both sexes there is a slight median ridge on the rear part of the dorsal surface of the pronotum, which divides, with the front end forming a 'y' shape. The adults vary from grey to light brown in ground colour, with fine blackish flecks that coalesce into patches in places, especially the sides of the pronotum (paranota). The paranota have pale borders, but these are obscured by darker flecks in adults. The outer surfaces of the hind femora frequently have a black 'fish-bone' marking. The underside is usually a very pale green or yellow. A form with green rather than grey or brown coloration of the pronotum is reported (e.g. Ragge, 1965), and the subspecies (*jerseyana*) that occurs in the Channel Islands often has more greenish coloration (Evans & Edmondson, 2007).

Similar species

There are three similar species.

(1) The dark bush-cricket (*P. griseoaptera*). This has only tiny wing stubs, and, in the male, has inner spines near the base of the cerci (not halfway along as in this species).
(2) Roesel's bush-cricket (*M. roeselii*) is usually brachypterous, and has well-marked cream-yellow borders to the paranota. The macropterous form of Roesel's bush-cricket has markedly longer wings than the grey.
(3) The bog bush-cricket (*M. brachyptera*) is also usually brachypterous, and has clear pale borders on the rear margin of the paranota.

In Britain the grey bush-cricket is mainly found in coastal sites, and not usually in association with any of the above (although occasionally with *M. roeselii* (B. Pinchen, pers. comm.). The song of the male is also distinctive (see below).

Life cycle

The eggs are laid singly or in small batches by the female in sand or soil, or sometimes in plant stems or crevices. They hatch in April or May, and there are six nymphal instars. The nymphs are brown, or green with brown head and pronotum. They have pale cream-yellow borders to the paranota, and variable black markings. The up-turned wing stubs are noticeable in the final two nymphal instars. Adults emerge from early July onwards, but do not usually survive much beyond the end of September or early October.

Habitat

In mainland Europe the grey bush-cricket inhabits rough grassland, but in Britain it can be found in a variety of coastal habitats such as among marram grass (*Ammophila arenaria*) tussocks on sand dunes, on grassy fringes of coastal cliffs, on stabilised shingle and among low scrub. Patches of loose soil or sand, interspersed with dense, low vegetative cover exposed to the sun seem to be characteristic of all habitat types.

Behaviour

The adults are very secretive, and sensitive to disturbance (a colleague remarked they should be re-named 'the shy bush-cricket'). They are active mainly in the warmer part of the day, and the patient observer can sometimes see them basking in sunny weather on taller vegetation, such as shrubby seablite (*Suaeda vera*) or sea purslane (*Halimione portulacoides*), and even on driftwood. Even here, however, they are never far from cover, and quickly descend into the depths of the vegetation if they detect the slightest movement. If alarmed when this is not a feasible option, they are effective in jumping and flying for the nearest cover. They are omnivorous, including other insects such as grasshopper nymphs in their diet, but, according to Ragge (1965), can be kept successfully in captivity on vegetable matter. In sand-dune habitats they feed on marram grass, often selecting desiccated stems. One was observed by the author lunging at a gatekeeper butterfly that settled some 5 cm away from it!

The males usually sing from cover and are very difficult to locate, even with the aid of a bat detector. The song consists of a brief chirp, repeated at a rate of 2 to 4 times per second, and continued in prolonged bursts lasting several minutes. The sound is rather quiet, and often obscured by the sound of the wind in its exposed habitat. However, when picked up with the aid of a bat detector it is quite distinctive. Males do not congregate, as males of the dark bush-cricket do, but 'duets' can often be heard when the song of one male interacts with that of another. However, in laboratory experiments such alternating duets have been shown to break down after some time, and the interaction may simply function to enable the males to space themselves out across the available habitat (Latimer, 1981a, 1981b). There is some evidence of at least temporary territoriality among the males, as there are brief skirmishes when they encounter one another (see DVD). The male delivers a spermatophore to the female on mating. This is given as approximately 5.5 per cent of the male's body weight (Vahed & Gilbert, 1996).

FIGS D–E. Singing male with 'mirror' partly exposed; underside of female with remains of spermatophore visible.

The females are more frequently found than the males away from deep cover on patches of unvegetated soil or sand, presumably seeking oviposition sites.

D

Enemies

None is reported in the literature, but their habit of retreating into cover suggests adaptation to avoid diurnal visual predators – possibly birds (such as ringed plover, dunlin, turnstone or kestrel) or mammals.

Distribution

This species is widespread in southern, south-western and central Europe, as well as north Africa. In Britain it is at the northern edge of its range, and this may

E

explain its rather specialised coastal and southerly distribution. Its distribution is almost continuous along the south coasts of England and Wales, and the south-west peninsula, with outliers further north along the east coast to Suffolk and, on the west, to north Wales. There is a small scattering of inland and more northerly reports. A site 14 km inland was reported from Ringwood, Hampshire (Widgery, 1998, 2001a) in the 1990s, but extension of an adjacent industrial estate may have been the cause of its subsequent demise (B. Pinchen, pers. corr.).

Status and conservation

The main threat to the grey bush-cricket is development for housing or tourism on its coastal habitats. On the east coast, in Essex and Suffolk, it is found in a small number of sand dune systems where it had been supposed extinct. Recent survey work suggests that it is currently increasing, and further colonisations along the east coast seem likely (Harvey *et al.*, 2005; Gardiner *et al.*, 2010). This might be aided by climate change, but coastal erosion might offset any such gains.

References: Evans & Edmondson, 2007; Harvey et al., *2005; Gardiner* et al., *2010; Latimer, 1981a, 1981b; Ragge, 1965; Vahed & Gilbert, 1996; Widgery, 1998, 2001a.*

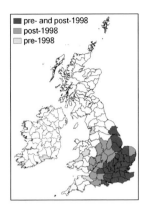

pre- and post-1998
post-1998
pre-1998

ROESEL'S BUSH-CRICKET
Metrioptera roeselii
(Hagenbach, 1822)

MEASUREMENTS: Male: 13–22 mm in length; female: 14–22 mm in length.

A   B   C   D

FIGS A–D. Male; female; green female; male, dorsal view.

FIG E. The macropterous f. *diluta*, male.

E

Description

Roesel's bush-cricket is a medium-
sized, sturdily built insect, in which the
wings are typically only part-developed
– reaching back over only the first five or six abdominal segments in the male,
fewer in the female. The fore wing stubs of the male are partially modified for
stridulation, and the long cerci have an inner projection halfway along. The
ovipositor is broad and up-turned, brown shading to black-brown towards the
tip. There is a continuous fine median ridge on the dorsal surface (discus) of the
pronotum, usually continued forward as a yellowish line over the head.

A minority of individuals of both sexes in most populations are of the long-
winged (macropterous) form (f. *diluta*). Although the wing tips in this form
soon become tattered, it is usually possible to see that the wings are very long –
sometimes extending beyond the tip of the abdomen by as much as one third to a
half of the total wing length.

The ground colour is usually grey-brown with darker markings. There is
often a fish-bone-shaped darker pattern on the outer surface of the rear femora,
and the side flaps (paranota) of the pronotum are usually black, with a continuous
cream-yellow border. The sides of the visible thoracic segments to the rear of the
pronotum also have yellow patches. The underside of the abdomen is yellow.

A variable proportion of most populations have pale green sides and hind
femora. In this form, the paranota are often greenish, with pale green borders.

Similar species

The pale yellowish (or greenish) borders to the paranota are distinctive. In the
bog bush-cricket (*M. brachyptera*), the pale borders are limited to the rear edges
only, and usually buff-cream in colour. The bog bush-cricket also lacks the
yellow patches on the sides of the thoracic segments, and the ovipositor of the
female bog bush-cricket is relatively longer, and less strongly up-curved.

For distinctions between Roesel's and the dark and grey bush-crickets (*P.
griseoaptera* and *P. albopunctata*), see the accounts of those species.

Life cycle

The female lays her eggs singly, in stems of coarse grasses or rushes. She
bites a hole in the outer layers of the plant with her mandibles and raises her

F   G

FIGS F–G. Early instar nymph; and final instar green nymph, female.

ovipositor under her abdomen to insert the tip into the cavity. The rest of the ovipositor is then pressed into the stem and she remains quiescent for some minutes while a single egg is placed in the plant tissue, parallel to the sides of the stem (see DVD). The egg is elongated, cylindrical and approximately 4 mm by 0.5 mm. Eggs laid early in the season may undergo sufficient embryonic development to hatch the following spring, while late-laid eggs pass two winters before hatching. The newly hatched nymphs appear in late May or early June, and pass through six nymphal instars before becoming adult from late June (Widgery, 2001b) or early July onwards. Adults and late instar nymphs can be found together through most of July. The adults persist until the end of September, and in declining numbers thereafter, until the end of October in most years.

The nymphs are usually pale brown, with a broad black band along each side of the abdomen, continued onto the paranota, with the pale border of the latter often more extensive than in the adults. A median black line runs along the whole dorsal surface of the insect, bordering the fine median ridge of the pronotum. The antennae are black. As in the adults, there is a form of the nymph with green sides, shading to brown dorsally. Up-turned wing stubs can be seen in the final two instars (see also Chapter 3, Fig 66).

Habitat

This is a species of open grassland with tall grasses. Although common on large expanses of grassland, such as south-facing downland and coastal grazing marshes, it is quite capable of surviving in small neglected field corners or roadside verges. It is common on sea walls and inner 'foldings', and is one of the few species to thrive in narrow conservation strips of coarse grasses at the edges of arable fields. However, it also occurs in overgrown and unmanaged sites, where there is succession to scrub, as well as along south-facing hedgerows, woodland edges and open woodland rides.

Behaviour

Roesel's bush-cricket is a sun-loving species, the females, especially, spending much of their time basking. They are omnivorous but feed mainly on vegetable matter, particularly grasses.

On sunny days the males sing in prolonged continuous bursts. Although the song is high-pitched, like that of most bush-crickets, it can be heard by most people as a distinctive 'buzz'. In most extensive grassland habitats the males are evenly spaced out, and sing from perches. These are usually exposed to the sun, but not conspicuous as they are surrounded by rank vegetation. However, there is some competition between males for song perches. Where wind or rain has broken clusters of grass stems to form a rough 'platform', three or more males may compete to occupy the perch, often emitting short bursts of song as they move about, and briefly skirmishing on contact. Clusters of both males and females may sometimes be seen on leaves of low scrub such as oak saplings or bramble.

At close quarters, courting males approach females, 'fencing' with their antennae, and continuing to emit bursts of stridulation (see DVD).

Long-winged forms appear to behave in similar ways to the typical one, but they are noticeably less mobile among the long grasses. The stridulation of the male seems to be unaffected by wing length. However, the long-winged

H

I

FIGS H–I. Singing male with raised fore wings; and courtship. Note the open wings of the singing male.

form, even where it is relatively common, soon declines as a proportion of the population. This may be simply because, as the dispersive form, they emigrate to colonise other suitable habitat. One remarkable description of this refers to many macropterous Roesel's bush-crickets taking to the wing in one field, the flight characterised as 'ponderous and straight, with no apparent means of steering to left or right – the legs protruding behind their bodies like twin tails' (Smith, 2007).

Clearly the macropterous form of *roeselii* is not a skillful flier, and as well as its disadvantage of lower mobility in tall vegetation, is also rendered vulnerable to predation when on the wing (see below). There is believed to be a trade-off between the dispersal ability of the long-winged form and its lower fecundity, compared with the more usual short-winged form (see Chapter 3).

Enemies

The simultaneous flight of numerous long-winged individuals described above was sufficient to attract the interest of avian predators – in the shape of two pairs of hobbys and another pair of kestrels. The kestrels, feeding lower down, could be seen plucking the crickets out of the air, partially dismembering them and swallowing the remainder. After feasting for about an hour, the raptors were joined by approximately sixty black-headed gulls and one common gull, which also could be seen catching flying bush-crickets.

History

Stephens recorded it from Hampstead in 1835, but until the beginning of the 20th century it had been recorded only from east coastal areas from Kent northwards to the Humber estuary (Marshall, 1974). Burr (1936) considered it to be restricted to the east coast – from Herne Bay, Kent in the south to the Humber estuary in the north. He had records from Kent, Essex, Lincoln and Yorkshire, with a 'doubtful suggestion' from Cambridgeshire. Pickard (1954) adds Hampshire, Surrey, and coastal areas of Suffolk. According to Ragge (1965) its 'liking for flat, estuarine localities' limited it to the areas around the Solent, Thames and Humber, with other records from south Suffolk, Cambridgeshire and Surrey. The reports from Kent and Surrey included downland localities, indicating that earlier assumptions associating it solely with low-lying damp grassland were perhaps too restrictive. It was discovered in West Wales in 1970 (Ragge, 1973), and subsequently in south-east Ireland.

Marshall & Haes (1988) argue that the species is probably a late arrival in Britain from Dogger Land in the North Sea, before that area's submergence, with the Thames estuary as the centre of its distribution in this country. They

note its recent rapid range expansion, aided by the macropterous form –
reported in exceptional numbers in London during the warm summers of 1983
and 1984. There is evidence that hot weather between April and July leads to
accelerated nymphal development and earlier sightings of macropterous forms
(Gardiner, 2009b; see also Chapter 2).

The expansion of range detected during the 1980s has continued apace.
Widgery (2001b) reported many new records for 1998–2000 from Norfolk,
Suffolk, Hampshire, Wiltshire (K. Rylands), Sussex (R. Becker) and Isle of Wight
(B. Pinchen). In 2001 there were new reports from Hertfordshire, Oxfordshire
and Gloucestershire, with evidence that at least some of these represented new
colonisation. Subsequent new county records include:

- Wiltshire 2003 (Sutton, 2010a)
- Dorset and Worcestershire (Sutton, 2005b)
- Derbyshire 2006 (Sutton, 2007b)
- Monmouth 2007 (Sutton, 2008a)

Distribution
This species is widespread in Europe, except for the south. In Britain and
southern Scandinavia it is close to the northern limit of its range. However, it
continues to extend its range in Britain from the south and eastern coastal areas
and is now common and widespread to the south and east of a line from the
Bristol Channel to the Wash, and a more scattered distribution west to north
Somerset, and north to Lancashire and Yorkshire. It is present in a restricted
area of west Wales, and also in the south of Ireland.

Status and conservation
It seems likely that the recent range extension of Roesel's bush-cricket will
be continued, and aided in the longer term by climate change. Its long-
grass habitats are likely to be a persistent, if marginal, feature of the farmed
landscape, as well as of neglected and relatively lightly managed land such
as roadside verges, flood defences and railway embankments. Agricultural
set-aside and subsequently grant-aided stewardship schemes have no doubt
favoured its range extension, and continue to provide both breeding habitat
and, probably, connectivity between subpopulations (Simmons & Thomas,
2004; Gardiner, 2009b).

*References: Gardiner, 2009b; Marshall & Haes, 1988; Simmons & Thomas, 2004; Smith,
2007; Sutton, 2005b, 2007b, 2008a, 2010a; Widgery, 2001b.*

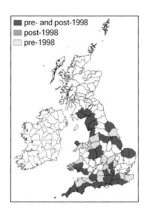

pre- and post-1998
post-1998
pre-1998

Metrioptera brachyptera
(Linnaeus, 1761)

MEASUREMENTS: Male: 11–18 mm in length; female: 13–21 mm in length.

FIGS A–D. Green male; green female; brown female; male, dorsal view.

A

B

C

D

FIG E. The rare macropterous form,
f. *marginata* (© P. Sutton).

E

Description

This medium-sized bush-cricket is
quite similar in appearance to its
relative, Roesel's bush-cricket. In the
typical form the hind wings are almost
absent, while the fore wings are reduced
to short stubs, reaching back only as
far as the third or fourth abdominal segment. In the male the fore wings (tegmina)
are modified for stridulation. There is a fine median longitudinal ridge along the
pronotum. The male cerci have a black inward-pointing spine about halfway along.
The ovipositor of the female is relatively long, and gently up-curved.

There are two basic colour forms, both of which occur quite frequently in
British populations. One form has a brown ground colour, with dark brown-
black markings. These are generally very fine speckles as well as larger patches
of blackish coloration on the sides of the head, pronotum and the abdominal
segments. There is often a fine pale line through the black around the eye,
leading back to the front edge of the pronotum, and there are usually black
stripes along the sides of the hind femora. The ovipositor is blackish for most of
its length, but paler towards the base. The underside of the abdomen, and, often,
the ventral surface of the hind femora, are green.

The other colour form is similar, except that the dorsal surface of the head
and pronotum, and both leading and hind edges of the tegmina, are bright green.

In all forms, the paranota (side flaps of the pronotum) have a pale buff or
cream-coloured hind margin.

There is a rare macropterous form (f. *marginata* (Thunberg)) in which both
pairs of wings are fully developed (Ragge, 1973).

Similar species

Roesel's bush-cricket has the pale border to the paranota running round the lower
and fore margins, but in the bog bush-cricket it is confined to the rear margin. The
ovipositor of the bog bush-cricket is longer relative to its body and more gently
up-curved than that of Roesel's bush-cricket. The subgenital plate of the female is
deeply notched in the latter species, but only very shallowly so in the female bog
bush-cricket (see the Key, Figs K8a and b, page 232). These species do occur together,
so it is important for recorders to have clear identifying characters.

FIG F. Final instar male nymph.

F

The dark bush-cricket is superficially very similar, especially to the brown form of the bog bush-cricket. However, the wings of the dark bush-cricket are much more drastically reduced than those of the bog bush-cricket – being virtually absent in females and reduced to the stridulatory apparatus in the males.

The grey bush-cricket is fully winged and so quite different in appearance to the typical form of the bog bush-cricket.

Life cycle

The eggs are probably laid in the stems of plants during the summer, and are thought to overwinter twice before hatching in May or early June. The resulting nymphs pass through six instars before completing their development during July or early August. The adults can be found through August and September, becoming more scarce through October, and sometimes surviving into November.

The up-turned wing stubs are just visible in the fifth instar nymphs, and more clearly so in the final instar. The nymphs are always brown in ground colour, and darker-brown to blackish on the paranota and sides of the abdomen. As in the adults, there is a pale rear border to the paranota.

Habitat

The bog bush-cricket, as its name implies, is an inhabitant of the wetter parts of heaths and moors, usually at low altitudes. It is associated in these habitats with tall, dense tufts of vegetation such as cross-leaved heath (*Erica tetralix*) and other heathers, bog myrtle (*Myrica gale*) and grasses such as purple moor-grass (*Molinia caerulea*). In the wet heaths of Dorset and the New Forest it is often found together with the large marsh grasshopper (*Stethophyma grossum*).

Behaviour

The adults feed on seed heads of heathers and grasses, and probably also on other invertebrates. They make good use of the shelter provided by the grass tufts and low shrubs they inhabit, the males usually singing from cover. When they bask on outer branches or leaves they are easily alarmed by a careless approach and disappear down into the depths of the vegetation. A patient (and often waterlogged!) wait will sometimes be rewarded by their reappearance, and the males do sometimes sing while moving around over more exposed patches of scrub (see DVD).

The males sing through the day, and will often sing in overcast conditions. Their song is a short chirp, repeated at a variable rate of 2 to 6 chirps per second. It is rather quiet, and for many people a bat detector is the best way of locating the males.

Distribution

The bog bush-cricket occurs in suitable habitat through central and northern Europe, but is absent from the south and from northern Scandinavia. It also occurs in temperate Asia. In Britain it has a scattered distribution because of its rather specialised habitat requirements. It is present in heaths of Dorset, Hampshire, Surrey, Sussex, Kent and the south-west peninsula, then more locally northwards to the mosses of Lancashire and Cumbria (e.g. Winmarleigh Moss, Lancashire, and Meathop Moss, Cumbria (Widgery, 2001a)). Its most northerly known location is Aucheninnes (Cloak) Moss, Kirkudbright, Scotland. Formerly under threat from habitat destruction, the habitat has been saved following an intervention by the charity 'Buglife' (Sutton, 2010a). Its most northerly English population is isolated at Wedholme Flow NNR (Sutton, 2008a), and it has a scattered distribution in Wales. In East Anglia it is apparently absent from the Suffolk heaths, but relatively widespread in Norfolk (rediscovered in west Norfolk after gap of more than 50 years (Richmond, via Sutton, 2007b)).

Status and conservation

The bog bush-cricket was presumably much more widely distributed in the past and must have suffered considerably from the loss of wet heath to 'development' and agricultural intensification. However, it is abundant in its remaining strongholds, such as the heaths of Dorset, Surrey and the New Forest. In the longer term, the effects of climate change on these more southerly habitats may pose a serious threat to this, as to other species of lowland damp heaths and bogs.

References: Ragge, 1973; Sutton, 2007d, 2008a, 2010a; Widgery, 2001a.

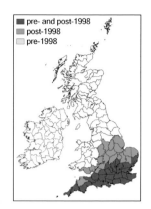

THE LONG-WINGED CONEHEAD

Conocephalus discolor
(Thunberg, 1815)

MEASUREMENTS: Male: 15–22 mm in length; female: 16–22 mm in length.

A   B

FIGS A–B. Male; female.

Description

The long-winged conehead is a rather delicately built species, with a distinctively triangular head (viewed from the side) that explains its vernacular name. Both pairs of wings are fully formed and extend back beyond the tip of the abdomen in both sexes (the hind wings usually projecting a little further back). The pronotum is saddle-shaped and without a median ridge on the dorsal surface. The basal area of the fore wings in males is modified for stridulation. The ovipositor is long, relatively narrow and almost straight, with minute serrations on the dorsal edge. The male cerci are almost straight at the tip.

There are two colour forms. The more common form is green with a dark brown dorsal band on the head and pronotum (and also usually on the abdomen, although this is largely obscured by the wings). This is bordered, at the sides, by a paler, yellowish band that shades into the green of the sides of the head and paranota. The wings are usually pale brown, with a transparent anterior section. The eyes are fawn, sometimes with a pinkish or violet tint, and the legs have tiny grey-black spots.

A minority of specimens have pale brown replacing the green coloration of the body, with darker brown on the dorsal surface of head and pronotum. The incidence of this form varies considerably from population to population (e.g up to 10 per cent of the population in the Plymouth area (Evans & Edmondson, 2007)), and also from year to year. In the south-east, 2009 was exceptionally dry, and this coincided with an apparent increase in numbers of the brown form.

There is also an extra-long-winged form of both sexes of this species, in which the wings reach almost to the tip of the ovipositor in females, and extend well beyond the tip of the abdomen in males. Ragge (1973) reports the discovery

C

D

FIGS C–D. Extra-macropterous form of male and female.

of this form by B. C. Pickard and S. House at Chapman's Pool, Dorset in 1969. This is presumably the first British record of the form, and it coincided with an 'enormous increase' in the size of the population. Simmons & Thomas (2004) found this form to be eight times more frequent in populations at the margin of their (expanding) range than in the core (see Chapter 3 for more detail).

Similar species
The long-winged conehead is much smaller than the great green bush-cricket, and is unlikely to be confused with any other established British species except its close relative, the short-winged conehead.

The short-winged conehead, as its name implies, is brachypterous in its typical form, and so confusion is unlikely. However, there is an uncommon long-winged form of the short-winged conehead which is very similar to C. discolor. In females, the shape of the ovipositor - almost straight in C. discolor, strongly up-curved in C. dorsalis - is the best guide to identification. Males of C. discolor are much more difficult to distinguish from the long-winged form of C. dorsalis. The shapes of the rear dorsal edge of the final abdominal segment and of the male cerci are different in the two species. In C. dorsalis there is a more prominent notched process on the final abdominal plate, and the male cerci narrow abruptly and are slightly up-turned at the tip. The male cerci in C. discolor narrow gradually towards the tip and are straight (see photographs under C. dorsalis, and the Key, Fig K4, page 231).

The songs of the two species are different (see DVD, and account of the following species).

The sickle-bearing bush-cricket (Phaneroptera falcata) has so far only a very tentative foothold in Britain, but could be confused with the long-winged conehead. However, P. falcata is much larger, is covered in tiny black spots, and both male cerci (strongly in-curved in P. falcata) and ovipositor (short, wide and strongly up-curved in P. falcata) are quite distinctive.

The large conehead (Ruspolia nitidula) is currently only doubtfully resident in mainland Britain, but may well become established in future years. It is much larger than the long-winged conehead, has a much more strongly conical head (i.e. the 'forehead' is sharply angled), and is bright green (without the dark brown on head and pronotum).

Life cycle
The cylindrical, buff-coloured eggs measure 6 mm by 1 mm, and are laid singly in plant stems during the summer and autumn. They hatch rather late the following year – in late April or May and into June. They develop through five

FIGS E–G. 4th instar female nymph; 5th instar male nymph; 5th instar female nymph.

nymphal instars to emerge as adults from late July onwards. Both late instar nymphs and adults can be found together at the end of August, and adults persist through October into November in most years.

The nymphs are bright green, with a dark brown to blackish band over the dorsal surface of the head, pronotum and abdominal segments. The up-turned wing stubs are clearly visible in the final two nymphal stages.

Habitat

This species inhabits a wide range of habitats – such as downland, coastal flood defences, conservation strips in agricultural land, roadside verges and unmanaged grassland – with long, coarse grasses, rushes or reeds, often with low scrub. In moist habitats it often coexists with the short-winged conehead, but it is also common in dry grassland, often in association with Roesel's bush-cricket within the geographical range of both species.

Behaviour

Both males and females are active in rank vegetation through the day. They feed on grasses, seed heads and pollen, as well as small invertebrates, including aphids and caterpillars. They can fly but are more likely to descend into the vegetation when disturbed.

H   I

FIGS H–I. Male eating pollen from flower of *Picris echioides*; singing male.

The males sing in long, continuous bursts. The frequency is at the limit of human hearing, and is rather quiet, so for most people a bat detector is the best way of locating singing males. Heard in this way, the song resembles a persistent 'chugging' motor. Singing males are usually evenly spread out in their habitat, although silent ('satellite') males can often be seen close to songsters. The females are attracted to the male song, and courtship begins with prolonged 'fencing' with the antennae, usually with the pair facing one another along the stem of a grass or rush. This is followed by a mutual approach, with male and female on opposite sides of the stem. As they slowly pass one another, the male curves round the tip of his abdomen in an attempt to 'lock' his genitalia onto their counterpart at the tip of the female's abdomen. However, even though she clearly co-operates in this, the pair usually break apart after a few seconds, and the exercise is repeated – with sometime two or more females being involved (see DVD). Numerous 'trial' or 'failed' mating attempts can be observed without full copulation occurring.

Vahed & Gilbert (1996) give the spermatophore in this species as 9.6 per cent of the male body weight. After mating and consumption of the spermatophylax, the female lays her eggs in the stems of a wide range of plants – including reeds, rushes, sedges, coarse grasses, and even bramble. Her usual practice is to hold onto a plant stem while raising the rear part of her abdomen and bending her ovipositor down so that it is roughly at right-angles to her body, with the point close to the surface of the plant stem. She then probes the plant stem with the tip of her ovipositor, often twirling round the stem as she does so, until she finds a weak point that will permit insertion of the ovipositor (see DVD). The eggs are then laid one at a time, although often with several within any stem, lying along the line of the stem. Females spend much of their time in the 'ovipositing mode' testing stems, often paying attention to leaf sheaths, and sometimes resorting to chewing a hole in a tough stem. This again involves prolonged trial and error, with the female often having some difficulty probing with her ovipositor to locate the hole she has chewed.

Distribution

The long-winged conehead is widely distributed in Europe (except the far north), North Africa and temperate Asia. In Britain it was first discovered in 1931, but only recognised as this species (under the name *C. fuscus*) some time later (Blair, 1936). Here it is at the northern limit of its range, and until the mid-1980s was known only from a few southern coastal counties in England. Ragge (1965) reported it from Dorset, Hampshire, Sussex, Kent and the Isle of Wight, and noted that it was 'seldom found far from tidal water'.

However, it began to expand its range beyond these limits during the 1980s – an extension that has accelerated since. It was first recorded from Hertfordshire in 1994, and from neighbouring Essex the following year (Wake, 1997). Widgery (2001b) reported new 10 km-square records from Hampshire and Kent, together with the first reports from Gloucestershire and Oxfordshire in 2001. The first Welsh record was from Cardiff in 1999, followed by Monmouth in 2004, with a report of it as widespread in Monmouthshire by 2007 (Sutton, 2008a). Its northward spread continued in the period from 2000, with new county records from Leicester (2001), Worcestershire and Norfolk (2003) (Sutton, 2004b), and Lincolnshire in 2006 (Sutton, 2007e).

Although the typical form is capable of flight (10–20 metres) (Sutton, 2003a), the extra-long-winged form is believed to have played a key role in its range expansion. (See Chapters 3 and 9 for more detail.)

Status and conservation

As it has spread from its former coastal habitats, this species seems to have become less specialised in its habitat requirements. Where it has become established it is found in almost all suitable habitat. Although many of its habitats are ephemeral, its proven dispersal ability indicates that it is unlikely to be at risk in Britain. It, like Roesel's bush-cricket, has probably been aided in its expansion by a combination of agricultural set-aside and stewardship schemes and a succession of warm summers. Its further spread is likely to be favoured by climate change.

References: Blair, 1936; Marshall, 1974; Ragge, 1965; Ragge, 1973; Simmons & Thomas, 2004; Sutton, 2003a, 2004b, 2007e, 2008a; Wake 1997; Widgery 2001b.

THE SHORT-WINGED CONEHEAD

Conocephalus dorsalis
(Latreille, 1804)

MEASUREMENTS:
Male: 11–15 mm in
length; female: 12–18
mm in length.

A

FIGS A–B. Male;
female.

B

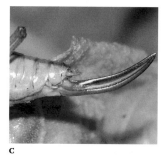

C

FIGS C–D. Ovipositor of female;
female f. *burri*.

D

Description

This small bush-cricket closely resembles its long-winged relative. In the typical
form the wings are short, but of variable length, reaching back over the first
three to five abdominal segments. The basal part of the fore wings is modified
for stridulation in the male. In both sexes the leading section of the fore wing is
transparent, sometimes with a greenish tint. The ovipositor is long, up-curved
and minutely serrated on the dorsal edge. The male cerci narrow abruptly close
to the tip, and the tip is slightly up-turned. The rear edge of the final dorsal plate
of the abdomen has a pronounced median notched projection.

The sides of the head, pronotum, abdomen and legs are green, and there is a
dark brown band running from the top of the head back over the dorsal surface of
the pronotum and abdomen. Often this band shades medially into paler reddish or
violet tints on the dorsal surface of the abdomen, and there is usually a narrow and
indistinct yellowish border between the brown band and the green of the sides of the
body. The ovipositor is pale brown shading to dark brown around the tip. The eyes are
fawn, often with pinkish or lilac tints, and there are tiny grey-black points on the legs.

There is a rare form in which the green coloration is replaced by brown. This
form was reportedly quite common in the females on the south side of Poole
Harbour in 1969 and 1970, although only one male was found (Payne, 1973; Ragge,
1973).

A small minority of specimens are of the long-winged form f. *burri* Ebner. In
this form, the wings extend well beyond the tip of the abdomen – and, in females,
beyond the tip of the ovipositor. The Colchester naturalist W. H. Harwood seems
to have been the first to recognise this form, on 'one hot day' near Clacton-on-Sea,
Essex, in August 1899 (Lucas, 1920; Marshall, 1974). There are also intermediate
forms, in which the wings reach back approximately to the tip of the abdomen.

Similar species

In its typical, brachypterous, form this species is unlikely to be confused with any other. However, the long-winged form f. *burri* could easily be confused with the typical form of the long-winged conehead. The shape of the ovipositor is a useful way of distinguishing the females, and the shape of the cerci and final abdominal plate can be used to distinguish the males. The songs of the males of the two species also differ.

The speckled bush-cricket (*Leptophyes punctatissima*) is also green and brachypterous. However, the body shape is quite different, and the wing stubs much more severely reduced. The shapes of the male cerci and of the ovipositor, too, are quite distinctive. The two species are unlikely to be found in the same habitat.

FIGS E–G. Male cerci: *C. discolor*; *C. dorsalis*, lateral; *C. dorsalis*, dorsal view.

Life cycle

The eggs are pale whitish-buff, elongated flask-shaped, and approximately 5 mm by 0.75 mm. They are laid in the sturdy stems of plants such as marram grass (*A. arenaria*) and sea club-rush (*Bolboschoenus maritimus*). This is where they spend the winter, emerging in late spring or early summer the following year. The resulting nymphs pass through five instars before emerging as adults in late July or August. However, nymphs continue to be seen well into September (and even into October) (Ragge, 1965; B. Pinchen, pers. comm.). August and September are the peak months for the adults, and numbers tail off through October.

The nymphs are green, or yellow-green, with a black or very dark brown band along the dorsal surface of the head, pronotum and abdomen. The up-turned wing stubs are just visible in the final two instars (see Chapter 3, Fig 52).

Habitat

This species is particularly abundant among the rushes, club-rushes, reeds and coarse grasses fringing coastal and estuarine ditches. It also occurs among

FIG H. Early instar nymph.

H

mature tussocks of marram grass (*Ammophila arenaria*) on exposed coastal sand dune systems. However, it can also be found inland in marshy areas in river flood plains and around fresh water ponds and lakes.

Behaviour

The short-winged conehead is omnivorous, feeding on small insects and also on vegetable matter, such as the seeds of rushes and reeds. According to Lucas (1920), it may also be cannibalistic.

When disturbed, the insects swivel round to the opposite side of a plant stem from the intruder, and adopt a posture that flattens the body against the plant stem – with hind legs stretched out behind, fore and mid legs aligned with the stem, and antennae pointing forwards. When slowly circled, they simply move around the stem to maintain their position relative to the observer, a game they seem able to play for quite some time!

They are active during the day. Females spend much of their time basking on the higher leaves of plants, or egg-laying, while the males are engaged in more active movement among the vegetation, or singing. The males stridulate for most of the day, with a song that superficially resembles that of the long-winged conehead. The sound is produced in prolonged, continuous bursts, but the more high-pitched 'chugging' (described as a 'hiss' by those who can hear it without the aid of a bat detector) alternates at irregular intervals with a lower-pitched 'clicking' sound (see DVD). This may be produced by alternately speeding up and slowing down the rate of vibration of the tegmina.

Although they sometimes move around as they stridulate, the males have favoured song perches. They can be seen to exude fluid from the tip of the abdomen and dab it along the surface of a leaf, in what appears to be a scent-marking activity. Singing males can often be seen competing physically for occupation of such a perch, sometimes by an intruder lunging at a defender, or sometimes by an approach that resembles a mating attempt – in which an intruder curves round his abdomen in the direction of his competitor. These interactions usually end very quickly with the retreat of one or other of them, but when two males are competing for the attentions of a female, the conflict can be much more prolonged, with repeated kicking, as well as the 'abdomen-curving' posture (see DVD). This seems to be counterproductive for both combatants, as the female invariably departs.

The females typically switch from basking in late afternoon and become more active, presumably searching for the singing males, although lunges by males at approaching females frequently result in the females' jumping away.

After mating, the females lay their eggs, one at a time, in holes in the stems of water-side plants. They spend a great deal of time chewing the holes, with repeated trials, followed by more chewing until, finally, the hole is large enough for the ovipositor to be inserted fully into it. This performance is slightly different from that of the long-winged conehead, because of the differently shaped ovipositor. In *C. dorsalis*, the ovipositor is lowered and bent round under the abdomen of the female, with the point sticking out. The point is then inserted into the hole in the plant stem, and the ovipositor stretched out from the female's body as she presses the shaft into the plant tissue and moves forwards (see DVD).

Enemies

Their excellent camouflage, and the hide-and-seek response to intruders, suggest adaptation to visual predators – possibly wetland birds such as reed and sedge warblers.

Distribution

Although somewhat localised because of its habitat requirements, this species is widespread through most of Europe, but absent from the south and far north.

The British distribution of the short-winged conehead seems to have remained stable until a significant extension of range began in the 1990s. Ragge's (1965) distribution maps show a mainly southern and south-eastern pattern, with records from the southern coastal counties, the south-west peninsula, including the Somerset Levels, and East Anglia. At that time, the range extended to west and north Wales, and, in the east, as far north as south Yorkshire, with a majority of records within a few kilometres of the coast. This pattern is retained in the maps prepared by the UK Biological Records Centre (BRC), using records collected up to mid-1988, and published in Marshall & Haes (1988). A subsequent atlas (Haes & Harding, 1997) showed a large increase in inland records, especially from central southern England. The authors note that this partly reflects past under-recording, but state that the species is 'certainly spreading in the vicinity of the Thames Valley and Hertfordshire'. This expansion into new areas in the south was confirmed by reports to Widgery, (2000b, 2001a), with a further extension to mainland west Cornwall (Haes, via Widgery, 2000c). This has been followed by a significant northward extension into Lancashire (2002 and 2005) (Sutton, 2005a; Smith & Newton, 2007), Cumbria (2006) (Sutton, 2007d), Leicestershire, Derbyshire and North Fife, in Scotland by 2009 (Sutton, 2010b). It has also been recorded from south-west Ireland.

Interestingly, the recently noted extension of range has not been accompanied by reports of increased numbers of the long-winged form, f. burri.

Status and conservation

Many of the habitats of this species are quite ephemeral, but partly as a result of human activity in maintaining flood defences and managing drainage ditches and ponds, suitable conditions are regularly reproduced. As many of its sites are quite isolated, it presumably has good powers of local dispersal, although it is unclear how this is achieved.

References: Haes & Harding, 1997; Lucas, 1920; Marshall, 1974; Marshall & Haes, 1988; Payne, 1973; Ragge, 1965, 1973; Smith & Newton, 2007; Sutton, 2005a, 2007d, 2010b; Widgery, 2000b, 2000c, 2001a.

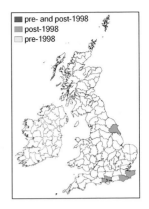

THE SICKLE-BEARING BUSH-CRICKET

Phaneroptera falcata
(Poda, 1761)

MEASUREMENTS: Male and female: 12–18 mm in length.

FIGS A–C. Male;
male dorsal view;
female.

Description

This relatively large bush-cricket is rather delicately built, with long thin legs, and very long wings. The fore wings reach back well beyond the tip of the abdomen, and the hind wings are significantly longer. The male cerci are long and upcurved, while the ovipositor is short, broad and strongly up-curved. The ground colour of the body and legs is pale yellowish green, with fine black speckles. The green shades to white on the ventral surface of the abdomen, and the face, too, is greenish white. The upper part of the eyes is red-brown, and the rear margin of the pronotum and rear edge of the wings are often also of this tint. There are two darker patches on the stridulatory apparatus on the male fore wing, and the dorsal surface of the abdomen (normally covered by the wings when at rest) shades from green to purple. The hearing organ at the base of the fore tibiae is very noticeable (see Chapter 1, Fig 9).

Similar species

The great green bush-cricket (*Tettigonia viridissima*) is also mainly green, fully winged and relatively long-bodied. However, that species is much more robust in appearance, lacks black spots on the body, and has a very differently shaped ovipositor (long and straight in *viridissima*) and male cerci (gently incurved in *viridissima*). The marked difference in length between fore wings (tegmina) and hind wings in *P. falcata* is also quite distinctive.

The long-winged conehead (*Conocephalus discolor*) is much smaller, and it, too, has very differently shaped ovipositor and male cerci.

The southern sickle-bearing bush-cricket (*Phaneroptera nana*) is very similar. The hind legs are thinner than those of *P. falcata*, and the side plates of the pronotum (paranota) are longer than deep (deeper than long in *P. nana*). However, *P. nana* has no known breeding colonies in Britain, and is an occasional accidental import only (e.g. a plant nursery in Nottinghamshire in 2007 (Sutton, 2008a)).

Life cycle

The eggs are laid between the surfaces of leaves. Adults emerge in July and last until October. In Britain August to September seems to be the peak period for finding the adults.

Habitat

P. falcata is regarded as an inhabitant of dry tall grassland and scrub on the mainland of Europe. The only currently known British population is confined to a substantial stand of rose-bay willowherb (*Chamerion angustifolium*) with a small tree in its midst, and some low bramble nearby and on an adjacent south-facing slope. The habitat is shared with *Conocephalus discolor*, *Pholidoptera griseoaptera* and *Chorthippus parallelus*.

Behaviour

The adults bask for brief periods on the higher leaves of the willowherb in sunshine, but retreat to the lower vegetation in cool weather. They rely greatly on their camouflage for protection, and move rather gingerly and deliberately through the vegetation. When seriously disturbed they can fly some distance and are then quite difficult to re-locate. The long back legs are stretched out and trail behind them when in flight.

The males sing from mid-afternoon into the night, the song being variously described as 'a faint tss tss tss' (Burr, 1936) and 'tzpp tzpp tzpp' (Evans & Edmondson, 2007). According to Ragge & Reynolds (1998) the calling song consists of single syllables repeated at irregular intervals, or, sometimes, more regularly at a rate of 1 to 4 per second. There is also a longer song consisting of 8 to 20 syllables. *Phaneroptera* seems to be unique in that the song is produced only during the opening strokes of the fore wings (Ragge & Reynolds, 1998).

History

This species is widespread in Europe north of the Mediterranean area, and its range extends eastwards through Turkey and central Asia to China and Japan. Despite occasional reports of single specimens, most commentators have not considered it to be a breeding species in Britain. However, Lucas (1920) reported two specimens that had been collected in Cornwall (in 1881 and 1884),

FIG D. Habitat: the only known locality in Britain.

D

and considered there was 'a chance' of it being included as a British species 'if some enterprising entomologist will search the Land's End district at the end of Summer' (Lucas, 1920: 199). Burr (1936) and Ragge (1965) both mention the Cornish records, and Ragge also mentions a 'dubious' sighting from Dorset. One 'enterprising entomologist', R. M. Payne, did follow Lucas's suggestion, and searched for the species in Cornwall without success (Payne, 1969).

However, the species has been extending its range in mainland Europe for several decades, and prior to its discovery in England had made 'spectacular' gains of territory in the Netherlands (Sutton, 2006b; Kleukers, 2002; Kleukers & Krekels, 2004).

Single individuals were reported in 2004 (from Yorkshire) and in 2006 (from Hampshire) but are presumed to be migrants or accidental introductions.

The first confirmed breeding colony in Britain was discovered by a group including P. Hodge, M. Edwards, G. Collins and A. Phillips at Hastings Country Park, in East Sussex on 11 August 2006 (Collins *et al.*, 2007; Sutton, 2006b). As many as 20 nymphs and adults were found in a patch of rose-bay willowherb at the corner of a rough, sloping meadow overlooking the sea. The presence of nymphs indicates that breeding had taken place at the site, implying that the species must have been present at least since the previous year. Visits to the site in subsequent years (2007, 2008) confirmed the survival of this breeding colony, but it is unclear whether it still survives.

However, there have been several reports of single specimens – either presumed migrants, or, just possibly, new colonists: one male, B. Pinchen, Hampshire, 2006 (Sutton, 2006b); one female (possibly of the closely related *P. nana*), Dungeness, 2009 (Sutton, 2010a); and one male, Humber estuary, east Yorkshire, 2010 (Sutton, 2010b). Also three nymphs were found in imported plants in Derbyshire (Sutton, 2007b).

Status and conservation
Repeated sightings of individuals of this species, together with its apparently successful breeding here for several years at one site, suggest that it is likely to establish itself in this country in the near future. In mainland Europe it appears not to be a habitat specialist and it flies readily, so there is no obvious reason why it should not spread to other localities in Britain.

References: Burr, 1936; Collins et al., 2007; Evans & Edmondson, 2007; Harz, 1969; Kleukers, 2002; Kleukers & Krekels, 2004; Lucas, 1920; Marshall & Haes, 1988; Payne, 1969; Ragge, 1965; Ragge & Reynolds, 1998; Sutton, 2006b, 2007b, 2008a, 2010a, 2010b.

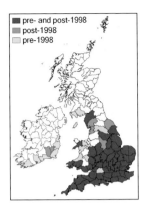

THE SPECKLED BUSH-CRICKET
Leptophyes punctatissima
(Bosc, 1792)

MEASUREMENTS: Male: 9–16 mm in length; female: 11–18 mm in length.

FIG A–D. Male; female; dorsal male; dorsal female showing wing-stubs.

Description

This small to medium-sized bush-cricket has a smoothly saddle-shaped pronotum, and long, spindly legs. The wings are greatly reduced to small flaps in both sexes. In the male, the wing-stubs overlap and are clearly modified for stridulation. In the female they are smaller, and project, side by side, behind the pronotum. The ovipositor is broad and scimitar-shaped, with minute serrations on both edges towards the tip. The male cerci are long and in-curved. The ground colour is pale green, densely flecked with tiny black spots (hence its vernacular name). The green shades paler towards the yellowish ventral surface. The male wing stubs are yellow-brown, as are the cerci, and there are similarly coloured patches on the pronotum. The tibiae and the eyes also tend to yellow-brown, and sometimes have a deeper, reddish tint. There is a dark band along the dorsal surface of the abdomen that varies from brown to violet-purple.

The female is similarly coloured except that the broad dorsal band on the abdomen is replaced in her case by a fine median yellow-brown (or violet) line. Her wing stubs are green with pale brown rear margins. The ovipositor is green with dark red-brown edging towards the tip. Both sexes have a yellow line along each edge of the dorsal surface of the pronotum (sometimes broken in the middle).

Similar species

Only two other British bush-crickets are green and brachypterous. One is the southern oak bush-cricket (*Meconema meridionale*). However, that species lacks the minute black spots, and has a yellow median line along its dorsal surface. The shape of the ovipositor also clearly distinguishes the females (long, narrow and gently up-curved in *M. meridionale*, short, broad and more strongly up-curved in *L. punctatissima*).

The other is the short-winged conehead (*Conocephalus dorsalis*). However, this species also lacks the black speckles of *L. punctatissima*, and, although usually brachypterous, has much less drastically reduced wings than *L. punctatissima*. The shapes of the male cerci and of the ovipositor are quite distinctive. *C. dorsalis* is unlikely to be found in the same habitat as *L. punctatissima*.

Nymphs of *L. punctatissima* could be confused with those – especially in the early instars – of the great green bush-cricket (*Tettigonia viridissima*), which often have black speckles on legs, abdomen and pronotum. However, the body shape of *T. viridissima* nymphs is more elongate, and the antennae are more or less uniformly brown (with strongly contrasting narrow bands of black and pale yellow-green in *L. punctatissima* nymphs).

Life cycle

The eggs are flat and ovoid in shape, approximately 1.5 mm by 3 mm. They are laid in the bark of trees or shrubs, or, where the bark is tough, in crevices. The nymphs emerge in May or early June and pass through six instars, before reaching adulthood from late July onwards. The adults persist into October, and even November in some years. In cooler parts of its range, the eggs undergo a double diapause, and the full life cycle takes two years (Deura & Hartley, 1982).

The nymphs are pale green, with quite prominent black spots on the body and legs. The antennae have distinctive alternating bands of black and pale yellow-green. The wing pads are visible in the final nymphal instar. The nymphs can often be seen sunning themselves on leaves of bramble or other low vegetation. They feed mainly on herbaceous plant species such as wood sage, dog's mercury, nettles and golden rod in the early instars, initially grazing on leaf cuticle, but later biting small holes in the leaf lamina and so leaving a distinctive feeding pattern. With maturity they migrate to higher vegetation and their diet shifts to tougher foliage, especially the leaves of bramble (Hall, Ash, Robinson, pers. comm.).

E

F

G

H

FIGS E–H. 1st instar nymph; 5th instar female nymph; 6th instar male nymph; 6th instar female nymph.

Habitat

This species inhabits trees and shrubs at various heights. Hedgerows, bramble patches, woodland edges and gardens may all be occupied. Although it may be found on a very wide range of woody plants, there is a strong association with bramble. A longstanding research project conducted by P. Ash, M. Hall and D. Robinson focused on this species has provided much new information on both its ecology and behaviour.

Behaviour

The adults are mainly vegetarian, feeding on the leaves of various plants. On sunny days they may be seen basking on open vegetation, especially on the upper surface of bramble leaves. The song of the male is a very quiet and high-pitched short chirp, which is repeated at variable intervals. Even at close quarters this is barely audible, and use of a bat detector enables detection of many more singing individuals. Modified by this device, the sound is a very brief 'tic'. They sing from vegetation at a wide range of heights above the ground – from 1.5 metres up to 14 metres in trees (Robinson *et al.*, 2009). Most frequently they sing from deep within foliage, but they will often walk around on exposed branches and leaves while singing. Singing males can be detected in this way at almost any time during the day, but they become more active from mid-afternoon onwards into the night.

The subfamily Phaneropterinae, to which this species belongs, is unusual in that receptive females respond to the male calling song with a song of their own. In *L. punctatissima*, this resembles that of the male, but without amplification it is even less audible to humans. The female response must occur within a very narrow 'time window' of 20 to 50 milliseconds. Allowing for the time the male song takes to reach the 'ear' of the female, her physiological processing of her response and the return of her stridulation to the male, the maximum distance across which effective communication can take place is approximately three metres (Heller & von Helversen, 1986; Robinson, 1980; Robinson *et al.*, 1990). On hearing an appropriately timed response from a

FIG 1. Male, showing tibial 'ears'.

I

female, the male increases his chirp rate, and by call and response he orientates himself to her location and moves towards her (Kostarakos *et al.*, 2007, Ofner *et al.*, 2007, Rheinlaender *et al.*, 2007, Zimmerman *et al.*, 1989. See Chapters 2 and 5 for more detail).

Mating generally takes place in the canopy, with the female mounting the male following antennal contact. The spermatophore is relatively small (approximately 4 per cent of the male body weight (Vahed & Gilbert, 1996). Following mating, the female consumes the spermatophore, taking some 30 minutes to do so, then descends to lower branches for oviposition (see Chapter 6, Fig 113). The eggs are laid at night, and are stuck to the substrate with a gum secreted by the female. Egg-laying sites at heights between 90 and 120 cm above the ground are usually chosen. Multiply-mated females lay more eggs than those with just one mating. This is not a function of how many spermatophores are consumed, and may be a consequence either of the female acquiring insufficient sperm at a single mating to fertilise all her eggs, or of stimulants transferred in the male ejaculate (Vahed, 2003b).

Enemies
There are four species of bats in Britain that forage by picking insects from vegetation at night. A legacy of predation by bats and other acoustically orienting predators may explain the extremely brief and relatively infrequent chirps emitted by this species as it moves through the vegetation (Robinson, 1990).

Distribution
This species is widespread through Europe, including southern Scandinavia, extending eastwards to the former Soviet Union.

In Britain it is common and widespread south of a line from the Wash to the Bristol Channel, including the south-west peninsula. Further north it has a more scattered distribution in England, but there are reports from south-western Scotland, the Isle of Man, western coastal districts of Wales, and in southern and eastern coastal areas of Ireland.

Status and Conservation
This is a common species and in many areas of southern Britain it is ubiquitous in gardens and hedgerows.

References: Deura & Hartley, 1982; Hartley & Robinson, 1976; Harz, 1969; Heller & von Helversen, 1986; Kostarakos et al., 2007; Offner et al., 2007; Rheinlaender et al., 2007; Robinson, 1980, 1990; Robinson, et al., 1986, 2009; Vahed, 2003b; Zimmerman et al., 1989.

FAMILY GRYLLIDAE: THE CRICKETS

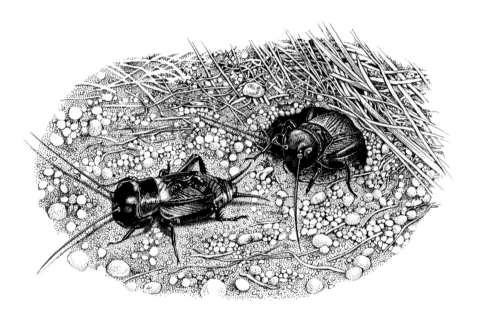

Field crickets (© Tim Bernhard)

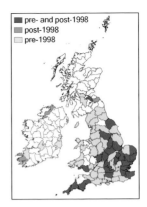

THE HOUSE CRICKET

Acheta domesticus
(Linnaeus, 1758)

MEASUREMENTS: Male: 14–20 mm in length; female: 14–18 mm in length.

FIG A–D. Male lateral; male dorsal; female lateral; female dorsal.

Description

Both sexes are fully winged, with the tegmina reaching back approximately to the tip of the abdomen in the female, and somewhat shorter in the male. The male tegmina are modified for stridulation. In both sexes the longer hind wings, when folded, project back well beyond the tip of the abdomen (and beyond the tip of the ovipositor in the female). Both sexes have long, straight tapering cerci that point back beyond the tip of the abdomen. The ovipositor is also long, straight and narrow, pointing directly back from the tip of the female abdomen.

The ground colour is pale fawn-brown, with dark brown patches and markings especially on the head and pronotum. The dark brown areas form lateral bands on the head. The dorsal areas of the tegmina are also tinted darker brown than the ground colour.

Similar species

There are two species that are commonly kept as food for reptiles or other exotic pets:

(1) The Jamaican Field Cricket (or 'brown' or 'silent' cricket), *Gryllus assimilis*. This is very similar to *A. domesticus*, but the dark markings on the head run longitudinally, rather than laterally.
(2) The Tropical House Cricket, *Gryllodes supplicans*. This species has short wings, especially in the female, and the cerci in both sexes are very long. In the female, they are longer than the ovipositor.

Life cycle

Given appropriate conditions, they reproduce continuously, so that all stages in the life cycle may be seen at any time of year. The eggs are white and cylindrical, about 2.5 mm by 0.5 mm. They are laid singly or in clusters loosely in the soil, and each female may lay several hundred eggs.

The eggs usually hatch in two or three weeks, but take longer at low temperatures. The resulting nymphs may develop to adulthood in as few as seven instars, but may pass through twelve or more. Development takes from three to eight months, depending on temperature and availability of food. The nymphs are similar to the adults in colour.

Habitat

In Britain house crickets are found almost exclusively in association with human settlements. Formerly they could be found in a range of habitats such as private homes, rubbish dumps, bakeries, hotel and restaurant kitchens, farm out-houses and factories – anywhere that offered a combination of winter warmth and scraps of food. They need artificial warmth during the winter, but in summer can live in habitats such as hedgerows, gardens and allotments. Precautions against rats, mice and cockroaches have eliminated them from many former sites.

Behaviour

The males sing mainly in the evening or at night, with a high-pitched, repeated chirp.

There is also a distinct courtship stridulation, which is softer and interspersed with 'clicks' like those of the courting male field cricket. The female mounts the male to mate, and he transfers a spermatophore to her.

They are omnivorous scavengers, consuming decaying vegetable matter and scraps of food waste. As Gilbert White noted: 'These crickets are not only very thirsty, but very voracious; for they will eat the scummings of pots, and yeast, salt, and crumbs of bread; and in any kitchen offal or sweepings.' (White, 1971 [1789]: 246)

They can be active during the day, and are able to fly. Again, on White's account: 'In the summer we have observed them to fly, when it became dusk, out of the windows, and over the neighbouring roofs. This feat of activity accounts for the sudden manner in which they often leave their haunts, as it does for the method by which they come to houses where they were not known before.'

Although unable to survive British winters, there are numerous reports of house crickets singing outdoors, with possible temporary colonisation of crevices in walls or pavements and domestic gardens (Gardiner, 2005, 2006a, 2007a).

Enemies

The main enemy of the house cricket seems to be our contemporary concern with hygiene, but it is possible that competition with other commensals of human habitation, such as the house mouse and brown rat, have contributed to its demise.

White describes other threats: 'Cats catch hearth-crickets, and, playing with them as they do with mice, devour them. Crickets may be destroyed, like wasps, by phials half-filled with beer or any liquid, and set in their haunts; for, being always eager to drink, they will crowd in till the bottles are full.' (White, 1971 [1789]: 247)

History

Although the species is now cosmopolitan in distribution, its origin was probably in dry areas of north Africa and south-west Asia (Ragge, 1965). One view is that it may have been brought back to Britain by Crusaders in the 13th century (Kevan, 1955; Marshall, 1974), but it was certainly here by the 16th century (Moffet, 1634). Forster (1770) included it in his list of British species, and, as we saw, it figures in Gilbert White's *Natural History of Selborne* (1971 [1789]). Given its close association with human habitation, it is not surprising that the house cricket (or 'cricket on the hearth') figured in poetry and folk lore. White quotes Milton's *Il Penseroso*: 'Far from all resort of mirth, save the cricket on the hearth.' He also refers to it as 'the housewife's barometer', foretelling rain, but also good or ill luck.

In Dickens's *The Cricket on the Hearth*, the house cricket symbolises and mediates the relations between the humans in the story: 'And it's sure to bring us good fortune, John! It always has done so. To have a cricket on the hearth is the luckiest thing in all the world!' (2004 [1845]). However, as some of the less savoury characters in Dickens' story indicate, and White's recipes for destroying them also suggest, the house cricket was not universally loved.

Lucas (1920) notes that not many British records of this species are 'to hand', and speculates that this may be owing to most entomologists' thinking that so common an insect does not need to be recorded. However, Lucas's view was that the species was undoubtedly declining at that time, possibly being displaced by the cockroach.

Burr (1936) refers to an inquest that came before the East Cheshire coroner in 1934, when '... it was officially stated that the sanitary inspector to Hale U.D.C. had been driven by crickets to desperation and suicide' (p. 121).

Pickard (1954) thought it 'not so common now as formerly'. Marshall & Haes (1988) comment on the loss of habitat owing to redevelopment of rubbish tips, the loss of many bakeries, and the use of insecticides such as DDT as responsible for a further decline in this species.

Distribution

There are historic records from almost all the English counties, as well as parts of Scotland, Wales and Ireland. The current distribution map shows it to be still widespread, although undoubtedly much less common than it once was.

Recent reports include its presence in manure heaps, a former landfill site, and along old railway track in Cambridgeshire (reported in Sutton, 2006b), a waste recycling plant in Pitsea, Essex (2009), manure heaps at West Stowe, Suffolk in 2002, and a pet-food factory in Suffolk in 2010 (A. Kettle, D. Underwood, pers. corr.)

Status and conservation

The house cricket is almost certainly an introduced species, once common and widespread, but now quite rarely found except for populations bred as food for reptiles. It seems likely that many of the frequent reports of new colonies of this species result from accidental or deliberate release of such captive populations.

References: Baldock, 1999; Burr, 1936; Dickens, 2004 [1845]; Forster, 1770; Gardiner, 2005, 2006a, 2007a; Kevan, 1955; Marshall, 1974; Marshall & Haes, 1988; Moffet, 1634; Pickard, 1954; Ragge, 1965; Sutton, 2006b; White, 1971 [1789].

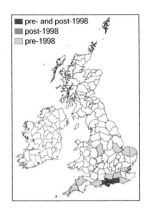

pre- and post-1998
post-1998
pre-1998

THE FIELD CRICKET

Gryllus campestris
(Linnaeus, 1758)

MEASUREMENTS:
Male and female: 18–23
mm in length.

A

FIGS A–B. Male; female.

B

Description

Both sexes have large, shiny rounded heads. The eyes and long antennae are dark brown to black. The fore and rear edges of the smoothly saddle-shaped pronotum are approximately parallel, giving a rectangular appearance when viewed from above. The fore wings reach back towards the tip of the abdomen, leaving 3-4 abdominal segments exposed, and fold down at the sides. Both fore wings (tegmina) of the male are modified for stridulation, with a clear area (the harp and mirror) on each, which augments the sound. There are two rows of spines on each hind tibia. Both sexes have long tapering cerci, and the female has a long, needle-shaped ovipositor.

The colour of head, pronotum and abdomen is black. The legs, too, are mainly black, although the hind tibiae may be dark red-brown. The tegmina are also brown, but with a yellow band across the base. This is most clearly marked in the male. Parts of the body, especially the sides of the abdomen, often have minute hairs that shine golden.

Similar species

No other native species is remotely similar. However, a close relative, the southern field cricket (*Gryllus bimaculatus*), occurs naturally further south in Europe and is occasionally introduced into Britain. Although any resulting populations appear to be short-lived, they may still cause confusion. In the southern field cricket, the hind wings are fully developed, and when at rest they are folded and reach back to a point well beyond the tip of the abdomen in both sexes. In addition, the tegmina of the male *G. bimaculatus* are relatively longer than those of *G. campestris*, reaching to the tip of the abdomen, or almost so. The wings of *G. bimaculatus* are also darker in colour, especially in the female.

Life cycle

The eggs are laid during June in soil, either on bare ground or among tufts of short grasses. They hatch a few weeks later, by mid-July, and the nymphs congregate on bare patches of ground through their first three instars – presumably because warmth is important for their rapid development. In their early stages they are believed to feed on fungi and small plant fragments, graduating to tougher plant material as they develop. In the sixth instar, reached by mid-August, the nymphs begin to establish their own burrows. This is done by digging with the large mandibles, and passing the sand or soil back by kicks of their legs. According to Ragge (1965) the burrows are as much as 20 mm in length, and usually have a sharp bend near the entrance. Development continues through the rest of the summer, and winter is usually spent in the tenth

C   D

FIGS C–D. 10th instar nymph; nymph entering its burrow.

(penultimate) nymphal instar. At this stage (see illustration) up-turned wing stubs are present, and, in females, the ovipositor is also just visible. Parts of the body, especially the dorsal surface of the abdomen, have a fine golden pubescence. Field crickets apparently may be seen foraging on mild winter days, but become fully active again in March or April. The ovipositor of the female becomes visible following the first spring moult, and the final moult, from which the fully adult insect emerges, takes place in mid-May.

Habitat

The field cricket requires warm, sunny conditions if it is to complete its annual life cycle in southern Britain, and its known sites have accordingly been open, south-facing but sheltered slopes, with areas of bare ground and short vegetation. Both over-wintering nymphs and adults dig burrows, and so require a loose, sandy or chalk soil substrate. They are vulnerable to shading out of their habitat by succession to scrub, but, in a few sites, colonies have survived in woodland that has been regularly clear-felled. Grazing by rabbits, or by sheep or cattle at appropriate stocking levels, seems to be essential to maintain sufficiently short turf.

Behaviour

Last instar nymphs chew hollow, boat-shaped 'platforms' at the entrance to their burrows and also establish 'runs' through adjacent grass tufts. The presence of droppings is an indication that a platform and its burrow are occupied. The males generally sing from the platform outside a burrow, but sometimes will sing from the cover of a nearby run. The song, as with other crickets, is produced by rubbing the right tegmen over the left, and is a pure-toned repetitive chirp. Although each

FIG E. Male producing 'courtship song' in contact with a female.

E

chirp is brief, it is repeated several times per second (usually 3–4), and when numerous individuals are singing simultaneously ('chorusing'), the effect is of an almost continuous sound, resembling the stridulation of cicadas. The song is produced during both day and night, but sometimes ceases in the middle of very hot days. The females, too, live in burrows, and emerge to wander about, feeding on grasses and seed heads of various kinds, as well as to approach singing males and to search for suitable sites for egg-laying.

The calling song of the male attracts females, which enter the platform area. Sometimes this results in a very speedy change on the part of the male from the calling song to a more subdued, repeated metallic 'click'. This is produced while he faces away from the female who, while probing him with her antennae, climbs onto his back. He meanwhile wriggles from side to side excitedly, and mating takes place. During this, a small white spermatophore is transferred to the female. This can be seen just below the base of her ovipositor (see DVD). However, on other occasions, male and female seem to spend extended periods of time together, sometimes motionless near the burrow entrance, sometimes moving in and out of the entrance. These periods are interspersed with persistent courtship activity on the part of the male, repeatedly edging, rear end first, towards the female, while making either the calling or courtship notes. In this mode, the females often retreat into a nearby 'run' among the grass stems, the male following on closely. The impression given is that male and female may cohabit in a burrow for substantial periods of time, with repeated matings or mating attempts on the part of the male. Edwards *et al.* (1996) reported instances of males using coercion to keep females in their burrows, and getting mauled by the females in return. However females often enter the burrows of males without any sign of coercion (pers. obs.). Formerly it was supposed that males were territorial, and would defend their burrow against other males. However, Edwards *et al.* demonstrated that individual crickets move frequently between burrows, and also dig new ones during the breeding season. Although they are not territorial, males can show aggression when they encounter one another. They may produce a more extended version of the calling chirp, and threaten one another with their large mandibles. Actual physical conflict may ensue, but usually neither male sustains injury. The adults emerge about the middle of May, and continue until the end of July or even early August. However, mating and egg-laying are mainly performed in the latter part of May and through June.

Enemies

During their research, Edwards *et al.* found two nymphs that had been attacked but then left by predators. In one of these examples there were bird bill feathers, suggesting that the insects were distasteful.

History

The field cricket was described by Thomas Moffet (1658, cited in Marshall, 1974), who noted the mechanism of its singing, and its habit of living in burrows. He also described a method of drawing it from its burrow by putting a tethered ant down the hole, but preferred the simpler technique, described later by White, and still used, of putting a twig or grass stem into the burrow and gently withdrawing it. Lucas (1920) included reports of this species from Devon and Cornwall, Norfolk and north Staffordshire, but expressed doubts about two Scottish reports. However, even at that time, it seems that the distribution of the field cricket was largely limited to the counties of Hampshire, Surrey and Sussex. Even here, he regarded it as 'very rare and local'. Gilbert White (1971 [1789]) regarded the insect as 'frequent in these parts', but also noted that it was not common in other counties (Letter XLVI). White's vivid descriptions of the habitat and behaviour of the field cricket have served to make it a well-known British insect – albeit one that is seldom encountered directly. Pickard (1954) added south Lincolnshire to the list of counties from which the field cricket had been reported, but Ragge (1965) commented that it was 'rapidly becoming one of our rarest Orthoptera', with flourishing colonies known only from south Hampshire, West Sussex and Surrey. Marshall (1974) reported several failed attempts to find the insect at sites where it had formerly been abundant, concluding that only two known breeding populations survived: one, near Arundel (discovered in 1956) and another, in West Sussex, discovered in 1971. The species was listed in Schedule 5 of the Wildlife and Countryside Act, 1981. Haes (1987) noted that there may have been a colony near Salisbury, in Wiltshire, up to the end of the 1960s, but confirmed the loss of all but two known colonies. One of these, on the chalk (presumably near Arundel) was reported as small and unmonitored. The other, on greensand, might produce over 100 singing males in warm years, but fewer than 30 in a cold one such as 1977.

In 1991, English Nature launched a 'species recovery programme', short-listing a small number of species for urgent conservation action on the basis of their impending extinction, their potential to recover given conservation measures, and their attractiveness to humans. Initially field crickets were not included, but survey work in 1991 demonstrated that they had not been seen for some years on one of their presumed sites, and were present in much smaller numbers than had been thought at the other. This led to the subsequent inclusion of the species in the 'target' list for urgent action (Edwards, et al., 1996). The introduction of an appropriate management regime at the remaining site, together with a captive breeding programme undertaken by the Invertebrate Conservation Centre, London Zoo, and reintroduction at a small number of sites within its historic range has so far yielded positive results, with three populations now well established (Edwards, 2008).

Distribution
The species is widespread in mainland Europe, south to North Africa, and east to the Caucasus and west Asia. However, it is much more localised than formerly in Europe, especially towards its northern limits (Kleukers & Krekels, 2004). As recounted above this long term trend of decline is also true of the British population, possibly as a result of a combination of climatic conditions and habitat loss. It has persisted in only one site, in Sussex, but there are now at least three surviving colonies at nearby re-introduction sites. There is also a plan to increase the area of its last native site (Edwards, pers. comm).

Status and conservation
It was assigned the highest conservation priority (in *British Red Data Books: 2*) by Haes (in Shirt, 1987). Thanks to the timely conservation work begun in 1991, and the co-operation of landowners, it now seems that this species is no longer in immediate danger of extinction. However, its future does depend on continued appropriate management of its small number of habitats. Edwards *et al.* (1996) note that for such a large insect to complete its life cycle in one year in the British climate requires favourable weather in spring and summer. Haes's report on annual fluctuations in numbers at one of its remaining sites through the 1970s supports the view of Edwards *et al.* that its remaining populations may undergo 'boom-and-bust' cycles in response to variations in weather from year to year. Local extinctions of isolated populations may have resulted from inclement weather through a succession of seasons, with no nearby populations to re-colonise the habitat.

References: Edwards, 2008; Edwards et al., 1996; Harz, 1969; Kleukers & Krekels, 2004; Lucas, 1920; Marshall, 1974; Ragge, 1965; Shirt, 1987; White, 1971 [1789].

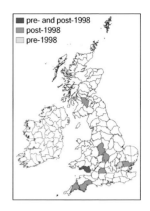

THE SOUTHERN FIELD CRICKET
Gryllus bimaculatus
(De Geer, 1773)

MEASUREMENTS: Male 19–23 mm in length; female 17–22 mm in length.

A

B

C

D

FIG A–D. Male dorsal; male lateral; female dorsal; female lateral.

Description
The head, pronotum and abdomen are black, as are the mouthparts, eyes and antennae. The legs are black, with variable amounts of reddish coloration. There are two rows of spines on the hind tibiae. Head and pronotum are approximately equal in width, and the pronotum is parallel sided, with a slightly wavy hind margin, especially in the female. The hind wings are long in both sexes – significantly projecting beyond the tip of the abdomen when furled. The tegmina are folded down over the sides of the abdomen. Both sexes have long cerci that curve outwards slightly. The ovipositor is straight and markedly longer than the cerci. The tegmina are black in the female, and dark brown in the male, with yellow towards the base – often reduced to a yellow patch on each tegmen.

Similar species
The field cricket (*G. campestris*) is very similar, but has shorter wings, not reaching the tip of the abdomen. The tegmina are paler in females of *G. campestris*.

Life cycle
In captivity it is continuously brooded, but in its natural habitat the adults emerge much later than those of the field cricket (*G. campestris*), and can be seen from July to September. The nymphs are pale fawn-brown, with dark brown to black markings, especially on head and pronotum. The dorsal surface of the abdomen is suffused blackish. In the final two nymphal instars the wing stubs are inverted, and in female nymphs the ovipositor can then be seen (see Chapter 3, Fig 55).

Habitat
Fabre (1917) says it does not burrow but lives in piles of rotting grass. According to Bellmann & Luquet (2009) it lives on the ground, taking shelter under crevices, stones and fragments of wood.

Distribution
It is present in all the French departments along the coast of the Mediterranean, west through the Iberian peninsula, and east into Greece. It is local, but sometimes abundant in dune habitats in France (Bellmann & Luquet, 2009).

In Britain there are occasional reports of short-lived colonies, presumably derived from crickets kept as food for reptiles. A colony was discovered in allotments near Epping, in Essex, by Mark Hanson (Sutton, 2006b). Another was reported from Chelmsford in 2008 (Sutton, 2008a).

Status and conservation

The current European distribution of this species remains close to the Mediterranean coast and it seems likely that climatic conditions will preclude its establishing a permanent population here.

References: Bellmann & Luquet, 2009; Fabre, 1917; Sutton, 2006b, 2008a.

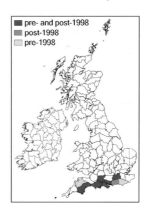

THE WOOD CRICKET
Nemobius sylvestris
(Bosc, 1792)

MEASUREMENTS: Male: 6.7–8.0 mm in length; female: 7.7–9.0 mm in length.

FIGS A–C. Male;
male dorsal view;
female.

Description

Both sexes are very small. The head is rounded and approximately as wide as the smoothly saddle-shaped pronotum (which looks broadly rectangular when viewed from above). The body is rather flattened dorso-ventrally, and both sexes have long, tapering cerci. The hind wings are absent, and the fore wings (tegmina) are short, but especially so in the female. The tegmina of the male reach back to cover roughly half of the abdomen, and are folded down at the sides. They are modified for stridulation, with the right tegmen overlapping the left when at rest. The female's tegmina are reduced to very short stubs projecting back from the rear edge of the pronotum. The ovipositor is long, straight and needle-shaped, as is typical in crickets. There is a double row of spines on the hind tibiae, and there are fine, long black hairs sparsely distributed on the body, especially on the hind margins of the abdominal segments and around the edges of the pronotum.

The colour is a somewhat variable mixture of pale fawn and dark brown. The pronotum is often predominantly fawn with darker brown patches, while the abdominal segments tend to be predominantly dark brown in the males, and patterned dark and pale brown in the females. The wing stubs in the female have the veins outlined in dark brown. In both sexes the head is dark brown and the antennae are black. The head has a distinctive diamond-shaped cream marking. The legs are mottled dark and pale brown, often with reddish tints on the hind femora.

Similar species

The small size, distinctive habitat and the presence of reduced wings distinguish the wood cricket from all other British species. The only species comparable in size and general colouration is the scaly cricket, but this is wingless, and is exceedingly unlikely to be found in the woodland haunts of the wood cricket.

Life cycle

In Britain this species takes two years to complete its life cycle. Eggs laid in summer or in autumn enter a resting stage through the winter. They hatch in spring or early summer the following year, and the resulting nymphs pass through their first five or six instars by autumn, when they enter another period of arrested development through the winter (although they do not hibernate, as they are reported to be active on mild winter days (B. Pinchen, pers. comm.)). They become fully active in April and go on to complete their development in June or, more usually, July. In early August both adults and some final instar nymphs can be found together, along with younger nymphs that have hatched from eggs laid the previous summer or autumn. The adults continue until November, or, in a few cases, last through yet another winter into early spring.

In all, the nymphs pass through eight instars. The wing rudiments are visible for the final two nymphal instars, as is the ovipositor in females.

Habitat

As its name implies, the wood cricket is a woodland species, living among deep leaf-litter in clearings, along the edges of rides, and among bracken around woodland edges. It is found primarily in broad-leaved woodland, especially large, ancient oak forests, but it also occurs in mixed woodland. Ragge (1965) adds: 'The wood cricket does occasionally occur in more open situations, such as on roadside banks or under a growth of bracken, but it is seldom found very far from trees'. Marshall & Haes (1988) also mention old stone walls, earthbanks and, on the Isle of Wight, crumbling sea cliffs, but it is always found close to trees or dense scrub.

Research on the Isle of Wight found it most abundant in older broad-leaved and mixed woodland, and associated with leaf litter, bare ground and low vegetation where the canopy cover was limited (in glades, rides and woodland edges.). The species was found to have good powers of dispersal in the absence of habitat barriers such as arable land (Brouwers & Newton, 2009a, 2009b; Brouwers, et al., 2011).

Behaviour

Wood crickets typically live among deep leaf-litter, and when disturbed disappear rapidly into it. They can run quite rapidly, and also jump when disappearing into the leaf litter is not an option. They feed on vegetable matter, supplemented by dead small invertebrates. According to Ragge (1965), in captivity they will eat a wide range of leaves, fruit, bread and dead insects. Although they will feed on the dead bodies of their own kind, there is little evidence of aggression even in crowded conditions.

The song is a low, churring sound, uttered in prolonged bursts. The crickets live in quite dense aggregations, and many males sing simultaneously ('chorusing'), giving a continuous sound. This is produced throughout the day in warm conditions, and sometimes into the night.

Ragge (ibid.) gives a detailed account of the extraordinary courtship and mating behaviour of this species, and this is the main source for the following. In the presence of a female, the male produces a courtship song that is more subdued than the calling song, and he jerks back and forth. Eventually a small spermatophore is produced at the tip of his extended abdomen. His jerking movements become more violent until the female climbs onto his back. He remains still while the spermatophore is transferred to the tip of the female's abdomen, below the base of the ovipositor. The pair then separate and the male resumes his jerky courtship movements until the female mounts him for a second time. This time they remain together for a longer period, and the female 'licks' an area on the right wing of the male that is covered in small hairs. The pair separate again, and a few minutes later the male produces a second, much larger, spermatophore. The male carries this with him for some time before resuming the jerky courtship movements, resulting in the female re-mounting him, mating for the second time, and taking the second spermatophore. The licking behaviour may be repeated. Sometimes the first spermatophore is removed and eaten by the female between the two matings, and sometimes it is retained, so that she carries both for some time. Eventually, the second spermatophore is rubbed off and eaten. Ragge notes that the female shows no inclination to remove and eat the spermatophore until at least a half hour has elapsed since she received it.

Current theoretical approaches suggest that edible spermatophores may function as nuptial gifts that convey nutrients to the female, as devices to give time for the male's sperm to fully enter the female's spermatheca, or as means of transferring stimulants to egg production or reduced receptivity to other males (see Chapter 6). The 'licking' behaviour, too, might perform any of these functions. However, this curious pattern of double mating with unequally sized spermatophores remains very puzzling.

Distribution

The wood cricket is widely distributed in Europe, including the Iberian peninsula, the Azores and Canary Islands, north Africa, and eastwards to the former Soviet Union. In the Alps it can be found up to an altitude of 1500 metres. In Britain, the Netherlands (where it is common in wooded areas) and Belgium it is close to the northern limit of its range.

In Britain it has a southerly distribution, south Devon, Hampshire and the Isle of Wight being its main strongholds. It has one population in Surrey, and there are previous records from Dorset and Sussex. Ragge (1965) mentions as 'doubtful' reports of the species from Cornwall, Worcestershire and Derbyshire.

Status and conservation

Widespread conversion of deciduous woodland to commercial conifer plantations must have caused many local extinctions of this species. Over-zealous woodland management, too, might lead to the elimination of the areas of warm, deep litter that they require. However, in their currently protected habitats, they remain very abundant and do not appear to be in immediate danger.

References: Baldock, 1999; Brouwers & Newton, 2009, 2010; Brouwers, Newton & Bailey, 2011; Harz, 1969; Marshall & Haes, 1988; Ragge, 1965.

FAMILY MOGOPLISTIDAE: SCALY CRICKETS

THE SCALY CRICKET
Pseudomogoplistes vicentae (Gorochov, 1996)

(Previously known as Mogoplistes squamiger, and Pseudomogoplistes squamiger.)

MEASUREMENTS: Male: 8–11 mm in length; female: 10–13 mm in length.

A

B

C

D

FIG A–D. Male; male lateral; female; female lateral.

Description
The scaly cricket has a slightly roughened appearance, especially on the abdomen, as a result of its covering of very fine scales. The head is as broad as the pronotum, narrowing at the front to a blunt 'face'. The pronotum is roughly rectangular when viewed from above, and smoothly curved down at the sides. The antennae are as long as, or longer than, the body. Wings are completely absent in both sexes. The cerci are long, tapering and slightly outwardly curved in both sexes. The ovipositor of the female is relatively broader than that of our other crickets and very slightly up-curved. The sexes differ considerably in body shape, the females having rounder, fatter abdomens, the males having straight-sided abdomens that gradually widen to the broad, blunt rear end. In most specimens the main coloration of the head, pronotum and abdomen is uniformly dark brown. However, some individuals, especially females, have lighter brown on the pronotum and rear portion of the head. In both sexes the antennae, mouthparts and legs are lighter brown, often with some darker patterning on the outer surface of the hind femora. There are variable amounts of very fine, short greyish hairs on the body, especially on the dorsal surface of the abdomen, and a row of short, erect ginger hairs between the pronotum and the head. There are often fine ginger hairs on the tip of the abdomen and a few on the legs.

Similar species
The only similarly small and brown cricket to be found in Britain is the wood cricket (N. sylvestris). However, although brachypterous, this does have obvious wing rudiments, and is extremely unlikely to be found in the habitat occupied by the scaly cricket.

Life cycle
As adults and variously developed nymphs are frequently found together it is now supposed that they have a two or three-year life cycle. One suggested pattern that explains the co-existence of various different developmental stages at various times of year has been provided by P. Sutton. On this proposal, eggs may be laid before or after a first winter, hatching to give early nymphal stages during the first spring and summer, and nymphs overwintering at various developmental stages. Nymphal development continues through the second spring and summer, some individuals reaching adulthood by the onset of winter, overwintering as adults and laying eggs by the following autumn (Sutton, 1999). Other patterns have been proposed, however (Timmins, 1994; Kirby, 1995), and it may be that the seasonal cycle of development is variable. The number of nymphal instars is so far unknown.

FIGS E–G. Eggs; first instar nymph; final instar male nymph.

The nymphs are often paler in colour than the adults, and frequently have regular patterns of pale and dark brown markings on the dorsal surface of the abdomen. The different body shapes of the sexes enable them to be distinguished even prior to the development of the ovipositor in the female.

Habitat

This species lives among the pebbles, or under rocks, concrete installations and larger stones on shingle beaches. Although they are sometimes found inland of the shingle ridge at their best known locality, Chesil Beach, Dorset, by far the greatest numbers (both here and at other more recently discovered sites) live just above the high-tide mark on the exposed seaward aspect of the beach. This is referred to as the 'seaweed strand line', but at Chesil Beach there is little or no vegetation of any kind. Instead, there is a scattering of sea-borne detritus and litter. Despite earlier views that it required sheltered conditions, this species is now known to favour very bleak, exposed aspects, with the shingle as its only protection.

Behaviour

Scaly crickets are nocturnal, but when disturbed and exposed to light during the day they can move with astonishing speed. They escape by flattening their bodies and wriggling between the pebbles or into rock crevices. They are virtually impossible to recapture once they have disappeared by this means. Their relatively short but powerful hind legs enable them to jump effectively.

Numbers caught in pit fall traps or trapped by accident in plastic containers among the beach litter suggest not only very large populations where they occur, but also that they may be gregarious. In captivity they roost close together during the day, and often remain in contact by stroking one another with their antennae when active at night. Courtship involves protracted 'fencing' with the antennae, followed by a receptive female raising her abdomen while the male runs under and out again. This may be repeated on numerous occasions without appearing to culminate in mating. The female oviposits by raising her abdomen and lowering her ovipositor, so that it is roughly at right-angles to a substrate, and pressing it into the sand. Approximately 60 eggs were laid by one captive female, some up to two millimetres under the surface of the sand, others simply laid in loose clusters on the surface. The eggs are pale cream to yellow, 3 mm by 0.5 mm, and elongated with a narrowing towards one end (uppermost in those laid under the surface).

History

P. Sutton (1999) has provided a thorough chronology of the scaly cricket in Britain, from which much of the following is drawn.

The scaly cricket was discovered in 1949 at the eastern end of Chesil Beach, west of Weymouth, Dorset. Initially it was considered that this may have been a casual introduction. However, in 1954 another female was discovered, suggesting that the species was established at this site – although probably not native to Britain. Five more individuals (all females) were found in 1955. Ragge (1965), assuming the identification of it as M. *squamiger* to be correct, noted that the species was an inhabitant of the Mediterranean area, and raised the possibility that it might have been introduced to Chesil Beach from ships calling at Portland harbour. However, he also speculated that, given its extraordinary habitat, it might yet be found to have a more extensive distribution.

Small numbers of females were found on various occasions between 1965 and 1976, and it was speculated that the species might be parthenogenetic. However, on several dates in October 1977, R. Hansford collected seven males from Chesil Beach and nearby Smallmouth Sands, Portland.

The species continued to be reported from only one 10 km square in Britain, and was still considered a rarity. In 1984, a Russian entomologist, A. V. Gorochov, published a revised classification of the crickets, as a result of which it was proposed that the scaly cricket, formerly in the genus 'Mogoplistes', should be assigned to a new genus 'Pseudomogoplistes'.

In 1985 extensive works were conducted to provide better pedestrian access to the reserve at the eastern end of Chesil Beach, and large numbers of the crickets (e.g. 100 reported by D. J. Moxom) were found under stones that were being laid to form a footpath. Further occasional reports of small numbers of specimens were received until 1992, when C. J. Timmins found 67 adult females, 22 adult males and a nymph, all dead in a margarine tub. This was the second indication that the Chesil Beach population could be much larger than previously thought. In 1994 a survey of the beach by P. Kirby confirmed this with the capture of 699 specimens using pitfall traps, and this was followed in 1995 by the capture of 207 crickets by Timmins using the same method. The co-existence of variously developed nymphs and adults led both observers to propose life-history patterns lasting more than one year. Kirby's study revealed the presence of the cricket further north and west along the shingle ridge at Chesil Beach, so that its British distribution now included two 10 km squares (SY67 and SY68).

Searches on other shingle beaches on the south coast of England were carried out by Timmins in 1996 and proved negative, leading Haes & Harding (1997) to conclude that it was: 'Probably introduced and successfully naturalised, occurring only at Chesil Beach, Dorset.' However, this view was soon to be overturned, as a colony of the scaly cricket was discovered on 5 June 1998 on the Channel Island of Sark by P. and E. Brown. At almost the same time, C. Ash, an Exeter student carrying out a survey on the stretch of shingle between Branscombe and Beer Head in Devon, found a single scaly cricket nymph. Subsequent searches and pitfall trapping on this site later in the same year by P. Sutton, D. Cooper and C. J. Timmins confirmed the presence of a substantial colony of the species along approximately 1 km of the beach. These finds support the view that the scaly cricket is, after all, a native British species. In the same year, Peter Stallegger, the Orthoptera recorder for Normandy, informed the then British Orthoptera Recorder, John Widgery, that the scaly cricket had been discovered at Glanville, on the Cherbourg Peninsula in France (Widgery, 1998).

These discoveries were followed by reports from two localities in Guernsey and from another French locality in 1999 (Widgery, 2000a). Then, in 1999, a 13-year old, Beth Knight, found a scaly cricket in south-west Wales at Marloes, Pembrokeshire. Her parents collected more specimens, and these were subsequently confirmed as belonging to this species (Widgery, 2000b, 2000c). The same year, there were reports of a new colony from Guernsey, and two more on the coast of Brittany. Most recently, another population has been located at Dale Bay, to the south-east of its known population at Marloes, Pembrokeshire. In addition, the continuing presence of a large population at Chesil Beach was confirmed by O. Leyshon, who captured 68 in May 2010 (Sutton, 2010b).

Meanwhile, further examination of the Normandy population led to the recognition that the scaly cricket had been wrongly identified. It is now recognised as *Pseudomogoplistes vicentae* (itself only distinguished by Gorochov in 1996). On the basis of small differences in the genitalia, Morère & Livory assigned these specimens to subspecies *septentrionalis*. Specimens from Sark and Chesil Beach were confirmed as also belonging to *P. vicentae* (Gorochov & Marshall, 2001).

Distribution

The species was first distinguished on the basis of specimens from Morocco and Portugal (Gorochov 1996). So far they have also been reported from coastal sites in northern France and the Channel Islands. In Britain its known distribution remains confined to a small number of shingle beaches in Dorset, Devon and south-west Wales.

Status and conservation

The scaly cricket was designated 'endangered' in the Nature Conservancy Council's *Red Data Book 2: Insects* (Haes, in Shirt 1987), and English Nature commissioned a survey carried out by C. J. Timmins in 1996. Since that time other populations have been discovered, and the large size of at least some of these has been demonstrated by trapping.

Despite its small number of localities, there has been concern that the large number of visitors to the first-discovered site might constitute a threat. The insect is potentially vulnerable to being crushed by people walking on the shingle, and there are reports of considerable numbers being killed by becoming accidentally trapped in litter. However, there is no evidence of a decline in the population at Chesil Beach, despite considerable visitor pressure. It has even been argued that there might be incidental benefits in the form of potential food items among litter (Gardiner, 2009c, and see also Chapter 9).

A more serious threat was illustrated by the off-shore grounding of the container ship NSC Napoli in January 2001. This resulted in oil pollution and large quantities of debris, some of it toxic, on Branscombe Beach. Both this and the subsequent clean-up operations, involving heavy vehicles and also physical cleaning of the shingle were a significant threat to the rich invertebrate fauna, and to the scaly cricket in particular (Sutton, 2007d). However, subsequent surveys revealed that the cricket had survived these operations (Sutton, 2008c), only to be challenged by winter storms in January 2010 that washed away large quantities of the shingle. Again, a visit by Beckman and Sutton in August that year confirmed the continued presence of the species there (Sutton, 2010b).

Sutton (2008a) reported the possibility of another threat to the population at Marloes from disturbance due to excavation for cables for a tidal energy installation.

Although such potential threats may well recur, the remarkable persistence of the species in its few favoured haunts gives grounds for optimism about its future. Although a number of shingle beaches on the south coast have been searched without success, it remains quite possible that the species will be discovered in further localities.

References: Gardiner, 2009c; Gorochov, 1996; Gorochov & Marshall, 2001; Haes & Harding, 1997; Morère & Livory, 1999; Shirt, 1987; Sutton, 1999, 2002, 2007d, 2008a, 2008c, 2010b; Timmins, 1994; Widgery, 1998, 2000a, 2000b, 2000c.

FAMILY GRYLLOTALPIDAE: THE MOLE-CRICKETS

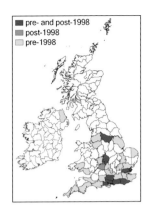

THE MOLE-CRICKET

Gryllotalpa gryllotalpa
(Linnaeus, 1758)

MEASUREMENTS: Male: 35–45 mm in length; female: 40–45 mm in length.

A

B

FIGS A–C. Male dorsal view (© B. Pinchen); male lateral view (© A. Kettle); head and pronotum, showing enlarged fore legs (© B. Pinchen).

C

Description

This species has a large, rather elongated body, with a tapering head, and an enlarged, rather funnel-shaped pronotum. The antennae are shorter than those of the crickets (approximately equalling the length of head plus pronotum). The fore wings are reduced, reaching back to about halfway along the abdomen in the male, and modified for stridulation in that sex. The hind wings are usually fully developed, and, furled up, they reach back beyond the tip of the abdomen. Both sexes have a pair of long, tapering cerci. The females do not have an external ovipositor, so that the simplest way of distinguishing males from females is by noting the different pattern of veins on the tegmina. Most of the body is covered by a fine pubescence. The colour is dark brown, paler below.

There is a rare form (f. *cophta* Haan) in which the hind wings are not fully developed, but this is apparently absent from Britain.

Similar species

There are no similar native species, but closely related mole-crickets are sometimes introduced accidentally in imported plant material. (e.g. an African mole-cricket *Gryllotalpa africana* found in York in 1999 (Widgery, 2000b), and *Gryllotalpa quindecim* found in Oxfordshire in 2005 (Pinchen, 2006)). Identification of species using morphological characters is extremely difficult.

Life cycle

Because of the difficulty in locating breeding colonies in Britain, most of the account below is drawn from mainland European studies of populations at similar latitudes. The information was collected together in Ragge (1965), which, together with Pinchen (2005), has been the main source used here.

Like the wood cricket, the mole-cricket has a two-year life cycle. The females begin to lay eggs from late April to early May. The eggs are laid over a one- to two-week period, in a heap within an underground chamber. Each batch may number from 30 to 50 eggs. However, a female may lay several egg batches during a summer, totalling 100 to 300, although as many as 640 have been recorded. Gilbert White described the accidentally exposed nest and eggs of a mole-cricket.

There were many caverns and winding passages leading to a kind of chamber, neatly smoothed and rounded, about the size of a moderate snuff-box. Within this secret nursery were deposited near an hundred eggs of a dirty yellow colour, and enveloped in a tough skin, but too lately excluded to contain any rudiments of young, being full of a viscous substance. The eggs lay but shallow, and within the influence of the sun, just under a little heap of fresh-moved mould... (G. White, 1971 [1789] letter XLVIII).

The eggs take from two to four weeks to hatch, depending on the temperature, and, uniquely among British Orthoptera, the mother engages in maternal care. She both guards the nest, and repeatedly cleans the eggs with her mouthparts – behaviour that is believed to protect them against mould.

After hatching, the small nymphs stay in the nest for a few weeks, feeding on humus and rootlets. When they emerge from the nest they continue for a while to be protected by the female, becoming independent by the fourth instar.

These nymphs continue to develop through the summer but do not reach the final instar before the onset of winter hibernation. As egg-laying continues into the summer, the offspring from later batches arrive at hibernation at earlier stages of development.

The following spring and summer the nymphs continue their development. The more advanced ones may reach adulthood by their second winter, but probably do not become sexually mature until the following spring. The nymphs that passed through their first winter in earlier developmental stages do not reach adulthood and sexual maturity until the summer after their second winter.

The number of nymphal instars appears to be variable, but Ragge gives ten as probably the most usual. Wing pads are just visible at the eighth instar, and clearly visible in the ninth and tenth.

Habitat

The mole-cricket makes its burrows in soft, moist soils, usually near rivers, streams canals or ponds. The edges of water meadows or river flood plains are its most common habitats, but it can be found in gardens and allotments. It prefers free-draining, loamy soils, with a fluctuating water table and with areas of short turf and occasionally disturbed soil, in open, sunny locations (Pinchen, 2005). An occasional source of records has been gardeners' complaints that its burrowing and feeding on roots is a cause of damage. When burrowing close to the surface of the soil, as it does in wet ground, its burrows cause ridges to appear on the surface, similar to those made by moles.

Behaviour

The mole-cricket is seldom seen, even when present in an area, as it spends most of its time underground. The burrows may be close to the soil surface, if the ground is wet, or to a depth of a metre or more when conditions are drier, and for hibernation.

The males sing below ground in a resonating chamber formed within the burrow system. The sound is a low, continuous 'churr' that has been likened to the call of the nightjar (*Caprimulgus europaeus*), and is emitted during warm evenings and nights in spring and early summer.

When a female arrives, the male continues to sing, while drooping its wings on either side of its body and swaying from side to side. Mating is reputedly accomplished by the female climbing onto the back of the male, while the male transfers a spermatophore to the female. However, video footage of an above-ground mating attempt shows the male attempting to reverse over the female (B. Pinchen, pers. comm.).

Both adults and nymphs are able to swim, and they are also able to run quickly backwards. Although they do not fly during the day, they do fly on some warm evenings. In Gilbert White's words, they 'move "*curso undoso*", rising and falling in curves' (G. White 1971 [1789]).

The song and habitat of the mole-cricket have given rise to an exceptional range of vernacular names for it: fen-cricket, churr-worm, eve-churr, jar-worm, Cambridge nightingale, and, in south Wales, rhing y les (Baldock, 1999; Marshall & Haes, 1988). Other local names include croaker, land crab, bog mole and jarr-bob. Eve-churr and jarr-bob are also local names for the nightjar (B. Pinchen, pers. comm.)

Enemies
Baldock (1999) cites an early comment by the eminent 19th-century Godalming naturalist, Edward Newman, to the effect that the mole-cricket was 'occasionally found in the craw of these birds [nightjars] when shot'. Newman's speculation was that the similar call of the nightjar served as a 'decoy' for the male mole-cricket (Baldock, 1999: 71). In the New Forest, B. Pinchen reports that fox and tawny owl came close to investigate the sound source when males were singing, while fox, magpie, nightjar and tawny owl were attracted to sound tapes of the mole-cricket. Song-tapes used in Guernsey attracted hobbys, and one householder spoke of mole-crickets being caught by her cat (B. Pinchen, pers. comm.).

Distribution
The mole-cricket is still widespread in much of Europe, except for Norway and Finland, and also occurs in north Africa and western Asia. However, in Britain it has undergone a long drawn-out decline, with what appears to be only one probably native population known on the mainland at the time of writing.

Lucas (1920) listed reports from Berkshire, Cambridgeshire, Cornwall, Derbyshire, Devon, Hampshire, Kent, Lancashire, Lincolnshire, Norfolk, Oxfordshire, Staffordshire, Surrey, Sussex and Wiltshire, although many of these were old records, and others referred to single specimens that may have been accidental introductions. The same may be true of the records from Scotland (Renfrewshire) and Ireland (Derry). He considered it likely that it was less common than formerly. According to Ragge, it had become 'very much rarer' by 1965, and he gave reports from the Avon and Test valleys in South Hampshire, and the River Wey and its tributaries in Surrey.

Marshall & Haes (1988) note the destruction of sites in Surrey, Dorset and Hampshire during the 1940s and 1950s, citing recent reports of colonies from the northern edge of the New Forest, on allotments close to the river Itchen near Southampton, and in East Sussex around Bucksted and Uckfield only.

By the 1960s and early 1970s only two small colonies were known, one in a Southampton garden, the other in a meadow on the Hampshire/Wiltshire border, but both are thought to have become extinct. There seem to have been no reports between that time and 1988, when a single male was dug up from a field near Wareham, Dorset (Pinchen, 2005). There were unconfirmed reports from central Hertfordshire up to the 1990s (Widgery, 2000a). These were followed by reports of single specimens from Macclesfield (1996), the Vauxhall car factory in Luton (1999), Chelmsford (2000), and a garden in South Woodham Ferrers, Essex (also in 2000) (Pinchen, 2003). Widgery (2001b) reported that mole-cricket stridulation was heard at Old Marsden, Oxfordshire, and burrows were found at a locality in south Wales. Credible reports of mole-cricket song include one from an Oxford allotment in 2001 (Sutton, 2004b and Pinchen, 2005). Subsequent investigation of these localities turned up no further evidence of the crickets. However, song was heard from a small area of the New Forest in 2003, and a survey of the site a month later revealed surface burrows. Mole-cricket song heard in 2008 gave evidence of the continuing presence of the species at this site (Pinchen, 2009).

There are other occasional reports, usually with evidence that the specimens concerned have been incidentally imported in plant material: Southend-on-Sea, Essex, in imported root vegetables at a greengrocers (Pinchen, 2004); Ashington, Sussex, in plant material imported from Italy, August 2003 (Sutton, 2003c); Gloucestershire, one male in plants imported from mainland Europe, September 2004 (Pinchen, 2006); Oxfordshire, nymphs and adults in a compost heap, almost certainly imports from mainland Europe; Hampshire, in the root stock of an imported palm; south Wales, one adult in a garden; Hampshire, a nymph in a garden centre (all 2005, Pinchen, 2006); and Winchelsea beach, East Sussex, one adult in 2006 (Pinchen, 2009).

Status and conservation
The mole-cricket is very elusive, spending most of its life underground, and males singing at the surface only on rare occasions. The native population may

now be close to extinction, but there remains the possibility that other surviving colonies await discovery. The mole-cricket was included in Schedule 5 of the Wildlife and Countryside Act, 1981, and listed as 'endangered' in the Nature Conservancy Council's *Red Data Book 2: Insects* (Haes, in Shirt 1987). The species was included in English Nature's Species Recovery Programme in 1994, and data was collected by M. Edwards. Searches for surviving colonies focused on the valley of the river Wey, where apparently suitable habitat still exists, but to no avail. It is also listed as a UK Biodiversity Action Plan priority species. Since 1999, the co-ordinator of the Species Recovery Project has been B. Pinchen, from whom much of the above information has been derived.

References: Baldock, 1999; Harz, 1969; Lucas, 1920; Pinchen, 2003, 2005, 2006, 2009; Ragge, 1965; Marshall & Haes, 1988; Shirt, 1987; Sutton, 2003c, 2004b; White, 1971 [1789]; Widgery, 2000a, 2001b.

CHAPTER 8

The British species, part 2: Caelifera
Groundhoppers and grasshoppers

GROUNDHOPPERS (TETRIGIDAE)

These are sometimes referred to as 'pygmy grasshoppers' or 'grouse locusts'. They are believed to have changed relatively little from the evolutionary ancestors of today's Orthoptera, and their preference for relatively simple plants such as soil algae and mosses as food sources can be understood as a legacy of their evolutionary ancestry (Blackith, 1987; Paranjape *et al.*, 1987).

There are only three British species of this fascinating group. They superficially resemble tiny grasshoppers, but on closer inspection one can see significant structural differences. The most obvious is that the pronotum section of the thorax projects back over the abdomen, tapering towards or beyond its tip. The tarsi of the fore and mid legs have only two segments (three in grasshoppers). The male genitalia and the female ovipositor are structured very differently from those of grasshoppers.

Slender groundhopper (© Tim Bernhard)

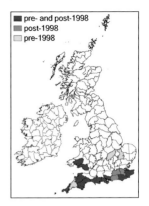

■ pre- and post-1998
■ post-1998
□ pre-1998

<small>CEPERO'S GROUNDHOPPER</small>
Tetrix ceperoi
(Bolivar, 1887)

MEASUREMENTS: Male: 9.5–10.5 mm in length; female: 11–13 mm in length.

A

B

FIGS A–C. Male; dorsal view; female

C

Description

Like the other groundhoppers, *T. ceperoi* is small and inconspicuous. The pronotum has a fine median ridge running along it and tapers back, usually reaching 2.5 mm to 4 mm beyond the tip of the abdomen. The fan-shaped hind wings are kept folded under the pronotum, and usually terminate just beyond the tip of the pronotum. The fore wings are vestigial and take the form of small pads at the side of the insect's body, just below the pronotum. The mid femora have wavy edges dorsally and ventrally, and the anterior edge of the vertex (front of the head) is approximately continuous with the front of the eyes.

Variation

Although they are generally quite cryptically coloured, there is considerable individual variation in both the ground colour and the patterning on the dorsal surface of the pronotum. Combining ground colour and pattern variation, Paul (1988) distinguished 10 varieties, while Hochkirch *et al.* (2007) distinguished 20 different colour forms, which they were able to reduce to a simpler 6-fold classification: light brown, dark brown, black, mottled green, red-brown and grey. Elsewhere, Hochkirch *et al.* (2008a) distinguished nine different pronotal patterns.

The colour forms are classified according to a mix of basic colour and pattern into nine categories, although some defied classification in such a simplified way:

(1) black with ochre patches on the femora, sides of the thorax and legs (Fig A above);
(2) brown with a pale median dorsal stripe;
(3) green with a pale dorsal stripe and lateral black markings on the pronotum;
(4) plain grey-brown;
(5) mottled green with pale 'shoulders' on the pronotum;
(6) mottled green;
(7) red-brown mottled;
(8) red-brown mottled with green;
(9) plain rust brown.

These variant colour patterns coexist in many populations, but differ in their relative frequency. Previous discussions in the literature have usually proposed explanations of the persistence of this diversity in terms of assortative mating, differential selective pressures and various genetic mechanisms on the assumption that colour patterns are strictly under genetic control (Nabours, 1929; Paul, 1988; Caesar *et al.*, 2007). A recent study by Hochkirch *et al.* (2008a) showed that some aspects of adult coloration are influenced by substrate colour during individual development, but their results are contested by Karlsson *et al.* (2009) (see Chapter 3 for more details).

FIGS D–K. Brown with pale median dorsal stripe; green with pale dorsal stripe; grey-brown; mottled green with pale shoulders; mottled green; red-brown mottled; red-brown mottled with green; rust brown.

Similar species

T. ceperoi could be confused with either of our other two groundhoppers.

T. undulata is larger bodied (more 'stocky' in appearance), and has a relatively much shorter pronotum, which reaches back approximately to the tip of the abdomen (significantly further in *T. ceperoi*). In addition, *T. undulata* has a more prominent raised keel down the middle of the dorsal surface of the pronotum.

The slender groundhopper, *T. subulata*, is very similar to *T. ceperoi* and careful examination is needed to separate them.

There are five main features.

(1) Size: on average, *T. ceperoi* is usually smaller than *T. subulata*, but this is useful only as an initial guide. Sizes can overlap, and in any case, the difference is only clear when you can compare the two.

(2) A good 'field' character, that can be seen with a ×10 hand lens, is the shape of the femora of the middle pair of legs. Viewed from the side these have wavy edges in *T. ceperoi*, and straight or smoothly curved ones in *T. subulata* (see the Key, Fig K12, page 234, and photos). However, care is needed in using this character: the legs of both species are often mottled dark and light; this can give the superficial impression of wavy edges in *T. subulata*.

(3) Also visible with a ×10 lens is the 'kink' in the dorsal ridge of the hind femur close to the 'knee' joint. This is straight in T. *subulata*.

(4) The characters most used in the literature have to do with the relative width of the eyes and vertex of the head (viewed from above) and also the shape of the face as seen from the side.

In *T. ceperoi* the width of the vertex is approximately 1.3 to 1.5 times the width of the eye. In *T. subulata* it is relatively wider, 1.5 to 1.8 or more times the width of the eye. These differences are, of course, difficult to determine with living insects in the field – but with experience the general impression of *T. ceperoi* is that its eyes are more prominent than those of *T. subulata*, when viewed from above.

In *T. ceperoi* the vertex does not project significantly in front of the eyes (giving the impression of a smoothly curved front edge when viewed from above). In *T. subulata* the vertex projects a small distance in front of the eyes. In profile, the front of the face is more vertical in *T. subulata* but curves back towards the top in *T. ceperoi*. One way of determining this is by observing (from the side) the angle formed by the meeting of the front of the face and the vertex. This is usually slightly obtuse in *T. ceperoi*, and acute in *T. subulata*.

(5)   The valves of the females of *T. ceperoi* have generally more deeply toothed serrations than those of *T. subulata* (Evans & Edmondson, 2007). Brown (1950) illustrated this feature, but conceded that, like some of the other characters used, there may be some overlap between individuals of the two species.

In all, it is probably advisable to check several characters – and, even better, several specimens – for confident identification. (See the Key, Figs K12–16, pages 234–5.)

Life cycle
The main period for mating and egg-laying in Britain is May and June. Eggs are laid in clusters held together by a sticky secretion, in damp ground or among low vegetation. They hatch in 3 to 4 weeks and the resulting nymphs pass through five (male) or six (female) instars, usually reaching adulthood by autumn. The winter is spent as either a late instar nymph or an immature adult. They may be active on warm days from early spring onwards, and reach full maturity by May.

Habitat
Despite its very restricted distribution in Britain, *T. ceperoi* occurs in a wide variety of habitats. These include the landward side of dune systems, on muddy or stony edges of ponds or lakes, on seepages from sea cliffs, on bare peat at the edge of streams and ponds, in wet sand pits and on muddy edges of drainage ditches. What all these habitats have in common is patches of damp or wet bare ground, interspersed with vegetation cover. The presence of soil algae, mosses or other small, delicate plants is also necessary. Most known sites in Britain are close to the coast.

Behaviour
Both sexes are inactive in dull or cool weather. In warm, sunny spells they graze on young shoots of mosses, on algae, or on decaying plant material. As they do so, their palps are continually in action, probing and 'testing' the substrate on which they feed. Females are relatively static, usually either feeding or occasionally moving around over mud, pebbles or larger plants. The males are more active, presumably in search of potential mates, and spend less of their time feeding. Hochkirch *et al.* (2007) showed that males spent more time than females did on bare ground and mosses, with greater intensity of incident sunlight. Females spent more time among leaf litter and higher plants than males did. There was a related difference in the frequency of two colour forms: black males were much more common than black females, and mottled-green females much

more common than males with that background colour. Black males would be better camouflaged on a muddy background, and females on their less exposed, more vegetated preferred microhabitat. Tentative evidence that males might also be more exposed to predation was the greater incidence of missing legs in the males. In the absence of stridulation, males find mates by visual searching, and it is supposed that the clear view they get by occupying bare ground enhances their chances of success, the resulting behaviour representing a 'trade-off' between natural and sexual selection.

Males of *T. ceperoi* have a distinctive 'courtship' display, referred to by Hochkirch *et al.* (2006) as 'pronotal bobbing'. This looks like a fast, deep 'bow' in the direction of the female (see DVD). The male simultaneously raises his hind legs and dips down his head, so raising the rest of his body at a steep angle, then returns to his usual stance and moves rapidly toward the female. In the analysis carried out by Hochkirch *et al.* the pronotal bobbing took on average only 0.8 of a second. The male next mounts the female and, if successful, holds on to her pronotum while curving his abdomen down between the rear portion of her pronotum and the nearside femur. Contact is then made by moving the open valves of his genitalia up to engage with the underside of the tip of the female's abdomen. Mating usually lasts only a few seconds and the male then moves on. However, two males often compete to mate with a single female, both attempting to mount her at once. Females are polyandrous and are often prepared to mate with rival males in quick succession. However, they also reject some males by not opening the space between the hind femur and pronotum, and sometimes by vibrating vigorously until a mounted but unwanted male is shaken off (see DVD).

Where *T. ceperoi* occurs together with *T. subulata* mating attempts and actual mating take place between the two species. Gröning *et al.* (2007) studied 'reproductive interference' between the two species both in the laboratory and in the field. In both situations males of both species appeared not to discriminate between the females of the two species. However, possibly because of the distinctive visual courtship signal of *T. ceperoi* ('pronotal bobbing'), females of that species rejected males of *T. subulata* more often than they rejected males of their own species (see Chapter 6).

Presumably their cryptic coloration, and tendency to rest on colour-matching substrates, is their main defence against predators. However, they can jump out of the way when disturbed (especially in warm weather), and they can augment their leaps with flight. They can also swim by powerful strokes of their hind legs if their escape attempts land them in open water, although there is no evidence of their entering the water independently of provocation.

Enemies

See under slender groundhopper (*T. subulata*).

Distribution

This species is quite widespread in western and southern Europe and North Africa. In Britain it is at the northern edge of its range. Here it is regarded as a localised and scarce species, although it can be abundant in suitable sites. Its known localities are mainly coastal and in the southern counties of England and Wales. It is present in coastal districts of Kent, Sussex, Hampshire and the Isle of Wight, Dorset, Devon and Cornwall in England and Carmarthenshire and Glamorgan in south Wales. There are also inland records from Surrey and Hampshire (New Forest), and isolated records from Northamptonshire and Cambridgeshire. It is not known from Ireland.

Status and conservation

Cepero's groundhopper was first distinguished from the slender groundhopper, *Tetrix subulata*, among British populations, and so recognised as a British species, by B. P. Uvarov (1940). The scarcity of *T. ceperoi* in Britain is probably the result of a combination of its rather specialised habitat preferences and its geographical range. It does not appear to be threatened, and, indeed, could well be under-recorded given its close similarity to *T. subulata*. The discovery of the species near Peterborough, many kilometres outside its previously known range, is of interest. It could be that this population is the result of an incidental introduction, but if it is not, then the possibility arises that the species may have been overlooked elsewhere outside its previously known range.

References: Brown, 1950; Caesar et al., 2007; Evans & Edmondson, 2007; Gröning et al., 2007; Hochkirch et al., 2006, 2007, 2008a; Karlsson et al., 2009; Nebours, 1929; Paul, 1988; Uvarov, 1940.

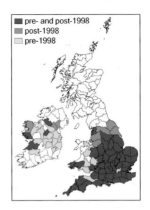

SLENDER GROUNDHOPPER

Tetrix subulata
(Linnaeus, 1758)

MEASUREMENTS: Male: 9–12.5 mm in length; Female: 11–15 mm in length.

FIGS A–C. Male;
dorsal view; female

A

B

C

FIG D. F. *bifasciata*

D

Description

This species, as its English name implies, is long and narrow in overall shape. The pronotum tapers back over the body and terminates several millimetres (3–4.5) beyond the tip of the abdomen. The fan-shaped wings, when not in use, are folded below and along the underside of the pronotum, and usually terminate just beyond its tip. The vertex is relatively broad and projects a small distance in front of the eyes. The edges of the mid femur, when viewed from the side, are straight or gently curved, not wavy, as in Cepero's groundhopper.

Variation

There is a form of the slender groundhopper (f. *bifasciata*) in which the pronotum and wings are shorter than they are in the typical form, terminating only just beyond the tip of the genitalia at the rear end of the abdomen. This form varies in frequency among populations (apparently one northern locality has mostly this form (see Widgery, 1998)), and there are intermediate forms.

As in other groundhoppers, there are many different colour patterns, and usually several in any population. Some common variants are illustrated.

(1) Black or dark brown pronotum, with paler, ochre patches on the femora (similar to form 1 of *T. ceperoi*).
(2) Grey or brown with a pale median stripe, sometimes with black markings flanking the pale stripe (similar to forms 2 and 3 of *T. ceperoi*).
(3) Grey, brown or green with pale outlining of the 'shoulders' of the pronotum (similar to form 5 of *T. ceperoi*).
(4) Indistinctly mottled forms, with various colourings of both mottling and ground-colour (similar to *T. ceperoi* forms 7 and 8).
(5) A distinctive form with brown or various shades of grey as ground colour and a wide, irregular patch of white across the middle of the pronotum. This form may also have black wedge-shaped marks flanking the white.
(6) Rust-brown pronotum with greyish or darker brown sides.
(7) Pale fawn pronotum with dark brown sides and legs.
(8) Dark grey with white flashes on the femora.
(9) Dark grey or brown without markings.

FIGS E–M. Dark brown with ochre patches; pale median stripe; pale shoulders; mottled form; white spot; rust-brown with dark sides; fawn with dark brown sides; dark with white flashes; dark grey unmarked.

Another colour form (not illustrated) was unmarked white, and found on exposed chalk in a disused chalk quarry (T. Tamblin, pers. obs.).

Similar species

The typical form is very similar to Cepero's groundhopper, and close examination with a hand lens is necessary for confirmation. (For details, see under that species.)

Form *bifasciata* could be confused with the common groundhopper (*T. undulata*), but the latter is a more 'stocky' insect, with a strongly raised median keel on the pronotum.

Life cycle

In early spring, slender groundhoppers become fully active a little later than their close relative, the common groundhopper. Initially, much of their time is spent basking or feeding. Courtship and mating take place from early April to June in sunny weather. The eggs are approximately 3 mm in length and are loosely sausage-shaped with a horn-like projection at one end. They are laid in small holes, usually in damp soil, in clutches of 10 to 20, stuck together with an adhesive secretion. They hatch in 3 to 4 weeks. As in other Orthoptera, the initial phase is a worm-like larva, which quickly sheds its outer coating to reveal the first instar nymph. Development takes place through the spring and summer months, males passing through five, females six, nymphal stages. The previous generation of adults dies out during the summer, so that later in the year only various nymphal stages are present. The winter is spent as a final instar nymph, or as an immature adult. Full sexual maturity is reached early in the following spring.

Habitat

The slender groundhopper is usually found in damp or marshy habitats such as river edges, pond margins, wet meadows, ditches and damp hollows in heathland. However, it can also be found well away from open water, in damp woodland rides, or cart tracks. Areas of bare ground, open to

FIG N. Nymph.

N

sunlight, but also damp, with simple plants such as soil algae, mosses and fungi are essential. The preference for damp conditions may be associated with the relatively specialised diet, but also may reflect water demands for the eggs (Hochkirch *et al.*, 2000). It may be that patches of bare ground are specifically required for courtship and mating, as, in many of the habitats, patches of open ground become shaded out by vigorous growth of grasses, sedges and rushes by late spring or early summer. At this time, especially, the groundhoppers climb up to sun themselves on exposed vegetation or other perches (see under 'Behaviour', below).

Behaviour

Although apparently dormant during the coldest months, the groundhoppers emerge to bask in sheltered spots during sunny weather from early March (in southern England). They are present in greater numbers by the beginning of April, and by the middle of April, courtship and mating are under way.

The groundhoppers are active mainly in warm and sunny weather and later in the season, when exposed patches of bare ground are often shaded out by denser vegetation, they climb onto the higher leaves and stems of grasses or sedges to bask. They can also be seen on the reflective surfaces of containers and other litter. In one former willow plantation by a small river they could be found resting or feeding on the raised platforms provided by the mossy and part-rotted stumps of the trees (pers. obs.).

They graze on soil algae and fresh, tender shoots of mosses, but will also consume detritus, and females sometimes eat young, tender shoots of grasses or other flowering plants. The somewhat different diets of males and females might be explained in terms of the nutritional needs of the latter for egg production (Hochkirch *et al.*, 2000). Feeding is generally accompanied by frequent antennation of the substrate, and probing with the palps (see DVD).

The females are relatively inactive, and spend most of their time resting or feeding on the ground or among detritus, while the males spend much of their time actively searching for potential mates, especially in the afternoon. Initial location of a female is probably visual, but, in close proximity, males frequently point their antennae directly towards the female and 'twirl' them in a way that suggests that scent may be involved. Commonly, but not always, the male faces the female and performs a very brief courtship signal. Hochkirch *et al.* (2006) distinguish two such signals which they term 'frontal swinging' and 'lateral swinging'. Both these signals are of very brief duration (around one second), and involve raising the body of the insect slightly by stretching the fore and mid legs and swinging forward, or stretching the legs on one side to produce a sideways motion. The amplitude of the signal is very small and it is easily missed by the human observer. However, on film it is readily detectable (see DVD).

The signal may be repeated several times as the male approaches the female. As the approach is usually from the front, he commonly mounts frontally, and climbs onto her pronotum, facing backwards. He then turns around, and, gripping her pronotum with fore and mid legs, curves his abdomen down between the side of the female's pronotum and the femur of that side. Females appear to vary in their receptiveness, and sometimes males attempt to force their way between these structures. Once this position has been achieved, the male searches with the tip of his abdomen for the genitalia of the female and mating takes place. This is usually very brief – a few seconds only – and is usually accompanied by antennal contact, the male curving his antennae down, the female raising hers. The male disconnects his genitalia from those of the female, dismounts and walks away. Frequently the female continues to feed throughout the operation.

However, this 'textbook' sequence is often varied. Competition between males for mates is quite intense, and it commonly happens that the mating attempts of one male are interrupted by the arrival of another suitor. The latter will often attempt to pull off the first, but, if that fails, he will simply clamber over it and attempt to mate from the other side of the female. Sometimes it appears that the second male successfully mates with the female as soon as the first completes copulation and dismounts. Often, if a male fails to elicit the appropriate response from a female he will resume the initial posture, facing backwards while standing on the pronotum of the female. This brings the tip of his abdomen over the antennae of the female. He then reverses to the standard position for copulation and is often successful. Another probable consequence of the intensity of male competition is that males often dash at and mount a female directly and without any observable courtship signal.

In addition to the two 'swing' signals described above, both males and females signal to one another by rapidly raising and then lowering one hind leg (or sometimes both). This 'leg flick' signal is most often used when males encounter one another, and is followed by one or both moving away.

Another pattern of movement that appears to have a communicative role is a rapid vibration of the whole body that looks like a brief fit of

FIG O. Mating pair.

O

rage or frustration. It could be that this is less a visual signal than a form of vibratory communication that is sensed either by direct physical contact or via the substrate (Benediktov, 2005). However, what appears to the human eye as the same 'vibration' signal is used in a range of different contexts. Most frequently it is used when two or more males encounter one another. In a head-on encounter, one or both may vibrate and one moves off. Sometimes one male climbs onto another, which then vibrates until the first dismounts. This is sometimes followed by a fit of vibration from the first. In fact, males frequently make physical contact with one another, sometimes climbing onto or over one another, and often with mutual antennation or vibratory signals. Hochkirch *et al.* (2006) interpret this as indicating that males will attempt to mate with more or less anything of roughly the right size. Occasionally, indeed, these encounters do look like mating attempts, but more often they have the appearance of mildly antagonistic or neutral contacts. The locations where individuals congregate and perform courtship and mating appear to be strongly physically delimited within the wider habitat. It could be that these contacts function in some way to maintain the cohesion of localised aggregations, which could be important for mate location in a species without sound communication that lives in habitats offering little long-distance visibility.

Where *T. ceperoi* and *T. subulata* occur together (as they do in some British localities, such as Rye Harbour), males of both species mis-direct courtship and mating attempts to females of the 'wrong' species (see under *T. ceperoi*).

In laboratory tests of reproductive interference between *T. subulata* and *T. undulata* (Hochkirch *et al.*, 2008a), males of both species showed a strong preference for females of *T. undulata*, while females of each species were equally receptive to males of either. This may be because of the close similarity of the courtship signals of the males. However, in the field, where the two species intermingle, males of *T. undulata* seem to court or mate with females of their own species and those of *T. subulata* in roughly equal proportions. Females of both species accept or resist mating attempts from males of either species without any obvious discrimination. In one extraordinary filmed sequence, a male *T. undulata* mounts a female *T. subulata*, but is pulled off by a rival male *T. subulata*, which then walks over the male *T. undulata* (eliciting a fit of vibration from the latter), to successfully mate with the female *T. subulata*. She then wanders off and re-encounters the original male *T. undulata*, who promptly mounts and successfully mates with her! (See Chapter 6 for more details, and the DVD.)

Enemies

There appear to be no literature reports of predation on groundhoppers, but it is possible that they are taken by water-side birds, amphibians or, like many other orthopterans, by spiders.

Loss of one of the back legs is common in most populations, and it is sometimes assumed that this is evidence of predation (autotomy is used by orthopterans as a means of escape from predators) but it may also be a result of imperfect moulting of nymphal cuticle during development. Cryptic coloration and the apparent tendency to select matching substrates must be an important defence against visual predators. However, when basking, and sometimes when feeding, they rest on contrasting substrates, presumably reflecting a trade-off between those priorities and predator avoidance. Their most common response to disturbance is to jump – often landing on a colour-matching surface. Especially in warm weather, they may respond by flying some four or five metres, and they can change direction to some extent while in flight. Like the other two groundhopper species, they are able to swim, using powerful kicks of the back legs. This is presumably an aid in escaping from terrestrial predators.

Distribution

This species has a very wide distribution throughout the temperate regions of the northern hemisphere, including most of Europe, temperate Asia, north Africa and north America. In Britain it is common and widespread in south-western, central-southern and south-eastern England and East Anglia. Kevan (1961) gives north Lincolnshire as its most northerly outpost, but it has since been recorded from Lancashire and Yorkshire (Drax power station, at Selby in 1998), and subsequently in a number of other localities in Yorkshire (Sutton, 2005a). There is also a scattering of records from southern and some eastern counties of Wales, and across Ireland.

Status and conservation

It seems likely that many of the slender groundhopper's localities are rather temporary and vulnerable to shading out of the required bare patches by vegetative succession, and to the drying out of ponds and damp hollows. Extensive drainage of wetlands for agriculture must also have greatly affected its populations. However, it appears to be a relatively effective coloniser of newly created habitats and is regarded as a 'pioneer' species. Careful searching of any apparently suitable habitat within its climatic range generally reveals its presence. In view of this, it seems unlikely that this species is significantly threatened in Britain.

References: Hochkirch et al., 2000, 2006, 2008a; Gröning et al., 2007; Kevan, 1961; Sutton, 2005a.

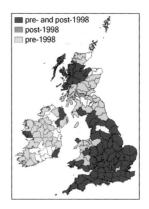

pre- and post-1998
post-1998
pre-1998

COMMON GROUNDHOPPER

Tetrix undulata
(Sowerby, 1806)

MEASUREMENTS: Male: 8–9 mm in length; female: 9–11 mm in length.

A

B

FIGS A–C. Male;
male dorsal view;
female.

C

Description

The common groundhopper is a more compact, robust insect than its two close relatives. This appearance is partly the result of the much shorter rear extension of the pronotum, the tip of which reaches back only so far as, or a little beyond, the rear end of the abdomen and genitalia. The reduced hind wings are largely concealed under the pronotum with just a narrow section of the leading edge visible below it, and to the rear of the small ridged pads that are the reduced vestiges of the fore wings. The longitudinal ridge on the dorsal surface of the pronotum forms a prominent keel in this species and has a convex outline when viewed from the side, giving a slightly 'hump-backed' appearance to the insect. The curvature is even in the male, but more abrupt towards the front of the pronotum in the female.

There is an uncommon fully-winged form (f. *macroptera* Haij) listed from two Scottish sites by Kevan (1952), and, more recently in 1991, also from Scotland (Haes & Harding, 1997).

As in the other groundhoppers, there is a great diversity of colour forms and many of these are similar in all three species – possibly reflecting their overlapping habitat preferences. (See Chapter 3, Fig 72.)

Similar species

The adults of this species can easily be distinguished from those of the other two British groundhopper species by the much shorter pronotum, and also by the raised central keel along the pronotum. However, confusion with the short-winged form *bifasciata* of the slender groundhopper is possible. The prominent keel in the common groundhopper is the most obvious distinguishing feature here. Early instar nymphs of all three species are very difficult to distinguish, but in the final nymphal instar the hind wing pads are clearly visible in the other two species, but not in *T. undulata*.

FIG D. Nymph.

D

Life cycle

Although they are reputed to be active in warm days through the year, common groundhoppers are rarely seen before the middle of March in southern Britain. However, by the end of that month they are very active in good weather. Courtship and mating begins at that time, and continues for much longer into the summer than is the case for the other two groundhopper species. The eggs, which are similar in form to those of the other groundhoppers (see under slender groundhopper), are laid into the ground or among low vegetation. They hatch in 3 to 4 weeks. Subsequent development is as in the other groundhoppers – an initial vermiform larva gives way to a series of five (in the male) or six (in the female) nymphal instars – but as the breeding season is more extended in this species, both adults and nymphs of various stages can be found together through the year. Overwintering nymphs complete their development the following spring, and so become fully adult later in the season than those that overwintered as adults.

Habitat

As noted by many observers, this species can be found in a much wider range of habitats than the other two British species of groundhopper. However, it does have markedly overlapping habitat preferences, so that the damp pond margins, stream edges and hollows where the slender groundhopper occurs frequently harbour this species too. It also inhabits a range of other biotopes: along path edges and in clearings in open woodland – especially among mosses and leaf litter, and on heathland among gorse and heathers. A key requirement seems to be patches of bare ground open to the sun, and plants such as algae and mosses that form its main diet. Even in apparently suitable habitat the population is often aggregated in small local patches.

Behaviour

Common groundhoppers are inactive in cool or overcast weather, and on warm, sunny days divide their time between basking, feeding and reproductive activity. Females are most often seen on the ground, feeding on various small plants, while males are generally more active. When not feeding or basking, they run in a rather jerky fashion on haphazard routes around open patches, or through leaf litter. This is presumably a mate-searching strategy, as when a female is approached the male generally stops, facing the female. Several brief and inconspicuous 'swinging' courtship signals may be given before the male moves forward, often making antennal contact with the female and mounting. Mounting is often from the front, so the male is initially standing on the pronotum of the female, facing backwards. He quickly turns around and probes with his abdomen to open a space between the hind femur and pronotum of the female. If the female is receptive, she allows this and the male then rubs his abdomen against that of the female and reaches down to make contact with her genitalia as she curves her abdomen in his direction. Mating usually lasts only a few seconds, and the male moves off, usually with the tip of his abdomen drooping, and the genital plates still parted.

However, there are many deviations from this pattern. Often males appear to approach directly, and mount and attempt to mate either without any obvious preliminaries, or with antennal contact only. In some examples, apparent female resistance is overcome by a mounted male reversing his position on the pronotum of the female, then reverting back to the normal mating position. One filmed sequence shows a female lacking one hind leg. A male who mounts her appears confused, dismounts, re-mounts and dismounts a further two times, despite her opening the space between her pronotum and the remaining hind femur. The sequence is completed by her walking over him, leaving him in a fit of vibration!

During their mate-searching activity, the males frequently encounter one another. When they do so, a variety of signals ensues. Commonly, two males exchange 'leg flick' signals with their hind legs. This usually results in one of

them departing. On other occasions one or both of two adjacent males will perform a rapid up-down vibration, followed by the departure of one of them. On still other occasions, the initial 'leg flick' signal is ignored by another approaching male who may simply climb onto the first. This usually elicits strong vibration from the underling until the other dismounts, and is often followed by a subsequent fit of vibration on the part of the 'abused' male. As in *T. subulata*, many of these interactions between males do not appear to involve

FIG E. Male slender groundhopper attempts to mate with female common groundhopper.

E

mating attempts, and may possibly have some function either in male-to-male competition, or in maintaining the cohesion of the local population.

These interactions between males are often replicated when males of *T. undulata* encounter male *T. subulata*. Where the two species mingle (as is very frequent in the damper parts of the habitat of *T. undulata*), courtship, mating attempts and mating between the two species are common (Hochkirch *at al.*, 2006, 2008a; see under *T. subulata*; and see also Chapter 6 for more detail, and the DVD).

Enemies

As in the other groundhopper species, the cryptic coloration, and the associated behavioural disposition to settle on colour-matching surfaces, suggests selection by visual predation. Although camouflage appears to be their best defence, they are effective jumpers and, like their relatives, good swimmers.

Distribution

This species is widespread throughout most of Europe, except for southern Spain and northern Scandinavia.

T. undulata is widespread throughout Britain, and has even been recorded in the Outer Hebrides (Barra and, more recently, South Uist (Sutton, 2007e)) and Orkney. In the Scottish highlands there are strong populations in ancient pine and birch woods (Marshall & Haes, 1988). In Monmouth it is recorded at altitudes up to 300m (Sutton, 2008a).

It also appears to be widespread in Ireland. Although there are gaps in the available distribution maps, this probably results from under-recording of this cryptic insect.

Status and conservation

Although *T. undulata* is a widespread and often abundant species, it has quite exacting habitat requirements and is vulnerable to vegetation succession as well as to habitat loss to agriculture and 'development'. Unlike its sister species, *T. subulata*, it cannot fly and is likely to be relatively poor at dispersal to new sites. It is unclear whether the rare occurrence of the macropterous form is related to dispersal ability.

References: Haes & Harding, 1997; Hodgson, 1963; Hochkirch et al., 2006, 2008a; Kevan, 1952; Marshall & Haes, 1988; Sutton, 2007e, 2008a.

GRASSHOPPERS (ACRIDIDAE)

There are eleven British species in this large family. They are familiar, often abundant, inhabitants of grassland and heath. The pronotum is saddle-shaped and usually has a median keel along the dorsal surface, and a keel on each side-edge. There is also a groove, or sulcus, that cuts across the dorsal surface of the pronotum at approximately the middle. The shape of the side-edge keels and the position of the transverse sulcus are often crucial characteristics for identification.

The head bears a pair of relatively short and thickened antennae (sometimes broadened at the tip). The mouthparts are adapted for chewing vegetable matter – usually grass-blades. The female has a short, inconspicuous ovipositor, composed of two pairs of valves, while the male has an up-turned subgenital plate at the rear end of its abdomen, so the different shape of the tip of the abdomen is a useful way of distinguishing the sexes.

Stripe-winged grasshopper (© Tim Bernhard)

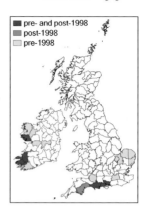

THE LARGE MARSH GRASSHOPPER

Stethophyma grossum
(Linnaeus, 1758)

MEASUREMENTS: Male: 22–9 mm in length; female: 29–36 mm in length.

FIGS A–E. Male; male dorsal view; female; female dorsal view; dark female.

Description

This is the largest of the British grasshoppers – and perhaps the most beautifully patterned. The wings are fully developed, although varying in length to some degree – extending almost to, or a few millimetres beyond, the tip of the abdomen. The leading edge of the fore wing bulges outwards towards the base. The side keels of the pronotum are gently incurved, and diverge laterally on the rear portion of the pronotum. The cerci are relatively long in the male, and the valves of the female ovipositor are long and distinctively shaped. The aperture of the hearing organ is wide, and clearly visible on each side at the anterior end of the abdomen.

In this species the colour patterns are quite distinctive, although variable. In both sexes the hind legs are ringed with black – usually around the 'knees', and often with other contrasting black patches on the femora or tibiae. The femora are bright red ventrally. The colour pattern of the males is usually more contrasting than that of the females. The dorsal surface of the head and pronotum is usually olive-green (sometimes brownish), shading to yellow laterally, and on the fore and mid legs and hind tibiae. The side keels of the pronota are outlined in yellow, and there is a black band along each side of the head behind the eye. The abdomen is green, shading to yellow ventrally, with variable black markings on each segment.

The females are usually olive green, shading to greenish yellow on the sides and underside of the abdomen, with the legs frequently green, rather than contrasting yellow, as in the males. In both sexes the fore wings are usually tinted brown, usually with a yellow stripe along the leading edge. There is often black on the paranota as well as on the sides of the head.

In some females the olive-green shades to greyish brown, and there is an uncommon purple form.

Similar species

This species is quite unlike any other British species. Its large size and colour pattern on the hind femora are unique.

Life cycle

The adults emerge rather late in the season, usually from the last week in July onwards. They continue through August and September, into October. The eggs are laid in batches of up to 14 at the base of grass tufts, enclosed in an elongated pod. They enter a resting-stage, and do not hatch until May or early June the following year. The nymphs pass through five instars before emerging as adults later in the summer.

Habitat

Earlier in the last century, this species inhabited a wider range of wet habitats than is the case now in Britain, including rough, wet meadows, marshes and moorland, as well as wet heaths. Further south, in Europe, it still does. According to Lucas (1920) it was found among rank grasses by the river Bure in Norfolk in 1892, and it formerly occurred in the Norfolk broads, the fens of Cambridgeshire, and the lower Thames marshes. In the west of Ireland it is still found by rivers and lakes, in Normandy it is found in 'fairly dry' riparian grassland (Sutton, 2007b), and in the Swiss Alps it occurs on rocky banks of mountain streams (pers. obs.).

Its current strongholds in England are acidic quaking bogs, often associated with purple moor-grass (*Molinia caerulea*), bog myrtle (*Myrica gale*), cross-leaved heath (*Erica tetralix*), *Sphagnum* mosses, broad-leaved cotton grass (*Eriophorum latifolium*) and white-beaked sedge (*Rhynchospora alba*). It is usually found in the wettest parts of such habitats, which it shares with few other orthopterans, although it is often found in the same habitat as the bog bush-cricket (*Metrioptera brachyptera*), especially in the New Forest and Dorset heaths.

Behaviour

For such a large and spectacular insect, the large marsh grasshopper is surprisingly difficult to spot. On warm days the males produce their unique 'ticking' stridulation by flicking one hind leg (sometimes both, but out of synchronisation) against a wing tip. The sound is repeated in bursts of four to ten at a rate of two to three per second. Usually the male is static while stridulating, but continues to

FIG F. Male on song perch.

F

move through the vegetation before delivering its next burst. However, sometimes a male delivers several bursts from the same perch, in alternation with a nearby competitor (see DVD). The 'song' is frequently produced from a perch as much as 20 or 30 cm above the ground, from the stem of a rush or small shrub. The male is very alert while stridulating, and any sudden movement from the observer sends it running backwards and down into the undergrowth. More active disturbance, especially in warm weather, results in the grasshopper taking to the wing, in a swift, direct flight path, often of 10 metres or more. Lucas's (1920) description of its flight and associated escape behaviour could hardly be bettered:

> One that flew near me had its long legs stretched out behind it, like those of a heron on the wing. When stalked it sometimes rises once or twice, but if thoroughly disturbed hides amongst the rank bog vegetation, with which its colours so harmonise that it is seldom again found... (Lucas, 1920: 228)

The females are usually less active, and are frequently seen lower down among low-growing plants such as *Sphagnum* moss. Both sexes are reluctant to fly in cool weather, and rely on their camouflage and ability to disappear into deep cover if alarmed.

They feed on blades and stems of grasses, rushes and sedges, sometimes biting through stems of rushes to access the more nutritious seed heads.

Enemies
Lucas (1920) reports having seen a male of this species being carried off by the hornet robber-fly, *Asilus crabroniformis*. Its cryptic coloration and the alertness of the males while stridulating suggest adaptation to visual or auditory predation – presumably from birds.

Distribution
This species is widespread (but not common, owing to its distinctive habitat requirements) throughout Europe north of the Alps, and northwards in Scandinavia to approximately 68 degrees latitude. It occurs in wet grassland and seepages in the Alps up to 2,400 metres. It is localised in northern Spain and north Italy. In the east, its range extends through eastern Europe and the former Soviet Union to Siberia.

This species has not been recorded in England north of a line from the Bristol Channel to the Wash, and even within its range it has always been restricted by its habitat requirements. It has not been recorded from Scotland or Wales, but is present in the west and south of Ireland.

It was regarded by Burr (1936) as extinct in the Cambridgeshire fens as a result of drainage, and has also been lost from its Norfolk and Thames-side localities (Marshall, 1974).

A population discovered in the Somerset Levels in 1942 was adversely affected by peat cutting and agricultural intensification. Since the 1980s there were records only from Shapwick Heath (1989) and Westhay Moor (1995), until a single specimen was reported in 2006. However, subsequent searches of the locality have proved unsuccessful (Sutton, 2007d).

It was deliberately introduced to Thursley Common, Surrey, in 1967 (Marshall & Haes, 1988) but appears to have become extinct both there, and also in what may have been a natural habitat in Surrey, where it was found in 1982. Subsequent searches of this locality have not been successful (Baldock, 1999; Sutton, 2003c).

Currently, the species appears to be confined to sphagnum-dominated mires in heathland in east Dorset and the New Forest, Hampshire. However, where suitable habitat exists in these areas, it maintains substantial populations.

Status and conservation
Haes (in Shirt 1987) rated it 'vulnerable', and considered the main threats to be drainage and shading of its habitat by afforestation.

As the species survives in a wider range of habitats in mainland Europe, it might be speculated that, with predicted warming of the UK climate, it might adopt a wider range here, and still be retained even if its current habitats in Dorset and Hampshire become too dry for it. Sutton (2007b) is sceptical about this possibility, however, as the Norfolk, Cambridgeshire, Surrey and Somerset populations were lost as habitat dried out.

However, reported extensions of its range in the Netherlands give rise to some cautious optimism (Sutton, 2008b), and the projected restoration of former East Anglian fens might allow for its reintroduction to that part of its range.

In the west of Ireland, it is threatened by peat extraction.

References: Baldock, 1999; Burr, 1936; Harz, 1975; Kleukers & Krekels, 2004; Lucas, 1920; Marshall, 1974; Marshall & Haes, 1988; Ragge, 1965; Shirt, 1987; Sutton, 2003c, 2007b, 2007d, 2008b.

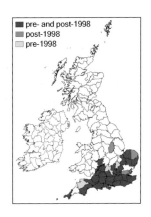

THE STRIPE-WINGED GRASSHOPPER
Stenobothrus lineatus
(Panzer, 1796)

MEASUREMENTS: Male: 15–19 mm in length; female: 17–22mm in length.

FIGS A–D. Male; male dorsal view; face; female.

Description

This handsome, medium-sized grasshopper is best identified by the unique pattern formed by the veins in the fore wings. The median area of each wing is enlarged, and the cross veins form an almost parallel series, giving a ladder-like impression. Both pairs of wings are fully developed; they reach to just beyond the tip of the abdomen in males, but are often significantly shorter in females. There is no bulge on the leading edge of the fore wing. The side keels of the pronotum are moderately inflexed or incurved, and diverge toward the rear edge of the pronotum. The males have from 300 to 450 minute stridulatory pegs on the inner surface of each hind femur, and a rather elongated subgenital plate that tapers to a point. In the female, the ovipositor valves (which usually protrude slightly from the rear end of the abdomen) have a small tooth (see the Key, Fig K21b, page 237).

There is considerable variation in colour pattern, but what is probably the most common form is green on the head, pronotum and rear edges of the wings (forming a tapering green dorsal 'roof' over the abdomen when the insect is at rest). The green shades paler down the sides of the pronotum and head, and may be considerably paler on the face, with palps sometimes white. The eyes vary from fawn to darker brown. The side keels of the pronotum are outlined in whitish to cream or pink, edged with black externally in the anterior part of the pronotum, and internally on the posterior part. The pale lines are continued forward onto the head and eventually meet at the front of the head. The wings often appear dark brown to black, but are paler in freshly emerged specimens. There is usually a white stripe close to the leading edge of the fore wing, and a white spot, or 'stigma' towards the outer tip. However, one or both of these may be absent. The upper (anterior) surface of the hind femora is commonly green, but may be fawn, brown, pinkish, or even purple.

A minority colour form has the green on the top of the head and pronotum and the rear margins of the fore wings replaced by brown or grey-brown, with a pale median longitudinal stripe on the top of the head and pronotum. In this form, the sides of the head and pronotum are green, but the anterior edge of the hind femora is generally brown. There is also a rare form in which the head, pronotum and hind legs are pink (B. Pinchen, pers. corr.)

In newly emerged individuals, the abdomen is pale grey, with dark brown patches on the sides of most segments. However, with sexual maturity, the hind three to four segments and genital plate become bright red in the male. The colour often extends further up the abdomen, and also suffuses the hind tibiae and posterior edge of the hind femora. Similar, but less spectacular colour changes also occur in the females, with orange coloration on several of the abdominal segments.

E   F

FIGS E–F. Two-colour forms.

Similar species

The wing venation is the best diagnostic feature to use, but this is not always obvious in the field. The male 'parsons nose' subgenital plate, and the toothed ovipositor valves in the female are also reliable characters, but still less easy to use in the field.

The most closely similar species, and one that often occurs together with the striped-winged, is the common green grasshopper (*Omocestus viridulus*). Many colour forms of this have brown or grey paranota, but in the stripe-winged grasshopper, these are always green, even in the 'brown' form. However, the fully green form of the common green grasshopper can look very similar indeed to the stripe-winged. Useful clues are:

- the common green never has the red or orange flush to the rear abdominal segments;
- the green on the rear margin of the fore wings is more extensive in the common green grasshopper – spreading down the sides especially in the basal half (as viewed when the insect is at rest);
- the pale outlining of the side keels of the pronotum is usually significantly narrower in the common green than in the stripe-winged, especially on the anterior part of the pronotum.

These indications are not entirely reliable, however, and for full confirmation anatomical characters should be used. In addition to the wing venation and shape of the male subgenital plate, these include the shape of the valves of the ovipositor in females: elongated and untoothed in the common green grasshopper.

Other species that could be confused with the stripe-winged grasshopper include the following:

(1) Its close relative, the lesser mottled grasshopper (*Stenobothrus stigmaticus*). This is very similar in general appearance, but as its only known locality is the southern tip of the Isle of Man, where the stripe-winged does not occur, confusion would be unlikely. The lesser mottled has rather shorter wings (rarely reaching back to the tip of the abdomen), and lacks the distinctive 'ladder' pattern of the fore-wing venation of the stripe-winged grasshopper. The male subgenital plate is less prominent in the lesser mottled, and there is usually a brownish rectangular area at the front of the paranota (which are completely green in the stripe-winged).

(2) The female of the woodland grasshopper (*Omocestus rufipes*) is often green dorsally, but does not have green paranota (always green in the stripe-winged), and lacks the distinctive 'ladder' pattern in the wing venation that is characteristic of the stripe-winged grasshopper.

(3) There is an uncommon wholly green form of the common field grasshopper (*Chorthippus brunneus*), but this has more strongly indented side keels to the pronotum, lacks the distinctive wing venation of the stripe-winged grasshopper and has a bulge on the leading edge of the fore wing.

Life cycle

The eggs are laid during the summer above the surface of the soil, among the bases of tufts of grasses. The pods contain up to eight eggs, and are oval in shape,

FIG G. Final instar nymph.

G

with plant fragments attached to the outer coating. The eggs remain dormant through the winter, and hatch in April or May the following year. The resulting nymphs pass through four instars prior to reaching adulthood by June or July. In favourable seasons and localities they may reach adulthood as early as the first week in June, becoming fully sexually mature a little later. The adults continue to be active through July, August and September, with a few surviving until October.

Habitat

The stripe-winged grasshopper favours rough, uncultivated and well-drained grasslands and heaths. It is often found, along with the rufous grasshopper (*Gomphocerippus rufus*), on south-facing, rabbit-grazed downland slopes. Elsewhere it is also found on the drier parts of heather heaths and on sandy, acid soils, as on the Suffolk heaths, and the Brecks of East Anglia. In the latter habitat it favours areas with bare ground and sparse vegetation, consisting of mosses, lichens and fine grasses, adjacent to areas of longer grass and scrub and often in association with rabbit activity.

Behaviour

Both sexes are well camouflaged in their habitat, the females, especially, being rather inactive and staying close to the ground. Both males and females retreat into deeper cover when disturbed, but also can fly effectively. If pursued, they frequently fly towards their tormenter, a very effective surprise tactic. The males are more active than the females, often wandering about and pausing every few seconds to produce a burst of stridulation. Because of the densely packed stridulatory pegs on the hind femora, the sound can be produced by a rather slow movement of the legs against the wings. Usually both legs are moved, usually out of synchronisation, and the resulting sound is a very distinctive 'wheezing' that lasts for some 10 to 20 seconds. Sometimes only one leg is used, and individuals that have lost a hind leg can still stridulate. The song is rather quiet and unobtrusive, and one frequently sees the slowly moving hind legs of a male before hearing the song. In the presence of a female, the character of the sound changes to a 'courtship' song.

In a prolonged film sequence of the courtship of this species, the male faced the female, a few centimetres away, and produced a quiet stridulation by rapid, low amplitude vibrations of the hind femora against the wings. This was continued for many minutes until the female moved off. She was soon re-found by the male who then continued with his low-amplitude stridulation (see DVD for clips of this). However, Ragge (1965) describes a more elaborate courtship pattern, consisting of an alternation between an extended version of the normal song, and a more subdued series of 'ticks' produced by more rapid leg movements. This continues for some time, culminating in a series of louder sounds produced by quick movements of the hind legs, followed by the male attempting to mate with the female. Ragge notes that the females, too, sometimes stridulate, but it is unclear what part this plays in the mating system of the species.

Distribution

The stripe-winged grasshopper is distributed throughout much of Europe, from Spain in the west, through to Siberia and Northern Mongolia in the east. Further south in Europe it is limited to moderate altitudes in mountains, for example, from 1,400 to 2,500 metres in the Alps.

In Britain, it is mainly confined to southern counties and East Anglia, with very few records from Cornwall and Devon. It occurs on the chalk downland of Dorset and the south of the Isle of Wight, and is common and widespread on south-facing slopes of the North and South Downs. Further north, it occurs, but is more localised, on the Mendips, the Cotswolds and the Chiltern hills, and (rarely) as far north as Nottinghamshire. It also occurs on heaths in Hampshire, Surrey and West Sussex, as well as in Suffolk and Norfolk. In the Brecks it is widespread, but thinly distributed on heather heath and dry grassland along rides and clearings in pine forest.

There are some indications that it is spreading into new localities, and possibly also expanding its range (Sutton, 2003c). Richmond reports new records that indicate that the species is spreading from its strongholds in the Brecks (Sutton, 2007d, 2008b, 2011), and it was discovered at a site in Epping Forest (the first Essex record) in 2010 (Wilde, 2009; Sutton, 2010a).

Status and conservation

It seems probable that a combination of agricultural intensification, afforestation and the decline of grazing by rabbits and livestock has rendered this species much more localised than in the past. However, as many of the remaining localities are managed by organisations with a conservation brief, it seems unlikely that this species is seriously endangered. In the Brecks, the open rides and large areas of clear fell associated with current management by the Forestry Commission appear to be very favourable to this species. The recent indications of range expansion could be a response to climate change, and close monitoring of suitable habitat away from its current range would be of interest.

References: Harz ,1975; Kleukers & Krekels, 2004; Lucas, 1920; Marshall & Haes, 1988; Ragge, 1965; Sutton, 2003c, 2007d, 2008b, 2010a, 2011; Wilde, 2009.

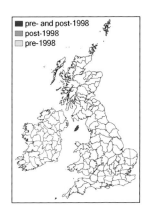

THE LESSER MOTTLED GRASSHOPPER

Stenobothrus stigmaticus
(Rambur, 1839)

MEASUREMENTS: Male: 10 to 12 mm in length; Female: 12 to 15 mm in length.

FIGS A–D. Male; male dorsal view; female; female dorsal view.

Description

The lesser mottled grasshopper is very small, with gently incurved side-keels
to the pronotum. Both pairs of wings are fully developed, but are usually
quite short. In the male they reach back almost to the tip of the abdomen, but
in females they are relatively shorter – often leaving two or three abdominal
segments exposed. The wings are also narrow, without the expanded median
zone characteristic of the stripe-winged grasshopper. The male antennae are
slightly thickened towards the tip. The ovipositor valves are toothed.

In the most frequent colour pattern, the head, pronotum, side plates of the
thorax to the rear of the paranota, and the anterior edges of the hind femora are
all bright green. The side keels of the pronotum are outlined in cream to pale
brown, with black edging externally on the anterior section of the pronotum, and,
somewhat widened as wedges, internally on the rear section of the pronotum.

The pale lines are carried forward onto the head and join at the front of the
head. The ground colour of the abdomen in freshly emerged specimens is grey.
The fore and mid legs, as well as the outer surfaces of the hind femora, are also
grey. The fore wings are fawn to cream in colour, often with a white stripe close
to the leading edge, and one or two white stigmata in the outer half of each fore
wing. There are often dark brown or black spots along the middle area of the fore
wing, and black patches at the sides of the first few abdominal segments. There is
a pale brownish rectangular patch at the front of the paranota, and the lower part
of the face is creamy white to pale brown.

As the adults become sexually mature, they develop a red tint to the
posterior segments of the abdomen, which sometimes extends to almost
the whole of the abdomen as well as the legs and wings. This is particularly
pronounced in the males.

Two minority colour forms have been noticed. In one of these, the green on
the dorsal surface of the head, pronotum and edges of the femora is replaced by
pale brown. In another form, all the green is replaced by brown. When this form
is suffused with red, the effect is very striking.

Similar species

In general appearance this species is quite similar to its close relative, the
stripe-winged grasshopper, although this does not occur in the Isle of Man.
The lesser mottled grasshopper lacks the expanded central area to the fore
wings, and the associated pattern in the wing venation, that characterise its
relative. The subgenital plate in the male is less pronounced in the lesser
mottled, and the grey or brownish patch at the front of the paranota in the
lesser mottled grasshopper is distinctive, but not evident in all colour forms.

The green form of the lesser mottled has fawn-brown rear edges to the fore wings (arched over the back at rest), while the green form of the stripe-winged always has green in this area.

Because of its small size, the lesser mottled grasshopper could be confused with the mottled grasshopper (*M. maculatus*), which does occur on the Isle of Man. However, that species has much more acutely inflexed side keels to the pronotum, and a noticeably larger head relative to the pronotum. The male antennae of the mottled grasshopper are clubbed, whereas those of the lesser mottled are only gradually thickened towards the tip.

The common green grasshopper (*O. viridulus*) is also quite similar, but lacks the grey or brownish patches on the paranota, has relatively longer wings, does not develop reddish tints with sexual maturity, and is considerably larger. Although *O. viridulus* does occur on the Isle of Man it has not been recorded in the habitats occupied by the lesser mottled.

The common field grasshopper (*C. brunneus*) does have an uncommon colour form that resembles the brown form of the lesser mottled grasshopper, but the field grasshopper has more strongly inflexed side keels and relatively longer wings, and is generally a much larger insect.

Life cycle
The eggs are laid during the summer, and enter a dormant stage over winter. Embryonic development has a high temperature threshold and so the eggs hatch late in the spring. Subsequent development is favoured by warm and sunny conditions that enable rapid 'catch-up' nymphal development (van Wingerden *et al.*, 1991; Cherrill & Selman, 2007). There are usually four nymphal instars, but (as in *C. brunneus*) females sometimes develop through five instars. The adults are present from late July until September.

Habitat
On the European mainland, the subspecies (ssp. *faberi*) to which the British population is assigned is reported to occur on *Calluna* heaths, dry meadows and steppe grassland, as well as inland dunes (Harz, 1975) and sheep pasture (Bellmann, 1988). In mainland Europe there is no special association with the coast. On the Isle of Man it exists in discrete colonies on patches of grass and heathers (*Calluna vulgaris*) and bell-heather (*Erica cinerea*), in the vicinity of rocky coastal outcrops. It occurs among shorter grasses in company with the mottled grasshopper (*M. maculatus*), but will tolerate tussocky grassland, where it occurs together with the common field grasshopper (*C. brunneus*). However, it does not occur in areas of taller grasses, or where heathers and other shrubs have more

than 50 per cent ground cover (Cherrill, 1994; Cherrill & Selman, 2007). The habitats favoured by this species have in common that they are warm and dry, with low-growing vegetation on nutrient-poor soils. In most localities moderate grazing by livestock, rabbits or deer seems to be required. Small populations were found close to the rough on the golf course that occupies the landward part of the Langness peninsula, on the Isle of Man (Cherrill & Selman, 2007; see also Chapter 9 for more detail.)

Behaviour

The Manx population seems to live in discrete colonies, with numerous males sharing favoured spots (e.g. a platform of flattened grass stems, or the flat top of a bank). In cool weather they remain inactive, but with an increase in temperature the males run actively through and over vegetation in their 'patch'. This seems to be a mate-location strategy, and when a female is encountered, males begin a courtship display. Ragge (1965) gives a detailed description of this. The process begins with a burst of soft stridulation lasting from four to six seconds in which one hind leg is moved more vigorously than the other. That leg is then moved quickly downwards to make a louder sound. After a pause of three to seven seconds there is a brief period of noiseless movement of the hind legs, followed by another burst of stridulation, which is like the first, only with the other leg moved more vigorously. The whole cycle is repeated several times, usually culminating with a mating attempt on the part of the male.

Most usually, the males are rejected, the female either jumping away, or moving off more slowly, in which case she is usually followed by the male, who then resumes courtship.

Frequently, two or more males compete with one another in courting a female, in which case antagonistic signals between the males disrupt the courtship routine described by Ragge, and brief bursts of stridulation in this context appear to have more to do with male-to-male communication than courtship (see DVD).

The calling song of the male is a rather subdued 'chirp' lasting from two to four seconds, starting soft and becoming louder. It is repeated at irregular intervals, but only in warm, sunny weather.

Distribution

Internationally, three subspecies are recognised, but the subspecies *faberi*, which includes the Isle of Man population, is widespread in central and western Europe, from lower altitudes in the Alps northwards, with north-west Germany marking the northern limit of its range on the European mainland. Eastwards, it occurs through eastern Europe to the western parts of the former Soviet Union.

In Britain it is known only from the southern tip (the Langness peninsula) of the Isle of Man, where it was first recognised in 1962 (Ragge, 1963). This is its northernmost outpost.

Status and conservation

The species is reputedly in decline in mainland Europe, where it is threatened by cessation of grazing on traditional pastures, with subsequent loss of its short-grass habitat through natural succession, and by agricultural intensification and 'improvement' of grassland (Bellmann & Luquet, 2009; van Wingerden & Dimmers, 1993).

Given the unique British distribution of this species, there has been some speculation that it might have been an accidental introduction. However, there is no obvious route by which this might have occurred. Also, Manx specimens are smaller than the ones from the continental mainland (the latter given as 11–13 mm (males) and 14–18 mm (females) in length), and this suggests that they may have been isolated for a long time. For both reasons, Ragge (1965) and Burton (1963) tentatively concluded that *S. stigmaticus* is probably a native species.

A species whose British distribution is as highly localised as that of the lesser mottled grasshopper must be considered vulnerable, despite its inclusion in the Isle of Man Wildlife Act of 1990, Section 5, and the inclusion of its habitat in a designated ASSI. An application to extend the existing golf course into the part of the peninsula occupied by the grasshopper was rejected at a public enquiry in 1990. However, the habitats continue to be privately owned, and there remains a question about appropriate management for the species. Grazing by sheep and cattle ceased around 1985, and it seems that parts of the habitat became unsuitable for *S. stigmaticus* as a result of the development of a tall, cool grass sward and encroachment by scrub (Cherrill & Selman, 2007). Resumption of grazing in one part of the peninsula in 2003 had resulted in recolonisation by the time the site was surveyed in 2006. Although rabbit grazing on habitat close to the rocky shore line may be adequate to maintain the habitat, the security of the species in its only known British locality will depend on appropriate management over the whole of the site. In the longer term, it is possible that some parts of the habitat will be threatened by sea-level rise.

References: Bellmann, 1988; Bellmann & Luquet, 2009; Burton, 1963; Cherrill, 1994; Cherrill & Selman, 2007; Evans & Edmondson, 2007; Harz, 1975; Marshall, 1974; Marshall & Haes, 1988; Ragge, 1963, 1965; van Wingerden et al., 1991; van Wingerden & Dimmers, 1993.

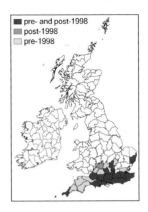

THE WOODLAND GRASSHOPPER

Omocestus rufipes
(Zetterstedt, 1821)

MEASUREMENTS: Male: 13 to17.5 mm in length; female: 18 to 22 mm in length.

FIGS A–G. Male; female dorsal; female; male face; female face; male; dark male dorsal.

Description

This is a medium-sized grasshopper, with both pairs of wings fully developed, reaching back to or beyond the tip of the abdomen in both sexes. There is no bulge on the leading edge of the fore wings. The transverse groove (sulcus) on the pronotum is anterior to the midpoint, and the side keels are strongly incurved. The ovipositor valves are short, and without teeth. The male has 90 to 130 stridulatory pegs on each hind femur.

In both sexes the side keels of the pronotum are finely outlined in white, but this may be obscured in very dark males (Fig G). When fully mature, males may be mainly black, with brown on the dorsal surface of the head, pronotum, rear-margins of the fore wings (folded over the abdomen when at rest), and the distal part of the hind femora. In these specimens, the final segments of the abdomen, the tibiae and sometimes part of the femora are bright red. The black of the face contrasts sharply with the chalk white of the palps.

The females are more variable in colour, but have two main colour forms: green and brown. In the green form, the top of the head, the pronotum and the rear edge of the fore wings are a rather dull green, sometimes shading paler medially. The white outlining of the side keels of the pronotum is clear, and bordered on the inner edge by black wedge-shaped marks on the rear section of the pronotum. The sides of the head, the pronotum and the hind femora vary from greyish through to chestnut brown. The palps, as in the male, are white, although they contrast less strongly with the face. The abdomen is greyish, with an orange-red flush on the hind segments in mature females, and black patches on the sides of the anterior segments. There are dark blackish blotches along the middle of the fore wings, usually with a white stigma towards the tip.

In the 'brown' form of the females, greyish or olive brown replaces the green dorsally, and the black wedge-shaped marks on the dorsal surface of the pronotum are larger, and continue to the rear margin of the pronotum.

E   F

FIGS E–F. Female with grey sides; brown female.

Similar species

The fully mature male is unmistakable, given its extensively black and red coloration, and the white palps are decisive in identification.

Either form of the female could be confused with one or other colour form of the common field grasshopper (*Chorthippus brunneus*). That species has more sharply inflexed side keels to the pronotum, and a small bulge on the leading edge of the fore wing which is absent in the woodland grasshopper.

The green form of the female could be confused with the following.

(1) The female common green grasshopper (*Omocestus viridulus*). This species does not develop the orange-red coloration of the rear abdominal segments, and does not have the pure white palps of *O. rufipes*. However, for confident identification, the shapes of the ovipositor in the two species are distinctive (but not easy to use as a field character) (see the Key, Figs K21a and c, page 237).

(2) The green form of the female of the stripe-winged grasshopper (*Stenobothrus lineatus*). In this species both green and brown forms of the female have the sides and front of the head and the paranota green. The palps are pale, but not pure white. Both sexes of the stripe-winged grasshopper have the expanded central section of the fore wings with the associated regular 'ladder-shaped' pattern of venation, not present in the woodland grasshopper.

The 'brown' form of the female can be confused with the heath grasshopper (*Chorthippus vagans*). This rare species is sometimes found close to woodland grasshopper habitat on heathland, and is very similar in appearance to the brown form of the female of the woodland grasshopper. A useful (but not entirely reliable) field character is that the anterior (upper, when at rest) edges of the hind femora of the heath grasshopper are usually pale brown and quite distinctly marked with dark brown blotches. The hind femora of the brown form of the woodland grasshopper are usually more uniformly coloured or mottled. More reliably, the transverse sulcus on the dorsal surface of the pronotum in the heath grasshopper cuts across the pronotum at the midpoint, or slightly posterior to it (so that the front section of the pronotum is equal to or slightly longer than the rear section), whereas in the common green grasshopper, the sulcus is further forward. Finally, the fore wings of the heath grasshopper have a small bulge on the leading edge, which is absent in the woodland grasshopper.

Life cycle

The eggs are laid from June to September in batches of five or six, and enclosed in a pod with a convex lid. The pods are deposited just below the surface of the soil, and the outer wall includes soil particles. The eggs hatch in April or May, depending on weather conditions, and the resulting nymphs pass through four instars to reach adulthood in June or early July. As the adults emerge early in this species, they are among the first to die off in late summer and early autumn. In southern France and Switzerland the species completes two full life cycles in the year, with adults present from April to June, and again from August to November (Bellmann & Luquet, 2009).

Habitat

In southern England the woodland grasshopper – as its name suggests – is to be found in open woodland, woodland edges, rides and clearings. For the first few years after clear felling or coppicing, numbers can increase very quickly. However, they decline again with woodland succession, and the species often seems to disappear altogether from a site. It appears to favour ancient deciduous woodland, but can also be found in conifer plantations.

An alternative habitat is moist or dry heathland, where it occurs in grassy hollows, often with heathers, but usually close to patches of gorse or other scrub, or stands of trees. This is characteristic of its habitat in the New Forest, Hampshire. In Cornwall it occurs on heathy areas and sea cliffs, away from woodland (Haes & Harding, 1997).

Further south in Europe, it is reported to live in a much wider range of habitats, including dry pine forests, dunes, and rocky slopes (Kleukers & Krekels, 2004; Bellmann & Luquet, 2009).

Behaviour

The calling song of the male is usually delivered from a perch above the ground – on low scrub or a tall grass stem. The hind legs move rapidly over the fore wings, almost synchronously (although in anticipation of a burst of song the male usually raises one leg). The stridulation begins noiselessly and slowly builds in intensity (although never becoming loud!) and stops suddenly. It may last from five to twenty seconds, and consists of a continuously repeated rapid series of 'ticks'. The resulting sound resembles that of a stick being drawn very rapidly across a set of railings (see DVD).

The courtship song consists of repetitions of the calling song, followed by a modified and quieter version of it 'in which the hind legs are vibrated in a rather ragged manner'. One or more quick downstrokes of the hind femora then follow and lead to the male's mating attempt (Ragge, 1965, 1986).

Virgin females apparently also stridulate, but it is not clear what role this has in their mating system.

Both sexes are inactive in overcast weather, and spend much of their time basking during sunny spells.

Distribution

The woodland grasshopper is widely distributed through Europe, especially in the south. It occurs in Spain and Portugal, through France and central Europe to Rumania and Bulgaria, and on to Turkey, Kazakhstan and southern Siberia. Its European distribution extends northwards into Norway and Finland.

In Britain it is confined to the southern counties, with some coastal records further north, in East Anglia. It has a scattered presence in coastal districts of Cornwall and in south Devon, one known locality in Somerset, and numerous sites in Dorset. However, its strongholds are in Hampshire (especially the New Forest) and in wooded areas of Surrey and Sussex, including the North and South Downs. It is common in parts of east Kent, but there is only one past record for Essex (from J. H. Flint, 1974, cited in Wake, 1997). However, after considerable unsuccessful searching of the area, Wake concluded that the record must be considered doubtful. Subsequent searches of coastal heathland in Suffolk, where the species were recorded in the 1990s by Mike Edwards (pers. corr.) proved unsuccessful, until the species was rediscovered by T. Gardiner in 2011 (pers. corr.). However, the tendency of this species to undergo wild fluctuations in population in response to heath and woodland management could well explain the failure to re-find it in these localities.

North of the river Thames, the woodland grasshopper is either absent or very localised. However, there are recent reports from north Gloucestershire – the northernmost known localities of the species in England – that indicate range expansion (Sutton, 2003c, 2010b).

Status and conservation

This species is abundant in its favoured localities, but is vulnerable to shading out of its woodland habitats. It may have benefited from modern forestry methods in the Weald of Kent and in east Kent (Marshall & Haes, 1988). As it is at the northern limit of its European range in southern England, its distribution is very localised in the northern fringes of its distribution in this country. However, with climate change it is possible that the reports of its range expansion in Gloucestershire herald a more general northerly spread. Suitable habitats at and beyond its range boundary should be carefully monitored.

References: Bellmann & Luquet, 2009; Haes & Harding, 1997; Harz, 1975; Kleukers & Krekels, 2004; Marshall & Haes, 1988; Ragge, 1965, 1986; Sutton, 2003c, 2010b; Wake, 1997.

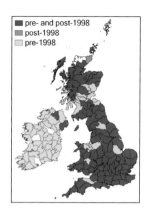

THE COMMON GREEN GRASSHOPPER
Omocestus viridulus
(Linnaeus, 1758)

MEASUREMENTS: Male 15 to 19mm in length; female 17 to 22 mm in length.

A

B

FIGS A–D. Green male; green female; brown male dorsal view; grey-sided female.

C

D

Description

This medium-sized grasshopper has fully developed wings, reaching back almost to the tip of the abdomen in females, and usually to a few millimetres beyond in males. There is no bulge on the leading edge of the fore wings. The side keels of the pronotum are strongly incurved, and the transverse sulcus is anterior to the midpoint of the dorsal surface of the pronotum. The ovipositor valves in the female are elongated and untoothed. The male has from 100 to 140 stridulatory pegs on each femur.

There is considerable variation in colour patterns, the males having 'green' or 'brown' forms.

The green form has a green head, pronotum (including paranota), hind femora, and rear edge of the fore wings (above when at rest). The side keels of the pronotum have a whitish outline, with black edging externally on the front section, and narrow wedge-shaped black markings internally on the rear section. The lower part of the face, and the antennae, palps and abdomen may be green, grey or brownish. The eyes are brown, and there are dark brown to black markings on the abdominal segments. The main central area of the wings is brown, shading to black towards the tip, often with a white stigma.

The 'brown' form of the male is more variable, possibly as a result of colour changes occurring with age. This form has brown replacing the green on the dorsal surface of the head and pronotum, and the rear edge of the fore wings. However, the side of the head and face, the paranota and the hind femora vary in colour from olive-green through grey to pale brown, often with black mottling. The sides of the abdomen often have larger areas of black on each segment in this form, and the black wedge-shaped markings on the dorsal surface of the pronotum are wider than in the green form, giving a rather striped appearance when viewed from above.

E

The females are green on the dorsal surface of the head, the pronotum and the rear edge of the fore wings (sometimes the green on the fore wings is more extensive, reaching the

FIGS E–F. Green female with brown side; brown male.

F

leading edge of the wing basally). There is sometimes a pale median line along
the dorsal surface of the head and pronotum. The side keels of the pronotum are
outlined in whitish, and they are edged with black, as in the male, but the black
edging is less extensive, especially on the rear section of the pronotum. There is
often a pale whitish or fawn median line along the head and the dorsal surface
of the pronotum. The sides and front of the head and the paranota may be of the
same green as the dorsal surfaces, or may be greyish or fawn-brown, sometimes
with darker mottling. The ground colour of the abdomen may be greyish or
very pale green, with black lateral markings on the first four or five segments.
The fore wings often have a white stripe close to the leading edge, and a faintly
marked white stigma.

There is also a rare form with purple coloration on the sides of the head, on
the paranota, and sometimes on the legs and the basal areas of the fore wings.

Similar species

(1) The stripe-winged grasshopper (*Stenobothrus lineatus*). The stripe-winged
grasshopper often occurs with the common green where their geographical
ranges overlap. The expanded middle part of the fore wings of the stripe-
winged grasshopper, and the associated 'ladder-formation' of the cross veins
serve to distinguish the two species. The untoothed ovipositor of the female
common green grasshopper is also a reliable character but is not easy to use
in the field. The stripe-winged grasshopper always has green paranota and
green sides of the head and face, distinguishing it from the colour forms of
the common green that have grey to brown sides. However, the fully green
form of *O. viridulus* can look very similar indeed to the green form of *S. lineatus*.
Mature adults of *S. lineatus* generally have bright red or orange coloration on
the rear portion of the abdomen, whereas those of *O. viridulus* do not (except
occasionally for a very slight tint on the final one or two segments). A useful
field character, when the wing venation cannot be clearly seen, is the more
extensive green on the fore wings in green forms of *O. viridulus*; when the
wings are folded over the back of the insect, the green coloration of the wings
extends down the sides basally in *O. viridulus*, but is sharply bounded along the
fold of the wings in *S. lineatus*, contrasting with the dark coloration of the rest
of the wings. See also under the stripe-winged grasshopper.

(2) The lesser mottled grasshopper (*Stenobothrus stigmaticus*). This species occurs
only on the Isle of Man in Britain, so confusion is likely to arise only there.

The lesser mottled grasshopper is noticeably smaller, and has shorter
wings, especially in the females. In all colour forms, the pale outlining of
the side keels of the pronotum is broader in *S. stigmaticus*, and also carried

forward onto the top of the head as broad, pale bands. (See also under lesser mottled grasshopper.)

(3) The female of the woodland grasshopper (*Omocestus rufipes*). The females of this species have red-orange tints on the abdomen when mature, and also have white palps, whereas the common green grasshopper rarely develops red on the abdomen, and may have pale-coloured, but not white, palps. The ovipositor valves are the most reliable character (see the Key, Figs 21a and c, page 237).

Life cycle

The egg pods are deposited during the summer at the bases of tufts of grass. They are broadly elliptical and contain up to ten eggs. These hatch the following spring, in April or early May in most years, and the resulting nymphs pass through four instars, emerging as adults from the end of May onwards. In the south the stridulation of the male can usually be heard from the first week in June onwards (as early as 19 May in the exceptionally warm spring of 2011 (pers. obs.)), later in the north and at higher altitudes. They are at their most abundant from mid-June through to early September, adults becoming scarcer into early October.

Habitat

This species is said to favour moist, grassy sites, including ditch banks, stream valleys, and damp meadows. Its habitats include parkland, open areas and ride edges in woodland, and, at higher altitudes, unimproved pastures and moorland up to 1,000 metres in Britain. It is regarded as an indicator species of unimproved pasture (Marshall & Haes, 1988). It prefers relatively tall, cool and moist grasslands, frequently with purple moor grass (*Molinea caerulea*) or Yorkshire fog (*Holcus lanatus*). It is regarded as physiologically adapted to cooler climates as it is relatively effective in raising its temperature above the ambient, and poor at cooling when ambient temperatures are high (Willott, 1997).

However, it also occurs in drier but tall grassland, and in woodland rides on well-drained soils in the East Anglian Brecks, as well as on heather heaths.

Behaviour

On sunny days the males stridulate from perches 50 cm or more above the ground on a tall grass stem or sprig of heather or gorse. The song is produced in quite extended bursts of 10 to 30 seconds or more. The movement of the hind legs against the wing veins is fast, and the whole insect may rock with the exertion involved (see DVD). The sound produced is a continuous series of rapidly repeated 'ticks', that sound very much like the song of the woodland grasshopper, only louder. The burst of song begins inaudibly and gradually gains in volume until it reaches a maximum about halfway through. Usually the insect moves to another perch after each burst of song, but it sometimes produces one or more subsequent bursts after a pause of 45 seconds or more. In open grassland, numerous males may be singing at the same time, spaced out evenly across the habitat. It is unclear whether this is chorusing behaviour or simply an incidental consequence of adjacent males alternating their songs with one another (see Chapter 5).

In the presence of a female, the male faces her and commences a prolonged and repetitive courtship performance. This consists of one or more bursts of a sharp clicking sound produced by striking the tip of the fore wings with the extended hind tibiae (a similar action to the stridulation of the large marsh grasshopper (*S. grossum*). Each burst of 'kick stridulation' consists of four to twelve kicks, and is followed directly by a prolonged but much quieter version of the normal stridulation. This is produced by low amplitude vibrations of the hind femora against the fore wings, with one hind leg working harder than its partner (either hind leg may play this role in successive repetitions). This phase of the courtship may last from 20 seconds to more than 90 seconds, after which the male remains motionless (except for twitching movements of the abdomen) for a few seconds before embarking on a new series of kick stridulations which, again, terminate in a prolonged low-intensity phase of stridulation. After many repetitions the male may move forwards, kick stridulating as he does so, to attempt mating (see clips on DVD).

According to Ragge (1965) a receptive female may respond by producing a short burst of quieter stridulation.

When stridulating, the males are very alert. Their favoured response to mild disturbance is to run backwards down a grass stem into the cover of deep vegetation. More vigorous disturbance will result in their taking to the wing, in low flights of 10 metres or more, after which they are usually extremely difficult to relocate.

Distribution

This species is widespread throughout almost all of Europe, including Scandinavia, to approximately 68 degrees north, from northern Spain in the west, and through central and eastern Europe to Siberia and Mongolia in the east. In southern Europe it is found at higher altitudes, up to 2,500 metres or more in the Alps, and as far south as central Italy.

It is present throughout almost the whole of the British Isles wherever its habitat persists. In the north it is present on the Hebrides, and the Orkneys (Sutton, 2003a), although it is absent from parts of mainland Scotland, including the north-west Highlands. It is widespread through Wales and reported to be the most widespread grasshopper in Ireland. In England it is particularly common in the northern and western uplands, the North and South Downs, Chilterns, Cotswolds and the downs of Wiltshire and Dorset. It is absent from parts of East Anglia and the south-east of England, such as parts of north Kent, East Essex and Suffolk.

Status and conservation

Although common and widespread in most parts of Britain, it has acquired conservation significance in those areas where it is scarce. Sutton (2003b and 2003c) reports its decline in parts of mainland Europe, the New Forest and also in Somerset and Devon and elsewhere in southern England. It is plausible that these declines in the southern parts of its range might be explained by warmer and drier conditions associated with climate change. Decline in the New Forest may have also occurred as part of an overall decline in orthopterans in the forest after fencing and gridding in the early 1960s led to overgrazing (Tubbs, 1986; Pinchen, pers. corr.). Significantly, it was reported to be thriving in Bushy Park, London (a humid habitat) and on Salisbury Plain (cool and damp).

In Essex its strongholds are in the west of the county, in Hatfield and Epping Forests. Elsewhere it is very local on remnants of old pasture, heaths and commons. It has not been recorded in the east of the county, which has a warmer, drier climate and predominantly sandy, well-drained soils. A decline of 50 per cent in its remaining sites in the county led to its inclusion in the county's Biodiversity Action Plan (Gardiner & Harvey, 2004; Thompson & Maclean, 1999). Gardiner & Gardiner (2009) provide an instructive account of its local extinction at a small area of relict heathland common in the ancient Writtle Forest, in mid-Essex. Formerly the species was 'widespread but local' on the common (Wake, 1997), but surveys from 2000 onwards have failed to encounter it. The lack of management of the site since the 1950s has led to encroachment by bracken, gorse scrub, and birch and oak woodland. These now occupy some 80 per cent of the site.

In some upland habitats (the Malvern Hills and the Cotswolds) a combination of lack of grazing at lower altitudes with intensive sheep grazing on hilltops limits the species to a narrow band of habitat between the two (Gardiner, 2011a).

Current evidence suggests that in most habitats some grazing is required to prevent shading out of the habitat, but that if this is so intense as to produce a short sward this, too, eliminates the grasshopper. Gardiner (2010b) notes that in Epping Forest low-intensity grazing (1–2 cows per 10 hectares) by English Longhorn cattle seems to be beneficial.

References: Gardiner, 2010b, 2011a; Gardiner & Gardiner, 2009; Gardiner & Harvey, 2004; Harz, 1975; Kleukers & Krekels, 2004; Marshall & Haes, 1988; Ragge, 1965; Sutton, 2003b, 2003c; Thompson & Maclean, 1999; Wake, 1997; Willott, 1997.

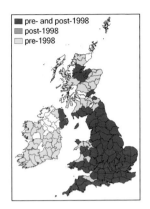

pre- and post-1998
post-1998
pre-1998

THE COMMON FIELD GRASSHOPPER

Chorthippus brunneus
(Thunberg, 1815)

MEASUREMENTS: Male 15–19 mm in length; Female 19–25 mm in length.

A

B

FIGS A–C. Male; dorsal view; female.

C

Description

This medium-sized grasshopper has strongly inflexed side keels to the pronotum, and the transverse sulcus on the pronotum is anterior to the midpoint. The wings are long, usually clearly reaching back beyond the hind knees and tip of the abdomen. Both sexes have a 'bulge' on the leading edge of each fore wing, located close to the opening of the hearing organ at the side of the abdomen when the wings are folded. The underside of the thorax is densely hairy. Males are generally noticeably smaller than females, with relatively longer antennae. They have 50 to 90 stridulatory pegs on each hind femur.

The colour patterns are extremely varied in both males and females. Ragge (1965) distinguishes the following 12 categories (with considerable detailed variation within each!).

(1) *Striped*: a very common form, usually brown, grey or straw-coloured, with side keels outlined pale, dark wedge-shaped marks on the pronotum, and the rear part of fore wings plain or striped (not mottled).
(2) *Mottled*: another common form, with mottling on the rear portion of the fore wings. Side keels not clearly outlined, and lacking wedge marks on the pronotum.
(3) *Semi-mottled*: also common, brown, grey or straw coloured, with side keels outlined in white and wedge marks on the pronotum.

FIGS D–G. Striped female; mottled male; semi-mottled female; green male.

FIGS H–N. Green brown sides female; green lilac sides female; purple female; purple brown sides female; buff female; black male; black pale sides.

(4) *Green*: head and pronotum entirely green.
(5) *Green brown sides*: green on the dorsal surface of the head and pronotum, and on the rear margin of the fore wings. The sides of the head, the pronotum and the main area of the fore wing may be brown (5a), rust-brown, or (5b) lilac.
(6) *Green brown wings*: as above, but lacking green on the fore wings (not illustrated).
(7) *Purple*: head and pronotum entirely pink, reddish or purple.
(8) *Purple brown sides*: dorsal surface of the head, pronotum and rear portion of the fore wings purple.
(9) *Purple brown wings*: as above, but without purple coloration of any part of the fore wings (not illustrated).
(10) *Buff*: head and pronotum orange, orange-brown or yellow.
(11) *Black*: head, pronotum and wings entirely black.
(12) *Black pale sides*: dorsal surface of the head and pronotum, and the rear portion of the wings black or dark grey, with the sides orange, orange-brown or yellow.

The mix and proportions of these colour forms varies greatly from one local population to another. However, in general it can be said that forms 1, 2, 3, 5 and 10 are relatively common, whereas the others are less so and may not occur at all in some populations.

Sexually mature males develop bright orange-red tints on the dorsal surface of the final four or five abdominal segments, and females, too, develop orange coloration on the rear abdominal segments, although this is not as striking as in the males. The underside of the abdomen is yellow or pale greenish yellow.

Some colour forms have a white stripe along the leading edge of the fore wings, and may also have a whitish stigma.

Similar species
The most closely similar British species is the very rare heath grasshopper (*Chorthippus vagans*). That species is so rare that in most localities confusion with the common field can be ruled out by location alone. However, where the heath grasshopper does occur (or might yet be discovered!) it is important to be able to separate the two species. The heath grasshopper is generally smaller than the common field, and less variable in its colour patterns. The most reliable character (not one easily used in the field, but quite clearly recognisable in sharp photographs) is the position of the transverse sulcus on the dorsal surface of the pronotum. This cuts across in front of the midpoint in *C. brunneus*, but at or behind the midpoint in *C. vagans* (i.e. the rear section of the pronotum is

distinctly longer than the front section in C. *brunneus*, equal or shorter in C. *vagans*). In C. *vagans* the wings are usually relatively shorter, rarely reaching beyond the hind knees, and the underside of the thorax is only sparsely hairy (densely so in C. *brunneus*). The width of the head is narrow relative to the distance from the tip of the head to hind margin of the pronotum in C. *vagans*, slightly wider in C. *brunneus* (giving C. *vagans*, especially in the males, a 'slimmer', more elongated appearance when viewed from above). A very useful field character that seems to be reliable is that the black wedge-shaped markings on the rear portion of the dorsal surface of the pronotum reach back to the rear margin of the pronotum in C. *vagans*, but stop short of the rear margin in C. *brunneus* (when present at all). C. *vagans* has alternating pale and dark brown areas on the upper edges of the hind femora – not a common feature in C. *brunneus*.

The various green forms of C. *brunneus* could be mistaken for green forms of stripe-winged, common green or lesser mottled grasshoppers. Often the resemblance in colour pattern can be remarkably close. However, the sharply inflexed side keels to the pronotum, the long wings and the bulge on the leading edge of the fore wings serve to distinguish it readily from these other species.

The very localised rufous grasshopper (*Gomphocerippus rufus*) also has similar colour forms to some of those exhibited by the common field, and also has rather similarly inflexed pronotal side keels. However, G. *rufus* has relatively shorter wings, and noticeably club-tipped antennae.

Life cycle
The eggs are laid in the soil, at a depth of about one centimetre, with up to 14 forming two or three rows in a large pod, equipped with a lid (see Chapter 3, Fig 61). They hatch from late April through to June the following year. Males pass through four nymphal instars before emerging as adults from the beginning of July onwards. Some females go through five nymphal stages, while others complete development in only four. Warmer conditions during early nymphal development and with abundant food increase the likelihood of females adding the extra nymphal stage. The switch between the four- or five-stage developmental pathways is the moult at the end of the second instar. In female nymphs destined to complete their development in four instars, this moult leads to the normal penultimate (third) stage of development, in which the wing stubs are inverted and point back with their leading edge along the midline of the dorsal surface of the abdomen. However, in female nymphs destined to develop through five nymphal instars, the moult gives rise to a larger nymph that retains the main features of the second instar. This then goes on to pass

through two further instars (fourth and fifth) that are broadly similar in stage of development of the genitalia and wings to stages 3 and 4 of the 'standard' four-stage developmental process. Normally the adult females that emerge from the five-stage process are larger than the others and capable of laying larger egg clutches (see Chapter 3, Fig 65, for images of nymphal stages).

Recent research has shown that there is a seasonal dimension to this variation in life-history strategies. It seems that eggs laid early in the summer are smaller than those that are laid later. The earlier-laid eggs develop at various rates, but all enter diapause at a certain stage of embryonic development, and overwinter at that stage. They hatch more or less synchronously early the following year. These early hatchlings are smaller than the offspring of eggs laid later the previous year, but given favourable early summer climatic conditions, the females are more likely to go on to develop through five nymphal instars. Conversely, eggs laid later in the summer tend to be larger, and do not reach the diapause stage by the onset of winter. As a consequence they avoid diapause, and go on to develop the following year with later, and more divergent hatching dates. These later hatchlings are larger than the earlier ones and the females of these are more likely to complete their development in just four nymphal stages.

This difference of developmental strategy can be explained in terms of a trade-off between, on the one hand, better survival chances of the offspring that develop earlier in the year, and on average greater fecundity of the larger females produced, and, on the other hand, the greater female 'parental investment' in the later-laid eggs, given the shorter period and less favourable conditions for development and reproduction that they are likely to encounter as they emerge later the following summer (Collins, 2001, 2006; Cherrill, 2002, 2004, 2005; Cherrill & Begon, 1989a, 1991; Cherrill & Haswell, 2006; see also Chapter 3 for more detail).

There is evidence that this seasonal difference in life-history strategies is also played out geographically, with larger, five-instar females being less frequent in more northerly localities (Telfer & Hassall, 1999).

Possibly owing to these complexities in its life history, adults of this species can be found from as early as the end of May (Pinchen, pers. corr.) through June, July, August and September, less commonly in October, and into early November in the south. An exceptionally late observation of a singing male was by J. Paul on 11 December 2004 (Sutton, 2005a).

Habitat

This species flourishes in a wide range of habitats – often ones that might appear hostile to the survival of any species. These include: roadside verges; sand dunes; dry rocky slopes; sandy or gravelly banks; the edges of car parks; recently disturbed land, such as eroding coastal cliffs, quarries or building sites; dry pastures; and open areas in woodland. However, these share common features: at least some sparse grasses, patches of bare ground with loose soil or fine gravel, and exposure to sunshine. Compared with other species, it is effective at raising its body temperature above the ambient, as well as avoiding overheating. For this it does require habitats open to sunshine, but it appears not to need tall, cooler grass tussocks for shelter from high temperatures (Willott, 1997). Although tolerant of a wide range of habitats, it is rarely found in moist or lush grassland. It is also absent from intensively managed and 'improved' farm grasslands (Gardiner, 2009a).

Behaviour

Both sexes spend much of their time on the ground or in low vegetation, frequently sunning themselves on exposed substrates such as rocks, items of litter, or concrete structures. Males are particularly active in warm conditions, and spend much of their time chasing females – often three or four in hot pursuit of a single female. Sometimes the males deliver a solitary calling song. This consists of a series of 6 to 10 short chirps (each chirp lasting half a second), with one or two seconds between chirps. The whole performance is repeated at regular intervals. However, the males are highly gregarious, and a still, silent male will be provoked into chirping by the approach of another male. Two males together will chirp alternately and the chirp rate becomes faster, producing an even more complex interaction when other males gather. Typically this happens as males assemble around a solitary female as she basks or feeds on grass blades. With rather little warning (sometimes by the male antennating the female, or by his producing a sharp noise by a quick downstroke of the hind legs) one of the males will make a mating attempt. If the female is not receptive she may kick him away with her hind legs, or she may hop away, in which case the males will usually follow and gather round her, chirping as before (see DVD).

Females, too, are able to stridulate, but their chirp is quieter than that of the male. Receptive females stridulate in response to the male stridulation.

There are reports of swarming behaviour, with numbers flying up to several hundred metres (Haes, 1976; Marshall & Haes, 1988). This is presumably a significant aid to colonisation of new sites.

Enemies

Eggs are attacked by parasitic wasps of the genus *Scelio*. Richards and Waloff (1954) reported 19 to 28 per cent of pods affected. A study of predation on this species and the mottled grasshopper (*M. maculatus*) in north-west England (Cherrill & Begon, 1989b) revealed very high rates of predation by wolf spiders of the genus *Pardosa* (Lycosidae) on early instars. Both nymphs and adults are taken by the solitary wasp *Tachysphex pompiliformis* (Richards & Waloff, 1954; N. Owens, pers. corr.).

The adults are frequent victims of large web-spinning spiders, such as the garden spider (*Araneus diadematus*) and wasp spider (*Argiope bruennichi*). Also, *C. brunneus* is among a small number of common species that form a significant part of the diet of declining farmland birds, such as cirl bunting (*Emberiza cirlus*), skylark (*Alauda arvensis*) and grey partridge (*Perdix perdix*) (Brickle et al., 2000; Robinson et al., 2001).

Distribution

This very widespread species occurs throughout Europe, eastwards through the middle-east to northern China, and southwards into north Africa.

In England the common field grasshopper is very common and widespread south of Yorkshire, but is more localised further north, becoming primarily a coastal species into Scotland. In Wales it is also widespread, but mainly in the lowland areas. It is present on the Isle of Man, the Scilly Isles and the Inner Hebrides.

Status and conservation

Although both common and widespread, this species does have definite habitat requirements. A survey of roadside verges in Essex, for example, found this species to be much more specialist in its habitat requirements than its relative, the common meadow grasshopper (*C. parallelus*) (pers. obs.). Dry, sparsely vegetated habitats with well drained nutrient poor substrates that are exposed to the sun – often on south-facing banks – are characteristic. Many of its habitats are provided as unintended consequences of human activity, and it could be locally threatened by excessive tidy-mindedness in the management of open spaces and marginal patches of land in urban and suburban areas. Fertilisation, frequent mowing, intensive grazing, and prolonged neglect leading to scrubbing over of habitat, are all threats to the survival of local populations. However, as it flies readily and well, it is likely to be effective at dispersal to new sites.

References: Brickle et al., 2000; Cherrill, 2002, 2004, 2005; Cherrill & Begon, 1989a, 1989b, 1991; Cherrill & Haswell, 2006; Collins, 2001, 2006; Gardiner, 2009a; Haes, 1976; Harz, 1975; Marshall & Haes, 1988; Ragge, 1965; Richards & Waloff, 1954; Robinson et al., 2001; Sutton, 2005a; Telfer & Hassall, 1999; Willott, 1997.

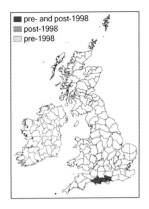

THE HEATH GRASSHOPPER

Chorthippus vagans
(Eversmann, 1848)

measurements: Male 13 to 16mm in length; females 16 to 21 mm in length.

FIGS A–D. Male; male dorsal view; female; female dorsal view.

FIG E. Grey form.

E

Description

This rare species has strongly inflexed side keels to the pronotum, fully developed wings which, however, are usually relatively short: reaching back to the hind knees, or just short of them. There is a slight bulge on the leading edge of each fore wing, close to the opening of the hearing organ on the abdomen when the wings are folded.

The transverse sulcus on the dorsal surface of the pronotum cuts across at the midpoint, or slightly posterior to it, so that the front section of the pronotum is equal to or longer than the rear section. The underside of the thorax is only sparsely hairy.

This species shows relatively little variation in colour pattern. The dorsal surface of the head and pronotum varies from olive-brown to grey, with the rear portion of the fore wings (uppermost when the wings are folded) usually of the same colour. The side keels on the pronotum are outlined in white or pale brown and edged externally dark brown to black, and internally on the rear portion by black wedges of varying width, but always reaching to the rear margin of the pronotum (in British specimens). In one common form, the sides of the head and thorax are plain grey, often with some shading to brown dorsally. In others there is irregular patterning of orange and chestnut-brown. The anterior segments of the abdomen have black patches at the sides, and in sexually mature specimens of both sexes, the rear segments of the abdomen are coloured orange-red, especially on the dorsal surface. This also tints the hind tibiae and femora. In most specimens there are dark blotches on a paler ground colour on the hind femora, especially on the anterior (upper) edge.

Similar species

There are two species that might be confused with the heath grasshopper.

(1) The common field grasshopper (*Chorthippus brunneus*). This species is usually larger than the heath grasshopper, and has longer wings in relation to the body. A reliable structural feature is the position of the transverse sulcus on the dorsal surface of the pronotum: anterior to the midpoint in *C. brunneus*, at or posterior to the middle in *C. vagans*. The underside of the thorax is densely hairy in *C. brunneus*, only sparsely so in *C. vagans*. A very useful field

FIGS F–G. Dorsal surface of the pronotum of C. *vagans*; dorsal surface of the pronotum of C. *brunneus*.

F   G

character in English specimens is the extent of the wedge-shaped black marks on the dorsal surface of the pronotum. These extend to the rear margin of the pronotum in C. *vagans*, but fall short of it in C. *brunneus*.

(2) The mottled grasshopper (*Myrmeleotettix maculatus*). This species does occur with the heath grasshopper in some sites, and could be confused with it – especially in the females. However, C. *vagans* is generally larger than *M. maculatus*. The latter species has much more strongly inflexed side keels on the pronotum, and also has the antennae thickened towards the tip in females, and distinctly clubbed in males. The transverse sulcus on the pronotum is anterior to the midpoint in *M. maculatus*, and that species also lacks the basal bulge on the leading edge of the fore wing.

Life cycle

The egg pods contain batches of approximately six to eight eggs, and they are deposited 0.5 to 1.5 cm below the surface of the soil. The eggs hatch during May or June the following year. The resulting nymphs pass through four instars and emerge as adults from early July and through August. They are at their peak in August, but can also be found in September, although in smaller numbers.

Habitat

In Britain this species occurs exclusively on dry heathland, often on the south-facing slopes of ridges or small hills, and associated with heathers as well as low-growing gorse scrub. Sparsely vegetated patches with bare, sandy ground appear also to be important.

Elsewhere in Europe it occurs in a wider range of habitats, including forest/dune transitional zones, arid grasslands, rocky slopes, quarries and railway embankments (Bellmann, 1988; Kleukers & Krekels, 2004). A German study found it positively associated with bare ground, and negatively with tree cover and leaf litter (Hochkirch *et al.*, 2008b) in a transitional zone between forest and inland dunes. The eggs are resistant to desiccation (Ingrisch, 1983), and the species seems adapted to hot, dry conditions. However, Hochkirch *et al.* found that nearby areas of taller vegetation and higher moisture content were used for shelter at high ambient temperatures.

Behaviour

They are active only during warm, sunny days. When weather conditions are favourable, and especially around the middle of the day, the males move around in vegetation and over bare ground, occasionally stopping to stridulate. The song is rather subdued, and consists of extended bursts of five seconds or more. It resembles the song of the meadow grasshopper, but is softer, and of longer duration. The song is repeated at irregular intervals. Interacting males exchange shorter, more frequent bursts of stridulation.

There is no distinct courtship song, but in the presence of a female the male makes a more abrupt sound by single down strokes of the hind legs.

Unusually for a British grasshopper, it feeds on plants such as heather and gorse as well as grasses (see DVD). Its preferred method of escape is to retreat into dense vegetation, except on hot days when it flies more readily. Hochkirch *et al.* (2008b) measured the dispersal ability of the species, showing that a proportion of their study population were able to disperse to an adjacent colony – the maximum distance moved by a single male being 180 metres.

History

The species was first thought to occur in Britain when a specimen labelled 'New Forest' was discovered in the collection of the Natural History Museum, London, by B. P. Uvarov (1922). Subsequently W. R. Frazer identified two specimens he had collected at Wareham, Dorset in 1934 (Frazer, 1944). Another collection, made at Studland, Dorset, in 1933, and subsequently passed to the Natural History Museum, was also found to contain this species. In 1947 others were found on Sopley Common, Hampshire. Subsequently Ragge was able to confirm and study these populations, reporting on the then-known status of the species (Ragge, 1954, 1965; Marshall, 1974).

Distribution

This species occurs from Denmark in the north, through Europe to Calabria in the south, and southern Spain in the west. To the east in occurs in Romania, Bulgaria, Slovenia, and the European part of the former Soviet Union as far as Kazakhstan.

In southern Britain it is at the northern edge of its climatic range, and confined to heathland in Dorset and Hampshire. In occurs locally on the heaths to the south and west of Poole Harbour, in a few remaining heathland sites in the Bournemouth area, and further east on the western fringe of the New Forest.

Status and conservation

This species is declining over much of its European range and regarded as vulnerable or endangered in a number of European countries (e.g. Germany, Switzerland, Belgium, the Netherlands and Luxemburg). Factors responsible for the decline include agricultural intensification, urbanisation, and conversion of some of its habitats for recreational use.

A study by Hochkirch *et al.* (2008b) on an inland dune in north-west Germany confirmed their view of it as a species of the transitional zone between forest and open dunes. A population on the open dune tended to seek out cooler, less dry microhabitats with taller grasses, whereas those in a recently cleared but previously forested area tended to occupy areas with greater irradiation and less leaf litter. Their conclusion was that the main threat to the species was the elimination of transitional zones between forest and dry, low-nutrient open habitats such as dunes (presumably also sandy heathland and other sparsely vegetated habitats). Sharp boundaries between these habitat types, as well as shading, either by succession or plantations, were seen as major threats. On their study site, thinning of forest trees and removal of leaf litter to increase both insolation and bare ground was followed by a large increase in population.

Marshall & Haes (1988) describe the species as vulnerable in Britain. Even at its favoured localities, numbers of this species fluctuate greatly from year to year, presumably in relation to weather. The main threats to it here have been loss and fragmentation of its heathland habitats, especially in the Bournmouth area, where heathland has been lost to agriculture and urban development. Afforestation of open heathland, as well as shading out by succession to scrub and secondary woodland is also a threat where heathland is not under conservation management.

Sutton (2003c) expressed concern about the threat of heathland fires, especially in hot, dry summers, although it was reported to have survived a recent fire on Upton Heath, Dorset. More research on the ecology of the few remaining UK populations and appropriate management regimes is required.

References: Bellmann, 1988; Frazer, 1944; Harz, 1975; Hochkirch et al., 2008b; Ingrisch, 1983; Kleukers & Krekels, 2004; Marshall, 1974; Marshall & Haes, 1988; Ragge, 1954; Ragge, 1965; Sutton, 2003c; Uvarov, 1922.

THE MEADOW GRASSHOPPER

Chorthippus parallelus
(Zetterstedt, 1821)

MEASUREMENTS: Male 10 to 17mm in length; female 16 to 23 mm in length.

A

B

C

FIGS A–C. Male; male dorsal view; female.

Description

This very common species is usually recognisable because of its very much reduced wings. This is particularly true of the females whose wings generally do not reach back beyond the rear margin of the second or third abdominal segment. The wings of the male are better developed, but still do not reach back as far as the hind 'knees'. There is a small bulge near the base of the leading edge of each fore wing. This is easier to make out in the male, but is also present in the female. The side keels of the pronotum are slightly incurved (not inflexed). The males are

FIGS D–I. Green female; green brown legs; green brown sides; dorsal stripe female; brown female; purple female (© J. Dobson).

considerably smaller than the females, and have noticeably longer antennae.

There is an uncommon form (f. *explicatus* (Sélys)) with fully developed wings, and, to make matters more complicated, there are also intermediate forms (see Chapter 3, Figs 68 and 70d).

This species, like its relative, the common field grasshopper, displays immense variability in its colour forms. The permutation of patterns includes various distributions of green, pink, purple, brown, rust-brown, grey, yellow and black.

Ragge (1965) offers a useful simplifying classification that fits each of these forms into six categories.

(1) *Green*: head, pronotum and the 'upper' edge of the hind femora green.
(2) *Green brown legs*: head and pronotum green, but the 'upper' edge of the femora other colours (brown, grey, etc.).
(3) *Green brown sides*: dorsal surface of the head and pronotum green, with the sides various other colours.
(4) *Dorsal stripe*: sides of the head and pronotum green, with the dorsal surfaces various colours. This includes striking forms with pink or purple on the top of the head and pronotum.
(5) *Brown*: various combinations of grey, brown or black, but no green on the head, pronotum or upper edge of the hind femora.
(6) *Purple*: head, pronotum and upper parts of the hind femora and abdomen pink-purple. This form occurs only in the females.

The eyes are usually chestnut to dark brown, and the side keels of the pronotum are often (but not always) outlined in whitish. Sometimes there is also a narrow black edging to the side keels, and occasionally this is extended internally to form wedge-shaped marks on the dorsal surface of the pronotum like those of the common field grasshopper. Either sex may also have a white stripe (usually indistinct) along the leading edge of each fore wing, and/or a white stigma towards the tip of the wing.

The abdomen often has a median dorsal stripe of a different colour (noticeable in females and nymphs), and there are black markings of variable extent on the sides of the abdominal segments.

The males almost always have black or very dark brown hind 'knees', which contrast with the rest of the visible parts of the femora.

Similar species

The very short wings of the females distinguish them from all other British species.

In both sexes, the slightly incurved, not inflexed, side keels of the pronotum distinguish this species from all others except the large and lesser marsh grasshopper (*Stethophyma grossum* and *Chorthippus albomarginatus*). This species is unlikely to be mistaken for the large marsh grasshopper on grounds of size and wing length. However, the lesser marsh grasshopper has parallel or sometimes slightly incurved side keels to the pronotum, and males of *C. parallelus* with relatively well-developed wings can be difficult to distinguish with confidence in the field from males of *C. albomarginatus*. Usually the wings of male *C. albomarginatus* reach almost to, or slightly beyond, the hind 'knees', while in normal forms of *C. parallelus* they fall well short of the hind 'knees'. Males of *C. parallelus* have a definite basal bulge on the leading edge of the fore wing, whereas this is absent (or vestigial) in male *C. albomarginatus* (but present in females). Males of *C. parallelus* also have a distinctive posture when at rest, with head and pronotum slightly upward sloping, as if they are 'sitting up'. Males of *C. albomarginatus* tend to align their bodies more closely with the vegetation they are resting on – 'sitting tight'. In sunny weather, of course, the songs of the two species are a very reliable diagnostic character.

Finally, a useful, if not entirely reliable, guide to field identification is the black-brown colour of the 'knees' of male *C. parallelus* – usually the same colour, or paler than the rest of the visible parts of the femora in *C. albomarginatus*. If in doubt, it is best to use a combination of the above characters.

The long-winged form of *C. parallelus* is often *very* long-winged – i.e., its wings are considerably longer than those of *C. albomarginatus*. For intermediate forms it is advisable to use other characters for identification.

Life cycle

Clutches of up to 10 eggs are enclosed in a pear-shaped pod, deposited just below the surface of the soil. The winter is passed in this stage, and the nymphs emerge early the following spring – usually from April onwards. The males pass through four nymphal stages, and the females either four or five, with adults usually emerging from the beginning of June onwards in the south (see Chapter 3, Fig 64). In the unusually warm spring of 2011 males were heard singing on Wanstead Flats, London, on 18 May (pers. obs.). They are abundant from July through to the end of September, with numbers declining in October.

Habitat

The meadow grasshopper can be found on most types of grassland, including quite small strips on roadside verges and central reservations, along the edges of arable fields as well as in flood meadows, rough pastures, open woodland

and rides, both dry and damp heathland, coastal and inland marshes, downs, and moorland up to 1,800 metres in the north of its range. It can be particularly abundant on lush, damp unimproved grassland. However, it is one of the few species that persists, albeit in reduced numbers, on farm grasslands. It favours grassland with intermediate sward heights of 10 to 20 cm. Although it is positively associated with fine grasses, such as *Agrostis* species, coarser grasses, such as *Lolium perenne*, are selected for food (Gardiner & Hill, 2004b), implying that sward structure is of greater significance than food source in shaping its habitat preferences.

Behaviour

The males sing from a perch, often 10 to 20 cm above the ground on a grass stem. The sound is a rather rough 'churring', delivered in distinct bursts (echemes) each of which lasts from one to three seconds, beginning quietly and increasing in volume. It consists of 10 to 15 pulses, each produced by a single up-down motion of the hind femora. The song is repeated, usually at irregular intervals of some fifteen to twenty seconds (longer at low temperatures), and usually from the same perch. Where populations are relatively dense, 'duets' may be established between adjacent singing males, each alternating with the chirps of the other. Such alternations can go on for several minutes, and the intervals between chirps become more regular than when a male sings solo (see DVD).

There is no distinct courtship song, but in the presence of a female the male faces her, with antennae pointing towards her, and delivers a quieter version of the calling song. This may persist for many minutes before the male eventually moves towards the female and attempts to mate. Usually (as with most species!) the female moves away, only to be followed by the male, with a repetition of the courtship sequence. According to Ragge (1965) receptive females make silent stridulatory movements with their hind legs, and males may make a sound with single down strokes of the hind femora prior to making a mating attempt. Females are polyandrous, probably mating once every six or seven days. Copulation lasts about 15 minutes (Reinhardt et al., 2007).

Females are relatively inactive, and usually rest or feed low down among grasses, or seek oviposition sites in patches of bare ground or among surface litter (see DVD).

A behavioural study carried out by Gardiner on a population in a grazed hay meadow showed directional patterns of dispersal. Adults, in particular, moved uphill from the short turf of the introduction site towards an area of longer grass some three metres away. It seems probable that the more favourable habitat was detected visually (Gardiner & Hill, 2004a; Gardiner, 2009a).

Enemies

The eggs are parasitised by wasps of the genus *Scelio*, with as many as 19 to 28 per cent of pods affected in the study by Richards & Waloff (1954). Adults and nymphs are taken by the wasp *Tachysphex pompiliformis*. The adults are among the most frequent prey of large, web-spinning spiders, including the garden spider (*Araneus diadematus*) and wasp spider (*Argiope bruennichi*).

Like *C. brunneus*, they form an important component of the diet of several declining farmland bird species, including skylark (*Alauda arvensis*), grey partridge (*Perdix perdix*) and cirl bunting (*Emberiza cirlus*).

Distribution

The meadow grasshopper is distributed throughout Europe, including Scandinavia, up to the Arctic circle, and eastwards to Turkey, Mongolia and Siberia. In southern Europe it may be found up to altitudes of 2,200 metres.

It is abundant and widespread in southern England, East Anglia, the Midlands and most of Wales. It persists more locally northwards to the north of Scotland, and has been recorded from the Orkneys and Inner Hebrides. However, it appears to be absent from the Isle of Man and from Ireland.

Form f. *explicatus* was reported to be particularly frequent in 1941 (Kevan, 1953).

Status and conservation

C. parallelus is possibly our most common and widespread species, surviving in most types of grassland apart from the most intensively grazed, cut or fertilised. However, its conservation is still important in those parts of southern and central England where the spread of intensive agriculture and silage production have greatly reduced the availability of habitat for this species. There is a further conservation significance in the importance of this as one of a small number of still common grasshopper species in the diet of several declining farmland birds. Studies by Tim Gardiner and co-workers have established the value of a range of locations – remaining patches of unimproved grassland; set-aside strips; various stewardship prescriptions; varied cutting and grazing regimes; hedgerows; and footpaths – for the survival of this species in the context of predominantly agricultural landscapes (Gardiner, 2007b, 2009a; Gardiner & Haines, 2008; Gardiner & Hill, 2005a, 2005b; Gardiner et al., 2002, 2008; and for a detailed discussion of this literature, see Chapter 9).

References: Gardiner, 2007b, 2009a; Gardiner & Haines, 2008, Gardiner & Hill, 2004a, 2004b, 2005a, 2005b; Gardiner et al., 2002, 2008; Harz, 1975; Kevan, 1953; Marshall & Haes, 1988; Ragge, 1965; Reinhardt et al., 2007.

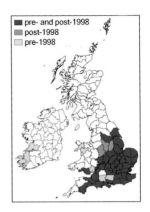

THE LESSER MARSH GRASSHOPPER

Chorthippus albomarginatus
(De Geer, 1773)

MEASUREMENTS: Male 14 to 16.5 mm in length; female 17 to 21 mm in length.

A

B

FIGS A–C. Male; dorsal view; female.

C

FIGS D–H. Brown male; green female; green brown sides male; dorsal stripe female; dorsal stripe (purple) female.

Description

This medium-sized grasshopper has fully developed, but rather short wings that reach back almost to, or just beyond, the hind 'knees'. There is a definite bulge towards the base of the leading edge of each fore wing in the female. This is either absent or vestigial in the male. The side keels of the pronotum are either straight and parallel to one another, or very slightly incurved. In some females the abdomen projects well beyond the hind knees and wing tips, giving the appearance of a short-winged species. Females are significantly larger than the males, and the latter have noticeably longer antennae. The males have 90 to 140 stridulatory pegs on each hind femur.

Although this species is not as variable in colour pattern as the common field and meadow grasshoppers, there is still a good deal of variation. Again, Ragge (1965) offers a useful classification.

(1) *Brown*: no green on the head or pronotum.
(2) *Green*: head, pronotum and 'upper' edge of the hind femora green.

(3) *Green brown legs*: head and pronotum green but 'upper' edge of the hind femora brown, grey, pink, etc. (not illustrated).
(4) *Green brown sides*: dorsal surface of the head and pronotum green, but the sides of the head and pronotum brown, grey, etc.
(5) *Dorsal stripe*: dorsal surface of the head and pronotum grey, brown, or purple, but the sides of head and pronotum green.

Within each of Ragge's categories there is considerable variation in ground colour. For example, the 'brown' form may be grey, brown or straw-coloured. The various green forms generally have predominantly green fore wings, too. Both green and brown forms tend to have well-marked white stripes close to the leading edge of the fore wings in the females, less commonly in the males. The side keels of the pronotum are usually outlined in white, and often have a narrow black edging externally. The hind femora are usually unmarked, lacking dark bands or spots.

Similar species
The parallel side keels on the pronotum and the fully developed wings should serve to distinguish this species from all other British grasshoppers. However, the pronotal side keels are slightly incurved in some individuals, and confusion with males of *C. parallelus* is quite possible. The black/dark-brown hind 'knees' in *C. parallelus* males are a useful field character, but for other, more reliable, features, see under that species.

Life cycle
The eggs are laid in batches of three to ten, enclosed in an irregularly-shaped pod deposited at the base of grass stems. They hatch in May the following year, and the nymphs pass through four instars, emerging as adults from the beginning of July onwards. The adults are most frequent from late July through to the end of September (see Chapter 3, Fig 63 for images of the life history stages).

Habitat
This species was formerly strongly associated with moist grasslands, especially coastal flood defences, grazing marshes, dune systems, and damp meadows in river flood plains. However, in recent decades it has been recorded frequently from dry habitats, including track sides on farmland, dry hillside pastures, roadside verges and dry grass heathland, such as the East Anglian Brecks. This may indicate a change in its habitat requirements, but earlier commentators also noted its ability to occupy dry grassland sites (e.g. Payne, 1957). In its coastal localities it is associated with grassland dominated by salt-marsh grasses (*Puccinellia* spp.), as well as among

marram grass (*Ammophila arenaria*) on dune systems, but a study of its Essex habitats found it commonly on lightly grazed and marginal areas of farm grassland, including agricultural set-aside, where it was associated with finer-leaved grasses such as creeping bent (*Agrostis stolonifera*) and rough meadow grass (*Poa trivialis*) (Gardiner *et al.*, 2002) with sward heights between 10 and 20 cm.

Behaviour

The males are active among the grasses in search of females, or, on warm, sunny days, singing from a perch on a grass stem. The song is a brief, unobtrusive 'burr' lasting about half a second, and repeated three or four times, with a pause of approximately one second between bursts. The insect usually moves to another perch before repeating its song.

In the vicinity of a female, the male produces a quite distinct courtship song. The male moves close to the female, facing her and spreading his long antennae wide in her direction. The courtship song begins as a prolonged and continuous stridulation, in which the hind legs are held low down, almost parallel with the line of the body, and vibrated through a very narrow arc. This phase is hardly, if at all, audible to humans. Eventually, the male shifts to a more vigorous stridulation, with the hind legs raised almost to the vertical. At this stage the insect's body begins to rock, and the stridulation is audible. From this point on there is a variable alternation between low- and raised-leg stridulation, eventually culminating in a mating attempt. This is (as is usual among grasshoppers!) generally rejected by the female moving off, or kicking the unfortunate male away (see clips from several courtship sequences on the DVD). The male then resumes the chase, takes up position and continues to court. According to Ragge (1965) a receptive female responds to the male courtship with a brief vibration of her hind femora, and mating ensues. In fact, courtship sequences are more often than not interrupted by other searching males, as groups of as many as ten individuals of both sexes tend to congregate. In these clusters there is frequent disturbance, with males making repeated direct mating attempts and being repulsed by females, while the males flick up their hind femora in response to one another.

Occasionally males perform the courtship sequence in the absence of a female (see DVD). Presumably, the calling song of the male functions to bring these groups together, rather than to locate or attract a receptive female.

Enemies

Along with *C. parallelus* and *C. brunneus*, this species forms a valuable component of the diet of declining farmland birds. Adults are frequent victims of large, web-spinning spiders, including *Argiope bruennichi* and *Araneus quadratus*.

Distribution

This species is widespread in mainland Europe from Spain in the west through to the former Soviet Union and Central Asia in the east. It occurs as far north as 64 degrees latitude in Scandinavia, and southwards to Italy and southern France. It occurs at altitudes up to 1,500 metres in the south. In the Netherlands it is common in the north and west, and in Belgium it is predominantly coastal (Kleukers & Krekels, 2004).

In Britain, the situation is confused by uncertainty about the validity of some earlier records, but it seems clear that the species has been extending its geographical range in recent years, possibly as a result of becoming more generalist in its habitat requirements (Wake, 1997; Evans & Edmondson, 2007). It is now widespread in southern, eastern and central counties of England, reaching north to Derbyshire (Sutton, 2003a) and south Yorkshire. Westwards it occurs in south Wales and is abundant around the Severn estuary. Further south and west it is much more localised in Dorset and Devon. In Ireland it appears to be confined to a small number of sites in the west.

Expansion of range from the south into greater London was reported by Sutton (2003c), and continued expansion north and west along a front from the Severn estuary to the Humber estuary was noted in 2004. New localities in Norfolk were discovered by Richmond and reported by Sutton (2007c). Range expansion seems to have been accompanied by readiness to occupy drier grassland habitats, including roadside verges. An intriguing report of one captured flying at 240 metres above the ground suggests a possible mode of dispersal (Sutton 2004b).

Status and conservation

The lesser marsh grasshopper is widespread and often abundant in southern and central Britain, and is possibly favoured by agricultural set-aside. With the cessation of set-aside, the fate of inland populations on farmland will be dependent on agri-environmental stewardship treatments that take account of its habitat requirements. Similar considerations apply to its habitats on flood defences, roadside verges, churchyards, cart tracks and other patches of unimproved and extensively managed grassland. It is adversely affected by hay-cutting, both suffering direct mortality, and becoming exposed to predation in short turf (see references to studies by Gardiner and colleagues under *C. parallelus*; see also Chapter 9).

References: Evans & Edmondson, 2007; Gardiner et al., 2002; Harz, 1975; Kleukers & Krekels, 2004; Mashall & Haes, 1988; Payne, 1957; Ragge, 1965; Sutton, 2003a, 2003c, 2004b, 2007c; Wake, 1997.

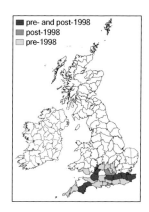

THE RUFOUS GRASSHOPPER
Gomphocerippus rufus
(Linnaeus, 1758)

MEASUREMENTS: Male: 14 to 18 mm. in length; female: 16 to 21 mm. in length.

A

B

FIGS A–C. Male;
dorsal view; female.

C

Description

The rufous grasshopper is one of only two British species with clubbed antennae. The antennae of the male are very long, and terminate with a pear-shaped club which tapers to a point at the tip. The female's antennae are shorter, and also thickend towards the tip but not as prominently as in the male. The side keels of the pronotum are strongly inflexed. The wings are fully developed, and in the male reach back to the hind 'knees' or a little beyond. In the female, the wings are relatively shorter, falling short of the tip of the abdomen and hind knees, so that the final two or three abdominal segments are exposed. There is a slight bulge basally on the leading edge of each fore wing in both sexes.

The eyes are usually dark red-brown, the antennal clubs black, with white tips, and, in sexually mature individuals, there is some reddish coloration on the rear segments of the abdomen (more vivid in the males) and on the hind tibiae and ventral edge of the hind femora. The face and palps of the male are pale greenish or fawn, and the palps, especially, are whitish.

The colour patterns of the wings and body are very variable, but Ragge (1965) organised the diversity into three main categories.

(1) *Purple*: head and pronotum purple.
(2) *Wedge*: various colour patterns, but with the side keels outlined in white, and black wedge-shaped markings on the dorsal surface of the pronotum.
(3) *Plain*: side keels of the pronotum not clearly outlined, and wedge-shaped markings absent.

D

E

F

FIGS D–E. purple; wedge; plain

Within these broad categories there is considerable variation of ground colour and patterning. The ground colour can vary from pale grey, through olive green and orange-brown, to a darker brown with black mottling. In some forms, especially the purple and brown varieties, the wings may be orange-brown with black spotting. In some forms the coloration of head and pronotum is plain, but in others there is darker mottling. In one striking form of the 'wedge' variety there is a dorsal cream stripe on the head, pronotum and rear margin of the fore wings.

In some localities, as well as the fully purple form distinguished by Ragge, there are forms in which the sides of the head and pronotum are purple, with various other colours dorsally.

Similar species
This is a distinctive species, unlikely to be confused with any other.

Some forms might be mistaken for the common field grasshopper (*Chorthippus brunneus*) on the basis of their inflexed pronotal side keels and comparable colour forms. However, the relatively longer wings and the lack of clubs to the antennae of that species are diagnostic.

The mottled grasshopper (*Myrmeleotettix maculatus*) also has clubbed antennae, but that species is very much smaller, and the side keels to the pronotum are much more acutely inflexed than those of *G. rufus*.

Life cycle
The egg pod is deposited just below the surface of the soil. It is roughly cylindrical with an apical lid, and contains up to 10 eggs. The eggs hatch rather late the following spring, from mid to late May, and the resulting nymphs pass through four instars before reaching adulthood in late July or August. Final instar nymphs can be seen as late as early September (Lucas, 1920; pers. obs.).

The antennal club is clearly visible in both sexes by the fourth nymphal instar.

Depending on weather conditions the adults persist through October, and into November. They have even been seen as late as the first week in December, and are reputed to take shelter under fallen leaves in cold weather (Marshall & Haes, 1988).

Habitat
This species is almost always found on calcareous grassland, especially south-facing slopes of chalk downland, although it is also reported from chalk sea cliffs and sand dunes as well as the edges of woodland. Where it occurs, the population is centred among patches of low scrub, notably dogwood or bramble among tall grasses. Male stridulation, courtship and mating, as well as basking, all seem to take place on the stems or broad leaves of woody plants in such patches. However,

as a sun-loving species, it depends on regular scrub management and is vulnerable to being shaded out. Bare patches of ground are also required for oviposition.

Further south in Europe it is also associated with wooded areas,being found in sunny clearings and along woodland rides as well as in dry grasslands.

Behaviour

This species is rather inactive except on warm, sunny days. Both sexes are frequently to be seen on a perch – usually in low, open scrub, basking in the sun. Like most basking orthopterans, they sit sideways to the sun, with the hind leg that faces the sun lowered, so that the side of the abdomen is exposed. The males sing from perches 10 to 20 cm or so above ground level. The typical song is a rather subdued trill, lasting some five seconds and repeated at irregular intervals. Males spend much of their time moving through vegetation in search of females.

Courtship and mating usually takes place in patches of low scrub, especially dogwood, with both male and female using the leaves as platforms.

In the presence of a female, the male performs the most extraordinary courtship song and dance of any British grasshopper. This consists of a series of distinct phases which are usually performed in a set sequence, although this is capable of modification under experimental manipulation (Riede, 1986; see also Chapter 6 for a detailed description; Ragge & Reynolds for an analysis, together with oscillograms; and the DVD for film clips illustrating the various phases of the courtship).

The female is largely motionless through the performance, and her only obvious signs of interest appear to be:

(1) abruptly turning round so that her rear end faces the male, and
(2) either raising her hind leg on the side from which the male makes his mating attempt (thus blocking his access), or lowering that leg.

Occasionally males run through the courtship routine in the absence of a female – as though practicing! (See the DVD.)

Enemies

Both sexes tend to remain in the loose cover of stands of dogwood or other low scrub, and either climb down into deeper cover or fly when disturbed. Males delivering the calling song are alert, but when engaged in the courtship performance they seem impervious to disturbance, and continue even when buffeted by rough winds. Some colour forms seem to match their substrates very closely, notably the purple, or partly purple forms, which are surprisingly well camouflaged against the early autumnal tints of dogwood leaves.

This, like other small and medium-sized grasshoppers, is vulnerable to predation by spiders, notably the wasp spider (*Argiope bruennichi*).

Distribution

This species occurs in mainland Europe from southern parts of Scandinavia, south-west through to France, especially the north, and eastwards through eastern Europe, the former Soviet Union, Siberia and Manchuria. In Italy it occurs in the Alps and Apennines, especially in forested zones. It is known from only one area in the Netherlands, but is more widespread in Belgium, especially in the south east.

In Britain this species is confined to the southern counties of England and a small area of south Wales. It is common on the North Downs in Surrey through to east Kent, but is less widespread on the South Downs. It has also been reported on calcareous grassland in Hampshire, Dorset and Wiltshire, on the Mendips (where it is rare) and in the Cotswolds, and on the south Devon coast. An isolated population is recorded from north Cornwall, where it occurs on calcareous dunes (Marshall & Haes, 1988).

The striking purple form is reported from Branscombe (Sutton, 2004a) and is also quite frequent on the North Downs (Baldock, 1999; pers. obs.)

Status and conservation

As this species is close to the northern limit of its geographical range in southern England, it is dependent on warm spring and summer weather, and so is highly vulnerable to prolonged poor weather, or successive poor summers, after which its numbers can be drastically reduced (Marshall & Haes, 1988). Many of its favoured habitats, such as on the North Downs and parts of the South Downs, are managed for conservation, but this is not necessarily favourable for this species. Many of the charismatic downland insects, notably butterflies such as the silver-spotted skipper (*Hesperia comma*) and Adonis blue (*Polyommatus bellargus*), require the hot microclimates produced by short turf. The rufous grasshopper, in contrast, favours areas of tall, tussocky grasses with low scrub. Haes and Harding (1997) suggest that this species benefited from the outbreak of myxomatosis in the 1950s, which reduced rabbit numbers and allowed coarser grasses to flourish. Despite the seeming incompatibility between management prescriptions for key downland butterflies and the rufous grasshopper, the management regime on the North Downs near Dorking seems favourable for both.

References: Baldock, 1999; Bellman & Luquet, 2009; Haes & Harding, 1997; Harz, 1975; Kleukers & Krekels, 2004; Lucas, 1920; Marshall & Haes, 1988; Ragge, 1965; Ragge & Reynolds, 1998; Riede, 1986; Sutton, 2004a.

THE MOTTLED GRASSHOPPER

Myrmeleotettix maculatus
(Thunberg, 1815)

MEASUREMENTS: Male: 12–15 mm in length; female: 13–19 mm in length.

FIGS A–D. male; dorsal view; face
and antennae (male); female

Description

The wings are fully developed in both sexes, reaching back to the hind 'knees' or just beyond in males and many females. In some females, however, the wings are slightly shorter in relation to the body, and the final one or two segments of the abdomen may be exposed. There is no bulge on the leading edge of the fore wings in either sex. The side keels of the pronotum are very strongly inflexed. The antennae of the male are very long, clubbed and turned outwards towards the tips. The female antennae are significantly shorter, and thickened towards the tips, rather than clearly clubbed.

There is a bewildering range of colour patterns, many individuals having irregular patterns of various colours that not only blend with the substrate, but also break up the outline of the insect's body. Constant features seem to be the pale coloured abdomen, with dark patches on the first three or four segments, and a diffuse reddish tint to the final few segments of the abdomen, and parts of the hind legs in sexually mature males.

Ragge (1965) offers a classification that reduces the colour variation to twelve broad categories.

(1) *Black*: dorsal surfaces of the head and pronotum and the 'upper' edge (when insect is at rest) of hind wings blackish (and not conspicuously mottled). No green, yellow/orange or red/purple on the head, pronotum or wings.
(2) *Semi-black*: as above, but with white/pale outlining of the pronotal side keels.
(3) *Mottled*: dorsal surfaces of the head and pronotum and the upper edge of fore wings black, brown, grey or straw-coloured, and upper edge of fore wings mottled. Side keels of pronotum not clearly outlined in white/pale coloration, and lacking dark wedge-shaped markings on the dorsal surface of the pronotum.
(4) *Semi-mottled*: as for mottled, except that the side keels of the pronotum are outlined, and there are wedge-shaped dark marks on the dorsal surface of the pronotum.
(5) *Plain*: dorsal surface of the head, pronotum and the upper edge of fore wings brown, grey or straw-coloured. Upper edges of the fore wings plain (not mottled or striped).
(6) *Striped*: as for plain, except that the upper edges of the fore wings are striped.
(7) *Green*: head and pronotum at least partly green dorsally.
(8) *Purple green sides*: pink to purple-brown on the dorsal surface of the head and pronotum, and some green on the sides of the head and pronotum.
(9) *Black green sides*: head, pronotum and upper edges of the fore wings black, with some green on the sides of the head and pronotum.

(10) *Brown green sides*: head, pronotum and upper edges of the fore wings brown, grey or straw-coloured, with some green on the sides of head and pronotum.

(11) *Purple*: head and pronotum with areas of pink to purple-brown on head and pronotum, but no green.

(12) *Buff*: areas of orange or yellow on the head and pronotum (but no green).

Forms 1 to 6 and 11 and 12 have no areas of green on the head or pronotum. (See Chapter 3, Fig 71 for images of a selection of these colour forms.)

There are some intermediate forms, especially between 1 and 2, and 3 and 4, where the side keels to the pronotum are faintly, but not clearly outlined pale, and vague outlines of the wedge-shaped markings on the dorsal surface of the pronotum are just visible.

As in the groundhoppers, the balance between different colour forms seems to vary with the character of the substrate, leading to speculation as to the causal mechanisms involved both in maintaining the diversity of colour forms and in modifying the proportions between them in local populations. An increase in the proportion of dark or black forms after heath fires ('fire melanism') is often noticed. For example, Baldock reported a population of this species as virtually all of the black form after a heath fire in Surrey (Sutton, 2003c). N. Owens made a quantitative study of the proportions of green and non-green individuals one year after a heath fire in Norfolk, comparing the populations on the burnt area with those on other substrates nearby. More than 75 per cent of those on the burnt area were 'non-green', compared with only 34 per cent non-green on a sandy cliff (Owens, 2010). There seem to be three possible explanations: high rates of selection by predators on non-matching insects over a single season; a phenotypic response to substrate colour during development; or selective movement into colour-matching areas by the different colour morphs. Initial results in 2011 suggest that the ratios of the colour morphs of early instars at different locations are very similar to those of the previous year (Owens, pers. corr.). This evidence tells against the explanation in terms of a phenotypic response to the substrate, but leaves open the other two possibilities. Selective movement across different parts of the habitat should not be ruled out in view of Gardiner's observations on the movements of *C. parallelus* (see under that species).

Similar species

This very small species is often recognisable by size alone.

On closer inspection, the clubbed or apically thickened antennae, as well as the rather more strongly inflexed side keels to the pronotum serve to distinguish this species from small specimens of the common field grasshopper (*Chorthippus brunneus*), which often occurs in the same habitats as the mottled. Also, the common field has a bulge on the leading edge of each fore wing, absent in the mottled grasshopper.

The only other British species with clubbed antennae is the rufous grasshopper (*Gomphocerippus rufus*), which is noticeably larger, is unlikely to be found in the same habitat as the mottled, and does have a basal bulge on the leading edge of the fore wing.

Confusion is also possible between females of the mottled grasshopper and the heath grasshopper (*Chorthippus vagans*) in the latter's very few localities. However, the heath grasshopper lacks the apical thickening of the antennae, has less markedly inflexed side-keels to the pronotum, and has a bulge on the leading edge of each fore wing (absent in *M. maculatus*).

Life cycle

The females deposit the egg-pods just below the surface of the soil on bare patches or among mosses or other low-growing plants. Each egg pod contains

E

F

G

H

FIGS E–H. Life-history stages: 2nd instar nymph; 3rd instar nymph; 4th instar nymph, green form; 4th instar nymph, semi-mottled form.

up to six eggs. These usually hatch in April or May the following year, and final instar nymphs are present as early as the second week in May, but also as late as mid-July. Adults begin to appear from late May in the south, and males can usually be heard as early as the first week in June. The adults are most abundant through July, but numbers begin to decline in the latter half of August, and continue to do so until early October.

Habitat

This is a species of dry, exposed habitats, with short vegetation, areas of bare ground, and maximum exposure to the sun. Among its favoured haunts are: south-facing hillsides on sand, chalk or limestone, especially where intensively grazed by rabbits; sparsely vegetated acidic grass heathlands; sandy heather heaths; coastal cliffs; and dune systems. In uplands of western Britain it is found commonly on moorland hillsides. Possibly because of its small size it is relatively poor at raising its body temperature above the ambient, and this may explain its strong association with habitats exposed to the sun with short turf and bare ground (Willott, 1997). Another consequence is that it is less liable to overheating than are species with better thermoregulatory ability, and so does not require adjacent stands of cooler longer grasses for shelter. However, its feeding preference is for coarser, broad-leaved grasses that are relatively scarce on the preferred habitat.

In many localities it is associated with rabbit grazing and with mosses typical of dry heathy habitats, such as *Polytrichum* species.

Behaviour

Males are especially active on sunny days, sometimes singing from a fixed location on the ground, or on mosses or other very low vegetation, but more often running rapidly on what appear to be random routes, criss-crossing a patch of open ground a square metre or so in area. As they do so, they stop occasionally to emit a short burst of song, then resume their 'patrol'. The song consists of a series of 10 to 30 soft 'burrs' that are repeated approximately every half-second, becoming louder towards the end. Females tend to be much more sedentary, spending much of their time feeding on grass blades, basking, or egg-laying. Once a male approaches a female he stops, points both antennae forward, then, after a short interval, approaches more closely, commencing his elaborate courtship sequence as he does so. Often this attracts the attention of other males and as many as three or four may assemble and collectively chase the female – normally without success.

The complexity of the male courtship performance almost matches that of the rufous grasshopper. (A detailed description of this is given in Chapter 6, and clips can be seen on the DVD; see also the analyses and oscillograms given in Ragge & Reynolds (1998).)

If there is no response from the female, or if, as frequently happens, she hops away a short distance, the whole process is repeated. Occasionally, during the male courtship sequence the female may make a few desultory stridulatory movements with her hind legs. However, it seems that the male is impervious to incoming sensory information in the course of the courtship performance, as, if the female leaves part way through, he continues to the end and then lunges at the empty space that was occupied by the desired female at the beginning of the sequence (see DVD).

Males often 'flick' a hind leg up and down when they encounter others during their perambulations. This has the appearance of an antagonistic signal, but may simply be a gender advertisement. This speculation is supported by an extraordinary event-sequence on film. A male was observed to perform a persistent courtship dance to what was visibly another male, but which remained still. The courting male eventually attempted to mate, jumping on to the back of the other male and then spinning around and leaving. On investigation, it was discovered that the motionless male was dead and in the grip of a spider. It seems likely that in this species at least, gender is indicated by behavioural signals, rather than by mere physical appearance.

Enemies

As the mottled grasshopper's usual habitats are relatively open and bare, they are presumably vulnerable to attack from birds and other vertebrate visual predators. Their exceptionally variable colour patterns and tendency to rest against matching substrates is likely to be their main defence against such predators. However, they also fly readily in warm weather when disturbed.

Adults and nymphs are subject to considerable predation from spiders (see above). Early-instar nymphs were found to be the main prey of wolf spiders of the genus *Pardosa* (Lycosidae) in a study of a population of this species and *C. brunneus* at a coastal locality in north-west England (Cherrill & Begon, 1989b). Both adults and nymphs are taken by the wasp *Tachysphex pompiliformis* (N. Owens, pers. corr.)

Distribution

This species is widely distributed throughout Europe as far as approximately 63 degrees north in Scandinavia, and eastwards to Turkey and Siberia. In southern Europe it can be found in mountains up to 2,000 metres or more.

In Britain it occurs almost throughout, wherever there is suitable habitat. In mainland Scotland it seems to be absent or very local in the west, but is widespread in the east and north. It is present on both the Inner and Outer Hebrides, and was recorded for the first time in Lewis in 2006 (Sutton, 2006b).

It is widespread throughout Wales, and has a scattered distribution in Ireland, being more frequent in the west. It is one of the few species that is present and common on the Isle of Man.

Status and conservation

This species seems to be able to maintain populations on relatively small and isolated relict patches of heathland, but is very vulnerable to succession to more vigorous grasses and scrub. Nutrient enrichment for agricultural purposes or cessation of grazing are therefore a threat to it. In many of its habitats active management is needed to maintain its key requirements of short turf and bare earth. Irregular disturbance by vehicles (as on Ministry of Defence land; see Gardiner & Benton, 2009) as well as rabbit-grazing disrupt natural succession and expose areas of bare ground.

In many lowland areas its marginal habitats are liable to be seen as ripe for building 'development', and many local extinctions must have resulted from this.

Although mineral extraction, road construction and other industrial activities often produce apparently suitable habitats for this species, its ability to colonise new sites seems to be very limited (Wake, 1997; Marshall & Haes, 1988). Although it is one of our most widespread species geographically, it is very localised in some parts of its range. In Essex, for example, Wake reported only five populations in the whole county, and county recorders T. Gardiner and P. Harvey included it in their Red Data list for the county (Gardiner & Harvey, 2004). In order to increase the number of Essex populations, Gardiner attempted translocation of the species from its strongest Essex population to nearby coastal habitat recently planted with marram grass as a flood prevention measure. Initial evidence suggests that the effort has been successful (Gardiner, 2010e)

References: Cherrill & Begon, 1989b; Gardiner, 2010e; Gardiner & Benton, 2009; Gardiner & Harvey, 2004; Harz, 1975; Marshall & Haes, 1988; Owens, 2010; Ragge, 1965; Ragge & Reynolds, 1998; Sutton, 2003c, 2006b; Wake, 1997; Willott, 1997.

CHAPTER 9

Ecology and conservation of the British species

The main focus of this chapter will be the ecology and conservation of the British Orthoptera. To set the issues in context the chapter begins with a theoretical discussion of the conditions affecting the survival or extinction of species in particular habitats or geographical areas, and the forces that influence the numbers of individuals, and their tendencies to retreat or disperse into new habitats. I hope this will offer some insights into the distinct patterns of distribution of the British species, their habitat preferences and changes over time in their status and distribution.

The research on the population ecology of orthopterans has been dominated by the peculiarities of those species that have had the greatest economic and human impact – most notably the locusts. The species of grasshopper that are known by this term exhibit massive population explosions periodically. These 'swarms' and 'plagues' are associated with increased population densities, often building up in an area over a number of seasons. The pheromonal interactions under these conditions induce marked physiological, morphological and behavioural changes. Among these are increased wing length in adults, and strong mutual attraction (gregarisation), leading nymphs to congregate and 'march', or adults to take to the wing, often in vast numbers. The swarms and plagues produced in this way may cover many thousands of square kilometres, devouring grasslands or food crops as they move over the land. Such outbreaks are characteristic of the arid grasslands of tropical or sub-tropical America, Australia, south-west Asia and Africa, and are rarely seen in temperate climates such as those of Britain and the rest of Europe where population densities are much lower (of the order of less than two per square metre in the UK (see Gardiner *et al.*, 2002)).

Nevertheless, the models of grasshopper population dynamics that have been developed in order to understand these dramatic events can be applied to the very different conditions that apply elsewhere (Joern & Gaines, 1990). At the most abstract level, the population dynamics of any species are a consequence of the relationship between mortality rates and reproductive rates, and immigration and emigration rates. The conditions affecting mortality and reproductive rates of insects can be divided into three sorts:

(1) evolved traits of the organisms themselves: the vulnerabilities of the various stages in their life cycle, how rapidly they develop under different conditions, the availability of alternative developmental pathways, their defensive reactions to predators or parasites, their reproductive behaviour and potential, their feeding preferences, their longevity, their ability to disperse and colonise new habitats, and so on;
(2) abiotic conditions, such as: rainfall, humidity, soil type, seasonal patterns of weather, temperature and topography;
(3) biotic factors, such as: vegetation structure, food availability, risk of disease, parasitism and predation, as well as competition both with other species sharing the same habitat and among members of the same species. Interactions between trends among these biotic factors may operate as regulators of populations. For example, increased population density may exacerbate competition for food, leading to reduced fecundity or even starvation, and so to decreasing population density. Increased density may also increase rates of disease or parasitism. Such density-dependent mortality may operate as a negative feedback, returning population density to a lower value, at which point parasites find it more difficult to locate hosts allowing population density to rise again. However, much will depend on whether natural enemies are generalists or specialists, and on the interactions between mortality from these causes or from others, such as adverse climatic conditions, or competition for food. Depending on the timescale over which populations respond to the many influences on fecundity and mortality, the result may be cyclical fluctuations in population, or long-run stability.

The significance of predation, parasitism and diseases for the dynamics of orthopteran populations has been the subject of a great deal of controversy. Dempster (1963) argued that the impact was likely to be relatively small, despite the fact that natural enemies of various kinds undoubtedly are a significant source of mortality. Grasshopper eggs are eaten by many invertebrates, and parasitised by some (Richards & Waloff, 1954; see below). Mortality rates are generally very high in the earliest instars, and are reduced with each successive stage of the life cycle. Adults, however, especially of the larger species, offer a nutritious meal to vertebrate predators such as birds and small mammals, and are subject to the attacks of parasitoid wasps as well as larger web-making spiders, robber-flies and fungal pathogens (Streett & McGuire, 1990). The range expansion of the wasp spider (*Argiope bruennichi*) has probably been aided by predation on common grasshoppers (Gardiner & Hill, 2005b). The stridulation of many species renders them vulnerable to attacks from acoustically orienting predators and parasitoids, and those that are active at night may also fall victim to bats (Robinson, 1980; Steiner, 1981; Belwood, 1990).

There are rather few quantitative studies of the impact of predation, parasitism and disease on the population dynamics of the British species. Cryptic colour patterns, behavioural responses to predation-risk, and such adaptations as the pattern and timing of stridulatory activity suggest that such threats have acted as powerful selective pressures in the evolution of many species. One study of spider predation on two species of grasshoppers (*Myrmeleotettix maculatus* and *Chorthippus brunneus*) on dune systems in north-west England used the presence of specific antigens in the gut contents of spiders to estimate rates of predation (Cherrill & Begon, 1989b). More than 90 per cent of the spiders (of six species) tested had fed on grasshopper nymphs, and the most prolific spider-predator group, the wolf spiders (*Pardosa* species, Lycosidae), were shown in laboratory tests to attack grasshopper nymphs almost exclusively in their first instar. This study suggests that predation by wandering spiders may be an important cause of mortality in early developmental stages of grasshoppers, but as these spiders also prey on other invertebrates, and grasshopper nymphs also fall prey to many other natural enemies as well as abiotic factors, the overall implications for their population dynamics remain to be fully explored. A study of the impact of lycosid spiders on populations of three grasshopper species in a grassland community in the USA also found very high rates of both spider predation and

FIG 124. Grasshoppers as prey of spiders: (left) garden spider, *Araneus diadematus*, with field grasshopper; (centre) wasp spider, *Argiope bruennichi*, with meadow grasshopper; (right) four-spotted spider, *Araneus quadratus*, with meadow grasshopper.

general mortality in early nymphal
stages, with spiders accounting for an
increasing proportion of the reduced
mortality rates at later developmental
stages (Oedekoven & Joern, 1998).
Again, however, although grasshopper
populations were clearly depressed by
spider predation, the overall effect on
population dynamics might depend on
other factors, including the possibility
that lower adult densities might
increase reproductive success.

Any careful examination of
orthopteran populations will reveal
individuals lacking legs or antennae or
parts of these structures. Although faulty
moulting undoubtedly is one cause of
such defects, it seems likely that another
significant cause is failed attacks by both
vertebrate and invertebrate predators.
Cherrill (1997) found 13 per cent of
nymph wartbiters and 31 per cent of

FIG 125. (top) Wartbiter with beak-marks
on head and pronotum; (above) mottled
grasshopper with missing hind leg.

adult wartbiters to be carrying sub-lethal injuries, including evidence of predation
by birds. It seems likely that these injuries reduce fitness by restricting mobility
and perceptual ability, as well as rendering the victim more susceptible to disease.

The impact of predation on the species diversity and relative abundance of
grasshoppers of different species has been studied in a few cases. For example,
Joern (1986) excluded bird predators from sections of a grassland habitat in
the USA, and measured the consequences for a community of 44 grasshopper
species. Most species showed lower population densities in areas subject to avian
predation, and species diversity was also lower. Another US study was carried
out on an area of prairie grassland with a grasshopper community comprising
15 species (Belovsky and Slade, 1993). Predation by spiders reduced numbers
of grasshopper nymphs at early stages, but this was compensated by greater
survival rates of later instar nymphs because of reduced population density.
Avian predation at this site resulted in actual increases in the overall grasshopper
population, but did so by selectively reducing the numbers of larger, more
competitive grasshoppers, while allowing medium-sized species to increase at
the expense of smaller ones.

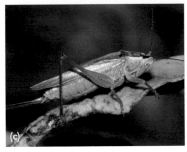

FIG 126. (a) Roesel's bush-cricket, normal form; (b) Roesel's bush-cricket, macropterous form, f. *diluta*; (c) long-winged conehead, normal form; (d) long-winged conehead, extra-macropterous form.

Dramatic population fluctuations and swarming are rarely encountered among the orthopterans of temperate climates, but some species still retain the potential to disperse over long distances when conditions arise for range expansion. Populations of these species include a minority of individuals that are morphologically adapted for long-range flight. This is most obvious in the case of species that are normally brachypterous, and so incapable of flight, but which retain the 'option' to develop as fully winged (macropterous) morphs. Two species that have extended their range dramatically in recent decades in Britain are the long-winged conehead (*Conocephalus discolor*) and Roesel's bush-cricket (*Metrioptera roeselii*). In the case of the long-winged conehead, the normal form is already macropterous, but it has a minority 'extra-macropterous' form.

A study of these species by Simmons and Thomas (2004) found that the macropterous (or extra-macropterous) forms constituted a higher proportion of the population at sites on the margins of the range-extension than at the core of their range – they were eight times more frequent in the case of the long-winged conehead, and four times more frequent in Roesel's bush-cricket. In some Essex populations the proportion of the macropterous form of *M. roeselii* is as high as 30 per cent (Gardiner, 2009b). Even in the case of the long-winged conehead, in which the normal form is able to fly, the increased proportion of the extra-macropterous form in expanding range-front populations is calculated to give a fourfold increase in long-distance dispersal (Thomas *et al.*, 2001).

Laboratory rearing of samples of both species from the two types of situation under common conditions produced much higher frequencies of the macropterous forms in those sourced from expanding range margins. This is consistent with the hypothesis that there may be a genetic component to the propensity to develop as a macropterous adult. Not only were the extra-macropterous morphs of the long-winged coneheads very much better at flying than the normal form, but extra-macropterous specimens sourced from the range margin flew further in laboratory tests than those sourced from towards the range centre.

Thomas *et al.* suggest that selective pressures favour the macropterous individuals that are disposed to be more dispersive during range expansions, and that greater gene-flow between populations may also contribute to greater habitat generalism. Towards the centre of the range, it is likely that selective pressures favour forms adapted to the local environment, and work against developmental pathways that enhance dispersal ability. The authors provide evidence that there is a trade-off between fecundity and macroptery (see also Roff, 1984; Roff *et al.*, 1999; Zera & Denno, 1997), but, at the expanding range margin, the ability to colonise new habitat outweighs the cost in terms of fecundity.

Another cost of actual dispersal is likely to be greater exposure to predation. Smith (2007) provides a vivid illustration of this: numerous long-winged Roesel's bush-crickets were flying over a field, only to be attacked by two pairs of hobbys and a pair of kestrels. These were soon joined by about sixty black-headed gulls and a common gull, and after about one-and-a-half hours there was no observable activity from predators or prey.

Evolved patterns of adaptation to a range of environmental conditions may result in relatively stable forms of population regulation, which continue to operate just as long as there are no major ecological disturbances. In the species that undergo periodic population explosions, a variety of such disturbances can be involved. In some species phase transformations, swarming and migration are an evolved adaptation to climates with extreme seasonal differences in availability of suitable food and ovipositing sites, notably arid zones with long dry seasons punctuated by shorter rainy seasons. In other cases, it seems these phenomena are associated with ephemeral habitats and unpredictable weather patterns, with migrating insects following wind currents to areas of likely rainfall (Farrow, 1990).

In Britain, and in large parts of lowland Europe, major external disruptive events and processes are more likely to be the result of human activity than extreme or unpredictable climatic conditions (although as global temperatures

FIG 127. (a) New development on Dorset heathland; (b) coastal development: bathing huts with close mown grass, but Orthoptera habitat on the slopes behind; (c) former grazing marsh, north east Essex; (d) intensive arable landscape, mid Essex.

rise, these may become more familiar). More often than not, the impact of these processes on orthopterans – along with other wildlife – is negative. Among the most significant of these human-induced changes are agricultural intensification, urbanisation and coastal development. These processes have led to the loss of much orthopteran habitat, most notably from diminished lowland grasslands and heaths, draining of wetlands, and loss of hedgerow and woodland-edge habitat. Even where patches of suitable habitat remain, these are too often isolated in an increasingly fragmented landscape, making local populations vulnerable and re-colonisation unlikely.

However, as far as many of the British Orthoptera are concerned, changes in land use have not been unremittingly negative. While not fully compensating for the loss of extensive areas of unimproved grassland, some infrastructural developments have incidentally provided both favourable habitat for some species (see, for example, Port & Thompson, 1980), and connectivity that has enabled dispersal and range extension for a few others. Two significant examples are the grass verges of the road network, and coastal flood defences. Measures designed to mitigate the negative economic and environmental impacts of agricultural intensification – such as set-aside and various agri-environmental programmes – have, again, benefited some species. Finally, a very small number of exceptionally vulnerable species have attracted conservation funding and ecological research that in at least one case has almost certainly averted extinction in the short term (e.g. Edwards *et al.*, 1996).

On the large scale, broad patterns of distribution of the British species are shaped by the interaction of three principal factors:

(1) the place and timing of their arrival, together with subsequent opportunities for dispersal and colonisation;
(2) species-specific climatic tolerances – especially with respect to temperature and rainfall; and
(3) any specialist habitat requirements, such as food specialisation, oviposition sites or vegetation structure.

A fourth possible factor – incidence of predation, parasitism and disease – may also have some significance, but a relative lack of quantitative studies, and the likely complexity and indirectness of its influence, make it difficult to take this fully into account. It is likely that its impact is, in any case, strongly mediated by climatic variables and other habitat features.

For certain species, such as the southern oak bush-cricket, *Meconema meridionale*, that have colonised mainland Britain quite recently (Hawkins, 2001), it is likely that there will continue to be further range extensions. However, the current broad pattern of distribution of the long-established or 'native' species is largely an expression of their climatic limits, combined, in some cases, with the distribution of specialised habitats such as coastal dunes or shingle, or lowland heaths and bogs. As a few long-established but alien species survive only in association with human habitation – notably the house cricket, *Acheta domesticus* (Kevan, 1955), and the greenhouse camel cricket, *Diestrammena asynamorus* – these, too, might be included in the group of habitat specialists, although I have not included them in the following classification.

With these considerations in mind, we can group most of the British species into four main divisions according to: (1) their geographical range (mainland/ southern); (2) their distribution within their range (widespread/local); and (3) their habitat requirements (habitat generalists/specialists). This gives the following grouping of the British species according to their ecology and distribution.

(1) **Mainland widespread habitat generalists**: the common groundhopper (*Tetrix undulata*); the common green grasshopper (*Omocestus viridulus*); the common field grasshopper (*Chorthippus brunneus*); the common meadow grasshopper (*Chorthippus parallelus*); and the mottled grasshopper (*Myrmeleotettix maculatus*) (? see below).

(2) **Southern widespread habitat generalists:** the oak bush-cricket (*Meconema thalassinum*); the dark bush-cricket (*Pholidoptera griseoaptera*); Roesel's bush-cricket (*Metrioptera roeselii*) since c.1970; the long-winged conehead (*Conocephalus discolor*) since c.1990; the speckled bush-cricket (*Leptophyes punctatissima*); and the lesser marsh grasshopper (*Chorthippus albomarginatus*).

(3) **Southern widespread habitat specialists:** the short-winged conehead (*Conocephalus dorsalis*); the slender groundhopper (*Tetrix subulata*); and the stripe-winged grasshopper (*Stenobothrus lineatus*).

(4) **Southern local habitat specialists:** the great green bush-cricket (*Tettigonia viridissima*); the wartbiter (*Decticus verrucivorus*); the grey bush-cricket (*Platycleis albopunctata*); bog bush-cricket (*Metrioptera brachyptera*); Roesel's bush-cricket (*Metrioptera roeselii*) before c.1970; long-winged conehead (*Conocephalus discolor*) before c.1990; the field cricket (*Gryllus campestris*); the wood cricket (*Nemobius sylvestris*); the scaly cricket (*Pseudomogoplistes vicentae*); the mole-cricket (*Gryllotalpa gryllotalpa*); Cepero's groundhopper (*Tetrix ceperoi*); the large marsh grasshopper (*Stethophyma grossum*); the woodland grasshopper (*Omocestus rufipes*); the heath grasshopper (*Chorthippus vagans*); the rufous grasshopper (*Gomphocerippus rufus*); and the lesser mottled grasshopper (*Stenobothrus stigmaticus*).

Not all species fit their allotted place equally well. As noted above, the long-winged conehead (*Conocephalus discolor*) and Roesel's bush-cricket (*Metrioptera roeselii*) have both extended their range in England very rapidly in recent decades, from very restricted former distributions close to the south coast (*C. discolor*) or in the south-east (*M. roeselii*), hence their representation in both the third and fourth divisions above.

In the 'mainland' category, I have included only species whose current distribution extends throughout mainland Britain, including northern Scotland. I have included as 'southern' a few species whose distribution extends into northern England but not beyond the Scottish borders, although a large proportion of the 'southern' species occur principally south of a line from the Bristol Channel to the Wash (often including coastal districts of South Wales). For species counted as 'mainland widespread' and many of the 'southern' species with more northerly limits, it is important to recognise that they typically become much more localised in the more northerly reaches of their range. It is generally true that species close to the northern edge of their range require particularly favourable habitat conditions if they are to survive, and this usually implies that their distribution becomes more sporadic and localised close to their climatic limit. This may help to explain the very localised distributions of several of the species that are very close to their northern, or north western, limit in the most southerly parts of Britain. These include the field cricket (*Gryllus campestris*), heath grasshopper (*Chorthippus vagans*) and wood cricket (*Nemobius sylvestris*).

Finally, what counts as 'habitat specialism' is debatable. The intention is to distinguish species that have stringent habitat requirements and so occupy only a restricted range of habitats, from those tolerant of a wider range of conditions. The distinction is not always clear as the degree of habitat generalism is often variable, depending on the position of a given population in relation to its overall range. It is possible for a habitat specialist to be quite widespread within its range if its preferred habitats are themselves widespread. It could be argued that the short-winged conehead and slender groundhopper fall into this category. More problematic is the case of the mottled grasshopper. This clearly has quite definite habitat requirements, but these are satisfied by several different habitat types (e.g. sparse acid grassland, coastal dune systems, calcareous grassland, or heather heath) so it figures above as a habitat generalist. It should also be remembered that the distinction is one of degree. For example, both the common field (*C. brunneus*) and meadow grasshoppers (*C. parallelus*) are treated as generalists because of their presence in a wide range of grassland habitats, but the common field grasshopper is distinctly more 'choosy' than its close relative, preferring hotter, drier habitats with patches of bare ground.

Another example is the common green grasshopper (*O. viridulus*) which is restricted in south-eastern England by low rainfall and limited availability of habitat, but is widespread elsewhere in Britain (see Gardiner, 2010b).

With these reservations, the above groupings do seem to suggest some interesting patterns. The first is that, excluding the established aliens that depend on human habitation, there are no ensiferans (bush-crickets and their allies) in the 'mainland' category. All three of the British cricket species are markedly southern, as are most of the bush-crickets, with only *M. brachyptera*, *M. thalassinum*, and *P. griseoaptera* extending into northern England or the Scottish border – and even then in very localised 'outlier' populations. This suggests that the crickets and bush-crickets are in general more limited by climatic factors than are at least some of the grasshoppers and groundhoppers. As we saw in Chapter 3, several of the bush-crickets take two or more years to complete their development, as an adaptation to their requirement for a sufficient number of days at temperatures above a critical threshold for that completion to occur (Hartley, 1990; Ingrisch, 1984a, 1984b, 1986a, 1986b, 1986c). In at least two of the mainland generalist grasshoppers it seems that their ability to survive at the more northerly latitudes is due to inherited differences in life-cycle traits across the geographically distributed sub-populations. In the common field grasshopper, northern populations have become adapted to shorter seasons and lower temperatures, with larger eggs and hatchling nymphs and faster development, but smaller adult size in the northern populations (Telfer & Hassall, 1999). Comparable genetic differences related to climatic conditions have also been found in the mottled grasshopper (Hewitt & Roscoe 1971).

Another notable pattern is the large proportion of the British orthopteran species that fall into the 'southern local habitat specialist' category. This is an indication of the geographical position of Britain close to the northerly, or north-westerly, limit of the climatic tolerance of so many of our species. Populations of these species can be self-sustaining only in habitat patches that are particularly favourable to them. Two apparent exceptions are the long-winged conehead and Roesel's bush cricket, which have broken out of their 'southern-local' status to become much more widespread. The reasons for this are not fully understood, but it seems likely that a combination of climate change, conservation measures and changes in the frequency of longer-winged forms may have been involved (see below). During the same period some species that have recently seen expansions on the nearby mainland of Europe have begun to colonise Britain. The southern oak bush cricket (*M. meridionale*) is so far the most successful of these, but the sickle-bearing bush-cricket (*Phaneroptera falcata*) seems able to maintain a foothold on the south coast (Sutton, 2006b; Evans & Edmondson, 2007; M. Edwards, pers. comm.), and the large conehead (*Ruspolia nitidula*) may be about to establish itself here (Hathway *et al.*, 2003). Again, it seems reasonable to guess that climate change is to some extent at work in this steady increase in the UK fauna. Changes in the British orthopteran fauna over a longer timescale are reviewed in Marshall (1974) (see also, for Essex: Gardiner, 2009d).

However, most of the 'southern local' habitat specialists remain local. Several of these appear to be declining, and at risk of extinction in the UK unless research and conservation effort continues to be committed to them. Among these species are the wartbiter (*D. verrucivorus*), field cricket (*G. campestris*), large marsh grasshopper (*S. grossum*), heath grasshopper (*C. vagans*) and lesser mottled grasshopper (*S. stigmaticus*). Other localised southern species that could become vulnerable if attention is not paid to their habitat requirements include the great green and grey bush-crickets (*T. viridissima* and *P. albopunctata*), the scaly and wood crickets (*P. vicentae, N. sylvestris*), Cepero's groundhopper (*T. ceperoi*), and the woodland and rufous grasshoppers (*O. rufipes* and *G. rufus*). I will return to discussion of current research and action in relation to the more vulnerable species later in this chapter.

Most of the mainland and southern widespread species favour open grassland habitats, and many can be found together in favoured sites in southern Britain.

FIG 128. Orthoptera-rich grassland, Suffolk Brecks.

It is not uncommon in some localities to find the common field, common meadow, lesser marsh and common green grasshoppers, together with the long-winged conehead and Roesel's bush crickets, within the same area of grassland – although usually occupying slightly different parts of the same territory.

CLASSIC STUDIES OF GRASSHOPPER ECOLOGY IN BRITAIN

Pioneering studies of orthopteran ecology in Britain have focused on such grassland communities as these, and subsequent research on grassland management and conservation strategies has often included orthopterans – especially the common grasshoppers – along with butterflies and farmland birds as suitable subjects for conservation. Two major studies that focused on grasshoppers were conducted around the middle of the 20th century, and their pioneering work has been influential for later research. However, the intensification of agriculture that has taken place since then has made it necessary in subsequent studies to give a much higher priority to the impact of methods of grassland management on orthopteran populations than was evident in the earlier work.

Clark (1948)

The early research on grasshopper ecology in Britain was to a considerable extent a spin-off from the much more focused research on tropical and subtropical grasslands affected by economically important outbreaks of orthopteran populations. The pioneering research of E. J. Clark in the years immediately following World War II (Clark 1948) would probably never have been published had it not been for the sponsorship of B. P. Uvarov, a leading specialist on locust ecology (Uvarov, 1928). However, Clark is explicit that in Britain and western Europe grasshopper populations never reach densities comparable to those that lead to locust swarms. Here, it is not food but climate that is likely to be the main determinant of both the survival and the relative abundance of grasshopper species.

Clark observed the feeding behaviour of seven (then!) widespread species of grasshopper, both under natural conditions and in captivity, concluding that, while each had a degree of preference for some grass species over others, no species displayed fixed or exclusive feeding preferences. Although all species showed a definite preference for grasses, some would also consume forbs such as trefoils and clovers. Clark argued that given relatively low population densities in Britain, and relatively general and flexible food preferences, food was unlikely to be a limiting factor for the survival of any species, or for its abundance in most habitats.

Overwhelmingly, the key determinant of grasshopper distribution here is climate – essentially temperature, humidity and rainfall. But the impact of climate on grasshopper survival is always mediated by specific local conditions affecting the microclimate, most important of which are vegetation structure (rather than species-composition), soil properties and topography (altitude, degree of slope, aspect, exposure, etc.). Admitting that parasites, predators and competitors might have some influence, Clark still insisted on the primary importance of climate and its local mediations.

Clark attempted to test these general theoretical expectations by quantitative studies at a large number of grassland and heathland sites, mainly in southern England. Vegetation structure was first interpreted in terms of height and density – the latter being assessed in terms of percentage of ground covered. Overall, population densities of grasshoppers were favoured by habitats with between 50 and 100 per cent vegetation cover, and heights of less than 20 cm – although there were wide tolerances on either side of this. His study methods did not make discriminations between species easy, but it seemed that in general, the common meadow and rufous grasshoppers tended to favour denser and taller grassland, while the mottled and common field grasshoppers tended to favour more sparsely vegetated habitats.

However, vegetation structure involves more than these two variables, and Clark includes in his discussion what he calls 'texture', meaning the growth form, leaf shapes and so on of the grassland community. He distinguishes three layers of vegetation – the scrub, herbaceous and ground layers – the last-mentioned comprising mainly mosses and low-growing forbs. He notes that many favourable habitats are characterised by unevenness in vegetation structure. Patches or 'enclaves' of short, sparse grasses, with bare earth, often sheltered by taller grasses and occasional shrubs often have the greatest density of grasshoppers, especially if they are in south-facing sheltered slopes. Shrubs may offer features (such as basking sites) for grasshoppers, but if the succession goes too far, and grassy areas become shaded from direct sunlight, this is adverse for grasshoppers. Grasshoppers showed no interest in feeding on mosses, and Clark argues that in general mosses in grassland indicate dense, tall vegetation and cool and damp conditions that are generally unfavourable to them.

It is the character of the herbaceous layer (mostly grasses of several species with some broad-leaved herbs and the occasional shrub such as gorse, juniper or bramble) that is most important for grasshoppers. As grasshoppers rarely move long distances, except in response to disturbance, and are greatly dependent on climatic conditions, it is important that they have available a sufficiently diverse habitat to provide them with access to a range of microclimates. Short, sparse grassland enclaves provide them with sunlit areas sheltered from wind, and, for those species that lay their eggs in soil, valuable ovipositing sites. If tall dense vegetation is close by, this can provide shelter from cold or rainy weather, cover from predators and resting places for the nights. Clark's notes on grasshopper movements indicate their diurnal patterns of local migration between habitat patches that are appropriate for their various needs for food, thermoregulation, shelter and reproduction.

As well as vegetation structure and exposure to sunlight, soil properties are also important – both directly and indirectly. Directly, soil texture must be suitable for egg-laying, so that pods can be placed at sufficient depth in the soil to avoid both extremes of temperature and the risk of excavation. Soil rich in nutrients and with relatively high moisture content favours the growth of the more vigorous tall grasses whose dense stands shade out the sunlight. Such swards are unsuitable for grasshoppers in general, although they may support some meadow and rufous grasshoppers. Poorer, well-drained soils favour the sort of uneven grassland, with areas of short grass and bare ground, that provides suitable habitat for most common grasshoppers.

Finally, Clark's studies included some consideration of the effects of various biotic (including agricultural) influences on grasshopper habitats. Ploughing, of course, was generally detrimental, but so also was cattle grazing, as it tended to produce a short, dense and even sward lacking the diversity of microclimates that grasshoppers need. By contrast, some sites that were heavily grazed by rabbits did provide some of the richest grasshopper habitat, and Clark speculates that excessive grazing pressures by domestic animals might break up the grass cover to produce suitable grasshopper habitat. A rotation system between hay production and grazing, as then practised, was also generally favourable. However, he pointed out that grasshopper abundance is usually a sign of poor soil or poor farming, and notes that the most favourable habitats in his study were 'agriculturally derelict or useless land'.

The timing of Clark's study is significant as there was a good deal of 'derelict' and 'useless' land prior to the long period of post-war agricultural intensification and mechanisation, and this would have been particularly favourable for grasshoppers. It is remarkable that while recognising some differences between the grasshopper species under study in their habitat preferences, he was still able to think in more general terms of grasshopper associations with up to seven species present. However, although the analysis of his grassland categories does not show great divergences between the preferences of individual species, there are great differences between the species in the absolute number of habitats from which they were recorded. This is not remarked upon by Clark, but of the 158 habitats surveyed, 81% and 73.4% respectively harboured *Chorthippus parallelus* and *C. 'bicolor'* (now called *C. brunneus*). This contrasts with 27.8% for each of *O. viridulus* and *G. rufus*, 21% for *S. lineatus*, 15% for *M. maculatus* and a mere 11% for *C. albomarginatus*. The woodland grasshopper (*Omocestus 'ventralis'*, now *O. rufipes*) was met with so rarely that it did not figure in Clark's analysis. This indicates that even some 60 years ago, *C. parallelus* and *C. brunneus* were very much more wide-ranging in their habitats than the other grassland species. Clark gives little indication of the criteria he used in selecting his survey sites, but it seems likely that any comparable survey conducted today would find *G. rufus* and *S. lineatus* much less commonly. *C. albomarginatus*, in contrast, would almost certainly figure much more prominently.

Richards & Waloff (1954)

Another notable contribution to the study of the ecology of British grasshoppers was conducted at Silwood Park – a field station of Imperial College – by O. W. Richards and N. Waloff between 1947 and 1951. Their study was, like Clark's, aided by Uvarov, and was published in the *Anti-Locust Bulletin* (Richards & Waloff, 1954). They studied three more-or-less distinct colonies in the park, with assemblages of four or five common grasshoppers. *C. parallelus, C. brunneus, O. viridulus* and *S.*

lineatus occurred in all locations studied, with M. *maculatus* sustaining only small and very localised populations. This study was confined to much more uniform habitats than was Clark's, but the researchers were able to quantify the effects of annual variations in weather on mortality and reproduction rates for at least the commonest of the species, and they also made interesting observations on the impact of predation and parasitism on their study populations. Important quantitative information was also obtained on differential mortality rates at various stages of the life cycle.

This study supported Clark's findings on the importance of climate as a determinant of grasshopper populations, the flexibility of their food preferences, and the significance of vegetation structure. The hot, dry summer of 1949 produced a peak in population density, most evidently in the two most abundant species, C. *parallelus* and C. *brunneus*. Populations of all species fell during the cool, damp summer of 1950. On the basis of international comparison, Richards and Waloff argue that while summer temperatures are important, sunshine hours can be decisive in determining the developmental and reproductive success of these grasshoppers. High rainfall was held to be an adverse influence, with very high nymphal mortality rates of 90 per cent in 1950, a year with exceptionally high summer rainfall, contrasting with very high survival rates in 1951, a year with very low rainfall in June and July.

Richards and Waloff's study also supported Clark's findings on the importance of complexity and unevenness of vegetation cover, and provided further insight into the way the grasshoppers make use of adjacent habitat patches. One of the colonies studied was located on a sloping area with shorter, sparse grasses with bare ground at the top, and more lush, long grasses at the bottom of the slope. Richards and Waloff showed that nymphs were more abundant in the sparsely vegetated habitat, but migrated to the lower habitat to feed, the adult females eventually returning to the higher area to lay their eggs. Interestingly, in the hot summer of 1949 females were more inclined to lay their eggs in the damper, better-vegetated patches, indicating considerable 'choosiness' and flexibility on the part of females in selecting their ovipositing sites.

Richards and Waloff lay considerable emphasis on the importance to overall population dynamics of the conditions for embryonic and nymphal development. Their study suggests that high levels of precipitation during the egg phase are detrimental to hatching rates, possibly because of waterlogging of the soil. Rapid nymphal development under favourable weather conditions, most significantly sunshine hours, reduces predation risk, and affects not just survival rates, but also adult weight. This is correlated in both C. *parallelus* and C. *brunneus* with fecundity. However, Richards and Waloff argue that the impact

of climatic variability on the population dynamics of the two species is different.
C. *brunneus* is subject to more year-by-year fluctuations in its population, and is
affected at each developmental stage by climatic conditions. These in turn affect
not only survival rates but also the number of pods laid by surviving females and
the number of eggs per pod. By contrast, females of C. *parallelus* vary much less
among themselves in fecundity, so that reproductive success of the population
depends primarily on nymphal survival rate, and thereby on the number of
female adults reaching the reproductive stage.

Unlike Clark, Richards and Waloff attempt to make some assessment of the
impact of predation and parasitism on the fluctuation of their study populations.
With one important exception, it proved difficult to acquire reliable quantitative
data, but they were able to provide an impressive list of the sheer diversity of
survival threats faced by grasshoppers. These range from infections of micro-
organisms and fungi at various life-history stages, through the attentions of
parasitic nematodes, Hymenoptera and Diptera to small mammals and birds.
They list seventeen species of the latter that were known to include grasshoppers
in their diet, but they were unable to devise a reliable method for assessing their
impact on grasshopper populations quantitatively.

They report some details of the life history and abundance of three
invertebrate enemies of grasshoppers that they encountered. Females of the
predatory sphecid wasp *Tachysphex pompiliformis* were observed carrying paralysed
adults and nymphs of both C. *brunneus* and C. *parallelus* back to their nests (see
Fig 15). The parasitoid fly *Blaesoxipha plumicornis* (reported as B. *laticornis*, but
probably in error) was presumably quite common at Silwood, and the authors
report finding it in all the species of grasshopper present. The female deposits
its newly-hatched larvae on the bodies – often the wings – of grasshoppers. The
larvae quickly burrow through the cuticle and feed on the body contents of the
grasshopper until, when full-grown, they emerge through a small hole behind the
head, and pupate in the soil. The infected grasshopper dies shortly afterwards.
The other enemy studied thoroughly was an egg parasite, the wasp *Scelio*. Females
of *Scelio* lay their eggs in grasshopper eggs, usually parasitising all eggs in a pod.
In the year of greatest abundance, as many as 19 to 28 per cent of the pods of
C. *brunneus* and C. *parallelus* were parasitized, and the authors suggest that the
increased abundance of *Scelio* in the year of peak abundance of the grasshoppers
must have played a significant part in the subsequent decline of the latter.

Although both Clark and Richards and Waloff were inclined to look for
common features of habitats and climatic conditions that favoured mixed
populations of grasshopper species, there was already evidence that the autecology
of the various species differed considerably, despite their sharing many sites. The

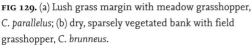

FIG 129. (a) Lush grass margin with meadow grasshopper, C. parallelus; (b) dry, sparsely vegetated bank with field grasshopper, C. brunneus.

striking differences in the proportion of sites occupied by the different species included in Clark's study suggest that there is significant differentiation in their ecological requirements. Richards and Waloff noted that *M. maculatus* was more restricted in its occurrence at Silwood than the other species, and made some attempt to characterise its distinctive habitat, noting its preference for areas of bare ground for egg-laying, and its association with heathy areas characterised by *Erica cinerea* and *Polytrichum* moss as well as sparse grasses. Some differentiation between the three commonest grasshoppers is also suggested, with *C. parallelus* and *O. viridulus* showing more tolerance of long grasses, continuity of grass cover and damp soil than *C. brunneus*, which preferred to oviposit in loose soil or sand.

ORTHOPTERA AND THE FARMED LANDSCAPE

Since these classic studies, there have been profound changes both in the extent of permanent grassland and in methods of grassland management. Agricultural intensification over large parts of lowland Britain has involved a marked shift away from mixed farming systems towards either intensive arable cultivation, or indoor rearing of cattle. Hay meadows and extensively grazed pastures have given way to arable fields, with remaining grassland managed for silage or 'improved' for more intensive livestock grazing (see, for example, Shoard, 1980; Harvey, 1997). The dramatic decline in farmland biodiversity that has resulted from these changes has resulted in a degree of public alarm, and, both in Britain and western Europe (van Wingerden *et al.*, 1992), incentives have been introduced to ameliorate some of the losses. In the main these have taken the form of compensatory payments to farmers in exchange for taking some land out of production. Initially the motivation at the level of the European Union was mainly economic. Agricultural intensification had been too successful, delivering a major problem of storage and disposal of massive surpluses. However, the areas to be 'set-aside' from production were also supposed to offer some environmental benefit – especially in terms of restoring some of the biodiversity that had been lost. This benefit was initially very limited, but the selection and management of set-aside eventually became more sensitive to the requirements of habitat provision, especially for farmland birds and butterflies. Alongside these developments, finance and advice became available in the shape of agri-environmental schemes that have been much more carefully targeted at conservation and the provision of wildlife habitat as well as countryside access.

Although these major changes in the farmed landscape and subsequent attempts to ameliorate their impact on wildlife have been the topic of a number of important studies, relatively few of these have paid attention to the Orthoptera. Prominent among those that have are numerous studies carried out, mainly in Essex, by Tim Gardiner and co-workers. One wide-ranging study (Gardiner *et al.*, 2002) was an attempt to investigate grassland structure in relation to the occurrence and abundance of three common *Chorthippus* species (*brunneus*, *parallelus* and *albomarginatus*). In addition to their intrinsic interest, these common grasshopper species are known to constitute a significant part of the diet of declining farmland birds such as the cirl bunting (*Emberiza cirlus*), the skylark (*Alauda arvensis*) and the grey partridge (*Perdix perdix*) (see, e.g., Brickle *et al.*, 2000; Robinson, *et al.* 2001). A range of grasshopper habitats was sampled, including dry and wet heathland, as well as intensively grazed agricultural grassland, lightly grazed horse pasture, roadside verge, cart track, hay meadow and conservation field margins. The inclusion of *C. albomarginatus* as a species sufficiently widespread in the study area (mid-Essex) is an indication of the range extension of this species since the earlier studies.

The broad conclusions of this study were that all three species had become very scarce in the intensively managed agricultural habitats, and two (*C. brunneus* and *C. parallelus*) were most abundant in the remaining fragments of heathland. In general, the three species considered collectively were more abundant in sward heights

FIG 131. (a) Intensively grazed sheep pasture, unsuitable for orthopterans; (b) heathland with intensive rabbit grazing – also unsuitable; (c) lightly cattle-grazed riverside meadow with uneven sward structure, favourable for some grassland orthopterans.

of between 10 and 20 cm, although in the favoured heathland sites, the two species that occurred there were more abundant even where the vegetation was taller than this. Although earlier studies had concluded that grass species composition of grassland was not a limiting condition in terms of food preferences, this study did find significant positive correlations between the abundance of *C. parallelus* and *C. brunneus* and the frequency of finer grasses (*Agrostis* species) and negative correlations with *Lolium perenne*. However, a study of feeding preferences of *C. parallelus* carried out by Gardiner and Hill (2004b) indicated that the coarser grasses were actually preferred to finer ones. This suggests that the preference for swards made up of fine grasses is not determined by food preferences but rather by the differences in sward structure associated with grasslands dominated by these different grass species. If the finer-leaved grasses tend to produce more sparse swards with more patches of bare soil, they may benefit grasshoppers by providing better ovipositing sites and opportunities for basking.

The grazing regimes included in the study enabled a comparison between intensive sheep and cattle grazing and more lightly grazed horse pasture. Both *C. albomarginatus* and *C. parallelus* were more abundant in the latter, suggesting that, given appropriate grazing levels, pasture can provide favourable habitat for at least some grasshoppers.

Subsequent work by Gardiner and others has also focused on the more common grassland orthopterans in relation to both the impact of intensively managed agricultural grasslands, and the prospects for conservation measures to ameliorate adverse impacts. Separate studies were conducted to investigate the impact of different grass-cutting and grazing regimes. Again, the studies dealt with common grassland species, but included two bush-crickets, the long-winged conehead (*Conocephalus discolor*) and Roesel's bush-cricket (*Metrioptera roeselii*), in addition to the grasshoppers. The two bush-crickets have both undergone striking range extensions since the studies that were conducted in the mid-20th century, possibly aided to some degree by agricultural change (see below). Interestingly, however, the common field grasshopper (*C. brunneus*), usually considered one of our commonest species, was not present in the agriculturally 'improved' grassland used for the first of these studies.

Gardiner (2009a) describes a study carried out from 2002 to 2004, in which the impact of four different grassland cutting regimes on four common orthopterans (*C. parallelus, C. albomarginatus, C. discolor* and *M. roeselii*) was investigated. The plots chosen for comparison were drawn from an area of improved grassland on the Writtle College estate in Essex. The grassland was dominated by *Lolium perenne* and, having previously been extensively grazed by horses, had moderately high populations of the four common orthopterans. The four management regimes included two that mimicked standard agricultural practice: a silage system, with cuts in late May and early July, and application of inorganic fertiliser; and a hay-making system that involved fertiliser application in May with mowing in early July. A third regime was designed as a 'conservation' system, with a cut at the beginning of May and another in late September, but no added fertiliser. The fourth treatment was a 'control' with no cutting or fertiliser application. In all years, all four common orthopterans were present in the conservation and control plots, with either three or four in the more intensive treatments. So, it seems that over this period of time, sheer number of species (very low in any case) was not affected. However, on measures of 'assemblage diversity' (i.e. taking into account the relative abundance of the different species) and overall abundance of individuals, the less intensively managed plots were clearly more favourable. In particular, the two bush-cricket species were present in significantly higher numbers in the conservation and control plots. Favourable weather conditions over the three years of the study seem to have enabled large increases in the populations of the two grasshopper species in the conservation and control plots, but not in the plots managed according to productive agricultural protocols.

More detailed analysis provided insights into these rather different patterns. The silage treatment, with its early cut, favoured abundance of the nymphs of the grasshopper species, while abundance of the adults was correlated with the taller grassland in late season provided by the conservation and control treatments. This might be interpreted in terms of the movements through the season noted in the study by Richards and Waloff – that nymphs favoured shorter, warmer swards, but migrated to adjacent areas of taller 'cool' grasses for food and shelter, then (in the case of females) back to the shorter, more sparse areas for egg-laying. However, in Gardiner's study, direct effects of the cutting process were taken into account. Marked reductions in density of both nymphs (in the early cut) and adults (in the July cut) in the silage treatment suggested high rates of mortality caused by machinery, combined (in the case of the later cut) with dispersal away from the newly cut sward (see Gardiner & Hill, 2005b, 2006; Gardiner, 2009a).

Gardiner's proposal is that these species would be favoured by cutting regimes that either were rotational, or combined areas of short, sparse turf to favour survival and rapid development of nymphs, with areas of taller grasses to provide shelter and food for adults. He notes that the two bush-cricket species lay their eggs in grass stems, and so might be eliminated altogether by early cutting regimes. In fact, it seems likely that any annual cutting regime involving removal of cuttings would severely affect these species, although both will lay their eggs in a variety of robust plant stems. Both species are widespread in tall, dense grasslands, and it may be that optimal conditions for them are provided by early stages of transition, with some scrub, especially bramble, present among the grasses. Both species are often the only orthopterans present in unmanaged long-grass field margins or roadside verges alongside hedgerows (pers. obs.). The absence of C. brunneus from this study confirms the impression given by the earlier study by Gardiner et al. (2002), that this species has a more stringent set of habitat requirements than its relatives. Sparse grassland on poor, well-drained soils, usually with a south-facing aspect, and patches of bare ground are characteristic features of habitats that support this species. In such habitats, individuals spend a high proportion of their time basking or indulging in competitive or courtship behaviour on the ground (see Fig 129b).

The influence of different grazing regimes on the common grassland orthopterans was the subject of another experimental study reported by Gardiner (2009a). The grassland used for this study had previously been intensively managed for livestock, and Orthoptera were very scarce at the start. Three different management regimes were compared for their Orthoptera assemblages over three years, from 2002 to 2004 inclusive. The 'control' plot was Lolium grassland, intensively grazed with fertiliser application in early Spring and again in late June. The grass was cut for silage in mid-June, with a second silage crop or intensive grazing with lambs and ewes thereafter. This treatment was intended to mimic widespread practice on productive farmland. The other two treatments involved extensive grazing with Red Poll cattle, a rare breed generally considered useful for conservation because of its tendency at low density to produce an uneven mosaic grassland structure. The stocking levels were higher (2–4 per hectare) than recommended for conservation grazing, to bring the comparison closer to economically viable levels. These two conservation treatments differed only in that one made use of the existing *Lolium* grassland, while the other was sown with a more diverse botanical mix.

Over the three years of the experiment, the species richness in the intensive plot fell from three to one species, but that in the extensive plots increased from three or four, to four or five. Abundance of all species combined, and of *C. parallelus* and *C. albomarginatus* individually, were much higher in the extensive plots, and the two grassland bush-crickets, although rare in all treatments, were virtually absent from the intensive one (one specimen of *M. roeselii* in 2002). Although population densities were generally higher in the botanically diverse treatment than in the *Lolium* extensive treatment, the extensive regimes were broadly comparable with one another.

Sward height in relation to the developmental stages of the insects was highlighted as a key factor explaining the differences between these management regimes. The fertiliser application and relatively late silage cut (mid-June) produced a tall, dense 'cold' vegetation structure in the intensive treatment, which was likely to slow down both egg and nymph development early in the year, while intensive grazing produced a short, even sward later in the year that would be unsuitable for shelter and feeding habitat for adults. Although the more extensive regimes tended to produce swards that were shorter than the 10 to 20 cm optimum for the *Chorthippus* species (Gardiner *et al.* 2002), they were more uneven than those produced by intensive grazing and silage cutting, leaving some 'rejected' patches of longer grasses that provided refuges for the grasshoppers, and were the only habitat suitable for the bush-crickets. In all treatments, numbers of orthopterans were low, a consequence of the Orthoptera-unfriendly management prior to the experiment. In effect, the study relied on colonisation of the habitats during the course of the experiment, and it is notable that *C. brunneus* turned up in very small numbers on the botanically diverse extensive treatment in the second year.

A study of sandy grasslands in the eastern Netherlands (van Wingerden *et al.*, 1992) compared fertilised with unfertilised areas in terms of the population densities and species diversity of orthopterans. The orthopteran communities in the study area (nine species of grasshoppers and one bush-cricket) were more species-rich than those studied by Gardiner, but the conclusions of the study were broadly similar. Fertilisation (increased nitrogen load) was associated with a reduction in both species diversity and overall population density. However, the complex methodology of the study enabled the authors to show that the effects of fertilisation were mediated by way of changed vegetation structure, humidity and microclimate. Dense, cool swards promoted by fertilisation reduced spring and autumn temperatures at soil level, and so slowed down egg development. For some species, late hatching limited their ability to complete their annual life cycle, especially in poor summers. Conversely, tall swards in summer favoured nymphs and adults by providing shelter. The implications are that grazing or cutting regimes should aim to reduce biomass in spring, but allow taller swards to develop during the summer. In unfertilised grasslands, the development of coarse grasses and scrub may also have adverse impacts on orthopteran communities.

These studies provide valuable insights into the reasons for the very low abundance and species richness of orthopterans in modern intensively managed farm grasslands, whether grazed or cut for hay or silage. They also provide indications of ways in which less-intensive but possibly still economically viable management regimes might produce grassland habitat somewhat less hostile to the common grassland species. As well as benefiting orthopteran assemblages, more extensive grazing regimes or rotational grass cutting would be likely to increase farmland biodiversity generally, both by favouring other invertebrates such as butterflies and beetles, and by providing crucial food sources for several species of declining or threatened farmland birds.

CONSERVING ORTHOPTERA IN THE FARMED LANDSCAPE?

As most of the British land surface is farmed, and, since the 1940s especially, intensification has involved loss of wildlife habitat on a devastating scale, efforts to ameliorate these losses are of great importance. Across Europe, concern about the costs of storage of agricultural surpluses coincided with growing public concern about the wide range of environmental and cultural losses associated with the newer agricultural regimes. Initially the policy response was to subsidise farmers for taking a proportion of productive land (usually 10 per cent) out of production as 'set-aside'. This was introduced into Britain in 1993, and took two forms: 'rotational', involving different plots of land each year; and 'permanent', with land taken out of production for ten years. With some modification, set-aside continued as a significant feature of UK agricultural landscapes until it was ended in 2008.

Meanwhile, as set-aside was increasingly acknowledged to provide relatively few environmental benefits, new forms of inducements for farmers to manage land 'sustainably' were introduced. In Britain, environmental concern had already by the late 1980s led to the designation of parts of the countryside that had high conservation value as 'environmentally sensitive areas' (ESAs) where farmers were encouraged to integrate environmental objectives into their management. This move was supplemented from the early 1990s by the Countryside Stewardship Scheme (CSS), coming fully into operation from 1996. This provided payments to farmers for environmental improvements such as providing grass field margins, and, ironically, restoring the hedgerows whose removal had previously also been massively grant-aided by the same bodies. Studies of the benefits of Countryside

Stewardship for farm biodiversity were initially rather equivocal, and in 2005 it was replaced by a more carefully designed and targeted Environmental Stewardship (ES) Scheme. This had several declared objectives: to conserve biodiversity, enhance landscape quality, protect historical features and natural resources, and to promote public access and understanding of the countryside. Under ES, land managers have three basic options: Entry Level Stewardship (open to all), Organic Entry Level Stewardship, and Higher Level Stewardship. The last of these is more

FIG 132. 'Set-aside' field, 1990s, with poppies and thistles.

FIG 133. Conservation strip for farmland birds, Essex 2003.

demanding in terms of detailed management requirements, and is available only to farmers in high-priority areas for conservation.

Entry Level Stewardship includes several options for maintaining marginal grass strips on cultivated land. These can be 2, 4 or 6 metres wide, involve minimal use of herbicides, no added fertiliser, and, after the first 12 months, no cutting except to remove woody growth at intervals of not less than 5 years. The 6-metre-wide strips additionally may be established by sowing fine-leaved grasses (rather than simply allowing natural regeneration), and have a cutting regime that allows for a diversity of sward heights. The 3-metre-wide swathe closest to the crop is cut annually in July, while the other 3-metre swathe is cut much less frequently, as with the 2 and 4 metre strips. Other options include permanent grassland managed with low or very low fertiliser, no ploughing or re-seeding, and very limited use of herbicide. These may be cut or grazed, but not between 1 April and 31 May.

Numerous empirical studies have been undertaken to evaluate these agri-environmental schemes for their impact on botanical diversity, farmland birds and various groups of invertebrates. However, very few of these have been directly focused on Orthoptera. Two studies that did monitor the influence on orthopteran populations of the Countryside Stewardship grass field margins yielded rather different conclusions. Marshall *et al.* (2006) concluded that grasshoppers were more abundant and diverse on 6-metre-wide field margins than on surrounding agricultural land. By contrast, Gardiner & Hill (Gardiner & Hill, 2005a) compared Countryside Stewardship grass margins in Essex with a range of other farm habitats and concluded that they offered little or nothing more than the surrounding more intensively managed land (see also Gardiner *et al.*, 2008, Gardiner & Hassall, 2009).

However, the two studies were not comparable in several respects, partly in terms of the methods used, and partly in terms of the nature of the surrounding habitat, soil conditions, climate and so on. Gardiner and Hill (2005a) compared their CSS margins with lightly grazed horse pasture, a disused farm track, and several more intensively managed grasslands and arable. The track was on well-drained soil, had more sparse, fine-leaved grasses, and supported three grasshopper species. The CSS margins supported only two, while the most intensively managed farmland supported just one – the ubiquitous *C. parallelus*. Most interesting was their monitoring of change through 7 years of the 10-year scheme, in surveys in 1999, 2001 and 2003. Initially the CSS margins supported three species in quite high densities, but thereafter the grasshopper fauna declined to only two, at low densities. Meanwhile, grasshopper populations in the lightly grazed horse pasture increased, indicating that the decline in grasshoppers on the CSS margins was not due to any general adverse conditions (such as weather) affecting local grasshopper populations.

Gardiner and Hill attribute the poor response of orthopterans to CSS in their study to a variety of factors. First, on the fertile soil in their locality, *Lolium perenne* was the dominant grass species, known to produce dense 'cold' sward relatively unsuitable for grasshoppers. Second, the requirement for an annual cut in July or August probably led to direct mortality from the cutting operation, combined with dispersal away from the short sward following the cut. A subsequent study of the effect of cutting for hay on microclimate confirmed much higher sward temperatures in the short, even sward after cutting, and dispersal of grasshoppers to uncut areas with tufts of longer grass that offered both shelter from predators and the opportunity to avoid overheating and water loss from exposure in the short grass (Gardiner & Hassall, 2009). The more favourable impact of CSS margins in the study by Marshall *et al.* highlights the importance of location of conservation measures in relation to other landscape features, source populations of target species, and general adaptation of the schemes to local climate, soil properties, field size and local farming practices (Gardiner *et al.*, 2008).

Conservation measures do, however, seem to have had a beneficial impact in enabling the range extension of Roesel's bush-cricket (and possibly of the long-winged conehead, too). Gardiner (2009b) was able to relate reported sightings of macropterous *M. roeselii* and landscape changes in Essex between 1980 and 2008 with successive phases of range expansion. From its historic range in the southern and eastern parts of the county, *M. roeselii* extended into central and western Essex during the 1980s and early 1990s. This part of the county had suffered less from hedgerow removal during that period than the north-west of the county, which was characterised by high rates of hedgerow loss, and large, arable monocultures. Increased reporting of macropters coincided closely with the introduction of agricultural set-aside in the early to mid-1990s, and also with a new phase of expansion of *M. roeselii* into the north-west of the county. This pattern is consistent with the hypothesis that the expansion of *M. roeselii* was facilitated by the increased landscape connectivity provided by long-grass set-aside strips. Although the period of expansion generally coincided with increased average air temperatures, Gardiner was unable to find significant correlations between specific climatic variables and the incidence of macropterism (see Chapter 3).

Although much of the research on farmland as habitat for orthopterans has concentrated on grassland, the farmed landscape includes habitats other than grassland. Features such as hedgerows, remnants of woodland, farm ponds, cart tracks and drainage ditches may also have actual or potential significance as orthopteran habitat. Several of these features have tended to become degraded

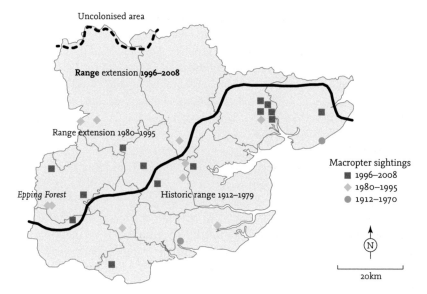

FIG 134. Range expansion of Roesel's bush-cricket in Essex showing the distribution of sightings of macropterous individuals. Range extensions show areas that have been colonised within the time period indicated (from Gardiner 2009b, fig 1:98).

through nutrient run-off or mechanised management, or eliminated in pursuit of more 'efficient' utilisation of land. Hedgerows and patches of woodland, for example, have been grubbed out to increase the total area available for intensive agriculture and to facilitate the use and movement of machinery. With the shift away from mixed farming towards arable and more intensive animal husbandry, farm ponds have been filled in or neglected, and cattle increasingly provided with piped water supply. Drainage ditches are often mechanically cleared of marginal and emergent vegetation, and polluted with chemical run-off, so that their value for aquatic wildlife has greatly diminished in many areas.

Nevertheless, such features do remain in the farmed landscape, albeit less frequently, and in a more fragmented pattern. Hedgerows, in particular, are an important habitat for several of our more widespread and tolerant bush-crickets. The oak, speckled and dark bush-crickets (*Meconema thalassinum, Leptophyes punctatissima* and *Pholidoptera griseoaptera*) fall into this grouping. All three species were recorded by Tim Gardiner in his study of the orthopteroids (including earwigs) of green lane hedgerows in Essex (Gardiner 2010a). The hedgerows surveyed formed belts of woody vegetation on both sides of footpaths, bridleways and byways, and Gardiner found that species richness of the bush-crickets was significantly correlated with the species richness of woody plants in the hedgerows, although not with their orientation (north/south or east/west), nor with the closure or openness of the canopy. Gardiner interprets the association of the bush-crickets with the more species-rich hedgerows in terms of the likely age – 500 years or more – of the green lane, suggesting continuity of usage and a great period of time during which the orthopterans could have dispersed and built up populations. Despite the lack of correlation with the orientation of the hedgerows, Gardiner notes that concentrations of bush-crickets were frequently found in shrubs in sun-spots. He also found that the bush-crickets were most abundant on stretches of 'ghost' hedgerow persisting as remnants of previously eliminated woodland.

Perhaps surprisingly, the oak and speckled bush-crickets were most frequently beaten from blackthorn and bramble, with such plants as dog rose, oak, field maple and hawthorn yielding fewer individuals. This may have been partly a function of the relative abundance of these woody species in the hedgerows, but may also have to do with the timing of the survey and the method of sampling. Gardiner chose the period 20 May to 4 July, as speckled bush-crickets tend to disperse upwards in vegetation later in their life-cycle (Hall, Ash & Robinson, unpub.), and the same is also supposed to apply to the oak bush-cricket. Beating would have missed insects in vegetation more than two metres above the ground, which would probably include the majority of speckled bush-crickets, by August. (Hall reports 10 out of 12 singing males above 2 metres in August in Oxfordshire (pers. comm.).)

Gardiner's study is valuable in demonstrating that old hedgerows are important habitats in the farmed landscape for these three bush-crickets, and also that hedgerows are successful substitute habitats for the oak bush-cricket, generally considered a species of mature woodland. However, what is

FIG 135. A green lane, with uneven shrub heights, mature trees and sun-spots.

known about the life-cycle and movements of these species suggests that other features of the hedgerows might be important. The early nymphal stages of the speckled bush-cricket require soft-leaved food plants such as wood sage or nettles, graduating to other herbaceous plants and bramble as they develop. Both speckled and oak bush-cricket females lay their eggs in bark or in crevices in tree-trunks, and the adults of both species are distributed at various heights up to high tree canopy. Although it seems that the speckled bush-cricket is mainly vegetarian, the oak bush-cricket lives mainly on small invertebrate prey. Finally, the dark bush-cricket is usually found low down in scrub and in adjacent herbaceous vegetation. It seems likely that the method of beating would have produced a significant under-estimate of its distribution and abundance.

These considerations point to a number of potentially important hedgerow features for the conservation of these species:

(1) as Gardiner shows, age and diversity of woody plant species;
(2) presence at the base of the hedgerow of a margin of uncut herbaceous vegetation, especially early in the season;
(3) sufficient unevenness in the hedgerow structure to give warm, sheltered 'sun-spots';
(4) sufficient abundance of invertebrate prey for the oak-bush cricket, possibly linked to age and diversity of the woody plants, but also to absence of insecticide spray drift;
(5) possibly also presence within the hedgerow of mature trees such as oak or lime as oviposition habitat. It is also possible that the movement of both speckled and oak bush-crickets high into the canopy plays some significant part in their life cycle. This is an interesting topic for research.

FIG 136. An Orthoptera-friendly hedgerow.

Footpaths through farmland, especially where they run alongside hedgerows, and are associated with a strip of uncultivated ground, can support several orthopteran species. Gardiner (2006b, 2007b; Gardiner & Dover, 2008) recorded six species on transect footpath walks in mid-Essex, and in this study they did find both more species and greater abundance on the leeward side of adjacent hedgerows. As well as expected species (*C. parallelus, C. brunneus, C. albomarginatus, M. roeselii, P. griseoaptera*) they found small numbers of the slender groundhopper (*Tetrix subulata*). This species, like *C. brunneus*, favours sparsely vegetated habitat with bare ground. These conditions are frequently provided by moderately well-walked footpaths, or those subject to sporadic vehicular traffic. Disturbance from vehicles on military training grounds may also benefit 'disturbance dependent' species such as the locally scarce mottled grasshopper, *M. maculatus* (Gardiner & Benton, 2009). Tyre tracks where the water table is high can also provide wet ground favourable to the colonisation of soil algae and mosses, the principal food of the groundhoppers. Where footpaths are bordered by ditches these, too, can provide marginal habitat suitable for both common and slender groundhoppers (*T. undulata* and *T. subulata*). Also, within its markedly south-eastern distribution (away from the coasts), the short-winged conehead (*Conocephalus dorsalis*) may be found in such habitats. Residual farm ponds, even where these have long been neglected, may also provide marginal habitat for the groundhoppers and short-winged conehead. Finally, patches of broad-leaved woodland, although not important for most orthopterans, may provide habitat for the oak bush-cricket (*Meconema thalassinum*).

FIG 137. Vehicle tracks on MoD training area, sparsely vegetated habitat for the mottled grasshopper.

FIG 138. (a) Intensive agricultural landscape, with remnant copse, and ditch bank; (b) pond margin with slender groundhopper and short-winged conehead; (c) vehicle tracks through open woodland providing habitat for the slender groundhopper.

BEYOND THE FARMED LANDSCAPE

However, from the point of view of the conservation of the Orthoptera more generally, it has to be conceded that many species either were never strongly represented on farmland, or have already been more or less fully excluded from the farmed countryside by the spread of modern mechanised, high-input agriculture.

A recent study of the distribution of orthopterans in three English counties in relation to patterns of land use bears this out (Cherrill 2010, 2011). Species richness on a landscape scale was inversely correlated with the proportion of arable land, and positively correlated with diversity of land-covers (Fig 139). The species found in the most intensively arable grid squares were *Meconema thalassinum, Leptophyes punctatissima, Omocestus viridulus, Chorthippus brunneus* and *C. parallelus*. A further 13 species all increased in frequency as the extent of arable cropping declined, but even the most intensively farmed area appeared to have sufficient land (at least by area) to support a wide range of species. This observation supports two points noted in other studies. First, the quality and connectivity of remnant semi-natural habitats in agricultural landscapes appears

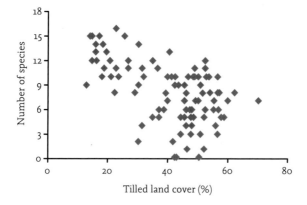

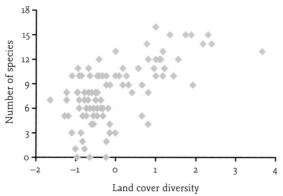

FIG 139. (a) The relationship between species richness and percentage of tilled land cover; (b) the relationship between species richness and land cover diversity (from Cherrill, 2010 Orthopterists' workshop, figs 2 and 5).

to be paramount, yet these habitats are frequently degraded and isolated. Second, such marginal habitats have, at least in theory, the potential to support a diversity of species. Indeed species adversely affected by agricultural change and other development pressures have in many instances survived in very small, localised populations, in habitats that have somehow escaped the ravages of intensive agriculture. These habitats can be divided into four broad and overlapping categories.

(1) Marginal land that has not been considered profitable for agricultural investment because of small area, adverse soil properties, inaccessibility, or lack of capital.

(2) Habitat produced as a (usually unintended) by-product of other human activities. This includes infrastructures such as road and rail verges, embankments and cuttings, flood defences, reservoir enclosures and the

like, drainage ditches and farm reservoirs, worked-out mineral extraction sites, land-fill, abandoned post-industrial brownfield sites, unmanaged land hoarded by property speculators or subject to planning blight, and so on.

(3) Habitat protected or created and managed explicitly for purposes of conservation or leisure use or both. This includes, in addition to the conservation measures introduced to agricultural land, areas designated as Areas or Sites of Special Scientific Interest, nature reserves owned or managed by voluntary or statutory bodies of various kinds, urban and rural parks and other green open spaces or corridors in towns and cities, margins of waterways, and various sensitive coastal habitats such as dune systems, shingle beaches, salt marshes and under-cliffs.

(4) Remaining broad-leaved woodland and forests, including the huge areas of heath and forests managed by the Forestry Commission. Much of this woodland is managed commercially for timber production, but there are significant holdings by conservation bodies such as the Woodland Trust, and the areas managed by the Forestry Commission have in recent years become increasingly important both for public recreational access and for wildlife conservation. This resource has been threatened by policies of several successive governments, but so far effectively defended by popular alliances.

Although much of the concern about loss of biodiversity has concentrated, understandably enough, on agricultural change, there are some compensatory by-products of other sorts of land use. In particular, these include infrastructural developments of two main sorts: roadside verges and flood defences. In both cases very extensive linear grasslands have the potential to provide both habitat in their own right and connectivity between otherwise fragmented semi-natural habitat. Little systematic research seems to have been carried out on the value of verges for orthopterans, but routine survey work carried out by local recorders in Essex found between three and seven (most commonly five) species in each of a series of randomly chosen short stretches of verge (Benton & Dobson, 2010, unpub.). In all, eight species were recorded (*L. punctatissima, P. griseoaptera, M. roeselii, C. discolor, T. subulata* (one site only), *C. parallelus, C. brunneus, C. albomarginatus*). Verges with adjacent hedgerows invariably had *L. punctatissima* (located by bat detector), and usually *P. griseoaptera*. The common method of verge management is to maintain a short grass sward close to the edge of the road, but to allow more rank grass and some scrub invasion away from the road on wider verges. Breaks in the short sward caused by machinery provided bare ground that was often occupied by *C. brunneus*, with *C. parallelus* and *C. albomarginatus* typically in longer grass tufts, while *C. discolor* and *M. roeselii* were exclusively found among the longer grasses.

It seems likely that in areas where roads have been cut through downland or heaths that harbour populations of more localised species, the potential value of appropriate verge management must be considerable, although work by Gardiner and others suggests that the common practice of intensive tree or shrub planting on trunk roads, as well as uniform mid-summer cutting are both likely to be detrimental. Systematic research into the optimal pattern of grassland management for orthopterans in roadside verges would be desirable.

Especially in eastern England, coastal and estuarine flood defences constitute a linear grassland refuge several thousand kilometres in extent. Like roadside verges, they provide important habitat in their own right, as well as connectivity, in this case between mainly coastal habitats such as salt marsh, sand dunes and

FIG 140. (a) Roadside verge with slender and common groundhoppers (© T. Gardiner); (b) wide verge with mowed edges, a bank with tussocky grasses and a rough hedgerow; (c) close-mown urban roadside verge, Orthoptera-hostile; (d) former railway cutting, now a chalk grassland nature reserve; (e) railway line with adjacent uncultivated rough grassland.

grazing marsh. Although structures vary, and along some stretches sea walls are hard surfaced, typical patterns are as described in Gardiner (2011b). An earth bank faces out towards the sea (or estuary) on one side, with a flat top, often managed as a footpath, and a steeply sloping bank on the landward side. Between the bank and adjacent land (usually arable, but formerly, and still, in places, grazing marsh) runs a flat strip of unimproved grassland (the 'folding') used for occasional vehicular access, and a ditch ('borrow dyke'). The sea walls and associated habitats provide important habitats for a wide range of invertebrates (Gardiner, 2011b; Benton, 2000, 2006) and have been the route for northerly migration of two threatened bumblebee species in recent years (Benton & Dobson, 2006, 2007). The diversity of aspects, elevations and treatments of the different components of the flood defence system results in a complex mosaic of microhabitats in close proximity to one another. The potential to satisfy the habitat preferences of a range of orthopterans is considerable, and up to ten species can be found on suitably managed defences in south-eastern England and East Anglia. C. brunneus tends to be confined to the shorter sward and bare ground along the tops of the sea walls, with C. albomarginatus in longer grass on the folding, or along the edges of the borrow dykes. C. discolor and M. roeselii, too, are frequently present in the longer grass strips. C. dorsalis is commonly present among marginal vegetation (especially stands of sea club-rush, Bolboschoenus maritimus) along the banks of the borrow dykes. The groundhoppers (T. undulata and T. subulata) can be found on heavily disturbed parts of the folding, in association with bare ground partially colonised by algae and mosses. Where the folding and associated dyke have been left unmanaged, the combination of rank, tussocky grasses and woody plants such as hawthorn, blackthorn and bramble may harbour populations of the scarce great green bush-cricket (Tettigonia viridissima).

However, grassland management on the sea walls is often unsuitable for Orthoptera. The encroachment of woody vegetation is resisted partly because of the risk to the integrity of the walls as flood defences, and partly to allow regular inspection. Although spring and early summer cutting is avoided so as not to disturb nesting birds, the resulting concentration of cutting in midsummer is likely to eliminate large numbers of orthopterans directly, as well as leaving behind short turf that is unsuitable for most species (Gardiner et al., 2002). An autumn cut, or rotational cutting of the different faces of the wall and folding, is provisionally recommended (Gardiner 2011b).

Other categories of potentially valuable orthopteran habitat created incidentally as a by-product of other human activities include worked-out mineral extraction sites, and so-called 'brown field' sites left by industrial decline. These share several common features: absence of treatment by fertiliser

FIG 141. (a) Flood defences, Essex coast; (b) flood defences, showing partly mown folding and ditch, habitat for Roesel's bush-cricket, long-winged conehead and lesser marsh grasshopper; (c) sparsely vegetated outer bank, habitat for field grasshopper; (d) uncut inner bank, habitat for great green bush-cricket; (e) ditch with sea club-rush, for great green bush-cricket and short-winged conehead; (f) insensitive ditch-management, eliminating all marginal vegetation on both sides.

or insecticide, diversity of aspects, irregular disturbance from walkers, motor-cycle scramblers and the like, nutrient-poor soils and, often, both wet and dry zones. On poor, well-drained soils the high proportion of bare ground, sparse vegetation and exposure to the sun favour *C. brunneus* and, in some places, the mottled grasshopper (*M. maculatus*). Damp corners and pool edges commonly harbour the two widespread groundhoppers, and sometimes the short-winged conehead (*C. dorsalis*). Where there is a more vigorous growth of common grasses, *C. parallelus*, *C. albomarginatus*, *C. discolor* and *M. roeselii* are often abundant.

Finally, urban parks and domestic gardens can be valuable refuges for a range of the commoner species. Trees, shrubs and hedgerows in these settings will commonly have populations of speckled and oak bush-crickets, and, as it continues to increase its range in England, the southern oak bush-cricket, *Meconema meridionale* (Hawkins, 2001; Gardiner *et al.*, 2009). Where management is not too severe, the dark bush-cricket, common field grasshopper and meadow grasshoppers can also usually survive.

Many of the species listed above as 'southern local habitat specialists' are unlikely to be present in much of the farmed landscape, and will occur on other human-made habitats such as sea walls, verges, flooded pits and so on only where these are situated close to remaining patches of suitable natural and seminatural habitat. These latter may persist where difficulties of access (such as small islands; see Gardiner & Ringwood, 2010) or lack of capital have prevented agricultural intensification or urbanisation, where expanses of land have been sequestered for other purposes, most notably military training (see Gardiner & Benton, 2009), or where management has been prescribed under a conservation designation. This last category might include land within national or local country parks, nature reserves, environmentally sensitive areas, sites designated for their scientific interest, and land protected for its value as historical or

FIG 142. A former gravel workings, now a nature reserve with common and slender groundhoppers.

FIG 143. (clockwise from above left) Urban park with close-mown grass but hay meadows beyond; suburban gardens, habitat for oak and speckled bush-crickets; hay meadow in a country park, with Orthoptera fauna limited by early cut.

cultural heritage. A significant recent trend has been to manage churchyards and cemeteries for conservation, with some mowing regimes specifically intended to boost orthopteran populations (see Cooper 2001; Gardiner *et al.*, 2011).

Flood plains of river valleys are also frequently retained as grassland, although how these are managed is crucially important for wildlife. One study has demonstrated the negative consequences for orthopterans of the short, even sward produced by intensive horse-grazing (Gardiner & Haines, 2008).

FIG 144. Churchyard with areas of long grass and shrubs, habitat for several common grasshoppers and bush-crickets.

THE SOUTHERN LOCAL AND RARE SPECIALISTS AND THEIR REFUGES

Five broad types of natural and semi-natural habitat are important for remaining populations of our southern local habitat specialists.

1. Woodland

The requirement of most orthopterans for exposure to solar radiation excludes most of the ground-living species from dense woodland. However, the oak bush-cricket lives mainly in the canopy, and the speckled bush-cricket thrives along wide woodland rides where the wood edge is bounded by shrubs and ground flora. Open but sheltered rides and wide junctions, such as are maintained by the Forestry Commission in Kings, Rendlesham and Thetford Forests in East Anglia, provide habitat for such localised grasshoppers as the stripe-winged, mottled and common green (Richmond, 2001).

The two species most closely associated with woodland are the woodland grasshopper (*Omocestus rufipes*) and wood cricket (*Nemobius sylvestris*).

The woodland grasshopper is found in open rides and clearings in woods, but also on grassland and heathland close to woods and scrub. It has a strictly southern distribution in England, centred on the New Forest, the western Weald and east of Kent. It is also found further west, and in Cornwall it inhabits heathy areas including sea cliffs (Marshall & Haes, 1988). It is rare north of the Thames (Paul, 1989). Further south in Europe it is not especially associated with woodland, but, rather, with wet heath, dunes, and even rocky slopes (Kleukers & Krekels, 2004). In its woodland habitats it may become abundant after coppicing or clear-fell, but disappears as the woodland floor becomes shaded out by regrowth of trees. It favours disturbed but sheltered locations, including heaths undergoing

FIG 145. An open ride in King's Forest, Suffolk, habitat for the stripe-winged and common green grasshoppers.

FIG 146. Habitat of the woodland grasshopper, New Forest.

restoration (Edwards, pers. comm.). It is also markedly less common in the New Forest woodlands where there are large populations of the wood ant, *Formica rufa* (B. Pinchen, pers. comm.). Systematic research on this probably declining species is needed. Its predilection for basking in sheltered sun-spots and its southerly distribution suggest that summer temperatures and availability of hot microclimates are important to its survival.

The wood cricket is another markedly southern species, with strongholds in the New Forest, the Isle of Wight, and south Devon. There is some uncertainty about its status as a British native species, but it is certainly long-established here. It favours sunny woodland rides and glades, wood edges and, in some parts of its distribution, more open heath or cliff habitats, but always close to scrub or woodland (Marshall & Haes, 1988). A study of populations in the Isle of Wight found that larger, ancient, mixed woodlands were more likely than others to harbour populations, and also that there was a correlation with irregularity of woodland shape (possibly indicating proportionally greater woodland-edge habitat). Habitat requirements include a well-developed leaf-litter layer, combined with relatively sparse, low-growing ground-flora and low canopy cover (as found in rides and wood edges). Like *O. rufipes*, it is also markedly less

FIG 147. Habitat of the wood cricket, New Forest.

common in New Forest woodlands where there are large populations of the wood ant (B. Pinchen, pers. comm.). Although the species has relatively good dispersal ability – being able to cross up to 55 metres of non-woodland habitat, and orient to woodland from 40 to 50 metres – habitat fragmentation is likely to be a barrier to dispersal. Provision of mature habitat corridors between patches of woodland would enable dispersal (Brouwers & Newton, 2009, 2010; Brouwers et al., 2011).

As these localised woodland species clearly depend on open areas with sunlight, a combination of active ride management with tree-felling or coppicing is essential (see Gardiner, 2010c). There is also good evidence that intensive horse-grazing is a significant threat to these species in the New Forest (Denton, 2006)

2. Unimproved grasslands (including acid grass heaths, commons and calcareous downland)

Where factors such as vegetation structure, aspect and climate are suitable, the common grassland orthopterans that are found in more intensively managed grasslands, roadside verges, sea walls and so on can also be expected to occur in unimproved grasslands. It is in the remaining fragments of common, grass heath and downland that the more localised and habitat-specialist species are to be found. However, even species that I characterised as generalist may be confined to such habitats in large parts of their range. The common green grasshopper (*Omocestus viridulus*) is one such species. It is distributed throughout almost the whole of the British Isles, and present at high altitude in uplands (reportedly up to 1000 metres (Marshall & Haes, 1988), 550 metres in Wales (Burton, 2010) and 410 metres in the Lake District (Horsfield, 2010), but it is quite scarce and localised in parts of the south east of England. Marshall & Haes (1988) regard it as an indicator species of unimproved pasture, with little ability to colonise roadside verges and other newer grasslands. The species is very local or absent from some south-eastern districts, and Tim Gardiner has recently surveyed its status in Essex (Gardiner, 2010b), where it has always been primarily confined to old grassland or heath habitats in the western half of the county (Wake, 1997). Current distribution patterns, and the 50 per cent decline evidenced by Gardiner's study, suggest that populations are vulnerable both to shading out of the habitat by natural succession to scrub and woodland (Gardiner & Gardiner, 2009), and to intensive grazing by rabbits. Preferred grassland habitats (such as many in its stronghold, Epping Forest) are tall, moist and cool swards, often dominated by purple moor grass (*Molinea caerulea*) or Yorkshire fog (*Holcus lanatus*). The higher rainfall, combined with more moisture-retentive clay soils, might help to explain the western distribution of the insect in the county. Remaining colonies outside Epping Forest are confined to isolated areas of old grassland, such as commons

FIG 148. Habitat of the common green grasshopper and common groundhopper, Danbury Common, Essex.

and remnants of heathland, where they are frequently threatened by lack of management. As indicated by its northerly distribution in Britain, preference for tall grassland and presence at high altitudes, *O. viridulus* is adapted to cool climates, and appears to be poor at cooling its body when ambient temperatures are high (Willott, 1997). It may also be susceptible to desiccation. It is also a scarce species in the New Forest where heavy grazing pressure prevents the establishment of taller swards (B. pinchen, pers. comm.).

Three other southern species are closely associated with unimproved grassland, and especially chalk or limestone downland. The most widespread of these is the stripe-winged grasshopper, *Stenobothrus lineatus* (which also thrives on acid grassland and sandy heaths; see below). This species is close to the northern edge of its European range in southern Britain, and occurs on dry, south-facing downland slopes south of a line from the Bristol Channel to the Wash, extending only very locally along the south-western peninsula (Marshall & Haes, 1988; Haes & Harding, 1997). It requires ambient temperatures between 20 and 25 degrees Celsius if it is to raise its body temperature above the threshold for development and reproduction (Willott, 1997). Like other thermophilous insects, such as the silver spotted skipper and Adonis blue butterflies (*Hesperia comma* and *Polyommatus bellargus*) which also occur on downland, it favours sheltered slopes and hollows with short turf (Asher *et al.*, 2001). Conservation grazing that favours these butterfly species is also likely to benefit *S. lineatus* (Baldock, 1999). Currently this species seems to be extending its range in East Anglia (N. Owens, pers. comm.). It was recently reported from Essex for the first time (Wilde, 2009), and has since been discovered in several sites in the west of the county (Gardiner 2011c).

Another denizen of south-facing downland slopes in the south of England is the rufous grasshopper (*Gomphocerippus rufus*). It ranges, increasingly locally, as far north as the Cotswolds, but its stronghold is the North Downs. Unlike the stripe-winged grasshopper, however, this species is associated with patches of tall, tussocky grasses and low scrub, often in the vicinity of woodland (Marshall & Haes, 1988; Baldock, 1999). It is said to have benefited from the introduction of myxomatosis in the 1950s, which led to a reduction of rabbit grazing in its downland habitats (Haes & Harding, 1997). Shrubs, especially dogwood, are used as platforms for basking and male calling song, as well as for prolonged and elaborate bouts of courtship (see the DVD). Further south in Europe, *G. rufus* occurs on woodland edges and sunny rides, indicating that there is a general association with woody vegetation (Bellmann, 1988). However, the eggs are laid in soil, and it may be that early stages of the life cycle benefit from the hotter microclimates of shorter turf and bare ground.

The third species is one of our rarest and most vulnerable orthopterans: the wartbiter (*Decticus verrucivorus*). It seems this species was always extremely

FIG 149. Chalk downland habitat of stripe-winged grasshopper and scarce grassland butterflies, Kent.

FIG 150. Habitat of the rufous grasshopper, North Downs, Surrey.

localised in southern Britain, and losses of populations through agricultural intensification and ubanisation led to its inclusion on Schedule 5 of the Wildlife and Countryside Act, 1981. It was classed as 'vulnerable' in the Nature Conservancy Council's *Red Data Book* (Shirt, 1987) and made the subject of an English Nature species-recovery project. By the early 1990s there were only four known English populations, three of them on chalk downland (and the fourth on heathland; see below). Research at the site holding the strongest population has provided detailed information on the habitat requirements of the species through its life-cycle phases (Cherrill & Brown, 1990a, 1990b). Final-instar nymphs and males are found mostly in patches of tall, tussocky grasses (*Bromopsis erecta* and *Brachypodium pinnatum*). However, in adjacent areas of short turf (around 5 cm tall) females are more likely to be seen than males. Earlier-instar nymphs, too, are most likely to be found in areas of short turf. Males use the sides of grass tufts for emitting their calling song, but readily dive into deep vegetation when disturbed. Females stray into areas of shorter turf, with patches of bare ground, to lay their eggs. Laboratory tests indicate that females are very selective in their use of oviposition sites, and warmer spots with fine soils are preferred (Cherrill *et al.*, 1991). It is probable that the prolonged embryonic development and subsequent nymphal growth and development benefit from the hotter microclimate of patches of short turf, while the larger nymphs and adults gain shelter from predators in nearby longer grass tufts. Also, given the much lower density of UK populations compared with those in mainland Europe, it is likely that mate-location depends on the better acoustic transmission offered by areas of short grass adjacent to the male calling perches.

The habitat requirements of all stages of development include a fine mosaic of short turf with areas of tall, tussocky grassland on warm, sunny downland slopes. The eggs require at least two years, and sometimes more, for embryonic development to be completed, an adaptation allowing populations to survive one or more years of poor weather and low reproductive success (Ingrisch, 1984a). Numbers of adults can fall close to zero in some summers, only to recover in the following year as a result of the hatching of eggs laid two years earlier (Haes *et al.*, 1990). However, as the species appears to be at its climatic limit in southern England, optimal habitat conditions are necessary for reproductive success in years when weather conditions are favourable for nymphal development in spring and summer, and for female longevity in late summer. Even in the strongest English population, Cherrill and Brown estimated more than 90 per cent mortality between hatching and adult emergence (1990a), but also found that the timing of adult emergence can vary by as much as five weeks owing to differences in the weather (1991b).

FIG 151. Habitat of the wartbiter, South Downs, Sussex.

Despite better understanding of the habitat requirements of the wartbiter, and some success at reintroduction using captive-reared insects, this remains one of our most vulnerable species. Future conservation efforts must rely on successful management of surviving populations. Captive-breeding, although successful, proved to be extremely labour-intensive. Unlike the field cricket (see below), the wartbiter is difficult to maintain in laboratory cultures and has a relatively low fecundity (Pearce-Kelly *et al.*, 1998). Cannibalism, high nymphal mortality, and the extended embryonic phase, alongside the difficulty of providing adequate supplies of suitable protein-rich food, made raising large numbers of individuals for release impossible. Outbreaks of fungal and gregarine disease also complicated the work and delayed or prevented releases of captive bred stock (Cunningham *et al.*, 1997). The Species Recovery Programme culminated with a successful re-introduction of the wartbiter to a downland site in Kent from which it had been lost in the 1970s (still present in 2010, pers. obs.). Introductions at two other sites were unsuccessful, probably because of the small numbers available for release.

Although management regimes suitable for the wartbiter are not identical to those for our other local species of downland, there are significant commonalities. A mosaic of short and long grass patches is consistent with the habitat requirements of the stripe-winged, common green, meadow and field grasshoppers as well as the very local great green bush-cricket (*Tettigonia viridissima*), all of which were recorded at the main downland locality for the wartbiter.

Finally, the field cricket (*Gryllus campestris*), one of our most vulnerable species, was formerly known from a small number of steep south-facing downland slopes, but occurred more frequently on sparsely vegetated grass heaths on fine, dry sandy soils. Always a highly localised species in south-central England, this species declined almost to extinction as a result of habitat destruction associated with conversion to arable, building development and recreational use of its habitats. Even where colonies survived these were mostly lost to invasion by heather, bracken, coarse grasses, or gorse and birch scrub in the absence of grazing. It could be that some sites were lost to the cessation of grazing by rabbits following the introduction of myxomatosis. Despite its listing in the Wildlife and Countryside Act, 1981, and its designation as 'vulnerable' (RDB1) in the Nature Conservancy Council's *Red Data Book* (Shirt, 1987), by 1988 only one remaining population was known. The cricket was made the subject of an English Nature Species Recovery project under the leadership of Mike Edwards in 1991, and this was followed by thorough study of the ecological requirements of the species and the establishment of a captive breeding programme at London Zoo. This has enabled reintroductions to sites where it was formerly known, as well as introductions to nearby sites that appeared suitable. Three of the reintroduction sites are so far successful, and there are plans to extend the original site (Haes & Harding, 1997; Edwards, *et al.*, 1996; Edwards, 2008, pers. comm.; Marshall, 2010).

Research on the autecology of the field cricket indicates the crucial importance of climatic variables. To complete its life cycle in a single year in a cool climate is a tall order for such a large insect, and both here and at other more northerly sites on the mainland of Europe the insect undergoes large fluctuations in population from year to year, depending on the temperatures and insolation in spring and summer. Eggs are laid in patches of bare earth or short turf in warm locations in June, and the resulting nymphs feed on fungi and plant material, frequently basking on bare soil, for their first three instars. From the sixth instar, they dig burrows, and they overwinter in the penultimate nymphal stage. It is thought that mild weather in winter presents a risk, as the overwintering nymphs become active, but cannot replenish their energy reserves. In spring the adults of both sexes occupy burrows, hollowing out a spoon-shaped 'platform' which they use for feeding and sunning themselves. The males often (but not always) sing from these platforms and – if lucky – court and mate here with females that they attract. The burrows provide a refuge from predators, and there are reports of predation by birds – notably corvids – as well as by small mammals. However, there is circumstantial evidence that they may be distasteful to birds. The crickets themselves are omnivorous (Edwards *et al.*, 1996).

The main habitat requirements seem to be light soil into which they can burrow; a warm, sheltered, south-facing situation open to the sun all year round; short, sparse turf, with areas of bare ground, and low tufts of grass or

FIG 152. Habitat of the field cricket.

heather; and a climate that provides enough sunshine and warmth through the summer to enable the nymphs to complete sufficient growth and development to overwinter successfully. Relatively cold winters are believed beneficial, although heavy downpours of rain even in favourable summers can be disastrous, as many drown in their burrows. It is possible that climate change may improve the prospects of this species in Britain, but it seems likely that it will continue to depend on active conservation management at its few known sites. It has limited powers of dispersal, and such features as hedges or streams may constitute insuperable barriers, so it seems likely that any expansion in its distribution will depend on deliberate introductions (Edwards *et al.*, 1996).

3. Lowland heaths

One of our rarest orthopterans, the heath grasshopper, *Chorthippus vagans*, is, as its vernacular name implies, in England found exclusively in dry, sandy heathland. It has probably always been confined to a small geographical area in Britain – notably the heathlands of east Dorset and west Hampshire. Unlike most grasshoppers, which feed mainly on grasses, the heath grasshopper readily eats both heather and gorse (see DVD). Further south, in mainland Europe, it is reported from a variety of habitats such as quarries, railway banks, rocky slopes and acid grassland as well as heaths (Kleukers & Krekels, 2004). The authors of one important study of a population in northern Germany regard it as a species of the transitional zone between pine forest and adjacent dry, sparsely vegetated habitats such as dunes, acid grasslands or heath (Hochkirch *et al.*, 2008). In this study the population at one site increased following tree-felling and clearance of leaf litter, and analysis of the distribution of the insects at their locality showed a strong negative correlation with both deciduous trees and leaf litter, but a positive correlation with patches of bare ground. Insects migrated to more open, sunny habitat later in the season as the lowering of the sun led to shading by an adjacent plantation. However, the population on the drier, more exposed habitat tended to seek out more humid and taller patches of vegetation.

According to Ingrisch (1983) the eggs are highly resistant to desiccation, and it seems this species is adapted to hot, dry, sparsely vegetated habitats, exposed to the sun. However, the evidence from Hochkirch et al., (2008b) suggests that the presence of tall vegetation, offering shelter from excessive temperatures and desiccation, may also be an important component of their habitat. The species is declining across much of its European range, partly owing to agricultural intensification, urbanisation and recreational use of its habitats. These processes have clearly been at work in extinguishing and fragmenting its habitats in Britain too, especially in the area around the Poole-Bournemouth conurbation. However, Hochkirch et al. also highlight other processes: the tendency to impose sharp boundaries to forested land; eliminating the transitional zone in which *C. vagans* flourishes; or, alternatively, neglect and loss of grazing pressure on adjacent habitats, leading to natural succession and shading out of the habitat. Although the UK habitats of this species do not conform exactly to the transitional zones identified by Hochkirch et al., it seems likely that shading out of their habitat by invasion of vigorous growths of heathers, gorse and other scrub is a serious threat to its survival at its few remaining British localities. Its small populations in the west of the New Forest appear to be dwindling rapidly. A possible explanation for this decline may be the change in heathland management away from turf-cutting to the more recent trend to burning. The former practice created patches of bare earth that would take up to seven years to regenerate, and would have provided transitional zones appropriate for this species. The cessation of regular and rotational cutting of birch scrub, bracken, heather and gorse will also have reduced the available transitional zones. Burning and flailing – which have replaced these

FIG 153. Habitat of the heath grasshopper, New Forest.

management practices – are both likely to be hostile to invertebrate populations, including the heath grasshopper (information from B. Pinchen, pers. comm.).

Heather and acid grass heathlands are also an alternative habitat for the stripe-winged grasshopper (*Stenobothrus lineatus*). It is widespread on dry, sandy heaths in Surrey, Hampshire and Dorset, as well as on

FIG 154. (a) Slepe heath, Dorset; (b) habitat of the woodland and mottled grasshoppers, New Forest; (c) detail of habitat of the common groundhopper, Danbury Common, Essex; (d) Cavenham Heath, Suffolk, habitat of stripe-winged and common green grasshoppers.

Breckland heaths and in open forest rides in East Anglia. Areas of bare soil, open, sunny conditions and early succession habitats are produced by occasional disturbance from forestry operations and clear-felling of large woodland compartments. Baldock (1999) notes that this species can commonly be found in the area between the rough and fairway on golf courses in Surrey. Other, more widespread orthopteran species can also be found on heathland, sometimes in association with either of these two more localised species. The mottled grasshopper (*M. maculatus*), the woodland grasshopper (*O. rufipes*), the common groundhopper (*Tetrix undulata*) and the field grasshopper (*C. brunneus*) are all likely to be found there, along with the common green grasshopper (*O. viridulus*) and the bog bush-cricket (*Metrioptera brachyptera*) in transitional zones between dry and wet heathland.

Finally, the wartbiter (*D. verrucivorus*) is known from one heathland site in Britain. Because of the very small population size, its habitat requirements on heathland have not been investigated in detail, but qualitative observations suggest that in terms of vegetation structure they are similar to those of the downland populations (Cherrill, 1993 and pers. comm.). The species is omnivorous and has a preference for protein-rich foods such as seed-heads and invertebrate prey (Cherrill & Brown 1990b). It is suggested that the critical factor in its ecology is the thermal demand of each developmental stage, rather than the availability of specific food sources. In mainland Europe the species is less of a habitat specialist than it is in southern England.

4. Wetlands

The characteristic species of wet heathlands is our largest grasshopper, the large marsh grasshopper (*Stethophyma grossum*). However, while never a widespread species in Britain, it is now markedly more limited in its distribution. It formerly occurred in the fens of Cambridgeshire and the Norfolk Broads, but apart from occasional artificial introductions, and the possibility of a surviving population on the Somerset Levels (Sutton, 2007a, 2007b, 2007c), it is now confined to wet heaths and bogs of Dorset and Hampshire. It was recorded early in the last century from Belton bog in east Norfolk, where a large area of heath and bog was subsequently destroyed by scrub encroachment and large-scale conifer plantation in the Waveney Forest area (Gardiner, 2010d; Richmond, 2001). The strong populations that persist in the New Forest inhabit the wettest parts of bogs, often indicated by the white heads of cotton-grass (Ragge, 1965), but are also associated with purple moor grass (*Molinea caerulea*), cross-leaved heath (*Erica tetralix*) and bog myrtle (*Myrica gale*) (Marshall & Haes, 1988). They feed on the stems of rushes and other tough marsh vegetation.

The main threat to this species has been drainage of its habitat and, in some areas, peat-cutting, although it retains significant populations in the west of Ireland (Sutton, 2007a). Its habitats in England are not under direct threats of this kind, but climate change could lead to a drying out of its remaining heathland bogs, with little prospect of its dispersing beyond its current very restricted geographical distribution without help (Gardiner *et al.*, unpub.; Sutton, 2007b). The trend towards burning as the favoured method of heathland management in the New Forest is likely to be detrimental to this species, with areas of valley mire/wet heath burnt in February or March. As the eggs of this species are laid in grass tufts, it is likely that they will be destroyed, and, as many bogs and mires are unconnected, local extinctions could follow. The large marsh grasshopper is currently the subject of a Natural England Species Recovery project, and the New Forest populations correlate strongly with *Sphagnum*-dominated mire habitat with open water. Restoration of large areas of former fen in East Anglia opens up the possibility of reintroduction of the species to this part of the country (Sutton, 2007a).

The habitats of the large marsh grasshopper are usually shared with the bog bush-cricket (*Metrioptera brachyptera*), although the geographical distribution of this species is much greater in extent. Although clearly a specialist of wet heathland and bog, the bog bush-cricket has scattered populations through most of England and into south-west Scotland (Haes & Harding, 1997; Evans & Edmondson, 2007; but see also Sutton, 2006a), so that its survival, even in the face of climate change, seems more certain than that of the large marsh grasshopper.

FIG 155. Habitat of the large marsh grasshopper and bog bush-cricket, New Forest.

Two other, inconspicuous, orthopterans of wetland habitats are the slender and Cepero's groundhoppers (*Tetrix subulata* and *T. ceperoi*). Although strongly associated with coastal habitats in Britain, Cepero's groundhopper is reported from some inland sites, most notably at the edges of pools and streams in the New Forest and Dorset heaths (Marshall & Haes, 1988). There appear to be no recent inland records from the New Forest, where it was always extremely localised. However, separation of these two species in the field is difficult, and it may be that Cepero's groundhopper is under-recorded.

Our final localised wetland species, the mole-cricket (*Gryllotalpa gryllotalpa*), was recorded from most counties in Britain until about the 1920s, but has become increasingly scarce until it was described as an 'extreme and elusive rarity' by Haes (in Shirt, 1987), listing it as 'endangered' (RDB1). Already, by the mid-1970s, only two small populations were known, and since then reports have been very sporadic. Many new reported sightings have turned out to be of other species, or, if *G. gryllotalpa*, then they were likely to have been incidentally imported with garden produce. The species was made the subject of an English Nature's Species Recovery Programme in 1994, and this is now co-ordinated by Bryan Pinchen, who has reported on a population in a clearing in the New Forest, first discovered in 2003 (Pinchen, 2005, 2006), with song heard here as recently as 2008 (B. Pinchen, pers. comm.). However, even here the species has proved elusive, and it remains uncertain whether the population is genuinely native.

Formerly the species inhabited the transitional areas on the edges of bogs and marshes, as well as wet pastures and meadows in river flood plains. Gardens

FIG 156. Water meadow, habitat of the slender groundhopper.

FIG 157. The only currently known mainland British site for the mole cricket.

and allotments have also been the source of many reports, and the species was sometimes regarded as a pest, damaging potatoes and carrots (Ragge, 1965). It remains common in some parts of Guernsey, and has been regarded there, too, as an agricultural pest. As there is only one known population on the British mainland, it is difficult to see what conservation measures are needed. However, as the crickets spend most of their lives underground, and the song of the male is heard so rarely, even when it is present, it is quite possible that populations persist undiscovered. It may be that protection of remaining unimproved wet pastures and peatlands that are of conservation value for other reasons offers the best hope for this species (Marshall, 2010).

5. Coastal habitats

Several of our most localised southern species are strongly associated with coastal habitats, and especially south-coastal habitats. These are, generally, species close

FIG 158. Habitat of Cepero's groundhopper, Kent.

FIG 159. Coastal habitats of the grey bush-cricket: (below left) vegetated dunes, north Essex; (below right) rocky outcrops, Sussex coast.

to, or at, the north-westerly limit of their geographical distribution in Europe. However, the term 'coastal' covers a great variety of very different habitats, including undercliffs, salt marshes, coastal flood defences, shingle spits and vegetated dune systems. These habitats are subject to modification by tidal action, sea-level rise, and, especially in the east, by coastal erosion. Loss and fragmentation of habitats has also been extensively caused by coastal developments for leisure activities, urban expansion, port facilities and the like. Populations of localised orthopterans, therefore, have become increasingly confined to habitats, such as undercliff and shingle spit, that are too challenging or not profitable enough to be 'developed', or which have been set aside as important for conservation. Cepero's groundhopper and the grey bush-cricket occupy a wide range of such habitats along the south coast of England. Cepero's groundhopper (like its more common close relative, the slender groundhopper) generally occupies thinly vegetated damp or muddy ground around the edges of pools and ditches, around seepages in undercliffs, in dune systems, shingle banks and by ditches next to salt marshes, where it is often accompanied by the slender groundhopper (Marshall & Haes, 1988; Haes & Harding, 1997; pers. obs.). It seems likely that its mainly coastal distribution is related to climatic conditions, as, like the slender groundhopper, it is capable of flight and is presumably quite capable of dispersal to new habitat. However, as its discovery at an inland site in Cambridgeshire suggests, it may be more widely distributed than is currently recognised.

The grey bush-cricket (*Platycleis albopunctata*) is distributed along the south coast of England and the south and west coasts of Wales, and has recently been rediscovered on the east coast of England as far north as Suffolk (Haes & Harding, 1997; N. Cuming, pers. comm.; Harvey *et al.*, 2005; Gardiner *et al.*, 2010). The grey bush-cricket occupies a wide variety of coastal habitats, including sandy and sparsely vegetated patches among rocky outcrops, undercliffs, shingle and dune systems. In Dorset, particularly on Purbeck, it occurs on the cliff-tops at heights of 50 metres or more above the sea (B. Pinchen, pers. comm.). Most sites have substantial areas of bare ground or sand, often used by the females for egg-laying. Both sexes bask on tall vegetation, such as the edges of stands of marram grass (*Ammophila arenaria*), or on shrubby seablite (*Suaeda vera*), but are apt to dive rapidly into deep vegetation if disturbed. As the species is not especially associated with coastal habitats further south in mainland Europe, it seems likely that its mainly southern-coastal distribution in Britain is determined by its high dependence on warmth and exposure to the sun. It is possible that the apparent increase in its population (if not actual range extension) on the east coast is related to climatic warming. In its coastal dune habitats on the east coast *P. albopunctata* is often accompanied by the short-winged conehead (*Conocephalus dorsalis*), lesser marsh grasshopper (*Chorthippus albomarginatus*), common field grasshopper (*Chorthippus brunneus*) and mottled grasshopper (*Myrmeleotettix maculatus*).

This leaves just two very highly localised and somewhat puzzling coastal species: the scaly cricket (*Pseudomogoplistes vicentae*) and the lesser mottled grasshopper (*Stenobothrus stigmaticus*). The scaly cricket (RDB1 in Shirt, 1987) was first discovered in Britain in 1949, and correctly identified as *P. vicentae* only some 50 years later (Gorochov & Marshall, 2001). For many years it was thought to occur among shingle and under rocks or concrete slabs at only one British site – Chesil Beach, Dorset. Controversy about its origins and UK status have been settled by the recent discovery of other populations between Branscombe and Beer Head in Devon, and in south west Wales (Sutton, 2004a). Early accounts supposed that the species survived in small numbers, favouring the more sheltered, landward bank of the shingle ridge at Chesil Beach. However, pit-fall trapping, combined with discoveries of numbers of dead specimens accidentally trapped in litter, have

FIG 160. Habitat of the scaly cricket, Chesil beach. (© T. Gardiner)

contributed to the realisation that the Dorset population, at least, must be very large, and is concentrated on the bleak, exposed and deeply inhospitable seaward flank of the shingle spit.

The population is extensive, but at its densest around and just above the seaweed strand line (although there is precious little seaweed at Chesil), and it appears to be confined to the eastern end of the spit, where the pebbles are larger. The insects remain in crevices among the pebbles or under larger stones or concrete slabs during the day, coming out to feed on decaying animal or plant material and detritus during the night. They are presumably unharmed by salt-water spray, and their habitat lacks growing vegetation. They move with great agility among the pebbles if disturbed during the day, and so are well defended against potential vertebrate predators. At night they are likely to be disturbed only by the occasional passing fisherman. To date, they have survived tourist pressure amounting to 100,000 visits per year. Short of large-scale engineering projects or marine pollution incidents, it is hard to see that they face any very significant threat, despite the tiny number of known localities (Sutton, 2004a). One possibility that has been discussed is the damage that might be caused by increased visitor numbers. Clearly some die from being trapped in items of litter, but it can be argued that litter may also constitute a significant food resource for them. It seems likely that the greater density of the cricket population at the eastern end of Chesil beach is to be explained by the greater freedom of access offered by the larger pebbles at this end, rather than any benefit conferred by greater visitor pressure (see Haes & Harding, 1997; Timmins, 1994; Sutton, 1999; Gardiner, 2009c). However, they are easily damaged by being crushed between pebbles, so trampling on the shingle might lead to some mortalities (pers. obs.).

FIG 161. Chesil beach, showing detritus.

Other threats include disturbance from engineering projects and, manifest at Branscombe in 2007, pollution of beaches from shipping accidents, and subsequent clean-up operations (Sutton, 2007b, 2010b; see also under species account, Chapter 7).

The lesser mottled grasshopper (*Stenobothrus stigmaticus*) is known from only one site in Britain, the Langness peninsula and its immediate vicinity on the Isle of Man. The origin of this population and its relationship with other populations on the near continent of Europe are so far unknown. Its European habitats are reported to include acidic grasslands, heaths, moorland and inland dunes, and it is not especially associated with coasts (Harz, 1975; Bellmann, 1988; van Wingerden & Dimmers, 1993). Its diverse habitats have in common that they are warm, dry, and open with low-growing vegetation on nutrient-poor soils (Cherrill, 1994; Cherrill & Selman, 2007). Livestock grazing appears to be important in maintaining suitable vegetation structure, but grazing by rabbits or deer may also be important in some locations. The species is in decline through most of its European range, partly due to 'improvement' of pastures, and partly as a result of abandonment of grazing and subsequent natural succession. The habitats occupied on Langness conform to the general European pattern, with populations concentrated on areas of unimproved short grassland, and among grasses and heather in the vicinity of rocky outcrops close to the sea. Embryonic development is slower in *S. stigmaticus* than in the other species with which it co-exists (*C. brunneus* and *M. maculatus*), the *C. stigmaticus* nymphs hatching later from the eggs, and subsequently depending on high ambient temperatures and the ability to bask in sunshine to 'catch up' in their development to adulthood (van Wingerden *et al.*, 1991, 1992). Comparison of numbers across several summers supported the view that warm, sunny springs and summers are favourable to the species (Cherrill & Selman, 2007).

FIG 162. (left) Habitat of the lesser mottled grasshopper, Langness, Isle of Man; (below) the same, showing detail of vegetation structure.

European studies suggest that *S. stigmaticus* is a selective grass feeder, probably preferring fine-leaved grasses. On Langness it was reported as feeding on the crested hair-grass (*Koeleria macrantha*), and occupying areas of short grass along with *M. maculatus*, but also tolerating more tussocky areas along with *C. brunneus*. However, it was not found among taller grasses or in heathy areas with more than 50 per

cent cover by heather and gorse scrub. Evidence from changing grazing regimes on Langness suggests that livestock grazing of areas of rank grasses is beneficial, although it may be disadvantageous if applied to areas of shorter grasses on nutrient-poor soils. Cherrill and Selman found small populations on the adjacent golf course, but these were confined to the edges of the rough, and were encouraged by reduced mowing. As with other grasshopper species, appropriate microclimate and opportunities for basking as well as shelter are likely to be important for growth and development, probably impacting differently at successive developmental stages. The species is relatively short-winged (especially in the females) and they are reluctant to fly. Such evidence as there is about their dispersal ability is equivocal, but they have shown little sign of spreading out beyond the confines of the peninsula since their discovery in 1962, so a precautionary view that they are vulnerable to fragmentation of their habitat may be advisable. Their habitat is now designated an Area of Special Scientific Interest, but its future will depend on continued suitable management.

DVD Commentary

Verbal introductions to each species are accompanied by images of typical habitat for the species. Where calling and courtship songs are included without modification using a bat detector, they might not be audible to many viewers. In some cases, this might be remedied by increasing the volume of the player, or tuning to enhanced high frequencies. Many sequences shown are brief clips from longer episodes of behaviour.

1. Introduction – 00:00:20

2. Great green bush-cricket – 00:03:15
A stationary female among tall vegetation – very difficult to see, despite its large size; a male stridulates from an elevated perch. The song is loud and metallic, delivered in long, continuous bursts with occasional brief pauses.

3. Wartbiter – 00:04:11
A female seeks an egg-laying site in short vegetation. A female catches a relatively large insect, and eats it – note the use of long palps. Views of stationary males, showing brown stridulatory apparatus at base of forewings. The male song is quiet, and so two sequences of male song modified using a bat detector are included. The first consists of distinct, short bursts, the second, more typical, consists of a prolonged, continuous repetition of echemes.

4. Dark bush-cricket – 00:06:19
A male and female bask on bramble, late afternoon. A male preens. A male delivers brief chirps as he moves through vegetation. Male delivers more prolonged chirp, associated with close encounters with other males – note the

response from a nearby female. A courtship sequence – note the 'fencing' with their antennae. Another pair: the female mounts the male, palpating the dorsal segments of his abdomen. He kicks her away, but continues to chirp, signalling he is still ready to mate. Two females remain close by. Modified sound of several nearby males chirping, followed by close-up of a singing male.

5. Grey bush-cricket – 00:09:40
A male patrols a tuft of marram grass, briefly engaging in hostile interaction with another male. A singing male – unmodified; sound very quiet. A stationary female among marram grass – note continuous monitoring with her antennae. A female basks and then returns to cover. A female feeds on dry stems of marram grass and other detritus. Recording of the modified song, which consists of prolonged sequences of repeated echemes. Close-up of singing male.

6. Bog Bush Cricket – 00:12:26
A green male dives for cover. A brown female basks and preens. Calling song of a male, sound modified, followed by another singing male, this time in view. Note the exposed mirror on the right fore wing.

7. Roesel's bush-cricket – 00:13:27
A freshly emerged male catches and eats a small invertebrate; note the continuous use of the antennae in navigation. A green female basks, cleans her ovipositor, and then returns to deep vegetation. A singing male. A long-winged form of the male, also singing. Antagonistic interactions between two males on a favoured song platform. A courtship sequence between a long-winged male and normal form of the female. He continues to sing, and 'strokes' the female with his antennae. She moves off, and he follows. Several clips from a longer sequence of a female biting a club-rush stem and using her curved ovipositor to lay an egg in the plant tissue. Sequences of modified sound of the calling song: a prolonged 'buzz', without clearly distinguishable echemes. Shorter bursts of song produced by rival males at close quarters.

8. Long-winged conehead – 00:17:09
A singing male. The unmodified song is very quiet. A female cleans her ovipositor. A male catches and eats a tiny insect running up a plant stem. Another male feeds on grass seeds . A male sings while searching for a potential mate. A courtship is interrupted by the arrival of a second male. Courtship is resumed, and the male succeeds in grasping the female. A second

female arrives and the male attempts to mate again. A female points her ovipositor down at approximately 90° to her body, and probes a plant stem. Competitive interaction between two females. Modified calling song of the male: a prolonged and usually uniform repetition of echemes, sounding like an electric motor.

9. Short-winged conehead – 00:21:02

A male sings as he moves through vegetation. Another male feeds on *Chenopodium* flower-heads. A male appears to scent-mark a leaf. A stationary singing male. Antagonistic interaction between a long-winged and a normal form of the male – note 'fencing' with antennae and the threat posture of one male, abdomen curved down as if intending to mate. Clips from a longer sequence, in which a courtship is interrupted by the arrival (from below) of a rival male. The two males fight by kicking with their hind legs, while the female makes off, left. One of the males rejoins the female and attempts to mate with her, but fails, despite her apparent cooperation. A courting male 'strokes' a female with his antennae and vibrates. A female chews a hole in a club-rush stem, attempts to insert her ovipositor, fails, and continues to chew. The quiet song is best heard with the use of a bat-detector. The song is a prolonged sequences of echemes, superficially similar to that of the long-winged conehead, but phases of rapidly repeated echemes are interspersed with (usually shorter) phases of slower 'ticking'.

10. Speckled bush-cricket – 00:25:28

A male basks on a leaf of bindweed. A female, close by. A male feeds from a desiccated blackberry. The (modified) male calling song; an irregularly spaced series of very brief chirps, or 'clicks'.

11. Field cricket – 00:27:19

A female makes a brief sortie from her burrow and returns, with a male singing in the background. A female leaves a burrow that she shares with a male, and subsequently returns to it. A male courts a female, without success. A male emerges from his burrow, tends the adjacent 'platform', and produces the prolonged sequence of repeated chirps of the calling song (note the raised position of the fore wings). A female arrives and the male song is modified to the courtship mode. She inspects the burrow, and then is induced to mount the male, who makes distinctive sideways twists as mating takes place. The female subsequently enters and then emerges from the burrow, rear-end first, showing the small white spermatophore.

DVD

12. Cepero's groundhopper – 00:30:43

A female feeds on detritus. A male searches among dead plant stems. A male (above) leans down in the direction of a female and delivers the 'pronotal bob' courtship signal (see Chapter 8). He then approaches and mounts the female, but is intercepted by a rival male. Two females are feeding on soil algae when one is approached by a male. He mounts her, but she vibrates so violently that he is shaken off. Directly afterwards, another male approaches, mounts and successfully mates with her.

13. Slender groundhopper – 00:32:43

A female feeds on soil algae, probing with her palpi. A female is approached by a male who performs several 'forward swing' courtship signals. He then mounts and mates with the female, while another male climbs over him and subsequently succeeds in mating with the female from her other side.

14. Common groundhopper – 00:34:31

A male feeds on small mosses. Interactions between males: a male approaches another, who gives a double 'leg-flick' signal, and vibrates as the first male mounts him and then dismounts. Two adjacent males give vibratory signals to one another. A male gives a series of 'forward-swing' signals and moves towards a female, mounts from the rear, and successfully mates with her.

15. Common and slender groundhoppers – 00:35:57

Sequences of interactions between the two species: complex interactions between three male common and one male slender groundhopper; an approaching male slender groundhopper elicits leg flick and vibratory responses from a male common groundhopper, and then mounts him; a male slender groundhopper is rejected by a female common groundhopper; a male slender groundhopper mounts and successfully mates with a female slender groundhopper; a male common groundhopper mounts a female slender groundhopper, who vibrates and eventually dislodges him. Clips from a longer sequence, in which: a male common groundhopper mounts a female slender groundhopper; a male slender groundhopper attempts to drag him off by the genitalia, and the female eventually shakes him off by moving forwards; the male slender groundhopper then walks to the female, eliciting a strong vibratory signal from the disappointed common groundhopper male as he does so; the male slender groundhopper then mates with the female and departs. (Not shown is the subsequent movement of the female slender groundhopper towards the male common groundhopper, who promptly mounts and mates with her.)

16. Large marsh grasshopper – 00:39:32

A female at rest on *Sphagnum* moss. A male preens his head and antenna. A male climbs through vegetation and delivers a sequence of the distinctive 'tick' stridulations. Another male stridulates and then bites off a section of the stem of a sedge – note the use of the fore legs in manipulating the stem. Another male stridulates from a perch, alternating with another close by.

17. Stripe-winged grasshopper – 00:41:28

'Brown' form of the female. A male climbs through grasses and stridulates. The leg movements are slow, and slightly out of sync. with one another. There are 26 syllables in the single, prolonged echeme of this particular song. The song is difficult to hear, but in this case is overwhelmed by the song of a nearby common green grasshopper. A male courts a female with rapid small amplitude vibrations of the hind legs, while she continues feeding and then departs. He follows and resumes courtship (many times!). The calling song of the male, as modified by a bat detector.

18. Lesser mottled grasshopper – 00:43:16

A male moves around on a grassy 'platform' by the sea. A female at rest on a patch of ling. A searching male finds a courting pair, attempts to mount the female, but is rejected and she departs. He follows but is then displaced by another male. The first male turns, preens and produces a brief stridulation, while his rival continues the chase.

19. Woodland grasshopper – 00:45:25

A female at rest on ling. A male basks in the sun. A male preens and tests a grass blade with its white palps. A male stridulates briefly. Another male cleans an antenna and then stridulates. The song is a single, brief echeme (in this case about 6 seconds), beginning quietly and increasing in intensity to the end.

20. Common green grasshopper – 00:47:04

A green female at rest. A male feeds on a grass blade. A green male stridulates from a perch in a gorse bush. The song is similar to that of the woodland grasshopper, but continues for longer at maximum intensity. This example is typical, lasting approximately 23 seconds . A brown form of the male sings and is joined by another, which continues to sing after the end of the song of the one in view. This song is longer than normal, possibly because of competition from the other male. A sequence of courtship behaviour of a male, showing a series of (12) leg flicks, resembling the 'ticking' stridulation of the large marsh grasshopper, followed by prolonged small-amplitude vibrations of the hind legs.

21. Common field grasshopper – 00:49:34
The male calling song – repeated brief chirps. Two males pursue an unwilling female, chirping as they go. Eventually they move off, chirping (to each other in rivalry?) as they go. A female is rapidly approached by a male, who attempts to mount and is repulsed by means of a double 'flick' with the hind legs. He continues to chirp as two other males arrive, one of them attempting to mount the female from the rear. This, too, is repulsed by the female, as is a second attempt by the first male. The males chirp frequently throughout. A mating pair.

22. Heath grasshopper – 00:51:06
A female at rest, cleans its antennae. A male feeds on gorse. Three episodes of male stridulation. This is quiet, and obscured by traffic noise (increasing the play-back volume might help). The first sequence illustrates the incidence of pauses in some performances of the song (Ragge & Reynolds 1998, 395).

23. Meadow grasshopper – 00:52:43
A female feeds from a grass blade. A female completes egg-laying. A male exchanges short bursts of song with a 'rival' male. The song consists of a single echeme lasting 1 to 2 seconds, beginning quietly and gaining intensity, and repeated at variable intervals. A complex sequence in which male 'A' (lower left) is approached by an 'intruder ('B'). B approaches and makes antennal contact with A, who then issues a series of signals which involve raising the head and stretching the fore legs, while drawing one antenna through a front tarsus. B backs slightly, stridulates, turns round and withdraws, while A continues to repeat the head-raising signal. As he leaves, B stridulates briefly, and so does A. B leaves, and A delivers two further stridulations, turns and repeats the 'head-raising' signal several times. A male approaches a female, antennae pointing forwards, and produces several brief stridulations. Eventually, he makes a lunge at the female, who moves off.

24. Lesser marsh grasshopper – 00:55:32
Typical escape behaviour – note the ability to run backwards. A male basks and preens, turning periodically to expose each side to the sun. A male feeds on plant material – note the use of the fore legs. Two examples of the male calling song; a brief echeme repeated from 2 to 6 times in a sequence. A searching

male locates a female, spreads his antennae wide, and begins the low-intensity courtship sequence. Three clips of phases in courtship – note the male vibrates his hind legs, alternating between femora held high and low, and later rocking his body. Finally, a female turns and repulses a male's brief attempt to mount. Two males are lined up behind a female, when a third male approaches and tries to mount the female. She kicks him away, while the other males respond to the approach of the rejected male with brief 'leg-flick' signals. A male makes repeated attempts to mount a female, who responds with sharp kicks. A male performs a courtship sequence in the absence of a female.

25. Rufous grasshopper – 00:59:29

A male feeds on a fine grass blade. A female of the purple form. Four examples of the brief, quiet male calling song. The short bursts lasting 3–10 seconds are easily masked by other ambient sounds (raising the play-back volume might help). A male produces his amazingly complex 'song and dance' courtship routine (for descriptions, see Ragge & Reynolds 1998: 374, or Chapter 8 in this volume). A mating pair. Two males compete for the same female. A courtship sequence, with the subdued sounds amplified using a bat detector.

26. Mottled grasshopper – 01:03:15

Three examples of the male calling song. Each burst might last up to 15 seconds, produced by alternating movements of the hind femora, beginning very quietly and increasing in volume towards the end (even then the sound is not loud, and high volume may be needed in play-back). An unusual male song, consisting of repeated short bursts produced by rapid movements of the hind femora. Apparently antagonistic interactions between two males, who exchange double hind 'leg-flick' signals. A courting male is approached by a rival, and the two exchange rapidly repeated leg-flick signals, while the female departs. Extracts from an extremely long courtship sequence, in which the male performs a complex 'song and dance' routine many times, and the female plays a 'cat and mouse' game, occasionally producing a brief stridulation before moving off a short distance. A male courts a female who departs part way through. The male continues to the end of the performance and then lunges at the empty space formerly occupied by the female. A male courts another male. The male was in fact dead and in the grip of a spider. It might be that males rely on the 'leg-flick' response from other males to distinguish the sexes.

References

Acosta, C. (2007). *No Way Home: A Cuban Dancer's Tale.* London: HarperCollins.

Ahnesjö, J. & Forsman, A. (2006). Differential habitat selection by pygmy grasshopper color morphs; interactive effects of temperature and predator avoidance. *Evolutionary Ecology* 20: 235–57.

Alexander, R. D & Otte, D. (1967). The evolution of genitalia and mating behavior in crickets (Gryllidae) and other Orthoptera. *University of Michigan Museum of Zoology Miscellaneous Publications* 121: 1–59.

Alexander, R. D. (1960). Sound communication in Orthoptera and Cicadidae. In W. E. Lanyon & W. N. Tavolga (Eds.) *Animal Sounds and Communication.* American Institute of Biological Science 7: 38–92.

Alexander, R. D. (1975). Natural selection and specialized chorusing behavior in acoustical insects. In D. Pimentel (Ed.) *Insects, Science and Society.* New York: Academic Press: 35–77.

Alexander, R. D., Marshall, D. C. & Cooley, J. R. (1997). Evolutionary perspectives on insect mating. In Choe & Crespi (Eds.) *op. cit.:* 4–31.

Allen, G. R. (2000). Call structure variability and field survival among bushcrickets exposed to phonotactic parasitoids. *Ethology* 106: 409–23.

Andersson, M. B. (1994). *Sexual Selection.* Princeton: Princeton University.

Andersson, M. B. & Iwasa, Y. (1996). Sexual Selection. *TREE:* 11(2): 53–8.

Arnqvist, G. & Rowe, L. (2005). *Sexual Conflict.* Princeton & Oxford: Princeton University.

Asher, J., Warren, M., Fox, R., Harding, P., Jeffcoate, G. and Jeffcoate, S. (2001). *The Millennium Atlas of Butterflies in Britain and Ireland.* Oxford: Oxford University.

Baccetti, B. M. (Ed.) (1987). *Evolutionary Biology of Orthopteroid Insects.* Chichester & New York: Ellis Horwood/John Wiley.

Bailey, N. W. (2008). Love will tear you apart: different components of female choice exert contrasting selection pressures on male field crickets. *Behavioral Ecology* 19(5): 960–6.

Bailey, N. W. & Zuk, M. (2008). Acoustic experience shapes female mate choice in field crickets. *Proceedings of the Royal Society* B 275: 2645–50.

Bailey, W. J. (1990). The ear of the bushcricket. In Bailey & Rentz (Eds.) *op. cit.:* 217–47.

Bailey, W. J. (1998). Do large bushcrickets have more sensitive ears? Natural variation in hearing thresholds within populations of the bushcricket *Requena verticalis* (Listroscelidinae: Tettigoniidae). *Physiological Entomology* 23: 105–12.

Bailey, W. J. (2006). Insect songs – the evolution of signal complexity. In Drosopoulos & Claridge (Eds.) *op. cit.*: 127–36.

Bailey, W. J. & Rentz, D. C. F. (Eds.) (1990). *The Tettigoniidae: Biology, Systematics and Evolution.* Berlin, etc.: Springer-Verlag.

Bailey, W. J. & Stephen, R. O. (1984). Auditory acuity in the orientation behaviour of the bushcricket *Pachysagella australis* Walker (Orthoptera, Tettigoniidae, Saginae). *Animal Behaviour* 32: 816–29

Bailey, W. J. & Thiele, D. R. (1983). Male spacing behaviour in the Tettigoniidae: an experimental approach. In Gwynne & Morris (Eds.) *op. cit.*: 163–84.

Bailey, W. J., Cunningham, R. J. & Lebel, L. (1990). Song power, spectral distribution and female phonotaxis in the bushcricket *Requena verticalis* (Orthoptera: Tettigoniidae): active choice or passive attraction. *Animal Behaviour* 40: 33–42.

Balakrishnan, R. & Pollack, G. S. (1997). The role of antennal sensory cues in female responses to courting males in the cricket *Teleogryllus oceanicus. Journal of Experimental Biology* 200: 511–22.

Baldock, D. W. (1999). *Grasshoppers and Crickets of Surrey.* Woking: Surrey Wildlife Trust.

Baldock, D. W. (2010). *Wasps of Surrey.* Woking: Surrey Wildlife Trust.

Barrientos, L. L. & Montes, M. T. (1997). Geographic distribution and singing activity of *Pterophylla beltrani* and *P. robertsi* (Orthoptera: Tettigoniidae), under field conditions. *Journal of Orthoptera Research* 6: 49–56.

Bateman, P. W. (1998). Mate preference for novel partners in the cricket *Gryllus bimaculatus. Ecological Entomology* 23: 473–5.

Bateman, P. W. (2001). Changes in phonotactic behaviour of a bushcricket with mating history. *Journal of Insect Behavior* 14: 333–43.

Bateman, P. W., Ferreira, M. & Ferguson J. W. H. (2001). Male size and sequential mate preference in the cricket *Gryllus bimaculatus. Animal Behaviour* 61: 631–7.

Battiston, R., Picciau, L., Fontana, P. and Marshall, J. (2010). *Mantids of the Euro-Mediterranean Area. WBA Handbooks* 2. Verona: World biodiversity Association.

Bellmann, H. (1985). *A Field Guide to the Grasshoppers and Crickets of Britain and Northern Europe.* London: Collins.

Bellmann, H. & Luquet, G. (2009). *Guide des Sauterelles, Grillons et Criquets d'Europe Occidentale.* Paris: Delachaux & Niestlé.

Belovsky, G. E. & Slade, J. B. (1993). The role of vertebrate and invertebrate predators in a grasshopper community. *Oikos* 68: 193–201.

Belovsky, G. E., Slade, J. B. & Chase, J. M. (1996). Mating strategies based on foraging ability: an experiment with grasshoppers. *Behavioral Ecology* 7: 438–444.

Belwood, J. J. (1990). Anti-predator defences and ecology of neotropical forest katydids, especially the Pseudophyllinae. In Bailey & Rentz (Eds.) *op. cit.*: 8–26.

Benediktov, A. A. (2005). Vibrational signals in the family Tetrigidae (Orthoptera). *Proceedings of the Russian Entomological Society* 76: 131–40.

Bennet-Clark, H. C. (1975). The energetics of the jump of the locust *Schistocerca gregaria. Journal of Experimental Biology* 63: 53–83.

Bennet-Clark, H. C. (1976). Energy storage in jumping insects. In H. R. Hepburn (Ed.) *The Insect Integument.* Amsterdam: Elsevier.

Bennet-Clark, H. C. (1990). Jumping in Orthoptera. In Chapman & Joern (Eds.)

Biology of Grasshoppers. New York, etc.: John Wiley & Sons.

Benton, T. (2000). *Bumblebees of Essex.* Wimbish: Lopinga.

Benton, T. (2006). *Bumblebess* (New Naturalist 98). London: HarperCollins.

Benton, T. (2010). Race, sex and the 'earthly paradise': Wallace versus Darwin on human evolution and prospects. In R. Carter & N. Charles (eds) *Nature, Society and Environmental Crisis. The Sociological Review* (Special Issue: Sociological Review Monograph Series) 57: 23–46

Benton, T. & Dobson, J. (2006). The shrill carder-bee on the move? *Essex Field Club Newsletter* 49: 12–14.

Benton, T. & Dobson, J. (2007). Bumblebee report for 2006–7. *Essex Naturalist (New Series)* 24: 66–9.

Bentsen, C. L., Hunt, J., Jennions, M. D. & Brooks, R. (2006). Complex multivariate selection on male acoustic signalling in a wild population of *Teleogryllus commodus. The American Naturalist* 167(4): 102–16.

Berger, D. (2008). *The Evolution of Complex Courtship Songs in the Genus* Stenobothrus *Fischer 1853 (Orthoptera, Caelifera, Gomphocerinae).* Ph.D thesis, University of Erlangen-Nuernberg, Germany.

Blackith, R. E. (1987). Primitive Orthoptera and primitive plants. In Baccetti (Ed.) *op. cit.:* Ch 3: 124–6.

Blair, K. G. (1936). *Conocephalus fuscus* Fab., a grasshopper new to Britain. *Entomologist's Monthly Magazine* 72: 273–4.

Blair, K. G. (1948). The egg of *Conocephalus dorsalis* Latr. (Orthoptera: Tettigoniidae) and its parasites. *Entomologist's Monthly Magazine* 84: 276–7.

Bland, R. G. & Rentz, D. C. F. (1991). External morphology and abundance of mouthpart sensilla in Australian Gryllacridiae, Stemopelmatidae, and Tettigoniidae. *Journal of Morphology* 207: 315–25.

Blaney, W. M. & Duckett, A. M. (1975). The significance of palpation by the maxillary palps of *Locusta migratoria* (L.): an electrophysiological and behavioural study. *Journal of Experimental Biology* 63: 701–12.

Blaney, W. M. & Simmonds, M. S. J. (1990). The chemoreceptors. In Chapman & Joern (Eds.) *op. cit.:* 1–38.

Boake, C. R. B. (1983). Mating systems and signals in crickets. In Gwynne & Morris (Eds.) *op. cit.:* 28–44.

Bowen, B. J., Codd, C. G. & Gwynne, D. T. (1984). The katydid spermatophore (Orthoptera: Tettigoniidae): male investment and its fate in the matcd female. *Australian Journal of Zoology* 32: 23–31.

Brickle, N. W., Harper, D. G. C., Aebischer, N. J. and Cockayne, S. H. (2000). Effects of agricultural intensification on the breeding success of corn buntings *Miliaria calandra*). *Journal of Applied Ecology* 37: 742–55.

Brooks, R., Hunt, J., Blows, M. W., Smith, M. J., Bussière, L. F. & Jennions, M. D. (2005). Experimental evidence for multivariate stabilizing sexual selection. *Evolution* 59: 871–80.

Brouwers, N. C. & Newton, A. C. (2009a). Habitat requirements for the conservation of wood cricket (*Nemobius sylvestris*) on the Isle of Wight, UK. *Journal of Insect Conservation* 13(5): 529–41.

Brouwers, N. C. & Newton, A. C. (2009b). The influence of barriers and orientation capacity on the dispersal ability of wood cricket (*Nemobius sylvestris*, Orthoptera: Gryllidae) *Journal of Insect Conservation* 14(3): 313–17.

Brouwers, N. C., Newton, A. C. and Bailey, S. (2011). Dispersal ability of wood cricket (*Nemobius sylvestris*, Orthoptera: Gryllidae) in a wooded landscape. *European Journal of Entomology* 108(1): 117–25.

Brown, E. S. (1950). Notes on the taxonomy, British distribution and ecology of *Tetrix subulata* (L.) and *T. ceperoi* I. Bolivar (Orthoptera, Tetrigidae). *Journal of the Society for British Entomology* 3(4) 189–200.

Brown, V. K. (1983). *Grasshoppers* (Naturalists' Handbooks 2). Cambridge: Cambridge University.

Brown, W. D. (1999). Mate choice in tree crickets and their kin. *Annual Review of Entomology* 44: 371–96.

Brown, W. D. & Gwynne, D. T. (1997). Evolution of mating in crickets, katydids and wetas (Ensifera). In Gangwere *et al., op. cit.*: 281–314.

Brown, W. D., Wideman, J., Andrade, M. C. B., Mason, A. C. & Gwynne, D. T. (1996). Female choice for an indicator of male size in the song of the black-horned tree cricket *Oecanthus nigricornis* (Orthoptera: Gryllidae: Oecanthinae). *Evolution* 50: 2400–11.

Bukhvalova, M. (2006). Partitioning of acoustic transmission channels in grasshopper communities. In Drosopoulos & Claridge (Eds.) *op. cit.*: 199–206.

Bull, C. M. (1979). The function of complexity in the courtship of the grasshopper *Myrmeleotettix maculatus*. *Behaviour* 69: 201–16.

Burk, T. (1983). Male aggression and female choice in a field cricket (*Teleogryllus oceanicus*): the importance of courtship song. In Gwynne & Morris (Eds.) *op. cit.*: 97–119.

Burr, M. (1936). *British Grasshoppers and their Allies: A Stimulus to their Study.* London: Philip Allan & Co.

Burton, J. F. (1963). Notes on the Orthoptera of the Isle of Man with special reference to *Stenobothrus stigmaticus* (Rambur) (Acrididae). *Entomologist's Monthly Magazine* 100: 193–7.

Burton, J. F. (2010). Altitudinal limits of the common green grasshopper *Omocestus*

viridulus (L.) (Orthoptera: Acrididae) in Britain. *Bulletin of the Amateur Entomologist's Society* 69: 137–8.

Bussière, L. F., Basit, H. A. & Gwynne, D. T. (2005a). Preferred males are not always good providers: female choice and male investment in tree crickets. *Behavioral Ecology* 16(1): 223–31.

Bussière, L. F., Clark, A. P. & Gwynne, D. T. (2005b). Precopulatory choice of material benefits in tree crickets. *Behavioral Ecology* 16(1): 255–9.

Butlin, R. K & Ritchie, M. G. (1991). variation in female mate preference across a grasshopper hybrid zone. *Journal of Evolutionary Biology* 4: 227–40.

Butlin, R. K., Woodhatch, C. W. & Hewitt, G. M. (1987). Male spermatophore investment increases female fecundity in a grasshopper. *Evolution* 41: 221–5.

Cade, W. (1975). Acoustically orienting parasitoids: fly phonotaxis to cricket song. *Science* 190: 1312–13.

Caesar, S. & Forsman, A. (2009). Do polyandrous pygmy grasshopper females obtain fitness benefits for their offspring? *Behavioral Ecology* 20: 354–61.

Caesar, S., Ahnesjö, J. & Forsman, A. (2007). Testing the role of coadapted genes versus bet-hedging for mating strategies of colour polymorphic pygmy grasshoppers. *Biological Journal of the Linnean Society*: 491–9.

Chamorro-R, J., Montealegre-Z, F. & Gonzalez-O, R. (2007). Determinants of male spacing behaviour in *Panacanthus pallicornis* (Orthoptera: Tettigoniidae). *Ethology* 113: 1158–72.

Champagnon, J. & del Castillo, R. C. (2008). Female mate choice, calling song and genetic variance in the cricket *Gryllodes sigillatus*. *Ethology* 114: 223–30.

Chapman, R. F. (1982). Insect chemoreceptors. *Advances in Insect Physiology* 16: 247–356.

Chapman, R. F. (1990). Food selection. In Chapman & Joern *op. cit.*: 39–72.

Chapman, R. F. & Joern, A. (Eds.) (1990). *Biology of Grasshoppers*. New York, etc.: John Wiley & Sons.

Chapman, R. F. & Sword, G. A. (1993). The importance of palpation in food selection by a polyphagous grasshopper (Orthoptera: Acrididae). *Journal of Insect Behavior* 6(1): 79–91.

Chapman, R. F. & Sword, G. A. (1994). The relationship between plant acceptability and suitability for survival and development of the polyphagous grasshopper, *Schistocerca americana* (Orthoptera: Acridiae). *Journal of Insect Behavior* 7(4): 411–31.

Chapman, R. F. & Thomas, J. G. (1978). The numbers and distribution of sensilla on the mouthparts of Acridoidea. *Acrida* 7: 115–48.

Chapman, R. F. & Whitham, F. (1968). The external morphogenesis of grasshopper embryos. *Proceedings of the Royal Entomological Society of London* A 43: 161–9.

Chapman, R. F., Page, W. W. & McCaffery, A. R. (1986). Bionomics of the variegated grasshopper (*Zonocerus variegatus*) in west and central Africa. *Annual Review of Entomology* 31: 479–505.

Chappell, M. A. & Whitman, D. W. (1990). Grasshopper thermoregulation. In Chapman & Joern *op. cit.*: 143–72

Cherrill, A. J. (1987). *The Development and Survival of the Eggs and Early Instars of the Grasshopper* Chorthippus brunneus *(Thun.) in North West England*. Ph.D. thesis: University of Liverpool.

Cherrill, A. J. (1993). The conservation of Britain's wart-biter bush-crickets. *British Wildlife* 5: 26–32.

Cherrill, A. J. (1994). The current status of the lesser mottled grasshopper *Stenobothrus stigmaticus* (Rambur) on the Isle of Man. *British Journal of Entomology and Natural History* 7: 53–7.

Cherrill, A. J. (1997). Sublethal injuries in a field population of the bush cricket *Decticus verrucivorus* (L.) in southern England. *Journal of Orthoptera Research* 6: 77–82.

Cherrill, A. (2002). Relationship between oviposition date, hatch date, and offspring size in the grasshopper *Chorthippus brunneus*. *Ecological Entomology* 27: 521–8.

Cherrill, A. (2004). Notation of the developmental stages of British grasshopper species (Orthoptera: Acrididae) with variable numbers of instars. *Entomologist's Gazette* 55: 181–3.

Cherrill, A. (2005). Body size and phenology of the grasshopper species *Chorthippus brunneus* with variable numbers of female instars (Orthoptera: Acrididae). *Entomologia Generalis* 28(3): 219–31.

Cherrill, A. J. (2010). Species richness of Orthoptera along gradients of agricultural intensification and urbanisation. *Journal of Orthoptera Research* 19(2): 293–301.

Cherrill, A. J. & Begon, M. (1989a). Timing of life-cycles in a seasonal environment: the temperature dependence of embryogenesis and diapause in a grasshopper (*Chorthippus brunneus*). *Oecologia* 78: 237–41.

Cherrill, A. J. & Begon, M. (1989b). Predation on grasshoppers by spiders in sand dune grasslands. *Entomologia Experimentalis et Applicata* 50: 225–31.

Cherrill, A. & Begon, M. (1991). Oviposition date and pattern of embryogenesis in the grasshopper *Chorthippus brunneus* (Orthoptera, Acrididae). *Holarctic Ecology* 14: 225–33.

Cherrill, A. J. & Brown, V. K. (1990a). The life-cycle and distribution of the wart-biter *Decticus verrucivorus* (L.) (Orthoptera: Tettigoniidae) in a chalk grassland in southern England. *Biological Conservation* 53: 125–43.

Cherrill, A. J. & Brown, V. K. (1990b). The habitat requirements of adults of the wart-biter *Decticus verrucivorus* (L.) (Orthoptera: Tettigoniidae) in southern England. *Biological Conservation* 53: 145–57.

Cherrill, A. J. & Brown, V. K. (1991a). Variation in colouration of *Decticus verrucivorus* (L.) (Orthoptera: Tettigoniidae) in southern England. *Entomologist's Gazette* 42: 175–83.

Cherrill, A. J. & Brown, V. K. (1991b). The effects of the summer of 1989 on the phenology of the wart-biter *Decticus verrucivorus* in Britain. *British Journal of Entomology and Natural History* 4: 163–8.

Cherrill, A. J. & Brown, V. K. (1992a). Ontogenetic changes in the micro-habitat preferences of *Decticus verrucivorus* (Orthoptera: Tettigoniidae) at the edge of its range. *Ecography* 15: 37–44.

Cherrill, A. J. & Brown, V. K. (1992b). Variation in body size between heathland and chalk grassland populations of the bush-cricket *Decticus verrucivorus* (L.) (Orthoptera: Tettigoniidae) in southern England. *Entomologist's Gazette* 43: 77–82.

Cherrill, A. & Haswell, M. (2006). Identifying the stage and developmental history of grasshoppers (Orthoptera: Acrididae) in a species with a variable number of instars. *Entomologist's Gazette* 57: 109–14.

Cherrill, A. J. & Selman, R. (2007). The lesser mottled grasshopper *Stenobothrus stigmaticus* on the Isle of Man: a review of the species' biology and habitat requirements. Unpublished report.

Cherrill, A. J., Shaughnessy, J. & Brown, V. K. (1991). Oviposition behaviour of the bush-cricket *Decticus verrucivorus* (L.) (Orthoptera: Tettigoniidae). *The Entomologist* 110(1): 37–42.

Choe, J. C & Crespi, B. J. (Eds.) (1997). *Mating Systems in Insects and Arachnids.* Cambridge: Cambridge University.

Clark, E. J. (1943). Colour variation in British Acrididae (orthopt.). *Entomologist's Monthly Magazine* 79: 91–104.

Clark, E. J. (1948). Studies in the ecology of British grasshoppers. *Transactions of the Royal Entomological Society of London* 99: 173–222.

Collins, G. A., Hodge, P. J., Edwards, M. and Phillips, A. (2007). Sickle-bearing bush-cricket, *Phaneroptera falcata* (Poda) (Orthoptera: Tettigoniidae), breeding in south-east England. *British Journal of Entomology and Natural History* 20: 133–7.

Collins, G. B. (2001). The nymphal stages of the field grasshopper, *Chorthippus brunneus* (Thunberg) (Orthoptera: Acrididae). *British Journal of Entomology and Natural History* 13: 203–13.

Collins, G. B. (2003). The nymphal development of the Large Marsh Grasshopper, *Stethophyma grossum* (Linnaeus, 1758). *Entomologist's Gazette* 54: 269–73.

Collins, G. B. (2006). Changes in antennal segmentation during the nymphal development of British grasshoppers (Orthoptera: Acrididea). *British Journal of Entomology and Natural History* 19: 209–16.

Cooper, N. S. (2001). *Wildlife in Church and Churchyard: Plants, Animals and their Management* (2nd edn.). London: Church House.

Crankshaw, O. S. (1979). Female choice in relation to calling and courtship songs in *Acheta domesticus*. *Animal Behaviour* 27: 1274–5.

Cronin, H. (1991). *The Ant and the Peacock.* Cambridge: Cambridge University.

Cunningham, A., Frank, J., Croft, P., Clarke, D. & Pearce-Kelly, P. (1997). Mortality of captive wartbiter crickets: implications for reintroduction programmes. *Journal of Wildlife Diseases* 33(3): 673–6.

Currie, P. W. E. (1953). The 'drumming' of *Meconema thalassinum* Fabre. *Entomologist's Record and Journal of Variation* 65: 93–4.

Dale, J. F. & Tobe, S. S. (1990). The endocrine basis of locust phase polymorphism. In Chapman & Joern (Eds.) *op. cit.*: 393–414.

Darwin, C. (1871). *The Descent of Man and Selection in Relation to Sex.* London: John Murray. (Page references are to the second (1874) edition.)

Darwin, C. (1968 [1859]). *On the Origin of Species by Means of Natural Selection.* Harmondsworth: Penguin.

De Souza Santos Jr., P. & Begon, M. (1987). Survival costs of reproduction in grasshoppers. *Functional Ecology* 1(3): 215–21.

Dearn, J. M. (1990). Colour pattern polymorphism. In Chapman & Joern (Eds.) *op. cit.*: 517– 49.

DEFA, Isle of Man (1990). *Wildlife Act.* Isle of Man Government.

Dempster, J. P. (1963). The population dynamics of grasshoppers and locusts. *Biological Reviews of the Cambridge Philosophical Society* 38: 490–529.

Denton, J. (2006). *Assessment of Potential Effects of Different grazing Regimes in Wootton Coppice and Holmsley Inclosures.* Unpublished report (cited in Gardiner & Haines 2008).

Deura, K. & Hartley, J. C. (1982). Initial diapause and embryonic development in the speckled bush-cricket, *Leptophyes punctatissima. Physiological Entomology* 7: 253–62.

Dickens, C. (2004 [1845]). The Cricket on the Hearth. In *A Christmas Carol and Two other Christmas Books.* London: CRW.

Dodson, G. N., Morris, G. K. & Gwynne, D. T. (1983). Mating behaviour of the primitive orthopteran genus *Cyphoderris* (Haglidae). In Gwynne & Morris (Eds.) *op. cit.*: 305–18.

Doherty, J. A & Howard, D. J. (1996). Lack of preference for conspecific calling songs in female crickets. *Animal Behaviour* 51: 981–90.

Drosopoulos, S. & Claridge, M. F. (Eds.) (2006). *Insect Sounds and Communication: Physiology, Behaviour and Ecology.* Boca Raton, London, New York: Taylor & Francis.

Eberhard, W. G. (1991). Copulatory courtship and cryptic female choice in insects. *Biological Reviews* 66: 1–31.

Eberhard, W. G. (1997). Sexual selection by cryptic female choice in insects and arachnids. In Choe & Crespi (Eds.) *op. cit.*: 32–57.

Edmondson, R. (2011). Southern oak bush-cricket (*Meconema meridionale* Costa 1860). Orthoptera: Tettigoniidae. *The Bulletin of the Amateur Entomologists' Society.* 70 (494): 15.

Edwards, M. (2008). *English Nature Species Recovery Programme, Field Cricket,* Gryllus campestris, *Project Report for 2008.* Peterborough: Natural England.

Edwards, M., Patmore, J. M. & Sheppard, D. (1996). The field cricket – preventing extinction. *British Wildlife* 8(2): 87–91.

Edwards, R. (Ed.) (1998). *Provisional Atlas of the aculeate Hymenoptera of Britain and Ireland. Part 2.* Huntingdon: Centre for Ecology and Hydrology (NERC).

Eggert, A.-K. & Sakaluk, S. K. (1994). Sexual cannibalism and its relation to male mating success in sagebrush crickets, *Cyphoderris strepitans* (Haglidae: Orthoptera). *Animal Behaviour* 47: 1171–7.

Emlen, S. T. & Oring, L. W. (1977). Ecology, sexual selection and the evolution of mating systems. *Science* 197: 215–23.

Evans, M. & Edmondson, R. A. (2007). *Photographic Guide to Grasshoppers and Crickets of Britain and Ireland.* Wildguides UK.

Fabre, J. H. (1917). *The Life of the Grasshopper* (tr. de Mattos). London, New York & Toronto: Hodder & Stoughton.

Fairbairn, D. J. & Yadlowski, D. E. (1997). Coevolution of traits determining migratory tendency: correlated response of a critical enzyme, juvenile hormone esterase, to selection on wing morphology. *Journal of Evolutionary Biology* 10: 495–513.

Farrow, R. A. (1990). Flight and migration in Acridoids. In Chapman & Joern (Eds.) *op. cit.*: 227–314.

Feaver, M. (1983). Pair formation in the katydid *Orchelimum nigripes* (Orthoptera: Tettigoniidae). In Gwynne & Morris (Eds.) *op. cit.*: 205–39.

Fedorka, K. M. & Mousseau, T. A. (2002). Tibial spur feeding in ground crickets: larger males contribute larger gifts (Orthoptera: Gryllidae). *Florida. Entomologist.* 85: 317–23.

Field, L. H. (1982). Stridulatory structures and acoustic spectra of seven species of New Zealand wetas (Orthoptera: Stenopelmatidae). *International Journal of Insect Morphology and Embryology* 11: 39–51.

Field, L. H. (Ed.) (2001). *The Biology of Wetas, King Crickets and their Allies.* Wallingford, UK & New York, USA: CABI.

Field, L. H & Bailey, W. J. (1997). Sound production in primitive Orthoptera from western Australia: sounds used in defence and social communication in *Ametrus* sp. and *Hadrogryllacris* sp. (Gryllacrididae: Orthoptera). *Journal of Natural History* 31(7): 1127–41.

Field, L. H. & Glasgow, S. (2001). Ch. 16: Defence behaviour. In L. H. Field (Ed.) *op. cit.*: 297–349.

Field, L. H. & Jarman, T. H. (2001). Ch 17: Mating behaviour. In L. H. Field (Ed.) *op. cit.*: 317–32.

Field, L. H. & Rind, F. C. (1992). Stridulatory behaviour in a New Zealand weta, *Hemideina crassidens. Journal of Zoology* 228: 371–94.

Field, L. H. & Sandlant, G. R. (1983). Aggression and mating behaviour in the Stenopelmatidae (Orthoptera, Ensifera), with reference to New Zealand Wetas. In Gwynne & Morris (Eds.) *op. cit.*: 120–46.

Field, L. H. & Sandlant, G. R. (2001). The gallery-related ecology of New Zealand tree wetas, *Hemideina femorata* and *Hemideina crassidens* (Orthoptera, Anostomatidae). In L. H. Field (Ed.) *op. cit.*: 243–58.

Fisher, R. A. (1915). The evolution of sexual preference. *Eugenics Review* 7: 184–92

Fisher, R. A. (1930a). *The Genetical Theory of Natural Selection.* Oxford: Clarendon.

Fisher, R. A. (1930b). The evolution of dominance in some polymorphic species. *American Naturalist* 64: 385–406.

Fisher, R. A. (1939). Selective forces in wild populations of *Paratettix texanus. Annals of Eugenics* 9: 109–22.

Forrest, T. G. (1983). Calling songs and mate choice in mole crickets. In Gwynne & Morris (Eds.) *op. cit.*: 185–204.

Forrest, T. G. (1987). Insect size tactics and developmental strategies. *Oecologia* 73: 187.

Forsman, A. (1997). Thermal capacity of different colour morphs in the pygmy grasshopper *Tetrix subulata. Ann-Zool Fennici* 34: 145–9.

Forsman, A. (1999a). Reproductive life history variation among colour morphs of the pygmy grasshopper *Tetrix subulata. Biological Journal of the Linnean Society* 67: 247–61.

Forsman, A. (1999b). Variation in thermal sensitivity of performance among colour morphs of a pygmy grasshopper. *Journal of Evolutionary Biology* 12: 869–78.

Forsman, A., Ringblom, K., Civantos, E. & Ahnesjö, J. (2002). Coevolution of colour pattern and thermoregulatory behaviour in polymorphic pygmy grasshoppers, *Tetrix undulata. Evolution* 56: 349–60.

Forster, J. R. (1770). *A Catalogue of British Insects.* Warrington: Eyres.

Frankino, W. A. & Sakaluk, S. K. (1994). Post-copulatory mate guarding delays promiscuous mating by female decorated crickets. *Animal Behaviour* 48: 1479–81.

Frazer, W. R. (1944). First authentic record of *Chorthippus vagans* Ev. (Orthopt., Acrididae) in Britain. *Journal of the Society of British Entomologists* 2(6): 224.

Friedel, T. & Gillott, C. (1976). Male accessory gland substance of *Melanoplus sanguinipes*: an oviposition stimulant under the control of the *corpus allatum*. *Journal of Insect Physiology* 22: 489–95.

Friedel, T. & Gillott, C. (1977). Contribution of male-produced proteins to vitellogenesis in *Melanopus sanguinipes*. *Journal of Insect Physiology* 23: 145–51.

Fuzeau-Braesch, S., Genin, E., Jullien, R., Knowles, E. & Papin, C. (1988). Composition and role of volatile substances in atmosphere surrounding two gregarious locusts, *Locusta migratoria* and *Schistocercus gregaria*. *Journal of Chemical Ecology* 14: 1023–32.

Galliart, P. L. & Shaw, K. C. (1996). The effect of variation in parameters of the male calling song of the katydid, *Amblycorypha parvipennis* (Orthoptera: Tettigoniidae), on female phonotaxis and phonoresponse. *Journal of Insect Behavior* 9: 841–55.

Gangwere, S. K., Muralirangan, M. C. & Muralirangan, M. (Eds.) (1997). *The Bionomics of Grasshoppers, Katydids and their Kin.* Wallingford, UK & New York, USA.: CAB International.

Gardiner, T. (2005). Orthoptera and allied insects of Essex 2004. *Essex Naturalist* 22: 60–64.

Gardiner, T. (2006a). Orthoptera and allied insects of Essex 2005. *Essex Naturalist* 23: 46–8.

Gardiner, T. (2006b). Insect highways. *Waymark* 19: 7–8.

Gardiner, T. (2007a). Orthoptera and allied insects of Essex 2006. *Essex Naturalist* 24: 71–6.

Gardiner, T. (2007b). Orthoptera of crossfield and headland footpaths in arable farmland. *Journal of Orthoptera Research* 16(2): 127–33.

Gardiner, T. (2009a). Hopping Back to Happiness. Saarbrücken: VDM Verlag Dr. Müller.

Gardiner, T. (2009b). Macropterism of Roesel's bushcricket *Metrioptera roeselii* in relation to climate change and landscape structure in eastern England. *Journal of Orthoptera Research* 18(1): 95–102.

Gardiner, T. (2009c). Distribution of the scaly cricket *Pseudomogoplistes vicentae* Gorochov (Orth: Gryllidae) in relation to public access at Chesil Beach in Dorset. *Entomologist's Record and Journal of Variation* 121: 292–5.

Gardiner, T. (2009d). Victoria County History update: the state of grasshoppers and crickets (Orthoptera) in Essex at the beginning of the 21st century. *Essex Naturalist* 26: 39–47.

Gardiner, T. (2009e). Observations of swimming grasshoppers in an acid pool in Epping Forest. *Journal of Orthoptera Research* 18(2): 237–9.

Gardiner, T. (2010a). Hedgerow species richness influences the presence of Orthoptera and Dermaptera along green lanes in Essex, UK. *Entomologist's Gazette* 61: 53–64.

Gardiner, T. (2010b). Precipitation and habitat degradation influence the occurrence of the common green grasshopper *Omocestus viridulus* in southeastern England. *Journal of Orthoptera Research* 19(2): 315–26.

Gardiner, T. (2010c). Essex Orthoptera update for 2009 including an assessment of heathland restoration at Tiptree Heath and Norton Heath Common. *Essex Naturalist* 27: 77–82.

Gardiner, T. (2010d). Insects of Waveney Forest (Fritton Warren) in east Norfolk. *Entomologist's Record and Journal of Variation* 122: 155–62.

Gardiner, T. (2010e). Successful translocation of the locally rare mottled grasshopper *Myrmeleotettix maculatus* to Jaywick flood defences in Essex, England. *Conservation Evidence* 7: 106–10.

Gardiner, T. (2011a). Altitudinal limits of grasshoppers in the Cotswolds and Malvern Hills in relation to livestock grazing of hilltops. *The Bulletin of the Amateur Entomologists' Society*. 70(no. 495): 77–81.

Gardiner, T. (2011b). How does mowing of grassland on sea wall flood defences affect insect assemblages in eastern England? In W.-J. Zheng (Ed.) *Grassland: Types, Biodiversity and Impacts.* Nova Science.

Gardiner, T. (2011c). Essex Orthoptera update for 2010 including new records of the Stripe-winged Grasshopper from Epping Forest and the great Mole Cricket escape. *Essex Naturalist* 28 (New Series): 37–42.

Gardiner, T. (in press). Waveney Forest rises like a phoenix from the ashes.

Gardiner, T. & Benton, T. (2009). Grasshoppers and bush-crickets (Orthoptera) of military training grounds near Colchester. *Entomologist's Record and Journal of Variation.* 121: 167–71.

Gardiner, T. & Dover, J. (2008). Is microclimate important for Orthoptera in open landscapes? *Journal of Insect Conservation* 12: 705–9.

Gardiner, T. & Gardiner, M. (2009). Scrub encroachment leads to the disappearance of the common green

grasshopper *Omocestus viridulus* (Orth: Acrididae) from heathland at Mill Green Common in Writtle Forest. *Entomologist's Record and Journal of Variation* 121: 63–7.

Gardiner, T. & Haines, K. (2008). Intensive grazing by horses detrimentally affects orthopteran assemblages in floodplain grassland along the Mardyke River Valley, Essex, England. *Conservation Evidence* 5: 38–44.

Gardiner, T. & Harvey, P. (2004). Red Data List for Essex Orthoptera and Allied Insects. *Bulletin of the Amateur Entomologist's Society* 63: 19–25.

Gardiner, T. & Hassall, M. (2009). Does microclimate affect grasshopper populations after cutting of hay in improved grassland? *Journal of Insect Conservation* 13: 97–102.

Gardiner, T. & Hill, J. (2004a). Directional dispersal patterns of *Chorthippus parallelus* (Orthoptera: Acrididae) in patches of grazed pastures. *Journal of Orthoptera Research* 13(1): 135–41.

Gardiner, T. & Hill, J. (2004b). Feeding preferences of *Chorthippus parallelus* (Orthoptera: Acrididae). *Journal of Orthoptera Research* 13(2): 197–203.

Gardiner, T. & Hill, J. (2005a). A study of grasshopper populations in Countryside Stewardship Scheme field margins in Essex. *British Journal of Entomology and Natural History* 18: 73–80.

Gardiner, T. & Hill, J. (2005b). Behavioural observations of *Chorthippus parallelus* (Orthoptera: Acrididae) adults in managed grassland. *British Journal of Entomology and Natural History* 18: 1–8.

Gardiner, T. & Hill, J. (2006). Mortality of Orthoptera caused by mechanised mowing of grassland. *British Journal of Entomology and Natural History* 19: 35–40.

Gardiner, T. & Ringwood, Z. (2010). Species richness of orthopteroid insects and incidence of a rare moth on an island nature reserve threatened by sea level rise in the Walton backwaters in eastern England. *Entomologist's Gazette* 61: 251–61.

Gardiner, T., Benton, T. & Harvey, P. (2009). Southern oak bush-cricket *Meconema meridionale* (Costa) new to Essex. *Essex Naturalist* 26: 62–3.

Gardiner, T., Gardiner, M. and Cooper, N. (2011). Grasshopper strips prove effective in enhancing grasshopper abundance in Rivenhall Churchyard, Essex, England. *Conservation Evidence* 8: 31–7.

Gardiner, T., Hill, J. & Chesmore, D. (2005). Review of the methods frequently used to estimate the abundance of Orthoptera in grassland ecosystems. *Journal of Insect Conservation* 9: 151–73.

Gardiner, T., Hill, J. & Marshall, E. J. P. (2008). Grass field margins and Orthoptera in eastern England. *Entomologist's Gazette* 59: 251–7.

Gardiner, T., Pye, M., Field, R. & Hill, J. (2002). The influence of sward height and vegetation composition in determining the habitat preferences of three *Chorthippus* species (Orthoptera: Acrididae) in Chelmsford, Essex, UK. *Journal of Orthoptera Research* 11(2): 207–13.

Gardiner, T., Seago, B., Benton, T. & Dobson, J. (2010). The use of bat detectors reveals a widespread population of grey bush-cricket *Platycleis albopunctata* at Colne Point and St. Osyth naturists' beach. *Essex Naturalist* (New Series) 27: 209–13.

Gerhardt, H. C. & Huber, F. (2002). *Acoustic Communication in Insects and Anurans*. Chicago & London: University of Chicago.

Gershman, S. N. (2007). Female *Gryllus vocalis* field crickets gain diminishing returns from increasing numbers of matings. *Ethology* 113: 1099–1106.

Gershman, S. N. (2010). Large numbers of matings give female crickets a direct benefit but not a genetic benefit. *Journal of Insect Behavior* 23: 59–68.

Gill, P. D. (1981). The genetics of colour patterns in the grasshopper *Chorthippus brunneus*. *Biological Journal of the Linnean Society* 16: 243–59.

Gillis, J. E. (1982). Substrate colour-matching cues in the cryptic grasshopper *Circotettix rabula rabula* (Rehn & Hebard). *Animal Behaviour* 30: 113–16.

Goldsworthy, G. J. (1990). Hormonal control of flight mechanism in locusts. In Chapman & Joern (Eds.) *op. cit.*: 205–25.

Gorochov, A. V. (1996). A new species of *Pseudomogoplistes* for Morocco and Portugal (Orthoptera: Mogoplistidae). *Zoosystematica Rossica* 4(2): 292.

Gorochov, A. V. & Marshall, J. A. (2001). New data on *Pseudomogoplistes* from atlantic islands (Orthoptera: Mogoplistidae). *Zoosystematica Rossica* 9(1): 76.

Gorochov, A. V., Jarzembowski, E. A. & Coram, R. A. (2006). Grasshoppers and crickets (Insecta: Orthoptera) from the lower Cretaceous of southern England. *Cretaceous Research* 27: 641–62.

Grant, A., Hassall, M. & Willott, S. J. (1993). An alternative theory of grasshopper life cycles. *Oikos* 66: 263–8.

Gray, D. A. (1997). Female house crickets, *Acheta domesticus*, prefer the chirps of large males. *Animal Behaviour* 54: 1553–62.

Greenfield, M. D. (1990). Evolution of acoustic communication in the genus *Neoconocephalus*: discontinuous songs, synchrony, and interspecific interaction. In Bailey & Rentz, *op. cit.*: 71–97.

Greenfield, M. D. (1997). Acoustic communication in Orthoptera. In S. K Gangwere, M. C. Muralirangan & M. Muralirangan (Eds.) *The Bionomics of Grasshoppers, Katydids and their Kin*. New York & Wallingford, Oxford: CAB International: 197–230

Greenfield, M. D. (1997). Sexual selection in resource defense polygyny: lessons from territorial grasshoppers. In Choe & Crespi (Eds.) *op. cit.*: 75–88.

Greenfield, M. D. & Minckley, R. L. (1993). Acoustic duelling in tarbrush grasshoppers: settlement of territorial contests via alternation of reliable signals. *Ethology* 95: 309–26.

Greenfield, M. D. & Roizen, I. (1993). Katydid synchronous chorusing is an evolutionarily stable outcome of female choice. *Nature* 364: 618–20.

Greenfield, M. D. & Shaw K. C. (1983). Adaptive significance of chorusing with special reference to the orthopteran mating systems. In Gwynne & Morris (Eds.) *op. cit.*: 1–27.

Greenfield, M. D., Tourtellot, K. K. & Snedden, W. A. (1997). Precedence effects and the evolution of chorusing. *Proceedings of the Royal Society of London* B 264: 1355–61.

Gröning, J., Lücke, N., Finger, A. & Hochkirch, A. (2007). Reproductive interference in two ground-hopper species: testing hypotheses of coexistence in the field. *Oikos* 116: 1449–60.

Grove, D. G. (1959). *The Natural History of the Angular-winged Katydid* Microcentrum rhombifolium. Ph.D. dissertation, Cornel University (cited in Alexander 1975, *op. cit.*).

Gwynne, D. T. (1984a). Courtship feeding increases female reproductive success in bushcrickets. *Nature* 307: 361–3.

Gwynne, D. T. (1984b). sexual selection and sexual differences in Mormon crickets (Orthoptera: Tettigoniidae, *Anabrus simplex*). *Evolution* 38: 1011–22.

Gwynne, D. T. (1988a). Courtship feeding and the fitness of female katydids (Orthoptera: Tettigoniidae) *Evolution* 42: 545–55.

Gwynne, D. T. (1988b). Courtship feeding in katydids benefits the male's offspring. *Behavioral Ecology and Sociobiology*. 23: 373–7.

Gwynne, D. T. (1990). Testing parental investment and the control of sexual selection in katydids: the operational sex ratio. *American Naturalist* 136: 474–84.

Gwynne, D. T. (1993). Food quality controls sexual selection in Mormon crickets by altering male mating investment. *Ecology* 74: 1406–13.

Gwynne, D. T. (1995). Phylogeny of the Ensifera (Orthoptera): a hypothesis supporting multiple origins of acoustical signalling, complex spermatophores and maternal care in crickets, katydids and weta. *Journal of Orthoptera Research* 4: 203–18.

Gwynne, D. T. (2001). *Katydids and Bush-Crickets: Reproductive Behavior and Evolution of the Tettigoniidae*. Ithaca & London: Cornell University.

Gwynne, D. (2004). The reproductive behaviour of ground weta (Orthoptera: Anostostomatidae): drumming, nuptial feeding, mate-guarding and maternal care. *Journal of the Kansas Entomological Society* 77(4); 414–28

Gwynne, D. T. (2008). Sexual conflict over nuptial gifts in insects. *Annual Review of Entomology* 53: 83–101.

Gwynne, D. T. & Bailey, W. J. (1988). Mating system, mate choice and ultrasonic calling in a zaprochiline katydid (Orthoptera: Tettigoniidae). *Behaviour* 105: 202–23.

Gwynne, D. T. & Bailey, W. J. (1999). Female-female competition in katydids: sexual selection for increased sensitivity to a male signal? *Evolution* 53: 546–51.

Gwynne, D. T. & Morris, G. K. (Eds.) (1983). *Orthopteran Mating Systems: Sexual Competition in a Diverse Group of Insects*. Boulder, Col.: Westview.

Gwynne, D. T. & Snedden, A. W. (1995). Paternity and female remating in *Requena verticalis* (Orthoptera:

Tettigoniidae). *Ecological Entomology* 20: 191–4.

Gwynne, D. T., Bailey, W. J. & Annells, A. (1998). The sex in short supply for matings varies over short spatial scales in a katydid (*Kawanaphila nartee*, Orthoptera: Tettigoniidae). *Behavioral Ecology and Sociobiology* 42: 157–62.

Haes, E. C. M. (1976). Orthoptera in Sussex. *Entomologist's Gazette* 27: 181–202.

Haes, E. C. M. (1987). Species account of the mole cricket in D. B. Shirt (Ed.) *British Red Data Books 2: Insects*. Nature Conservancy Council: 52.

Haes, E. C. M. & Harding, P. T. (1997). *Atlas of Grasshoppers, Crickets and Allied Insects of Britain and Ireland*. Huntingdon: NERC/ITE.

Haes, E. C. M., Cherrill, A. J. & Brown, V. K. (1990). Meteorological correlates of wart-biter (Orthoptera: Tettigoniidae) abundance. *The Entomologist* 109(2): 93–9.

Hardy, T. N. & Shaw, K. C. (1983). The role of chemoreception in sex recognition by male crickets: *Acheta domesticus* and *Teleogryllus oceanicus*. *Physiological Entomology* 8: 151–66.

Hartbauer, M., Kratzer, S. and Römer, H. (2006). Chirp rate is independent of male condition in a synchronising bushcricket. *Journal of Insect Physiology* 52: 221–30.

Hartley, J. C. (1964). The structure of the eggs of the British Tettigoniidae (Orthoptera). *Proceedings of the Royal Entomological Society of London* 39: 111–17.

Hartley, J. C. (1967). Some notes on hatching the eggs of *Pholidoptera griseoaptera* (Deggear) (Orthoptera, Tettigoniidae). *Entomologist's Monthly Magazine* 103: 123–4.

Hartley, J. C. (1990). Egg biology of the Tettigoniidae. In Bailey & Rentz (Eds.) *op. cit.*: 41–70.

Hartley, J. C. (1993). Acoustic behaviour and phonotaxis in the duetting ephippigerines, *Steropleurus nobrei* and *Steropleurus stali* (Tettigoniidae). *Zoological Journal of the Linnaean Society* 107: 155–67.

Hartley, J. C. & Robinson, D. J. (1976). Acoustic behaviour of both sexes of the speckled bush cricket *Leptophyes punctatissima*. *Physiological Entomology* 1: 21–5.

Hartley, J. C. & Warne, A. C. (1972). The developmental biology of the egg stage of Western European Tettigoniidae (Orthoptera). *Journal of Zoology* 168: 267–98.

Hartley, J. C. & Warne, A. C. (1973). The distribution of *Pholidoptera griseoaptera* (DEG.) (Orth., Tett.) in England and Wales related to accumulated temperatures. *Journal of Animal Ecology* 42: 531–7.

Hartley, J. C., Jatho, M., Kalmring, K., Stephen, R. O. & Schorder, H. (2000). Contrasting sound production in Tettigoniidae. *Journal of Orthoptera Research* 9: 121–7.

Harvey, G. (1997). *The Killing of the Countryside*. London: Jonathan Cape.

Harvey, P., & Gardiner, T. (2006). Pitfall trapping of scarce Orthoptera at a coastal nature reserve in Essex, UK. *Journal of Insect Conservation* 10: 371–3.

Harvey, P., Gardiner, T. & Smith, D. (2005). Grey bush-cricket *Platycleis albopunctata* (Goeze) rediscovered in Essex. *Essex Naturalist* (New Series) 22: 289–96.

Harz, K. (1969). *The Orthoptera of Europe* Vol. 1. The Hague: Dr. W. Junk N. V.

Harz, K. (1975). *The Orthoptera of Europe* Vol. 2. The Hague: Dr. W. Junk B. V.

Hassall, M. & Grayson, F. W. L. (1987). The occurrence of an additional instar in the development of *Chorthippus brunneus* (Orthoptera: Gomphocerinae). *Journal of Natural History* 21: 329–37.

Hathway, R., Stancliffe, P. & Goodey, M. (2003). The discovery of large conehead bush-cricket in the Isles of Scilly. *British Wildlife* 15(1) October: 45–6.

Hawkins, R. D. (2001). The southern oak bush-cricket *Meconema meridionale* Costa (Orthoptera: Tettigoniidae), new to Britain. *British Journal of Entomology and Natural History* 14(4): 207–13.

Hedwig, B. (2001). Singing and hearing: neuronal mechanisms of acoustic communication in Orthopterans. *Zoology* 103: 140–9.

Hedwig, B. (2006). Pulses, patterns and paths: neurobiology of acoustic behaviour in crickets. *Journal of Comparative Physiology* A 192(7): 677–89

Hedwig, B. (2007). Pulses patterns paths; auditory processing in crickets. *Proceedings of the Institute of Acoustics* 29(3): 1–8

Hedwig, B. & Poulet, J. F. A. (2004). Complex auditory behaviour emerges from simple reactive steering. *Nature* 430: 781–5.

Hedwig, B. & Poulet, J. F. A. (2005). Mechanisms underlying phonotactic steering in the cricket *Gryllus bimaculatus* revealed with a fast trackball system. *Journal of Experimental Biology* 208: 915–27.

Helfert, B. V. & Sänger, K. (1995). Ant-mimicking in larvae of *Macroxiphus siamsensis* (Orthoptera: Tettigoniidae). *Z. Arbeit Österr. Ent.* 47: 41–8.

Heller, K.-G. (1990). Evolution of song pattern in east mediterranean Phaneropterinae: constraints by the communication system. In Bailey & Rentz (Eds.) *op. cit.*: 130–51.

Heller, K.-G. (1995). Acoustic signalling in palaeotropical bush-crickets (Orthoptera, Tettigonioidea, Pseudophyllidae): does predation pressure by eavesdropping enemies differ in the palaeotropics and neotropics? *Journal of Zoology* 237: 469–85.

Heller, K.-G. (2006). Song evolution and speciation in bush crickets. In Drosopoulos & Claridge (Eds.) *op. cit.*: 137–54.

Heller, K.-G. & von Helversen, D. (1986). Acoustic communication in phaneropterid bushcrickets: species-specific delay of female stridulatory response and matching male sensory time window. *Behavioural Ecology and Sociobiology* 18: 189–98.

Hewitt, G. & Roscoe, C. (1971). Changes in microclimate correlated with a cline for B-chromosomes in the grasshopper *Myrmeleotettix maculatus* (Thunb.) (Orthoptera: Acrididae). *Journal of Animal Ecology* 40: 753–65.

Hilbert, D. W., Logan, J. A. & Swift, D. M. (1985). A unifying hypothesis of temperature effects on egg development and diapause of the migratory grasshopper, *Melanoplus sanguinipes* (Orthoptera: Acrididae). *Journal of Theoretical Biology* 112(4): 827–38.

Hingston, R. W. G. (1933). *The Meaning of Animal Colour and Adornment*. London: Edward Arnold.

Hochkirch, A., Bücker, A. & Gröning, J. (2008). Reproductive interference between the Common Ground-hopper *Tetrix undulata* and the Slender Ground-hopper *Tetrix subulata* (Orthoptera, Tetrigidae). *Bulletin of Entomological Research* 98: 605–12.

Hochkirch, A., Deppermann, J. & Gröning, J. (2006). Visual communication behaviour as a mechanism behind reproductive interference in three pygmy grasshopers (Genus *Tetrix*, Tetrigidae, Orthoptera). *Journal of Insect Behavior* 19(5): 559–71.

Hochkirch, A., Deppermann, J. & Gröning, J. (2008a). Phenotypic plasticity in insects: the effects of substrate colour on the coloration of two groundhopper species. *Evolution and Development* 10(3): 350–9.

Hochkirch, A., Gärtner, A.-C. & Brandt, T. (2008b). Effects of forest-dune ecotone managment on the endangered heath grasshopper, *Chorthippus vagans* (Orthoptera: Acrididae). *Bulletin of Entomological Research* 98: 449–56.

Hochkirch, A., Gröhning, J., Loos, T., Metzing, C. & Reichelt, M. (2000). Specialized diet and feeding habits as key factors for the habitat requirements of the grasshopper species *Tetrix subulata* (Orthoptera: Tetrigidae). *Entomologia Generalis* 25(1): 39–51.

Hochkirch, A., Gröning, J and Krause, S. (2007). Intersexual niche segregation in Cepero's ground-hopper, *Tetrix ceperoi*. *Evolutionary Ecology* 21: 727–38.

Hockham, L. R. & Vahed, K. (1997). The function of mate guarding in a field cricket (Orthoptera: Gryllidae; *Teleogryllus natalis* Otte & Cade). *Journal of Insect Behavior* 10: 247–56.

Hodgson, C. J. (1963). Some observations on the habits and life history of *Tetrix undulata*. *Proceedings of the Royal Entomological Society of London* A 38: 200–5.

Holzer, B., Jacot, A. & Brinkhof, M. W. G. (2003). Condition-dependent signalling affects male sexual attractiveness in field crickets, *Gryllus campestris*. *Behavioral Ecology* 14(3): 353–9.

Honěk, A. (1993). Intraspecific variation in body size and fecundity in insects: a general relationship. *Oikos* 66: 483–92.

Horsfield, D. (2010). Altitudinal limits of grasshoppers in the Lake District. *Bulletin of the Amateur Entomologist's Society* 69: 108–10.

Hoy, R. R. (1992). The evolution of hearing in insects as an adaptation to predation from bats. In D. B. Webster, R. R. Fay & A. N. Popper (Eds.) *The Evolutionary Biology of Hearing*. New York: Springer-Verlag.

Huber, F. (1964). The role of the central nervous system in Orthoptera during the co-ordination and control of stridulation. In R. G. Busnel (Ed.) *Acoustic Behaviour of Animals*. Amsterdam: Elsevier: 440–87.

Huber, F., Moore, T. E. & Loher, W. (Eds.) (1989). *Cricket Behaviour and Neurobiology*. New York: Cornell University.

Hunt, J., Brooks, R. & Jennions, M. D. (2005). Female mate choice as a condition-dependent life-history trait. *American Naturalist* 166: 79–92.

Hutchinson, J. M. C., McNamara, J. M., Houston, A. I. & Vollrath, F. (1997). Dyer's rule and the investment principle: optimal moulting strategies if feeding rate is size-dependent and growth is discontinuous. *Philosophical Transactions of the Royal Society of London* B 352: 113–38.

Huxley, J. S. (1914). The courtship habits of the great crested grebe (*Podiceps cristatus*); with an addition to the theory of sexual selection. *Proceedings of the Zoological Society of London* 84(3): 491–562

Huxley, J. S. (1938). Darwin's theory of sexual selection and the data subsumed by it, in the light of recent research. *American Naturalist* 72: 416–33.

Ingrisch, S. (1983). Zum Einfluß der Feuchte auf die Schlupfrate und Entwicklungsdauer der Eier mitteleuropäischer Feldheuschrecken. *Deutsche Entomologische Zeitschrift* 30: 1–15.

Ingrisch, S. (1984a). Embryonic development of *Decticus verrucivorus* (Orthoptera: Tettigoniidae). *Entomologia Generalis* 10(1): 1–9.

Ingrisch, S. (1984b). The influence of environmental factors on dormancy and duration of egg development in *Metrioptera roeselii* (Orthoptera: Tettigoniidae). *Oecologia* 61: 254–8.

Ingrisch, S. (1986a). The plurennial life cycles of the European Tettigoniidae (Insecta: Orthoptera) I. The effect of temperature on embryonic development and hatching. *Oecologia* 70: 606–16.

Ingrisch, S. (1986b). The plurennial life cycles of the European Tettigoniidae (insecta: Tettigoniidae) 2. The effect of photoperiod on the induction of an initial diapause. *Oecologia* 70: 617–23.

Ingrisch, S. (1986c). The plurennial life cycles of the European Tettigoniidae (Insecta: Orthoptera) 3. The effect of drought and the variable duration of the initial diapause. *Oecologia* 70: 624–30.

Ingrisch, S. (1996). Evidence of an embryonic diapause in a tropical Phanopterinae (Insecta: Ensifera, Tettigonioidea). *Tropical Zoology* 9: 431–9.

Ivy, T. M. & Sakaluk, S. K. (2005). Polyandry promotes enhanced offspring survival in decorated crickets. *Evolution* 59: 152–9.

Jang, Y. & Gerhardt, H. C. (2006). Divergence in the calling songs between sympatric and allopatric populations of the southern wood cricket *Gryllus fultoni* (Orthoptera: Gryllidae). *Journal of Evolutionary Biology* 19: 459–72.

Jang, Y., Gerhardt, C. & Choe, J. C. (2008). A comparative study of aggressiveness in eastern North American field cricket species (genus *Gryllus*). *Behavioral Ecology and Sociobiology* 62: 1397–1407.

Jarman, T. H. (1982). *Mating behaviour and its releasers in* Hemideina crassidens *(Orthoptera: Stenopelmatidae)*. Thesis, University of Canterbury, N. Z. (cited in Greenfield & Jarman 2001, *op. cit.*).

Jennions, M. D., Drayton, J. M, Brooks, R. & Hunt, J. (2007). Do female black field crickets *Teleogryllus commodus* benefit from polyandry? *Journal of Evolutionary Biology* 20(4): 1469–77.

Jin, X.-B. & Yen, A. L. (1998). Conservation and the cricket culture in China. *Journal of Insect Conservation* 2: 211–16.

Joern, A. (1982). Importance of behaviour and coloration in the control of body temperature by *Brachystola magna* Girard (Orthoptera: Acrididae). *Acrida* 10: 117–30.

Joern, A. (1986). Experimental study of avian predation on coexisting grasshopper populations (Orthoptera: Acrididae) in a sandhills grassland. *Oikos* 46: 243–9.

Joern, A. & Gaines, S. B. (1990). Population dynamics and regulation in grasshoppers. In Chapman & Joern (Eds.) *op. cit.*: 415–82.

Jones, M. D. R. (1963). Sound signals and alternation behaviour in *Pholidoptera*. *Nature* 199: 928–9.

Jones, M. D. R. (1966). The acoustic behaviour of the bush cricket *Pholidoptera griseoaptera*. 2. Interaction with artificial sound signals. *Journal of Experimental Biology* 45: 31–44.

Kalmring, K., Keuper, A. & Kaiser, W. (1990). Aspects of acoustic and vibratory communication in seven European bushcrickets. In Bailey & Rentz (Eds.) *op. cit.*: 191–216.

Karlsson, M., Johansson, J., Caesar, S. and Forsman, A. (2009). No evidence for developmental plasticity of color patterns in response to rearing substrate in pygmy grasshoppers. *Canadian Journal of Zoology* 87: 1044–51.

Kelly, C. D. (2006). Resource quality or harem size: what influences male tenure at refuge sites in tree weta (Orthoptera: Anostostomatidae)? *Behavioral Ecology and Sociobiology* 60: 175–83.

Kelly, C. D. (2008). Why do male tree weta aggressively evict females from galleries after mating? *Ethology* 114: 203–8.

Kerr, A. M., Gershman, S. N. & Sakaluk, S. K. (2010). Experimentally induced spermatophore production and immune responses reveal a trade-off in crickets. *Behavioral Ecology* 21: 647–54.

Kevan, D. K. McE. (1952). A summary of the recorded distribution of British orthopteroids. *Transactions of the Society for British Entomology* 11(8): 173.

Kevan, D. K. McE. (1953). Notes on the distribution of British orthopteroids. *Journal of the Society for British Entomology* 4(6): 120.

Kevan, D. K. McE. (1955). The home of the house cricket, *Acheta domesticus* (L.) (Orth., Gryllidae). *Entomologist's Monthly Magazine* 91: 263.

Kevan, D. K. McE. (1961). A revised summary of the known distribution of British orthopteroids. *Transactions of the Society for British Entomology.* 14(8): 195.

Kevan, D. K. McE. (1979). The place of grasshoppers and crickets in amerinidian cultures. *Proceedings of the Pan American Acridological Society* 1979: 8–74.

Key, K. H. & Day, M. F. (1954). A temperature controlled physiological colour change in the grasshopper *Kosciuscola tristis* Sjost. (Orthoptera: Acrididae). *Australian Journal of Zoology* 2: 340–63.

Kirby, P. (1995). *Lyme Bay Environmental Study: Volume 13 (Terrestrial Ecology: Invertebrates of Chesil Beach).* Ambios Environmental Consultants Ltd.

Kleukers, R. (2002). Niewe Waarnemingen aan Sprinkhanen en Krekels in Nederland (Orthoptera). *Nederlandse Faunistische Mededelingen* 17: 87–102.

Kleukers, R. & Krekels, R. (2004). *Veldgids Sprinkhanen en Krekels.* Utrecht: KNNV Uitgeverij.

Kostarakos, K., Rheinlaender, J. & Römer, H. (2007). Spatial orientation in the bushcricket *Leptophyes punctatissima* (Phaneropterinae; Orthoptera): III.

Peripheral directionality and central nervous processing of spatial cues. *Journal of Comparative Physiology A* 193: 1115–23.

Kral, K. (2010). Escape behaviour in blue-winged grasshoppers (*Oedipoda caerulescens*). *Physiological Entomology* 35(3): 240–8.

Labhart, T. (1999). How polarization-sensitive neurones of crickets see the polarization patterns of the sky: a field study with an opto-electronic model neurone. *Journal of Experimental Biology* 202: 757–70.

Labhart, T. & Meyer, E. P. (2002). Neural mechanisms in insect navigation: polarization compass and odometer. *Current Opinion in Neurobiology* 12: 707–14.

Lange, A. B. & Loughton, B. G. (1985). An oviposition-stimulating factor in the male accessory reproductive gland of the locust, *Locusta migratoria. General Comparative Endocrinology* 57: 208–15.

Latimer, W. (1981a). The acoustic behaviour of *Platycleis albopunctata* (Goeze) (Orthoptera: Tettigoniidae). *Behaviour* 76: 182–206.

Latimer, W. (1981b). Variation in the song of the bush cricket *Platycleis albopunctata* (Orthoptera, Tettigoniidae). *Journal of Natural History* 15: 245–263.

Lehmann, G. U. C. & Lehmann, A. W. (2008). Bushcricket song as a clue for spermatophore size? *Behavioral Ecology and Sociobiology* 62: 569–578.

Loher, W. (1990). Pheromones and phase transformation in locusts. In Chapman & Joern (Eds.) *op. cit.*: 331–55.

Lucas, W. J. (1920). *A Monograph of the British Orthoptera.* London: the Ray Society.

Marshall, E. J. P., West, T. M. & Kleijn, D. (2006). Impacts of an agri-environmeent field margin prescription on the flora and fauna of arable farmland in different landscapes. *Agriculture, Ecosystems and Environment* 113: 36–44.

Marshall, J. A. (1974). The British Orthoptera since 1800. In D. L. Hawksworth (Ed.) *The Changing Flora and Fauna of Britain* (Systematics Association Special Volume no. 6). London & New York: Academic Press: 307–22.

Marshall, J. A. (2010). Grasshoppers, crickets and allied insects. In N. Maclean (Ed.) *Silent Summer: The State of Wildlife in Britain and Ireland.* Cambridge: Cambridge University.

Marshall, J. A. & Haes, E. C. M. (1988). *Grasshoppers and Allied Insects of Great Britain and Ireland.* Great Horkesley: Harley.

Masaki, S. (1978). Seasonal and latitudinal adaptations in the life cycles of crickets. In: Dingle H. (Ed.) *Evolution of Insect Migration and Diapause.* New York, Heidelberg & Berlin: Springer: 72–100.

Masaki, S. (1980). Summer diapause. *Annual Review of Entomology* 25: 1–25.

McVean, A. & Field, L. H. (1996). Communication by substrate vibration in the New Zealand tree weta, *Hemideina femorata* (Stenopelmatidae: Orthoptera). *Journal of Zoology* 239: 101–22.

Minckley, R. L. & Greenfield, M. D. (1995). Psychoacoustics of female phonotaxis and the evolution of male signal interactions in Orthoptera. *Ethology Ecology and Evolution* 7: 235–43.

Minckley, R. l., Greenfield, M. D. & Tourtellot, M. K. (1995). Chorus structure in tarbrush grasshoppers: inhibition, selective phonoresponse, and signal competition. *Animal Behaviour* 50: 579–94.

Moffet, T. (1634). *Theatrum Insectorum.* London: Cotes.

Møller, A. P. (2001). Female preference for symmetric calls in a grasshopper. *Ethology Ecology and Evolution* 13: 261–72.

Morère, J.-J. & Livory, A. (1999). Le grillon maritime de la manche: une espéce nouvelle pour la France. *L'Argiope* 23: 29–37.

Moriarty, F. (1969a). Water uptake and embryonic development in eggs of *Chorthippus brunneus* Thunberg (Saltatoria: Acrididae). *Journal of Experimental Biology* 50: 327–33.

Moriarty, F. (1969b). Egg diapause and water absorbtion in the grasshopper *Chorthippus brunneus. Journal of Insect Physiology* 15: 2069–74.

Morris, G. K, Kerr, G. E. & Fullard, J. H. (1978). Phonotactic preferences of female meadow katydids (Orthoptera: Tettigoniidae, *Conocephalus nigropleurum*). *Canadian Journal of Zoology* 56: 1479–87.

Morris, G. K. & Fullard, J. H. (1983). Random noise and congeneric discrimination in *Conocephalus* (Orthoptera; Tettigoniidae). In Gwynne & Morris *op. cit.*: 73–96.

Morris, G. K., Gwynne, D. T., Klimas, D. E. & Sakaluk, S. K. (1989). Virgin male mating advantage in a primitive acoustic insect (Orthoptera:Haglidae). *Journal of Insect Behavior* 2(2): 173–85.

Murakami, S. & Itoh, M. T. (2003). Removal of both antennae influences the courtship and aggressive behaviours in male crickets. *Journal of Neurobiology* 57: 110–18.

Nabours, R. K. (1929). *The genetics of the Tetrigidae (grouse locusts). Bibliographica Genetica*: 27–104

Neems, R. M. & Butlin, R. K. (1992). Divergence in mate finding behaviour between two subspecies of the meadow grasshopper *Chorthippus parallelus* (Orthoptera:Acrididae). *Journal of Insect Behavior* 6(4): 421–30.

Neems, R. M. & Butlin, R. K. (1995). Divergence in cuticular hydrocarbons between parapatric subspecies of the meadow grasshopper, *Chorthippus parallelus* (Orthoptera, Acrididae). *Biological Journal of the Linnaean Society* 54: 139–49.

Nityananda, V. & Balakrishnan, R. (2008). Leaders and followers in katydid choruses in the field: call intensity, spacing and consistency. *Animal Behaviour* 76: 723–35.

Nityananda, V. & Balakrishnan, R. (2009). Modeling the role of competition and cooperation in the evolution of kaydid acoustic synchrony. *Behavioral Ecology* 20: 484–9.

Nityanander, V., Stradner, J., Balakrishnan, R. & Römer, H. (2007). Selective attention in a synchronising bushcricket: physiology, behaviour and ecology. *Journal of Comparative Physiology A* 193: 983–91.

Norris, M. J. (1970). Aggregation response in ovipositing females of the desert locust, with special reference to the chemical factor. *Journal of Insect Physiology* 16: 1493–1515.

Oedekoven, M. A. & Joern, A. (1998). Stage-based mortality of grassland grasshoppers (Acrididae) from wandering spider (Lycosidae) predation. *Acta Oecologica* 19(6): 507–15.

Ofner, E., Rheinlaender, J. & Römer, H. (2007). Spatial orientation in the bushcricket *Leptophyes punctatissima* (Phaneropterinae; Orthoptera): II. Phonotaxis to elevated sound sources on a walking compensator. *Journal of Comparative Physiology A* 193: 321–30.

Okelo, O. (1979). Influence of male presence on clutch size in *Schistocerca vaga* Scudder (Orthoptera: Acrididae). *International Journal of Invertebrate Reproduction* 1: 317–21.

Oldfield, B. (1980). Accuracy of orientation in female crickets, *Teleogryllus oceanicus* (Gryllidae): dependence on song spectrum. *Journal of Comparative Physiology* 147: 461–9.

Ostrowski, T. D., Sradnick, J., Stumpner, A. & Elsner, N. (2009). The elaborate courtship behaviour of *Stenobothrus clavatus* Willemse 1979 (Acrididae: Gomphocerinae). *Journal of Orthoptera Research* 18(2): 171–82.

Otte, D. (1977). Communication in Orthoptera. In T. A. Sebeok (Ed.) *How Animals Communicate*. Bloomington & London: Indiana University: 334–61.

Owens, N. (2010). The chameleon grasshopper. *Natterjack* (Norfolk and Norwich Naturalists' Society): 10–11.

Panter G. (2007). The end of one cricket season and the start of another? *Leicester Literary and Philosophical Society [Natural History Section]* 84, Spring.

Paranjape, S. Y., Balerao, A. M. & Naidu, N. M. (1987). On etho-ecological characteristics and phylogeny of Tetrigidae. In B. M. Baccetti (Ed.) *op. cit.*: 386–95.

Pardo, M. C., Camacho, J. P. M., & Hewitt, G. M. (1994). Dynamics of ejaculate nutrient transfer in *Locusta migratoria*. *Heredity* 73: 190–7.

Pardo, M. C., Lopez-Leon, M. D., Hewitt, G. M. & Camacho, J. P. M. (1995). Female fitness is increased by frequent mating in grasshoppers. *Heredity* 74: 654–60.

Parker, D. J. & Vahed, K. (2010). The intensity of pre- and post-copulatory mate guarding in relation to spermatophore transfer in the cricket, *Gryllus bimaculatus*. *Journal of Ethology* 28: 245–9.

Parker, G. A. (1979). Sexual selection and sexual conflict. In M. S. Blum & N. A. Blum (Eds.) *Sexual Selection and Reproductive Competition in Insects*. New York: Academic: 123–66.

Paul, J. (1988). Colour and pattern variation in *Tetrix ceperoi* Bolivar (Orthoptera: Tetrigidae): an aid to identification. *Entomologist's Gazette* 39: 133–9.

Paul, J. (1989). *Grasshoppers and Crickets of Berkshire, Buckinghamshire and Oxfordshire*. Oxford: Pisces.

Payne, K. (1973). A survey of the *Spartina*-feeding insects in Poole harbour, Dorset. *Entomologist's Monthly Magazine* 108: 66–79.

Payne, R. M. (1957). The distribution of grasshoppers and allied Insects in the London area. *The London Naturalist:* 102–15.

Payne, R. M. (1969). A disappointing day at Porthgwarra. *Entomologist's Record and Journal of Variation* 81: 91–2.

Pearce-Kelly, P., Jones, R., Clarke, D., Walker, C., Atkin, P. & Cunningham, A. (1998). The captive rearing of threatened Orthoptera: a comparison of the conservation potential and practical considerations of two species' breeding programmes at the Zoological Society of London. *Journal of Insect Conservation* 2: 201–10.

Pemberton, R. W. (1990). The selling of *Gampsocleis gratiosa* Brunner (Orthoptera: Tettigoniidae) as singing pets in China. *Pan-Pacific Entomologist* 66: 93–5.

Pickard, B. C. (1954). *Grasshoppers and Crickets of Great Britain and the Channel Islands.* Ilkley: Rowan House.

Pinchen, B. J. (2003). Searching for the mole cricket – an elusive monster. *The Bulletin of the Amateur Entomologists' Society* 62 (447): 45–7.

Pinchen, B. J. (2005). Recent records of the mole cricket *Gryllotalpa gryllotalpa* Linn. in Britain. *Atropos* 24: 36–40.

Pinchen, B. J. (2006). Records of the mole cricket *Gryllotalpa gryllotalpa* Linn. during 2005 *Atropos* 27: 39–41.

Pinchen, B. J. (2009). An update on the occurrences of various mole cricket species *Gryllotalpa* spp. in the British Isles since 2005. *Atropos* 36: 12–15.

Pool, J. E. & Aquandro, C. F. (2007). The genetic basis of adaptive pigmentation variation in *Drosophyla melanogaster*. *Molecular Ecology* 16: 2844–51.

Port, G. R. & Thompson, J. R. (1980). Outbreaks of insect herbivores on plants along motorways in the United Kingdom. *Journal of Applied Ecology* 17: 649–56.

Poulet, J. F. A. & Hedwig, B. (2005). Auditory orientation in crickets: pattern recognition controls reactive steering. *Proceedings of the National Academy of Sciences of the USA* 102(43): 15665–9.

Prestwich, K. N. (1994). The energetics of acoustic signalling in anurans and insects. *American Zoologist* 34: 625–43.

Prokop, P. & Maxwell, M. R. (2008). Interactions between multiple forms of nuptial feeding in the wood cricket *Nemobius sylvestris* (Bosc): dual spermatophores and male forewings. *Ethology* 114: 1173–82.

Ragge, D. R. (1954). The distribution of *Chorthippus vagans* (Eversmann) in Dorset and Hampshire (Orth., Acrididae). *Entomologist* 89: 200.

Ragge, D. R. (1963). First record of the grasshopper *Stenobothrus stigmaticus* (Rambur) (Acrididae) in the British Isles, with other new distribution records and notes on the origin of the British Orthoptera. *Entomologist* 96: 211–7

Ragge, D. R. (1965). *Grasshoppers, Crickets and Cockroaches of the British Isles.* London & New York: Frederick Warne.

Ragge, D. R. (1973). The British Orthoptera: a supplement. *Entomologist's Gazette* 24: 227–45.

Ragge, D. R. (1986). The Songs of the Western European Grasshoppers of the Genus *Omocestus* in Relation to their Taxonomy (Orthoptera: Acrididae). *Bulletin of the British Museum (Natural History). Entomology Series* 53(4): 227.

Ragge, D. R. (1987). Speciation and biogeography of some southern European Orthoptera, as revealed by their songs. In B. M. Baccetti (Ed.) *op. cit.*: 418–26.

Ragge, D. R. (1988). The distribution and history of the British Orthoptera. In J. A. Marshall & E. C. M. Haes *op. cit.*: 25–33.

Ragge, D. R. & Reynolds, W. J. (1998). *The Songs of the Grasshoppers and Crickets of Western Europe.* London & Great Horkesley: The Natural History Museum/Harley Books.

Reinhardt, K. (2000). Variation in sperm precedence in *Chorthippus* grasshoppers. (Caelifera:Gomphocerinae). *Physiological Entomology* 25(4): 324–9.

Reinhardt, K, Köhler, G. & Schumacher, J. (1999). Females of the grasshopper *Chorthippus parallelus* (Zett.) do not remate for fresh sperm. *Proceedings of the Royal Society B* 266: 2003–9.

Reinhardt, K., Köhler, G., Webb, S. and Childs, D. (2007). Field mating rate of female meadow grasshoppers, *Chorthippus parallelus*, estimated from sperm counts. *Ecological Entomology* 32(6): 637–42.

Reinhold, K. (1999). Paternal investment in *Poecilimon veluchianus* bushcrickets: beneficial effects of nuptial feeding on offspring viability. *Behavioral Ecology and Sociobiology* 45: 293–9.

Rence, B., & Loher, W. (1977). Contact chemoreceptive sex recognition in the male cricket, *Teleogryllus commodus*. *Physiological Entomology* 2: 225–36.

Rentz, D. C. & Gurney, A. B. (1985). The shield-backed katydids of South America (Orthoptera: Tettigoniidae, Tettigoniidae) and a new tribe of Conocephalinae with genera in Chile and Australia. *Entomologica Scandinavica* 16: 69–119.

Rheinlaender, J. & Römer, H. (1990). Acoustic cues for sound localisation and spacing in orthopteran insects. In Bailey & Rentz (Eds.) *op. cit.*: 248–64.

Rheinlaender, J., Hartbauer, M. & Römer, H. (2007). Spatial orientation in the bushcricket *Leptophyes punctatissima*

(Phaneropterinae: Orthoptera): I. Phonotaxis to elevated and depressed sound sources. *Journal of Comparative Physiology A* 193: 313–20.

Richards, O. W. & Waloff, N. (1954). Studies on the biology and population dynamics of British grasshoppers. *Anti-Locust Bulletin* 17: 1–186.

Richmond, D. (2001). *Grasshoppers and Allied Insects of Norfolk.* Norwich: Norfolk and Norwich Naturalists' Society.

Riede, K. (1986). Modification of the courtship song by visual stimuli in the grasshopper *Gomphocerus rufus* (Acrididae). *Physiological Entomology* 11: 61–74.

Ritchie, M. G. (1990). Are differences in song responsible for assortative mating between subspecies of the grasshopper *Chorthippus parallelus* (Orthoptera: Acrididae)? *Animal behaviour* 39: 685–91.

Ritchie, M. G., Butlin, R. K. & Hewitt, G. M. (1987). Causation, fitness effects and morphology of macropterism in *Chorthippus parallelus* (Orthoptera: Acrididae). *Ecological Entomology* 12: 209–18.

Ritchie, M. G., Sunter, D. and Hockham, L. R. (1998). Behavioral components of sex role reversal in the tettigoniid bushcricket *Ephippiger ephippiger*. *Journal of Insect Behavior* 11(4): 481–91.

Robinson, D. J. (1980). Acoustic communication between the sexes of the bush cricket, *Leptophyes punctatissima*. *Physiological Entomology* 5: 183–9.

Robinson, D. J. (1990). Acoustic communication between the sexes in bush crickets. In Bailey & Rentz (Eds.) *op. cit.*: 112–29.

Robinson, D. J. & Hall, M. J. (2002). Sound signalling in Orthoptera. In Evans, P. (Ed.) *Advances in Insect Physiology* 29: 151–278.

Robinson, D. J., Ash, P. J. & Hall, M. J. (2009). Calling heights chosen by male speckled bush crickets (*Leptophyes punctatissima*). *Comparative Biochemistry and Physiology* 153(2), supp. 1: S95.

Robinson, D. J., Rheinlaender, J. & Hartley, J. C. (1986). Temporal parameters of male-female sound communication in *Leptophyes punctatissima*. *Physiological Entomology* 11: 317–23.

Robinson, R. A., Wilson, J. D. & Crick, H. Q. P. (2001). The importance of arable habitat for farmland birds in grassland landscapes. *Journal of Applied Ecology* 38: 1059–69.

Robson, L. J. & Gwynne, D. J. (2010). Measuring sexual selection on females in sex-role-reversed mormon crickets (*Anabrus simplex*, Orthoptera: Tettigoniidae). *Journal of Evolutionary Biology* 23(7): 1528–31.

Roff, D. A. (1984). The cost of being able to fly: a study of wing polymorphism in two species of crickets. *Oecologia* 63: 30–37.

Roff, D. A., Tucker, J., Stirling, G. & Fairbairn, D. J. (1999). The evolution of threshold traits: effects of selection on fecundity and correlated response in wing dimorphism in the sand cricket. *Journal of Evolutionary Biology* 535–46.

Römer, H. (1992). Evolutionary constraints for the evolution of hearing and sound communication in insects. In D. B. Webster, R. R. Fay & A. N. Popper (Eds.) *The Evolutionary Biology of Hearing*. New York: Springer-Verlag: 79–93.

Rowell, C. H. F. (1971). The variable coloration of the acridoid grasshoppers. *Advances in Insect Physiology* 8: 145–98.

Roy, A. (2009). *Listening to Grasshoppers: Field Notes on Democracy*. London, etc.: Penguin/Hamish Hamilton.

Ryan, K. M. & Sakaluk, S. K. (2009). Dulling the senses: the role of the antennae in mate recognition, copulation and mate guarding in decorated crickets. *Animal Behaviour* 77: 1345–50.

Sakaluk, S. K. (1984). Male crickets feed females to ensure complete sperm transfer. *Science* 223: 609–10.

Sakaluk, S. K. & Eggert, A.-K. (2009). Coping with the cold: temperature and mating activity of male sagebrush crickets *Cyphoderris strepitans* (Orthoptera: Haglidae). *Physiological Entomology* 34: 251–5.

Sakaluk, S. K., Campbell, M. T. H., Clark, A. P., Johnson, J. C. and Keorpes, P. A. (2004). Haemolymph loss during nuptial feeding constrains male mating success in sagebrush crickets. *Behavioral Ecology* 15(5): 845–9.

Schädler & Witsak (1999). Variation of post-embryonic development time and number of nymphal instars on a small spatial scale in central European grasshoppers (Califera: Acrididae). *Entomologia Generalis* 24: 125–35.

Schatral, A. (1990). Body size, song frequency and mating success of male bush-crickets *Requena verticalis* (Orthoptera, Tettigoniidae, Listrocelidinae) in the field. *Animal Behaviour* 40: 982–4.

Schmidt, G. H. & Osman, K. S. A. (1988). Male pheromones and egg production in Acrididae. In F. Sehnal, A. Dabza & D. L. Denlinger (Eds.) *Endocrinological Frontiers in Physiological Insect Ecology*. Wroctaw: Wroctaw Technological University: 701–6.

Schul, J., von Helversen, D. & von Helversen, O. (1998). Selective phonotaxis in *Tettigonia cantans* and *T. viridissima* in song recognition and discrimination. *Journal of Comparative Physiology* A 182: 687–94.

Sharov, A. G. (1968). Phylogeny of orthopteroid insects. *Proceedings of the Palaeontological Institute*. Russian Academy of Sciences 118: 1–216.

Shelly, T. E. (1993). Effects of female deprivation on mating propensity and mate selectivity by male *Requena verticalis* (Orthoptera: Tettigoniidae). *Journal of Insect Behavior* 6: 689–98.

Shelly, T. E. & Greenfield, M. D. (1991). Dominions and desert clickers (Orthoptera: Acrididae): influences of resources and male signalling on female settlement patterns. *Behavioral Ecology and Sociobiology* 28: 133–40.

Shirt, D. B. (Ed.) (1987). *British Red Data Books: 2. Insects*. Peterborough: Nature Conservancy Council.

Shoard, M. (1980). *The Theft of the Countryside*. London: Temple.

Sibly, R. & Monk, K. (1987). A theory of grasshopper life cycles. *Oikos* 48: 186–94.

Siddiqi, J. I & Kahn, M. A. (1981). The secretion and perception of a sex pheromone in the grasshopper *Hieroglyphus nigrorepletus* Bolivar (Orthoptera: Acrididae). *Acrida* 10: 233–42.

Simmons, A. D. & Thomas, C. D. (2004). Changes in dispersal during species' range expansions. *The American Naturalist* 164(3): 378–95.

Simmons, L. W. (1986). Female choice in the field cricket, *Gryllus bimaculatus* (De Geer). *Animal Behaviour* 34: 1463–70.

Simmons, L. W. (1987). Female choice contributes to offspring fitness in the field cricket, *Gryllus bimaculatus* (De Geer) *Behavioral Ecology and Sociobiology* 21: 313–21.

Simmons, L. W. (1988). The calling song of the field cricket, *Gryllus bimaculatus* (De Geer): constraints on transmission and the role in intermale competition and female choice. *Animal Behaviour* 36: 380–94.

Simmons, L. W. (1989). Kin recognition and its influence on mating preferences of the field cricket, *Gryllus bimaculatus* (De Geer). *Animal Behaviour* 38: 68–77.

Simmons, L. W. (1990). Nuptial feeding in tettigoniids: male costs and rates of fecundity increase. *Behavioral Ecology and Sociobiology*. 27: 43–7.

Simmons, L. W. (1991). Female choice and the relatedness of mates in the field cricket *Gryllus bimaculatus*. *Animal Behaviour* 41: 493–501.

Simmons, L. W. (1994). Reproductive energetics of the role reversing bushcricket, *Kawanaphila nartee* (Orthoptera: Tettigoniidae: Zaprochilinae). *Journal of Evolutionary Biology* 7(2): 189–200.

Simmons, L. W. (1995). Relative parental expenditure, potential reproductive rates and the control of sexual selection in Katydids. *American Naturalist* 145: 797–808.

Simmons, L. W. (2001). The evolution of polyandry: an examination of the genetic incompatibility and good-sperm hypotheses. *Journal of Evolutionary Biology* 14: 585–94.

Simmons, L. W. (2005). The evolution of polyandry: sperm competition, sperm selection, and offspring viability. *Annual Review of Ecology, Evolution and Systematics* 36: 125–46.

Simmons, L. W. & Bailey, W. J. (1990). Resource influenced sex roles of zaprochiline tettigoniids (Orthoptera: Tettigoniidae). *Evolution* 44: 1853–68.

Simmons, L. W. & Gwynne, D. T. (1991). The refractory period of female katydids (Orthoptera: Tettigoniidae): sexual conflict over the remating interval? *Behavioral Ecology* 2: 276–82.

Simmons, L. W. & Parker, G. A. (1989). Nuptial feeding in insects: mating effort versus paternal investment. *Ethology* 81: 332–43.

Simmons, L. W., Zuk, M. & Rotenberry, J. T. (2001). Geographic variation in preference functions and male songs of the field cricket *Teleogryllus oceanicus*. *Evolution* 55: 1386–94.

Smith, G. (2007). Bush crickets on the menu. *Essex Field Club Newsletter* 54: 8–9.

Smith, P. H. & Newton, J. M. (2007). *Conocephalus dorsalis* (Latreille) (Orthoptera: Tettigoniidae) in Merseyside and Lancashire *British Journal of Entomology and Natural History* 20: 46–8.

Smith, S. C. H. (1972). Goldcrests feeding young with Oak bush crickets. *British Birds* 65: 33.

Snedden, W. A. & Greenfield, M. D. (1998). Females prefer leading males: relative call timing and sexual selection in katydid choruses. *Animal Behaviour* 56: 1091–8.

Solulu, T. M., Simpson, S. J. & Kathirithambi, J. (1998). The effect of strepsipteran parasitism on a tettigoniid pest of oil palm in Papua New Guinea. *Physiological Entomology* 23: 388–98.

Somerset Maugham, W. (1963). *Collected Short Stories.* Vol. 1. Harmondsworth: Penguin.

Steinberg, J. B. & Willey, R. B. (1983). The mating system of *Trimerotropis maritima* (Acrididae: Oedipodinae). In Gwynne & Morris (Eds.) *op. cit.*: 285–304.

Steiner, A. L. (1981). Anti-predator strategies II. Grasshoppers (Orthoptera, Acrididae) attacked by *Prionyx parkeri* and some *Tachysphex* wasps (Hymenoptera, Sphecinae and Larrinae): a descriptive study. *Psyche* 88: 1–24.

Streett, D. A. & McGuire, M. R. (1990). Pathogenic diseases of grasshoppers. In Chapman & Joern (Eds.) *op. cit.*: 483–516.

Sutton, P. G. (1999). The scaly cricket in Britain: a complete history from discovery to citizenship. *British Wildlife* 10(3): 145–51.

Sutton, P. G. (2002). Wildlife reports: grasshoppers and relatives. *British Wildlife* 14(1): 55–6.

Sutton, P. G. (2003a). Wildlife reports: grasshoppers and relatives. *British Wildlife* 14(3): 208–9.

Sutton, P. G. (2003b). Wildlife reports: grasshoppers and relatives. *British Wildlife* 14(5): 358–9.

Sutton, P. G. (2003c). Wildlife reports: grasshoppers and relatives. *British Wildlife* 15(1): 56–8.

Sutton, P. G. (2004a). Classic entomological sites: Branscombe beach and undercliff, East Devon. *Bulletin of the Amateur Entomologist's Society* 63: 47–67.

Sutton, P. G. (2004b). Wildlife reports: grasshoppers and relatives. *British Wildlife* 15(3): 209–10.

Sutton, P. G. (2004c). Wildlife reports: grasshoppers and relatives. *British Wildlife* 16(1): 55–6.

Sutton, P. G. (2004d). Wildlife reports: grasshoppers and relatives. *British Wildlife* 16(3): 203–5.

Sutton, P. G. (2005a). Wildlife reports: grasshoppers and relatives. *British Wildlife* 16(3): 203–5.

Sutton, P. G. (2005b). Wildlife reports: grasshoppers and relatives. *British Wildlife* 17(2): 125–7.

Sutton, P. G. (2006a). Wildlife reports: grasshoppers and relatives. *British Wildlife* 17(5): 355–6.

Sutton, P. G. (2006b). Wildlife reports: grasshoppers and relatives. *British Wildlife* 18(1): 53–4.

Sutton, P. G. (2007a). Wildlife reports: grasshoppers and relatives. *British Wildlife* 18(2): 203–5.

Sutton, P. G. (2007b). Wildlife reports: grasshoppers and relatives. *British Wildlife* 18(3): 203–5.

Sutton, P. G. (2007c). Wildlife reports: grasshoppers and relatives. *British Wildlife* 18(4): 354–6.

Sutton, P. G. (2007d). Wildlife reports: grasshoppers and relatives. *British Wildlife* 18(5): 354–6.

Sutton, P. G. (2007e). Wildlife reports: grasshoppers and relatives. *British Wildlife* 19(1): 54–5.

Sutton, P. G. (2008a). Wildlife reports: grasshoppers and relatives. *British Wildlife* 19(3): 206–7.

Sutton, P. G. (2008b). Wildlife reports: grasshoppers and relatives. *British Wildlife* 19(6): 432–3.

Sutton, P. G. (2008c). Wildlife reports: grasshoppers and relatives. *British Wildlife* 20(2): 124–5.

Sutton, P. G. (2009). Wildlife reports: grasshoppers and relatives. *British Wildlife* 20(6): 432–3.

Sutton, P. G. (2010a). Wildlife reports: grasshoppers and relatives. *British Wildlife* 21(3): 200–202.

Sutton, P. G. (2010b). Wildlife reports: grasshoppers and relatives. *British Wildlife* 22(1): 49–51.

Sutton, P. G. (2011). Wildlife reports: grasshoppers and relatives. *British Wildlife* 22(4): 280–1.

Sutton, P. G. & Brown, D. E. (1992). The purple form of the wart-biter, *Decticus verrucivorus*. *Bulletin of the Amateur Entomologists' Society* 51: 27–9.

Tauber, E. (2001). Bidirectional communication system in katydids: the effect on chorus structure. *Behavioral Ecology* 12: 308–12.

Tauber, E., Cohen, D., Greenfield, M. D. & Pener, M. P. (2001). Duet singing and female choice in the bushcricket *Phaneroptera nana*. *Behaviour* 138: 411–30.

Telfer, M. G. & Hassall, M. (1999). Ecotypic differentiation in the grasshopper *Chorthippus brunneus*: life history varies in relation to climate. *Oecologia* 121: 245–54.

ter Hofstede, H. M., Ratcliffe, J. M. & Fullard, J. H. (2008). The effectiveness of katydid (*Neoconocephalus ensiger*) song cessation as antipredator defence against the gleaning bat *Myotis*

septentrionalis. *Behavioral Ecology and Sociobiology* 63: 217–226

Thomas, C. D., Bodsworth, E. J., Wilson, R. J., Simmons, A. D., Davies, Z. G., Musche, M. & Conradt, L. (2001). Ecological and evolutionary processes at expanding range margins. *Nature* 411: 577–81.

Thomas, M. C. & Simmons, L. W. (2009). Male dominance influences pheromone expression, ejaculate quality and fertilization success in the Australian field cricket *Teleogryllus oceanicus*. *Behavioral Ecology* 20(5): 1111–17.

Thomas, M. L. & Simmons, L. W. (2008). Sexual dimorphism in cuticular hydrocarbons of the Australian field cricket *Teleogryllus oceanicus* (Orthoptera: Gryllidae). *Journal of Insect Physiology* 54: 1081–9.

Thomas-Bailey, C. (2010). 'It's not just cricket...' *The Guardian Weekend*, 13th November: 31–5.

Thompson, G. & Maclean, B. (1999). *Essex Biodiversity Action Plan*. Chelmsford: Essex County Council.

Timmins, C. J. (1994). The population size of *Pseudomogoplistes squamiger* Fischer (Orthop. Gryllidae) on Chesil Beach, Dorset. *Entomologist's Monthly Magazine* 130: 66.

Tinghitella, R. M., Wang, J. M. & Zuk, M. (2009). Preexisting behavior renders a mutation adaptive: flexibility in male phonotaxis behavior and the loss of singing ability in the field cricket *Teleogryllus oceanicus*. *Behavioral Ecology* 20(4): 722–8.

Tregenza, T. & Wedell, N. (1997). Definitive evidence for cuticular pheromones in a cricket. *Animal Behaviour* 54: 979–84.

Tregenza, T. & Wedell, N. (1998). Benefits of multiple mates in the cricket *Gryllus bimaculatus*. *Evolution* 52: 1726–30.

Trivers, R. L. (1972). Parental investment and sexual selection. In B. Campbell (Ed.) *Sexual Selection and the Descent of Man, 1871–1971.* Chicago: Aldine: 136–79.

Tubbs, C. R. (1986). *The New Forest.* London: Collins.

Tuckerman, J. F., Gwynne, D. T. & Morris, G. K. (1993). Reliable acoustic cues for female mate preference in a katydid (*Scudderia curvicauda*, Orthoptera, Tettigoniidae). *Behavioral Ecology* 4: 106–13.

Uvarov, B. P. (1922). A grasshopper new to Britain. *Entomologist's Monthly Magazine* 58: 211.

Uvarov, B. P. (1928). *Grasshoppers and Locusts: A Handbook of General Acridology* vol. 2. London: Imperial Bureau of Entomology.

Uvarov, B. P. (1940). *Tetrix ceperoi*, I. Bolivar new to British fauna (Orthoptera, Tetrigidae). *Journal of the Society for British Entomology* 2(2): 72–5.

Vahed, K. (1994). *The Evolution and Function of the Spermatophylax in Bushcrickets (Orthoptera: Tettigoniidae).* Ph.D. Thesis, University of Nottingham.

Vahed, K. (1996). Prolonged copulation in oak bushcrickets (Tettigoniidae: Meconematinae: *Meconema thalassinum* and *M. meridionale*). *Journal of Orthoptera Research* 5: 199–204.

Vahed, K. (1998). The function of nuptial feeding in insects: a review of empirical studies. *Biological Reviews* 73: 43–78.

Vahed, K. (2002). Coercive copulation in the alpine bushcricket *Anonconotus alpinus* Yersin (Tettigoniidae: Tettigoniinae: Platycleidini) *Ethology* 108: 1065–75.

Vahed, K. (2003a). Structure of spermatodoses in shield-back crickets (Tettigoniidae: Tettigoniinae). *Journal of Morphology* 257: 45–52.

Vahed, K. (2003b). Increases in egg production in multiply mated female bushcrickets *Leptophyes punctatissima* are not due to substances in the nuptial gift. *Ecological Entomology* 28: 124–8.

Vahed, K. (2006). Larger ejaculate volumes are associated with a lower degree of polyandry across bushcricket taxa. *Proceedings of the Royal Society* B 273: 2387–94.

Vahed, K. (2007). Comparative evidence for a cost to males of manipulating females in bushcrickets. *Behavioral Ecology* 18: 507–12.

Vahed, K. (2011). Titanic testicles in tettigoniids add weight to the male mating rate hypothesis. *Bulletin of the Entomological Society of Canada* 43:136–140.

Vahed, K. & Carron, G. (2008). Comparison of forced mating behaviour in four taxa of *Anonconotus*, the Alpine bushcricket. *Journal of Zoology* 276: 313–21.

Vahed, K. & Gilbert, F. S. (1996). Differences across taxa in nuptial gift size correlate with differences in sperm number and ejaculate volume in bushcrickets (Orthoptera: Tettigoniidae). *Proceedings of the Royal Society* B 263: 1257–65.

Vahed, K. & Gilbert, F. S. (1997). No effect of nuptial gift consumption on female reproductive output in the bush-cricket *Leptophyes laticauda* Friv. *Ecological Entomology* 22: 479–82.

Vahed, K. & Parker, D. J. (2012). The evolution of large testes: sperm competition or male mating rate? *Ethology*, in press.

Vahed, K, Parker, D. J., & Gilbert, J. D. J. (2011). Larger testes are associated with a higher level of polyandry, but a smaller ejaculate volume , across bushcricket species (Tettigoniidae). *Biology Letters* 7(2): 261–4.

van Wingerden, W. K. R. E. & Dimmers, W. J. (1993). Effect of rabbit and cattle grazing on grasshoppers (Orthoptera: Acrididae) of river dunes. *Proceedings of the section Experimental and Applied Entomology* 4: 127–36.

van Wingerden, W. K. R. E., Musters, J. C. M. & Maaskamp, F. I. M. (1991). The influence of temperature on the duration of egg development in West European Grasshoppers (Orthoptera: Acrididae). *Oecologia* 87: 417–23.

van Wingerden, W. K. R. E., van Kreveld, A. R. & Bongers, W. (1992). Analysis of species composition and abundance of grasshoppers (Orth., Acrididae) in natural and fertilized grasslands. *Journal of Applied Entomology* 113: 138–52.

Velando, A, Torres, R. & Alonzo-Alvarez, C. (2008). Avoiding bad genes: oxidatively damaged DNA in germ line and mate choice. *Bio essays* 30: 1212–19.

Verburgt, L., Ferreira, M. & Ferguson, J. W. H. (2011). Male field cricket song reflects age, allowing females to prefer young males. *Animal Behaviour* 81: 19–29.

von Helversen, D. & Wendler, D. (2000). Coupling of visual to auditory cues during phonotactic approach in the phaneropterine bushcricket *Poecilimon affinis*. *Journal of Comparative Physiology A* 186: 729–36.

von Helversen, O. & von Helversen, D. (1994). Forces driving coevolution of song and song recognition in grasshoppers. In K. Schildberger & N. Elsner (Eds.) *Neural Basis of Behavioural Adaptations*. Stuttgart: Gustav Fischer Verlag: 253–84.

Wagner, W. E., Jr. & Hoback, W. W. (1999). Nutritional effects on male calling behaviour in the variable field cricket. *Animal Behaviour* 57: 89–95

Wagner, W. E., Murray, A, M. & Cade, W. H. (1995). Phenotypic variation in the mating preferences of female field crickets, *Gryllus integer*. *Animal Behaviour* 49: 1269–81.

Wagner, W. E., Smeds, M. R. & Wiegmann, D. D. (2001). Experience affects female responses to male song in the variable field cricket *Gryllus lineaticeps* (Orthoptera, Gryllidae). *Ethology* 107: 769–76.

Wake, A. J. (1997). *Grasshoppers and Crickets of Essex*. Colchester: Colchester Natural History Society.

Walker, T. J & Masaki, S. (1989). Natural history. In F. Huber *et al.* (Eds.) *op. cit.*: 1–42.

Walker, T. J. (1979). Calling crickets (*Anurogryllus arboreus*) over pitfalls: females, males, and predators. *Environmental Entomology* 8: 441–3.

Walker, T. J. (1983a). Diel patterns of calling in nocturnal Orthoptera. In Gwynne &. Morris (Eds.) *op. cit.*: 45–72.

Walker, T. J. (1983b). Mating modes and female choice in short-tailed crickets (*Anurogryllus arboreus*). In Gwynne & Morris (Eds.) *op. cit.*: 241–67.

Wall, R. & Begon, M. (1987). Individual variation and the effects of population density in the grasshopper *Chorthippus brunneus*. *Oikos* 49: 15–27.

Wallace, A. R. (1871). Darwin's 'The Descent of Man and Selection in Relation to Sex'. *The Academy*, 15 March 1871: 177–83.

Wallace, A. R. (1875a [1864]). The Malayan Papilionidae, or swallowtailed butterflies, as illustrative of the theory of natural selection. In Wallace, A. R. (Ed.) *op. cit.* (Originally published as: 'On the phenomena of variation and geographical distribution, as illustrated by the Papilionidae of the Malayan region', in *Transactions of the Linnaean Society* XXV.)

Wallace, A. R. (1875b [1867]). Mimicry and other protective resemblances among animals. In A. R. Wallace (Ed.) *Contributions to the Theory of Natural Selection*. London: Macmillan. (Originally published in the *Westminster Review*, July 1867.)

Wallace, A. R. (1875c [1868]). A theory of birds' nests. In A. R. Wallace (Ed.) *op. cit.* (Originally published in the *Journal of Travel and Natural History* 2: 1868.)

Wallace, A. R. (1889). *Darwinism: An Exposition of the Theory of Natural Selection with Some of its Applications.* London & New York: Macmillan.

Waloff, N. (1950). The egg-pods of the British short-horned grasshoppers. *Proceedings of the Royal Entomological Society of London* (A) 25: 115–26.

Warwick, S., Vahed, K., Raubenheimer, D. & Simpson, S. J. (2009). Free amino acids as phagostimulants in cricket nuptial gifts: support for the 'Candymaker' hypothesis. *Biology Letters* 5: 194–6.

Weaver, J. E. & Sommers, R. A. (1969). Life history and habits of the short-tailed cricket, *Anurogryllus muticus,* in Central Louisiana. *Annals of the Entomological Society of America* 62(2): 337–42.

Wedell, N. & Arak, A. (1989). The wartbiter spermatophore and its effect on female reproductive output (Orthoptera: Tettigoniidae, *Decticus verrucivorus*). *Behavioral Ecology and Sociobiology* 24: 117–25.

Wedell, N. (1993). Spermatophore size in bushcrickets: comparative evidence for nuptial gifts as sperm protection devices. *Evolution* 47: 1203–12.

Wedell, N. (1994). Variation in nuptial gift quality in bushcrickets (Orthoptera: Tettigoniidae). *Proceedings of the Royal Society of London* B 258: 181–5.

West-Eberhard, M. J. (2003). *Developmental Plasticity and Evolution.* Oxford: Oxford University.

West, M. J. & Alexander, R. D. (1963). Sub-social behaviour in a burrowing cricket *Anurogryllus muticus* (De Geer) Orthoptera: Gryllidae. *Ohio Journal of Science* 63: 19–24.

White, G. (1971 [1789]). *The Natural History of Selborne.* London: Oxford University.

Whitman, D. W. (1982). Grasshopper sexual pheromone: a component of the defensive secretion in *Taeniopoda eques. Physiological Entomology* 7: 111–15.

Whitman, D. W. (1986). Developmental thermal requirements for the grasshopper *Taeniopoda eques* (Orthoptera: Acrididae). *Animal Behaviour* 35: 1814–26.

Whitman, D. W. (1988). Function and evolution of thermoregulation in the desert grasshopper *Taeniopoda eques. Animal Ecology* 57: 369–83.

Whitman, D. W. (1990). Grasshopper chemical communication. In R. F. Chapman & A. Joern (Eds.) *op. cit.:* 357–91.

Widgery, J. (1998). Wildlife reports: grasshoppers and relatives. *British Wildlife* 10(1): 51–2.

Widgery, J. (2000a). Wildlife reports: grasshoppers and relatives. *British Wildlife* 11(3): 211–12

Widgery, J. (2000b). Wildlife reports: grasshoppers and relatives. *British Wildlife* 11(5): 362.

Widgery, J. (2000c). Wildlife reports: grasshoppers and relatives. *British Wildlife* 12(1): 54–5.

Widgery, J. (2001a). Wildlife reports: grasshoppers and relatives. *British Wildlife* 12(5): 359–60.

Widgery, J. (2001b). Wildlife reports: grasshoppers and relatives. *British Wildlife* 13(1): 59–60.

Widgery, J. (2002). Wildlife reports. Grasshoppers and relatives. *British Wildlife* 13(3): 207–8.

Wilde, I. (2009). The stripe-winged grasshopper *Stenobothrus lineatus* (Panzer 1796) (Orthoptera: Gomphocerinae) new to Essex. *Essex Naturalist* 26 (New Series): 61–2.

Willott, S. J. (1997). Thermoregulation in four species of British grasshoppers (Orthoptera: Acrididae). *Functional Ecology* 11: 705–13.

Wynne-Edwards, V. C. (1962). *Animal Dispersion in Relation to Social Behaviour.* Edinburgh: Oliver & Boyd.

Wynne, H. & Vahed, K. (2004). Male *Gryllus bimaculatus* guard females to delay them from mating with rival males and to obtain repeated copulations. *Journal of Insect Behavior* 17(1): 53–66.

Zera, A. J. & Denno, R. F. (1997). Physiology and ecology of dispersal polymorphism in insects. *Annual Review of Entomology* 42: 207–30.

Zera, A. J., Strambi, C., Tiebel, K. C., Strambi, A. & Rankin, M. A. (1989). Juvenile hormone and ecdysteroid titers during critical periods of wing morph determination in *Gryllus rubens. Journal of Insect Physiology* 35: 501–11.

Zimmermann, U., Rheinlaender, J. & Robinson, D. (1989). Cues for male phonotaxis in the duetting bushcricket *Leptophyes punctatissima. Journal of Comparative Physiology* A 164: 621–8.

Zufall, F., Schmitt, M. & Menzel, R. (1989). Spectral and polarized light sensitivity of photoreceptors in the compound eye of the cricket (*Gryllus bimaculatus*). *Journal of Comparative Physiology* A 164: 597–608.

Zuk, M. & Simmons, L. W. (1997). Reproductive strategies of the crickets (Orthoptera: Gryllidae). In Choe & Crespi (Eds.) *op. cit.*: 89–109.

Zuk, M., Rebar, D. & Scott, S. P. (2008). Courtship song is more variable than calling song in the field cricket *Teleogryllus oceanicus. Animal Behaviour* 76: 1065–71.

Zuk, M., Rotenberry, J. T. & Tinghitella, R. M. (2006). Silent night: adaptive disappearance of a sexual signal in a parasitized population of field crickets. *Biological Letters* 2: 521–4.

Index